Zend Framework

The Official Programmer's Reference Guide
Volume 2 of 2

Zend, Inc.

Apress®

**The Zend Press
Series**

President and Publisher: Paul Manning
Lead Editor: Jeffrey Pepper
Editorial Board: Clay Andres, Steve Anglin, Mark Beckner, Ewan Buckingham, Tony Campbell, Gary Cornell, Jonathan Gennick, Michelle Lowman, Matthew Moodie, Jeffrey Pepper, Frank Pohlmann, Ben Renow-Clarke, Dominic Shakeshaft, Matt Wade, Tom Welsh
Compositor: StanInfo Solutions and Zend Technologies USA, Inc
Cover Designer: Anna Ishchenko

Distributed to the book trade worldwide by Springer-Verlag New York, Inc., 233 Spring Street, 6th Floor, New York, NY 10013. Phone 1-800-SPRINGER, fax 201-348-4505, e-mail orders-ny@springer-sbm.com, or visit http://www.springeronline.com.

For information on translations, please e-mail info@apress.com, or visit http://www.apress.com.

Apress and friends of ED books may be purchased in bulk for academic, corporate, or promotional use. eBook versions and licenses are also available for most titles. For more information, reference our Special Bulk Sales—eBook Licensing web page at http://www.apress.com/info/bulksales.

About Zend Press

Zend Press publishes books that are authored by leaders in the PHP community, PHP engineers & consultants, employees of Zend, and all those knowledgeable about PHP and its use to deliver powerful, scalable, and reliable web-based applications and infrastructure. Zend Press is a joint publishing relationship between Zend and Apress, the leading publisher on emerging technologies.

As the market leader in PHP related technology, Zend will utilize Zend Press to deliver books on Zend-related projects or products and also on thought leading topics in professional PHP as well. Zend Press will publish books at all levels to meet the needs of a diverse PHP community with relevant, cutting edge know-how. Regardless of the audience, we are committed to publishing books that best serve the needs of users at any targeted level.

Through this publishing program, we are committed to bringing you more and better information, to help you use our products more effectively, with the professionalism that you have come to expect from Zend, from the PHP community at large, and from Apress.

Zeev Suraski
Zend Technologies Co-founder and Chief Technology Officer

Foreword

These two volumes contain the full Zend Framework Reference Guide in a handy format for quick reference (this same material can also be viewed online at http://framework.zend.com/manual). You may want to keep it next to you while developing or invest your time in a more thorough review to improve your ZF expertise in general. Much like the framework itself, it can be read in a 'use-at-will' fashion; that is, you can read each section of the guide without having to read other sections in advance. As its name implies, typically this reference guide would not be read cover-to-cover, but if you are dedicated to learning about every component in ZF it will also lend itself well to this purpose.

One of Zend Framework's core strengths is the fact that all contributors to the project have to supply documentation along with their code. As a result, every feature is called out and documented in detail. And with over 500 code examples, this reference guide will show you exactly how to use these features in your applications.

The guide documents each feature and API in full, with plenty of examples to make easy work of adding ZF components to your applications. In particular, this guide features:

- A chapter dedicated to every component in Zend Framework
- Quick Starts for key components such as Zend_Controller and Zend_Form
- Over a thousand pages of Zend Framework material written by hundreds of ZF contributors
- Edited and reviewed by the Zend Framework team at Zend Technologies

We hope you find this guide as useful as the Zend Framework components themselves while writing the next generation of PHP applications. The Zend Framework community has invested countless hours to make this guide as helpful as possible, but if you find improvements to be made, please join us at http://framework.zend.com to add your voice to our growing community!

Matthew Weier O'Phinney
Project Lead, Zend Framework

List of Tables

List of Examples

Chapter 1. Zend_InfoCard

Introduction

The `Zend_InfoCard` component implements relying-party support for Information Cards. Information Cards are used for identity management on the internet and authentication of users to web sites. The web sites that the user ultimately authenticates to are called *relying-parties*.

Detailed information about information cards and their importance to the internet identity metasystem can be found on the IdentityBlog [http://www.identityblog.com/].

Basic Theory of Usage

Usage of `Zend_InfoCard` can be done one of two ways: either as part of the larger `Zend_Auth` component via the `Zend_InfoCard` authentication adapter or as a stand-alone component. In both cases an information card can be requested from a user by using the following HTML block in your HTML login form:

```
<form action="http://example.com/server" method="POST">
  <input type='image' src='/images/ic.png' align='center'
         width='120px' style='cursor:pointer' />
  <object type="application/x-informationCard"
          name="xmlToken">
   <param name="tokenType"
          value="urn:oasis:names:tc:SAML:1.0:assertion" />
   <param name="requiredClaims"
          value="http://.../claims/privatepersonalidentifier
          http://.../claims/givenname
          http://.../claims/surname" />
  </object>
</form>
```

In the example above, the `requiredClaims` <param> tag is used to identify pieces of information known as claims (i.e. person's first name, last name) which the web site (a.k.a "relying party") needs in order a user to authenticate using an information card. For your reference, the full URI (for instance the givenname claim) is as follows: `http://schemas.xmlsoap.org/ws/2005/05/identity/claims/givenname`

When the above HTML is activated by a user (clicks on it), the browser will bring up a card selection program which not only shows them which information cards meet the requirements of the site, but also allows them to select which information card to use if multiple meet the criteria. This information card is transmitted as an XML document to the specified `POST` URL and is ready to be processed by the `Zend_InfoCard` component.

Note, Information cards can only be `HTTP  POSTed` to SSL-encrypted URLs. Please consult your web server's documentation on how to set up SSL encryption.

Using as part of Zend_Auth

In order to use the component as part of the `Zend_Auth` authentication system, you must use the provided `Zend_Auth_Adapter_InfoCard` to do so (not available in the standalone `Zend_InfoCard` distribution). An example of its usage is shown below:

```
<?php
if (isset($_POST['xmlToken'])) {
```

```php
$adapter = new Zend_Auth_Adapter_InfoCard($_POST['xmlToken']);

$adapter->addCertificatePair('/usr/local/Zend/apache2/conf/server.key',
                             '/usr/local/Zend/apache2/conf/server.crt');

$auth = Zend_Auth::getInstance();

$result = $auth->authenticate($adapter);

switch ($result->getCode()) {
    case Zend_Auth_Result::SUCCESS:
        $claims = $result->getIdentity();
        print "Given Name: {$claims->givenname}<br />";
        print "Surname: {$claims->surname}<br />";
        print "Email Address: {$claims->emailaddress}<br />";
        print "PPI: {$claims->getCardID()}<br />";
        break;
    case Zend_Auth_Result::FAILURE_CREDENTIAL_INVALID:
        print "The Credential you provided did not pass validation";
        break;
    default:
    case Zend_Auth_Result::FAILURE:
        print "There was an error processing your credentials.";
        break;
}

if (count($result->getMessages()) > 0) {
    print "<pre>";
    var_dump($result->getMessages());
    print "</pre>";
}

}
?>
<hr />
<div id="login" style="font-family: arial; font-size: 2em;">
<p>Simple Login Demo</p>
 <form method="post">
  <input type="submit" value="Login" />
   <object type="application/x-informationCard" name="xmlToken">
    <param name="tokenType"
          value="urn:oasis:names:tc:SAML:1.0:assertion" />
    <param name="requiredClaims"
          value="http://.../claims/givenname
                 http://.../claims/surname
                 http://.../claims/emailaddress
                 http://.../claims/privatepersonalidentifier" />
  </object>
 </form>
</div>
```

In the example above, we first create an instance of the Zend_Auth_Adapter_InfoCard and pass the XML data posted by the card selector into it. Once an instance has been created you must then provide at least one SSL certificate public/private key pair used by the web server that received the HTTP POST. These files are used to validate the destination of the information posted to the server and are a requirement when using Information Cards.

Once the adapter has been configured, you can then use the standard Zend_Auth facilities to validate the provided information card token and authenticate the user by examining the identity provided by the getIdentity() method.

Using the Zend_InfoCard component standalone

It is also possible to use the Zend_InfoCard component as a standalone component by interacting with the Zend_InfoCard class directly. Using the Zend_InfoCard class is very similar to its use with the Zend_Auth component. An example of its use is shown below:

```php
<?php
if (isset($_POST['xmlToken'])) {
    $infocard = new Zend_InfoCard();
    $infocard->addCertificatePair('/usr/local/Zend/apache2/conf/server.key',
                                  '/usr/local/Zend/apache2/conf/server.crt');

    $claims = $infocard->process($_POST['xmlToken']);

    if($claims->isValid()) {
        print "Given Name: {$claims->givenname}<br />";
        print "Surname: {$claims->surname}<br />";
        print "Email Address: {$claims->emailaddress}<br />";
        print "PPI: {$claims->getCardID()}<br />";
    } else {
        print "Error Validating identity: {$claims->getErrorMsg()}";
    }
}
?>
<hr />
<div id="login" style="font-family: arial; font-size: 2em;">
 <p>Simple Login Demo</p>
 <form method="post">
  <input type="submit" value="Login" />
   <object type="application/x-informationCard" name="xmlToken">
    <param name="tokenType"
          value="urn:oasis:names:tc:SAML:1.0:assertion" />
    <param name="requiredClaims"
          value="http://.../claims/givenname
                 http://.../claims/surname
                 http://.../claims/emailaddress
                 http://.../claims/privatepersonalidentifier" />
   </object>
 </form>
</div>
```

In the example above, we use the Zend_InfoCard component independently to validate the token provided by the user. As was the case with the Zend_Auth_Adapter_InfoCard, we create an instance of Zend_InfoCard and then set one or more SSL certificate public/private key pairs used by the web server. Once configured, we can use the process() method to process the information card and return the results.

Working with a Claims object

Regardless of whether the Zend_InfoCard component is used as a standalone component or as part of Zend_Auth via Zend_Auth_Adapter_InfoCard, the ultimate result of the processing of an information card is a Zend_InfoCard_Claims object. This object contains the assertions (a.k.a. claims) made by the submitting user based on the data requested by your web site when the user authenticated. As shown in the examples above, the validity of the information card can be ascertained by calling the Zend_InfoCard_Claims::isValid() method. Claims themselves can either be retrieved by simply accessing the identifier desired (i.e. givenname) as a property of the object or through the getClaim() method.

In most cases you will never need to use the getClaim() method. However, if your requiredClaims mandate that you request claims from multiple different sources/namespaces then you will need to extract them explicitly using this method (simply pass it the full URI of the claim to retrieve its value from within the information card). Generally speaking however, the Zend_InfoCard component will set the default URI for claims to be the one used the most frequently within the information card itself and the simplified property-access method can be used.

As part of the validation process, it is the developer's responsibility to examine the issuing source of the claims contained within the information card and to decide if that source is a trusted source of information. To do so, the getIssuer() method is provided within the Zend_InfoCard_Claims object which returns the URI of the issuer of the information card claims.

Attaching Information Cards to existing accounts

It is possible to add support for information cards to an existing authentication system by storing the private personal identifier (PPI) to a previously traditionally-authenticated account and including at least the http://schemas.xmlsoap.org/ws/2005/05/identity/claims/private personalidentifier claim as part of the requiredClaims of the request. If this claim is requested then the Zend_InfoCard_Claims object will provide a unique identifier for the specific card that was submitted by calling the getCardID() method.

An example of how to attach an information card to an existing traditional-authentication account is shown below:

```
// ...
public function submitinfocardAction()
{
    if (!isset($_REQUEST['xmlToken'])) {
        throw new ZBlog_Exception('Expected an encrypted token ' .
                                  'but was not provided');
    }

    $infoCard = new Zend_InfoCard();
    $infoCard->addCertificatePair(SSL_CERTIFICATE_PRIVATE,
                                  SSL_CERTIFICATE_PUB);

    try {
        $claims = $infoCard->process($request['xmlToken']);
    } catch(Zend_InfoCard_Exception $e) {
        // TODO Error processing your request
        throw $e;
    }

    if ($claims->isValid()) {
        $db = ZBlog_Data::getAdapter();

        $ppi = $db->quote($claims->getCardID());
        $fullname = $db->quote("{$claims->givenname} {$claims->surname}");

        $query = "UPDATE blogusers
                    SET ppi = $ppi,
                        real_name = $fullname
                  WHERE username='administrator'";

        try {
            $db->query($query);
        } catch(Exception $e) {
            // TODO Failed to store in DB
        }

        $this->view->render();
        return;
    } else {
        throw new
```

```
                ZBlog_Exception("Infomation card failed security checks");
        }
}
```

Creating Zend_InfoCard Adapters

The Zend_InfoCard component was designed to allow for growth in the information card standard through the use of a modular architecture. At this time, many of these hooks are unused and can be ignored, but there is one class that should be written for any serious information card implementation: the Zend_InfoCard adapter.

The Zend_InfoCard adapter is used as a callback mechanism within the component to perform various tasks, such as storing and retrieving Assertion IDs for information cards when they are processed by the component. While storing the assertion IDs of submitted information cards is not necessary, failing to do so opens up the possibility of the authentication scheme being compromised through a replay attack.

To prevent this, one must implement the Zend_InfoCard_Adapter_Interface and set an instance of this interface prior to calling either the process() (standalone) or authenticate() method as a Zend_Auth adapter. To set this interface, the setAdapter() method should be used. In the example below, we set a Zend_InfoCard adapter and use it in our application:

```
class myAdapter implements Zend_InfoCard_Adapter_Interface
{
    public function storeAssertion($assertionURI,
                                   $assertionID,
                                   $conditions)
    {
        /* Store the assertion and its conditions by ID and URI */
    }

    public function retrieveAssertion($assertionURI, $assertionID)
    {
        /* Retrieve the assertion by URI and ID */
    }

    public function removeAssertion($assertionURI, $assertionID)
    {
        /* Delete a given assertion by URI/ID */
    }
}

$adapter  = new myAdapter();

$infoCard = new Zend_InfoCard();
$infoCard->addCertificatePair(SSL_PRIVATE, SSL_PUB);
$infoCard->setAdapter($adapter);

$claims = $infoCard->process($_POST['xmlToken']);
```

Chapter 2. Zend_Json

Introduction

Zend_Json provides convenience methods for serializing native PHP to JSON and decoding JSON to native PHP. For more information on JSON, visit the JSON project site [http://www.json.org/].

JSON, JavaScript Object Notation, can be used for data interchange between JavaScript and other languages. Since JSON can be directly evaluated by JavaScript, it is a more efficient and lightweight format than XML for exchanging data with JavaScript clients.

In addition, Zend_Json provides a useful way to convert any arbitrary XML formatted string into a JSON formatted string. This built-in feature will enable PHP developers to transform the enterprise data encoded in XML format into JSON format before sending it to browser-based Ajax client applications. It provides an easy way to do dynamic data conversion on the server-side code thereby avoiding unnecessary XML parsing in the browser-side applications. It offers a nice utility function that results in easier application-specific data processing techniques.

Basic Usage

Usage of Zend_Json involves using the two public static methods available: Zend_Json::encode() and Zend_Json::decode().

```
// Retrieve a value:
$phpNative = Zend_Json::decode($encodedValue);

// Encode it to return to the client:
$json = Zend_Json::encode($phpNative);
```

Advanced Usage of Zend_Json

JSON Objects

When encoding PHP objects as JSON, all public properties of that object will be encoded in a JSON object.

JSON does not allow object references, so care should be taken not to encode objects with recursive references. If you have issues with recursion, Zend_Json::encode() and Zend_Json_Encoder::encode() allow an optional second parameter to check for recursion; if an object is serialized twice, an exception will be thrown.

Decoding JSON objects poses an additional difficulty, however, since Javascript objects correspond most closely to PHP's associative array. Some suggest that a class identifier should be passed, and an object instance of that class should be created and populated with the key/value pairs of the JSON object; others feel this could pose a substantial security risk.

By default, Zend_Json will decode JSON objects as associative arrays. However, if you desire an object returned, you can specify this:

```
// Decode JSON objects as PHP objects
$phpNative = Zend_Json::decode($encodedValue, Zend_Json::TYPE_OBJECT);
```

Any objects thus decoded are returned as StdClass objects with properties corresponding to the key/value pairs in the JSON notation.

The recommendation of Zend Framework is that the individual developer should decide how to decode JSON objects. If an object of a specified type should be created, it can be created in the developer code and populated with the values decoded using Zend_Json.

Encoding PHP objects

If you are encoding PHP objects by default the encoding mechanism can only access public properties of these objects. When a method toJson() is implemented on an object to encode, Zend_Json calls this method and expects the object to return a JSON representation of its internal state.

Internal Encoder/Decoder

Zend_Json has two different modes depending if ext/json is enabled in your PHP installation or not. If ext/json is installed by default json_encode() and json_decode() functions are used for encoding and decoding JSON. If ext/json is not installed a Zend Framework implementation in PHP code is used for en-/decoding. This is considerably slower than using the php extension, but behaves exactly the same.

Still sometimes you might want to use the internal encoder/decoder even if you have ext/json installed. You can achieve this by calling:

```
Zend_Json::$useBuiltinEncoderDecoder = true:
```

JSON Expressions

Javascript makes heavy use of anonymnous function callbacks, which can be saved within JSON object variables. Still they only work if not returned inside double qoutes, which Zend_Json naturally does. With the Expression support for Zend_Json support you can encode JSON objects with valid javascript callbacks. This works for both json_encode() or the internal encoder.

A javascript callback is represented using the Zend_Json_Expr object. It implements the value object pattern and is immutable. You can set the javascript expression as the first constructor argument. By default Zend_Json::encode does not encode javascript callbacks, you have to pass the option 'enableJsonExprFinder' = true into the encode function. If enabled the expression support works for all nested expressions in large object structures. A usage example would look like:

```
$data = array(
    'onClick' => new Zend_Json_Expr('function() {'
                . 'alert("I am a valid javascript callback '
                . 'created by Zend_Json"); }'),
    'other' => 'no expression',
);
$jsonObjectWithExpression = Zend_Json::encode(
    $data,
    false,
    array('enableJsonExprFinder' => true)
);
```

XML to JSON conversion

Zend_Json provides a convenience method for transforming XML formatted data into JSON format. This feature was inspired from an IBM developerWorks article [http://www.ibm.com/developerworks/xml/library/x-xml2jsonphp/].

Zend_Json includes a static function called Zend_Json::fromXml(). This function will generate JSON from a given XML input. This function takes any arbitrary XML string as an input parameter. It also takes an optional boolean input parameter to instruct the conversion logic to ignore or not ignore the XML attributes during the conversion process. If this optional input parameter is not given, then the default behavior is to ignore the XML attributes. This function call is made as shown below:

```
// fromXml function simply takes a String containing XML contents
// as input.
$jsonContents = Zend_Json::fromXml($xmlStringContents, true);
```

Zend_Json::fromXml() function does the conversion of the XML formatted string input parameter and returns the equivalent JSON formatted string output. In case of any XML input format error or conversion logic error, this function will throw an exception. The conversion logic also uses recursive techniques to traverse the XML tree. It supports recursion upto 25 levels deep. Beyond that depth, it will throw a Zend_Json_Exception. There are several XML files with varying degree of complexity provided in the tests directory of Zend Framework. They can be used to test the functionality of the xml2json feature.

The following is a simple example that shows both the XML input string passed to and the JSON output string returned as a result from the Zend_Json::fromXml() function. This example used the optional function parameter as not to ignore the XML attributes during the conversion. Hence, you can notice that the resulting JSON string includes a representation of the XML attributes present in the XML input string.

XML input string passed to Zend_Json::fromXml() function:

```
<books>
    <book id="1">
        <title>Code Generation in Action</title>
        <author><first>Jack</first><last>Herrington</last></author>
        <publisher>Manning</publisher>
    </book>

    <book id="2">
        <title>PHP Hacks</title>
        <author><first>Jack</first><last>Herrington</last></author>
        <publisher>O'Reilly</publisher>
    </book>

    <book id="3">
        <title>Podcasting Hacks</title>
        <author><first>Jack</first><last>Herrington</last></author>
        <publisher>O'Reilly</publisher>
    </book>
</books>
```

JSON output string returned from Zend_Json::fromXml() function:

```
{
    "books" : {
        "book" : [ {
            "@attributes" : {
                "id" : "1"
            },
            "title" : "Code Generation in Action",
            "author" : {
                "first" : "Jack", "last" : "Herrington"
            },
            "publisher" : "Manning"
        }, {
            "@attributes" : {
                "id" : "2"
            },
```

```
        "title" : "PHP Hacks", "author" : {
           "first" : "Jack", "last" : "Herrington"
        },
        "publisher" : "O'Reilly"
     }, {
        "@attributes" : {
           "id" : "3"
        },
        "title" : "Podcasting Hacks", "author" : {
           "first" : "Jack", "last" : "Herrington"
        },
        "publisher" : "O'Reilly"
     }
   ] }
}
```

More details about this xml2json feature can be found in the original proposal itself. Take a look at the Zend_xml2json proposal [http://tinyurl.com/2tfa8z].

Zend_Json_Server - JSON-RPC server

Zend_Json_Server is a JSON-RPC [http://groups.google.com/group/json-rpc/] server implementation. It supports both the JSON-RPC version 1 specification [http://json-rpc.org/wiki/specification] as well as the version 2 specification [http://groups.google.com/group/json-rpc/web/json-rpc-1-2-proposal]; additionally, it provides a PHP implementation of the Service Mapping Description (SMD) specification [http://groups.google.com/group/json-schema/web/service-mapping-description-proposal] for providing service metadata to service consumers.

JSON-RPC is a lightweight Remote Procedure Call protocol that utilizes JSON for its messaging envelopes. This JSON-RPC implementation follows PHP's SoapServer [http://us.php.net/manual/en/function.soap-soapserver-construct.php] API. This means that in a typical situation, you will simply:

• Instantiate the server object

• Attach one or more functions and/or classes/objects to the server object

• handle() the request

Zend_Json_Server utilizes the section called "Zend_Server_Reflection" to perform reflection on any attached classes or functions, and uses that information to build both the SMD and enforce method call signatures. As such, it is imperative that any attached functions and/or class methods have full PHP docblocks documenting, minimally:

• All parameters and their expected variable types

• The return value variable type

Zend_Json_Server listens for POST requests only at this time; fortunately, most JSON-RPC client implementations in the wild at the time of this writing will only POST requests as it is. This makes it simple to utilize the same server end point to both handle requests as well as to deliver the service SMD, as is shown in the next example.

Example 2.1. Zend_Json_Server Usage

First, let's define a class we wish to expose via the JSON-RPC server. We'll call the class 'Calculator', and define methods for 'add', 'subtract', 'multiply', and 'divide':

```
/**
 * Calculator - sample class to expose via JSON-RPC
 */
class Calculator
{
    /**
     * Return sum of two variables
     *
     * @param  int $x
     * @param  int $y
     * @return int
     */
    public function add($x, $y)
    {
        return $x + $y;
    }

    /**
     * Return difference of two variables
     *
     * @param  int $x
     * @param  int $y
     * @return int
     */
    public function subtract($x, $y)
    {
        return $x - $y;
    }

    /**
     * Return product of two variables
     *
     * @param  int $x
     * @param  int $y
     * @return int
     */
    public function multiply($x, $y)
    {
        return $x * $y;
    }

    /**
     * Return the division of two variables
     *
     * @param  int $x
     * @param  int $y
     * @return float
     */
    public function divide($x, $y)
    {
        return $x / $y;
    }
}
```

Note that each method has a docblock with entries indicating each parameter and its type, as well as an entry for the return value. This is *absolutely critical* when utilizing Zend_Json_Server -- or any other server component in Zend Framework, for that matter.

Now we'll create a script to handle the requests:

```
$server = new Zend_Json_Server();

// Indicate what functionality is available:
```

```
$server->setClass('Calculator');

// Handle the request:
$server->handle();
```

However, this will not address the issue of returning an SMD so that the JSON-RPC client can autodiscover methods. That can be accomplished by determining the HTTP request method, and then specifying some server metadata:

```
$server = new Zend_Json_Server();
$server->setClass('Calculator');

if ('GET' == $_SERVER['REQUEST_METHOD']) {
    // Indicate the URL endpoint, and the JSON-RPC version used:
    $server->setTarget('/json-rpc.php')
            ->setEnvelope(Zend_Json_Server_Smd::ENV_JSONRPC_2);

    // Grab the SMD
    $smd = $server->getServiceMap();

    // Return the SMD to the client
    header('Content-Type: application/json');
    echo $smd;
    return;
}

$server->handle();
```

If utilizing the JSON-RPC server with Dojo toolkit, you will also need to set a special compatibility flag to ensure that the two interoperate properly:

```
$server = new Zend_Json_Server();
$server->setClass('Calculator');

if ('GET' == $_SERVER['REQUEST_METHOD']) {
    $server->setTarget('/json-rpc.php')
            ->setEnvelope(Zend_Json_Server_Smd::ENV_JSONRPC_2);
    $smd = $server->getServiceMap();

    // Set Dojo compatibility:
    $smd->setDojoCompatible(true);

    header('Content-Type: application/json');
    echo $smd;
    return;
}

$server->handle();
```

Advanced Details

While most functionality for Zend_Json_Server is spelled out in Example 2.1, "Zend_Json_Server Usage", more advanced functionality is available.

Zend_Json_Server

Zend_Json_Server is the core class in the JSON-RPC offering; it handles all requests and returns the response payload. It has the following methods:

- `addFunction($function)`: Specify a userland function to attach to the server.

- `setClass($class)`: Specify a class or object to attach to the server; all public methods of that item will be exposed as JSON-RPC methods.

- `fault($fault = null, $code = 404, $data = null)`: Create and return a `Zend_Json_Server_Error` object.

- `handle($request = false)`: Handle a JSON-RPC request; optionally, pass a `Zend_Json_Server_Request` object to utilize (creates one by default).

- `getFunctions()`: Return a list of all attached methods.

- `setRequest(Zend_Json_Server_Request $request)`: Specify a request object for the server to utilize.

- `getRequest()`: Retrieve the request object used by the server.

- `setResponse(Zend_Json_Server_Response $response)`: Set the response object for the server to utilize.

- `getResponse()`: Retrieve the response object used by the server.

- `setAutoEmitResponse($flag)`: Indicate whether the server should automatically emit the response and all headers; by default, this is true.

- `autoEmitResponse()`: Determine if auto-emission of the response is enabled.

- `getServiceMap()`: Retrieve the service map description in the form of a `Zend_Json_Server_Smd` object

Zend_Json_Server_Request

The JSON-RPC request environment is encapsulated in the `Zend_Json_Server_Request` object. This object allows you to set necessary portions of the JSON-RPC request, including the request ID, parameters, and JSON-RPC specification version. It has the ability to load itself via JSON or a set of options, and can render itself as JSON via the `toJson()` method.

The request object has the following methods available:

- `setOptions(array $options)`: Specify object configuration. `$options` may contain keys matching any 'set' method: `setParams()`, `setMethod()`, `setId()`, and `setVersion()`.

- `addParam($value, $key = null)`: Add a parameter to use with the method call. Parameters can be just the values, or can optionally include the parameter name.

- `addParams(array $params)`: Add multiple parameters at once; proxies to `addParam()`

- `setParams(array $params)`: Set all parameters at once; overwrites any existing parameters.

- `getParam($index)`: Retrieve a parameter by position or name.

- `getParams()`: Retrieve all parameters at once.

- `setMethod($name)`: Set the method to call.

- `getMethod()`: Retrieve the method that will be called.

- `isMethodError()`: Determine whether or not the request is malformed and would result in an error.

- `setId($name)`: Set the request identifier (used by the client to match requests to responses).

- `getId()`: Retrieve the request identifier.

- `setVersion($version)`: Set the JSON-RPC specification version the request conforms to. May be either '1.0' or '2.0'.

- `getVersion()`: Retrieve the JSON-RPC specification version used by the request.

- `loadJson($json)`: Load the request object from a JSON string.

- `toJson()`: Render the request as a JSON string.

An HTTP specific version is available via `Zend_Json_Server_Request_Http`. This class will retrieve the request via `php://input`, and allows access to the raw JSON via the `getRawJson()` method.

Zend_Json_Server_Response

The JSON-RPC response payload is encapsulated in the `Zend_Json_Server_Response` object. This object allows you to set the return value of the request, whether or not the response is an error, the request identifier, the JSON-RPC specification version the response conforms to, and optionally the service map.

The response object has the following methods available:

- `setResult($value)`: Set the response result.

- `getResult()`: Retrieve the response result.

- `setError(Zend_Json_Server_Error $error)`: Set an error object. If set, this will be used as the response when serializing to JSON.

- `getError()`: Retrieve the error object, if any.

- `isError()`: Whether or not the response is an error response.

- `setId($name)`: Set the request identifier (so the client may match the response with the original request).

- `getId()`: Retrieve the request identifier.

- `setVersion($version)`: Set the JSON-RPC version the response conforms to.

- `getVersion()`: Retrieve the JSON-RPC version the response conforms to.

- `toJson()`: Serialize the response to JSON. If the response is an error response, serializes the error object.

- `setServiceMap($serviceMap)`: Set the service map object for the response.

- `getServiceMap()`: Retrieve the service map object, if any.

An HTTP specific version is available via `Zend_Json_Server_Response_Http`. This class will send the appropriate HTTP headers as well as serialize the response as JSON.

Zend_Json_Server_Error

JSON-RPC has a special format for reporting error conditions. All errors need to provide, minimally, an error message and error code; optionally, they can provide additional data, such as a backtrace.

Error codes are derived from those recommended by the XML-RPC EPI project [http://xmlrpc-epi.sourceforge.net/specs/rfc.fault_codes.php]. `Zend_Json_Server` appropriately assigns the code based on the error condition. For application exceptions, the code '-32000' is used.

`Zend_Json_Server_Error` exposes the following methods:

- `setCode($code)`: Set the error code; if the code is not in the accepted XML-RPC error code range, -32000 will be assigned.

- `getCode()`: Retrieve the current error code.

- `setMessage($message)`: Set the error message.

- `getMessage()`: Retrieve the current error message.

- `setData($data)`: Set auxiliary data further qualifying the error, such as a backtrace.

- `getData()`: Retrieve any current auxiliary error data.

- `toArray()`: Cast the error to an array. The array will contain the keys 'code', 'message', and 'data'.

- `toJson()`: Cast the error to a JSON-RPC error representation.

Zend_Json_Server_Smd

SMD stands for Service Mapping Description, a JSON schema that defines how a client can interact with a particular web service. At the time of this writing, the specification [http://groups.google.com/group/json-schema/web/service-mapping-description-proposal] has not yet been formally ratified, but it is in use already within Dojo toolkit as well as other JSON-RPC consumer clients.

At its most basic, a Service Mapping Description indicates the method of transport (POST, GET, TCP/IP, etc), the request envelope type (usually based on the protocol of the server), the target URL of the service provider, and a map of services available. In the case of JSON-RPC, the service map is a list of available methods, which each method documenting the available parameters and their types, as well as the expected return value type.

`Zend_Json_Server_Smd` provides an object oriented way to build service maps. At its most basic, you pass it metadata describing the service using mutators, and specify services (methods and functions).

The service descriptions themselves are typically instances of `Zend_Json_Server_Smd_Service`; you can also pass all information as an array to the various service mutators in `Zend_Json_Server_Smd`, and it will instantiate a service object for you. The service objects contain information such as the name of the service (typically the function or method name), the parameters (names, types, and position), and the return value type. Optionally, each service can have its own target and envelope, though this functionality is rarely used.

`Zend_Json_Server` actually does all of this behind the scenes for you, by using reflection on the attached classes and functions; you should create your own service maps only if you need to provide custom functionality that class and function introspection cannot offer.

Methods available in `Zend_Json_Server_Smd` include:

- `setOptions(array $options)`: Setup an SMD object from an array of options. All mutators (methods beginning with 'set') can be used as keys.

- `setTransport($transport)`: Set the transport used to access the service; only POST is currently supported.

- `getTransport()`: Get the current service transport.

- `setEnvelope($envelopeType)`: Set the request envelope that should be used to access the service. Currently, supports the constants `Zend_Json_Server_Smd::ENV_JSONRPC_1` and `Zend_Json_Server_Smd::ENV_JSONRPC_1`.

- `getEnvelope()`: Get the current request envelope.

- `setContentType($type)`: Set the content type requests should use (by default, this is 'application/json').

- `getContentType()`: Get the current content type for requests to the service.

- `setTarget($target)`: Set the URL endpoint for the service.

- `getTarget()`: Get the URL endpoint for the service.

- `setId($id)`: Typically, this is the URL endpoint of the service (same as the target).

- `getId()`: Retrieve the service ID (typically the URL endpoint of the service).

- `setDescription($description)`: Set a service description (typically narrative information describing the purpose of the service).

- `getDescription()`: Get the service description.

- `setDojoCompatible($flag)`: Set a flag indicating whether or not the SMD is compatible with Dojo toolkit. When true, the generated JSON SMD will be formatted to comply with the format that Dojo's JSON-RPC client expects.

- `isDojoCompatible()`: Returns the value of the Dojo compatibility flag (false, by default).

- `addService($service)`: Add a service to the map. May be an array of information to pass to the constructor of `Zend_Json_Server_Smd_Service`, or an instance of that class.

- `addServices(array $services)`: Add multiple services at once.

- `setServices(array $services)`: Add multiple services at once, overwriting any previously set services.

- `getService($name)`: Get a service by its name.

- `getServices()`: Get all attached services.

- `removeService($name)`: Remove a service from the map.

- `toArray()`: Cast the service map to an array.

- `toDojoArray()`: Cast the service map to an array compatible with Dojo Toolkit.

- `toJson()`: Cast the service map to a JSON representation.

`Zend_Json_Server_Smd_Service` has the following methods:

- `setOptions(array $options)`: Set object state from an array. Any mutator (methods beginning with 'set') may be used as a key and set via this method.

- `setName($name)`: Set the service name (typically, the function or method name).

- `getName()`: Retrieve the service name.

- `setTransport($transport)`: Set the service transport (currently, only transports supported by `Zend_Json_Server_Smd` are allowed).

- `getTransport()`: Retrieve the current transport.

- `setTarget($target)`: Set the URL endpoint of the service (typically, this will be the same as the overall SMD to which the service is attached).

- `getTarget()`: Get the URL endpoint of the service.

- `setEnvelope($envelopeType)`: Set the service envelope (currently, only envelopes supported by `Zend_Json_Server_Smd` are allowed).

- `getEnvelope()`: Retrieve the service envelope type.

- `addParam($type, array $options = array(), $order = null)`: Add a parameter to the service. By default, only the parameter type is necessary. However, you may also specify the order, as well as options such as:

  - *name*: the parameter name

  - *optional*: whether or not the parameter is optional

  - *default*: a default value for the parameter

  - *description*: text describing the parameter

- `addParams(array $params)`: Add several parameters at once; each param should be an assoc array containing minimally the key 'type' describing the parameter type, and optionally the key 'order'; any other keys will be passed as `$options` to `addOption()`.

- `setParams(array $params)`: Set many parameters at once, overwriting any existing parameters.

- `getParams()`: Retrieve all currently set parameters.

- `setReturn($type)`: Set the return value type of the service.

- `getReturn()`: Get the return value type of the service.

- `toArray()`: Cast the service to an array.

- `toJson()`: Cast the service to a JSON representation.

Chapter 3. Zend_Layout

Introduction

Zend_Layout implements a classic Two Step View pattern, allowing developers to wrap application content within another view, usually representing the site template. Such templates are often termed *layouts* by other projects, and Zend Framework has adopted this term for consistency.

The main goals of Zend_Layout are as follows:

- Automate selection and rendering of layouts when used with the Zend Framework MVC components.

- Provide separate scope for layout related variables and content.

- Allow configuration, including layout name, layout script resolution (inflection), and layout script path.

- Allow disabling layouts, changing layout scripts, and other states; allow these actions from within action controllers and view scripts.

- Follow same script resolution rules (inflection) as the ViewRenderer, but allow them to also use different rules.

- Allow usage without Zend Framework MVC components.

Zend_Layout Quick Start

There are two primary use cases for Zend_Layout: with the Zend Framework MVC, and without.

Layout scripts

In both cases, however, you'll need to create a layout script. Layout scripts simply utilize Zend_View (or whatever view implementation you are using). Layout variables are registered with a Zend_Layout placeholder, and may be accessed via the placeholder helper or by fetching them as object properties of the layout object via the layout helper.

As an example:

```
<!DOCTYPE html
    PUBLIC "-//W3C//DTD XHTML 1.0 Transitional//EN"
    "http://www.w3.org/TR/xhtml1/DTD/xhtml1-transitional.dtd">
<html>
<head>
    <meta http-equiv="Content-Type" content="text/html; charset=utf-8" />
    <title>My Site</title>
</head>
<body>
<?php
    // fetch 'content' key using layout helper:
    echo $this->layout()->content;

    // fetch 'foo' key using placeholder helper:
    echo $this->placeholder('Zend_Layout')->foo;

    // fetch layout object and retrieve various keys from it:
    $layout = $this->layout();
    echo $layout->bar;
```

```
    echo $layout->baz;
?>
</body>
</html>
```

Because `Zend_Layout` utilizes `Zend_View` for rendering, you can also use any view helpers registered, and also have access to any previously assigned view variables. Particularly useful are the various placeholder helpers, as they allow you to retrieve content for areas such as the <head> section, navigation, etc.:

```
<!DOCTYPE html
    PUBLIC "-//W3C//DTD XHTML 1.0 Transitional//EN"
    "http://www.w3.org/TR/xhtml1/DTD/xhtml1-transitional.dtd">
<html>
<head>
    <meta http-equiv="Content-Type" content="text/html; charset=utf-8" />
    <?php echo $this->headTitle() ?>
    <?php echo $this->headScript() ?>
    <?php echo $this->headStyle() ?>
</head>
<body>
    <?php echo $this->render('header.phtml') ?>

    <div id="nav"><?php echo $this->placeholder('nav') ?></div>

    <div id="content"><?php echo $this->layout()->content ?></div>

    <?php echo $this->render('footer.phtml') ?>
</body>
</html>
```

Using Zend_Layout with the Zend Framework MVC

`Zend_Controller` offers a rich set of functionality for extension via its front controller plugins and action controller helpers. `Zend_View` also has helpers. `Zend_Layout` takes advantage of these various extension points when used with the MVC components.

`Zend_Layout::startMvc()` creates an instance of `Zend_Layout` with any optional configuration you provide it. It then registers a front controller plugin that renders the layout with any application content once the dispatch loop is done, and registers an action helper to allow access to the layout object from your action controllers. Additionally, you may at any time grab the layout instance from within a view script using the `layout` view helper.

First, let's look at how to initialize Zend_Layout for use with the MVC:

```
// In your bootstrap:
Zend_Layout::startMvc();
```

`startMvc()` can take an optional array of options or `Zend_Config` object to customize the instance; these options are detailed in the section called "Zend_Layout Configuration Options".

In an action controller, you may then access the layout instance as an action helper:

```
class FooController extends Zend_Controller_Action
{
    public function barAction()
    {
        // disable layouts for this action:
        $this->_helper->layout->disableLayout();
```

```
    }

    public function bazAction()
    {
        // use different layout script with this action:
        $this->_helper->layout->setLayout('foobaz');
    };
}
```

In your view scripts, you can then access the layout object via the `layout` view helper. This view helper is slightly different than others in that it takes no arguments, and returns an object instead of a string value. This allows you to immediately call methods on the layout object:

```
<?php $this->layout()->setLayout('foo'); // set alternate layout ?>
```

At any time, you can fetch the `Zend_Layout` instance registered with the MVC via the `getMvcInstance()` static method:

```
// Returns null if startMvc() has not first been called
$layout = Zend_Layout::getMvcInstance();
```

Finally, `Zend_Layout`'s front controller plugin has one important feature in addition to rendering the layout: it retrieves all named segments from the response object and assigns them as layout variables, assigning the 'default' segment to the variable 'content'. This allows you to access your application content and render it in your view scripts.

As an example, let's say your code first hits `FooController::indexAction()`, which renders some content to the default response segment, and then forwards to `NavController::menuAction()`, which renders content to the 'nav' response segment. Finally, you forward to `CommentController::fetchAction()` and fetch some comments, but render those to the default response segment as well (which appends content to that segment). Your view script could then render each separately:

```
<body>
    <!-- renders /nav/menu -->
    <div id="nav"><?php echo $this->layout()->nav ?></div>

    <!-- renders /foo/index + /comment/fetch -->
    <div id="content"><?php echo $this->layout()->content ?></div>
</body>
```

This feature is particularly useful when used in conjunction with the ActionStack action helper and plugin, which you can use to setup a stack of actions through which to loop, and thus create widgetized pages.

Using Zend_Layout as a Standalone Component

As a standalone component, Zend_Layout does not offer nearly as many features or as much convenience as when used with the MVC. However, it still has two chief benefits:

- Scoping of layout variables.

- Isolation of layout view script from other view scripts.

When used as a standalone component, simply instantiate the layout object, use the various accessors to set state, set variables as object properties, and render the layout:

```
$layout = new Zend_Layout();

// Set a layout script path:
$layout->setLayoutPath('/path/to/layouts');

// set some variables:
$layout->content = $content;
$layout->nav     = $nav;

// choose a different layout script:
$layout->setLayout('foo');

// render final layout
echo $layout->render();
```

Sample Layout

Sometimes a picture is worth a thousand words. The following is a sample layout script showing how it might all come together.

```
<?= $this->docType('XHTML1_STRICT') ?>
<html>
  <head>
    <?= $this->headTitle() ?>
    <?= $this->headScript() ?>
    <?= $this->headStylesheet() ?>
  </head>
  <body>
```

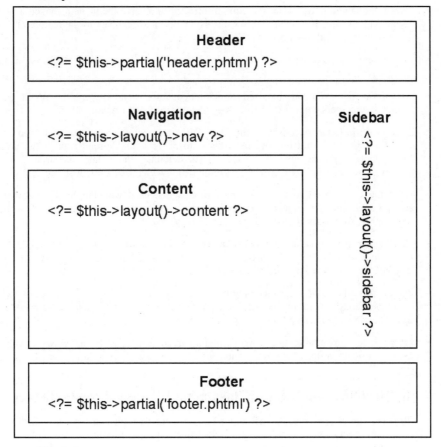

```
  </body>
</html>
```

The actual order of elements may vary, depending on the CSS you've setup; for instance, if you're using absolute positioning, you may be able to have the navigation displayed later in the document, but still show up at the top; the same could be said for the sidebar or header. The actual mechanics of pulling the content remain the same, however.

Zend_Layout Configuration Options

Zend_Layout has a variety of configuration options. These may be set by calling the appropriate accessors, passing an array or Zend_Config object to the constructor or startMvc(), passing an array of options to setOptions(), or passing a Zend_Config object to setConfig().

- *layout*: the layout to use. Uses the current inflector to resolve the name provided to the appropriate layout view script. By default, this value is 'layout' and resolves to 'layout.phtml'. Accessors are setLayout() and getLayout().

- *layoutPath*: the base path to layout view scripts. Accessors are setLayoutPath() and getLayoutPath().

- *contentKey*: the layout variable used for default content (when used with the MVC). Default value is 'content'. Accessors are setContentKey() and getContentKey().

- *mvcSuccessfulActionOnly*: when using the MVC, if an action throws an exception and this flag is true, the layout will not be rendered (this is to prevent double-rendering of the layout when the ErrorHandler plugin is in use). By default, the flat is true. Accessors are setMvcSuccessfulActionOnly() and getMvcSuccessfulActionOnly().

- *view*: the view object to use when rendering. When used with the MVC, Zend_Layout will attempt to use the view object registered with the ViewRenderer if no view object has been passed to it explicitly. Accessors are setView() and getView().

- *helperClass*: the action helper class to use when using Zend_Layout with the MVC components. By default, this is Zend_Layout_Controller_Action_Helper_Layout. Accessors are setHelperClass() and getHelperClass().

- *pluginClass*: the front controller plugin class to use when using Zend_Layout with the MVC components. By default, this is Zend_Layout_Controller_Plugin_Layout. Accessors are setPluginClass() and getPluginClass().

- *inflector*: the inflector to use when resolving layout names to layout view script paths; see the Zend_Layout inflector documentation for more details. Accessors are setInflector() and getInflector().

helperClass and pluginClass must be passed to startMvc()

In order for the helperClass and pluginClass settings to have effect, they must be passed in as options to startMvc(); if set later, they have no affect.

Examples

The following examples assume the following $options array and $config object:

```
$options = array(
    'layout'     => 'foo',
    'layoutPath' => '/path/to/layouts',
    'contentKey' => 'CONTENT',              // ignored when MVC not used
);


/**
```

```
[layout]
layout = "foo"
layoutPath = "/path/to/layouts"
contentKey = "CONTENT"
*/
$config = new Zend_Config_Ini('/path/to/layout.ini', 'layout');
```

Example 3.1. Passing options to the constructor or startMvc()

Both the constructor and the `startMvc()` static method can accept either an array of options or a `Zend_Config` object with options in order to configure the `Zend_Layout` instance.

First, let's look at passing an array:

```
// Using constructor:
$layout = new Zend_Layout($options);

// Using startMvc():
$layout = Zend_Layout::startMvc($options);
```

And now using a config object:

```
$config = new Zend_Config_Ini('/path/to/layout.ini', 'layout');

// Using constructor:
$layout = new Zend_Layout($config);

// Using startMvc():
$layout = Zend_Layout::startMvc($config);
```

Basically, this is the easiest way to customize your `Zend_Layout` instance.

Example 3.2. Using setOption() and setConfig()

Sometimes you need to configure the `Zend_Layout` object after it has already been instantiated; `setOptions()` and `setConfig()` give you a quick and easy way to do so:

```
// Using an array of options:
$layout->setOptions($options);

// Using a Zend_Config object:
$layout->setConfig($options);
```

Note, however, that certain options, such as `pluginClass` and `helperClass`, will have no affect when passed using this method; they need to be passed to the constructor or `startMvc()` method.

Example 3.3. Using Accessors

Finally, you can also configure your `Zend_Layout` instance via accessors. All accessors implement a fluent interface, meaning their calls may be chained:

```
$layout->setLayout('foo')
        ->setLayoutPath('/path/to/layouts')
        ->setContentKey('CONTENT');
```

Zend_Layout Advanced Usage

Zend_Layout has a number of use cases for the advanced developer who wishes to adapt it for different view implementations, file system layouts, and more.

The major points of extension are:

- *Custom view objects.* Zend_Layout allows you to utilize any class that implements Zend_View_Interface.

- *Custom front controller plugins.* Zend_Layout ships with a standard front controller plugin that automates rendering of layouts prior to returning the response. You can substitute your own plugin.

- *Custom action helpers.* Zend_Layout ships with a standard action helper that should be suitable for most needs as it is a dumb proxy to the layout object itself.

- *Custom layout script path resolution.* Zend_Layout allows you to use your own inflector for layout script path resolution, or simply to modify the attached inflector to specify your own inflection rules.

Custom View Objects

Zend_Layout allows you to use any class implementing Zend_View_Interface or extending Zend_View_Abstract for rendering your layout script. Simply pass in your custom view object as a parameter to the constructor/startMvc(), or set it using the setView() accessor:

```
$view = new My_Custom_View();
$layout->setView($view);
```

Not all Zend_View implementations are equal

While Zend_Layout allows you to use any class implementing Zend_View_Interface, you may run into issues if they can not utilize the various Zend_View helpers, particularly the layout and placeholder helpers. This is because Zend_Layout makes variables set in the object available via itself and placeholders.

If you need to use a custom Zend_View implementation that does not support these helpers, you will need to find a way to get the layout variables to the view. This can be done by either extending the Zend_Layout object and altering the render() method to pass variables to the view, or creating your own plugin class that passes them prior to rendering the layout.

Alternately, if your view implementation supports any sort of plugin capability, you can access the variables via the 'Zend_Layout' placeholder, using the placeholder helper:

```
$placeholders = new Zend_View_Helper_Placeholder();
$layoutVars   = $placeholders->placeholder('Zend_Layout')->getArrayCopy();
```

Custom Front Controller Plugins

When used with the MVC components, Zend_Layout registers a front controller plugin that renders the layout as the last action prior to exiting the dispatch loop. In most cases, the default plugin will be suitable, but should you desire to write your own, you can specify the name of the plugin class to load by passing the `pluginClass` option to the `startMvc()` method.

Any plugin class you write for this purpose will need to extend `Zend_Controller_Plugin_Abstract`, and should accept a layout object instance as an argument to the constructor. Otherwise, the details of your implementation are up to you.

The default plugin class used is `Zend_Layout_Controller_Plugin_Layout`.

Custom Action Helpers

When used with the MVC components, `Zend_Layout` registers an action controller helper with the helper broker. The default helper, `Zend_Layout_Controller_Action_Helper_Layout`, acts as a dumb proxy to the layout object instance itself, and should be suitable for most use cases.

Should you feel the need to write custom functionality, simply write an action helper class extending `Zend_Controller_Action_Helper_Abstract` and pass the class name as the `helperClass` option to the `startMvc()` method. Details of the implementation are up to you.

Custom Layout Script Path Resolution: Using the Inflector

`Zend_Layout` uses `Zend_Filter_Inflector` to establish a filter chain for translating a layout name to a layout script path. By default, it uses the rules 'Word_CamelCaseToDash' followed by 'StringToLower', and the suffix 'phtml' to transform the name to a path. As some examples:

- 'foo' will be transformed to 'foo.phtml'.

- 'FooBarBaz' will be transformed to 'foo-bar-baz.phtml'.

You have three options for modifying inflection: modify the inflection target and/or view suffix via `Zend_Layout` accessors, modify the inflector rules and target of the inflector associated with the `Zend_Layout` instance, or create your own inflector instance and pass it to `Zend_Layout::setInflector()`.

Example 3.4. Using Zend_Layout accessors to modify the inflector

The default `Zend_Layout` inflector uses static references for the target and view script suffix, and has accessors for setting these values.

```
// Set the inflector target:
$layout->setInflectorTarget('layouts/:script.:suffix');

// Set the layout view script suffix:
$layout->setViewSuffix('php');
```

Example 3.5. Direct modification of Zend_Layout inflector

Inflectors have a target and one or more rules. The default target used with `Zend_Layout` is ':script.:suffix'; ':script' is passed the registered layout name, while ':suffix' is a static rule of the inflector.

Let's say you want the layout script to end in the suffix 'html', and that you want to separate MixedCase and camelCased words with underscores instead of dashes, and not lowercase the name. Additionally, you want it to look in a 'layouts' subdirectory for the script.

```
$layout->getInflector()->setTarget('layouts/:script.:suffix')
                        ->setStaticRule('suffix', 'html')
                        ->setFilterRule(array('Word_CamelCaseToUnderscore'));
```

Example 3.6. Custom inflectors

In most cases, modifying the existing inflector will be enough. However, you may have an inflector you wish to use in several places, with different objects of different types. Zend_Layout supports this.

```
$inflector = new Zend_Filter_Inflector('layouts/:script.:suffix');
$inflector->addRules(array(
    ':script' => array('Word_CamelCaseToUnderscore'),
    'suffix'  => 'html'
));
$layout->setInflector($inflector);
```

Inflection can be disabled

Inflection can be disabled and enabled using accessors on the Zend_Layout object. This can be useful if you want to specify an absolute path for a layout view script, or know that the mechanism you will be using for specifying the layout script does not need inflection. Simply use the enableInflection() and disableInflection() methods.

Chapter 4. Zend_Ldap

Introduction

Minimal Functionality

Currently this class is designed only to satisfy the limited functionality necessary for the `Zend_Auth_Adapter_Ldap` authentication adapter. Operations such as searching, creating, modifying or renaming entries in the directory are currently not supported and will be defined at a later time.

`Zend_Ldap` is a class for performing LDAP operations including but not limited to binding, searching and modifying entries in an LDAP directory.

Theory of Operation

This component currently consists of two classes, `Zend_Ldap` and `Zend_Ldap_Exception`. The `Zend_Ldap` class conceptually represents a binding to a single LDAP server. The parameters for binding may be provided explicitly or in the form of an options array.

Using the `Zend_Ldap` class depends on the type of LDAP server and is best summarized with some simple examples.

If you are using OpenLDAP, a simple example looks like the following (note that the `bindRequiresDn` option is important if you are *not* using AD):

```
$options = array(
    'host' => 's0.foo.net',
    'username' => 'CN=user1,DC=foo,DC=net',
    'password' => 'pass1',
    'bindRequiresDn' => true,
    'accountDomainName' => 'foo.net',
    'baseDn' => 'OU=Sales,DC=foo,DC=net',
);
$ldap = new Zend_Ldap($options);
$acctname = $ldap->getCanonicalAccountName('abaker',
                                           Zend_Ldap::ACCTNAME_FORM_DN);
echo "$acctname\n";
```

If you are using Microsoft AD a simple example is:

```
$options = array(
    'host' => 'dc1.w.net',
    'useStartTls' => true,
    'username' => 'user1@w.net',
    'password' => 'pass1',
    'accountDomainName' => 'w.net',
    'accountDomainNameShort' => 'W',
    'baseDn' => 'CN=Users,DC=w,DC=net',
);
$ldap = new Zend_Ldap($options);
$acctname = $ldap->getCanonicalAccountName('bcarter',
                                           Zend_Ldap::ACCTNAME_FORM_DN);
echo "$acctname\n";
```

Note that we use the `getCanonicalAccountName()` method to retrieve the account DN here only because that is what exercises the most of what little code is currently present in this class.

Automatic Username Canonicalization When Binding

If `bind()` is called with a non-DN username but `bindRequiresDN` is `true` and no username in DN form was supplied as an option, the bind will fail. However, if a username in DN form is supplied in the options array, `Zend_Ldap` will first bind with that username, retrieve the account DN for the username supplied to `bind()` and then re- bind with that DN.

This behavior is critical to `Zend_Auth_Adapter_Ldap`, which passes the username supplied by the user directly to `bind()`.

The following example illustrates how the non-DN username `'abaker'` can be used with `bind()`:

```
$options = array(
        'host' => 's0.foo.net',
        'username' => 'CN=user1,DC=foo,DC=net',
        'password' => 'pass1',
        'bindRequiresDn' => true,
        'accountDomainName' => 'foo.net',
        'baseDn' => 'OU=Sales,DC=foo,DC=net',
);
$ldap = new Zend_Ldap($options);
$ldap->bind('abaker', 'moonbike55');
$acctname = $ldap->getCanonicalAccountName('abaker',
                                        Zend_Ldap::ACCTNAME_FORM_DN);
echo "$acctname\n";
```

The `bind()` call in this example sees that the username `'abaker'` is not in DN form, finds `bindRequiresDn` is `true`, uses `'CN=user1,DC=foo,DC=net'` and `'pass1'` to bind, retrieves the DN for `'abaker'`, unbinds and then rebinds with the newly discovered `'CN=Alice Baker,OU=Sales,DC=foo,DC=net'`.

Zend_Ldap Options

The `Zend_Ldap` component accepts an array of options either supplied to the constructor or through the `setOptions()` method. The permitted options are as follows:

Table 4.1. Zend_Ldap Options

Name	Description
host	The default hostname of LDAP server if not supplied to `connect()` (also may be used when trying to canonicalize usernames in `bind()`).
port	Default port of LDAP server if not supplied to `connect()`.
useStartTls	Whether or not the LDAP client should use TLS (aka SSLv2) encrypted transport. A value of `true` is strongly favored in production environments to prevent passwords from be transmitted in clear text. The default value is `false`, as servers frequently require that a certificate be installed separately after installation. The `useSsl` and `useStartTls` options are mutually exclusive. The `useStartTls` option should be favored over `useSsl` but not all servers support this newer mechanism.
useSsl	Whether or not the LDAP client should use SSL encrypted transport. The `useSsl` and

Name	Description
	useStartTls options are mutually exclusive.
username	The default credentials username. Some servers require that this be in DN form.
password	The default credentials password (used only with username above).
bindRequiresDn	If true, this instructs Zend_Ldap to retrieve the DN for the account used to bind if the username is not already in DN form. The default value is false.
baseDn	The default base DN used for searching (e.g., for accounts). This option is required for most account related operations and should indicate the DN under which accounts are located.
accountCanonicalForm	A small integer indicating the form to which account names should be canonicalized. See the *Account Name Canonicalization* section below.
accountDomainName	The FQDN domain for which the target LDAP server is an authority (e.g., example.com).
accountDomainNameShort	The 'short' domain for which the target LDAP server is an authority. This is usually used to specify the NetBIOS domain name for Windows networks but may also be used by non-AD servers.
accountFilterFormat	The LDAP search filter used to search for accounts. This string is a printf() [http://php.net/printf] style expression that must contain one '%s' to accommodate the username. The default value is '(&(objectClass =user)(sAMAccount Name=%s))' unless bindRequiresDn is set to true, in which case the default is '(&(objectClass=posix Account)(uid=%s))'. Users of custom schemas may need to change this option.
allowEmptyPassword	Some LDAP servers can be configured to accept an empty string password as an anonymous bind. This behavior is almost always undesirable. For this reason, empty passwords are explicitly disallowed. Set this value to true to allow an empty string password to be submitted during the bind.
optReferrals	If set to true, this option indicates to the LDAP client that referrals should be followed. The default value is false.

Account Name Canonicalization

The accountDomainName and accountDomainNameShort options are used for two purposes: (1) they facilitate multi-domain authentication and failover capability, and (2) they are also used to canonicalize usernames. Specifically, names are canonicalized to the form specified by the accountCanonicalForm option. This option may one of the following values:

Table 4.2. accountCanonicalForm

Name	Value	Example
ACCTNAME_FORM_DN	1	CN=Alice Baker,CN=Users,DC=example, DC=com
ACCTNAME_FORM_USERNAME	2	abaker
ACCTNAME_FORM_BACKSLASH	3	EXAMPLE\abaker
ACCTNAME_FORM_PRINCIPAL	4	abaker@example.com

The default canonicalization depends on what account domain name options were supplied. If `accountDomainNameShort` was supplied, the default `accountCanonicalForm` value is `ACCTNAME_FORM_BACKSLASH`. Otherwise, if `accountDomainName` was supplied, the default is `ACCTNAME_FORM_PRINCIPAL`.

Account name canonicalization ensures that the string used to identify an account is consistent regardless of what was supplied to `bind()`. For example, if the user supplies an account name of *abaker@example.com* or just *abaker* and the `accountCanonicalForm` is set to 3, the resulting canonicalized name would be *EXAMPLE\abaker*.

Multi-domain Authentication and Failover

The `Zend_Ldap` component by itself makes no attempt to authenticate with multiple servers. However, `Zend_Ldap` is specifically designed to handle this scenario gracefully. The required technique is to simply iterate over an array of arrays of server options and attempt to bind with each server. As described above `bind()` will automatically canonicalize each name, so it does not matter if the user passes `abaker@foo.net` or `W\bcarter` or `cdavis` - the `bind()` method will only succeed if the credentials were successfully used in the bind.

Consider the following example that illustrates the technique required to implement multi-domain authentication and failover:

```
$acctname = 'W\\user2';
$password = 'pass2';

$multiOptions = array(
    'server1' => array(
        'host' => 's0.foo.net',
        'username' => 'CN=user1,DC=foo,DC=net',
        'password' => 'pass1',
        'bindRequiresDn' => true,
        'accountDomainName' => 'foo.net',
        'accountDomainNameShort' => 'FOO',
        'accountCanonicalForm' => 4, // ACCT_FORM_PRINCIPAL
        'baseDn' => 'OU=Sales,DC=foo,DC=net',
    ),
    'server2' => array(
        'host' => 'dc1.w.net',
        'useSsl' => true,
        'username' => 'user1@w.net',
        'password' => 'pass1',
        'accountDomainName' => 'w.net',
        'accountDomainNameShort' => 'W',
        'accountCanonicalForm' => 4, // ACCT_FORM_PRINCIPAL
        'baseDn' => 'CN=Users,DC=w,DC=net',
    ),
);
```

```
$ldap = new Zend_Ldap();

foreach ($multiOptions as $name => $options) {

    echo "Trying to bind using server options for '$name'\n";

    $ldap->setOptions($options);
    try {
        $ldap->bind($acctname, $password);
        $acctname = $ldap->getCanonicalAccountName($acctname);
        echo "SUCCESS: authenticated $acctname\n";
        return;
    } catch (Zend_Ldap_Exception $zle) {
        echo '  ' . $zle->getMessage() . "\n";
        if ($zle->getCode() === Zend_Ldap_Exception::LDAP_X_DOMAIN_MISMATCH) {
            continue;
        }
    }
}
```

If the bind fails for any reason, the next set of server options is tried.

The getCanonicalAccountName call gets the canonical account name that the application would presumably use to associate data with such as preferences. The accountCanonicalForm = 4 in all server options ensures that the canonical form is consistent regardless of which server was ultimately used.

The special LDAP_X_DOMAIN_MISMATCH exception occurs when an account name with a domain component was supplied (e.g., abaker@foo.net or FOO\abaker and not just abaker) but the domain component did not match either domain in the currently selected server options. This exception indicates that the server is not an authority for the account. In this case, the bind will not be performed, thereby eliminating unnecessary communication with the server. Note that the continue instruction has no effect in this example, but in practice for error handling and debugging purposes, you will probably want to check for LDAP_X_DOMAIN_MISMATCH as well as LDAP_NO_SUCH_OBJECT and LDAP_INVALID_CREDENTIALS.

The above code is very similar to code used within Zend_Auth_Adapter_Ldap. In fact, we recommend that you simply use that authentication adapter for multi-domain + failover LDAP based authentication (or copy the code).

Chapter 5. Zend_Loader

Loading Files and Classes Dynamically

The Zend_Loader class includes methods to help you load files dynamically.

Zend_Loader vs. require_once()

The Zend_Loader methods are best used if the filename you need to load is variable. For example, if it is based on a parameter from user input or method argument. If you are loading a file or a class whose name is constant, there is no benefit to using Zend_Loader over using traditional PHP functions such as require_once() [http://php.net/require_once].

Loading Files

The static method Zend_Loader::loadFile() loads a PHP file. The file loaded may contain any PHP code. The method is a wrapper for the PHP function include() [http://php.net/include]. This method returns boolean false on failure, for example if the specified file does not exist.

Example 5.1. Example of the loadFile() Method

```
Zend_Loader::loadFile($filename, $dirs=null, $once=false);
```

The $filename argument specifies the filename to load, which must not contain any path information. A security check is performed on $filename. The $filename may only contain alphanumeric characters, dashes ("-"), underscores ("_"), or periods ("."). No such restriction is placed on the $dirs argument.

The $dirs argument specifies which directories to search for the file in. If the value is NULL, only the include_path is searched; if the value is a string or an array, the directory or directories specified will be searched, followed by the include_path.

The $once argument is a boolean. If TRUE, Zend_Loader::loadFile() uses the PHP function include_once() [http://php.net/include] for loading the file, otherwise the PHP function include() [http://php.net/include_once] is used.

Loading Classes

The static method Zend_Loader::loadClass($class, $dirs) loads a PHP file and then checks for the existence of the class.

Example 5.2. Example of the loadClass() Method

```
Zend_Loader::loadClass('Container_Tree',
    array(
        '/home/production/mylib',
        '/home/production/myapp'
    )
);
```

The string specifying the class is converted to a relative path by substituting underscores with directory separators for your OS, and appending '.php'. In the example above, 'Container_Tree' becomes 'Container/Tree.php' on Windows.

If $dirs is a string or an array, Zend_Loader::loadClass() searches the directories in the order supplied. The first matching file is loaded. If the file does not exist in the specified $dirs, then the include_path for the PHP environment is searched.

If the file is not found or the class does not exist after the load, Zend_Loader::loadClass() throws a Zend_Exception.

Zend_Loader::loadFile() is used for loading, so the class name may only contain alphanumeric characters and the hyphen ('-'), underscore ('_'), and period ('.').

Testing if a File is Readable

The static method Zend_Loader::isReadable($pathname) returns TRUE if a file at the specified pathname exists and is readable, FALSE otherwise.

Example 5.3. Example of isReadable() method

```
if (Zend_Loader::isReadable($filename)) {
    // do something with $filename
}
```

The $filename argument specifies the filename to check. This may contain path information. This method is a wrapper for the PHP function is_readable() [http://php.net/is_readable]. The PHP function does not search the include_path, while Zend_Loader::isReadable() does.

Using the Autoloader

The Zend_Loader class contains a method you can register with the PHP SPL autoloader. Zend_Loader::autoload() is the callback method. As a convenience, Zend_Loader provides the registerAutoload() function to register its autoload() method. If the spl_autoload extension is not present in your PHP environment, then the registerAutoload() method throws a Zend_Exception.

Example 5.4. Example of registering the autoloader callback method

```
Zend_Loader::registerAutoload();
```

After registering the Zend Framework autoload callback, you can reference classes from Zend Framework without having to load them explicitly. The autoload() method uses Zend_Loader::loadClass() automatically when you reference a class.

If you have extended the Zend_Loader class, you can give an optional argument to registerAutoload(), to specify the class from which to register an autoload() method.

Example 5.5. Example of registering the autoload callback method from an extended class

Because of the semantics of static function references in PHP, you must implement code for both `loadClass()` and `autoload()`, and the `autoload()` must call `self::loadClass()`. If your `autoload()` method delegates to its parent to call `self::loadClass()`, then it calls the method of that name in the parent class, not the subclass.

```
class My_Loader extends Zend_Loader
{
    public static function loadClass($class, $dirs = null)
    {
        parent::loadClass($class, $dirs);
    }

    public static function autoload($class)
    {
        try {
            self::loadClass($class);
            return $class;
        } catch (Exception $e) {
            return false;
        }
    }
}

Zend_Loader::registerAutoload('My_Loader');
```

You can remove an autoload callback. The `registerAutoload()` has an optional second argument, which is `true` by default. If this argument is `false`, the autoload callback is unregistered from the SPL autoload stack.

The Autoloader

`Zend_Loader_Autoloader` introduces a comprehensive autoloading solution for Zend Framework. It has been designed with several goals in mind:

• Provide a true namespace autoloader. (Previous incarnations intercepted all userland namespaces.)

• Allow registering arbitrary callbacks as autoloaders, and manage them as a stack. (At the time of this writing, this overcomes some issues with `spl_autoload`, which does not allow re-registering a callback that utilizes an instance method.)

• Allow optimistic matching of namespaces to provide faster class resolution.

`Zend_Loader_Autoloader` implements a singleton, making it unversally accessible. This provides the ability to register additional autoloaders from anywhere in your code as necessary.

Using the Autoloader

The first time an instance of the autoloader is retrieved, it registers itself with `spl_autoload`. You retrieve an instance using the `getInstance()` method:

```
$autoloader = Zend_Loader_Autoloader::getInstance();
```

By default, the autoloader is configured to match the "Zend_" and "ZendX_" namespaces. If you have your own library code that uses your own namespace, you may register it with the autoloader using the `registerNamespace()` method. For instance, if your library code is prefixed with "My_", you could do so as follows:

```
$autoloader->registerNamespace('My_');
```

Namespace Prefixes

You'll note that the previous example uses "My_" and not "My". This is because `Zend_Loader_Autoloader` is intended as a general purpose autoloader, and does not make the assumption that a given class prefix namespace includes an underscore. If your class namespace *does* include one, you should include it when registering your namespace.

You can also register arbitrary autoloader callbacks, optionally with a specific namespace (or group of namespaces). `Zend_Loader_Autoloader` will attempt to match these first before using its internal autoloading mechanism.

As an example, you may want to utilize one or more eZcomponents components with your Zend Framework application. To use its autoloading capabilities, push it onto the autoloader stack using `pushAutoloader()`:

```
$autoloader->pushAutoloader(array('ezcBase', 'autoload'), 'ezc');
```

This tells the autoloader to use the eZcomponents autoloader for classes beginning with "ezc".

You can use the `unshiftAutoloader()` method to add the autoloader to the beginning of the autoloader chain.

By default, `Zend_Loader_Autoloader` does no error suppression when using its internal autoloader, which utilizes `Zend_Loader::loadClass()`. Most of the time, this is exactly what you want. However, there may be cases where you want to suppress them. You can do this using `suppressNotFoundWarnings()`:

```
$autoloader->suppressNotFoundWarnings(true);
```

Finally, there may be times when you want the autoloader to load any namespace. For instance, PEAR libraries do not share a common namespace, making specifying individual namespaces difficult when many PEAR components are in use. You can use the `setFallbackAutoloader()` method to have the autoloader act as a catch-all:

```
$autoloader->setFallbackAutoloader(true);
```

The Autoloader Interface

Besides being able to specify arbitrary callbacks as autoloaders, Zend Framework also defines an interface autoloading classes may imlement, `Zend_Loader_Autoloader_Interface`:

```
interface Zend_Loader_Autoloader_Interface
{
    public function autoload($class);
}
```

When using this interface, you can simply pass a class instance to `Zend_Loader_Autoloader`'s `pushAutoloader()` and `unshiftAutoloader()` methods:

```
// Assume Foo_Autoloader implements Zend_Loader_Autoloader_Interface:
$foo = new Foo_Autoloader();

$autoloader->pushAutoloader($foo, 'Foo_');
```

Autoloader Reference

Below, please find a guide to the methods available in `Zend_Loader_Autoloader`.

Table 5.1. Zend_Loader_Autoloader Methods

Method	Return Value	Parameters	Description
`getInstance()`	`Zend_Loader_Autoloader`	N/A	Retrieve the `Zend_Loader_Autoloader` singleton instance. On first retrieval, it registers itself with `spl_autoload`. This method is static.
`resetInstance()`	void	N/A	Resets the state of the `Zend_Loader_Autoloader` singleton instance to it's original state, unregistering all autoloader callbacks and all registered namespaces.
`autoload($class)`	`string|false`	• `$class`, *required*. A string class name to load.	Attempt to resolve a class name to a file and load it.
`setDefault Autoloader ($callback)`	`Zend_Loader_Autoloader`	• `$callback`, *required*.	Specify an alternate PHP callback to use for the default autoloader implementation.
`getDefault Autoloader()`	callback	N/A	Retrieve the default autoloader implementation; by default, this is `Zend_Loader::loadClass()`.
`setAutoloaders (array $autoloaders)`	`Zend_Loader_Autoloader`	• `$autoloaders`, *required*.	Set a list of concrete autoloaders to use in the autoloader stack. Each item in the autoloaders array must be a PHP callback.
`getAutoloaders()`	array	N/A	Retrieve the internal autoloader stack.
`getNamespace Autoloaders ($namespace)`	array	• `$namespace`, *required*	Fetch all autoloaders that have registered to load a specific namespace.
`registerNamespace`	`Zend_Loader`	• `$namespace`,	Register one or more

Method	Return Value	Parameters	Description
($namespace)	_Autoloader	*required.*	namespaces with the default autoloader. If $namespace is a string, it registers that namespace; if it's an array of strings, registers each as a namespace.
unregister Namespace ($namespace)	Zend_Loader _Autoloader	• $namespace, *required.*	Unregister one or more namespaces from the default autoloader. If $namespace is a string, it unregisters that namespace; if it's an array of strings, unregisters each as a namespace.
getRegistered Namespace()	array	N/A	Returns an array of all namespaces registered with the default autoloader.
suppressNot FoundWarnings ($flag = null)	boolean|Zend_ Loader_Autoloader	• $flag, *optional.*	Set or retrieve the value of the flag used to indicate whether the default autoloader implementation should suppress "file not found" warnings. If no arguments or a null value is passed, returns a boolean indicating the status of the flag; if a boolean is passed, the flag is set to that value and the autoloader instance is returned (to allow method chaining).
setFallback Autoloader($flag)	Zend_Loader_Autoloader	• $flag, *required.*	Set the value of the flag used to indicate whether or not the default autoloader should be used as a fallback or catch-all autoloader for all namespaces.
isFallback Autoloader()	boolean	N/A	Retrieve the value of the flag used to indicate whether or not the default autoloader should be used as a fallback or catch-all autoloader for all namespaces. By default, this is false.
getClass Autoloaders ($class)	array	• $class, *required.*	Get the list of namespaced autoloaders that could potentially match the provided

Method	Return Value	Parameters	Description
			class. If none match, all global (non-namespaced) auto-loaders are returned.
unshiftAutoloader ($callback, $namespace = '')	Zend_Loader _Autoloader	• $callback, *required*. A valid PHP callback • $namespace, *optional*. A string representing a class prefix namespace.	Add a concrete autoload-er implementation to the beginning of the internal autoloader stack. If a namespace is provided, that namespace will be used to match optimist-ically; otherwise, the autoloader will be con-sidered a global auto-loader.
pushAutoloader ($callback, $namespace = '')	Zend_Loader _Autoloader	• $callback, *required*. A valid PHP callback • $namespace, *optional*. A string representing a class prefix namespace.	Add a concrete autoload-er implementation to the end of the internal auto-loader stack. If a namespace is provided, that namespace will be used to match optimist-ically; otherwise, the autoloader will be con-sidered a global auto-loader.
removeAutoloader ($callback, $namespace = '')	Zend_Loader _Autoloader	• $callback, *required*. A valid PHP callback • $namespace, *optional*. A string representing a class prefix namespace, or an array of namespace strings.	Remove a concrete auto-loader implementation from the the internal autoloader stack. If a namespace or namespaces are provided, the callback will be removed from that namespace or namespaces only.

Resource Autoloaders

Resource autoloaders are intended to manage namespaced library code that follow Zend Framework coding standard guidelines, but which do not have a 1:1 mapping between the class name and the directory structure. Their primary purpose is to facilitate autoloading application resource code, such as application-specific models, forms, and ACLs.

Resource autoloaders register with the autoloader on instantiation, with the namespace to which they are associated. This allows you to easily namespace code in specific directories, and still reap the benefits of autoloading.

Resource autoloader usage

Let's consider the following directory structure:

```
path/to/some/directory/
    acls/
```

```
    Site.php
forms/
    Login.php
models/
    User.php
```

Within this directory, all code is prefixed with the namespace "My_". Within the "acls" subdirectory, the component prefix "Acl_" is added, giving a final class name of "My_Acl_Site". Similarly, the "forms" subdirectory maps to "Form_", giving "My_Form_Login". The "models" subdirectory has no component namespace, giving "My_User".

You can use a resource autoloader to autoload these classes. To instantiate the resource autoloader, you are required to pass at the minimum the base path and namespace for the resources it will be responsible for:

```
$resourceLoader = new Zend_Loader_Autoloader_Resource(array(
    'basePath'  => 'path/to/some/directory',
    'namespace' => 'My',
));
```

Base namespace

In Zend_Loader_Autoloader, you are expected to provide the trailing underscore ("_") in your namespace if your autoloader will use it to match the namespace. Zend_Loader_Autoloader_Resource makes the assumption that all code you are autoloading will use an underscore separator between namespaces, components, and classes. As a result, you do not need to use the trailing underscore when registering a resource autoloader.

Now that we have setup the base resource autoloader, we can add some components to it to autoload. This is done using the addResourceType() method, which accepts three arguments: a resource "type", used internally as a reference name; the subdirectory path underneath the base path in which these resources live; and the component namespace to append to the base namespace. As an example, let's add each of our resource types.

```
$resourceLoader->addResourceType('acl', 'acls/', 'Acl')
               ->addResourceType('form', 'forms/', 'Form')
               ->addResourceType('model', 'models/');
```

Alternately, you could pass these as an array to addResourceTypes(); the following is equivalent to the above:

```
$resourceLoader->addResourceTypes(array(
    'acl' => array(
        'path'      => 'acls/',
        'namespace' => 'Acl',
    ),
    'form' => array(
        'path'      => 'forms/',
        'namespace' => 'Form',
    ),
    'model' => array(
        'path'      => 'models/',
    ),
));
```

Finally, you can specify all of this when instantiating the object, by simply specifying a "resourceTypes" key in the options passed and a structure like that above:

```
$resourceLoader = new Zend_Loader_Autoloader_Resource(array(
    'basePath'      => 'path/to/some/directory',
    'namespace'     => 'My',
    'resourceTypes' => array(
        'acl' => array(
            'path'      => 'acls/',
            'namespace' => 'Acl',
        ),
        'form' => array(
            'path'      => 'forms/',
            'namespace' => 'Form',
        ),
        'model' => array(
            'path'      => 'models/',
        ),
    ),
));
```

The Module Resource Autoloader

Zend Framework ships with a concrete implementation of `Zend_Loader_Autoloader_Resource` that contains resource type mappings that cover the default recommended directory structure for Zend Framework MVC applications. This loader, `Zend_Application_Module_Autoloader`, comes with the following mappings:

```
api/          => Api
forms/        => Form
models/       => Model
    DbTable/  => Model_DbTable
plugins/      => Plugin
```

As an example, if you have a module with the prefix of "Blog_", and attempted to instantiate the class "Blog_Form_Entry", it would look in the resource directory's "forms/" subdirectory for a file named "Entry.php".

When using module bootstraps with `Zend_Application`, an instance of `Zend_Application_Module_Autoloader` will be created by default for each discrete module, allowing you to autoload module resources.

Using Resource Autoloaders as Object Factories

Resource Autoloader Reference

Loading Plugins

A number of Zend Framework components are pluggable, and allow loading of dynamic functionality by specifying a class prefix and path to class files that are not necessarily on the `include_path` or do not necessarily follow traditional naming conventions. `Zend_Loader_PluginLoader` provides common functionality for this process.

The basic usage of the `PluginLoader` follows Zend Framework naming conventions of one class per file, using the underscore as a directory separator when resolving paths. It allows passing an optional class prefix to prepend when determining if a particular plugin class is loaded. Additionally, paths are searched in LIFO order. Due to the LIFO search and the class prefixes, this allows you to define namespaces for your plugins, and thus override plugins from paths registered earlier.

Basic Use Case

First, let's assume the following directory structure and class files, and that the top level directory and library directory are on the include_path:

```
application/
    modules/
        foo/
            views/
                helpers/
                    FormLabel.php
                    FormSubmit.php
        bar/
            views/
                helpers/
                    FormSubmit.php
library/
    Zend/
        View/
            Helper/
                FormLabel.php
                FormSubmit.php
                FormText.php
```

Now, let's create a plugin loader to address the various view helper repositories available:

```
$loader = new Zend_Loader_PluginLoader();
$loader->addPrefixPath('Zend_View_Helper', 'Zend/View/Helper/')
     ->addPrefixPath('Foo_View_Helper',
                         'application/modules/foo/views/helpers')
     ->addPrefixPath('Bar_View_Helper',
                         'application/modules/bar/views/helpers');
```

We can then load a given view helper using just the portion of the class name following the prefixes as defined when adding the paths:

```
// load 'FormText' helper:
$formTextClass = $loader->load('FormText'); // 'Zend_View_Helper_FormText';

// load 'FormLabel' helper:
$formLabelClass = $loader->load('FormLabel'); // 'Foo_View_Helper_FormLabel'

// load 'FormSubmit' helper:
$formSubmitClass = $loader->load('FormSubmit'); // 'Bar_View_Helper_FormSubmi
```

Once the class is loaded, we can now instantiate it.

Note

In some cases, you may use the same prefix for multiple paths. Zend_Loader_PluginLoader actually registers an array of paths for each given prefix; the last one registered will be the first one checked. This is particularly useful if you are utilizing incubator components.

Paths may be defined at instantiation

You may optionally provide an array of prefix / path pairs (or prefix / paths -- plural paths are allowed) as a parameter to the constructor:

```
$loader = new Zend_Loader_PluginLoader(array(
    'Zend_View_Helper' => 'Zend/View/Helper/',
    'Foo_View_Helper' => 'application/modules/foo/views/helpers',
    'Bar_View_Helper' => 'application/modules/bar/views/helpers'
));
```

Zend_Loader_PluginLoader also optionally allows you to share plugins across plugin-aware objects, without needing to utilize a singleton instance. It does so via a static registry. Indicate the registry name at instantiation as the second parameter to the constructor:

```
// Store plugins in static registry 'foobar':
$loader = new Zend_Loader_PluginLoader(array(), 'foobar');
```

Other components that instantiate the PluginLoader using the same registry name will then have access to already loaded paths and plugins.

Manipulating Plugin Paths

The example in the previous section shows how to add paths to a plugin loader. What if you want to determine the paths already loaded, or remove one or more?

- getPaths($prefix = null) returns all paths as prefix / path pairs if no $prefix is provided, or just the paths registered for a given prefix if a $prefix is present.

- clearPaths($prefix = null) will clear all registered paths by default, or only those associated with a given prefix, if the $prefix is provided and present in the stack.

- removePrefixPath($prefix, $path = null) allows you to selectively remove a specific path associated with a given prefix. If no $path is provided, all paths for that prefix are removed. If a $path is provided and exists for that prefix, only that path will be removed.

Testing for Plugins and Retrieving Class Names

Sometimes you simply want to determine if a plugin class has been loaded before you perform an action. isLoaded() takes a plugin name, and returns the status.

Another common use case for the PluginLoader is to determine fully qualified plugin class names of loaded classes; getClassName() provides this functionality. Typically, this would be used in conjunction with isLoaded():

```
if ($loader->isLoaded('Adapter')) {
    $class   = $loader->getClassName('Adapter');
    $adapter = call_user_func(array($class, 'getInstance'));
}
```

Getting Better Performance for Plugins

Plugin loading can be an expensive operation. At its heart, it needs to loop through each prefix, then each path on the prefix, until it finds a file that matches -- and which defines the class expected. In cases where the file exists but does not define the class, an error will be added to the PHP error stack, which is also an expensive operation. The question then turns to: how can you keep the flexibility of plugins and also address performance?

Zend_Loader_PluginLoader offers an opt-in feature for just this situation, a class file include cache. When enabled, it will create a file that contains all successful includes which you can then call from your bootstrap. Using this strategy, you can greatly improve the performance of your production servers.

Example 5.6. Using the PluginLoader class file include cache

To use the class file include cache, simply drop the following code into your bootstrap:

```
$classFileIncCache = APPLICATION_PATH . '/../data/pluginLoaderCache.php';
if (file_exists($classFileIncCache)) {
    include_once $classFileIncCache;
}
Zend_Loader_PluginLoader::setIncludeFileCache($classFileIncCache);
```

Obviously, the path and filename will vary based on your needs. This code should come as early as possible, to ensure that plugin-based components can make use of it.

During development, you may wish to disable the cache. One method for doing so is to use a configuration key for determining whether or not the plugin loader should cache.

```
$classFileIncCache = APPLICATION_PATH . '/../data/pluginLoaderCache.php';
if (file_exists($classFileIncCache)) {
    include_once $classFileIncCache;
}
if ($config->enablePluginLoaderCache) {
    Zend_Loader_PluginLoader::setIncludeFileCache($classFileIncCache);
}
```

This technique allows you to keep your modifications to your configuration file rather than code.

Chapter 6. Zend_Locale

Introduction

Zend_Locale is the Frameworks answer to the question, "How can the same application be used around the whole world?" Most people will say, "That's easy. Let's translate all our output to several languages." However, using simple translation tables to map phrases from one language to another is not sufficient. Different regions will have different conventions for first names, surnames, salutory titles, formatting of numbers, dates, times, currencies, etc.

We need Localization [http://en.wikipedia.org/wiki/L10n] and complementary Internationalization [http://en.wikipedia.org/wiki/L10n] . Both are often abbreviated to L10n and I18n. Internationalization refers more to support for use of systems, regardless of special needs unique to groups of users related by language, region, number format conventions, financial conventions, time and date conventions, etc. Localization involves adding explicit support to systems for special needs of these unique groups, such as language translation, and support for local customs or conventions for communicating plurals, dates, times, currencies, names, symbols, sorting and ordering, etc. L10n and I18n compliment each other. Zend Framework provides support for these through a combination of components, including Zend_Locale, Zend_Date, Zend_Measure, Zend_Translate, Zend_Currency, and Zend_TimeSync.

Zend_Locale and setLocale()

PHP's documentation [http://php.net/setlocale] states that setlocale() is not threadsave because it is maintained per process and not per thread. This means that, in multithreaded environments, you can have the problem that the locale changes while the script never has changed the locale itself. This can lead to unexpected behaviour when you use setlocale() in your scripts.

When you are using Zend_Locale you will not have this limitations, because Zend_Locale is not related to or coupled with PHP's setlocale().

What is Localization

Localization means that an application (or homepage) can be used from different users which speak different languages. But as you already have expected Localization means more than only translating strings. It includes

- Zend_Locale - Backend support of locales available for localization support within other ZF components.

- Zend_Translate - Translating of strings.

- Zend_Date - Localization of dates, times.

- Zend_Calendar - Localization of calendars (support for non-Gregorian calendar systems)

- Zend_Currency - Localization of currencies.

- Zend_Locale_Format - Parsing and generating localized numbers.

- Zend_Locale_Data - Retrieve localized standard strings as country names, language names and more from the CLDR [http://unicode.org/cldr/] .

- TODO - Localization of collations

What is a Locale?

Each computer user makes use of Locales, even when they don't know it. Applications lacking localization support, normally have implicit support for one particular locale (the locale of the author). When a class or function makes use of localization, we say it is `locale-aware`. How does the code know which localization the user is expecting?

A locale string or object identifying a supported locale gives `Zend_Locale` and its subclasses access to information about the language and region expected by the user. Correct formatting, normalization, and conversions are made based on this information.

How are Locales Represented?

Locale identifiers consist of information about the user's language and preferred/primary geographic region (e.g. state or province of home or workplace). The locale identifier strings used in Zend Framework are internationally defined standard abbreviations of language and region, written as `language_REGION`. Both the language and region parts are abbreviated to alphabetic, ASCII characters.

Note

Be aware that there exist not only locales with 2 characters as most people think. Also there are languages and regions which are not only abbreviated with 2 characters. Therefor you should NOT strip the region and language yourself, but use `Zend_Locale` when you want to strip language or region from a locale string. Otherwise you could have unexpected behaviour within your code when you do this yourself.

A user from USA would expect the language `English` and the region `USA`, yielding the locale identifier "en_US". A user in Germany would expect the language `German` and the region `Germany`, yielding the locale identifier "de_DE". See the list of pre-defined locale and region combinations [http://unicode.org/cldr/data/diff/supplemental/languages_and_territories.html], if you need to select a specific locale within Zend Framework.

Example 6.1. Choosing a specific locale

```
$locale = new Zend_Locale('de_DE'); // German language _ Germany
```

A German user in America might expect the language `German` and the region `USA`, but these non-standard mixes are not supported directly as recognized "locales". Instead, if an invalid combination is used, then it will automatically be truncated by dropping the region code. For example, "de_IS" would be truncated to "de", and "xh_RU" would be truncated to "xh", because neither of these combinations are valid. Additionally, if the base language code is not supported (e.g. "zz_US") or does not exist, then a default "root" locale will be used. The "root" locale has default definitions for internationally recognized representations of dates, times, numbers, currencies, etc. The truncation process depends on the requested information, since some combinations of language and region might be valid for one type of data (e.g. dates), but not for another (e.g. currency format).

Beware of historical changes, as ZF components do not know about or attempt to track the numerous timezone changes made over many years by many regions. For example, we can see a historical list [http://www.statoids.com/tus.html] showing dozens of changes made by governments to when and if a particular region observes Daylight Savings Time, and even which timezone a particular geographic area belongs. Thus, when performing date math, the math performed by ZF components will not adjust for these changes, but instead will give the correct time for the timezone using current, modern rules for DST and timezone assignment for geographic regions.

Selecting the Right Locale

For most situations, new `Zend_Locale()` will automatically select the correct locale, with preference given to information provided by the user's web browser. However, if new `Zend_Locale(Zend_Locale::ENVIRONMENT)` is used, then preference will be given to using the host server's environment configuration, as described below.

Example 6.2. Automatically selecting a locale

```
$locale  = new Zend_Locale();

// default behavior, same as above
$locale1 = new Zend_Locale(Zend_Locale::BROWSER);

// prefer settings on host server
$locale2 = new Zend_Locale(Zend_Locale::ENVIRONMENT);

// perfer framework app default settings
$locale3 = new Zend_Locale(Zend_Locale::FRAMEWORK);
```

The search algorithm used by `Zend_Locale` for automatic selection of a locale uses three sources of information:

1. const `Zend_Locale::BROWSER` - The user's Web browser provides information with each request, which is published by PHP in the global variable `HTTP_ACCEPT_LANGUAGE`. If no matching locale can be found, then preference is given to ENVIRONMENT and lastly FRAMEWORK.

2. const `Zend_Locale::ENVIRONMENT` - PHP publishes the host server's locale via the PHP internal function `setlocale()`. If no matching locale can be found, then preference is given to FRAMEWORK and lastly BROWSER.

3. const `Zend_Locale::FRAMEWORK` - When Zend Framework has a standardized way of specifying component defaults (planned, but not yet available), then using this constant during instantiation will give preference to choosing a locale based on these defaults. If no matching locale can be found, then preference is given to ENVIRONMENT and lastly BROWSER.

Usage of automatic Locales

`Zend_Locale` provides three additionally locales. These locales do not belong to any language or region. They are "automatic" locales which means that they have the same effect as the method `getDefault()` but without the negative effects like creating an instance. These "automatic" locales can be used anywhere, where also a standard locale and also the definition of a locale, its string representation, can be used. This offers simplicity for situations like working with locales which are provided by a browser.

There are three locales which have a slightly different behaviour:

1. `'browser'` - Zend_Locale should work with the information which is provided by the user's Web browser. It is published by PHP in the global variable `HTTP_ACCEPT_LANGUAGE`.

    If a user provides more than one locale within his browser, `Zend_Locale` will use the first found locale. If the user does not provide a locale or the script is being called from the command line the automatic locale `'environment'` will automatically be used and returned.

2. `'environment'` - Zend_Locale should work with the information which is provided by the host server. It is published by PHP via the internal function `setlocale()`.

If a environment provides more than one locale, Zend_Locale will use the first found locale. If the host does not provide a locale the automatic locale 'browser' will automatically be used and returned.

3. 'auto' - Zend_Locale should automatically detect any locale which can be worked with. It will first search for a users locale and then, if not successful, search for the host locale.

If no locale can be detected, it will throw an exception and tell you that the automatic detection has been failed.

Example 6.3. Using automatic locales

```
// without automatic detection
//$locale = new Zend_Locale(Zend_Locale::BROWSER);
//$date = new Zend_Date($locale);

// with automatic detection
$date = new Zend_Date('auto');
```

Using a default Locale

In some environments it is not possible to detect a locale automatically. You can expect this behaviour when you get an request from command line or the requesting browser has no language tag set and additionally your server has the default locale 'C' set or another proprietary locale.

In such cases Zend_Locale will normally throw an exception with a message that the automatic detection of any locale was not successful. You have two options to handle such a situation. Either through setting a new locale per hand, or defining a default locale.

Example 6.4. Handling locale exceptions

```
// within the bootstrap file
try {
    $locale = new Zend_Locale('auto');
} catch (Zend_Locale_Exception $e) {
    $locale = new Zend_Locale('de');
}

// within your model/controller
$date = new Zend_Date($locale);
```

But this has one big negative effect. You will have to set your locale object within every class using Zend_Locale. This could become very unhandy if you are using multiple classes.

Since Zend Framework Release 1.5 there is a much better way to handle this. You can set a default locale which the static setDefault() method. Of course, every unknown or not full qualified locale will also throw an exception. setDefault() should be the first call before you initiate any class using Zend_Locale. See the following example for details:

Example 6.5. Setting a default locale

```
// within the bootstrap file
Zend_Locale::setDefault('de');

// within your model/controller
$date = new Zend_Date();
```

In the case that no locale can be detected, automatically the locale *de* will be used. Otherwise, the detected locale will be used.

ZF Locale-Aware Classes

In the ZF, locale-aware classes rely on `Zend_Locale` to automatically select a locale, as explained above. For example, in a ZF web application, constructing a date using `Zend_Date` without specifying a locale results in an object with a locale based on information provided by the current user's web browser.

Example 6.6. Dates default to correct locale of web users

```
$date = new Zend_Date('2006',Zend_Date::YEAR);
```

To override this default behavior, and force locale-aware ZF components to use specific locales, regardless of the origin of your website visitors, explicitly specify a locale as the third argument to the constructor.

Example 6.7. Overriding default locale selection

```
$usLocale = new Zend_Locale('en_US');
$date = new Zend_Date('2006', Zend_Date::YEAR, $usLocale);
$temp = new Zend_Measure_Temperature('100,10',
                                     Zend_Measure::TEMPERATURE,
                                     $usLocale);
```

If you know many objects should all use the same default locale, explicitly specify the default locale to avoid the overhead of each object determining the default locale.

Example 6.8. Performance optimization when using a default locale

```
$locale = new Zend_Locale();
$date = new Zend_Date('2006', Zend_Date::YEAR, $locale);
$temp = new Zend_Measure_Temperature('100,10',
                                     Zend_Measure::TEMPERATURE,
                                     $locale);
```

Application wide locale

Zend Framework allows the usage of an application wide locale. You simply set an instance of Zend_Locale to the registry with the key 'Zend_Locale'. Then this instance will be used within all locale aware classes of Zend Framework. This way you set one locale within your registry and then you can forget about setting it again. It will automatically be used in all other classes. See the below example for the right usage:

Example 6.9. Usage of an application wide locale

```
// within your bootstrap
$locale = new Zend_Locale('de_AT');
Zend_Registry::set('Zend_Locale', $locale);

// within your model or controller
$date = new Zend_Date();
// print $date->getLocale();
echo $date->getDate();
```

Zend_Locale_Format::setOptions(array $options)

The 'precision' option of a value is used to truncate or stretch extra digits. A value of '-1' disables modification of the number of digits in the fractional part of the value. The 'locale' option helps when parsing numbers and dates using separators and month names. The date format 'format_type' option selects between CLDR/ISO date format specifier tokens and PHP's date() tokens. The 'fix_date' option enables or disables heuristics that attempt to correct invalid dates. The 'number_format' option specifies a default number format for use with toNumber() (see the section called "Number localization").

The 'date_format' option can be used to specify a default date format string, but beware of using getDate(), checkdateFormat() and getTime() after using setOptions() with a 'date_format'. To use these four methods with the default date format for a locale, use array('date_format' => null, 'locale' => $locale) for their options.

Example 6.10. Dates default to correct locale of web users

```
Zend_Locale_Format::setOptions(array('locale' => 'en_US',
                                     'fix_date' => true,
                                     'format_type' => 'php'));
```

For working with the standard definitions of a locale the option Zend_Locale_Format::STANDARD can be used. Setting the option Zend_Locale_Format::STANDARD for date_format uses the standard definitions from the actual set locale. Setting it for number_format uses the standard number format for this locale. And setting it for locale uses the standard locale for this environment or browser.

Example 6.11. Using STANDARD definitions for setOptions()

```
Zend_Locale_Format::setOptions(array('locale' => 'en_US',
                                     'date_format' => 'dd.MMMM.YYYY'));
// overriding the global set date format
$date = Zend_Locale_Format::getDate('2007-04-20',
```

```
                                          array('date_format' =>
                                              Zend_Locale_Format::STANDARD);

// global setting of the standard locale
Zend_Locale_Format::setOptions(array('locale' => Zend_Locale_Format::
                      STANDARD,'date_format' => 'dd.MMMM.YYYY'));
```

Speed up Zend_Locale and its subclasses

Zend_Locale and its subclasses can be speed up by the usage of Zend_Cache. Use the static method Zend_Locale::setCache($cache) if you are using Zend_Locale. Zend_Locale_Format can be speed up the using the option cache within Zend_Locale_Format::setOptions(array('cache' => $adapter));. If you are using both classes you should only set the cache for Zend_Locale, otherwise the last set cache will overwrite the previous set cache. For convenience there are also the static methods getCache(), hasCache(), clearCache() and removeCache().

Using Zend_Locale

Zend_Locale also provides localized information about locales for each locale, including localized names for other locales, days of the week, month names, etc.

Copying, Cloning, and Serializing Locale Objects

Use object cloning [http://php.net/language.oop5.cloning] to duplicate a locale object exactly and efficiently. Most locale-aware methods also accept string representations of locales, such as the result of $locale->toString().

Example 6.12. clone

```
$locale = new Zend_Locale('ar');

// Save the $locale object as a serialization
$serializedLocale = $locale->serialize();
// re-create the original object
$localeObject = unserialize($serializedLocale);

// Obtain a string identification of the locale
$stringLocale = $locale->toString();

// Make a cloned copy of the $local object
$copiedLocale = clone $locale;

print "copied: ", $copiedLocale->toString();

// PHP automatically calls toString() via __toString()
print "copied: ", $copiedLocale;
```

Equality

Zend_Locale also provides a convenience function to compare two locales. All locale-aware classes should provide a similar equality check.

Example 6.13. Check for equal locales

```
$locale = new Zend_Locale();
$mylocale = new Zend_Locale('en_US');

// Check if locales are equal
if ($locale->equals($mylocale)) {
    print "Locales are equal";
}
```

Default locales

The method getDefault() returns an array of relevant locales using information from the user's web browser (if available), information from the environment of the host server, and ZF settings. As with the constructor for Zend_Locale, the first parameter selects a preference of which information to consider (BROWSER, ENVIRONMENT, or FRAMEWORK) first. The second parameter toggles between returning all matching locales or only the first/best match. Locale-aware components normally use only the first locale. A quality rating is included, when available.

Example 6.14. Get default locales

```
$locale = new Zend_Locale();

// Return all default locales
$found = $locale->getDefault();
print_r($found);

// Return only browser locales
$found2 = $locale->getDefault(Zend_Locale::BROWSER,TRUE);
print_r($found2);
```

To obtain only the default locales relevant to the BROWSER, ENVIRONMENT, or FRAMEWORK , use the corresponding method:

- getEnvironment()

- getBrowser()

- getLocale()

Set a new locale

A new locale can be set with the function setLocale(). This function takes a locale string as parameter. If no locale is given, a locale is automatically selected. Since Zend_Locale objects are "light", this method exists primarily to cause side-effects for code that have references to the existing instance object.

Example 6.15. setLocale

```
$locale = new Zend_Locale();

// Actual locale
```

```
print $locale->toString();

// new locale
$locale->setLocale('aa_DJ');
print $locale->toString();
```

Getting the language and region

Use `getLanguage()` to obtain a string containing the two character language code from the string locale identifier. Use `getRegion()` to obtain a string containing the two character region code from the string locale identifier.

Example 6.16. getLanguage and getRegion

```
$locale = new Zend_Locale();

// if locale is 'de_AT' then 'de' will be returned as language
print $locale->getLanguage();

// if locale is 'de_AT' then 'AT' will be returned as region
print $locale->getRegion();
```

Obtaining localized strings

`getTranslationList()` gives you access to localized informations of several types. These information are useful if you want to display localized data to a customer without the need of translating it. They are already available for your usage.

The requested list of information is always returned as named array. If you want to give more than one value to a explicit type where you wish to receive values from, you have to give an array instead of multiple values.

Example 6.17. getTranslationList

```
$list = Zend_Locale::getTranslationList('language', 'de_AT');

print_r ($list);
// example key -> value pairs...
// [de] -> Deutsch
// [en] -> Englisch

// use one of the returned key as value for the getTranslation() method
// of another language
print Zend_Locale::getTranslation('de', 'language', 'zh');
// returns the translation for the language 'de' in chinese
```

You can receive this informations for all languages. But not all of the informations are completely available for all languages. Some of these types are also available through an own function for simplicity. See this list for detailed informations.

Table 6.1. Details for getTranslationList($type = null, $locale = null, $value = null)

Type	Description
Language	Returns a localized list of all languages. The language part of the locale is returned as key and the translation as value. For your convenience use the `getLanguageTranslationList()` method
Script	Returns a localized list of all scripts. The script is returned as key and the translation as value. For your convenience use the `getScriptTranslationList()` method
Territory	Returns a localized list of all territories. This contains countries, continents and territories. To get only territories and continents use '1' as value. To get only countries use '2' as value. The country part of the locale is used as key where applicable. In the other case the official ISO code for this territory is used. The translated territory is returned as value. For your convenience use the `getCountryTranslationList()` method to receive all countries and the `getTerritoryTranslationList()` method to receive all territories without countries. When you omit the value you will get a list with both.
Variant	Returns a localized list of known variants of scripts. The variant is returned as key and the translation as value
Key	Returns a localized list of known keys. This keys are generic values used in translation. These are normally calendar, collation and currency. The key is returned as array key and the translation as value
Type	Returns a localized list of known types of keys. These are variants of types of calendar representations and types of collations. When you use 'collation' as value you will get all types of collations returned. When you use 'calendar' as value you will get all types of calendars returned. When you omit the value you will get a list all both returned. The type is used as key and the translation as value
Layout	Returns a list of rules which describes how to format special text parts
Characters	Returns a list of allowed characters within this locale
Delimiters	Returns a list of allowed quoting characters for this locale
Measurement	Returns a list of known measurement values. This list is depreciated
Months	Returns a list of all month representations within this locale. There are several different

Type	Description
	representations which are all returned as sub array. If you omit the value you will get a list of all months from the 'gregorian' calendar returned. You can give any known calendar as value to get a list of months from this calendar returned. Use Zend_Date for simplicity
Month	Returns a localized list of all month names for this locale. If you omit the value you will get the normally used gregorian full name of the months where each month number is used as key and the translated month is returned as value. You can get the months for different calendars and formats if you give an array as value. The first array entry has to be the calendar, the second the used context and the third the width to return. Use Zend_Date for simplicity
Days	Returns a list of all day representations within this locale. There are several different representations which are all returned as sub array. If you omit the value you will get a list of all days from the 'gregorian' calendar returned. You can give any known calendar as value to get a list of days from this calendar returned. Use Zend_Date for simplicity
Day	Returns a localized list of all day names for this locale. If you omit the value you will get the normally used gregorian full name of the days where the english day abbreviation is used as key and the translated day is returned as value. You can get the days for different calendars and formats if you give an array as value. The first array entry has to be the calendar, the second the used context and the third the width to return. Use Zend_Date for simplicity
Week	Returns a list of values used for proper week calculations within a locale. Use Zend_Date for simplicity
Quarters	Returns a list of all quarter representations within this locale. There are several different representations which are all returned as sub array. If you omit the value you will get a list of all quarters from the 'gregorian' calendar returned. You can give any known calendar as value to get a list of quarters from this calendar returned
Quarter	Returns a localized list of all quarter names for this locale. If you omit the value you will get the normally used gregorian full name of the quarters where each quarter number is used as key and the translated quarter is returned as value. You can get the quarters for different calendars and formats if you give an array as value. The first array entry has to be the calendar, the second the used context and the third the width to return
Eras	Returns a list of all era representations within this

Type	Description
	locale. If you omit the value you will get a list of all eras from the 'gregorian' calendar returned. You can give any known calendar as value to get a list of eras from this calendar returned
Era	Returns a localized list of all era names for this locale. If you omit the value you will get the normally used gregorian full name of the eras where each era number is used as key and the translated era is returned as value. You can get the eras for different calendars and formats if you give an array as value. The first array entry has to be the calendar and the second the width to return
Date	Returns a localized list of all date formats for this locale. The name of the dateformat is used as key and the format itself as value.If you omit the value you will get the date formats for the gregorian calendar returned. You can get the date formats for different calendars if you give the wished calendar as string. Use Zend_Date for simplicity
Time	Returns a localized list of all time formats for this locale. The name of the timeformat is used as key and the format itself as value. If you omit the value you will get the time formats for the gregorian calendar returned. You can get the time formats for different calendars if you give the wished calendar as string. Use Zend_Date for simplicity
DateTime	Returns a localized list of all known date-time formats for this locale. The name of the date-time format is used as key and the format itself as value. If you omit the value you will get the date-time formats for the gregorian calendar returned. You can get the date-time formats for different calendars if you give the wished calendar as string. Use Zend_Date for simplicity
Field	Returns a localized list of date fields which can be used to display calendars or date strings like 'month' or 'year' in a wished language. If you omit the value you will get this list for the gregorian calendar returned. You can get the list for different calendars if you give the wished calendar as string
Relative	Returns a localized list of relative dates which can be used to display textual relative dates like 'yesterday' or 'tomorrow' in a wished language. If you omit the value you will get this list for the gregorian calendar returned. You can get the list for different calendars if you give the wished calendar as string
Symbols	Returns a localized list of characters used for number representations
NameToCurrency	Returns a localized list of names for currencies. The currency is used as key and the translated name as value. Use Zend_Currency for simplicity
CurrencyToName	Returns a list of currencies for localized names.

Type	Description
	The translated name is used as key and the currency as value. Use Zend_Currency for simplicity
CurrencySymbol	Returns a list of known localized currency symbols for currencies. The currency is used as key and the symbol as value. Use Zend_Currency for simplicity
Question	Returns a list of localized strings for acceptance ('yes') and negation ('no'). Use Zend_Locale's getQuestion method for simplicity
CurrencyFraction	Returns a list of fractions for currency values. The currency is used as key and the fraction as integer value. Use Zend_Currency for simplicity
CurrencyRounding	Returns a list of how to round which currency. The currency is used as key and the rounding as integer value. Use Zend_Currency for simplicity
CurrencyToRegion	Returns a list of currencies which are known to be used within a region. The ISO3166 value ('region') is used as array key and the ISO4217 value ('currency') as array value. Use Zend_Currency for simplicity
RegionToCurrency	Returns a list of regions where a currency is used . The ISO4217 value ('currency') is used as array key and the ISO3166 value ('region') as array value. When a currency is used in several regions these regions are separated with a whitespace. Use Zend_Currency for simplicity
RegionToTerritory	Returns a list of territories with the countries or sub territories which are included within that territory. The ISO territory code ('territory') is used as array key and the ISO3166 value ('region') as array value. When a territory contains several regions these regions are separated with a whitespace
TerritoryToRegion	Returns a list of regions and the territories where these regions are located. The ISO3166 code ('region') is used as array key and the ISO territory code ('territory') as array value. When a region is located in several territories these territories are separated with a whitespace
ScriptToLanguage	Returns a list of scripts which are used within a language. The language code is used as array key and the script code as array value. When a language contains several scripts these scripts are separated with a whitespace
LanguageToScript	Returns a list of languages which are using a script. The script code is used as array key and the language code as array value. When a script is used in several languages these languages are separated with a whitespace
TerritoryToLanguage	Returns a list of countries which are using a language. The country code is used as array key and the language code as array value. When a

Type	Description
	language is used in several countries these countries are separated with a whitespace
LanguageToTerritory	Returns a list of countries and the languages spoken within these countries. The country code is used as array key and the language code as array value. When a territory is using several languages these languages are separated with a whitespace
TimezoneToWindows	Returns a list of windows timezones and the related ISO timezone. The windows timezone is used as array key and the ISO timezone as array value
WindowsToTimezone	Returns a list of ISO timezones and the related windows timezone. The ISO timezone is used as array key and the windows timezone as array value
TerritoryToTimezone	Returns a list of regions or territories and the related ISO timezone. The ISO timezone is used as array key and the territory code as array value
TimezoneToTerritory	Returns a list of timezones and the related region or territory code. The region or territory code is used as array key and the ISO timezone as array value
CityToTimezone	Returns a localized list of cities which can be used as translation for a related timezone. Not for all timezones is a translation available, but for a user is the real city written in his languages more accurate than the ISO name of this timezone. The ISO timezone is used as array key and the translated city as array value
TimezoneToCity	Returns a list of timezones for localized city names. The localized city is used as array key and the ISO timezone name as array value
PhoneToTerritory	Returns a list of phone codes which are known to be used within a territory. The territory (region) is used as array key and the telephone code as array value
TerritoryToPhone	Returns a list of territories where a phone is used . The phone code is used as array key and the territory (region) as array value. When a phone code is used in several territories these territories are separated with a whitespace
NumericToTerritory	Returns a list of 3 digit number codes for territories. The territory (region) is used as array key and the 3 digit number code as array value
TerritoryToNumeric	Returns a list of territories with their 3 digit number code. The 3 digit number code is used as array key and the territory (region) as array value
Alpha3ToTerritory	Returns a list of 3 sign character codes for territories. The territory (region) is used as array key and the 3 sign character code as array value
TerritoryToAlpha3	Returns a list of territories with their 3 sign character code. The 3 sign character code is used as array key and the territory (region) as array value

If you are in need of a single translated value, you can use the getTranslation() method. It returns always a string but it accepts some different types than the getTranslationList() method. Also value is the same as before with one difference. You have to give the detail you want to get returned as additional value.

Note

Because you have almost always give a value as detail this parameter has to be given as first parameter. This differs from the getTranslationList() method.

See the following table for detailed information:

Table 6.2. Details for getTranslation($value = null, $type = null, $locale = null)

Type	Description
Language	Returns a translation for a language. To select the wished translation you must give the language code as value. For your convenience use the getLanguageTranslation($value) method
Script	Returns a translation for a script. To select the wished translation you must give the script code as value. For your convenience use the getScriptTranslation($value) method
Territory or *Country*	Returns a translation for a territory. This can be countries, continents and territories. To select the wished variant you must give the territory code as value. For your convenience use the getCountryTranslation($value) method.
Variant	Returns a translation for a script variant. To select the wished variant you must give the variant code as value
Key	Returns translation for a known keys. This keys are generic values used in translation. These are normally calendar, collation and currency. To select the wished key you must give the key code as value
DateChars	Returns a character table which contains all characters used when displaying dates
DefaultCalendar	Returns the default calendar for the given locale. For most locales this will be 'gregorian'. Use Zend_Date for simplicity
MonthContext	Returns the default context for months which is used within the given calendar. If you omit the value the 'gregorian' calendar will be used. Use Zend_Date for simplicity
DefaultMonth	Returns the default format for months which is used within the given calendar. If you omit the value the 'gregorian' calendar will be used. Use Zend_Date for simplicity
Month	Returns a translation for a month. You have to give the number of the month as integer value. It has to

Type	Description
	be between 1 and 12. If you want to receive data for other calendars, contexts or formats, then you must give an array instead of an integer with the expected values. The array has to look like this: `array( 'calendar', 'context', 'format', 'month number')`. If you give only an integer then the default values are the 'gregorian' calendar, the context 'format' and the format 'wide'. Use Zend_Date for simplicity
DayContext	Returns the default context for ´days which is used within the given calendar. If you omit the value the 'gregorian' calendar will be used. Use Zend_Date for simplicity
DefaultDay	Returns the default format for days which is used within the given calendar. If you omit the value the 'gregorian' calendar will be used. Use Zend_Date for simplicity
Day	Returns a translation for a day. You have to give the english abbreviation of the day as string value ('sun', 'mon', etc.). If you want to receive data for other calendars, contexts or format, then you must give an array instead of an integer with the expected values. The array has to look like this: `array('calendar', 'context', 'format', 'day abbreviation')`. If you give only an string then the default values are the 'gregorian' calendar, the context 'format' and the format 'wide'. Use Zend_Date for simplicity
Quarter	Returns a translation for a quarter. You have to give the number of the quarter as integer and it has to be between 1 and 4. If you want to receive data for other calendars, contexts or formats, then you must give an array instead of an integer with the expected values. The array has to look like this: `array('calendar', 'context', 'format', 'quarter number')`. If you give only an string then the default values are the 'gregorian' calendar, the context 'format' and the format 'wide'
Am	Returns a translation for 'AM' in a expected locale. If you want to receive data for other calendars an string with the expected calendar. If you omit the value then the 'gregorian' calendar will be used. Use Zend_Date for simplicity
Pm	Returns a translation for 'PM' in a expected locale. If you want to receive data for other calendars an string with the expected calendar. If you omit the value then the 'gregorian' calendar will be used. Use Zend_Date for simplicity
Era	Returns a translation for an era within a locale. You have to give the era number as string or integer. If you want to receive data for other calendars or formats, then you must give an array instead of the era number with the expected values.

Type	Description
	The array has to look like this: `array('calendar', 'format', 'era number')`. If you give only an string then the default values are the 'gregorian' calendar and the 'abbr' format
DefaultDate	Returns the default date format which is used within the given calendar. If you omit the value the 'gregorian' calendar will be used. Use Zend_Date for simplicity
Date	Returns the date format for an given calendar or format within a locale. If you omit the value then the 'gregorian' calendar will be used with the 'medium' format. If you give a string then the 'gregorian' calendar will be used with the given format. Or you can also give an array which will have to look like this: `array('calendar', 'format')`. Use Zend_Date for simplicity
DefaultTime	Returns the default time format which is used within the given calendar. If you omit the value the 'gregorian' calendar will be used. Use Zend_Date for simplicity
Time	Returns the time format for an given calendar or format within a locale. If you omit the value then the 'gregorian' calendar will be used with the 'medium' format. If you give a string then the 'gregorian' calendar will be used with the given format. Or you can also give an array which will have to look like this: `array('calendar', 'format')`. Use Zend_Date for simplicity
DateTime	Returns the datetime format for the given locale which indicates how to display date with times in the same string within the given calendar. If you omit the value the 'gregorian' calendar will be used. Use Zend_Date for simplicity
Field	Returns a translated date field which can be used to display calendars or date strings like 'month' or 'year' in a wished language. You must give the field which has to be returned as string. In this case the 'gregorian' calendar will be used. You can get the field for other calendar formats if you give an array which has to look like this: `array('calendar', 'date field')`
Relative	Returns a translated date which is relative to today which can include date strings like 'yesterday' or 'tomorrow' in a wished language. You have to give the number of days relative to tomorrow to receive the expected string. Yesterday would be '-1', tomorrow '1' and so on. This will use the 'gregorian' calendar. If you want to get relative dates for other calendars you will have to give an array which has to look like this: `array('calendar', 'relative days')`. Use Zend_Date for simplicity
DecimalNumber	Returns the format for decimal numbers within a

Type	Description
	given locale. Use Zend_Locale_Format for simplicity
ScientificNumber	Returns the format for scientific numbers within a given locale
PercentNumber	Returns the format for percentage numbers within a given locale
CurrencyNumber	Returns the format for displaying currency numbers within a given locale. Use Zend_Currency for simplicity
NameToCurrency	Returns the translated name for a given currency. The currency has to be given in ISO format which is for example 'EUR' for the currency 'euro'. Use Zend_Currency for simplicity
CurrencyToName	Returns a currency for a given localized name. Use Zend_Currency for simplicity
CurrencySymbol	Returns the used symbol for a currency within a given locale. Not for all currencies exists a symbol. Use Zend_Currency for simplicity
Question	Returns a localized string for acceptance ('yes') and negotation ('no'). You have to give either 'yes' or 'no' as value to receive the expected string. Use Zend_Locale's getQuestion method for simplicity
CurrencyFraction	Returns the fraction to use for a given currency. You must give the currency as ISO value. Use Zend_Currency for simplicity
CurrencyRounding	Returns how to round a given currency. You must give the currency as ISO value. If you omit the currency then the 'DEFAULT' rounding will be returned. Use Zend_Currency for simplicity
CurrencyToRegion	Returns the currency for a given region. The region code has to be given as ISO3166 string for example 'AT' for austria. Use Zend_Currency for simplicity
RegionToCurrency	Returns the regions where a currency is used. The currency has to be given as ISO4217 code for example 'EUR' for euro. When a currency is used in multiple regions, these regions are separated with a whitespace character. Use Zend_Currency for simplicity
RegionToTerritory	Returns the regions for a given territory. The territory has to be given as ISO4217 string for example '001' for world. The regions within this territory are separated with a whitespace character
TerritoryToRegion	Returns the territories where a given region is located. The region has to be given in ISO3166 string for example 'AT' for austria. When a region is located in multiple territories then these territories are separated with a whitespace character
ScriptToLanguage	Returns the scripts which are used within a given language. The language has to be given as ISO language code for example 'en' for english. When

Type	Description
	multiple scripts are used within a language then these scripts are separated with a whitespace character
LanguageToScript	Returns the languages which are used within a given script. The script has to be given as ISO script code for example 'Latn' for latin. When a script is used in multiple languages then these languages are separated with a whitespace character
TerritoryToLanguage	Returns the territories where a given language is used. The language has to be given as ISO language code for example 'en' for english. When multiple territories exist where this language is used then these territories are separated with a whitespace character
LanguageToTerritory	Returns the languages which are used within a given territory. The territory has to be given as ISO3166 code for example 'IT' for italia. When a language is used in multiple territories then these territories are separated with a whitespace character
TimezoneToWindows	Returns a ISO timezone for a given windows timezone
WindowsToTimezone	Returns a windows timezone for a given ISO timezone
TerritoryToTimezone	Returns the territory for a given ISO timezone
TimezoneToTerritory	Returns the ISO timezone for a given territory
CityToTimezone	Returns the localized city for a given ISO timezone. Not for all timezones does a city translation exist
TimezoneToCity	Returns the ISO timezone for a given localized city name. Not for all cities does a timezone exist
PhoneToTerritory	Returns the telephone code for a given territory (region). The territory code has to be given as ISO3166 string for example 'AT' for austria
TerritoryToPhone	Returns the territory (region) where a telephone code is used. The telephone code has to be given as plain integer code for example '43' for +43. When a telephone code is used in multiple territories (regions), these territories are separated with a whitespace character
NumericToTerritory	Returns the 3 digit number code for a given territory (region). The territory code has to be given as ISO3166 string for example 'AT' for austria
TerritoryToNumeric	Returns the territory (region) for a 3 digit number code. The 3 digit number code has to be given as plain integer code for example '43'
Alpha3ToTerritory	Returns the 3 sign character code for a given territory (region). The territory code has to be given as ISO3166 string for example 'AT' for austria

Type	Description
TerritoryToAlpha3	Returns the territory (region) for a 3 sign character code

Note

With Zend Framework 1.5 several old types have been renamed. This has to be done because of several new types, some misspelling and to increase the usability. See this table for a list of old to new types:

Table 6.3. Differences between ZF 1.0 and ZF 1.5

Old type	New type
Country	Territory (with value '2')
Calendar	Type (with value 'calendar')
Month_Short	Month (with array('gregorian', 'format', 'abbreviated')
Month_Narrow	Month (with array('gregorian', 'stand-alone', 'narrow')
Month_Complete	Months
Day_Short	Day (with array('gregorian', 'format', 'abbreviated'))
Day_Narrow	Day (with array('gregorian', 'stand-alone', 'narrow'))
DateFormat	Date
TimeFormat	Time
Timezones	CityToTimezone
Currency	NameToCurrency
Currency_Sign	CurrencySymbol
Currency_Detail	CurrencyToRegion
Territory_Detail	TerritoryToRegion
Language_Detail	LanguageToTerritory

The example below demonstrates how to obtain the names of things in different languages.

Example 6.18. getTranslationList

```
// prints the names of all countries in German language
print_r(Zend_Locale::getTranslationList('country', 'de'));
```

The next example shows how to find the name of a language in another language, when the two letter iso country code is not known.

Example 6.19. Converting country name in one language to another

```
$code2name = Zend_Locale::getLanguageTranslationList('en_US');
$name2code = array_flip($code2name);
$frenchCode = $name2code['French'];
echo Zend_Locale::getLanguageTranslation($frenchCode, 'de_AT');
// output is the German name of the French language
```

To generate a list of all languages known by Zend_Locale, with each language name shown in its own language, try the example below in a web page. Similarly, getCountryTranslationList() and getCountryTranslation() could be used to create a table mapping your native language names for regions to the names of the regions shown in another language. Use a try .. catch block to handle exceptions that occur when using a locale that does not exist. Not all languages are also locales. In the example, below exceptions are ignored to prevent early termination.

Example 6.20. All Languages written in their native language

```
$list = Zend_Locale::getLanguageTranslationList('auto');

foreach($list as $language => $content) {
    try {
        $output = Zend_Locale::getLanguageTranslation($language, $language);
        if (is_string($output)) {
            print "\n<br>[".$language."] ".$output;
        }
    } catch (Exception $e) {
        continue;
    }
}
```

Obtaining translations for "yes" and "no"

Frequently, programs need to solicit a "yes" or "no" response from the user. Use getQuestion() to obtain an array containing the correct word(s) or regex strings to use for prompting the user in a particular $locale (defaults to the current object's locale). The returned array will contain the following informations :

- *yes and no*: A generic string representation for yes and no responses. This will contain the first and most generic response from yesarray and noarray.

  yesarray and noarray: An array with all known yes and no responses. Several languages have more than just two responses. In general this is the full string and its abbreviation.

  yesexpr and noexpr: An generated regex which allows you to handle user response, and search for yes or no.

All of this informations are of course localized and depend on the set locale. See the following example for the informations you can receive:

Example 6.21. getQuestion()

```
$locale = new Zend_Locale();
// Question strings
print_r($locale->getQuestion('de'));

- - - Output - - -

Array
(
    [yes] => ja
    [no] => nein
    [yesarray] => Array
        (
            [0] => ja
            [1] => j
        )

    [noarray] => Array
        (
            [0] => nein
            [1] => n
        )

    [yesexpr] => ^([jJ][aA]?)|([jJ]?)
    [noexpr] => ^([nN]([eE][iI][nN])?)|([nN]?)
)
```

Note

Until 1.0.3 *yesabbr* from the underlaying locale data was also available. Since 1.5 this information is no longer standalone available, but you will find the information from it within *yesarray*.

Get a list of all known locales

Sometimes you will want to get a list of all known locales. This can be used for several tasks like the creation of a selectbox. For this purpose you can use the static getLocaleList() method which will return a list of all known locales.

Example 6.22. getLocaleList()

```
$localelist = Zend_Locale::getLocaleList();
```

Note

Note that the locales are returned as key of the array you will receive. The value is always a boolean true.

Detecting locales

When you want to detect if a given input, regardless of its source, is a locale you should use the static isLocale() method. The first parameter of this method is the string which you want to check.

Example 6.23. Simple locale detection

```
$input = 'to_RU';
if (Zend_Locale::isLocale($input)) {
    print "'{$input}' is a locale";
} else {
    print "Sorry... the given input is no locale";
}
```

As you can see, the output of this method is always a boolean. There is only one reason you could get an exception when calling this method. When your system does not provide any locale and Zend Framework is not able to detect it automatically. Normally this shows that there is a problem with your OS in combination with PHP's setlocale().

You should also note that any given locale string will automatically be degraded if the region part does not exist for this locale. In our previous example the language 'to' does not exist in the region 'RU', but you will still get true returned as Zend_Locale can work with the given input.

Still it's sometimes usefull to prevent this automatic degrading, and this is where the second parameter of isLocale() comes in place. The strict parameter defaults to false and can be used to prevent degrading when set to true.

Example 6.24. Strict locale detection

```
$input = 'to_RU';
if (Zend_Locale::isLocale($input, true)) {
    print "'{$input}' is a locale";
} else {
    print "Sorry... the given input is no locale";
}
```

Now that you are able to detect if a given string is a locale you could add locale aware behaviour to your own classes. But you will soon detect that this will always leads to the same 15 lines of code. Something like the following example:

Example 6.25. Implement locale aware behaviour

```
if ($locale === null) {
    $locale = new Zend_Locale();
}

if (!Zend_Locale::isLocale($locale, true, false)) {
    if (!Zend_Locale::isLocale($locale, false, false)) {
        throw new Zend_Locale_Exception(
            "The locale '$locale' is no known locale");
    }

    $locale = new Zend_Locale($locale);
}

if ($locale instanceof Zend_Locale) {
    $locale = $locale->toString();
}
```

With Zend Framework 1.8 we added a static `findLocale()` method which returns you a locale string which you can work with. It processes the following tasks:

- Detects if a given string is a locale

- Degrades the locale if it does not exist in the given region

- Returns a previous set application wide locale if no input is given

- Detects the locale from browser when the previous detections failed

- Detects the locale from environment when the previous detections failed

- Detects the locale from framework when the previous detections failed

- Returns always a string which represents the found locale.

The following example shows how these checks and the above code can be simplified with one single call:

Example 6.26. Locale aware behaviour as with ZF 1.8

```
$locale = Zend_Locale::findLocale($inputstring);
```

Normalization and Localization

`Zend_Locale_Format` is a internal component used by `Zend_Locale`. All locale aware classes use `Zend_Locale_Format` for normalization and localization of numbers and dates. Normalization involves parsing input from a variety of data representations, like dates, into a standardized, structured representation, such as a PHP array with year, month, and day elements.

The exact same string containing a number or a date might mean different things to people with different customs and conventions. Disambiguation of numbers and dates requires rules about how to interpret these strings and normalize the values into a standardized data structure. Thus, all methods in `Zend_Locale_Format` require a locale in order to parse the input data.

Default "root" Locale

If no locale is specified, then normalization and localization will use the standard "root" locale, which might yield unexpected behavior, if the input originated in a different locale, or output for a specific locale was expected.

Number normalization: getNumber($input, Array $options)

There are many number systems [http://en.wikipedia.org/wiki/Numeral] different from the common decimal system [http://en.wikipedia.org/wiki/Decimal] (e.g. "3.14"). Numbers can be normalized with the `getNumber()` function to obtain the standard decimal representation. for all number-related discussions in this manual, Arabic/European numerals (0,1,2,3,4,5,6,7,8,9) [http://en.wikipedia.org/wiki/Arabic_numerals] are implied, unless explicitly stated otherwise. The options array may contain a 'locale' to define grouping and decimal characters. The array may also have a 'precision' to truncate excess digits from the result.

Example 6.27. Number normalization

```
$locale = new Zend_Locale('de_AT');
$number = Zend_Locale_Format::getNumber('13.524,678',
                                        array('locale' => $locale,
                                              'precision' => 3)
                                       );

print $number; // will return 13524.678
```

Precision and Calculations

Since `getNumber($value, array $options = array())` can normalize extremely large numbers, check the result carefully before using finite precision calculations, such as ordinary PHP math operations. For example, `if ((string)int_val($number) != $number) {` use BCMath [http://www.php.net/bc] or GMP [http://www.php.net/gmp] . Most PHP installations support the BCMath extension.

Also, the precision of the resulting decimal representation can be rounded to a desired length with `getNumber()` with the option `'precision'`. If no precision is given, no rounding occurs. Use only PHP integers to specify the precision.

If the resulting decimal representation should be truncated to a desired length instead of rounded the option `'number_format'` can be used instead. Define the length of the decimal representation with the desired length of zeros. The result will then not be rounded. So if the defined precision within number_format is zero the value "1.6" will return "1", not "2. See the example nearby:

Example 6.28. Number normalization with precision

```
$locale = new Zend_Locale('de_AT');
$number = Zend_Locale_Format::getNumber('13.524,678',
                                        array('precision' => 1,
                                              'locale' => $locale)
                                       );
print $number; // will return 13524.7

$number = Zend_Locale_Format::getNumber('13.524,678',
                                        array('number_format' => '#.00',
                                              'locale' => $locale)
                                       );
print $number; // will return 13524.67
```

Number localization

`toNumber($value, array $options = array())` can localize numbers to the following supported locales . This function will return a localized string of the given number in a conventional format for a specific locale. The 'number_format' option explicitly specifies a non-default number format for use with `toNumber()`.

Example 6.29. Number localization

```
$locale = new Zend_Locale('de_AT');
$number = Zend_Locale_Format::toNumber(13547.36,
                                       array('locale' => $locale));

// will return 13.547,36
print $number;
```

Unlimited length

toNumber() can localize numbers with unlimited length. It is not related to integer or float limitations.

The same way as within getNumber(), toNumber() handles precision. If no precision is given, the complete localized number will be returned.

Example 6.30. Number localization with precision

```
$locale = new Zend_Locale('de_AT');
$number = Zend_Locale_Format::toNumber(13547.3678,
                                       array('precision' => 2,
                                             'locale' => $locale));

// will return 13.547,37
print $number;
```

Using the option 'number_format' a self defined format for generating a number can be defined. The format itself has to be given in CLDR format as described below. The locale is used to get separation, precision and other number formatting signs from it. German for example defines ',' as precision separation and in English the '.' sign is used.

Table 6.4. Format tokens for self generated number formats

Token	Description	Example format	Generated output
#0	Generates a number without precision and separation	#0	1234567
,	Generates a separation with the length from separation to next separation or to 0	#,##0	1,234,567
#,##,##0	Generates a standard separation of 3 and all following separations with 2	#,##,##0	12,34,567
.	Generates a precision	#0.#	1234567.1234
0	Generates a precision with a defined length	#0.00	1234567.12

Example 6.31. Using a self defined number format

```
$locale = new Zend_Locale('de_AT');
$number = Zend_Locale_Format::toNumber(13547.3678,
                                       array('number_format' => '#,#0.00',
                                             'locale' => 'de')
                                      );

// will return 1.35.47,36
print $number;

$number = Zend_Locale_Format::toNumber(13547.3,
                                       array('number_format' => '#,##0.00',
                                             'locale' => 'de')
                                      );

// will return 13.547,30
print $number;
```

Number testing

isNumber($value, array $options = array()) checks if a given string is a number and returns true or false.

Example 6.32. Number testing

```
$locale = new Zend_Locale();
if (Zend_Locale_Format::isNumber('13.445,36', array('locale' => 'de_AT')) {
    print "Number";
} else {
    print "not a Number";
}
```

Float value normalization

Floating point values can be parsed with the getFloat($value, array $options = array()) function. A floating point value will be returned.

Example 6.33. Floating point value normalization

```
$locale = new Zend_Locale('de_AT');
$number = Zend_Locale_Format::getFloat('13.524,678',
                                       array('precision' => 2,
                                             'locale' => $locale)
                                      );

// will return 13524.68
print $number;
```

Floating point value localization

toFloat() can localize floating point values. This function will return a localized string of the given number.

Example 6.34. Floating point value localization

```
$locale = new Zend_Locale('de_AT');
$number = Zend_Locale_Format::toFloat(13547.3655,
                                      array('precision' => 1,
                                            'locale' => $locale)
                                     );

// will return 13.547,4
print $number;
```

Floating point value testing

isFloat($value, array $options = array()) checks if a given string is a floating point value and returns true or false.

Example 6.35. Floating point value testing

```
$locale = new Zend_Locale('de_AT');
if (Zend_Locale_Format::isFloat('13.445,36', array('locale' => $locale)) {
    print "float";
} else {
    print "not a float";
}
```

Integer value normalization

Integer values can be parsed with the getInteger() function. A integer value will be returned.

Example 6.36. Integer value normalization

```
$locale = new Zend_Locale('de_AT');
$number = Zend_Locale_Format::getInteger('13.524,678',
                                         array('locale' => $locale));

// will return 13524
print $number;
```

Integer point value localization

toInteger($value, array $options = array()) can localize integer values. This function will return a localized string of the given number.

Example 6.37. Integer value localization

```
$locale = new Zend_Locale('de_AT');
$number = Zend_Locale_Format::toInteger(13547.3655,
                                        array('locale' => $locale));

// will return 13.547
print $number;
```

Integer value testing

isInteger($value, array $options = array()) checks if a given string is a integer value and returns true or false.

Example 6.38. Integer value testing

```
$locale = new Zend_Locale('de_AT');
if (Zend_Locale_Format::isInteger('13.445', array('locale' => $locale)) {
    print "integer";
} else {
    print "not a integer";
}
```

Numeral System Conversion

Zend_Locale_Format::convertNumerals() converts digits between different numeral systems [http://en.wikipedia.org/wiki/Arabic_numerals] , including the standard Arabic/European/Latin numeral system (0,1,2,3,4,5,6,7,8,9), not to be confused with Eastern Arabic numerals [http://en.wikipedia.org/wiki/Eastern_Arabic_numerals] sometimes used with the Arabic language to express numerals. Attempts to use an unsupported numeral system will result in an exception, to avoid accidentally performing an incorrect conversion due to a spelling error. All characters in the input, which are not numerals for the selected numeral system, are copied to the output with no conversion provided for unit separator characters. Zend_Locale* components rely on the data provided by CLDR (see their list of scripts grouped by language [http://unicode.org/cldr/data/diff/supplemental/languages_and_scripts.html?sortby=date]).

In CLDR and hereafter, the Europena/Latin numerals will be referred to as "Latin" or by the assigned 4-letter code "Latn". Also, the CLDR refers to this numeral systems as "scripts".

Suppose a web form collected a numeric input expressed using Eastern Arabic digits "####". Most software and PHP functions expect input using Arabic numerals. Fortunately, converting this input to its equivalent Latin numerals "100" requires little effort using convertNumerals($inputNumeralString, $sourceNumeralSystem, $destNumeralSystem) , which returns the $input with numerals in the script $sourceNumeralSystem converted to the script $destNumeralSystem.

Example 6.39. Converting numerals from Eastern Arabic scripts to European/Latin scripts

```
$arabicScript = "####";   // Arabic for "100" (one hundred)
$latinScript = Zend_Locale_Format::convertNumerals($arabicScript,
```

```
                                                        'Arab',
                                                        'Latn');

print "\nOriginal:   " . $arabicScript;
print "\nNormalized: " . $latinScript;
```

Similarly, any of the supported numeral systems may be converted to any other supported numeral system.

Example 6.40. Converting numerals from Latin script to Eastern Arabic script

```
$latinScript = '123';
$arabicScript = Zend_Locale_Format::convertNumerals($latinScript,
                                                     'Latn',
                                                     'Arab');

print "\nOriginal:  " . $latinScript;
print "\nLocalized: " . $arabicScript;
```

Example 6.41. Getting 4 letter CLDR script code using a native-language name of the script

```
function getScriptCode($scriptName, $locale)
{
    $scripts2names = Zend_Locale_Data::getList($locale, 'script');
    $names2scripts = array_flip($scripts2names);
    return $names2scripts[$scriptName];
}
echo getScriptCode('Latin', 'en'); // outputs "Latn"
echo getScriptCode('Tamil', 'en'); // outputs "Taml"
echo getScriptCode('tamoul', 'fr'); // outputs "Taml"
```

List of supported numeral systems

Table 6.5. List of supported numeral systems

Notation Name	Script
Arabic	Arab
Balinese	Bali
Bengali	Beng
Devanagari	Deva
Gujarati	Gujr
Gurmukhi	Guru
Kannada	Knda
Khmer	Khmr
Lao	Laoo

Notation Name	Script
Limbu	Limb
Malayalam	Mlym
Mongolian	Mong
Myanmar	Mymr
New_Tai_Lue	Talu
Nko	Nkoo
Oriya	Orya
Tamil	Taml
Telugu	Telu
Thai	Tale
Tibetan	Tibt

Working with Dates and Times

`Zend_Locale_Format` provides several methods for working with dates and times to help convert and normalize between different formats for different locales. Use `Zend_Date` for manipulating dates, and working with date strings that already conform to one of the many internationally recognized standard formats, or one of the localized date formats supported by `Zend_Date`. Using an existing, pre-defined format offers advantages, including the use of well-tested code, and the assurance of some degree of portability and interoperability (depending on the standard used). The examples below do not follow these recommendations, since using non-standard date formats would needlessly increase the difficulty of understanding these examples.

Normalizing Dates and Times

The `getDate()` method parses strings containing dates in localized formats. The results are returned in a structured array, with well-defined keys for each part of the date. In addition, the array will contain a key 'date_format' showing the format string used to parse the input date string. Since a localized date string may not contain all parts of a date/time, the key-value pairs are optional. For example, if only the year, month, and day is given, then all time values are suppressed from the returned array, and vice-versa if only hour, minute, and second were given as input. If no date or time can be found within the given input, an exception will be thrown.

If `setOption(array('fix_date' => true))` is set the `getDate()` method adds a key 'fixed' with a whole number value indicating if the input date string required "fixing" by rearranging the day, month, or year in the input to fit the format used.

Table 6.6. Key values for getDate() with option 'fix_date'

value	meaning
0	nothing to fix
1	fixed false month
2	swapped day and year
3	swapped month and year
4	swapped month and day

For those needing to specify explicitly the format of the date string, the following format token specifiers are supported. If an invalid format specifier is used, such as the PHP 'i' specifier when in ISO format mode, then an error will be thrown by the methods in `Zend_Locale_Format` that support user-defined formats.

These specifiers (below) are a small subset of the full "ISO" set supported by `Zend_Date`'s `toString()`. If you need to use PHP `date()` compatible format specifiers, then first call `setOptions(array('format_type' => 'php'))`. And if you want to convert only one special format string from PHP `date()` compatible format to "ISO" format use `convertPhpToIsoFormat()`. Currently, the only practical difference relates to the specifier for minutes ('m' using the ISO default, and 'i' using the PHP date format).

Table 6.7. Return values

getDate() format character	Array key	Returned value	Minimum	Maximum
d	day	integer	1	31
M	month	integer	1	12
y	year	integer	no limit	PHP integer's maximum
h	hour	integer	0	PHP integer's maximum
m	minute	integer	0	PHP integer's maximum
s	second	integer	0	PHP integer's maximum

Example 6.42. Normalizing a date

```
$dateString = Zend_Locale_Format::getDate('13.04.2006',
                                  array('date_format' =>
                                          'dd.MM.yyyy')
                              );

// creates a Zend_Date object for this date
$dateObject = Zend_Date('13.04.2006',
                    array('date_format' => 'dd.MM.yyyy'));

print_r($dateString); // outputs:

Array
(
    [format] => dd.MM.yyyy
    [day] => 13
    [month] => 4
    [year] => 2006
)

// alternatively, some types of problems with input data can be
// automatically corrected
$date = Zend_Locale_Format::getDate('04.13.2006',
                              array('date_format' => 'dd.MM.yyyy',
                                    'fix_date' => true)
                          );
```

```
print_r($date); // outputs:

Array
(
    [format] => dd.MM.yyyy
    [day] => 13
    [month] => 4
    [year] => 2006
    [fixed] => 4
)
```

Since getDate() is "locale-aware", specifying the $locale is sufficient for date strings adhering to that locale's format. The option 'fix_date' uses simple tests to determine if the day or month is not valid, and then applies heuristics to try and correct any detected problems. Note the use of 'Zend_Locale_Format::STANDARD' as the value for 'date_format' to prevent the use of a class-wide default date format set using setOptions(). This forces getDate to use the default date format for $locale.

Example 6.43. Normalizing a date by locale

```
$locale = new Zend_Locale('de_AT');
$date = Zend_Locale_Format::getDate('13.04.2006',
                                    array('date_format' =>
                                              Zend_Locale_Format::STANDARD,
                                          'locale' => $locale)
                                   );
print_r ($date);
```

A complete date and time is returned when the input contains both a date and time in the expected format.

Example 6.44. Normalizing a date with time

```
$locale = new Zend_Locale('de_AT');
$date = Zend_Locale_Format::getDate('13.04.2005 22:14:55',
                                    array('date_format' =>
                                              Zend_Locale_Format::STANDARD,
                                          'locale' => $locale)
                                   );

print_r ($date);
```

If a specific format is desired, specify the $format argument, without giving a $locale. Only single-letter codes (H, m, s, y, M, d), and MMMM and EEEE are supported in the $format.

Example 6.45. Normalizing a userdefined date

```
$date = Zend_Locale_Format::getDate('13200504T551422',
                                    array('date_format' =>
                                              'ddyyyyMM ssmmHH')
                                   );

print_r ($date);
```

The format can include the following signs :

Table 6.8. Format definition

Format Letter	Description
d or dd	1 or 2 digit day
M or MM	1 or 2 digit month
y or yy	1 or 2 digit year
yyyy	4 digit year
h	1 or 2 digit hour
m	1 or 2 digit minute
s	1 or 2 digit second

Examples for proper formats are

Table 6.9. Example formats

Formats	Input	Output
dd.MM.yy	1.4.6	['day'] => 1, ['month'] => 4, ['year'] => 6
dd.MM.yy	01.04.2006	['day'] => 1, ['month'] => 4, ['year'] => 2006
yyyyMMdd	1.4.6	['day'] => 6, ['month'] => 4, ['year'] => 1

Database date format

To parse a database date value (f.e. MySql or MsSql), use Zend_Date's ISO_8601 format instead of getDate().

The option 'fix_date' uses simple tests to determine if the day or month is not valid, and then applies heuristics to try and correct any detected problems. getDate() automatically detects and corrects some kinds of problems with input, such as misplacing the year:

Example 6.46. Automatic correction of input dates

```
$date = Zend_Locale_Format::getDate('41.10.20',
                          array('date_format' => 'ddMMyy',
                                'fix_date' => true)
                      );

// instead of 41 for the day, the 41 will be returned as year value
print_r ($date);
```

Testing Dates

Use checkDateFormat($inputString, array('date_format' => $format, $locale)) to check if a given string contains all expected date parts. The checkDateFormat() method uses getDate(), but without the option 'fixdate' to avoid returning true when the input fails to conform to the date format. If errors are detected in the input, such as swapped values for months and days, the option 'fixdate' method will apply heuristics to "correct" dates before determining their validity.

Example 6.47. Date testing

```
$locale = new Zend_Locale('de_AT');
// using the default date format for 'de_AT', is this a valid date?
if (Zend_Locale_Format::checkDateFormat('13.Apr.2006',
                                        array('date_format' =>
                                                      Zend_Locale_Format::
                                                      STANDARD, $locale)
                          ) {
    print "date";
} else {
    print "not a date";
}
```

Normalizing a Time

Normally, a time will be returned with a date, if the input contains both. If the proper format is not known, but the locale relevant to the user input is known, then getTime() should be used, because it uses the default time format for the selected locale.

Example 6.48. Normalize an unknown time

```
$locale = new Zend_Locale('de_AT');
if (Zend_Locale_Format::getTime('13:44:42',
                                array('date_format' =>
                                          Zend_Locale_Format::STANDARD,
                                          'locale' => $locale)) {
    print "time";
} else {
    print "not a time";
}
```

Testing Times

Use checkDateFormat() to check if a given string contains a proper time. The usage is exact the same as with checking Dates, only date_format should contain the parts which you expect to have.

Example 6.49. Testing a time

```
$locale = new Zend_Locale('de_AT');
if (Zend_Locale_Format::checkDateFormat('13:44:42',
                                        array('date_format' => 'HH:mm:ss',
                                              'locale' => $locale)) {
    print "time";
} else {
    print "not a time";
}
```

Supported locales

Zend_Locale provides information on several locales. The following table shows all languages and their related locales, sorted by language:

Table 6.10. List of all supported languages

Language	Locale	Region
Afar	aa	---
	aa_DJ	Djibouti
	aa_ER	Eritrea
	aa_ET	Ethiopia
Afrikaans	af	---
	af_NA	Namibia
	af_ZA	South Africa
Akan	ak	---
	ak_GH	Ghana
Amharic	am	---
	am_ET	Ethiopia

Language	Locale	Region
Arabic	ar	---
	ar_AE	United Arab Emirates
	ar_BH	Bahrain
	ar_DZ	Algeria
	ar_EG	Egypt
	ar_IQ	Iraq
	ar_JO	Jordan
	ar_KW	Kuwait
	ar_LB	Lebanon
	ar_LY	Libya
	ar_MA	Morocco
	ar_OM	Oman
	ar_QA	Qatar
	ar_SA	Saudi Arabia
	ar_SD	Sudan
	ar_SY	Syria
	ar_TN	Tunisia
	ar_YE	Yemen
Assamese	as	---
	as_IN	India
Azerbaijani	az	---
	az_AZ	Azerbaijan
Belarusian	be	---
	be_BY	Belarus
Bulgarian	bg	---
	bg_BG	Bulgaria
Bengali	bn	---
	bn_BD	Bangladesh
	bn_IN	India
Bosnian	bs	---
	bs_BA	Bosnia and Herzegovina
Blin	byn	---
	byn_ER	Eritrea
Catalan	ca	---
	ca_ES	Spain
Atsam	cch	---
	cch_NG	Nigeria
Coptic	cop	---
Czech	cs	---
	cs_CZ	Czech Republic

Language	Locale	Region
Welsh	cy	---
	cy_GB	United Kingdom
Danish	da	---
	da_DK	Denmark
German	de	---
	de_AT	Austria
	de_BE	Belgium
	de_CH	Switzerland
	de_DE	Germany
	de_LI	Liechtenstein
	de_LU	Luxembourg
Divehi	dv	---
	dv_MV	Maldives
Dzongkha	dz	---
	dz_BT	Bhutan
Ewe	ee	---
	ee_GH	Ghana
	ee_TG	Togo
Greek	el	---
	el_CY	Cyprus
	el_GR	Greece

Language	Locale	Region
English	en	---
	en_AS	American Samoa
	en_AU	Australia
	en_BE	Belgium
	en_BW	Botswana
	en_BZ	Belize
	en_CA	Canada
	en_GB	United Kingdom
	en_GU	Guam
	en_HK	Hong Kong
	en_IE	Ireland
	en_IN	India
	en_JM	Jamaica
	en_MH	Marshall Islands
	en_MP	Northern Mariana Islands
	en_MT	Malta
	en_NA	Namibia
	en_NZ	New Zealand
	en_PH	Philippines
	en_PK	Pakistan
	en_SG	Singapore
	en_TT	Trinidad and Tobago
	en_UM	United States Minor Outlying Islands
	en_US	United States
	en_VI	U.S. Virgin Islands
	en_ZA	South Africa
	en_ZW	Zimbabwe
Esperanto	eo	---

Language	Locale	Region
Spanish	es	---
	es_AR	Argentina
	es_BO	Bolivia
	es_CL	Chile
	es_CO	Colombia
	es_CR	Costa Rica
	es_DO	Dominican Republic
	es_EC	Ecuador
	es_ES	Spain
	es_GT	Guatemala
	es_HN	Honduras
	es_MX	Mexico
	es_NI	Nicaragua
	es_PA	Panama
	es_PE	Peru
	es_PR	Puerto Rico
	es_PY	Paraguay
	es_SV	El Salvador
	es_US	United States
	es_UY	Uruguay
	es_VE	Venezuela
Estonian	et	---
	et_EE	Estonia
Basque	eu	---
	eu_ES	Spain
Persian	fa	---
	fa_AF	Afghanistan
	fa_IR	Iran
Finnish	fi	---
	fi_FI	Finland
Filipino	fil	---
	fil_PH	Philippines
Faroese	fo	---
	fo_FO	Faroe Islands

Language	Locale	Region
French	fr	---
	fr_BE	Belgium
	fr_CA	Canada
	fr_CH	Switzerland
	fr_FR	France
	fr_LU	Luxembourg
	fr_MC	Monaco
	fr_SN	Senegal
Friulian	fur	---
	fur_IT	Italy
Irish	ga	---
	ga_IE	Ireland
Ga	gaa	---
	gaa_GH	Ghana
Geez	gez	---
	gez_ER	Eritrea
	gez_ET	Ethiopia
Gallegan	gl	---
	gl_ES	Spain
Gujarati	gu	---
	gu_IN	India
Manx	gv	---
	gv_GB	United Kingdom
Hausa	ha	---
	ha_GH	Ghana
	ha_NE	Niger
	ha_NG	Nigeria
	ha_SD	Sudan
Hawaiian	haw	---
	haw_US	United States
Hebrew	he	---
	he_IL	Israel
Hindi	hi	---
	hi_IN	India
Croatian	hr	---
	hr_HR	Croatia
Hungarian	hu	---
	hu_HU	Hungary
Armenian	hy	---
Interlingua	ia	---

Language	Locale	Region
Indonesian	id	---
	id_ID	Indonesia
Igbo	ig	---
	ig_NG	Nigeria
Sichuan Yi	ii	---
	ii_CN	China
Indonesian	in	---
Icelandic	is	---
	is_IS	Iceland
Italian	it	---
	it_CH	Switzerland
	it_IT	Italy
Inuktitut	iu	---
Hebrew	iw	---
Japanese	ja	---
	ja_JP	Japan
Georgian	ka	---
	ka_GE	Georgia
Jju	kaj	---
	kaj_NG	Nigeria
Kamba	kam	---
	kam_KE	Kenya
Tyap	kcg	---
	kcg_NG	Nigeria
Koro	kfo	---
	kfo_CI	Ivory Coast
Kazakh	kk	---
	kk_KZ	Kazakhstan
Kalaallisut	kl	---
	kl_GL	Greenland
Khmer	km	---
	km_KH	Cambodia
Kannada	kn	---
	kn_IN	India
Korean	ko	---
	ko_KR	South Korea
Konkani	kok	---
	kok_IN	India
Kpelle	kpe	---
	kpe_GN	Guinea
	kpe_LR	Liberia

Language	Locale	Region
Kurdish	ku	---
	ku_TR	Turkey
Cornish	kw	---
	kw_GB	United Kingdom
Kirghiz	ky	---
	ky_KG	Kyrgyzstan
Lingala	ln	---
	ln_CD	Congo - Kinshasa
	ln_CG	Congo - Brazzaville
Lao	lo	---
	lo_LA	Laos
Lithuanian	lt	---
	lt_LT	Lithuania
Latvian	lv	---
	lv_LV	Latvia
Macedonian	mk	---
	mk_MK	Macedonia
Malayalam	ml	---
	ml_IN	India
Mongolian	mn	---
	mn_CN	China
	mn_MN	Mongolia
Romanian	mo	---
Marathi	mr	---
	mr_IN	India
Malay	ms	---
	ms_BN	Brunei
	ms_MY	Malaysia
Maltese	mt	---
	mt_MT	Malta
Burmese	my	---
	my_MM	Myanmar
Norwegian Bokmal	nb	---
	nb_NO	Norway
Nepali	ne	---
	ne_IN	India
	ne_NP	Nepal
Dutch	nl	---
	nl_BE	Belgium
	nl_NL	Netherlands

Language	Locale	Region
Norwegian Nynorsk	nn	---
	nn_NO	Norway
Norwegian	no	---
South Ndebele	nr	---
	nr_ZA	South Africa
Northern Sotho	nso	---
	nso_ZA	South Africa
Nyanja	ny	---
	ny_MW	Malawi
Oromo	om	---
	om_ET	Ethiopia
	om_KE	Kenya
Oriya	or	---
	or_IN	India
Punjabi	pa	---
	pa_IN	India
	pa_PK	Pakistan
Polish	pl	---
	pl_PL	Poland
Pashto	ps	---
	ps_AF	Afghanistan
Portuguese	pt	---
	pt_BR	Brazil
	pt_PT	Portugal
Romanian	ro	---
	ro_MD	Moldova
	ro_RO	Romania
Russian	ru	---
	ru_RU	Russia
	ru_UA	Ukraine
Kinyarwanda	rw	---
	rw_RW	Rwanda
Sanskrit	sa	---
	sa_IN	India
Northern Sami	se	---
	se_FI	Finland
	se_NO	Norway
Serbo-Croatian	sh	---
	sh_BA	Bosnia and Herzegovina
	sh_CS	Serbia and Montenegro
	sh_YU	Serbia

Language	Locale	Region
Sinhala	si	---
	si_LK	Sri Lanka
Sidamo	sid	---
	sid_ET	Ethiopia
Slovak	sk	---
	sk_SK	Slovakia
Slovenian	sl	---
	sl_SI	Slovenia
Somali	so	---
	so_DJ	Djibouti
	so_ET	Ethiopia
	so_KE	Kenya
	so_SO	Somalia
Albanian	sq	---
	sq_AL	Albania
Serbian	sr	---
	sr_BA	Bosnia and Herzegovina
	sr_CS	Serbia and Montenegro
	sr_ME	Montenegro
	sr_RS	Serbia
	sr_YU	Serbia
Swati	ss	---
	ss_SZ	Swaziland
	ss_ZA	South Africa
Southern Sotho	st	---
	st_LS	Lesotho
	st_ZA	South Africa
Swedish	sv	---
	sv_FI	Finland
	sv_SE	Sweden
Swahili	sw	---
	sw_KE	Kenya
	sw_TZ	Tanzania
Syriac	syr	---
	syr_SY	Syria
Tamil	ta	---
	ta_IN	India
Telugu	te	---
	te_IN	India
Tajik	tg	---
	tg_TJ	Tajikistan

Language	Locale	Region
Thai	th	---
	th_TH	Thailand
Tigrinya	ti	---
	ti_ER	Eritrea
	ti_ET	Ethiopia
Tigre	tig	---
	tig_ER	Eritrea
Tagalog	tl	---
Tswana	tn	---
	tn_ZA	South Africa
Tonga	to	---
	to_TO	Tonga
Turkish	tr	---
	tr_TR	Turkey
Tsonga	ts	---
	ts_ZA	South Africa
Tatar	tt	---
	tt_RU	Russia
Uighur	ug	---
	ug_CN	China
Ukrainian	uk	---
	uk_UA	Ukraine
Urdu	ur	---
	ur_IN	India
	ur_PK	Pakistan
Uzbek	uz	---
	uz_AF	Afghanistan
	uz_UZ	Uzbekistan
Venda	ve	---
	ve_ZA	South Africa
Vietnamese	vi	---
	vi_VN	Vietnam
Walamo	wal	---
	wal_ET	Ethiopia
Wolof	wo	---
	wo_SN	Senegal
Xhosa	xh	---
	xh_ZA	South Africa
Yoruba	yo	---
	yo_NG	Nigeria

Language	Locale	Region
Chinese	zh	---
	zh_CN	China
	zh_HK	Hong Kong
	zh_MO	Macau
	zh_SG	Singapore
	zh_TW	Taiwan
Zulu	zu	---
	zu_ZA	South Africa

Migrating from previous versions

The API of Zend_Locale has changed from time to time. If you started to use Zend_Locale and its subcomponents in earlier versions follow the guidelines below to migrate your scripts to use the new API.

Migrating from 1.6 to 1.7 or newer

Changes when using isLocale()

According to the coding standards isLocale() had to be changed to return a boolean. In previous releases a string was returned on success. For release 1.7 a compatibility mode has been added which allows to use the old behaviour of a returned string, but it triggers a user warning to mention you to change to the new behaviour. The rerouting which the old behaviour of isLocale() could have done is no longer neccessary as all I18N will now process a rerouting themself.

To migrate your scripts to the new API, simply use the method as shown below.

Example 6.50. How to change isLocale() from 1.6 to 1.7

```
// Example for 1.6
if ($locale = Zend_Locale::isLocale($locale)) {
    // do something
}

// Same example for 1.7

// You should change the compatiblity mode to prevent user warnings
// But you can do this in your bootstrap
Zend_Locale::$compatibilityMode = false;

if (Zend_Locale::isLocale($locale)) {
}
```

Note that you can use the second parameter to see if the locale is correct without processing a rerouting.

```
// Example for 1.6
if ($locale = Zend_Locale::isLocale($locale, false)) {
    // do something
}

// Same example for 1.7
```

```
// You should change the compatiblity mode to prevent user warnings
// But you can do this in your bootstrap
Zend_Locale::$compatibilityMode = false;

if (Zend_Locale::isLocale($locale, false)) {
    if (Zend_Locale::isLocale($locale, true)) {
        // no locale at all
    }

    // original string is no locale but can be rerouted
}
```

Changes when using getDefault()

The meaning of the getDefault() method has been change due to the fact that we integrated a framework locale which can be set with setDefault(). It does no longer return the locale chain but only the set framework locale.

To migrate your scripts to the new API, simply use the method as shown below.

Example 6.51. How to change getDefault() from 1.6 to 1.7

```
// Example for 1.6
$locales = $locale->getDefault(Zend_Locale::BROWSER);

// Same example for 1.7

// You should change the compatiblity mode to prevent user warnings
// But you can do this in your bootstrap
Zend_Locale::$compatibilityMode = false;

$locale = Zend_Locale::getOrder(Zend_Locale::BROWSER);
```

Note that the second parameter of the old getDefault() implementation is not available anymore, but the returned values are the same.

Note

Per default the old behaviour is still active, but throws a user warning. When you have changed your code to the new behaviour you should also change the compatibility mode to false so that no warning is thrown anymore.

Chapter 7. Zend_Log

Overview

Zend_Log is a component for general purpose logging. It supports multiple log backends, formatting messages sent to the log, and filtering messages from being logged. These functions are divided into the following objects:

- A Log (instance of Zend_Log) is the object that your application uses the most. You can have as many Log objects as you like; they do not interact. A Log object must contain at least one Writer, and can optionally contain one or more Filters.

- A Writer (inherits from Zend_Log_Writer_Abstract) is responsible for saving data to storage.

- A Filter (implements Zend_Log_Filter_Interface) blocks log data from being saved. A filter may be applied to an individual Writer, or to a Log where it is applied before all Writers. In either case, filters may be chained.

- A Formatter (implements Zend_Log_Formatter_Interface) can format the log data before it is written by a Writer. Each Writer has exactly one Formatter.

Creating a Log

To get started logging, instantiate a Writer and then pass it to a Log instance:

```
$logger = new Zend_Log();
$writer = new Zend_Log_Writer_Stream('php://output');

$logger->addWriter($writer);
```

It is important to note that the Log must have at least one Writer. You can add any number of Writers using the Log's addWriter() method.

Alternatively, you can pass a Writer directly to constructor of Log as a shortcut:

```
$writer = new Zend_Log_Writer_Stream('php://output');
$logger = new Zend_Log($writer);
```

The Log is now ready to use.

Logging Messages

To log a message, call the log() method of a Log instance and pass it the message with a corresponding priority:

```
$logger->log('Informational message', Zend_Log::INFO);
```

The first parameter of the log() method is a string message and the second parameter is an integer priority. The priority must be one of the priorities recognized by the Log instance. This is explained in the next section.

A shortcut is also available. Instead of calling the `log()` method, you can call a method by the same name as the priority:

```
$logger->log('Informational message', Zend_Log::INFO);
$logger->info('Informational message');

$logger->log('Emergency message', Zend_Log::EMERG);
$logger->emerg('Emergency message');
```

Destroying a Log

If the Log object is no longer needed, set the variable containing it to `null` to destroy it. This will automatically call the `shutdown()` instance method of each attached Writer before the Log object is destroyed:

```
$logger = null;
```

Explicitly destroying the log in this way is optional and is performed automatically at PHP shutdown.

Using Built-in Priorities

The `Zend_Log` class defines the following priorities:

```
EMERG   = 0;   // Emergency: system is unusable
ALERT   = 1;   // Alert: action must be taken immediately
CRIT    = 2;   // Critical: critical conditions
ERR     = 3;   // Error: error conditions
WARN    = 4;   // Warning: warning conditions
NOTICE  = 5;   // Notice: normal but significant condition
INFO    = 6;   // Informational: informational messages
DEBUG   = 7;   // Debug: debug messages
```

These priorities are always available, and a convenience method of the same name is available for each one.

The priorities are not arbitrary. They come from the BSD `syslog` protocol, which is described in RFC-3164 [http://tools.ietf.org/html/rfc3164]. The names and corresponding priority numbers are also compatible with another PHP logging system, PEAR Log [http://pear.php.net/package/log], which perhaps promotes interoperability between it and `Zend_Log`.

Priority numbers descend in order of importance. EMERG (0) is the most important priority. DEBUG (7) is the least important priority of the built-in priorities. You may define priorities of lower importance than DEBUG. When selecting the priority for your log message, be aware of this priority hierarchy and choose appropriately.

Adding User-defined Priorities

User-defined priorities can be added at runtime using the Log's `addPriority()` method:

```
$logger->addPriority('FOO', 8);
```

The snippet above creates a new priority, FOO, whose value is 8. The new priority is then available for logging:

```
$logger->log('Foo message', 8);
$logger->foo('Foo Message');
```

New priorities cannot overwrite existing ones.

Understanding Log Events

When you call the `log()` method or one of its shortcuts, a log event is created. This is simply an associative array with data describing the event that is passed to the writers. The following keys are always created in this array: `timestamp`, `message`, `priority`, and `priorityName`.

The creation of the `event` array is completely transparent. However, knowledge of the `event` array is required for adding an item that does not exist in the default set above.

To add a new item to every future event, call the `setEventItem()` method giving a key and a value:

```
$logger->setEventItem('pid', getmypid());
```

The example above sets a new item named `pid` and populates it with the PID of the current process. Once a new item has been set, it is available automatically to all writers along with all of the other data event data during logging. An item can be overwritten at any time by calling the `setEventItem()` method again.

Setting a new event item with `setEventItem()` causes the new item to be sent to all writers of the logger. However, this does not guarantee that the writers actually record the item. This is because the writers won't know what to do with it unless a formatter object is informed of the new item. Please see the section on Formatters to learn more.

Writers

A Writer is an object that inherits from `Zend_Log_Writer_Abstract`. A Writer's responsibility is to record log data to a storage backend.

Writing to Streams

`Zend_Log_Writer_Stream` sends log data to a PHP stream [http://www.php.net/stream].

To write log data to the PHP output buffer, use the URL `php://output`. Alternatively, you can send log data directly to a stream like `STDERR` (`php://stderr`).

```
$writer = new Zend_Log_Writer_Stream('php://output');
$logger = new Zend_Log($writer);

$logger->info('Informational message');
```

To write data to a file, use one of the Filesystem URLs [http://www.php.net/manual/en/wrappers.php#wrappers.file]:

```
$writer = new Zend_Log_Writer_Stream('/path/to/logfile');
$logger = new Zend_Log($writer);

$logger->info('Informational message');
```

By default, the stream opens in the append mode ("a"). To open it with a different mode, the `Zend_Log_Writer_Stream` constructor accepts an optional second parameter for the mode.

The constructor of `Zend_Log_Writer_Stream` also accepts an existing stream resource:

```
$stream = @fopen('/path/to/logfile', 'a', false);
if (! $stream) {
    throw new Exception('Failed to open stream');
}

$writer = new Zend_Log_Writer_Stream($stream);
```

```
$logger = new Zend_Log($writer);

$logger->info('Informational message');
```

You cannot specify the mode for existing stream resources. Doing so causes a Zend_Log_Exception to be thrown.

Writing to Databases

Zend_Log_Writer_Db writes log information to a database table using Zend_Db. The constructor of Zend_Log_Writer_Db receives a Zend_Db_Adapter instance, a table name, and a mapping of database columns to event data items:

```
$params = array ('host'     => '127.0.0.1',
                 'username' => 'malory',
                 'password' => '******',
                 'dbname'   => 'camelot');
$db = Zend_Db::factory('PDO_MYSQL', $params);

$columnMapping = array('lvl' => 'priority', 'msg' => 'message');
$writer = new Zend_Log_Writer_Db($db, 'log_table_name', $columnMapping);

$logger = new Zend_Log($writer);

$logger->info('Informational message');
```

The example above writes a single row of log data to the database table named log_table_name table. The database column named lvl receives the priority number and the column named msg receives the log message.

Writing to Firebug

Zend_Log_Writer_Firebug sends log data to the Firebug [http://www.getfirebug.com/] Console [http://getfirebug.com/logging.html].

All data is sent via the Zend_Wildfire_Channel_HttpHeaders component which uses HTTP headers to ensure the page content is not disturbed. Debugging AJAX requests that require clean JSON and XML responses is possible with this approach.

Requirements:

- Firefox Browser ideally version 3 but version 2 is also supported.

- Firebug Firefox Extension which you can download from https://addons.mozilla.org/en-US/firefox/addon/1843.

- FirePHP Firefox Extension which you can download from https://addons.mozilla.org/en-US/firefox/addon/6149.

Example 7.1. Logging with Zend_Controller_Front

```
// Place this in your bootstrap file before dispatching your front controller
$writer = new Zend_Log_Writer_Firebug();
$logger = new Zend_Log($writer);

// Use this in your model, view and controller files
$logger->log('This is a log message!', Zend_Log::INFO);
```

Example 7.2. Logging without Zend_Controller_Front

```
$writer = new Zend_Log_Writer_Firebug();
$logger = new Zend_Log($writer);

$request = new Zend_Controller_Request_Http();
$response = new Zend_Controller_Response_Http();
$channel = Zend_Wildfire_Channel_HttpHeaders::getInstance();
$channel->setRequest($request);
$channel->setResponse($response);

// Start output buffering
ob_start();

// Now you can make calls to the logger

$logger->log('This is a log message!', Zend_Log::INFO);

// Flush log data to browser
$channel->flush();
$response->sendHeaders();
```

Setting Styles for Priorities

Built-in and user-defined priorities can be styled with the setPriorityStyle() method.

```
$logger->addPriority('FOO', 8);
$writer->setPriorityStyle(8, 'TRACE');
$logger->foo('Foo Message');
```

The default style for user-defined priorities can be set with the setDefaultPriorityStyle() method.

```
$writer->setDefaultPriorityStyle('TRACE');
```

The supported styles are as follows:

Table 7.1. Firebug Logging Styles

Style	Description
LOG	Displays a plain log message
INFO	Displays an info log message
WARN	Displays a warning log message
ERROR	Displays an error log message that increments Firebug's error count
TRACE	Displays a log message with an expandable stack trace
EXCEPTION	Displays an error long message with an expandable stack trace
TABLE	Displays a log message with an expandable table

Preparing data for Logging

While any PHP variable can be logged with the built-in priorities, some special formatting is required if using some of the more specialized log styles.

The LOG, INFO, WARN, ERROR and TRACE styles require no special formatting.

Exception Logging

To log a Zend_Exception simply pass the exception object to the logger. It does not matter which priority or style you have set as the exception is automatically recognized.

```
$exception = new Zend_Exception('Test exception');
$logger->err($exception);
```

Table Logging

You can also log data and format it in a table style. Columns are automatically recognized and the first row of data automatically becomes the header.

```
$writer->setPriorityStyle(8, 'TABLE');
$logger->addPriority('TABLE', 8);

$table = array('Summary line for the table',
            array(
                array('Column 1', 'Column 2'),
                array('Row 1 c 1',' Row 1 c 2'),
                array('Row 2 c 1',' Row 2 c 2')
            )
            );
$logger->table($table);
```

Writing to Email

Zend_Log_Writer_Mail writes log entries in an email message by using Zend_Mail. The Zend_Log_Writer_Mail constructor takes a Zend_Mail object, and an optional Zend_Layout object.

The primary use case for `Zend_Log_Writer_Mail` is notifying developers, systems administrators, or any concerned parties of errors that might be occurring with PHP-based scripts. `Zend_Log_Writer_Mail` was born out of the idea that if something is broken, a human being needs to be alerted of it immediately so they can take corrective action.

Basic usage is outlined below:

```
$mail = new Zend_Mail();
$mail->setFrom('errors@example.org')
    ->addTo('project_developers@example.org');

$writer = new Zend_Log_Writer_Mail($mail);

// Set subject text for use; summary of number of errors is appended to the
// subject line before sending the message.
$writer->setSubjectPrependText('Errors with script foo.php');

// Only email warning level entries and higher.
$writer->addFilter(Zend_Log::WARN);

$log = new Zend_Log();
$log->addWriter($writer);

// Something bad happened!
$log->error('unable to connect to database');

// On writer shutdown, Zend_Mail::send() is triggered to send an email with
// all log entries at or above the Zend_Log filter level.
```

`Zend_Log_Writer_Mail` will render the email body as plain text by default.

One email is sent containing all log entries at or above the filter level. For example, if warning-level entries an up are to be emailed, and two warnings and five errors occur, the resulting email will contain a total of seven log entries.

Zend_Layout Usage

A `Zend_Layout` instance may be used to generate the HTML portion of a multipart email. If a `Zend_Layout` instance is in use, `Zend_Log_Writer_Mail` assumes that it is being used to render HTML and sets the body HTML for the message as the `Zend_Layout`-rendered value.

When using `Zend_Log_Writer_Mail` with a `Zend_Layout` instance, you have the option to set a custom formatter by using the `setLayoutFormatter()` method. If no `Zend_Layout`-specific entry formatter was specified, the formatter currently in use will be used. Full usage of `Zend_Layout` with a custom formatter is outlined below.

```
$mail = new Zend_Mail();
$mail->setFrom('errors@example.org')
    ->addTo('project_developers@example.org');
// Note that a subject line is not being set on the Zend_Mail instance!

// Use a simple Zend_Layout instance with its defaults.
$layout = new Zend_Layout();

// Create a formatter that wraps the entry in a listitem tag.
$layoutFormatter = new Zend_Log_Formatter_Simple(
    '<li>' . Zend_Layout::DEFAULT_FORMAT . '</li>'
);

$writer = new Zend_Log_Writer_Mail($mail, $layout);
```

```
// Apply the formatter for entries as rendered with Zend_Layout.
$writer->setLayoutFormatter($layoutFormatter);
$writer->setSubjectPrependText('Errors with script foo.php');
$writer->addFilter(Zend_Log::WARN);

$log = new Zend_Log();
$log->addWriter($writer);

// Something bad happened!
$log->error('unable to connect to database');

// On writer shutdown, Zend_Mail::send() is triggered to send an email with
// all log entries at or above the Zend_Log filter level. The email will
// contain both plain text and HTML parts.
```

Subject Line Error Level Summary

The `setSubjectPrependText()` method may be used in place of `Zend_Mail::setSubject()` to have the email subject line dynamically written before the email is sent. For example, if the subject prepend text reads "Errors from script", the subject of an email generated by `Zend_Log_Writer_Mail` with two warnings and five errors would be "Errors from script (warn = 2; error = 5)". If subject prepend text is not in use via `Zend_Log_Writer_Mail`, the `Zend_Mail` subject line, if any, is used.

Caveats

Sending log entries via email can be dangerous. If error conditions are being improperly handled by your script, or if you're misusing the error levels, you might find yourself in a situation where you are sending hundreds or thousands of emails to the recipients depending on the frequency of your errors.

At this time, `Zend_Log_Writer_Mail` does not provide any mechanism for throttling or otherwise batching up the messages. Such functionallity should be implemented by the consumer if necessary.

Again, `Zend_Log_Writer_Mail`'s primary goal is to proactively notify a human being of error conditions. If those errors are being handled in a timely fashion, and safeguards are being put in place to prevent those circumstances in the future, then email-based notification of errors can be a valuable tool.

Stubbing Out the Writer

The `Zend_Log_Writer_Null` is a stub that does not write log data to anything. It is useful for disabling logging or stubbing out logging during tests:

```
$writer = new Zend_Log_Writer_Null;
$logger = new Zend_Log($writer);

// goes nowhere
$logger->info('Informational message');
```

Testing with the Mock

The `Zend_Log_Writer_Mock` is a very simple writer that records the raw data it receives in an array exposed as a public property.

```
$mock = new Zend_Log_Writer_Mock;
$logger = new Zend_Log($mock);

$logger->info('Informational message');
```

```
var_dump($mock->events[0]);

// Array
// (
//     [timestamp] => 2007-04-06T07:16:37-07:00
//     [message] => Informational message
//     [priority] => 6
//     [priorityName] => INFO
// )
```

To clear the events logged by the mock, simply set `$mock->events = array()`.

Compositing Writers

There is no composite Writer object. However, a Log instance can write to any number of Writers. To do this, use the `addWriter()` method:

```
$writer1 = new Zend_Log_Writer_Stream('/path/to/first/logfile');
$writer2 = new Zend_Log_Writer_Stream('/path/to/second/logfile');

$logger = new Zend_Log();
$logger->addWriter($writer1);
$logger->addWriter($writer2);

// goes to both writers
$logger->info('Informational message');
```

Formatters

A Formatter is an object that is responsible for taking an `event` array describing a log event and outputting a string with a formatted log line.

Some Writers are not line-oriented and cannot use a Formatter. An example is the Database Writer, which inserts the event items directly into database columns. For Writers that cannot support a Formatter, an exception is thrown if you attempt to set a Formatter.

Simple Formatting

`Zend_Log_Formatter_Simple` is the default formatter. It is configured automatically when you specify no formatter. The default configuration is equivalent to the following:

```
$format = '%timestamp% %priorityName% (%priority%): %message%' . PHP_EOL;
$formatter = new Zend_Log_Formatter_Simple($format);
```

A formatter is set on an individual Writer object using the Writer's `setFormatter()` method:

```
$writer = new Zend_Log_Writer_Stream('php://output');
$formatter = new Zend_Log_Formatter_Simple('hello %message%' . PHP_EOL);
$writer->setFormatter($formatter);

$logger = new Zend_Log();
$logger->addWriter($writer);

$logger->info('there');

// outputs "hello there"
```

The constructor of `Zend_Log_Formatter_Simple` accepts a single parameter: the format string. This string contains keys surrounded by percent signs (e.g. `%message%`). The format string may contain any key from the event data array. You can retrieve the default keys by using the `DEFAULT_FORMAT` constant from `Zend_Log_Formatter_Simple`.

Formatting to XML

`Zend_Log_Formatter_Xml` formats log data into XML strings. By default, it automatically logs all items in the event data array:

```
$writer = new Zend_Log_Writer_Stream('php://output');
$formatter = new Zend_Log_Formatter_Xml();
$writer->setFormatter($formatter);

$logger = new Zend_Log();
$logger->addWriter($writer);

$logger->info('informational message');
```

The code above outputs the following XML (space added for clarity):

```
<logEntry>
  <timestamp>2007-04-06T07:24:37-07:00</timestamp>
  <message>informational message</message>
  <priority>6</priority>
  <priorityName>INFO</priorityName>
</logEntry>
```

It's possible to customize the root element as well as specify a mapping of XML elements to the items in the event data array. The constructor of `Zend_Log_Formatter_Xml` accepts a string with the name of the root element as the first parameter and an associative array with the element mapping as the second parameter:

```
$writer = new Zend_Log_Writer_Stream('php://output');
$formatter = new Zend_Log_Formatter_Xml('log',
                                        array('msg' => 'message',
                                              'level' => 'priorityName')
                                        );
$writer->setFormatter($formatter);

$logger = new Zend_Log();
$logger->addWriter($writer);

$logger->info('informational message');
```

The code above changes the root element from its default of `logEntry` to `log`. It also maps the element msg to the event data item `message`. This results in the following output:

```
<log>
  <msg>informational message</msg>
  <level>INFO</level>
</log>
```

Filters

A Filter object blocks a message from being written to the log.

Filtering for All Writers

To filter before all writers, you can add any number of Filters to a Log object using the addFilter()
method:

```
$logger = new Zend_Log();

$writer = new Zend_Log_Writer_Stream('php://output');
$logger->addWriter($writer);

$filter = new Zend_Log_Filter_Priority(Zend_Log::CRIT);
$logger->addFilter($filter);

// blocked
$logger->info('Informational message');

// logged
$logger->emerg('Emergency message');
```

When you add one or more Filters to the Log object, the message must pass through all of the Filters
before any Writers receives it.

Filtering for a Writer Instance

To filter only on a specific Writer instance, use the addFilter method of that Writer:

```
$logger = new Zend_Log();

$writer1 = new Zend_Log_Writer_Stream('/path/to/first/logfile');
$logger->addWriter($writer1);

$writer2 = new Zend_Log_Writer_Stream('/path/to/second/logfile');
$logger->addWriter($writer2);

// add a filter only to writer2
$filter = new Zend_Log_Filter_Priority(Zend_Log::CRIT);
$writer2->addFilter($filter);

// logged to writer1, blocked from writer2
$logger->info('Informational message');

// logged by both writers
$logger->emerg('Emergency message');
```

Chapter 8. Zend_Mail

Introduction

Getting started

`Zend_Mail` provides generalized functionality to compose and send both text and MIME-compliant multipart e-mail messages. Mail can be sent with `Zend_Mail` via the default `Zend_Mail_Transport_Sendmail` transport or via `Zend_Mail_Transport_Smtp`.

Example 8.1. Simple E-Mail with Zend_Mail

A simple e-mail consists of some recipients, a subject, a body and a sender. To send such a mail using `Zend_Mail_Transport_Sendmail`, do the following:

```
$mail = new Zend_Mail();
$mail->setBodyText('This is the text of the mail.');
$mail->setFrom('somebody@example.com', 'Some Sender');
$mail->addTo('somebody_else@example.com', 'Some Recipient');
$mail->setSubject('TestSubject');
$mail->send();
```

Minimum definitions

In order to send an e-mail with `Zend_Mail` you have to specify at least one recipient, a sender (e.g., with `setFrom()`), and a message body (text and/or HTML).

For most mail attributes there are "get" methods to read the information stored in the mail object. For further details, please refer to the API documentation. A special one is `getRecipients()`. It returns an array with all recipient e-mail addresses that were added prior to the method call.

For security reasons, `Zend_Mail` filters all header fields to prevent header injection with newline (\n) characters. Double quotation is changed to single quotation and angle brackets to square brackets in the name of sender and recipients. If the marks are in email address, the marks will be removed.

You also can use most methods of the `Zend_Mail` object with a convenient fluent interface.

```
$mail = new Zend_Mail();
$mail->setBodyText('This is the text of the mail.')
    ->setFrom('somebody@example.com', 'Some Sender')
    ->addTo('somebody_else@example.com', 'Some Recipient')
    ->setSubject('TestSubject')
    ->send();
```

Configuring the default sendmail transport

The default transport for a `Zend_Mail` instance is `Zend_Mail_Transport_Sendmail`. It is essentially a wrapper to the PHP `mail()` [http://php.net/mail] function. If you wish to pass additional parameters to the `mail()` [http://php.net/mail] function, simply create a new transport instance and pass your parameters to the constructor. The new transport instance can then act as the default `Zend_Mail` transport, or it can be passed to the `send()` method of `Zend_Mail`.

Example 8.2. Passing additional parameters to the Zend_Mail_Transport_Sendmail transport

This example shows how to change the Return-Path of the `mail()` [http://php.net/mail] function.

```
$tr = new Zend_Mail_Transport_Sendmail('-freturn_to_me@example.com');
Zend_Mail::setDefaultTransport($tr);

$mail = new Zend_Mail();
$mail->setBodyText('This is the text of the mail.');
$mail->setFrom('somebody@example.com', 'Some Sender');
$mail->addTo('somebody_else@example.com', 'Some Recipient');
$mail->setSubject('TestSubject');
$mail->send();
```

Safe mode restrictions

The optional additional parameters will be cause the `mail()` [http://php.net/mail] function to fail if PHP is running in safe mode.

Sending via SMTP

To send mail via SMTP, `Zend_Mail_Transport_Smtp` needs to be created and registered with `Zend_Mail` before the `send()` method is called. For all remaining `Zend_Mail::send()` calls in the current script, the SMTP transport will then be used:

Example 8.3. Sending E-Mail via SMTP

```
$tr = new Zend_Mail_Transport_Smtp('mail.example.com');
Zend_Mail::setDefaultTransport($tr);
```

The `setDefaultTransport()` method and the constructor of `Zend_Mail_Transport_Smtp` are not expensive. These two lines can be processed at script setup time (e.g., config.inc or similar) to configure the behavior of the `Zend_Mail` class for the rest of the script. This keeps configuration information out of the application logic - whether mail is sent via SMTP or `mail()` [http://php.net/mail], what mail server is used, etc.

Sending Multiple Mails per SMTP Connection

By default, a single SMTP transport creates a single connection and re-uses it for the lifetime of the script execution. You may send multiple e-mails through this SMTP connection. A RSET command is issued before each delivery to ensure the correct SMTP handshake is followed.

Example 8.4. Sending Multiple Mails per SMTP Connection

```
// Create transport
$transport = new Zend_Mail_Transport_Smtp('localhost');
```

```
// Loop through messages
for ($i = 0; $i > 5; $i++) {
    $mail = new Zend_Mail();
    $mail->addTo('studio@peptolab.com', 'Test');
    $mail->setFrom('studio@peptolab.com', 'Test');
    $mail->setSubject(
        'Demonstration - Sending Multiple Mails per SMTP Connection'
    );
    $mail->setBodyText('...Your message here...');
    $mail->send($transport);
}
```

If you wish to have a separate connection for each mail delivery, you will need to create and destroy your transport before and after each send() method is called. Or alternatively, you can manipulate the connection between each delivery by accessing the transport's protocol object.

Example 8.5. Manually controlling the transport connection

```
// Create transport
$transport = new Zend_Mail_Transport_Smtp();

$protocol = new Zend_Mail_Protocol_Smtp('localhost');
$protocol->connect();
$protocol->helo('localhost');

$transport->setConnection($protocol);

// Loop through messages
for ($i = 0; $i > 5; $i++) {
    $mail = new Zend_Mail();
    $mail->addTo('studio@peptolab.com', 'Test');
    $mail->setFrom('studio@peptolab.com', 'Test');
    $mail->setSubject(
        'Demonstration - Sending Multiple Mails per SMTP Connection'
    );
    $mail->setBodyText('...Your message here...');

    // Manually control the connection
    $protocol->rset();
    $mail->send($transport);
}

$protocol->quit();
$protocol->disconnect();
```

Using Different Transports

In case you want to send different e-mails through different connections, you can also pass the transport object directly to send() without a prior call to setDefaultTransport(). The passed object will override the default transport for the actual send() request.

Example 8.6. Using Different Transports

```
$mail = new Zend_Mail();
// build message...
$tr1 = new Zend_Mail_Transport_Smtp('server@example.com');
$tr2 = new Zend_Mail_Transport_Smtp('other_server@example.com');
$mail->send($tr1);
$mail->send($tr2);
$mail->send();  // use default again
```

Additional transports

Additional transports can be written by implementing
Zend_Mail_Transport_Interface.

HTML E-Mail

To send an e-mail in HTML format, set the body using the method setBodyHTML() instead of
setBodyText(). The MIME content type will automatically be set to text/html then. If you use
both HTML and Text bodies, a multipart/alternative MIME message will automatically be generated:

Example 8.7. Sending HTML E-Mail

```
$mail = new Zend_Mail();
$mail->setBodyText('My Nice Test Text');
$mail->setBodyHtml('My Nice <b>Test</b> Text');
$mail->setFrom('somebody@example.com', 'Some Sender');
$mail->addTo('somebody_else@example.com', 'Some Recipient');
$mail->setSubject('TestSubject');
$mail->send();
```

Attachments

Files can be attached to an e-mail using the createAttachment() method. The default behavior of
Zend_Mail is to assume the attachment is a binary object (application/octet-stream), that it should be
transferred with base64 encoding, and that it is handled as an attachment. These assumptions can be
overridden by passing more parameters to createAttachment():

Example 8.8. E-Mail Messages with Attachments

```
$mail = new Zend_Mail();
// build message...
$mail->createAttachment($someBinaryString);
$mail->createAttachment($myImage,
                        'image/gif',
                        Zend_Mime::DISPOSITION_INLINE,
                        Zend_Mime::ENCODING_8BIT);
```

If you want more control over the MIME part generated for this attachment you can use the return value of createAttachment() to modify its attributes. The createAttachment() method returns a Zend_Mime_Part object:

```
$mail = new Zend_Mail();

$at = $mail->createAttachment($myImage);
$at->type        = 'image/gif';
$at->disposition = Zend_Mime::DISPOSITION_INLINE;
$at->encoding    = Zend_Mime::ENCODING_8BIT;
$at->filename    = 'test.gif';

$mail->send();
```

An alternative is to create an instance of Zend_Mime_Part and add it with addAttachment():

```
$mail = new Zend_Mail();

$at = new Zend_Mime_Part($myImage);
$at->type        = 'image/gif';
$at->disposition = Zend_Mime::DISPOSITION_INLINE;
$at->encoding    = Zend_Mime::ENCODING_8BIT;
$at->filename    = 'test.gif';

$mail->addAttachment($at);

$mail->send();
```

Adding Recipients

Recipients can be added in three ways:

- addTo(): Adds a recipient to the mail with a "To" header

- addCc(): Adds a recipient to the mail with a "Cc" header

- addBcc(): Adds a recipient to the mail not visible in the header.

getRecipients() serves list of the recipients. clearRecipients() clears the list.

Additional parameter

addTo() and addCc() accept a second optional parameter that is used as a human-readable name of the recipient for the header. Double quotation is changed to single quotation and angle brackets to square brackets in the parameter.

Controlling the MIME Boundary

In a multipart message, a MIME boundary for separating the different parts of the message is normally generated at random. In some cases, however, you might want to specify the MIME boundary that is used. This can be done using the setMimeBoundary() method, as in the following example:

Example 8.9. Changing the MIME Boundary

```
$mail = new Zend_Mail();
$mail->setMimeBoundary('=_' . md5(microtime(1) . $someId++));
// build message...
```

Additional Headers

Arbitrary mail headers can be set by using the addHeader() method. It requires two parameters containing the name and the value of the header field. A third optional parameter determines if the header should have only one or multiple values:

Example 8.10. Adding E-Mail Message Headers

```
$mail = new Zend_Mail();
$mail->addHeader('X-MailGenerator', 'MyCoolApplication');
$mail->addHeader('X-greetingsTo', 'Mom', true); // multiple values
$mail->addHeader('X-greetingsTo', 'Dad', true);
```

Character Sets

Zend_Mail does not check for the correct character set of the mail parts. When instantiating Zend_Mail, a charset for the e-mail itself may be given. It defaults to iso-8859-1. The application has to make sure that all parts added to that mail object have their content encoded in the correct character set. When creating a new mail part, a different charset can be given for each part.

Only in text format

Character sets are only applicable for message parts in text format.

Encoding

Text and HTML message bodies are encoded with the quotedprintable mechanism by default. Message headers are also encoded with the quotedprintable mechanism if you do not specify base64 in setHeaderEncoding(). All other attachments are encoded via base64 if no other encoding is given in the addAttachment() call or assigned to the MIME part object later. 7Bit and 8Bit encoding currently only pass on the binary content data.

Zend_Mail_Transport_Smtp encodes lines starting with one dot or two dots so that the mail does not violate the SMTP protocol.

SMTP Authentication

Zend_Mail supports the use of SMTP authentication, which can be enabled be passing the 'auth' parameter to the configuration array in the Zend_Mail_Transport_Smtp constructor. The available built-in authentication methods are PLAIN, LOGIN and CRAM-MD5 which all expect a 'username' and 'password' value in the configuration array.

Example 8.11. Enabling authentication within Zend_Mail_Transport_Smtp

```
$config = array('auth' => 'login',
                'username' => 'myusername',
                'password' => 'password');

$transport = new Zend_Mail_Transport_Smtp('mail.server.com', $config);

$mail = new Zend_Mail();
$mail->setBodyText('This is the text of the mail.');
$mail->setFrom('sender@test.com', 'Some Sender');
$mail->addTo('recipient@test.com', 'Some Recipient');
$mail->setSubject('TestSubject');
$mail->send($transport);
```

Authentication types

The authentication type is case-insensitive but has no punctuation. E.g. to use CRAM-MD5 you would pass 'auth' => 'crammd5' in the Zend_Mail_Transport_Smtp constructor.

Securing SMTP Transport

Zend_Mail also supports the use of either TLS or SSL to secure a SMTP connection. This can be enabled be passing the 'ssl' parameter to the configuration array in the Zend_Mail_Transport_Smtp constructor with a value of either 'ssl' or 'tls'. A port can optionally be supplied, otherwise it defaults to 25 for TLS or 465 for SSL.

Example 8.12. Enabling a secure connection within Zend_Mail_Transport_Smtp

```
$config = array('ssl' => 'tls',
                'port' => 25); // Optional port number supplied

$transport = new Zend_Mail_Transport_Smtp('mail.server.com', $config);

$mail = new Zend_Mail();
$mail->setBodyText('This is the text of the mail.');
$mail->setFrom('sender@test.com', 'Some Sender');
$mail->addTo('recipient@test.com', 'Some Recipient');
$mail->setSubject('TestSubject');
$mail->send($transport);
```

Reading Mail Messages

Zend_Mail can read mail messages from several local or remote mail storages. All of them have the same basic API to count and fetch messages and some of them implement additional interfaces for not so common features. For a feature overview of the implemented storages see the following table.

Table 8.1. Mail Read Feature Overview

Feature	Mbox	Maildir	Pop3	IMAP
Storage type	local	local	remote	remote
Fetch message	Yes	Yes	Yes	Yes
Fetch MIME-part	emulated	emulated	emulated	emulated
Folders	Yes	Yes	No	Yes
Create message/folder	No	todo	No	todo
Flags	No	Yes	No	Yes
Quota	No	Yes	No	No

Simple example using Pop3

```
$mail = new Zend_Mail_Storage_Pop3(array('host'     => 'localhost',
                                          'user'     => 'test',
                                          'password' => 'test'));

echo $mail->countMessages() . " messages found\n";
foreach ($mail as $message) {
    echo "Mail from '{$message->from}': {$message->subject}\n";
}
```

Opening a local storage

Mbox and Maildir are the two supported formats for local mail storages, both in their most simple formats.

If you want to read from a Mbox file you only need to give the filename to the constructor of Zend_Mail_Storage_Mbox:

```
$mail = new Zend_Mail_Storage_Mbox(array('filename' =>
                                         '/home/test/mail/inbox'));
```

Maildir is very similar but needs a dirname:

```
$mail = new Zend_Mail_Storage_Maildir(array('dirname' =>
                                            '/home/test/mail/'));
```

Both constructors throw a Zend_Mail_Exception if the storage can't be read.

Opening a remote storage

For remote storages the two most popular protocols are supported: Pop3 and Imap. Both need at least a host and a user to connect and login. The default password is an empty string, the default port as given in the protocol RFC.

```
// connecting with Pop3
$mail = new Zend_Mail_Storage_Pop3(array('host'     => 'example.com',
                                         'user'     => 'test',
```

```
                                             'password' => 'test'));

// connecting with Imap
$mail = new Zend_Mail_Storage_Imap(array('host'     => 'example.com',
                                         'user'     => 'test',
                                         'password' => 'test'));

// example for a none standard port
$mail = new Zend_Mail_Storage_Pop3(array('host'     => 'example.com',
                                         'port'     => 1120
                                         'user'     => 'test',
                                         'password' => 'test'));
```

For both storages SSL and TLS are supported. If you use SSL the default port changes as given in the RFC.

```
// examples for Zend_Mail_Storage_Pop3, same works for Zend_Mail_Storage_Imap

// use SSL on different port (default is 995 for Pop3 and 993 for Imap)
$mail = new Zend_Mail_Storage_Pop3(array('host'     => 'example.com',
                                         'user'     => 'test',
                                         'password' => 'test',
                                         'ssl'      => 'SSL'));

// use TLS
$mail = new Zend_Mail_Storage_Pop3(array('host'     => 'example.com',
                                         'user'     => 'test',
                                         'password' => 'test',
                                         'ssl'      => 'TLS'));
```

Both constructors can throw Zend_Mail_Exception or Zend_Mail_Protocol_Exception (extends Zend_Mail_Exception), depending on the type of error.

Fetching messages and simple methods

Messages can be fetched after you've opened the storage . You need the message number, which is a counter starting with 1 for the first message. To fetch the message, you use the method getMessage():

```
$message = $mail->getMessage($messageNum);
```

Array access is also supported, but this access method won't supported any additional parameters that could be added to getMessage(). As long as you don't mind, and can live with the default values, you may use:

```
$message = $mail[$messageNum];
```

For iterating over all messages the Iterator interface is implemented:

```
foreach ($mail as $messageNum => $message) {
    // do stuff ...
}
```

To count the messages in the storage, you can either use the method countMessages() or use array access:

```
// method
$maxMessage = $mail->countMessages();

// array access
$maxMessage = count($mail);
```

To remove a mail, you use the method removeMessage() or again array access:

```
// method
$mail->removeMessage($messageNum);

// array access
unset($mail[$messageNum]);
```

Working with messages

After you fetch the messages with getMessage() you want to fetch headers, the content or single parts of a multipart message. All headers can be accessed via properties or the method getHeader() if you want more control or have unusual header names. The header names are lower-cased internally, thus the case of the header name in the mail message doesn't matter. Also headers with a dash can be written in camel-case. If no header is found for both notations an exception is thrown. To encounter this the method headerExists() can be used to check the existance of a header.

```
// get the message object
$message = $mail->getMessage(1);

// output subject of message
echo $message->subject . "\n";

// get content-type header
$type = $message->contentType;

// check if CC isset:
if( isset($message->cc) ) { // or $message->headerExists('cc');
    $cc = $message->cc;
}
```

If you have multiple headers with the same name- i.e. the Received headers- you might want an array instead of a string. In this case, use the getHeader() method.

```
// get header as property - the result is always a string,
// with new lines between the single occurrences in the message
$received = $message->received;

// the same via getHeader() method
$received = $message->getHeader('received', 'string');

// better an array with a single entry for every occurrences
$received = $message->getHeader('received', 'array');
foreach ($received as $line) {
    // do stuff
}

// if you don't define a format you'll get the internal representation
// (string for single headers, array for multiple)
$received = $message->getHeader('received');
if (is_string($received)) {
    // only one received header found in message
}
```

The method getHeaders() returns all headers as array with the lower-cased name as key and the value as and array for multiple headers or as string for single headers.

```
// dump all headers
foreach ($message->getHeaders() as $name => $value) {
    if (is_string($value)) {
        echo "$name: $value\n";
        continue;
    }
    foreach ($value as $entry) {
        echo "$name: $entry\n";
    }
}
```

If you don't have a multipart message, fetching the content is easily done via getContent(). Unlike the headers, the content is only fetched when needed (aka late-fetch).

```
// output message content for HTML
echo '<pre>';
echo $message->getContent();
echo '</pre>';
```

Checking for multipart messages is done with the method isMultipart(). If you have multipart message you can get an instance of Zend_Mail_Part with the method getPart(). Zend_Mail_Part is the base class of Zend_Mail_Message, so you have the same methods: getHeader(), getHeaders(), getContent(), getPart(), isMultipart and the properties for headers.

```
// get the first none multipart part
$part = $message;
while ($part->isMultipart()) {
    $part = $message->getPart(1);
}
echo 'Type of this part is ' . strtok($part->contentType, ';') . "\n";
echo "Content:\n";
echo $part->getContent();
```

Zend_Mail_Part also implements RecursiveIterator, which makes it easy to scan through all parts. And for easy output, it also implements the magic method __toString(), which returns the content.

```
// output first text/plain part
$foundPart = null;
foreach (new RecursiveIteratorIterator($mail->getMessage(1)) as $part) {
    try {
        if (strtok($part->contentType, ';') == 'text/plain') {
            $foundPart = $part;
            break;
        }
    } catch (Zend_Mail_Exception $e) {
        // ignore
    }
}
if (!$foundPart) {
    echo 'no plain text part found';
} else {
    echo "plain text part: \n" . $foundPart;
}
```

Checking for flags

Maildir and IMAP support storing flags. The class Zend_Mail_Storage has constants for all known maildir and IMAP system flags, named Zend_Mail_Storage::FLAG_<flagname>. To check for flags Zend_Mail_Message has a method called hasFlag(). With getFlags() you'll get all set flags.

```
// find unread messages
echo "Unread mails:\n";
foreach ($mail as $message) {
    if ($message->hasFlag(Zend_Mail_Storage::FLAG_SEEN)) {
        continue;
    }
    // mark recent/new mails
    if ($message->hasFlag(Zend_Mail_Storage::FLAG_RECENT)) {
        echo '! ';
    } else {
        echo '  ';
    }
    echo $message->subject . "\n";
}

// check for known flags
$flags = $message->getFlags();
echo "Message is flagged as: ";
foreach ($flags as $flag) {
    switch ($flag) {
        case Zend_Mail_Storage::FLAG_ANSWERED:
            echo 'Answered ';
            break;
        case Zend_Mail_Storage::FLAG_FLAGGED:
            echo 'Flagged ';
            break;

        // ...
        // check for other flags
        // ...

        default:
            echo $flag . '(unknown flag) ';
    }
}
```

As IMAP allows user or client defined flags, you could get flags that don't have a constant in Zend_Mail_Storage. Instead, they are returned as strings and can be checked the same way with hasFlag().

```
// check message for client defined flags $IsSpam, $SpamTested
if (!$message->hasFlag('$SpamTested')) {
    echo 'message has not been tested for spam';
} else if ($message->hasFlag('$IsSpam')) {
    echo 'this message is spam';
} else {
    echo 'this message is ham';
}
```

Using folders

All storages, except Pop3, support folders, also called mailboxes. The interface implemented by all storages supporting folders is called Zend_Mail_Storage_Folder_Interface. Also all of these classes have an additional optional parameter called folder, which is the folder selected after login, in the constructor.

For the local storages you need to use separate classes called Zend_Mail_Storage_Folder_Mbox or Zend_Mail_Storage_Folder_Maildir. Both need one parameter called dirname with the name of the base dir. The format for maildir is as defined in maildir++ (with a dot as default delimiter), Mbox is a directory hierarchy with Mbox files. If you don't have a Mbox file called INBOX in your Mbox base dir you need to set another folder in the constructor.

Zend_Mail_Storage_Imap already supports folders by default. Examples for opening these storages:

```
// mbox with folders
$mail = new Zend_Mail_Storage_Folder_Mbox(array('dirname' =>
                                    '/home/test/mail/'));

// mbox with a default folder not called INBOX, also works
// with Zend_Mail_Storage_Folder_Maildir and Zend_Mail_Storage_Imap
$mail = new Zend_Mail_Storage_Folder_Mbox(array('dirname' =>
                                    '/home/test/mail/',
                              'folder'  =>
                                  'Archive'));

// maildir with folders
$mail = new Zend_Mail_Storage_Folder_Maildir(array('dirname' =>
                                    '/home/test/mail/'));

// maildir with colon as delimiter, as suggested in Maildir++
$mail = new Zend_Mail_Storage_Folder_Maildir(array('dirname' =>
                                    '/home/test/mail/',
                              'delim'   => ':'));

// imap is the same with and without folders
$mail = new Zend_Mail_Storage_Imap(array('host'     => 'example.com',
                                   'user'     => 'test',
                                   'password' => 'test'));
```

With the method getFolders($root = null) you can get the folder hierarchy starting with the root folder or the given folder. It's returned as an instance of Zend_Mail_Storage_Folder, which implements RecursiveIterator and all children are also instances of Zend_Mail_Storage_Folder. Each of these instances has a local and a global name returned by the methods getLocalName() and getGlobalName(). The global name is the absolute name from the root folder (including delimiters), the local name is the name in the parent folder.

Table 8.2. Mail Folder Names

Global Name	Local Name
/INBOX	INBOX
/Archive/2005	2005
List.ZF.General	General

If you use the iterator, the key of the current element is the local name. The global name is also returned by the magic method __toString(). Some folders may not be selectable, which means they can't store messages and selecting them results in an error. This can be checked with the method isSelectable(). So it's very easy to output the whole tree in a view:

```
$folders = new RecursiveIteratorIterator($this->mail->getFolders(),
                                         RecursiveIteratorIterator::
                                            SELF_FIRST);
echo '<select name="folder">';
foreach ($folders as $localName => $folder) {
    $localName = str_pad('', $folders->getDepth(), '-', STR_PAD_LEFT) .
                 $localName;
    echo '<option';
    if (!$folder->isSelectable()) {
        echo ' disabled="disabled"';
    }
    echo ' value="' . htmlspecialchars($folder) . '">'
        . htmlspecialchars($localName) . '</option>';
}
echo '</select>';
```

The current selected folder is returned by the method getSelectedFolder(). Changing the folder is done with the method selectFolder(), which needs the global name as parameter. If you want to avoid to write delimiters you can also use the properties of a Zend_Mail_Storage_Folder instance:

```
// depending on your mail storage and its settings $rootFolder->Archive->2005
// is the same as:
//    /Archive/2005
//    Archive:2005
//    INBOX.Archive.2005
//    ...
$folder = $mail->getFolders()->Archive->2005;
echo 'Last folder was '
   . $mail->getSelectedFolder()
   . "new folder is $folder\n";
$mail->selectFolder($folder);
```

Advanced Use

Using NOOP

If you're using a remote storage and have some long tasks you might need to keep the connection alive via noop:

```
foreach ($mail as $message) {

    // do some calculations ...

    $mail->noop(); // keep alive

    // do something else ...

    $mail->noop(); // keep alive

}
```

Caching instances

Zend_Mail_Storage_Mbox,   Zend_Mail_Storage_Folder_Mbox,
Zend_Mail_Storage_Maildir and Zend_Mail_Storage_Folder_Maildir implement
the magic methods __sleep() and __wakeup(), which means they are serializable. This avoids
parsing the files or directory tree more than once. The disadvantage is that your Mbox or Maildir storage
should not change. Some easy checks may be done, like reparsing the current Mbox file if the
modification time changes, or reparsing the folder structure if a folder has vanished (which still results
in an error, but you can search for another folder afterwards). It's better if you have something like a
signal file for changes and check it before using the cached instance.

```
// there's no specific cache handler/class used here,
// change the code to match your cache handler
$signal_file = '/home/test/.mail.last_change';
$mbox_basedir = '/home/test/mail/';
$cache_id = 'example mail cache ' . $mbox_basedir . $signal_file;

$cache = new Your_Cache_Class();
if (!$cache->isCached($cache_id) ||
    filemtime($signal_file) > $cache->getMTime($cache_id)) {
    $mail = new Zend_Mail_Storage_Folder_Pop3(array('dirname' =>
                                                $mbox_basedir));
} else {
    $mail = $cache->get($cache_id);
}

// do stuff ...

$cache->set($cache_id, $mail);
```

Extending Protocol Classes

Remote   storages   use   two   classes: Zend_Mail_Storage_<Name>   and
Zend_Mail_Protocol_<Name>. The protocol class translates the protocol commands and
responses from and to PHP, like methods for the commands or variables with different structures for
data. The other/main class implements the common interface.

If you need additional protocol features, you can extend the protocol class and use it in the constructor
of the main class. As an example, assume we need to knock different ports before we can connect to
POP3.

```
class Example_Mail_Exception extends Zend_Mail_Exception
{

}

class Example_Mail_Protocol_Exception extends Zend_Mail_Protocol_Exception
{

}

class Example_Mail_Protocol_Pop3_Knock extends Zend_Mail_Protocol_Pop3
{
    private $host, $port;

    public function __construct($host, $port = null)
    {
        // no auto connect in this class
        $this->host = $host;
        $this->port = $port;
```

```
    }

    public function knock($port)
    {
        $sock = @fsockopen($this->host, $port);
        if ($sock) {
            fclose($sock);
        }
    }

    public function connect($host = null, $port = null, $ssl = false)
    {
        if ($host === null) {
            $host = $this->host;
        }
        if ($port === null) {
            $port = $this->port;
        }
        parent::connect($host, $port);
    }
}

class Example_Mail_Pop3_Knock extends Zend_Mail_Storage_Pop3
{
    public function __construct(array $params)
    {
        // ... check $params here! ...
        $protocol = new Example_Mail_Protocol_Pop3_Knock($params['host']);

        // do our "special" thing
        foreach ((array)$params['knock_ports'] as $port) {
            $protocol->knock($port);
        }

        // get to correct state
        $protocol->connect($params['host'], $params['port']);
        $protocol->login($params['user'], $params['password']);

        // initialize parent
        parent::__construct($protocol);
    }
}

$mail = new Example_Mail_Pop3_Knock(array('host'         => 'localhost',
                                          'user'         => 'test',
                                          'password'     => 'test',
                                          'knock_ports' =>
                                              array(1101, 1105, 1111)));
```

As you see, we always assume we're connected, logged in and, if supported, a folder is selected in the constructor of the main class. Thus if you assign your own protocol class, you always need to make sure that's done or the next method will fail if the server doesn't allow it in the current state.

Using Quota (since 1.5)

Zend_Mail_Storage_Writable_Maildir has support for Maildir++ quotas. It's disabled by default, but it's possible to use it manually, if the automatic checks are not desired (this means appendMessage(), removeMessage() and copyMessage() do no checks and do not add entries to the maildirsize file). If enabled, an exception is thrown if you try to write to the maildir and it's already over quota.

There are three methods used for quotas: getQuota(), setQuota() and checkQuota():

```
$mail = new Zend_Mail_Storage_Writable_Maildir(array('dirname' =>
                                              '/home/test/mail/'));
$mail->setQuota(true); // true to enable, false to disable
echo 'Quota check is now ', $mail->getQuota() ? 'enabled' :
        'disabled', "\n";
// check quota can be used even if quota checks are disabled
echo 'You are ', $mail->checkQuota() ? 'over quota' : 'not
        over quota', "\n";
```

checkQuota() can also return a more detailed response:

```
$quota = $mail->checkQuota(true);
echo 'You are ', $quota['over_quota'] ? 'over quota' : 'not
        over quota', "\n";
echo 'You have ',
     $quota['count'],
     ' of ',
     $quota['quota']['count'],
     ' messages and use ';
echo $quota['size'], ' of ', $quota['quota']['size'], ' octets';
```

If you want to specify your own quota instead of using the one specified in the maildirsize file you can
do with setQuota():

```
// message count and octet size supported, order does matter
$quota = $mail->setQuota(array('size' => 10000, 'count' => 100));
```

To add your own quota checks use single letters as keys, and they will be preserved (but obviously not
checked). It's also possible to extend Zend_Mail_Storage_Writable_Maildir to define your
own quota only if the maildirsize file is missing (which can happen in Maildir++):

```
class Example_Mail_Storage_Maildir extends Zend_Mail_Storage_Writable
    _Maildir {
    // getQuota is called with $fromStorage = true by quota checks
    public function getQuota($fromStorage = false) {
        try {
            return parent::getQuota($fromStorage);
        } catch (Zend_Mail_Storage_Exception $e) {
            if (!$fromStorage) {
                // unknown error:
                throw $e;
            }
            // maildirsize file must be missing

            list($count, $size) = get_quota_from_somewhere_else();
            return array('count' => $count, 'size' => $size);
        }
    }
}
```

Chapter 9. Zend_Measure

Introduction

`Zend_Measure_*` classes provide a generic and easy way for working with measurements. Using `Zend_Measure_*` classes, you can convert measurements into different units of the same type. They can be added, subtracted and compared against each other. From a given input made in the user's native language, the unit of measurement can be automatically extracted. Numerous units of measurement are supported.

Example 9.1. Converting measurements

The following introductory example shows automatic conversion of units of measurement. To convert a measurement, its value and its type have to be known. The value can be an integer, a float, or even a string containing a number. Conversions are only possible for units of the same type (mass, area, temperature, velocity, etc.), not between types.

```
$locale = new Zend_Locale('en');
$unit = new Zend_Measure_Length(100, Zend_Measure_Length::METER, $locale);

// Convert meters to yards
echo $unit->convertTo(Zend_Measure_Length::YARD);
```

`Zend_Measure_*` includes support for many different units of measurement. The units of measurement all have a unified notation: `Zend_Measure_<TYPE>::NAME_OF_UNIT`, where `<TYPE>` corresponds to a well-known physical or numerical property. . Every unit of measurement consists of a conversion factor and a display unit. A detailed list can be found in the chapter `Types of measurements`.

Example 9.2. The meter measurement

The `meter` is used for measuring lengths, so its type constant can be found in the `Length` class. To refer to this unit of measurement, the notation `Length::METER` must be used. The display unit is m.

```
echo Zend_Measure_Length::STANDARD;   // outputs 'Length::METER'
echo Zend_Measure_Length::KILOMETER;  // outputs 'Length::KILOMETER'

$unit = new Zend_Measure_Length(100,'METER');
echo $unit;
// outputs '100 m'
```

Creation of Measurements

When creating a measurement object, `Zend_Measure_*` methods expect the input/original measurement data value as the first parameter. This can be a `numeric argument`, a `string` without units, or a `localized string` with unit(s) specified. The second parameter defines the type of the measurement. Both parameters are mandatory. The language may optionally be specified as the third parameter.

Creating measurements from integers and floats

In addition to integer data values, floating point types may be used, but "simple decimal fractions like 0.1 or 0.7 cannot be converted into their internal binary counterparts without a little loss of precision," [http://www.php.net/float] sometimes giving surprising results. Also, do not compare two "float" type numbers for equality.

Example 9.3. Creation using integer and floating values

```
$measurement = 1234.7;
$unit = new Zend_Measure_Length((integer)$measurement,
                                 Zend_Measure_Length::STANDARD);
echo $unit;
// outputs '1234 m' (meters)

$unit = new Zend_Measure_Length($measurement, Zend_Measure_Length::STANDARD)
echo $unit;
// outputs '1234.7 m' (meters)
```

Creating measurements from strings

Many measurements received as input to ZF applications can only be passed to Zend_Measure_* classes as strings, such as numbers written using roman numerals [http://en.wikipedia.org/wiki/Roman_numerals] or extremely large binary values that exceed the precision of PHP's native integer and float types. Since integers can be denoted using strings, if there is any risk of losing precision due to limitations of PHP's native integer and float types, using strings instead. Zend_Measure_Number uses the BCMath extension to support arbitrary precision, as shown in the example below, to avoid limitations in many PHP functions, such as bin2dec() [http://php.net/bin2dec] .

Example 9.4. Creation using strings

```
$mystring = "10010100111010111010100001011011101010001";
$unit = new Zend_Measure_Number($mystring, Zend_Measure_Number::BINARY);

echo $unit;
```

Usually, Zend_Measure_* can automatically extract the desired measurement embedded in an arbitrary string. Only the first identifiable number denoted using standard European/Latin digits (0,1,2,3,4,5,6,7,8,9) will be used for measurement creation. If there are more numerals later in the string, the rest of these numerals will be ignored.

Example 9.5. Arbitrary text input containing measurements

```
$mystring = "My house is 125m² in size";
$unit = new Zend_Measure_Area($mystring, Zend_Measure_Area::STANDARD);
echo $unit; // outputs "125 m²in size";

$mystring = "My house is 125m² in size, it has 5 rooms of 25m² each.";
```

```
$unit = new Zend_Measure_Area($mystring, Zend_Measure_Area::STANDARD);
echo $unit; // outputs "125 m² in size";
```

Measurements from localized strings

When a string is entered in a localized notation, the correct interpretation can not be determined without knowing the intended locale. The division of decimal digits with "." and grouping of thousands with "," is common in the English language, but not so in other languages. For example, the English number "1,234.50" would be interpreted as meaning "1.2345" in German. To deal with such problems, the locale-aware Zend_Measure_* family of classes offer the possibility to specify a language or region to disambiguate the input data and properly interpret the intended semantic value.

Example 9.6. Localized string

```
$locale = new Zend_Locale('de');
$mystring = "The boat is 1,234.50 long.";
$unit = new Zend_Measure_Length($mystring,
                                Zend_Measure_Length::STANDARD,
                                $locale);
echo $unit; // outputs "1.234 m"

$mystring = "The boat is 1,234.50 long.";
$unit = new Zend_Measure_Length($mystring,
                                Zend_Measure_Length::STANDARD,
                                'en_US');
echo $unit; // outputs "1234.50 m"
```

Since Zend Framework 1.7.0 Zend_Measure does also support the usage of an application wide locale. You can simply set a Zend_Locale instance to the registry like shown below. With this notation you can forget about setting the locale manually with each instance when you want to use the same locale multiple times.

```
// in your bootstrap file
$locale = new Zend_Locale('de_AT');
Zend_Registry::set('Zend_Locale', $locale);

// somewhere in your application
$length = new Zend_Measure_Length(Zend_Measure_Length::METER());
```

Outputting measurements

Measurements can be output in a number of different ways.

```
Automatic output
```

```
Outputting values
```

```
Output with unit of measurement
```

```
Output as localized string
```

Automatic output

Zend_Measure supports outputting of strings automatically.

Example 9.7. Automatic output

```
$locale = new Zend_Locale('de');
$mystring = "1.234.567,89 Meter";
$unit = new Zend_Measure_Length($mystring,
                                Zend_Measure_Length::STANDARD,
                                $locale);

echo $unit;
```

Measurement output

Output can be achieved simply by using echo [http://php.net/echo] or print [http://php.net/print] .

Outputting values

The value of a measurement can be output using getValue().

Example 9.8. Output a value

```
$locale = new Zend_Locale('de');
$mystring = "1.234.567,89 Meter";
$unit = new Zend_Measure_Length($mystring,
                                Zend_Measure_Length::STANDARD,
                                $locale);

echo $unit->getValue();
```

The getValue() method accepts an optional parameter 'round' which allows to define a precision for the generated output. The standard precision is '2'.

Output with unit of measurement

The function getType() returns the current unit of measurement.

Example 9.9. Outputting units

```
$locale = new Zend_Locale('de');
$mystring = "1.234.567,89";
$unit = new Zend_Measure_Weight($mystring,
                                Zend_Measure_Weight::POUND,
                                $locale);

echo $unit->getType();
```

Output as localized string

Outputting a string in a format common in the users' country is usually desirable. For example, the measurement "1234567.8" would become "1.234.567,8" for Germany. This functionality will be supported in a future release.

Manipulating Measurements

Parsing and normalization of input, combined with output to localized notations makes data accessible to users in different locales. Many additional methods exist in Zend_Measure_* components to manipulate and work with this data, after it has been normalized.

*   Convert

*   Add and subtract

*   Compare to boolean

*   Compare to greater/smaller

*   Manually change values

*   Manually change types

Convert

Probably the most important feature is the conversion into different units of measurement. The conversion of a unit can be done any number of times using the method convertTo(). Units of measurement can only be converted to other units of the same type (class). Therefore, it is not possible to convert (e.g.) a length into a weight, which would might encourage poor programming practices and allow errors to propagate without exceptions.

The convertTo method accepts an optional parameter. With this parameter you can define an precision for the returned output. The standard precision is '2'.

Example 9.10. Convert

```
$locale = new Zend_Locale('de');
$mystring = "1.234.567,89";
$unit = new Zend_Measure_Weight($mystring,'POND', $locale);

print "Kilo:".$unit->convertTo('KILOGRAM');

// constants are considered "better practice" than strings
print "Ton:".$unit->convertTo(Zend_Measure_Weight::TON);

// define a precision for the output
print "Ton:".$unit->convertTo(Zend_Measure_Weight::TON, 3);
```

Add and subtract

Measurements can be added together using add() and subtracted using sub(). Each addition will create a new object for the result. The actual object will never be changed by the class. The new object will be of the same type as the originating object. Dynamic objects support a fluid style of programming, where complex sequences of operations can be nested without risk of side-effects altering the input objects.

Example 9.11. Adding units

```
// Define objects
$unit = new Zend_Measure_Length(200, Zend_Measure_Length::CENTIMETER);
$unit2 = new Zend_Measure_Length(1, Zend_Measure_Length::METER);

// Add $unit2 to $unit
$sum = $unit->add($unit2);

echo $sum; // outputs "300 cm"
```

Automatic conversion

Adding one object to another will automatically convert it to the correct unit. It is not necessary to call convertTo() before adding different units.

Example 9.12. Subtract

Subtraction of measurements works just like addition.

```
// Define objects
$unit = new Zend_Measure_Length(200, Zend_Measure_Length::CENTIMETER);
$unit2 = new Zend_Measure_Length(1, Zend_Measure_Length::METER);

// Subtract $unit2 from $unit
$sum = $unit->sub($unit2);

echo $sum;
```

Compare

Measurements can also be compared, but without automatic unit conversion. Thus, equals() returns TRUE, only if both the value and the unit of measure are identical.

Example 9.13. Different measurements

```
// Define measurements
$unit = new Zend_Measure_Length(100, Zend_Measure_Length::CENTIMETER);
$unit2 = new Zend_Measure_Length(1, Zend_Measure_Length::METER);

if ($unit->equals($unit2)) {
    print "Both measurements are identical";
} else {
    print "These are different measurements";
}
```

Example 9.14. Identical measurements

```
// Define measurements
$unit = new Zend_Measure_Length(100, Zend_Measure_Length::CENTIMETER);
$unit2 = new Zend_Measure_Length(1, Zend_Measure_Length::METER);

$unit2->setType(Zend_Measure_Length::CENTIMETER);

if ($unit->equals($unit2)) {
    print "Both measurements are identical";
} else {
    print "These are different measurements";
}
```

Compare

To determine if a measurement is less than or greater than another, use compare(), which returns 0, -1 or 1 depending on the difference between the two objects. Identical measurements will return 0. Lesser ones will return a negative, greater ones a positive value.

Example 9.15. Difference

```
$unit = new Zend_Measure_Length(100, Zend_Measure_Length::CENTIMETER);
$unit2 = new Zend_Measure_Length(1, Zend_Measure_Length::METER);
$unit3 = new Zend_Measure_Length(1.2, Zend_Measure_Length::METER);

print "Equal:".$unit2->compare($unit);
print "Lesser:".$unit2->compare($unit3);
print "Greater:".$unit3->compare($unit2);
```

Manually change values

To change the value of a measurement explicitly, use setValue(). to overwrite the current value. The parameters are the same as the constructor.

Example 9.16. Changing a value

```
$locale = new Zend_Locale('de_AT');
$unit = new Zend_Measure_Length(1,Zend_Measure_Length::METER);

$unit->setValue(1.2);
echo $unit;

$unit->setValue(1.2, Zend_Measure_Length::KILOMETER);
echo $unit;
```

```
$unit->setValue("1.234,56", Zend_Measure_Length::MILLIMETER,$locale);
echo $unit;
```

Manually change types

To change the type of a measurement without altering its value use setType().

Example 9.17. Changing the type

```
$unit = new Zend_Measure_Length(1,Zend_Measure_Length::METER);
echo $unit; // outputs "1 m"

$unit->setType(Zend_Measure_Length::KILOMETER);
echo $unit; // outputs "1000 km"
```

Types of measurements

All supported measurement types are listed below, each with an example of the standard usage for such measurements.

Table 9.1. List of measurement types

Type	Class	Standardunit	Description
Acceleration	Zend_Measure _Acceleration	Meter per square second | m/s²	Zend_Measure _Acceleration covers the physical factor of acceleration.
Angle	Zend_Measure_Angle	Radiant | rad	Zend_Measure _Angle covers angular dimensions.
Area	Zend_Measure_Area	Square meter | m²	Zend_Measure_Area covers square measures.
Binary	Zend_Measure_Binary	Byte | b	Zend_Measure _Binary covers binary conversions.
Capacitance	Zend_Measure _Capacitance	Farad | F	Zend_Measure _Capacitance covers physical factor of capacitance.
Cooking volumes	Zend_Measure _Cooking_Volume	Cubic meter | m³	Zend_Measure _Cooking_Volume covers volumes which are used for cooking or written in cookbooks.
Cooking weights	Zend_Measure _Cooking_Weight	Gram | g	Zend_Measure _Cooking_Weight covers the weights which are used for

Type	Class	Standardunit	Description
			cooking or written in cookbooks.
Current	Zend_Measure_Current	Ampere | `A`	`Zend_Measure _Current` covers the physical factor of current.
Density	Zend_Measure_Density	Kilogram per cubic meter | `kg/m³`	`Zend_Measure _Density` covers the physical factor of density.
Energy	Zend_Measure_Energy	Joule | `J`	`Zend_Measure _Energy` covers the physical factor of energy.
Force	Zend_Measure_Force	Newton | `N`	`Zend_Measure _Force` covers the physical factor of force.
Flow (mass)	Zend_Measure _Flow_Mass	Kilogram per second | `kg/s`	`Zend_Measure _Flow_Mass` covers the physical factor of flow rate. The weight of the flowing mass is used as reference point within this class.
Flow (mole)	Zend_Measure _Flow_Mole	Mole per second | `mol/s`	`Zend_Measure _Flow_Mole` covers the physical factor of flow rate. The density of the flowing mass is used as reference point within this class.
Flow (volume)	Zend_Measure _Flow_Volume	Cubic meter per second | `m³/s`	`Zend_Measure _Flow_Volume` covers the physical factor of flow rate. The volume of the flowing mass is used as reference point within this class.
Frequency	Zend_Measure _Frequency	Hertz | `Hz`	`Zend_Measure _Frequency` covers the physical factor of frequency.
Illumination	Zend_Measure _Illumination	Lux | `lx`	`Zend_Measure _Illumination` covers the physical factor of light density.
Length	Zend_Measure_Length	Meter | `m`	`Zend_Measure _Length` covers the physical factor of length.
Lightness	Zend_Measure _Lightness	Candela per square meter | `cd/m²`	`Zend_Measure _Ligntness` covers the physical factor of light energy.

Type	Class	Standardunit	Description
Number	Zend_Measure_Number	Decimal | (10)	`Zend_Measure _Number` converts between number formats.
Power	Zend_Measure_Power	Watt | W	`Zend_Measure _Power` covers the physical factor of power.
Pressure	Zend_Measure_Pressure	Newton per square meter | N/m²	`Zend_Measure _Pressure` covers the physical factor of pressure.
Speed	Zend_Measure_Speed	Meter per second | m/s	`Zend_Measure _Speed` covers the physical factor of speed.
Temperature	Zend_Measure _Temperature	Kelvin | K	`Zend_Measure _Temperature` covers the physical factor of temperature.
Time	Zend_Measure_Time	Second | s	`Zend_Measure_Time` covers the physical factor of time.
Torque	Zend_Measure_Torque	Newton meter | Nm	`Zend_Measure _Torque` covers the physical factor of torque.
Viscosity (dynamic)	Zend_Measure _Viscosity_Dynamic	Kilogram per meter second | kg/ms	`Zend_Measure _Viscosity _Dynamic` covers the physical factor of viscosity. The weight of the fluid is used as reference point within this class.
Viscosity (kinematic)	Zend_Measure _Viscosity_Kinematic	Square meter per second | m²/s	`Zend_Measure _Viscosity _Kinematic` covers the physical factor of viscosity. The distance of the flown fluid is used as reference point within this class.
Volume	Zend_Measure_Volume	Cubic meter | m³	`Zend_Measure _Volume` covers the physical factor of volume (content).
Weight	Zend_Measure_Weight	Kilogram | kg	`Zend_Measure _Weight` covers the physical factor of weight.

Hints for Zend_Measure_Binary

Some popular binary conventions, include terms like kilo-, mega-, giga, etc. in normal language use imply base 10, such as 1000 or 10^3. However, in the binary format for computers these terms have to be seen for a conversion factor of 1024 instead of 1000. To preclude confusions a few years ago the notation BI was introduced. Instead of kilobyte, kibibyte for kilo-binary-byte should be used.

In the class BINARY both notations can be found, such as `KILOBYTE = 1024 - binary conputer conversion KIBIBYTE = 1024 - new notation KILO_BINARY_BYTE = 1024 -` new, or the notation, long format `KILOBYTE_SI = 1000 - SI notation for kilo (1000)`. DVDs for example are marked with the SI-notation, but almost all harddisks are marked in computer binary notation.

Hints for Zend_Measure_Number

The best known number format is the decimal system. Additionally this class supports the octal system, the hexadecimal system, the binary system, the roman number system and some other less popular systems. Note that only the decimal part of numbers is handled. Any fractional part will be stripped.

Roman numbers

For the roman number system digits greater 4000 are supported. In reality these digits are shown with a crossbeam on top of the digit. As the crossbeam can not be shown within the computer, an underline has to be used instead of it.

```
$great = '_X';
$locale = new Zend_Locale('en');
$unit = new Zend_Measure_Number($great,Zend_Measure_Number::ROMAN, $locale);

// convert to the decimal system
echo $unit->convertTo(Zend_Measure_Number::DECIMAL);
```

Chapter 10. Zend_Memory

Overview

Introduction

The Zend_Memory component is intended to manage data in an environment with limited memory.

Memory objects (memory containers) are generated by memory manager by request and transparently swapped/loaded when it's necessary.

For example, if creating or loading a managed object would cause the total memory usage to exceed the limit you specify, some managed objects are copied to cache storage outside of memory. In this way, the total memory used by managed objects does not exceed the limit you need to enforce.

The memory manager uses Zend_Cache backends as storage providers.

Example 10.1. Using Zend_Memory component

Zend_Memory::factory() instantiates the memory manager object with specified backend options.

```
$backendOptions = array(
    'cache_dir' => './tmp/' // Directory where to put the swapped
        memory blocks
);

$memoryManager = Zend_Memory::factory('File', $backendOptions);

$loadedFiles = array();

for ($count = 0; $count < 10000; $count++) {
    $f = fopen($fileNames[$count], 'rb');
    $data = fread($f, filesize($fileNames[$count]));
    $fclose($f);

    $loadedFiles[] = $memoryManager->create($data);
}

echo $loadedFiles[$index1]->value;

$loadedFiles[$index2]->value = $newValue;

$loadedFiles[$index3]->value[$charIndex] = '_';
```

Theory of Operation

Zend_Memory component operates with the following concepts:

* Memory manager

* Memory container

* Locked memory object

* Movable memory object

Memory manager

The memory manager generates memory objects (locked or movable) by request of user application and returns them wrapped into a memory container object.

Memory container

The memory container has a virtual or actual `value` attribute of string type. This attribute contains the data value specified at memory object creation time.

You can operate with this `value` attribute as an object property:

```
$memObject = $memoryManager->create($data);

echo $memObject->value;

$memObject->value = $newValue;

$memObject->value[$index] = '_';

echo ord($memObject->value[$index1]);

$memObject->value = substr($memObject->value, $start, $length);
```

Note

If you are using a PHP version earlier than 5.2, use the getRef() method instead of accessing the value property directly.

Locked memory

Locked memory objects are always stored in memory. Data stored in locked memory are never swapped to the cache backend.

Movable memory

Movable memory objects are transparently swapped and loaded to/from the cache backend by Zend_Memory when it's necessary.

The memory manager doesn't swap objects with size less than the specified minimum, due to performance considerations. See the section called "MinSize" for more details.

Memory Manager

Creating a Memory Manager

You can create new a memory manager (Zend_Memory_Manager object) using the Zend_Memory::factory($backendName [, $backendOprions]) method.

The first argument $backendName is a string that names one of the backend implementations supported by Zend_Cache.

The second argument $backendOptions is an optional backend options array.

```
$backendOptions = array(
    'cache_dir' => './tmp/' // Directory where to put the swapped
```

```
        memory blocks
);

$memoryManager = Zend_Memory::factory('File', $backendOptions);
```

Zend_Memory uses Zend_Cache backends as storage providers.

You may use the special name 'None' as a backend name, in addition to standard Zend_Cache backends.

```
$memoryManager = Zend_Memory::factory('None');
```

If you use 'None' as the backend name, then the memory manager never swaps memory blocks. This is useful if you know that memory is not limited or the overall size of objects never reaches the memory limit.

The 'None' backend doesn't need any option specified.

Managing Memory Objects

This section describes creating and destroying objects in the managed memory, and settings to control memory manager behavior.

Creating Movable Objects

Create movable objects (objects, which may be swapped) using the Zend_Memory_Manager::create([$data]) method:

```
$memObject = $memoryManager->create($data);
```

The $data argument is optional and used to initialize the object value. If the $data argument is omitted, the value is an empty string.

Creating Locked Objects

Create locked objects (objects, which are not swapped) using the Zend_Memory_Manager::createLocked([$data]) method:

```
$memObject = $memoryManager->createLocked($data);
```

The $data argument is optional and used to initialize the object value. If the $data argument is omitted, the value is an empty string.

Destroying Objects

Memory objects are automatically destroyed and removed from memory when they go out of scope:

```
function foo()
{
    global $memoryManager, $memList;

    ...

    $memObject1 = $memoryManager->create($data1);
    $memObject2 = $memoryManager->create($data2);
    $memObject3 = $memoryManager->create($data3);
```

```
...

$memList[] = $memObject3;

...

unset($memObject2); // $memObject2 is destroyed here

...
// $memObject1 is destroyed here
// but $memObject3 object is still referenced by $memList
// and is not destroyed
}
```

This applies to both movable and locked objects.

Memory Manager Settings

Memory Limit

Memory limit is a number of bytes allowed to be used by loaded movable objects.

If loading or creation of an object causes memory usage to exceed of this limit, then the memory manager swaps some other objects.

You can retrieve or set the memory limit setting using the getMemoryLimit() and setMemoryLimit($newLimit) methods:

```
$oldLimit = $memoryManager->getMemoryLimit();  // Get memory limit in bytes
$memoryManager->setMemoryLimit($newLimit);     // Set memory limit in bytes
```

A negative value for memory limit means 'no limit'.

The default value is two-thirds of the value of 'memory_limit' in php.ini or 'no limit' (-1) if 'memory_limit' is not set in php.ini.

MinSize

MinSize is a minimal size of memory objects, which may be swapped by memory manager. The memory manager does not swap objects that are smaller than this value. This reduces the number of swap/load operations.

You can retrieve or set the minimum size using the getMinSize() and setMinSize($newSize) methods:

```
$oldMinSize = $memoryManager->getMinSize();  // Get MinSize in bytes
$memoryManager->setMinSize($newSize);        // Set MinSize limit in bytes
```

The default minimum size value is 16KB (16384 bytes).

Memory Objects

Movable

Create movable memory objects using the create([$data]) method of the memory manager:

```
$memObject = $memoryManager->create($data);
```

"Movable" means that such objects may be swapped and unloaded from memory and then loaded when application code accesses the object.

Locked

Create locked memory objects using the `createLocked([$data])` method of the memory manager:

```
$memObject = $memoryManager->createLocked($data);
```

"Locked" means that such objects are never swapped and unloaded from memory.

Locked objects provides the same interface as movable objects (`Zend_Memory_Container_Interface`). So locked object can be used in any place instead of movable objects.

It's useful if an application or developer can decide, that some objects should never be swapped, based on performance considerations.

Access to locked objects is faster, because the memory manager doesn't need to track changes for these objects.

The locked objects class (`Zend_Memory_Container_Locked`) guarantees virtually the same performance as working with a string variable. The overhead is a single dereference to get the class property.

Memory container 'value' property.

Use the memory container (movable or locked) `'value'` property to operate with memory object data:

```
$memObject = $memoryManager->create($data);

echo $memObject->value;

$memObject->value = $newValue;

$memObject->value[$index] = '_';

echo ord($memObject->value[$index1]);

$memObject->value = substr($memObject->value, $start, $length);
```

An alternative way to access memory object data is to use the `getRef()` method. This method *must* be used for PHP versions before 5.2. It also may have to be used in some other cases for performance reasons.

Memory container interface

Memory container provides the following methods:

getRef() method

```
public function &getRef();
```

The `getRef()` method returns reference to the object value.

Movable objects are loaded from the cache at this moment if the object is not already in memory. If the object is loaded from the cache, this might cause swapping of other objects if the memory limit would be exceeded by having all the managed objects in memory.

The getRef() method *must* be used to access memory object data for PHP versions before 5.2.

Tracking changes to data needs additional resources. The getRef() method returns reference to string, which is changed directly by user application. So, it's a good idea to use the getRef() method for value data processing:

```
$memObject = $memoryManager->create($data);

$value = &$memObject->getRef();

for ($count = 0; $count < strlen($value); $count++) {
    $char = $value[$count];
    ...
}
```

touch() method

```
public function touch();
```

The touch() method should be used in common with getRef(). It signals that object value has been changed:

```
$memObject = $memoryManager->create($data);
...

$value = &$memObject->getRef();

for ($count = 0; $count < strlen($value); $count++) {
    ...
    if ($condition) {
        $value[$count] = $char;
    }
    ...
}

$memObject->touch();
```

lock() method

```
public function lock();
```

The lock() methods locks object in memory. It should be used to prevent swapping of some objects you choose. Normally, this is not necessary, because the memory manager uses an intelligent algorithm to choose candidates for swapping. But if you exactly know, that at at this part of code some objects should not be swapped, you may lock them.

Locking objects in memory also guarantees that reference returned by the getRef() method is valid until you unlock the object:

```
$memObject1 = $memoryManager->create($data1);
$memObject2 = $memoryManager->create($data2);
...

$memObject1->lock();
$memObject2->lock();
```

```
$value1 = &$memObject1->getRef();
$value2 = &$memObject2->getRef();

for ($count = 0; $count < strlen($value2); $count++) {
    $value1 .= $value2[$count];
}

$memObject1->touch();
$memObject1->unlock();
$memObject2->unlock();
```

unlock() method

```
public function unlock();
```

unlock() method unlocks object when it's no longer necessary to be locked. See the example above.

isLocked() method

```
public function isLocked();
```

The isLocked() method can be used to check if object is locked. It returns true if the object is locked, or false if it is not locked. This is always true for "locked" objects, and may be either true or false for "movable" objects.

Chapter 11. Zend_Mime

Zend_Mime

Introduction

Zend_Mime is a support class for handling multipart MIME messages. It is used by Zend_Mail and Zend_Mime_Message and may be used by applications requiring MIME support.

Static Methods and Constants

Zend_Mime provides a simple set of static helper methods to work with MIME:

- Zend_Mime::isPrintable(): Returns TRUE if the given string contains no unprintable characters, FALSE otherwise.

- Zend_Mime::encodeBase64(): Encodes a string into base64 encoding.

- Zend_Mime::encodeQuotedPrintable(): Encodes a string with the quoted-printable mechanism.

Zend_Mime defines a set of constants commonly used with MIME Messages:

- Zend_Mime::TYPE_OCTETSTREAM: 'application/octet-stream'

- Zend_Mime::TYPE_TEXT: 'text/plain'

- Zend_Mime::TYPE_HTML: 'text/html'

- Zend_Mime::ENCODING_7BIT: '7bit'

- Zend_Mime::ENCODING_8BIT: '8bit'

- Zend_Mime::ENCODING_QUOTEDPRINTABLE: 'quoted-printable'

- Zend_Mime::ENCODING_BASE64: 'base64'

- Zend_Mime::DISPOSITION_ATTACHMENT: 'attachment'

- Zend_Mime::DISPOSITION_INLINE: 'inline'

Instantiating Zend_Mime

When Instantiating a Zend_Mime Object, a MIME boundary is stored that is used for all subsequent non-static method calls on that object. If the constructor is called with a string parameter, this value is used as a MIME boundary. If not, a random MIME boundary is generated during construction time.

A Zend_Mime object has the following Methods:

- boundary(): Returns the MIME boundary string.

- boundaryLine(): Returns the complete MIME boundary line.

- mimeEnd(): Returns the complete MIME end boundary line.

Zend_Mime_Message

Introduction

Zend_Mime_Message represents a MIME compliant message that can contain one or more separate Parts (Represented as Zend_Mime_Part objects). With Zend_Mime_Message, MIME compliant multipart messages can be generated from Zend_Mime_Part objects. Encoding and Boundary handling are handled transparently by the class. Zend_Mime_Message objects can also be reconstructed from given strings (experimental). Used by Zend_Mail .

Instantiation

There is no explicit constructor for Zend_Mime_Message.

Adding MIME Parts

Zend_Mime_Part Objects can be added to a given Zend_Mime_Message object by calling ->addPart($part)

An array with all Zend_Mime_Part objects in the Zend_Mime_Message is returned from the method ->getParts(). The Zend_Mime_Part objects can then be changed since they are stored in the array as references. If parts are added to the array or the sequence is changed, the array needs to be given back to the Zend_Mime_Part object by calling ->setParts($partsArray).

The function ->isMultiPart() will return true if more than one part is registered with the Zend_Mime_Message object and thus the object would generate a Multipart-Mime-Message when generating the actual output.

Boundary handling

Zend_Mime_Message usually creates and uses its own Zend_Mime Object to generate a boundary. If you need to define the boundary or want to change the behaviour of the Zend_Mime object used by Zend_Mime_Message, you can instantiate the Zend_Mime object yourself and then register it to Zend_Mime_Message. Usually you will not need to do this. ->setMime(Zend_Mime $mime) sets a special instance of Zend_Mime to be used by this Zend_Mime_Message

->getMime() returns the instance of Zend_Mime that will be used to render the message when generateMessage() is called.

->generateMessage() renders the Zend_Mime_Message content to a string.

parsing a string to create a Zend_Mime_Message object (experimental)

A given MIME compliant message in string form can be used to reconstruct a Zend_Mime_Message Object from it. Zend_Mime_Message has a static factory Method to parse this String and return a Zend_Mime_Message Object.

Zend_Mime_Message::createFromMessage($str, $boundary) decodes the given string and returns a Zend_Mime_Message Object that can then be examined using ->getParts()

Zend_Mime_Part

Introduction

This class represents a single part of a MIME message. It contains the actual content of the message part plus information about its encoding, content type and original filename. It provides a method for generating a string from the stored data. Zend_Mime_Part objects can be added to Zend_Mime_Message to assemble a complete multipart message.

Instantiation

Zend_Mime_Part is instantiated with a string that represents the content of the new part. The type is assumed to be OCTET-STREAM, encoding is 8Bit. After instantiating a Zend_Mime_Part, meta information can be set by accessing its attributes directly:

```
public $type = Zend_Mime::TYPE_OCTETSTREAM;
public $encoding = Zend_Mime::ENCODING_8BIT;
public $id;
public $disposition;
public $filename;
public $description;
public $charset;
public $boundary;
public $location;
public $language;
```

Methods for rendering the message part to a string

getContent() returns the encoded content of the MimePart as a string using the encoding specified in the attribute $encoding. Valid values are Zend_Mime::ENCODING_* Characterset conversions are not performed.

getHeaders() returns the Mime-Headers for the MimePart as generated from the information in the publicly accessible attributes. The attributes of the object need to be set correctly before this method is called.

- $charset has to be set to the actual charset of the content if it is a text type (Text or HTML).

- $id may be set to identify a content-id for inline images in a HTML mail.

- $filename contains the name the file will get when downloading it.

- $disposition defines if the file should be treated as an attachment or if it is used inside the (HTML-) mail (inline).

- $description is only used for informational purposes.

- $boundary defines string as boundary.

- $location can be used as resource URI that has relation to the content.

- $language defines languages in the content.

Chapter 12. Zend_Navigation

Introduction

Zend_Navigation is a component for managing trees of pointers to web pages. Simply put: It can be used for creating menus, breadcrumbs, links, and sitemaps, or serve as a model for other navigation related purposes.

Pages and Containers

There are two main concepts in Zend_Navigation:

Pages

A page (Zend_Navigation_Page) in Zend_Navigation – in its most basic form – is an object that holds a pointer to a web page. In addition to the pointer itself, the page object contains a number of other properties that are typically relevant for navigation, such as label, title, etc.

Read more about pages in the pages section.

Containers

A navigation container (Zend_Navigation_Container) is a container class for pages. It has methods for adding, retrieving, deleting and iterating pages. It implements the SPL [http://php.net/spl] interfaces RecursiveIterator and Countable, and can thus be iterated with SPL iterators such as RecursiveIteratorIterator.

Read more about containers in the containers section.

> **Note**
>
> Zend_Navigation_Page extends Zend_Navigation_Container, which means that a page can have sub pages.

Separation of data (model) and rendering (view)

Classes in the Zend_Navigation namespace do not deal with rendering of navigational elements. Rendering is done with navigational view helpers. However, pages contain information that is used by view helpers when rendering, such as; label, CSS class, title, lastmod and priority properties for sitemaps, etc.

Read more about rendering navigational elements in the manual section on navigation helpers.

Pages

Zend_Navigation ships with two page types:

- MVC pages – using the class Zend_Navigation_Page_Mvc

- URI pages – using the class Zend_Navigation_Page_Uri
MVC pages are link to on-site web pages, and are defined using MVC parameters (action, controller, module, route, params). URI pages are defined by a single property uri, which give you the full flexibility to link off-site pages or do other things with the generated links (e.g. an URI that turns into <a href="#">foo<a>).

Common page features

All page classes must extend `Zend_Navigation_Page`, and will thus share a common set of features and properties. Most notably they share the options in the table below and the same initialization process.

Option keys are mapped to `set` methods. This means that the option `order` maps to the method `setOrder()`, and `reset_params` maps to the method `setResetParams()`. If there is no setter method for the option, it will be set as a custom property of the page.

Read more on extending Zend_Navigation_Page in Creating custom page types.

Table 12.1. Common page options

Key	Type	Default	Description
label	string	null	A page label, such as 'Home' or 'Blog'.
id	string|int	null	An id tag/attribute that may be used when rendering the page, typically in an anchor element.
class	string	null	A CSS class that may be used when rendering the page, typically in an anchor element.
title	string	null	A short page description, typically for using as the `title` attribute in an anchor.
target	string	null	Specifies a target that may be used for the page, typically in an anchor element.
rel	array	array()	Specifies forward relations for the page. Each element in the array is a key-value pair, where the key designates the relation/link type, and the value is a pointer to the linked page. An example of a key-value pair is `'alternate' => 'format/plain.html'`. To allow full flexbility, there are no restrictions on relation values. The value does not have to be a string. Read more about `rel` and `rev` in the section on the Links helper..
rev	array	array()	Specifies reverse relations for the page.

Key	Type	Default	Description
			Works exactly like `rel`.
order	`string`|`int`|`null`	`null`	Works like order for elements in `Zend_Form` . If specified, the page will be iterated in a specific order, meaning you can force a page to be iterated before others by setting the order attribute to a low number, e.g. -100. If a `string` is given, it must parse to a valid `int`. If `null` is given, it will be reset, meaning the order in which the page was added to the container will be used.
resource	`string` | `Zend_Acl_Resource_Interface` | `null`	`null`	ACL resource to associate with the page. Read more in the section on ACL integration in view helpers..
privilege	`string`|`null`	`null`	ACL privilege to associate with the page. Read more in the section on ACL integration in view helpers..
active	`bool`	`false`	Whether the page should be considered active for the current request. If active is `false` or not given, MVC pages will check its properties against the request object upon calling `$page->isActive()`
visible	`bool`	`true`	Whether page should be visible for the user, or just be a part of the structure. Invisible pages are skipped by view helpers.
pages	`array` | `Zend_Config`|`null`	`null`	Child pages of the page. This could be an `array` or `Zend_Config` object containing either page options that can be passed to the `factory()` method, or actual `Zend_Navigation_Page` instances, or a mixture of both.

Custom properties

All pages support setting and getting of custom properties by use of the magic methods
`__set($name,      $value)`,   `__get($name)`,   `__isset($name)`   and
`__unset($name)`. Custom properties may have any value, and will be included in the array
that is returned from `$page->toArray()`, which means that pages can be
serialized/deserialized successfully even if the pages contains properties that are not native in
the page class.

Both native and custom properties can be set using `$page->set($name,  $value)` and
retrieved using `$page->get($name)`, or by using magic methods.

Example 12.1. Custom page properties

This example shows how custom properties can be used.

```
$page = new Zend_Navigation_Page_Mvc();
$page->foo = 'bar';
$page->meaning = 42;

echo $page->foo;

if ($page->meaning != 42) {
    // action should be taken
}
```

Zend_Navigation_Page_Mvc

MVC pages are defined using MVC parameters known from the `Zend_Controller` component. An
MVC page will use `Zend_Controller_Action_Helper_Url` internally in the `getHref()`
method   to   generate   hrefs,   and   the   `isActive()`   method   will   intersect   the
`Zend_Controller_Request_Abstract` params with the page's params to determine if the page
is active.

Table 12.2. MVC page options

Key	Type	Default	Description
action	string	null	Action name to use when generating href to the page.
controller	string	null	Controller name to use when generating href to the page.
module	string	null	Module name to use when generating href to the page.
params	array	array()	User params to use when generating href to the page.
route	string	null	Route name to use when generating href to the

Key	Type	Default	Description
			page.
reset_params	bool	true	Whether user params should be reset when generating href to the page.

Note

The three examples below assume a default MVC setup with the `default` route in place.

The URI returned is relative to the `baseUrl` in `Zend_Controller_Front`. In the examples, the baseUrl is '/' for simplicity.

Example 12.2. getHref() generates the page URI

This example show that MVC pages use `Zend_Controller_Action_Helper_Url` internally to generate URIs when calling `$page->getHref()`.

```
// getHref() returns /
$page = new Zend_Navigation_Page_Mvc(array(
    'action'     => 'index',
    'controller' => 'index'
));

// getHref() returns /blog/post/view
$page = new Zend_Navigation_Page_Mvc(array(
    'action'     => 'view',
    'controller' => 'post',
    'module'     => 'blog'
));

// getHref() returns /blog/post/view/id/1337
$page = new Zend_Navigation_Page_Mvc(array(
    'action'     => 'view',
    'controller' => 'post',
    'module'     => 'blog',
    'params'     => array('id' => 1337)
));
```

Example 12.3. isActive() determines if page is active

This example show that MVC pages determine whether they are active by using the params found in the request object.

```
/*
 * Dispatched request:
 * - module:     default
 * - controller: index
 * - action:     index
 */
$page1 = new Zend_Navigation_Page_Mvc(array(
    'action'     => 'index',
    'controller' => 'index'
```

```
));

$page2 = new Zend_Navigation_Page_Mvc(array(
    'action'     => 'bar',
    'controller' => 'index'
));

$page1->isActive(); // returns true
$page2->isActive(); // returns false

/*
 * Dispatched request:
 * - module:     blog
 * - controller: post
 * - action:     view
 * - id:         1337
 */
$page = new Zend_Navigation_Page_Mvc(array(
    'action'     => 'view',
    'controller' => 'post',
    'module'     => 'blog'
));

// returns true, because request has the same module, controller and action
$page->isActive();

/*
 * Dispatched request:
 * - module:     blog
 * - controller: post
 * - action:     view
 */
$page = new Zend_Navigation_Page_Mvc(array(
    'action'     => 'view',
    'controller' => 'post',
    'module'     => 'blog',
    'params'     => array('id' => null)
));

// returns false, because page requires the id param to be set in the request
$page->isActive(); // returns false
```

Example 12.4. Using routes

Routes can be used with MVC pages. If a page has a route, this route will be used in `getHref()` to generate the URL for the page.

Note

Note that when using the `route` property in a page, you should also specify the default params that the route defines (module, controller, action, etc.), otherwise the `isActive()` method will not be able to determine if the page is active. The reason for this is that there is currently no way to get the default params from a `Zend_Controller_Router_Route_Interface` object, nor to retrieve the current route from a `Zend_Controller_Router_Interface` object.

```
// the following route is added to the ZF router
Zend_Controller_Front::getInstance()->getRouter()->addRoute(
```

```
        'article_view', // route name
        new Zend_Controller_Router_Route(
            'a/:id',
            array(
                'module'     => 'news',
                'controller' => 'article',
                'action'     => 'view',
                'id'         => null
            )
        )
    )
);

// a page is created with a 'route' option
$page = new Zend_Navigation_Page_Mvc(array(
    'label'      => 'A news article',
    'route'      => 'article_view',
    'module'     => 'news',      // required for isActive(), see note above
    'controller' => 'article',   // required for isActive(), see note above
    'action'     => 'view',      // required for isActive(), see note above
    'params'     => array('id' => 42)
));

// returns: /a/42
$page->getHref();
```

Zend_Navigation_Page_Uri

Pages of type Zend_Navigation_Page_Uri can be used to link to pages on other domains or sites, or to implement custom logic for the page. URI pages are simple; in addition to the common page options, a URI page takes only one option — uri. The uri will be returned when calling $page->getHref(), and may be a string or null.

Note

Zend_Navigation_Page_Uri will not try to determine whether it should be active when calling $page->isActive(). It merely returns what currently is set, so to make a URI page active you have to manually call $page->setActive() or specifying active as a page option when constucting.

Table 12.3. URI page options

Key	Type	Default	Description
uri	string	null	URI to page. This can be any string or null.

Creating custom page types

When extending Zend_Navigation_Page, there is usually no need to override the constructor or the methods setOptions() or setConfig(). The page constructor takes a single parameter, an array or a Zend_Config object, which is passed to setOptions() or setConfig() respectively. Those methods will in turn call set() method, which will map options to native or custom properties. If the option internal_id is given, the method will first look for a method named setInternalId(), and pass the option to this method if it exists. If the method does not exist, the option will be set as a custom property of the page, and be accessible via $internalId = $page->internal_id; or $internalId = $page->get('internal_id');.

Example 12.5. The most simple custom page

The only thing a custom page class needs to implement is the `getHref()` method.

```
class My_Simple_Page extends Zend_Navigation_Page
{
    public function getHref()
    {
        return 'something-completely-different';
    }
}
```

Example 12.6. A custom page with properties

When adding properties to an extended page, there is no need to override/modify `setOptions()` or `setConfig()`.

```
class My_Navigation_Page extends Zend_Navigation_Page
{
    private $_foo;
    private $_fooBar;

    public function setFoo($foo)
    {
        $this->_foo = $foo;
    }

    public function getFoo()
    {
        return $this->_foo;
    }

    public function setFooBar($fooBar)
    {
        $this->_fooBar = $fooBar;
    }

    public function getFooBar()
    {
        return $this->_fooBar;
    }

    public function getHref()
    {
        return $this->foo . '/' . $this->fooBar;
    }
}

// can now construct using
$page = new My_Navigation_Page(array(
    'label'   => 'Property names are mapped to setters',
    'foo'     => 'bar',
    'foo_bar' => 'baz'
));

// ...or
$page = Zend_Navigation_Page::factory(array(
```

```
    'type'    => 'My_Navigation_Page',
    'label'   => 'Property names are mapped to setters',
    'foo'     => 'bar',
    'foo_bar' => 'baz'
));
```

Creating pages using the page factory

All pages (also custom classes), can be created using the page factory, Zend_Navigation_Page::factory(). The factory can take an array with options, or a Zend_Config object. Each key in the array/config corresponds to a page option, as seen in the section on Pages. If the option uri is given and no MVC options are given (action, controller, module, route), an URI page will be created. If any of the MVC options are given, an MVC page will be created.

If type is given, the factory will assume the value to be the name of the class that should be created. If the value is mvc or uri and MVC/URI page will be created.

Example 12.7. Creating an MVC page using the page factory

```
$page = Zend_Navigation_Page::factory(array(
    'label'  => 'My MVC page',
    'action' => 'index'
));

$page = Zend_Navigation_Page::factory(array(
    'label'      => 'Search blog',
    'action'     => 'index',
    'controller' => 'search',
    'module'     => 'blog'
));

$page = Zend_Navigation_Page::factory(array(
    'label'      => 'Home',
    'action'     => 'index',
    'controller' => 'index',
    'module'     => 'index',
    'route'      => 'home'
));

$page = Zend_Navigation_Page::factory(array(
    'type'   => 'mvc',
    'label'  => 'My MVC page'
));
```

Example 12.8. Creating a URI page using the page factory

```
$page = Zend_Navigation_Page::factory(array(
    'label' => 'My URI page',
    'uri'   => 'http://www.example.com/'
));

$page = Zend_Navigation_Page::factory(array(
    'label'  => 'Search',
```

```
    'uri'    => 'http://www.example.com/search',
    'active' => true
));

$page = Zend_Navigation_Page::factory(array(
    'label' => 'My URI page',
    'uri'   => '#'
));

$page = Zend_Navigation_Page::factory(array(
    'type'   => 'uri',
    'label'  => 'My URI page'
));
```

Example 12.9. Creating a custom page type using the page factory

To create a custom page type using the factory, use the option type to specify a class name to instantiate.

```
class My_Navigation_Page extends Zend_Navigation_Page
{
    protected $_fooBar = 'ok';

    public function setFooBar($fooBar)
    {
        $this->_fooBar = $fooBar;
    }
}

$page = Zend_Navigation_Page::factory(array(
    'type'    => 'My_Navigation_Page',
    'label'   => 'My custom page',
    'foo_bar' => 'foo bar'
));
```

Containers

Containers have methods for adding, retrieving, deleting and iterating pages. Containers implement the SPL [http://php.net/spl] interfaces RecursiveIterator and Countable, meaning that a container can be iterated using the SPL RecursiveIteratorIterator class.

Creating containers

Zend_Navigation_Container is abstract, and can not be instantiated directly. Use Zend_Navigation if you want to instantiate a container.

Zend_Navigation can be constructed entirely empty, or take an array or a Zend_Config object with pages to put in the container. Each page in the given array/config will eventually be passed to the addPage() method of the container class, which means that each element in the array/config can be an array or a config object, or a Zend_Navigation_Page instance.

Example 12.10. Creating a container using an array

```
/*
 * Create a container from an array
 *
 * Each element in the array will be passed to
 * Zend_Navigation_Page::factory() when constructing.
 */
$container = new Zend_Navigation(array(
    array(
        'label' => 'Page 1',
        'id' => 'home-link'
    ),
    array(
        'label' => 'Zend',
        'uri' => 'http://www.zend-project.com/',
        'order' => 100
    ),
    array(
        'label' => 'Page 2',
        'controller' => 'page2',
        'pages' => array(
            array(
                'label' => 'Page 2.1',
                'action' => 'page2_1',
                'controller' => 'page2',
                'class' => 'special-one',
                'title' => 'This element has a special class',
                'active' => true
            ),
            array(
                'label' => 'Page 2.2',
                'action' => 'page2_2',
                'controller' => 'page2',
                'class' => 'special-two',
                'title' => 'This element has a special class too'
            )
        )
    ),
    array(
        'label' => 'Page 2 with params',
        'action' => 'index',
        'controller' => 'page2',
        // specify a param or two
        'params' => array(
            'format' => 'json',
            'foo' => 'bar'
        )
    ),
    array(
        'label' => 'Page 2 with params and a route',
        'action' => 'index',
        'controller' => 'page2',
        // specify a route name and a param for the route
        'route' => 'nav-route-example',
        'params' => array(
            'format' => 'json'
        )
    ),
    array(
        'label' => 'Page 3',
```

```
        'action' => 'index',
        'controller' => 'index',
        'module' => 'mymodule',
        'reset_params' => false
    ),
    array(
        'label' => 'Page 4',
        'uri' => '#',
        'pages' => array(
            array(
                'label' => 'Page 4.1',
                'uri' => '/page4',
                'title' => 'Page 4 using uri',
                'pages' => array(
                    array(
                        'label' => 'Page 4.1.1',
                        'title' => 'Page 4 using mvc params',
                        'action' => 'index',
                        'controller' => 'page4',
                        // let's say this page is active
                        'active' => '1'
                    )
                )
            )
        )
    ),
    array(
        'label' => 'Page 0?',
        'uri' => '/setting/the/order/option',
        // setting order to -1 should make it appear first
        'order' => -1
    ),
    array(
        'label' => 'Page 5',
        'uri' => '/',
        // this page should not be visible
        'visible' => false,
        'pages' => array(
            array(
                'label' => 'Page 5.1',
                'uri' => '#',
                'pages' => array(
                    array(
                        'label' => 'Page 5.1.1',
                        'uri' => '#',
                        'pages' => array(
                            array(
                                'label' => 'Page 5.1.2',
                                'uri' => '#',
                                // let's say this page is active
                                'active' => true
                            )
                        )
                    )
                )
            )
        )
    ),
    array(
        'label' => 'ACL page 1 (guest)',
        'uri' => '#acl-guest',
        'resource' => 'nav-guest',
        'pages' => array(
            array(
```

```
                    'label' => 'ACL page 1.1 (foo)',
                    'uri' => '#acl-foo',
                    'resource' => 'nav-foo'
                ),
                array(
                    'label' => 'ACL page 1.2 (bar)',
                    'uri' => '#acl-bar',
                    'resource' => 'nav-bar'
                ),
                array(
                    'label' => 'ACL page 1.3 (baz)',
                    'uri' => '#acl-baz',
                    'resource' => 'nav-baz'
                ),
                array(
                    'label' => 'ACL page 1.4 (bat)',
                    'uri' => '#acl-bat',
                    'resource' => 'nav-bat'
                )
            )
        ),
        array(
            'label' => 'ACL page 2 (member)',
            'uri' => '#acl-member',
            'resource' => 'nav-member'
        ),
        array(
            'label' => 'ACL page 3 (admin',
            'uri' => '#acl-admin',
            'resource' => 'nav-admin',
            'pages' => array(
                array(
                    'label' => 'ACL page 3.1 (nothing)',
                    'uri' => '#acl-nada'
                )
            )
        ),
        array(
            'label' => 'Zend Framework',
            'route' => 'zf-route'
        )
));
```

Example 12.11. Creating a container using a config object

```
/* CONTENTS OF /path/to/navigation.xml:
<config>
    <nav>

        <zend>
            <label>Zend</label>
            <uri>http://www.zend-project.com/</uri>
            <order>100</order>
        </zend>

        <page1>
            <label>Page 1</label>
            <uri>page1</uri>
            <pages>
```

```
            <page1_1>
                <label>Page 1.1</label>
                <uri>page1/page1_1</uri>
            </page1_1>

        </pages>
    </page1>

    <page2>
        <label>Page 2</label>
        <uri>page2</uri>
        <pages>

            <page2_1>
                <label>Page 2.1</label>
                <uri>page2/page2_1</uri>
            </page2_1>

            <page2_2>
                <label>Page 2.2</label>
                <uri>page2/page2_2</uri>
                <pages>

                    <page2_2_1>
                        <label>Page 2.2.1</label>
                        <uri>page2/page2_2/page2_2_1</uri>
                    </page2_2_1>

                    <page2_2_2>
                        <label>Page 2.2.2</label>
                        <uri>page2/page2_2/page2_2_2</uri>
                        <active>1</active>
                    </page2_2_2>

                </pages>
            </page2_2>

            <page2_3>
                <label>Page 2.3</label>
                <uri>page2/page2_3</uri>
                <pages>

                    <page2_3_1>
                        <label>Page 2.3.1</label>
                        <uri>page2/page2_3/page2_3_1</uri>
                    </page2_3_1>

                    <page2_3_2>
                        <label>Page 2.3.2</label>
                        <uri>page2/page2_3/page2_3_2</uri>
                        <visible>0</visible>
                        <pages>

                            <page2_3_2_1>
                                <label>Page 2.3.2.1</label>
                                <uri>page2/page2_3/page2_3_2/1</uri>
                                <active>1</active>
                            </page2_3_2_1>

                            <page2_3_2_2>
                                <label>Page 2.3.2.2</label>
                                <uri>page2/page2_3/page2_3_2/2</uri>
                                <active>1</active>
```

```
                                        <pages>
                                            <page_2_3_2_2_1>
                                                <label>Ignore</label>
                                                <uri>#</uri>
                                                <active>1</active>
                                            </page_2_3_2_2_1>      .
                                        </pages>
                                    </page2_3_2_2>

                        </pages>
                    </page2_3_2>

                    <page2_3_3>
                        <label>Page 2.3.3</label>
                        <uri>page2/page2_3/page2_3_3</uri>
                        <resource>admin</resource>
                        <pages>

                                <page2_3_3_1>
                                    <label>Page 2.3.3.1</label>
                                    <uri>page2/page2_3/page2_3_3/1</uri>
                                    <active>1</active>
                                </page2_3_3_1>

                                <page2_3_3_2>
                                    <label>Page 2.3.3.2</label>
                                    <uri>page2/page2_3/page2_3_3/2</uri>
                                    <resource>guest</resource>
                                    <active>1</active>
                                </page2_3_3_2>

                        </pages>
                    </page2_3_3>

                </pages>
            </page2_3>

        </pages>
    </page2>

    <page3>
        <label>Page 3</label>
        <uri>page3</uri>
        <pages>

            <page3_1>
                <label>Page 3.1</label>
                <uri>page3/page3_1</uri>
                <resource>guest</resource>
            </page3_1>

            <page3_2>
                <label>Page 3.2</label>
                <uri>page3/page3_2</uri>
                <resource>member</resource>
                <pages>

                    <page3_2_1>
                        <label>Page 3.2.1</label>
                        <uri>page3/page3_2/page3_2_1</uri>
                    </page3_2_1>

                    <page3_2_2>
                        <label>Page 3.2.2</label>
```

```
                                <uri>page3/page3_2/page3_2_2</uri>
                                <resource>admin</resource>
                            </page3_2_2>

                        </pages>
                    </page3_2>

                    <page3_3>
                        <label>Page 3.3</label>
                        <uri>page3/page3_3</uri>
                        <resource>special</resource>
                        <pages>

                            <page3_3_1>
                                <label>Page 3.3.1</label>
                                <uri>page3/page3_3/page3_3_1</uri>
                                <visible>0</visible>
                            </page3_3_1>

                            <page3_3_2>
                                <label>Page 3.3.2</label>
                                <uri>page3/page3_3/page3_3_2</uri>
                                <resource>admin</resource>
                            </page3_3_2>

                        </pages>
                    </page3_3>

                </pages>
            </page3>

            <home>
                <label>Home</label>
                <order>-100</order>
            </home>

        </nav>
    </config>
 */

$config = new Zend_Config_Xml('/path/to/navigation.xml', 'nav');
$container = new Zend_Navigation($config);
```

Adding pages

Adding pages to a container can be done with the methods addPage(), addPages(), or setPages(). See examples below for explanation.

Example 12.12. Adding pages to a container

```
// create container
$container = new Zend_Navigation();

// add page by giving a page instance
$container->addPage(Zend_Navigation_Page::factory(array(
    'uri' => 'http://www.example.com/'
)))

// add page by giving an array
```

```
$container->addPage(array(
    'uri' => 'http://www.example.com/'
)))

// add page by giving a config object
$container->addPage(new Zend_Config(array(
    'uri' => 'http://www.example.com/'
)))

$pages = array(
    array(
        'label'  => 'Save'
        'action' => 'save',
    ),
    array(
        'label'  =>  'Delete',
        'action' => 'delete'
    )
);

// add two pages
$container->addPages($pages);

// remove existing pages and add the given pages
$container->setPages($pages);
```

Removing pages

Removing pages can be done with removePage() or removePages(). The first method accepts a an instance of a page, or an integer. The integer corresponds to the order a page has. The latter method will remove all pages in the container.

Example 12.13. Removing pages from a container

```
$container = new Zend_Navigation(array(
    array(
        'label'  => 'Page 1',
        'action' => 'page1'
    ),
    array(
        'label'  => 'Page 2',
        'action' => 'page2',
        'order'  => 200
    ),
    array(
        'label'  => 'Page 3',
        'action' => 'page3'
    )
));

// remove page by implicit page order
$container->removePage(0);        // removes Page 1

// remove page by instance
$page3 = $container->findOneByAction('Page 3');
$container->removePage($page3); // removes Page 3

// remove page by explicit page order
$container->removePage(200);      // removes Page 2
```

```
// remove all pages
$container->removePages();        // removes all pages
```

Finding pages

Containers have finder methods for retrieving pages. They are findOneBy($property, $value), findAllBy($property, $value), and findBy($property, $value, $all = false). Those methods will recursively search the container for pages matching the given $page->$property == $value. The first method, findOneBy(), will return a single page matching the property with the given value, or null if it cannot be found. The second method will return all pages with a property matching the given value. The third method will call one of the two former methods depending on the $all flag.

The finder methods can also be used magically by appending the property name to findBy, findOneBy, or findAllBy, e.g. findOneByLabel('Home') to return the first matching page with label Home. Other combinations are findByLabel(...), findOnyByTitle(...), findAllByController(...), etc. Finder methods also work on custom properties, such as findByFoo('bar').

Example 12.14. Finding pages in a container

```
$container = new Zend_Navigation(array(
    array(
        'label' => 'Page 1',
        'uri'   => 'page-1',
        'foo'   => 'bar',
        'pages' => array(
            array(
                'label' => 'Page 1.1',
                'uri'   => 'page-1.1',
                'foo'   => 'bar',
            ),
            array(
                'label' => 'Page 1.2',
                'uri'   => 'page-1.2',
                'class' => 'my-class',
            ),
            array(
                'type'   => 'uri',
                'label'  => 'Page 1.3',
                'uri'    => 'page-1.3',
                'action' => 'about'
            )
        )
    ),
    array(
        'label'      => 'Page 2',
        'id'         => 'page_2_and_3',
        'class'      => 'my-class',
        'module'     => 'page2',
        'controller' => 'index',
        'action'     => 'page1'
    ),
    array(
        'label'      => 'Page 3',
        'id'         => 'page_2_and_3',
        'module'     => 'page3',
```

```
                'controller' => 'index'
        )
));

// The 'id' is not required to be unique, but be aware that
// having two pages with the same id will render the same id attribute
// in menus and breadcrumbs.
$found = $container->findBy('id',
                           'page_2_and_3');          // returns Page 2
$found = $container->findOneBy('id',
                              'page_2_and_3');     // returns Page 2
$found = $container->findBy('id',
                           'page_2_and_3',
                           true);                    // returns Page 2 and
                                                     //         Page 3
$found = $container->findById('page_2_and_3');      // returns Page 2
$found = $container->findOneById('page_2_and_3');   // returns Page 2
$found = $container->findAllById('page_2_and_3');   // returns Page 2 and
                                                    //         Page 3


// Find all matching CSS class my-class
$found = $container->findAllBy('class',
                              'my-class');           // returns Page 1.2 and
                                                     //         Page 2
$found = $container->findAllByClass('my-class');    // returns Page 1.2 and
                                                    //         Page 2

// Find first matching CSS class my-class
$found = $container->findOneByClass('my-class');    // returns Page 1.2

// Find all matching CSS class non-existant
$found = $container->findAllByClass('non-existant'); // returns array()

// Find first matching CSS class non-existant
$found = $container->findOneByClass('non-existant'); // returns null

// Find all pages with custom property 'foo' = 'bar'
$found = $container->findAllBy('foo', 'bar'); // returns Page 1 and
                                              //         Page 1.1

// To achieve the same magically, 'foo' must be in lowercase.
// This is because 'foo' is a custom property, and thus the
// property name is not normalized to 'Foo'
$found = $container->findAllByfoo('bar');

// Find all with controller = 'index'
$found = $container->findAllByController('index'); // returns Page 2 and
                                                   //         Page 3
```

Iterating containers

Zend_Navigation_Container implements RecursiveIteratorIterator, and can be iterated using any Iterator class. To iterate a container recursively, use the RecursiveIteratorIterator class.

Example 12.15. Iterating a container

```
/*
 * Create a container from an array
```

```
 */
$container = new Zend_Navigation(array(
    array(
        'label' => 'Page 1',
        'uri'   => '#'
    ),
    array(
        'label' => 'Page 2',
        'uri'   => '#',
        'pages' => array(
            array(
                'label' => 'Page 2.1',
                'uri'   => '#'
            ),
            array(
                'label' => 'Page 2.2',
                'uri'   => '#'
            )
        )
    )
    array(
        'label' => 'Page 3',
        'uri'   => '#'
    )
));

// Iterate flat using regular foreach:
// Output: Page 1, Page 2, Page 3
foreach ($container as $page) {
    echo $page->label;
}

// Iterate recursively using RecursiveIteratorIterator
$it = new RecursiveIteratorIterator(
        $container, RecursiveIteratorIterator::SELF_FIRST);

// Output: Page 1, Page 2, Page 2.1, Page 2.2, Page 3
foreach ($it as $page) {
    echo $page->label;
}
```

Other operations

The method hasPage(Zend_Navigation_Page $page) checks if the container has the given page. The method hasPages() checks if there are any pages in the container, and is equivalent to count($container) > 1.

The toArray() method converts the container and the pages in it to an array. This can be useful for serializing and debugging.

Example 12.16. Converting a container to an array

```
$container = new Zend_Navigation(array(
    array(
        'label' => 'Page 1',
        'uri'   => '#'
    ),
    array(
        'label' => 'Page 2',
```

```
            'uri'    => '#',
            'pages' => array(
                array(
                    'label' => 'Page 2.1',
                    'uri'    => '#'
                ),
                array(
                    'label' => 'Page 2.2',
                    'uri'    => '#'
                )
            )
        )
    )
));

var_dump($container->toArray());

/* Output:
array(2) {
   [0]=> array(15) {
     ["label"]=> string(6) "Page 1"
     ["id"]=> NULL
     ["class"]=> NULL
     ["title"]=> NULL
     ["target"]=> NULL
     ["rel"]=> array(0) {
     }
     ["rev"]=> array(0) {
     }
     ["order"]=> NULL
     ["resource"]=> NULL
     ["privilege"]=> NULL
     ["active"]=> bool(false)
     ["visible"]=> bool(true)
     ["type"]=> string(23) "Zend_Navigation_Page_Uri"
     ["pages"]=> array(0) {
     }
     ["uri"]=> string(1) "#"
   }
   [1]=> array(15) {
     ["label"]=> string(6) "Page 2"
     ["id"]=> NULL
     ["class"]=> NULL
     ["title"]=> NULL
     ["target"]=> NULL
     ["rel"]=> array(0) {
     }
     ["rev"]=> array(0) {
     }
     ["order"]=> NULL
     ["resource"]=> NULL
     ["privilege"]=> NULL
     ["active"]=> bool(false)
     ["visible"]=> bool(true)
     ["type"]=> string(23) "Zend_Navigation_Page_Uri"
     ["pages"]=> array(2) {
       [0]=> array(15) {
         ["label"]=> string(8) "Page 2.1"
         ["id"]=> NULL
         ["class"]=> NULL
         ["title"]=> NULL
         ["target"]=> NULL
         ["rel"]=> array(0) {
         }
         ["rev"]=> array(0) {
```

```
        }
        ["order"]=> NULL
        ["resource"]=> NULL
        ["privilege"]=> NULL
        ["active"]=> bool(false)
        ["visible"]=> bool(true)
        ["type"]=> string(23) "Zend_Navigation_Page_Uri"
        ["pages"]=> array(0) {
        }
        ["uri"]=> string(1) "#"
      }
      [1]=>
      array(15) {
        ["label"]=> string(8) "Page 2.2"
        ["id"]=> NULL
        ["class"]=> NULL
        ["title"]=> NULL
        ["target"]=> NULL
        ["rel"]=> array(0) {
        }
        ["rev"]=> array(0) {
        }
        ["order"]=> NULL
        ["resource"]=> NULL
        ["privilege"]=> NULL
        ["active"]=> bool(false)
        ["visible"]=> bool(true)
        ["type"]=> string(23) "Zend_Navigation_Page_Uri"
        ["pages"]=> array(0) {
        }
        ["uri"]=> string(1) "#"
      }
    }
    ["uri"]=> string(1) "#"
  }
}
*/
```

Chapter 13. Zend_OpenId

Introduction

Zend_OpenId is a Zend Framework component that provides a simple API for building OpenID-enabled sites and identity providers.

What is OpenID?

OpenID is a set of protocols for user-centric digital identities. These protocols allows users to create an identity online, using an identity provider. This identity can be used on any site that supports OpenID. Using OpenID-enabled sites, users do not need to remember traditional authentication tokens such as usernames and passwords for each site. All OpenID-enabled sites accept a single OpenID identity. This identity is typically a URL. It may be the URL of the user's personal page, blog or other resource that may provide additional information about them. That mean a user needs just one identifier for all sites he or she uses. services. OpenID is an open, decentralized, and free user-centric solution. Users may choose which OpenID provider to use, or even create their own personal identity server. No central authority is required to approve or register OpenID-enabled sites or identity providers.

For more information about OpenID visit the OpenID official site [http://www.openid.net/].

How Does it Work?

The purpose of the Zend_OpenId component is to implement the OpenID authentication protocol as described in the following sequence diagram:

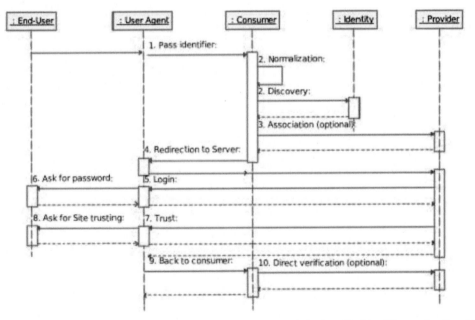

1. Authentication is initiated by the end user, who passes their OpenID identifier to the OpenID consumer through a User-Agent.

2. The OpenID consumer performs normalization and discovery on the user-supplied identifier. Through this process, the consumer obtains the claimed identifier, the URL of the OpenID provider

and an OpenID protocol version.

3. The OpenID consumer establishes an optional association with the provider using Diffie-Hellman keys. As a result, both parties have a common "shared secret" that is used for signing and verification of the subsequent messages.

4. The OpenID consumer redirects the User-Agent to the URL of the OpenID provider with an OpenID authentication request.

5. The OpenID provider checks if the User-Agent is already authenticated and, if not, offers to do so.

6. The end user enters the required password.

7. The OpenID provider checks if it is allowed to pass the user identity to the given consumer, and asks the user if necessary.

8. The user allows or disallows passing his identity.

9. The OpenID Provider redirects the User-Agent back to the OpenID consumer with an "authentication approved" or "failed" request.

10. The OpenID consumer verifies the information received from the provider by using the shared secret it got in step 3 or by sending an additional direct request to the OpenID provider.

Zend_OpenId Structure

Zend_OpenId consists of two sub-packages. The first one is Zend_OpenId_Consumer for developing OpenID-enabled sites, and the second is Zend_OpenId_Provider for developing OpenID servers. They are completely independent of each other and may be used separately.

The only common code used by these sub-packages are the OpenID Simple Registration Extension implemented by Zend_OpenId_Extension_Sreg class and a set of utility functions implemented by the Zend_OpenId class.

Note

Zend_OpenId takes advantage of the GMP extension [http://php.net/gmp], where available. Consider enabling the GMP extension for enhanced performance when using Zend_OpenId.

Supported OpenID Standards

The Zend_OpenId component supports the following standards:

- OpenID Authentication protocol version 1.1
- OpenID Authentication protocol version 2.0 draft 11
- OpenID Simple Registration Extension version 1.0
- OpenID Simple Registration Extension version 1.1 draft 1

Zend_OpenId_Consumer Basics

Zend_OpenId_Consumer can be used to implement OpenID authentication for web sites.

OpenID Authentication

From a web site developer's point of view, the OpenID authentication process consists of three steps:

1. Show OpenID authentication form

2. Accept OpenID identity and pass it to the OpenID provider

3. Verify response from the OpenID provider

The OpenID authentication protocol actually requires more steps, but many of them are encapsulated inside Zend_OpenId_Consumer and are therefore transparent to the developer.

The end user initiates the OpenID authentication process by submitting his or her identification credentials with the appropriate form. The following example shows a simple form that accepts an OpenID identifier. Note that the example only demonstrates a login.

Example 13.1. The Simple OpenID Login form

```
<html><body>
<form method="post" action="example-1_2.php"><fieldset>
<legend>OpenID Login</legend>
<input type="text" name="openid_identifier">
<input type="submit" name="openid_action" value="login">
</fieldset></form></body></html>
```

This form passes the OpenID identity on submission to the following PHP script that performs the second step of authentication. The PHP script need only call the Zend_OpenId_Consumer::login() method in this step. The first argument of this method is an accepted OpenID identity, and the second is the URL of a script that handles the third and last step of authentication.

Example 13.2. The Authentication Request Handler

```
$consumer = new Zend_OpenId_Consumer();
if (!$consumer->login($_POST['openid_identifier'], 'example-1_3.php')) {
    die("OpenID login failed.");
}
```

The Zend_OpenId_Consumer::login() method performs discovery on a given identifier, and, if successful, obtains the address of the identity provider and its local identifier. It then creates an association to the given provider so that both the site and provider share a secret that is used to sign the subsequent messages. Finally, it passes an authentication request to the provider. This request redirects the end user's web browser to an OpenID server site, where the user can continue the authentication process.

An OpenID provider usually asks users for their password (if they weren't previously logged-in), whether the user trusts this site and what information may be returned to the site. These interactions are not visible to the OpenID consumer, so it can not obtain the user's password or other information that the user did not has not directed the OpenID provider to share with it.

On success, Zend_OpenId_Consumer::login() does not return, instead performing an HTTP redirection. However, if there is an error it may return false. Errors may occur due to an invalid identity, unresponsive provider, communication error, etc.

The third step of authentication is initiated by the response from the OpenID provider, after it has authenticated the user's password. This response is passed indirectly, as an HTTP redirection using the end user's web browser. The consumer must now simply check that this response is valid.

Example 13.3. The Authentication Response Verifier

```php
$consumer = new Zend_OpenId_Consumer();
if ($consumer->verify($_GET, $id)) {
    echo "VALID " . htmlspecialchars($id);
} else {
    echo "INVALID " . htmlspecialchars($id);
}
```

This check is performed using the Zend_OpenId_Consumer::verify method, which takes an array of the HTTP request's arguments and checks that this response is properly signed by the OpenID provider. It may assign the claimed OpenID identity that was entered by end user in the first step using a second, optional argument.

Combining all Steps in One Page

The following example combines all three steps in one script. It doesn't provide any new functionality. The advantage of using just one script is that the developer need not specify URL's for a script to handle the next step. By default, all steps use the same URL. However, the script now includes some dispatch code to execute the appropriate code for each step of authentication.

Example 13.4. The Complete OpenID Login Script

```php
<?php
$status = "";
if (isset($_POST['openid_action']) &&
    $_POST['openid_action'] == "login" &&
    !empty($_POST['openid_identifier'])) {

    $consumer = new Zend_OpenId_Consumer();
    if (!$consumer->login($_POST['openid_identifier'])) {
        $status = "OpenID login failed.";
    }
} else if (isset($_GET['openid_mode'])) {
    if ($_GET['openid_mode'] == "id_res") {
        $consumer = new Zend_OpenId_Consumer();
        if ($consumer->verify($_GET, $id)) {
            $status = "VALID " . htmlspecialchars($id);
        } else {
            $status = "INVALID " . htmlspecialchars($id);
        }
    } else if ($_GET['openid_mode'] == "cancel") {
        $status = "CANCELLED";
    }
}
?>
<html><body>
<?php echo "$status<br>" ?>
<form method="post">
<fieldset>
<legend>OpenID Login</legend>
<input type="text" name="openid_identifier" value=""/>
<input type="submit" name="openid_action" value="login"/>
</fieldset>
</form>
</body></html>
```

In addition, this code differentiates between cancelled and invalid authentication responses. The provider returns a cancelled response if the identity provider is not aware of the supplied identity, the user is not logged in, or the user doesn't trust the site. An invalid response indicates that the response is not conformant to the OpenID protocol or is incorrectly signed.

Consumer Realm

When an OpenID-enabled site passes authentication requests to a provider, it identifies itself with a realm URL. This URL may be considered a root of a trusted site. If the user trusts the realm URL, he or she should also trust matched and subsequent URLs.

By default, the realm URL is automatically set to the URL of the directory in which the login script resides. This default value is useful for most, but not all, cases. Sometimes an entire domain, and not a directory should be trusted. Or even a combination of several servers in one domain.

To override the default value, developers may pass the realm URL as a third argument to the Zend_OpenId_Consumer::login method. In the following example, a single interaction asks for trusted access to all php.net sites.

Example 13.5. Authentication Request for Specified Realm

```
$consumer = new Zend_OpenId_Consumer();
if (!$consumer->login($_POST['openid_identifier'],
                      'example-3_3.php',
                      'http://*.php.net/')) {
    die("OpenID login failed.");
}
```

This example implements only the second step of authentication; the first and third steps are similar to the examples above.

Immediate Check

In some cases, an application need only check if a user is already logged in to a trusted OpenID server without any interaction with the user. The Zend_OpenId_Consumer::check method does precisely that. It is executed with the same arguments as Zend_OpenId_Consumer::login, but it doesn't display any OpenID server pages to the user. From the users point of view this process is transparent, and it appears as though they never left the site. The third step succeeds if the user is already logged in and trusted by the site, otherwise it will fail.

Example 13.6. Immediate Check without Interaction

```
$consumer = new Zend_OpenId_Consumer();
if (!$consumer->check($_POST['openid_identifier'], 'example-4_3.php')) {
    die("OpenID login failed.");
}
```

This example implements only the second step of authentication; the first and third steps are similar to the examples above.

Zend_OpenId_Consumer_Storage

There are three steps in the OpenID authentication procedure, and each step is performed by a separate HTTP request. To store information between requests, Zend_OpenId_Consumer uses internal storage.

Developers do not necessarily have to be aware of this storage because by default Zend_OpenId_Consumer uses file-based storage under the temporary directory- similar to PHP sessions. However, this storage may be not suitable in all cases. Some developers may want to store information in a database, while others may need to use common storage suitable for server farms. Fortunately, developers may easily replace the default storage with their own. To specify a custom storage mechanism, one need only extend the Zend_OpenId_Consumer_Storage class and pass this subclass to the Zend_OpenId_Consumer constructor in the first argument.

The following example demonstrates a simple storage mechanism that uses Zend_Db as its backend and exposes three groups of functions. The first group contains functions for working with associations, while the second group caches discovery information, and the third group can be used to check whether a response is unique. This class can easily be used with existing or new databases; if the required tables don't exist, it will create them.

Example 13.7. Database Storage

```
class DbStorage extends Zend_OpenId_Consumer_Storage
{
    private $_db;
    private $_association_table;
    private $_discovery_table;
    private $_nonce_table;

    // Pass in the Zend_Db_Adapter object and the names of the
    // required tables
    public function __construct($db,
                               $association_table = "association",
                               $discovery_table = "discovery",
                               $nonce_table = "nonce")
    {
        $this->_db = $db;
        $this->_association_table = $association_table;
        $this->_discovery_table = $discovery_table;
        $this->_nonce_table = $nonce_table;
        $tables = $this->_db->listTables();

        // If the associations table doesn't exist, create it
        if (!in_array($association_table, $tables)) {
            $this->_db->getConnection()->exec(
                "create table $association_table (" .
                " url     varchar(256) not null primary key," .
                " handle  varchar(256) not null," .
                " macFunc char(16) not null," .
                " secret  varchar(256) not null," .
                " expires timestamp" .
                ")");
        }

        // If the discovery table doesn't exist, create it
        if (!in_array($discovery_table, $tables)) {
            $this->_db->getConnection()->exec(
                "create table $discovery_table (" .
                " id      varchar(256) not null primary key," .
```

```
                " realId  varchar(256) not null," .
                " server  varchar(256) not null," .
                " version float," .
                " expires timestamp" .
                ")");
        }

        // If the nonce table doesn't exist, create it
        if (!in_array($nonce_table, $tables)) {
            $this->_db->getConnection()->exec(
                "create table $nonce_table (" .
                " nonce   varchar(256) not null primary key," .
                " created timestamp default current_timestamp" .
                ")");
        }
    }

    public function addAssociation($url,
                                   $handle,
                                   $macFunc,
                                   $secret,
                                   $expires)
    {
        $table = $this->_association_table;
        $secret = base64_encode($secret);
        $this->_db
            ->query('insert into ' .
                    $table (url, handle, macFunc, secret, expires) " .
                    "values ('$url', '$handle', '$macFunc', " .
                    "'$secret', $expires)");
        return true;
    }

    public function getAssociation($url,
                                   &$handle,
                                   &$macFunc,
                                   &$secret,
                                   &$expires)
    {
        $table = $this->_association_table;
        $this->_db->query("delete from $table where expires < " . time());
        $res = $this->_db->fetchRow('select handle, macFunc, secret,
            expires ' .
                                    "from $table where url = '$url'");
        if (is_array($res)) {
            $handle  = $res['handle'];
            $macFunc = $res['macFunc'];
            $secret  = base64_decode($res['secret']);
            $expires = $res['expires'];
            return true;
        }
        return false;
    }

    public function getAssociationByHandle($handle,
                                           &$url,
                                           &$macFunc,
                                           &$secret,
                                           &$expires)
    {
        $table = $this->_association_table;
        $this->_db->query("delete from $table where expires < " . time());
        $res = $this->_db
                    ->fetchRow('select url, macFunc, secret, expires ' .
```

```
                                  "from $table where handle = '$handle'");
        if (is_array($res)) {
            $url     = $res['url'];
            $macFunc = $res['macFunc'];
            $secret  = base64_decode($res['secret']);
            $expires = $res['expires'];
            return true;
        }
        return false;
    }

    public function delAssociation($url)
    {
        $table = $this->_association_table;
        $this->_db->query("delete from $table where url = '$url'");
        return true;
    }

    public function addDiscoveryInfo($id,
                                     $realId,
                                     $server,
                                     $version,
                                     $expires)
    {
        $table = $this->_discovery_table;
        $this->_db
            ->query("insert into $table " .
                    "(id, realId, server, version, expires) " .
                    "values " .
                    "('$id', '$realId', '$server', $version, $expires)");
        return true;
    }

    public function getDiscoveryInfo($id,
                                     &$realId,
                                     &$server,
                                     &$version,
                                     &$expires)
    {
        $table = $this->_discovery_table;
        $this->_db->query("delete from $table where expires < " . time());
        $res = $this->_db
                    ->fetchRow('select realId, server, version, expires ' .
                               "from $table where id = '$id'");
        if (is_array($res)) {
            $realId  = $res['realId'];
            $server  = $res['server'];
            $version = $res['version'];
            $expires = $res['expires'];
            return true;
        }
        return false;
    }

    public function delDiscoveryInfo($id)
    {
        $table = $this->_discovery_table;
        $this->_db->query("delete from $table where id = '$id'");
        return true;
    }

    public function isUniqueNonce($nonce)
    {
        $table = $this->_nonce_table;
```

```
        try {
            $ret = $this->_db
                        ->query("insert into $table (nonce) values
                            ('$nonce')");
        } catch (Zend_Db_Statement_Exception $e) {
            return false;
        }
        return true;
    }

    public function purgeNonces($date=null)
    {

    }
}

$db = Zend_Db::factory('Pdo_Sqlite',
    array('dbname'=>'/tmp/openid_consumer.db'));
$storage = new DbStorage($db);
$consumer = new Zend_OpenId_Consumer($storage);
```

This example doesn't list the OpenID authentication code itself, but this code would be the same as that for other examples in this chapter. examples.

Simple Registration Extension

In addition to authentication, the OpenID standard can be used for lightweight profile exchange to make information about a user portable across multiple sites. This feature is not covered by the OpenID authentication specification, but by the OpenID Simple Registration Extension protocol. This protocol allows OpenID-enabled sites to ask for information about end users from OpenID providers. Such information may include:

- *nickname* - any UTF-8 string that the end user uses as a nickname

- *email* - the email address of the user as specified in section 3.4.1 of RFC2822

- *fullname* - a UTF-8 string representation of the user's full name

- *dob* - the user's date of birth in the format 'YYYY-MM-DD'. Any values whose representation uses fewer than the specified number of digits in this format should be zero-padded. In other words, the length of this value must always be 10. If the end user does not want to reveal any particular part of this value (i.e., year, month or day), it must be set to zero. For example, if the user wants to specify that his date of birth falls in 1980, but not specify the month or day, the value returned should be '1980-00-00'.

- *gender* - the user's gender: "M" for male, "F" for female

- *postcode* - a UTF-8 string that conforms to the postal system of the user's country

- *country* - the user's country of residence as specified by ISO3166

- *language* - the user's preferred language as specified by ISO639

- *timezone* - an ASCII string from a TimeZone database. For example, "Europe/Paris" or "America/Los_Angeles".

An OpenID-enabled web site may ask for any combination of these fields. It may also strictly require some information and allow users to provide or hide additional information. The following example instantiates the Zend_OpenId_Extension_Sreg class, requiring a *nickname* and optionally requests an *email* and a *fullname*.

Example 13.8. Sending Requests with a Simple Registration Extension

```
$sreg = new Zend_OpenId_Extension_Sreg(array(
    'nickname'=>true,
    'email'=>false,
    'fullname'=>false), null, 1.1);
$consumer = new Zend_OpenId_Consumer();
if (!$consumer->login($_POST['openid_identifier'],
                      'example-6_3.php',
                      null,
                      $sreg)) {
    die("OpenID login failed.");
}
```

As you can see, the Zend_OpenId_Extension_Sreg constructor accepts an array of OpenID fields. This array has the names of fields as indexes to a flag indicating whether the field is required; *true* means the field is required and *false* means the field is optional. The Zend_OpenId_Consumer::login method accepts an extension or an array of extensions as its fourth argument.

On the third step of authentication, the Zend_OpenId_Extension_Sreg object should be passed to Zend_OpenId_Consumer::verify. Then on successful authentication the Zend_OpenId_Extension_Sreg::getProperties method will return an associative array of requested fields.

Example 13.9. Verifying Responses with a Simple Registration Extension

```
$sreg = new Zend_OpenId_Extension_Sreg(array(
    'nickname'=>true,
    'email'=>false,
    'fullname'=>false), null, 1.1);
$consumer = new Zend_OpenId_Consumer();
if ($consumer->verify($_GET, $id, $sreg)) {
    echo "VALID " . htmlspecialchars($id) ."<br>\n";
    $data = $sreg->getProperties();
    if (isset($data['nickname'])) {
        echo "nickname: " . htmlspecialchars($data['nickname']) . "<br>\n";
    }
    if (isset($data['email'])) {
        echo "email: " . htmlspecialchars($data['email']) . "<br>\n";
    }
    if (isset($data['fullname'])) {
        echo "fullname: " . htmlspecialchars($data['fullname']) . "<br>\n";
    }
} else {
    echo "INVALID " . htmlspecialchars($id);
}
```

If the Zend_OpenId_Extension_Sreg object was created without any arguments, the user code should check for the existence of the required data itself. However, if the object is created with the same list of required fields as on the second step, it will automatically check for the existence of required data. In this case, Zend_OpenId_Consumer::verify will return *false* if any of the required fields are missing.

Zend_OpenId_Extension_Sreg uses version 1.0 by default, because the specification for version 1.1 is not yet finalized. However, some libraries don't fully support version 1.0. For example, www.myopenid.com requires an SREG namespace in requests which is only available in 1.1. To work with such a server, you must explicitly set the version to 1.1 in the Zend_OpenId_Extension_Sreg constructor.

The second argument of the Zend_OpenId_Extension_Sreg constructor is a policy URL, that should be provided to the user by the identity provider.

Integration with Zend_Auth

Zend Framework provides a special class to support user authentication: Zend_Auth. This class can be used together with Zend_OpenId_Consumer. The following example shows how OpenIdAdapter implements the Zend_Auth_Adapter_Interface with the authenticate method. This performs an authentication query and verification.

The big difference between this adapter and existing ones, is that it works on two HTTP requests and includes a dispatch code to perform the second or third step of OpenID authentication.

Example 13.10. Zend_Auth Adapter for OpenID

```php
<?php
class OpenIdAdapter implements Zend_Auth_Adapter_Interface {
    private $_id = null;

    public function __construct($id = null) {
        $this->_id = $id;
    }

    public function authenticate() {
        $id = $this->_id;
        if (!empty($id)) {
            $consumer = new Zend_OpenId_Consumer();
            if (!$consumer->login($id)) {
                $ret = false;
                $msg = "Authentication failed.";
            }
        } else {
            $consumer = new Zend_OpenId_Consumer();
            if ($consumer->verify($_GET, $id)) {
                $ret = true;
                $msg = "Authentication successful";
            } else {
                $ret = false;
                $msg = "Authentication failed";
            }
        }
        return new Zend_Auth_Result($ret, $id, array($msg));
    }
}

$status = "";
$auth = Zend_Auth::getInstance();
if ((isset($_POST['openid_action']) &&
     $_POST['openid_action'] == "login" &&
     !empty($_POST['openid_identifier'])) ||
    isset($_GET['openid_mode'])) {
    $adapter = new OpenIdAdapter(@$_POST['openid_identifier']);
    $result = $auth->authenticate($adapter);
    if ($result->isValid()) {
```

```
            Zend_OpenId::redirect(Zend_OpenId::selfURL());
        } else {
            $auth->clearIdentity();
            foreach ($result->getMessages() as $message) {
                $status .= "$message<br>\n";
            }
        }
    } else if ($auth->hasIdentity()) {
        if (isset($_POST['openid_action']) &&
            $_POST['openid_action'] == "logout") {
            $auth->clearIdentity();
        } else {
            $status = "You are logged in as " . $auth->getIdentity() . "<br>\n";
        }
    }
}
?>
<html><body>
<?php echo htmlspecialchars($status);?>
<form method="post"><fieldset>
<legend>OpenID Login</legend>
<input type="text" name="openid_identifier" value="">
<input type="submit" name="openid_action" value="login">
<input type="submit" name="openid_action" value="logout">
</fieldset></form></body></html>
```

With `Zend_Auth` the end-user's identity is saved in the session's data. It may be checked with `Zend_Auth::hasIdentity` and `Zend_Auth::getIdentity`.

Integration with Zend_Controller

Finally a couple of words about integration into Model-View-Controller applications: such Zend Framework applications are implemented using the `Zend_Controller` class and they use objects of the `Zend_Controller_Response_Http` class to prepare HTTP responses and send them back to the user's web browser.

`Zend_OpenId_Consumer` doesn't provide any GUI capabilities but it performs HTTP redirections on success of `Zend_OpenId_Consumer::login` and `Zend_OpenId_Consumer::check`. These redirections may work incorrectly or not at all if some data was already sent to the web browser. To properly perform HTTP redirection in MVC code the real `Zend_Controller_Response_Http` should be sent to `Zend_OpenId_Consumer::login` or `Zend_OpenId_Consumer::check` as the last argument.

Zend_OpenId_Provider

`Zend_OpenId_Provider` can be used to implement OpenID servers. This chapter provides examples that demonstrate how to build a very basic server. However, for implementation of a production OpenID server (such as www.myopenid.com [http://www.myopenid.com]) you may have to deal with more complex issues.

Quick Start

The following example includes code for creating a user account using `Zend_OpenId_Provider::register`. The link element with `rel="openid.server"` points to our own server script. If you submit this identity to an OpenID-enabled site, it will perform authentication on this server.

The code before the <html> tag is just a trick that automatically creates a user account. You won't need such code when using real identities.

Example 13.11. The Identity

```php
<?php
// Set up test identity
define("TEST_SERVER", Zend_OpenId::absoluteURL("example-8.php"));
define("TEST_ID", Zend_OpenId::selfURL());
define("TEST_PASSWORD", "123");
$server = new Zend_OpenId_Provider();
if (!$server->hasUser(TEST_ID)) {
    $server->register(TEST_ID, TEST_PASSWORD);
}
?>
<html><head>
<link rel="openid.server" href="<?php echo TEST_SERVER;?>" />
</head><body>
<?php echo TEST_ID;?>
</body></html>
```

The following identity server script handles two kinds of requests from OpenID-enabled sites (for association and authentication). Both of them are handled by the same method: `Zend_OpenId_Provider::handle`. The two arguments to the `Zend_OpenId_Provider` constructor are URLs of login and trust pages, which ask for input from the end user.

On success, the method `Zend_OpenId_Provider::handle` returns a string that should be passed back to the OpenID-enabled site. On failure, it returns `false`. This example will return an HTTP 403 response if `Zend_OpenId_Provider::handle` fails. You will get this response if you open this script with a web browser, because it sends a non-OpenID conforming request.

Example 13.12. Simple Identity Provider

```php
$server = new Zend_OpenId_Provider("example-8-login.php",
                                   "example-8-trust.php");
$ret = $server->handle();
if (is_string($ret)) {
    echo $ret;
} else if ($ret !== true) {
    header('HTTP/1.0 403 Forbidden');
    echo 'Forbidden';
}
```

Note

It is a good idea to use a secure connection (HTTPS) for these scripts- especially for the following interactive scripts- to prevent password disclosure.

The following script implements a login screen for an identity server using `Zend_OpenId_Provider` and redirects to this page when a required user has not yet logged in. On this page, a user will enter his password to login.

You should use the password "123" that was used in the identity script above.

On submit, the script calls `Zend_OpenId_Provider::login` with the accepted user's identity and password, then redirects back to the main identity provider's script. On success, the `Zend_OpenId_Provider::login` establishes a session between the user and the identity provider and stores the information about the user, who is now logged in. All following requests from the same user won't require a login procedure- even if they come from another OpenID enabled web site.

Note

Note that this session is between end-user and identity provider only. OpenID enabled sites know nothing about it.

Example 13.13. Simple Login Screen

```php
<?php
$server = new Zend_OpenId_Provider();

if ($_SERVER['REQUEST_METHOD'] == 'POST' &&
    isset($_POST['openid_action']) &&
    $_POST['openid_action'] === 'login' &&
    isset($_POST['openid_identifier']) &&
    isset($_POST['openid_password'])) {
    $server->login($_POST['openid_identifier'],
                   $_POST['openid_password']);
    Zend_OpenId::redirect("example-8.php", $_GET);
}
?>
<html>
<body>
<form method="post">
<fieldset>
<legend>OpenID Login</legend>
<table border=0>
<tr>
<td>Name:</td>
<td>
<input type="text"
       name="openid_identifier"
       value="<?php echo htmlspecialchars($_GET['openid_identity']);?>">
</td>
</tr>
<tr>
<td>Password:</td>
<td>
<input type="text"
       name="openid_password"
       value="">
</td>
</tr>
<tr>
<td> </td>
<td>
<input type="submit"
       name="openid_action"
       value="login">
</td>
</tr>
</table>
</fieldset>
</form>
</body>
</html>
```

The fact that the user is now logged in doesn't mean that the authentication must necessarily succeed. The user may decide not to trust particular OpenID enabled sites. The following trust screen allows the end user to make that choice. This choice may either be made only for current requests or forever. In the second case, information about trusted/untrusted sites is stored in an internal database, and all following authentication requests from this site will be handled automatically without user interaction.

Example 13.14. Simple Trust Screen

```php
<?php
$server = new Zend_OpenId_Provider();

if ($_SERVER['REQUEST_METHOD'] == 'POST' &&
    isset($_POST['openid_action']) &&
    $_POST['openid_action'] === 'trust') {

    if (isset($_POST['allow'])) {
        if (isset($_POST['forever'])) {
            $server->allowSite($server->getSiteRoot($_GET));
        }
        $server->respondToConsumer($_GET);
    } else if (isset($_POST['deny'])) {
        if (isset($_POST['forever'])) {
            $server->denySite($server->getSiteRoot($_GET));
        }
        Zend_OpenId::redirect($_GET['openid_return_to'],
                              array('openid.mode'=>'cancel'));
    }
}
?>
<html>
<body>
<p>A site identifying as
<a href="<?php echo htmlspecialchars($server->getSiteRoot($_GET));?>">
<?php echo htmlspecialchars($server->getSiteRoot($_GET));?>
</a>
has asked us for confirmation that
<a href="<?php echo htmlspecialchars($server->getLoggedInUser());?>">
<?php echo htmlspecialchars($server->getLoggedInUser());?>
</a>
is your identity URL.
</p>
<form method="post">
<input type="checkbox" name="forever">
<label for="forever">forever</label><br>
<input type="hidden" name="openid_action" value="trust">
<input type="submit" name="allow" value="Allow">
<input type="submit" name="deny" value="Deny">
</form>
</body>
</html>
```

Production OpenID servers usually support the Simple Registration Extension that allows consumers to request some information about the user from the provider. In this case, the trust page can be extended to allow entering requested fields or selecting a specific user profile.

Combined Provide Scripts

It is possible to combine all provider functionality in one script. In this case login and trust URLs are omitted, and `Zend_OpenId_Provider` assumes that they point to the same page with the additional "openid.action" GET argument.

Note

The following example is not complete. It doesn't provide GUI code for the user, instead performing an automatic login and trust relationship instead. This is done just to simplify the example; a production server should include some code from previous examples.

Example 13.15. Everything Together

```php
$server = new Zend_OpenId_Provider();

define("TEST_ID", Zend_OpenId::absoluteURL("example-9-id.php"));
define("TEST_PASSWORD", "123");

if ($_SERVER['REQUEST_METHOD'] == 'GET' &&
    isset($_GET['openid_action']) &&
    $_GET['openid_action'] === 'login') {
    $server->login(TEST_ID, TEST_PASSWORD);
    unset($_GET['openid_action']);
    Zend_OpenId::redirect(Zend_OpenId::selfUrl(), $_GET);
} else if ($_SERVER['REQUEST_METHOD'] == 'GET' &&
    isset($_GET['openid_action']) &&
    $_GET['openid_action'] === 'trust') {
    unset($_GET['openid_action']);
    $server->respondToConsumer($_GET);
} else {
    $ret = $server->handle();
    if (is_string($ret)) {
        echo $ret;
    } else if ($ret !== true) {
        header('HTTP/1.0 403 Forbidden');
        echo 'Forbidden';
    }
}
```

If you compare this example with previous examples split in to separate pages, you will see only the one difference besides the dispatch code: unset($_GET['openid_action']). This call to unset is necessary to route the next request to main handler.

Simple Registration Extension

Again, the code before the <html> tag is just a trick to demonstrate functionality. It creates a new user account and associates it with a profile (nickname and password). Such tricks aren't needed in deployed providers where end users register on OpenID servers and fill in their profiles. Implementing this GUI is out of scope for this manual.

Example 13.16. Identity with Profile

```php
<?php
define("TEST_SERVER", Zend_OpenId::absoluteURL("example-10.php"));
define("TEST_ID", Zend_OpenId::selfURL());
define("TEST_PASSWORD", "123");
$server = new Zend_OpenId_Provider();
if (!$server->hasUser(TEST_ID)) {
    $server->register(TEST_ID, TEST_PASSWORD);
```

```
    $server->login(TEST_ID, TEST_PASSWORD);
    $sreg = new Zend_OpenId_Extension_Sreg(array(
        'nickname' =>'test',
        'email' => 'test@test.com'
    ));
    $root = Zend_OpenId::absoluteURL(".");
    Zend_OpenId::normalizeUrl($root);
    $server->allowSite($root, $sreg);
    $server->logout();
}
?>
<html>
<head>
<link rel="openid.server" href="<?php echo TEST_SERVER;?>" />
</head>
<body>
<?php echo TEST_ID;?>
</body>
</html>
```

You should now pass this identity to the OpenID-enabled web site (use the Simple Registration Extension example from the previous section), and it should use the following OpenID server script.

This script is a variation of the script in the "Everything Together" example. It uses the same automatic login mechanism, but doesn't contain any code for a trust page. The user already trusts the example scripts forever. This trust was established by calling the Zend_OpenId_Provider::allowSite() method in the identity script. The same method associates the profile with the trusted URL. This profile will be returned automatically for a request from the trusted URL.

To make Simple Registration Extension work, you must simply pass an instance of Zend_OpenId_Extension_Sreg as the second argument to the Zend_OpenId_Provider::handle() method.

Example 13.17. Provider with SREG

```
$server = new Zend_OpenId_Provider();
$sreg = new Zend_OpenId_Extension_Sreg();

define("TEST_ID", Zend_OpenId::absoluteURL("example-10-id.php"));
define("TEST_PASSWORD", "123");

if ($_SERVER['REQUEST_METHOD'] == 'GET' &&
    isset($_GET['openid_action']) &&
    $_GET['openid_action'] === 'login') {
    $server->login(TEST_ID, TEST_PASSWORD);
    unset($_GET['openid_action']);
    Zend_OpenId::redirect(Zend_OpenId::selfUrl(), $_GET);
} else if ($_SERVER['REQUEST_METHOD'] == 'GET' &&
    isset($_GET['openid_action']) &&
    $_GET['openid_action'] === 'trust') {
    echo "UNTRUSTED DATA" ;
} else {
    $ret = $server->handle(null, $sreg);
    if (is_string($ret)) {
        echo $ret;
    } else if ($ret !== true) {
        header('HTTP/1.0 403 Forbidden');
        echo 'Forbidden';
    }
}
```

Anything Else?

Building OpenID providers is much less common than building OpenID-enabled sites, so this manual doesn't cover all `Zend_OpenId_Provider` features exhaustively, as was done for `Zend_OpenId_Consumer`.

To summamize, `Zend_OpenId_Provider` contains:

- A set of methods to build an end-user GUI that allows users to register and manage their trusted sites and profiles

- An abstract storage layer to store information about users, their sites and their profiles. It also stores associations between the provider and OpenID-enabled sites. This layer is very similar to that of the `Zend_OpenId_Consumer` class. It also uses file storage by default, but may used with another backend.

- An abstract user-association layer that may associate a user's web browser with a logged-in identity

The `Zend_OpenId_Provider` class doesn't attempt to cover all possible features that can be implemented by OpenID servers, e.g. digital certificates, but it can be extended easily using `Zend_OpenId_Extensions` or by standard object-oriented extension.

Chapter 14. Zend_Paginator

Introduction

`Zend_Paginator` is a flexible component for paginating collections of data and presenting that data to users.

The primary design goals of `Zend_Paginator` are as follows:

- Paginate arbitrary data, not just relational databases

- Fetch only the results that need to be displayed

- Do not force users to adhere to only one way of displaying data or rendering pagination controls

- Loosely couple `Zend_Paginator` to other Zend Framework components so that users who wish to use it independently of `Zend_View`, `Zend_Db`, etc. can do so

Usage

Paginating data collections

In order to paginate items into pages, `Zend_Paginator` must have a generic way of accessing that data. For that reason, all data access takes place through data source adapters. Several adapters ship with Zend Framework by default:

Table 14.1. Adapters for Zend_Paginator

Adapter	Description
Array	Use a PHP array
DbSelect	Use a `Zend_Db_Select` instance, which will return an array
DbTableSelect	Use a `Zend_Db_Table_Select` instance, which will return an instance of `Zend_Db_Table_Rowset_Abstract`. This provides additional information about the result set, such as column names.
Iterator	Use an `Iterator` [http://www.php.net/~helly/php/ext/spl/interfaceIterator.html] instance
Null	Do not use `Zend_Paginator` to manage data pagination. You can still take advantage of the pagination control feature.

Note

Instead of selecting every matching row of a given query, the DbSelect and DbTableSelect adapters retrieve only the smallest amount of data necessary for displaying the current page.

Because of this, a second query is dynamically generated to determine the total number of matching rows. However, it is possible to directly supply a count or count query yourself. See the `setRowCount()` method in the DbSelect adapter for more information.

To create an instance of Zend_Paginator, you must supply an adapter to the constructor:

```
$paginator = new Zend_Paginator(new Zend_Paginator_Adapter_Array($array));
```

For convenience, you may take advantage of the static factory() method for the adapters packaged with Zend Framework:

```
$paginator = Zend_Paginator::factory($array);
```

Note

In the case of the Null adapter, in lieu of a data collection you must supply an item count to its constructor.

Although the instance is technically usable in this state, in your controller action you'll need to tell the paginator what page number the user requested. This allows him to advance through the paginated data.

```
$paginator->setCurrentPageNumber($page);
```

The simplest way to keep track of this value is through a URL. Although we recommend using a Zend_Controller_Router_Interface-compatible router to handle this, it is not a requirement.

The following is an example route you might use in an INI configuration file:

```
routes.example.route = articles/:articleName/:page
routes.example.defaults.controller = articles
routes.example.defaults.action = view
routes.example.defaults.page = 1
routes.example.reqs.articleName = \w+
routes.example.reqs.page = \d+
```

With the above route (and using Zend Framework MVC components), you might set the current page number like this:

```
$paginator->setCurrentPageNumber($this->_getParam('page'));
```

There are other options available; see Configuration for more on them.

Finally, you'll need to assign the paginator instance to your view. If you're using Zend_View with the ViewRenderer action helper, the following will work:

```
$this->view->paginator = $paginator;
```

Rendering pages with view scripts

The view script is used to render the page items (if you're using Zend_Paginator to do so) and display the pagination control.

Because Zend_Paginator implements the SPL interface IteratorAggregate [http://www.php.net/~helly/php/ext/spl/interfaceIteratorAggregate.html], looping over your items and displaying them is simple.

```
<html>
<body>
<h1>Example</h1>
<?php if (count($this->paginator)): ?>
<ul>
<?php foreach ($this->paginator as $item): ?>
  <li><?php echo $item; ?></li>
<?php endforeach; ?>
</ul>
<?php endif; ?>

<?php echo $this->paginationControl($this->paginator,
                    'Sliding',
                    'my_pagination_control.phtml'); ?>

</body>
</html>
```

Notice the view helper call near the end. PaginationControl accepts up to four parameters: the paginator instance, a scrolling style, a view partial, and an array of additional parameters.

The second and third parameters are very important. Whereas the view partial is used to determine how the pagination control should *look*, the scrolling style is used to control how it should *behave*. Say the view partial is in the style of a search pagination control, like the one below:

Results Page:

Prev ◀ 2 3 4 5 6 7 8 9 10 11 ▶ **Next**

What happens when the user clicks the "next" link a few times? Well, any number of things could happen. The current page number could stay in the middle as you click through (as it does on Yahoo!), or it could advance to the end of the page range and then appear again on the left when the user clicks "next" one more time. The page numbers might even expand and contract as the user advances (or "scrolls") through them (as they do on Google).

There are four scrolling styles packaged with Zend Framework:

Table 14.2. Scrolling styles for Zend_Paginator

Scrolling style	Description
All	Returns every page. This is useful for dropdown menu pagination controls with relatively few pages. In these cases, you want all pages available to the user at once.
Elastic	A Google-like scrolling style that expands and contracts as a user scrolls through the pages.
Jumping	As users scroll through, the page number advances to the end of a given range, then starts again at the beginning of the new range.
Sliding	A Yahoo!-like scrolling style that positions the current page number in the center of the page range, or as close as possible. This is the default style.

The fourth and final parameter is reserved for an optional associative array of additional variables that you want available in your view partial (available via $this). For instance, these values could include extra URL parameters for pagination links.

By setting the default view partial, default scrolling style, and view instance, you can eliminate the calls to PaginationControl completely:

```
Zend_Paginator::setDefaultScrollingStyle('Sliding');
Zend_View_Helper_PaginationControl::setDefaultViewPartial(
    'my_pagination_control.phtml'
);
$paginator->setView($view);
```

When all of these values are set, you can render the pagination control inside your view script with a simple echo statement:

```
<?php echo $this->paginator; ?>
```

Note

Of course, it's possible to use Zend_Paginator with other template engines. For example, with Smarty you might do the following:

```
$smarty->assign('pages', $paginator->getPages());
```

You could then access paginator values from a template like so:

```
{$pages.pageCount}
```

Example pagination controls

The following example pagination controls will hopefully help you get started:

Search pagination

```
<!--
See http://developer.yahoo.com/ypatterns/pattern.php?pattern=searchpagination
-->

<?php if ($this->pageCount): ?>
<div class="paginationControl">
<!-- Previous page link -->
<?php if (isset($this->previous)): ?>
  <a href="<?php echo $this->url(array('page' => $this->previous)); ?>">
    &lt; Previous
  </a> |
<?php else: ?>
  <span class="disabled">&lt; Previous</span> |
<?php endif; ?>

<!-- Numbered page links -->
<?php foreach ($this->pagesInRange as $page): ?>
  <?php if ($page != $this->current): ?>
    <a href="<?php echo $this->url(array('page' => $page)); ?>">
        <?php echo $page; ?>
    </a> |
  <?php else: ?>
    <?php echo $page; ?> |
```

```php
  <?php endif; ?>
<?php endforeach; ?>

<!-- Next page link -->
<?php if (isset($this->next)): ?>
  <a href="<?php echo $this->url(array('page' => $this->next)); ?>">
    Next &gt;
  </a>
<?php else: ?>
  <span class="disabled">Next &gt;</span>
<?php endif; ?>
</div>
<?php endif; ?>
```

Item pagination

```php
<!--
See http://developer.yahoo.com/ypatterns/pattern.php?pattern=itempagination
-->

<?php if ($this->pageCount): ?>
<div class="paginationControl">
<?php echo $this->firstItemNumber; ?> - <?php echo $this->lastItemNumber; ?>
of <?php echo $this->totalItemCount; ?>

<!-- First page link -->
<?php if (isset($this->previous)): ?>
  <a href="<?php echo $this->url(array('page' => $this->first)); ?>">
    First
  </a> |
<?php else: ?>
  <span class="disabled">First</span> |
<?php endif; ?>

<!-- Previous page link -->
<?php if (isset($this->previous)): ?>
  <a href="<?php echo $this->url(array('page' => $this->previous)); ?>">
    &lt; Previous
  </a> |
<?php else: ?>
  <span class="disabled">&lt; Previous</span> |
<?php endif; ?>

<!-- Next page link -->
<?php if (isset($this->next)): ?>
  <a href="<?php echo $this->url(array('page' => $this->next)); ?>">
    Next &gt;
  </a> |
<?php else: ?>
  <span class="disabled">Next &gt;</span> |
<?php endif; ?>

<!-- Last page link -->
<?php if (isset($this->next)): ?>
  <a href="<?php echo $this->url(array('page' => $this->last)); ?>">
    Last
  </a>
<?php else: ?>
  <span class="disabled">Last</span>
<?php endif; ?>

</div>
<?php endif; ?>
```

Dropdown pagination

```php
<?php if ($this->pageCount): ?>
<select id="paginationControl" size="1">
<?php foreach ($this->pagesInRange as $page): ?>
  <?php $selected = ($page == $this->current) ? ' selected="selected"' :
        ''; ?>
  <option value="<?php
        echo $this->url(array('page' => $page));?>"<?php echo $selected ?>>
    <?php echo $page; ?>
  </option>
<?php endforeach; ?>
</select>
<?php endif; ?>

<script type="text/javascript"
    src="http://ajax.googleapis.com/ajax/libs/prototype/1.6.0.2/prototype.j
</script>
<script type="text/javascript">
$('paginationControl').observe('change', function() {
    window.location = this.options[this.selectedIndex].value;
})
</script>
```

Listing of properties

The following options are available to pagination control view partials:

Table 14.3. Properties available to view partials

Property	Type	Description
first	integer	First page number (i.e., 1)
firstItemNumber	integer	Absolute number of the first item on this page
firstPageInRange	integer	First page in the range returned by the scrolling style
current	integer	Current page number
currentItemCount	integer	Number of items on this page
itemCountPerPage	integer	Maximum number of items available to each page
last	integer	Last page number
lastItemNumber	integer	Absolute number of the last item on this page
lastPageInRange	integer	Last page in the range returned by the scrolling style
next	integer	Next page number
pageCount	integer	Number of pages
pagesInRange	array	Array of pages returned by the scrolling style
previous	integer	Previous page number
totalItemCount	integer	Total number of items

Configuration

Zend_Paginator has several configuration methods that can be called:

Table 14.4. Configuration methods for Zend_Paginator

Method	Description
setCurrentPageNumber	Sets the current page number (default 1).
setItemCountPerPage	Sets the maximum number of items to display on a page (default 10).
setPageRange	Sets the number of items to display in the pagination control (default 10). Note: Most of the time this number will be adhered to exactly, but scrolling styles do have the option of only using it as a guideline or starting value (e.g., Elastic).
setView	Sets the view instance, for rendering convenience.

Advanced usage

Custom data source adapters

At some point you may run across a data type that is not covered by the packaged adapters. In this case, you will need to write your own.

To do so, you must implement Zend_Paginator_Adapter_Interface. There are two methods required to do this:

- count()

- getItems($offset, $itemCountPerPage)

Additionally, you'll want to implement a constructor that takes your data source as a parameter and stores it as a protected or private property. How you wish to go about doing this specifically is up to you.

If you've ever used the SPL interface Countable [http://www.php.net/~helly/php/ext/spl/interfaceCountable.html], you're familiar with count(). As used with Zend_Paginator, this is the total number of items in the data collection. Additionally, the Zend_Paginator instance provides a method countAllItems() that proxies to the adapter count() method.

The getItems() method is only slightly more complicated. For this, your adapter is supplied with an offset and the number of items to display per page. You must return the appropriate slice of data. For an array, that would be:

```
return array_slice($this->_array, $offset, $itemCountPerPage);
```

Take a look at the packaged adapters (all of which implement the Zend_Paginator_Adapter_Interface) for ideas of how you might go about implementing your own.

Custom scrolling styles

Creating your own scrolling style requires that you implement Zend_Paginator_ScrollingStyle_Interface, which defines a single method, getPages(). Specifically,

```
public function getPages(Zend_Paginator $paginator, $pageRange = null);
```

This method should calculate a lower and upper bound for page numbers within the range of so-called "local" pages (that is, pages that are nearby the current page).

Unless it extends another scrolling style (see Zend_Paginator_ScrollingStyle_Elastic for an example), your custom scrolling style will inevitably end with something similar to the following line of code:

```
return $paginator->getPagesInRange($lowerBound, $upperBound);
```

There's nothing special about this call; it's merely a convenience method to check the validity of the lower and upper bound and return an array of the range to the paginator.

When you're ready to use your new scrolling style, you'll need to tell Zend_Paginator what directory to look in. To do that, do the following:

```
$prefix = 'My_Paginator_ScrollingStyle';
$path   = 'My/Paginator/ScrollingStyle/';
Zend_Paginator::addScrollingStylePrefixPath($prefix, $path);
```

Caching features

Zend_Paginator can be told to cache the data it has already passed on, preventing the adapter from fetching them each time they are used. To tell paginator to automatically cache the adapter's data, just pass to its setCache() method a Zend_Cache_Core instance.

```
$paginator = Zend_Paginator::factory($someData);
$fO = array('lifetime' => 3600, 'automatic_serialization' => true);
$bO = array('cache_dir'=>'/tmp');
$cache = Zend_cache::factory('Core', 'File', $fO, $bO);
Zend_Paginator::setCache($cache);
```

As far as Zend_Paginator has got a Zend_Cache_Core instance, data will be cached. Sometimes you would like not to cache data even if you already passed a cache instance. You should then use setCacheEnable() for that.

```
$paginator = Zend_Paginator::factory($someData);
// $cache is a Zend_Cache_Core instance
Zend_Paginator::setCache($cache);
// ... later on the script
$paginator->setCacheEnable(false);
// cache is now disabled
```

When a cache is set, data are automatically stored in it and pulled out from it. It then can be useful to empty the cache manually. You can get this done by calling clearPageItemCache($pageNumber). If you don't pass any parameter, the whole cache will be empty. You can optionally pass a parameter representing the page number to empty in the cache:

```
$paginator = Zend_Paginator::factory($someData);
Zend_Paginator::setCache($cache);
$items = $paginator->getCurrentItems();
// page 1 is now in cache
$page3Items = $paginator->getItemsByPage(3);
// page 3 is now in cache

// clear the cache of the results for page 3
$paginator->clearPageItemCache(3);

// clear all the cache data
$paginator->clearPageItemCache();
```

Changing the item count per page will empty the whole cache as it would have become invalid:

```
$paginator = Zend_Paginator::factory($someData);
Zend_Paginator::setCache($cache);
// fetch some items
$items = $paginator->getCurrentItems();

// all the cache data will be flushed:
$paginator->setItemCountPerPage(2);
```

It is also possible to see the data in cache and ask for them directly. getPageItemCache() can be used for that:

```
$paginator = Zend_Paginator::factory($someData);
$paginator->setItemCountPerPage(3);
Zend_Paginator::setCache($cache);

// fetch some items
$items = $paginator->getCurrentItems();
$otherItems = $paginator->getItemsPerPage(4);

// see the cached items as a two-dimension array:
var_dump($paginator->getPageItemCache());
```

Chapter 15. Zend_Pdf

Introduction

The `Zend_Pdf` component is a PDF (Portable Document Format) manipulation engine. It can load, create, modify and save documents. Thus it can help any PHP application dynamically create PDF documents by modifying existing documents or generating new ones from scratch. `Zend_Pdf` offers the following features:

- Create a new document or load existing one. [*]

- Retrieve a specified revision of the document.

- Manipulate pages within a document. Change page order, add new pages, remove pages from a document.

- Different drawing primitives (lines, rectangles, polygons, circles, ellipses and sectors).

- Text drawing using any of the 14 standard (built-in) fonts or your own custom TrueType fonts.

- Rotations.

- Image drawing. [§]

- Incremental PDF file update.

Creating and Loading PDF Documents

The `Zend_Pdf` class represents PDF documents and provides document-level operations.

To create a new document, a new `Zend_Pdf` object should first be created.

`Zend_Pdf` class also provides two static methods to load an existing PDF document. These are the `Zend_Pdf::load()` and `Zend_Pdf::parse()` methods. Both of them return `Zend_Pdf` objects as a result or throw an exception if an error occurs.

Example 15.1. Create new or load existing PDF document.

```
...
// Create a new PDF document
$pdf1 = new Zend_Pdf();

// Load a PDF document from a file
$pdf2 = Zend_Pdf::load($fileName);

// Load a PDF document from a string
$pdf3 = Zend_Pdf::parse($pdfString);
...
```

The PDF file format supports incremental document update. Thus each time a document is updated, then a new revision of the document is created. `Zend_Pdf` component supports the retrieval of a specified revision.

---

[*] Loading PDF V1.4 (Acrobat 5) documents is now supported.
[§] JPG, PNG [Up to 8bit per channel+Alpha] and TIFF images are supported.

A revision can be specified as a second parameter to the Zend_Pdf::load() and Zend_Pdf::parse() methods or requested by calling the Zend_Pdf::rollback() method. [†] call.

Example 15.2. Requesting Specific Revisions of a PDF Document

```
. . .
// Load the previous revision of the PDF document
$pdf1 = Zend_Pdf::load($fileName, 1);

// Load the previous revision of the PDF document
$pdf2 = Zend_Pdf::parse($pdfString, 1);

// Load the first revision of the PDF document
$pdf3 = Zend_Pdf::load($fileName);
$revisions = $pdf3->revisions();
$pdf3->rollback($revisions - 1);
. . .
```

Save Changes to PDF Documents

There are two methods that save changes to PDF documents: the Zend_Pdf::save() and Zend_Pdf::render() methods.

Zend_Pdf::save($filename, $updateOnly = false) saves the PDF document to a file. If $updateOnly is true, then only the new PDF file segment is appended to a file. Otherwise, the file is overwritten.

Zend_Pdf::render($newSegmentOnly = false) returns the PDF document as a string. If $newSegmentOnly is true, then only the new PDF file segment is returned.

Example 15.3. Saving PDF Documents

```
. . .
// Load the PDF document
$pdf = Zend_Pdf::load($fileName);
. . .
// Update the PDF document
$pdf->save($fileName, true);
// Save document as a new file
$pdf->save($newFileName);

// Return the PDF document as a string
$pdfString = $pdf->render();

. . .
```

[†] Zend_Pdf::rollback() method must be invoked before any changes are applied to the document, otherwise the behavior is not defined.

Working with Pages

Page Creation

The pages in a PDF document are represented as `Zend_Pdf_Page` instances in `Zend_Pdf`.

PDF pages either are loaded from an existing PDF or created using the `Zend_Pdf` API.

New pages can be created by instantiating new `Zend_Pdf_Page` objects directly or by calling the `Zend_Pdf::newPage()` method, which returns a `Zend_Pdf_Page` object. `Zend_Pdf::newPage()` creates a page that is already attached to a document. Unattached pages can't be used with multiple PDF documents, but they are somewhat more performant. [‡]

The `Zend_Pdf::newPage()` method and the `Zend_Pdf_Page` constructor take the same parameters specifying page size. They can take either the size of page ($x, $y) in points (1/72 inch) or a predefined constant representing a page type:

* Zend_Pdf_Page::SIZE_A4

* Zend_Pdf_Page::SIZE_A4_LANDSCAPE

* Zend_Pdf_Page::SIZE_LETTER

* Zend_Pdf_Page::SIZE_LETTER_LANDSCAPE

Document pages are stored in the `$pages` public attribute of the `Zend_Pdf` class. The attribute holds an array of `Zend_Pdf_Page` objects and completely defines the instances and order of pages. This array can be manipulated like any other PHP array:

Example 15.4. PDF document pages management.

```
...
// Reverse page order
$pdf->pages = array_reverse($pdf->pages);
...
// Add new page
$pdf->pages[] = new Zend_Pdf_Page(Zend_Pdf_Page::SIZE_A4);
// Add new page
$pdf->pages[] = $pdf->newPage(Zend_Pdf_Page::SIZE_A4);

// Remove specified page.
unset($pdf->pages[$id]);

...
```

Page cloning.

Existing PDF page can be cloned by creating new `Zend_Pdf_Page` object with existing page as a parameter:

Example 15.5. Cloning existing page.

[‡] It's a limitation of current ZF version. It will be eliminated in future versions. But unattached pages will always give better (more optimal) result for sharing pages between documents.

```
. . .
// Store template page in a separate variable
$template = $pdf->pages[$templatePageIndex];
. . .
// Add new page
$page1 = new Zend_Pdf_Page($template);
$pdf->pages[] = $page1;
. . .

// Add another page
$page2 = new Zend_Pdf_Page($template);
$pdf->pages[] = $page2;
. . .

// Remove source template page from the documents.
unset($pdf->pages[$templatePageIndex]);

. . .
```

It's useful if you need several pages to be created using one template.

Caution

Important! Cloned page shares some PDF resources with a template page, so it can be used only within the same document as a template page. Modified document can be saved as new one.

Drawing

Geometry

PDF uses the same geometry as PostScript. It starts from bottom-left corner of page and by default is measured in points (1/72 of an inch).

Page size can be retrieved from a page object:

```
$width  = $pdfPage->getWidth();
$height = $pdfPage->getHeight();
```

Colors

PDF has a powerful capabilities for colors representation. Zend_Pdf module supports Gray Scale, RGB and CMYK color spaces. Any of them can be used in any place, where Zend_Pdf_Color object is required. Zend_Pdf_Color_GrayScale, Zend_Pdf_Color_Rgb and Zend_Pdf_Color_Cmyk classes provide this functionality:

```
// $grayLevel (float number). 0.0 (black) - 1.0 (white)
$color1 = new Zend_Pdf_Color_GrayScale($grayLevel);

// $r, $g, $b (float numbers). 0.0 (min intensity) - 1.0 (max intensity)
$color2 = new Zend_Pdf_Color_Rgb($r, $g, $b);

// $c, $m, $y, $k (float numbers). 0.0 (min intensity) - 1.0 (max intensity)
$color3 = new Zend_Pdf_Color_Cmyk($c, $m, $y, $k);
```

HTML style colors are also provided with `Zend_Pdf_Color_Html` class:

```
$color1 = new Zend_Pdf_Color_Html('#3366FF');
$color2 = new Zend_Pdf_Color_Html('silver');
$color3 = new Zend_Pdf_Color_Html('forestgreen');
```

Shape Drawing

All drawing operations can be done in a context of PDF page.

`Zend_Pdf_Page` class provides a set of drawing primitives:

```
/**
 * Draw a line from x1,y1 to x2,y2.
 *
 * @param float $x1
 * @param float $y1
 * @param float $x2
 * @param float $y2
 * @return Zend_Pdf_Page
 */
public function drawLine($x1, $y1, $x2, $y2);



/**
 * Draw a rectangle.
 *
 * Fill types:
 * Zend_Pdf_Page::SHAPE_DRAW_FILL_AND_STROKE - fill rectangle
 *                                             and stroke (default)
 * Zend_Pdf_Page::SHAPE_DRAW_STROKE         - stroke rectangle
 * Zend_Pdf_Page::SHAPE_DRAW_FILL           - fill rectangle
 *
 * @param float $x1
 * @param float $y1
 * @param float $x2
 * @param float $y2
 * @param integer $fillType
 * @return Zend_Pdf_Page
 */
public function drawRectangle($x1, $y1, $x2, $y2,
                    $fillType = Zend_Pdf_Page::SHAPE_DRAW_FILL_AND_STROKE);



/**
 * Draw a polygon.
 *
 * If $fillType is Zend_Pdf_Page::SHAPE_DRAW_FILL_AND_STROKE or
 * Zend_Pdf_Page::SHAPE_DRAW_FILL, then polygon is automatically closed.
 * See detailed description of these methods in a PDF documentation
 * (section 4.4.2 Path painting Operators, Filling)
 *
 * @param array $x  - array of float (the X co-ordinates of the vertices)
 * @param array $y  - array of float (the Y co-ordinates of the vertices)
 * @param integer $fillType
 * @param integer $fillMethod
 * @return Zend_Pdf_Page
 */
public function drawPolygon($x, $y,
                        $fillType =
                            Zend_Pdf_Page::SHAPE_DRAW_FILL_AND_STROKE,
```

```
                                        $fillMethod =
                                            Zend_Pdf_Page::FILL_METHOD_NON_ZERO_WINDING)


/**
 * Draw a circle centered on x, y with a radius of radius.
 *
 * Angles are specified in radians
 *
 * Method signatures:
 * drawCircle($x, $y, $radius);
 * drawCircle($x, $y, $radius, $fillType);
 * drawCircle($x, $y, $radius, $startAngle, $endAngle);
 * drawCircle($x, $y, $radius, $startAngle, $endAngle, $fillType);
 *
 *
 * It's not a really circle, because PDF supports only cubic Bezier
 * curves. But very good approximation.
 * It differs from a real circle on a maximum 0.00026 radiuses (at PI/8,
 * 3*PI/8, 5*PI/8, 7*PI/8, 9*PI/8, 11*PI/8, 13*PI/8 and 15*PI/8 angles).
 * At 0, PI/4, PI/2, 3*PI/4, PI, 5*PI/4, 3*PI/2 and 7*PI/4 it's exactly
 * a tangent to a circle.
 *
 * @param float $x
 * @param float $y
 * @param float $radius
 * @param mixed $param4
 * @param mixed $param5
 * @param mixed $param6
 * @return Zend_Pdf_Page
 */
public function  drawCircle($x,
                            $y,
                            $radius,
                            $param4 = null,
                            $param5 = null,
                            $param6 = null);


/**
 * Draw an ellipse inside the specified rectangle.
 *
 * Method signatures:
 * drawEllipse($x1, $y1, $x2, $y2);
 * drawEllipse($x1, $y1, $x2, $y2, $fillType);
 * drawEllipse($x1, $y1, $x2, $y2, $startAngle, $endAngle);
 * drawEllipse($x1, $y1, $x2, $y2, $startAngle, $endAngle, $fillType);
 *
 * Angles are specified in radians
 *
 * @param float $x1
 * @param float $y1
 * @param float $x2
 * @param float $y2
 * @param mixed $param5
 * @param mixed $param6
 * @param mixed $param7
 * @return Zend_Pdf_Page
 */
public function drawEllipse($x1,
                            $y1,
                            $x2,
                            $y2,
```

```
                            $param5 = null,
                            $param6 = null,
                            $param7 = null);
```

Text Drawing

Text drawing operations also exist in the context of a PDF page. You can draw a single line of text at any position on the page by supplying the x and y coordinates of the baseline. Current font and current font size are used for text drawing operations (see detailed description below).

```
/**
 * Draw a line of text at the specified position.
 *
 * @param string $text
 * @param float $x
 * @param float $y
 * @param string $charEncoding (optional) Character encoding of source
 *                text.Defaults to current locale.
 * @throws Zend_Pdf_Exception
 * @return Zend_Pdf_Page
 */
public function drawText($text, $x, $y, $charEncoding = '');
```

Example 15.6. Draw a string on the page

```
...
$pdfPage->drawText('Hello world!', 72, 720);
...
```

By default, text strings are interpreted using the character encoding method of the current locale. If you have a string that uses a different encoding method (such as a UTF-8 string read from a file on disk, or a MacRoman string obtained from a legacy database), you can indicate the character encoding at draw time and Zend_Pdf will handle the conversion for you. You can supply source strings in any encoding method supported by PHP's iconv() [http://www.php.net/manual/function.iconv.php] function:

Example 15.7. Draw a UTF-8-encoded string on the page

```
...
// Read a UTF-8-encoded string from disk
$unicodeString = fread($fp, 1024);

// Draw the string on the page
$pdfPage->drawText($unicodeString, 72, 720, 'UTF-8');
...
```

Using fonts

Zend_Pdf_Page::drawText() uses the page's current font and font size, which is set with the Zend_Pdf_Page::setFont() method:

```
/**
 * Set current font.
 *
 * @param Zend_Pdf_Resource_Font $font
 * @param float $fontSize
 * @return Zend_Pdf_Page
 */
public function setFont(Zend_Pdf_Resource_Font $font, $fontSize);
```

PDF documents support PostScript Type 1 and TrueType fonts, as well as two specialized PDF types, Type 3 and composite fonts. There are also 14 standard Type 1 fonts built-in to every PDF viewer: Courier (4 styles), Helvetica (4 styles), Times (4 styles), Symbol, and Zapf Dingbats.

Zend_Pdf currently supports the standard 14 PDF fonts as well as your own custom TrueType fonts. Font objects are obtained via one of two factory methods: Zend_Pdf_Font::fontWithName($fontName) for the standard 14 PDF fonts or Zend_Pdf_Font::fontWithPath($filePath) for custom fonts.

Example 15.8. Create a standard font

```
...
// Create new font
$font = Zend_Pdf_Font::fontWithName(Zend_Pdf_Font::FONT_HELVETICA);

// Apply font
$pdfPage->setFont($font, 36);
...
```

Constants for the standard 14 PDF font names are defined in the Zend_Pdf_Font class:

- Zend_Pdf_Font::FONT_COURIER

- Zend_Pdf_Font::FONT_COURIER_BOLD

- Zend_Pdf_Font::FONT_COURIER_ITALIC

- Zend_Pdf_Font::FONT_COURIER_BOLD_ITALIC

- Zend_Pdf_Font::FONT_TIMES

- Zend_Pdf_Font::FONT_TIMES_BOLD

- Zend_Pdf_Font::FONT_TIMES_ITALIC

- Zend_Pdf_Font::FONT_TIMES_BOLD_ITALIC

- Zend_Pdf_Font::FONT_HELVETICA

- Zend_Pdf_Font::FONT_HELVETICA_BOLD

- Zend_Pdf_Font::FONT_HELVETICA_ITALIC

- Zend_Pdf_Font::FONT_HELVETICA_BOLD_ITALIC

- Zend_Pdf_Font::FONT_SYMBOL

- Zend_Pdf_Font::FONT_ZAPFDINGBATS

You can also use any individual TrueType font (which usually has a '.ttf' extension) or an OpenType font ('.otf' extension) if it contains TrueType outlines. Currently unsupported, but planned for a future release are Mac OS X .dfont files and Microsoft TrueType Collection ('.ttc' extension) files.

To use a TrueType font, you must provide the full file path to the font program. If the font cannot be read for some reason, or if it is not a TrueType font, the factory method will throw an exception:

Example 15.9. Create a TrueType font

```
...
// Create new font
$goodDogCoolFont = Zend_Pdf_Font::fontWithPath('/path/to/GOODDC__.TTF');

// Apply font
$pdfPage->setFont($goodDogCoolFont, 36);
...
```

By default, custom fonts will be embedded in the resulting PDF document. This allows recipients to view the page as intended, even if they don't have the proper fonts installed on their system. If you are concerned about file size, you can request that the font program not be embedded by passing a 'do not embed' option to the factory method:

Example 15.10. Create a TrueType font, but do not embed it in the PDF document.

```
...
// Create new font
$goodDogCoolFont = Zend_Pdf_Font::fontWithPath('/path/to/GOODDC__.TTF',
                                               Zend_Pdf_Font::EMBED
                                                 _DONT_EMBED);

// Apply font
$pdfPage->setFont($goodDogCoolFont, 36);
...
```

If the font program is not embedded but the recipient of the PDF file has the font installed on their system, they will see the document as intended. If they do not have the correct font installed, the PDF viewer application will do its best to synthesize a replacement.

Some fonts have very specific licensing rules which prevent them from being embedded in PDF documents. So you are not caught off-guard by this, if you try to use a font that cannot be embedded, the factory method will throw an exception.

You can still use these fonts, but you must either pass the do not embed flag as described above, or you can simply suppress the exception:

Example 15.11. Do not throw an exception for fonts that cannot be embedded.

```
...
$font = Zend_Pdf_Font::fontWithPath(
            '/path/to/unEmbeddableFont.ttf',
         Zend_Pdf_Font::EMBED_SUPPRESS_EMBED_EXCEPTION
```

```
            );
...
```

This suppression technique is preferred if you allow an end-user to choose their own fonts. Fonts which can be embedded in the PDF document will be; those that cannot, won't.

Font programs can be rather large, some reaching into the tens of megabytes. By default, all embedded fonts are compressed using the Flate compression scheme, resulting in a space savings of 50% on average. If, for some reason, you do not want to compress the font program, you can disable it with an option:

Example 15.12. Do not compress an embedded font.

```
...
$font = Zend_Pdf_Font::fontWithPath('/path/to/someReallyBigFont.ttf',
                                     Zend_Pdf_Font::EMBED_DONT_COMPRESS);
...
```

Finally, when necessary, you can combine the embedding options by using the bitwise OR operator:

Example 15.13. Combining font embedding options.

```
...
$font = Zend_Pdf_Font::fontWithPath(
          $someUserSelectedFontPath,
          (Zend_Pdf_Font::EMBED_SUPPRESS_EMBED_EXCEPTION |
          Zend_Pdf_Font::EMBED_DONT_COMPRESS));
...
```

Standard PDF fonts limitations.

Standard PDF fonts use several single byte encodings internally (see PDF Reference, Sixth Edition, version 1.7 [http://www.adobe.com/devnet/acrobat/pdfs/pdf_reference_1-7.pdf] Appendix D for details). They are generally equal to Latin1 character set (except Symbol and ZapfDingbats fonts).

Zend_Pdf uses CP1252 (WinLatin1) for drawing text with standard fonts.

Text still can be provided in any other encoding, which must be specified if it differs from a current locale. Only WinLatin1 characters will be actually drawn.

Example 15.14. Combining font embedding options.

```
...
$font = Zend_Pdf_Font::fontWithName(Zend_Pdf_Font::FONT_COURIER);
$pdfPage->setFont($font, 36)
        ->drawText('Euro sign - €', 72, 720, 'UTF-8')
        ->drawText('Text with umlauts - à è ì', 72, 650, 'UTF-8');
...
```

Extracting fonts.

Zend_Pdf module provides a possibility to extract fonts from loaded documents.

It may be useful for incremental document updates. Without this functionality you have to attach and possibly embed font into a document each time you want to update it.

Zend_Pdf and Zend_Pdf_Page objects provide special methods to extract all fonts mentioned within a document or a page:

Example 15.15. Extracting fonts from a loaded document.

```
...
$pdf = Zend_Pdf::load($documentPath);
...
// Get all document fonts
$fontList = $pdf->extractFonts();
$pdf->pages[] = ($page = $pdf->newPage(Zend_Pdf_Page::SIZE_A4));
$yPosition = 700;
foreach ($fontList as $font) {
    $page->setFont($font, 15);
    $fontName = $font->getFontName(Zend_Pdf_Font::NAME_POSTSCRIPT,
                                   'en',
                                   'UTF-8');
    $page->drawText($fontName . ': The quick brown fox jumps over the
                                lazy dog',
                    100,
                    $yPosition,
                    'UTF-8');
    $yPosition -= 30;
}
...
// Get fonts referenced within the first document page
$firstPage = reset($pdf->pages);
$firstPageFonts = $firstPage->extractFonts();
...
```

Example 15.16. Extracting font from a loaded document by specifying font name.

```
...
$pdf = new Zend_Pdf();
...
$pdf->pages[] = ($page = $pdf->newPage(Zend_Pdf_Page::SIZE_A4));

$font = Zend_Pdf_Font::fontWithPath($fontPath);
$page->setFont($font, $fontSize);
$page->drawText($text, $x, $y);
...
// This font name should be stored somewhere...
$fontName = $font->getFontName(Zend_Pdf_Font::NAME_POSTSCRIPT,
                               'en',
                               'UTF-8');
...
$pdf->save($docPath);
```

```
. . .

. . .
$pdf = Zend_Pdf::load($docPath);
. . .
$pdf->pages[] = ($page = $pdf->newPage(Zend_Pdf_Page::SIZE_A4));

/* $srcPage->extractFont($fontName) can also be used here */
$font = $pdf->extractFont($fontName);

$page->setFont($font, $fontSize);
$page->drawText($text, $x, $y);
. . .
$pdf->save($docPath, true /* incremental update mode */);
. . .
```

Extracted fonts can be used in the place of any other font with the following limitations:

- Extracted font can be used only in the context of the document from which it was extracted.

- Possibly embedded font program is actually not extracted. So extracted font can't provide correct font metrics and original font has to be used for text width calculations:

```
. . .
$font = $pdf->extractFont($fontName);
$originalFont = Zend_Pdf_Font::fontWithPath($fontPath);

$page->setFont($font /* use extracted font for drawing */, $fontSize);
$xPosition = $x;
for ($charIndex = 0; $charIndex < strlen($text); $charIndex++) {
    $page->drawText($text[$charIndex], xPosition, $y);

    // Use original font for text width calculation
    $width = $originalFont->widthForGlyph(
                $originalFont->glyphNumberForCharacter($text[$charIndex])
            );
    $xPosition += $width/$originalFont->getUnitsPerEm()*$fontSize;
}
. . .
```

Image Drawing

Zend_Pdf_Page class provides drawImage() method to draw image:

```
/**
 * Draw an image at the specified position on the page.
 *
 * @param Zend_Pdf_Resource_Image $image
 * @param float $x1
 * @param float $y1
 * @param float $x2
 * @param float $y2
 * @return Zend_Pdf_Page
 */
public function drawImage(Zend_Pdf_Resource_Image $image, $x1, $y1, $x2, $y2)
```

Image objects should be created with `Zend_Pdf_Image::imageWithPath($filePath)` method (JPG, PNG and TIFF images are supported now):

Example 15.17. Image drawing

```
...
// load image
$image = Zend_Pdf_Image::imageWithPath('my_image.jpg');

$pdfPage->drawImage($image, 100, 100, 400, 300);
...
```

Important! JPEG support requires PHP GD extension to be configured. Important! PNG support requires ZLIB extension to be configured to work with Alpha channel images.

Refer to the PHP documentation for detailed information (http://www.php.net/manual/en/ref.image.php). (http://www.php.net/manual/en/ref.zlib.php).

Line drawing style

Line drawing style is defined by line width, line color and line dashing pattern. All of this parameters can be assigned by `Zend_Pdf_Page` class methods:

```
/** Set line color. */
public function setLineColor(Zend_Pdf_Color $color);

/** Set line width. */
public function setLineWidth(float $width);

/**
 * Set line dashing pattern.
 *
 * Pattern is an array of floats:
 *     array(on_length, off_length, on_length, off_length, ...)
 * Phase is shift from the beginning of line.
 *
 * @param array $pattern
 * @param array $phase
 * @return Zend_Pdf_Page
 */
public function setLineDashingPattern($pattern, $phase = 0);
```

Fill style

`Zend_Pdf_Page::drawRectangle()`, `Zend_Pdf_Page::drawPolygon()`, `Zend_Pdf_Page::drawCircle()` and `Zend_Pdf_Page::drawEllipse()` methods take `$fillType` argument as an optional parameter. It can be:

- Zend_Pdf_Page::SHAPE_DRAW_STROKE - stroke shape

- Zend_Pdf_Page::SHAPE_DRAW_FILL - only fill shape

- Zend_Pdf_Page::SHAPE_DRAW_FILL_AND_STROKE - fill and stroke (default behavior)

`Zend_Pdf_Page::drawPolygon()` methods also takes an additional parameter `$fillMethod`:

- Zend_Pdf_Page::FILL_METHOD_NON_ZERO_WINDING (default behavior)

PDF reference describes this rule as follows:

> The nonzero winding number rule determines whether a given point is inside a path by conceptually drawing a ray from that point to infinity in any direction and then examining the places where a segment of the path crosses the ray. Starting with a count of 0, the rule adds 1 each time a path segment crosses the ray from left to right and subtracts 1 each time a segment crosses from right to left. After counting all the crossings, if the result is 0 then the point is outside the path; otherwise it is inside. Note: The method just described does not specify what to do if a path segment coincides with or is tangent to the chosen ray. Since the direction of the ray is arbitrary, the rule simply chooses a ray that does not encounter such problem intersections. For simple convex paths, the nonzero winding number rule defines the inside and outside as one would intuitively expect. The more interesting cases are those involving complex or self-intersecting paths like the ones shown in Figure 4.10 (in a PDF Reference). For a path consisting of a five-pointed star, drawn with five connected straight line segments intersecting each other, the rule considers the inside to be the entire area enclosed by the star, including the pentagon in the center. For a path composed of two concentric circles, the areas enclosed by both circles are considered to be inside, provided that both are drawn in the same direction. If the circles are drawn in opposite directions, only the "doughnut" shape between them is inside, according to the rule; the "doughnut hole" is outside.

- Zend_Pdf_Page::FILL_METHOD_EVEN_ODD

    PDF reference describes this rule as follows:

    > An alternative to the nonzero winding number rule is the even-odd rule. This rule determines the "insideness" of a point by drawing a ray from that point in any direction and simply counting the number of path segments that cross the ray, regardless of direction. If this number is odd, the point is inside; if even, the point is outside. This yields the same results as the nonzero winding number rule for paths with simple shapes, but produces different results for more complex shapes. Figure 4.11 (in a PDF Reference) shows the effects of applying the even-odd rule to complex paths. For the five-pointed star, the rule considers the triangular points to be inside the path, but not the pentagon in the center. For the two concentric circles, only the "doughnut" shape between the two circles is considered inside, regardless of the directions in which the circles are drawn.

Linear Transformations

Rotations.

PDF page can be rotated before applying any draw operation. It can be done by Zend_Pdf_Page::rotate() method:

```
/**
 * Rotate the page.
 *
 * @param float $x     - the X co-ordinate of rotation point
 * @param float $y     - the Y co-ordinate of rotation point
 * @param float $angle - rotation angle
 * @return Zend_Pdf_Page
 */
public function rotate($x, $y, $angle);
```

Starting from ZF 1.8, scaling.

Scaling transformation is provided by Zend_Pdf_Page::scale() method:

```
/**
 * Scale coordination system.
 *
 * @param float $xScale - X dimention scale factor
 * @param float $yScale - Y dimention scale factor
 * @return Zend_Pdf_Page
 */
public function scale($xScale, $yScale);
```

Starting from ZF 1.8, translating.

Coordinate system shifting is performed by Zend_Pdf_Page::translate() method:

```
/**
 * Translate coordination system.
 *
 * @param float $xShift - X coordinate shift
 * @param float $yShift - Y coordinate shift
 * @return Zend_Pdf_Page
 */
public function translate($xShift, $yShift);
```

Starting from ZF 1.8, skewing.

Page skewing can be done using Zend_Pdf_Page::skew() method:

```
/**
 * Translate coordination system.
 *
 * @param float $x   - the X co-ordinate of axis skew point
 * @param float $y   - the Y co-ordinate of axis skew point
 * @param float $xAngle - X axis skew angle
 * @param float $yAngle - Y axis skew angle
 * @return Zend_Pdf_Page
 */
public function skew($x, $y, $xAngle, $yAngle);
```

Save/restore graphics state

At any time page graphics state (current font, font size, line color, fill color, line style, page rotation, clip area) can be saved and then restored. Save operation puts data to a graphics state stack, restore operation retrieves it from there.

There are two methods in Zend_Pdf_Page class for these operations:

```
/**
 * Save the graphics state of this page.
 * This takes a snapshot of the currently applied style, position,
 * clipping area and any rotation/translation/scaling that has been
 * applied.
 *
 * @return Zend_Pdf_Page
 */
public function saveGS();
```

```
/**
 * Restore the graphics state that was saved with the last call to
 * saveGS().
 *
 * @return Zend_Pdf_Page
 */
public function restoreGS();
```

Clipping draw area

PDF and Zend_Pdf module support clipping of draw area. Current clip area limits the regions of the page affected by painting operators. It's a whole page initially.

Zend_Pdf_Page class provides a set of methods for clipping operations.

```
/**
 * Intersect current clipping area with a rectangle.
 *
 * @param float $x1
 * @param float $y1
 * @param float $x2
 * @param float $y2
 * @return Zend_Pdf_Page
 */
public function clipRectangle($x1, $y1, $x2, $y2);
```

```
/**
 * Intersect current clipping area with a polygon.
 *
 * @param array $x   - array of float (the X co-ordinates of the vertices)
 * @param array $y   - array of float (the Y co-ordinates of the vertices)
 * @param integer $fillMethod
 * @return Zend_Pdf_Page
 */
public function clipPolygon($x,
                            $y,
                            $fillMethod =
                                Zend_Pdf_Page::FILL_METHOD_NON_ZERO
                                    _WINDING);
```

```
/**
 * Intersect current clipping area with a circle.
 *
 * @param float $x
 * @param float $y
 * @param float $radius
 * @param float $startAngle
 * @param float $endAngle
 * @return Zend_Pdf_Page
 */
public function clipCircle($x,
                           $y,
                           $radius,
                           $startAngle = null,
                           $endAngle = null);
```

```
/**
```

```
 * Intersect current clipping area with an ellipse.
 *
 * Method signatures:
 * drawEllipse($x1, $y1, $x2, $y2);
 * drawEllipse($x1, $y1, $x2, $y2, $startAngle, $endAngle);
 *
 * @todo process special cases with $x2-$x1 == 0 or $y2-$y1 == 0
 *
 * @param float $x1
 * @param float $y1
 * @param float $x2
 * @param float $y2
 * @param float $startAngle
 * @param float $endAngle
 * @return Zend_Pdf_Page
 */
public function clipEllipse($x1,
                            $y1,
                            $x2,
                            $y2,
                            $startAngle = null,
                            $endAngle = null);
```

Styles

Zend_Pdf_Style class provides styles functionality.

Styles can be used to store a set of graphic state parameters and apply it to a PDF page by one operation:

```
/**
 * Set the style to use for future drawing operations on this page
 *
 * @param Zend_Pdf_Style $style
 * @return Zend_Pdf_Page
 */
public function setStyle(Zend_Pdf_Style $style);

/**
 * Return the style, applied to the page.
 *
 * @return Zend_Pdf_Style|null
 */
public function getStyle();
```

Zend_Pdf_Style class provides a set of methods to set or get different graphics state parameters:

```
/**
 * Set line color.
 *
 * @param Zend_Pdf_Color $color
 * @return Zend_Pdf_Page
 */
public function setLineColor(Zend_Pdf_Color $color);


/**
 * Get line color.
 *
 * @return Zend_Pdf_Color|null
 */
public function getLineColor();
```

```
/**
 * Set line width.
 *
 * @param float $width
 * @return Zend_Pdf_Page
 */
public function setLineWidth($width);


/**
 * Get line width.
 *
 * @return float
 */
public function getLineWidth();


/**
 * Set line dashing pattern
 *
 * @param array $pattern
 * @param float $phase
 * @return Zend_Pdf_Page
 */
public function setLineDashingPattern($pattern, $phase = 0);


/**
 * Get line dashing pattern
 *
 * @return array
 */
public function getLineDashingPattern();


/**
 * Get line dashing phase
 *
 * @return float
 */
public function getLineDashingPhase();


/**
 * Set fill color.
 *
 * @param Zend_Pdf_Color $color
 * @return Zend_Pdf_Page
 */
public function setFillColor(Zend_Pdf_Color $color);


/**
 * Get fill color.
 *
 * @return Zend_Pdf_Color|null
 */
public function getFillColor();
```

```
/**
 * Set current font.
 *
 * @param Zend_Pdf_Resource_Font $font
 * @param float $fontSize
 * @return Zend_Pdf_Page
 */
public function setFont(Zend_Pdf_Resource_Font $font, $fontSize);
```

```
/**
 * Modify current font size
 *
 * @param float $fontSize
 * @return Zend_Pdf_Page
 */
public function setFontSize($fontSize);
```

```
/**
 * Get current font.
 *
 * @return Zend_Pdf_Resource_Font $font
 */
public function getFont();
```

```
/**
 * Get current font size
 *
 * @return float $fontSize
 */
public function getFontSize();
```

Transparency

Zend_Pdf module supports transparency handling.

Transparency may be set using Zend_Pdf_Page::setAlpha() method:

```
/**
 * Set the transparency
 *
 * $alpha == 0  - transparent
 * $alpha == 1  - opaque
 *
 * Transparency modes, supported by PDF:
 * Normal (default), Multiply, Screen, Overlay, Darken, Lighten,
 * ColorDodge, ColorBurn, HardLight, SoftLight, Difference, Exclusion
 *
 * @param float $alpha
 * @param string $mode
 * @throws Zend_Pdf_Exception
 * @return Zend_Pdf_Page
 */
public function setAlpha($alpha, $mode = 'Normal');
```

Document Info and Metadata.

A PDF document may include general information such as the document's title, author, and creation and modification dates.

Historically this information is stored using special Info structure. This structure is available for read and writing as an associative array using `properties` public property of `Zend_Pdf` objects:

```
$pdf = Zend_Pdf::load($pdfPath);

echo $pdf->properties['Title'] . "\n";
echo $pdf->properties['Author'] . "\n";

$pdf->properties['Title'] = 'New Title.';
$pdf->save($pdfPath);
```

The following keys are defined by PDF v1.4 (Acrobat 5) standard:

- *Title* - string, optional, the document's title.

- *Author* - string, optional, the name of the person who created the document.

- *Subject* - string, optional, the subject of the document.

- *Keywords* - string, optional, keywords associated with the document.

- *Creator* - string, optional, if the document was converted to PDF from another format, the name of the application (for example, Adobe FrameMaker®) that created the original document from which it was converted.

- *Producer* - string, optional, if the document was converted to PDF from another format, the name of the application (for example, Acrobat Distiller) that converted it to PDF..

- *CreationDate* - string, optional, the date and time the document was created, in the following form: "D:YYYYMMDDHHmmSSOHH'mm'", where:

  - *YYYY* is the year.

  - *MM* is the month.

  - *DD* is the day (01–31).

  - *HH* is the hour (00–23).

  - *mm* is the minute (00–59).

  - *SS* is the second (00–59).

  - *O* is the relationship of local time to Universal Time (UT), denoted by one of the characters +, #, or Z (see below).

  - *HH* followed by ' is the absolute value of the offset from UT in hours (00–23).

  - *mm* followed by ' is the absolute value of the offset from UT in minutes (00–59).
  The apostrophe character (') after HH and mm is part of the syntax. All fields after the year are optional. (The prefix D:, although also optional, is strongly recommended.) The default values for MM and DD are both 01; all other numerical fields default to zero values. A plus sign (+) as the value of the O field signifies that local time is later than UT, a minus sign (#) that local time is earlier than UT, and the letter Z that local time is equal to UT. If no UT information is specified, the relationship of the specified time to UT is considered to be unknown. Whether or not the time zone is known, the rest of the date should be specified in local time.

For example, December 23, 1998, at 7:52 PM, U.S. Pacific Standard Time, is represented by the string "D:199812231952#08'00'".

- *ModDate* - string, optional, the date and time the document was most recently modified, in the same form as *CreationDate*.

- *Trapped* - boolean, optional, indicates whether the document has been modified to include trapping information.

  - *true* - The document has been fully trapped; no further trapping is needed.

  - *false* - The document has not yet been trapped; any desired trapping must still be done.

  - *null* - Either it is unknown whether the document has been trapped or it has been partly but not yet fully trapped; some additional trapping may still be needed.

Since PDF v 1.6 metadata can be stored in the special XML document attached to the PDF (XMP - Extensible Metadata Platform [http://www.adobe.com/products/xmp/]).

This XML document can be retrieved and attached to the PDF with `Zend_Pdf::getMetadata()` and `Zend_Pdf::setMetadata($metadata)` methods:

```
$pdf = Zend_Pdf::load($pdfPath);
$metadata = $pdf->getMetadata();
$metadataDOM = new DOMDocument();
$metadataDOM->loadXML($metadata);

$xpath = new DOMXPath($metadataDOM);
$pdfPreffixNamespaceURI = $xpath->query('/rdf:RDF/rdf:Description')
                                ->item(0)
                                ->lookupNamespaceURI('pdf');
$xpath->registerNamespace('pdf', $pdfPreffixNamespaceURI);

$titleNode = $xpath->query('/rdf:RDF/rdf:Description/pdf:Title')->item(0);
$title = $titleNode->nodeValue;
...

$titleNode->nodeValue = 'New title';
$pdf->setMetadata($metadataDOM->saveXML());
$pdf->save($pdfPath);
```

Common document properties are duplicated in the Info structure and Metadata document (if presented). It's user application responsibility now to keep them synchronized.

Zend_Pdf module usage example

This section provides an example of module usage.

This example can be found in a `demos/Zend/Pdf/demo.php` file.

There are also `test.pdf` file, which can be used with this demo for test purposes.

Example 15.18. Zend_Pdf module usage demo

```
/**
 * @package Zend_Pdf
 * @subpackage demo
 */
```

```php
if (!isset($argv[1])) {
    echo "USAGE: php demo.php <pdf_file> [<output_pdf_file>]\n";
    exit;
}

try {
    $pdf = Zend_Pdf::load($argv[1]);
} catch (Zend_Pdf_Exception $e) {
    if ($e->getMessage() == 'Can not open \'' . $argv[1] .
                            '\' file for reading.') {
        // Create new PDF if file doesn't exist
        $pdf = new Zend_Pdf();

        if (!isset($argv[2])) {
            // force complete file rewriting (instead of updating)
            $argv[2] = $argv[1];
        }
    } else {
        // Throw an exception if it's not the "Can't open file
        // exception
        throw $e;
    }
}

//-----------------------------------------------------------------------
// Reverse page order
$pdf->pages = array_reverse($pdf->pages);

// Create new Style
$style = new Zend_Pdf_Style();
$style->setFillColor(new Zend_Pdf_Color_Rgb(0, 0, 0.9));
$style->setLineColor(new Zend_Pdf_Color_GrayScale(0.2));
$style->setLineWidth(3);
$style->setLineDashingPattern(array(3, 2, 3, 4), 1.6);
$fontH = Zend_Pdf_Font::fontWithName(Zend_Pdf_Font::FONT_HELVETICA_BOLD);
$style->setFont($fontH, 32);

try {
    // Create new image object
    $imageFile = dirname(__FILE__) . '/stamp.jpg';
    $stampImage = Zend_Pdf_Image::imageWithPath($imageFile);
} catch (Zend_Pdf_Exception $e) {
    // Example of operating with image loading exceptions.
    if ($e->getMessage() != 'Image extension is not installed.' &&
        $e->getMessage() != 'JPG support is not configured properly.') {
        throw $e;
    }
    $stampImage = null;
}

// Mark page as modified
foreach ($pdf->pages as $page){
    $page->saveGS()
         ->setAlpha(0.25)
         ->setStyle($style)
         ->rotate(0, 0, M_PI_2/3);

    $page->saveGS();
    $page->clipCircle(550, -10, 50);
    if ($stampImage != null) {
        $page->drawImage($stampImage, 500, -60, 600, 40);
    }
    $page->restoreGS();
```

```
    $page->drawText('Modified by Zend Framework!', 150, 0)
         ->restoreGS();
}

// Add new page generated by Zend_Pdf object
// (page is attached to the specified the document)
$pdf->pages[] = ($page1 = $pdf->newPage('A4'));

// Add new page generated by Zend_Pdf_Page object
// (page is not attached to the document)
$page2 = new Zend_Pdf_Page(Zend_Pdf_Page::SIZE_LETTER_LANDSCAPE);
$pdf->pages[] = $page2;

// Create new font
$font = Zend_Pdf_Font::fontWithName(Zend_Pdf_Font::FONT_HELVETICA);

// Apply font and draw text
$page1->setFont($font, 36)
      ->setFillColor(Zend_Pdf_Color_Html::color('#9999cc'))
      ->drawText('Helvetica 36 text string', 60, 500);

// Use font object for another page
$page2->setFont($font, 24)
      ->drawText('Helvetica 24 text string', 60, 500);

// Use another font
$fontT = Zend_Pdf_Font::fontWithName(Zend_Pdf_Font::FONT_TIMES);
$page2->setFont($fontT, 32)
      ->drawText('Times-Roman 32 text string', 60, 450);

// Draw rectangle
$page2->setFillColor(new Zend_Pdf_Color_GrayScale(0.8))
      ->setLineColor(new Zend_Pdf_Color_GrayScale(0.2))
      ->setLineDashingPattern(array(3, 2, 3, 4), 1.6)
      ->drawRectangle(60, 400, 400, 350);

// Draw circle
$page2->setLineDashingPattern(Zend_Pdf_Page::LINE_DASHING_SOLID)
      ->setFillColor(new Zend_Pdf_Color_Rgb(1, 0, 0))
      ->drawCircle(85, 375, 25);

// Draw sectors
$page2->drawCircle(200, 375, 25, 2*M_PI/3, -M_PI/6)
      ->setFillColor(new Zend_Pdf_Color_Cmyk(1, 0, 0, 0))
      ->drawCircle(200, 375, 25, M_PI/6, 2*M_PI/3)
      ->setFillColor(new Zend_Pdf_Color_Rgb(1, 1, 0))
      ->drawCircle(200, 375, 25, -M_PI/6, M_PI/6);

// Draw ellipse
$page2->setFillColor(new Zend_Pdf_Color_Rgb(1, 0, 0))
      ->drawEllipse(250, 400, 400, 350)
      ->setFillColor(new Zend_Pdf_Color_Cmyk(1, 0, 0, 0))
      ->drawEllipse(250, 400, 400, 350, M_PI/6, 2*M_PI/3)
      ->setFillColor(new Zend_Pdf_Color_Rgb(1, 1, 0))
      ->drawEllipse(250, 400, 400, 350, -M_PI/6, M_PI/6);

// Draw and fill polygon
$page2->setFillColor(new Zend_Pdf_Color_Rgb(1, 0, 1));
$x = array();
$y = array();
for ($count = 0; $count < 8; $count++) {
    $x[] = 140 + 25*cos(3*M_PI_4*$count);
    $y[] = 375 + 25*sin(3*M_PI_4*$count);
```

```
}
$page2->drawPolygon($x, $y,
                    Zend_Pdf_Page::SHAPE_DRAW_FILL_AND_STROKE,
                    Zend_Pdf_Page::FILL_METHOD_EVEN_ODD);

// ---------- Draw figures in modified coordination system --------------

// Coordination system movement
$page2->saveGS();
$page2->translate(60, 250); // Shift coordination system

// Draw rectangle
$page2->setFillColor(new Zend_Pdf_Color_GrayScale(0.8))
      ->setLineColor(new Zend_Pdf_Color_GrayScale(0.2))
      ->setLineDashingPattern(array(3, 2, 3, 4), 1.6)
      ->drawRectangle(0, 50, 340, 0);

// Draw circle
$page2->setLineDashingPattern(Zend_Pdf_Page::LINE_DASHING_SOLID)
      ->setFillColor(new Zend_Pdf_Color_Rgb(1, 0, 0))
      ->drawCircle(25, 25, 25);

// Draw sectors
$page2->drawCircle(140, 25, 25, 2*M_PI/3, -M_PI/6)
      ->setFillColor(new Zend_Pdf_Color_Cmyk(1, 0, 0, 0))
      ->drawCircle(140, 25, 25, M_PI/6, 2*M_PI/3)
      ->setFillColor(new Zend_Pdf_Color_Rgb(1, 1, 0))
      ->drawCircle(140, 25, 25, -M_PI/6, M_PI/6);

// Draw ellipse
$page2->setFillColor(new Zend_Pdf_Color_Rgb(1, 0, 0))
      ->drawEllipse(190, 50, 340, 0)
      ->setFillColor(new Zend_Pdf_Color_Cmyk(1, 0, 0, 0))
      ->drawEllipse(190, 50, 340, 0, M_PI/6, 2*M_PI/3)
      ->setFillColor(new Zend_Pdf_Color_Rgb(1, 1, 0))
      ->drawEllipse(190, 50, 340, 0, -M_PI/6, M_PI/6);

// Draw and fill polygon
$page2->setFillColor(new Zend_Pdf_Color_Rgb(1, 0, 1));
$x = array();
$y = array();
for ($count = 0; $count < 8; $count++) {
    $x[] = 80 + 25*cos(3*M_PI_4*$count);
    $y[] = 25 + 25*sin(3*M_PI_4*$count);
}
$page2->drawPolygon($x, $y,
                    Zend_Pdf_Page::SHAPE_DRAW_FILL_AND_STROKE,
                    Zend_Pdf_Page::FILL_METHOD_EVEN_ODD);

// Draw line
$page2->setLineWidth(0.5)
      ->drawLine(0, 25, 340, 25);

$page2->restoreGS();

// Coordination system movement, skewing and scaling
$page2->saveGS();
$page2->translate(60, 150)      // Shift coordination system
      ->skew(0, 0, 0, -M_PI/9)  // Skew coordination system
      ->scale(0.9, 0.9);        // Scale coordination system

// Draw rectangle
$page2->setFillColor(new Zend_Pdf_Color_GrayScale(0.8))
      ->setLineColor(new Zend_Pdf_Color_GrayScale(0.2))
```

```
        ->setLineDashingPattern(array(3, 2, 3, 4), 1.6)
        ->drawRectangle(0, 50, 340, 0);

// Draw circle
$page2->setLineDashingPattern(Zend_Pdf_Page::LINE_DASHING_SOLID)
        ->setFillColor(new Zend_Pdf_Color_Rgb(1, 0, 0))
        ->drawCircle(25, 25, 25);

// Draw sectors
$page2->drawCircle(140, 25, 25, 2*M_PI/3, -M_PI/6)
        ->setFillColor(new Zend_Pdf_Color_Cmyk(1, 0, 0, 0))
        ->drawCircle(140, 25, 25, M_PI/6, 2*M_PI/3)
        ->setFillColor(new Zend_Pdf_Color_Rgb(1, 1, 0))
        ->drawCircle(140, 25, 25, -M_PI/6, M_PI/6);

// Draw ellipse
$page2->setFillColor(new Zend_Pdf_Color_Rgb(1, 0, 0))
        ->drawEllipse(190, 50, 340, 0)
        ->setFillColor(new Zend_Pdf_Color_Cmyk(1, 0, 0, 0))
        ->drawEllipse(190, 50, 340, 0, M_PI/6, 2*M_PI/3)
        ->setFillColor(new Zend_Pdf_Color_Rgb(1, 1, 0))
        ->drawEllipse(190, 50, 340, 0, -M_PI/6, M_PI/6);

// Draw and fill polygon
$page2->setFillColor(new Zend_Pdf_Color_Rgb(1, 0, 1));
$x = array();
$y = array();
for ($count = 0; $count < 8; $count++) {
    $x[] = 80 + 25*cos(3*M_PI_4*$count);
    $y[] = 25 + 25*sin(3*M_PI_4*$count);
}
$page2->drawPolygon($x, $y,
                    Zend_Pdf_Page::SHAPE_DRAW_FILL_AND_STROKE,
                    Zend_Pdf_Page::FILL_METHOD_EVEN_ODD);

// Draw line
$page2->setLineWidth(0.5)
        ->drawLine(0, 25, 340, 25);

$page2->restoreGS();

//----------------------------------------------------------------------

if (isset($argv[2])) {
    $pdf->save($argv[2]);
} else {
    $pdf->save($argv[1], true /* update */);
}
```

Chapter 16. Zend_ProgressBar

Zend_ProgressBar

Introduction

Zend_ProgressBar is a component to create and update progressbars in different environments. It consists of a single backend, which outputs the progress through one of the multiple adapters. On every update, it takes an absolute value and optionally a status message, and then calls the adapter with some precalculated values like percentage and estimated time left.

Basic Usage of Zend_Progressbar

Zend_ProgressBar is quite easy in its usage. You simply create a new instance of Zend_Progressbar, defining a min- and a max-value, and choose an adapter to output the data. If you want to process a file, you would do something like:

```
$progressBar = new Zend_ProgressBar($adapter, 0, $fileSize);

while (!feof($fp)) {
    // Do something

    $progressBar->update($currentByteCount);
}

$progressBar->finish();
```

In the first step, an instance of Zend_ProgressBar is created, with a specific adapter, a min-value of 0 and a max-value of the total filesize. Then a file is processed and in every loop the progressbar is updated with the current byte count. At the end of the loop, the progressbar status is set to finished.

You can also call the update() method of Zend_ProgressBar without arguments, which just recalculates ETA and notifies the adapter. This is useful when there is no data update but you want the progressbar to be updated.

Persistent progress

If you want the progressbar to be persistent over multiple requests, you can give the name of a session namespace as fourth argument to the constructor. In that case, the progressbar will not notify the adapter within the constructor, but only when you call update() or finish(). Also the current value, the status text and the start time for ETA calculation will be fetched in the next request run again.

Standard adapters

Zend_ProgressBar comes with the following three adapters:

- the section called "Zend_ProgressBar_Adapter_Console"

- the section called "Zend_ProgressBar_Adapter_JsPush"

- the section called "Zend_ProgressBar_Adapter_JsPull"

Zend_ProgressBar_Adapter_Console

Zend_ProgressBar_Adapter_Console is a text-based adapter for terminals. It can automatically detect terminal widths but supports custom widths as well. You can define which elements are displayed with the progressbar and as well customize the order of them. You can also define the style of the progressbar itself.

Automatic console width recognition

shell_exec is required for this feature to work on *nix based systems. On windows, there is always a fixed terminal width of 80 character, so no recognition is required there.

You can set the adapter options either via the set* methods or give an array or a Zend_Config instance with options as first parameter to the constructor. The available options are:

- outputStream: A different output-stream, if you don't want to stream to STDOUT. Can be any other stream like php://stderr or a path to a file.

- width: Either an integer or the AUTO constant of Zend_Console_ProgressBar.

- elements: Either NULL for default or an array with at least one of the following constants of Zend_Console_ProgressBar as value:

  - ELEMENT_PERCENT: The current value in percent.

  - ELEMENT_BAR: The visual bar which display the percentage.

  - ELEMENT_ETA: The automatic calculated ETA. This element is firstly displayed after five seconds, because in this time, it is not able to calculate accurate results.

  - ELEMENT_TEXT: An optional status message about the current process.

- textWidth: Width in characters of the ELEMENT_TEXT element. Default is 20.

- charset: Charset of the ELEMENT_TEXT element. Default is utf-8.

- barLeftChar: A string which is used left-hand of the indicator in the progressbar.

- barRightChar: A string which is used right-hand of the indicator in the progressbar.

- barIndicatorChar: A string which is used for the indicator in the progressbar. This one can be empty.

Zend_ProgressBar_Adapter_JsPush

Zend_ProgressBar_Adapter_JsPush is an adapter which let's you update a progressbar in a browser via Javascript Push. This means that no second connection is required to gather the status about a running process, but that the process itself sends its status directly to the browser.

You can set the adapter options either via the set* methods or give an array or a Zend_Config instance with options as first parameter to the constructor. The available options are:

- updateMethodName: The javascript method which should be called on every update. Default value is Zend_ProgressBar_Update.

- finishMethodName: The javascript method which should be called after finish status was set. Default value is NULL, which means nothing is done.

The usage of this adapter is quite simple. First you create a progressbar in your browser, either with JavaScript or previously created with plain HTML. Then you define the update method and optionally the finish method in JavaScript, both taking a json object as single argument. Then you call a webpage with the long-running process in a hidden iframe or object tag. While the process is running, the adapter will call the update method on every update with a json object, containing the following parameters:

- current: The current absolute value

- max: The max absolute value

- `percent`: The calculated percentage

- `timeTaken`: The time how long the process ran yet

- `timeRemaining`: The expected time for the process to finish

- `text`: The optional status message, if given

Example 16.1. Basic example for the client-side stuff

This example illustrates a basic setup of HTML, CSS and JavaScript for the JsPush adapter

```
<div id="zend-progressbar-container">
    <div id="zend-progressbar-done"></div>
</div>

<iframe src="long-running-process.php" id="long-running-process">
    </iframe>
```

```
#long-running-process {
    position: absolute;
    left: -100px;
    top: -100px;

    width: 1px;
    height: 1px;
}

#zend-progressbar-container {
    width: 100px;
    height: 30px;

    border: 1px solid #000000;
    background-color: #ffffff;
}

#zend-progressbar-done {
    width: 0;
    height: 30px;

    background-color: #000000;
}
```

```
function Zend_ProgressBar_Update(data)
{
    document.getElementById('zend-progressbar-done').style.width =
        data.percent + '%';
}
```

This will create a simple container with a black border and a block which indicates the current process. You should not hide the `iframe` or `object` by `display: none;`, as some browsers like Safari 2 will not load the actual content then.

Instead of creating your custom progressbar, you may want to use one of the available JavaScript libraries like Dojo, jQuery etc. For example, there are:

- Dojo:
  http://dojotoolkit.org/book/dojo-book-0-9/part-2-dijit/user-assistance-and-feedback/progress-bar

- jQuery: http://t.wits.sg/2008/06/20/jquery-progress-bar-11/

- MooTools: http://davidwalsh.name/dw-content/progress-bar.php

- Prototype: http://livepipe.net/control/progressbar

Interval of updates

You should take care of not sending too many updates, as every update has a min-size of 1kb. This is a requirement for the Safari browser to actually render and execute the function call. Internet Explorer has a similar limitation of 256 bytes.

Zend_ProgressBar_Adapter_JsPull

Zend_ProgressBar_Adapter_JsPull is the opposite of jsPush, as it requires to pull for new updates, instead of pushing updates out to the browsers. Generally you should use the adapter with the persistence option of the Zend_ProgressBar. On notify, the adapter sends a JSON string to the browser, which looks exactly like the JSON string which is send by the jsPush adapter. The only difference is, that it contains an additional parameter, finished, which is either false when update() is called or true, when finish() is called.

You can set the adapter options either via the set* methods or give an array or a Zend_Config instance with options as first parameter to the constructor. The available options are:

- exitAfterSend: Exits the current request after the data were send to the browser. Default is true.

Chapter 17. Zend_Reflection

Introduction

`Zend_Reflection` is a drop-in extension to PHP's own Reflection API [http://php.net/reflection], providing several additional features:

- Ability to retrieve return values types.

- Ability to retrieve method and function parameter types.

- Ability to retrieve class property types.

- DocBlocks gain a Reflection class, allowing introspection of docblocks. This provides the ability to determine what annotation tags have been defined as well as to retrieve their values, and the ability to retrieve the short and long descriptions.

- Files gain a Reflection class, allowing introspection of PHP files. This provides the ability to determine what functions and classes are defined in a given file, as well as to introspect them.

- Ability to override any Reflection class with your own variant, for the entire reflection tree you create.

In general, `Zend_Reflection` works just like the standard Reflection API, but provides a few additional methods for retrieving artifacts not defined in the Reflection API.

Zend_Reflection Examples

Example 17.1. Performing reflection on a file

```
$r = new Zend_Reflection_File($filename);
printf(
    "===> The %s file\n".
    "     has %d lines\n",
    $r->getFileName(),
    $r->getEndLine()
);

$classes = $r->getClasses();
echo "    It has " . count($classes) . ":\n";
foreach ($classes as $class) {
    echo "        " . $class->getName() . "\n";
}

$functions = $r->getFunctions();
echo "    It has " . count($functions) . ":\n";
foreach ($functions as $function) {
    echo "        " . $function->getName() . "\n";
}
```

Example 17.2. Performing reflection on a class

```
$r = new Zend_Reflection_Class($class);

printf(
    "The class level docblock has the short description: %s\n".
    "The class level docblock has the long description:\n%s\n",
    $r->getDocblock()->getShortDescription(),
    $r->getDocblock()->getLongDescription(),
);

// Get the declaring file reflection
$file = $r->getDeclaringFile();
```

Example 17.3. Performing reflection on a method

```
$r = new Zend_Reflection_Method($class, $name);

printf(
"The method '%s' has a return type of %s",
    $r->getName(),
    $r->getReturn()
);

foreach ($r->getParameters() as $key => $param) {
    printf(
        "Param at position '%d' is of type '%s'\n",
        $key,
        $param->getType()
    );
}
```

Example 17.4. Performing reflection on a docblock

```
$r = new Zend_Reflection_Method($class, $name);
$docblock = $r->getDocblock();

printf(
    "The short description: %s\n".
    "The long description:\n%s\n",
    $r->getDocblock()->getShortDescription(),
    $r->getDocblock()->getLongDescription(),
);

foreach ($docblock->getTags() as $tag) {
    printf(
        "Annotation tag '%s' has the description '%s'\n",
        $tag->getName(),
        $tag->getDescription()
    );
}
```

Zend_Reflection Reference

The various classes in `Zend_Reflection` mimic the API of PHP's Reflection API [http://php.net/reflection] - with one important difference. PHP's Reflection API does not provide introspection into docblock annotation tags, nor into parameter variable types or return types.

`Zend_Reflection` analyzes method docblock annotations to determine parameter variable types and the return type. Specifically, the `@param` and `@return` annotations are used. However, you can also check for any other annotation tags, as well as the standard "short" and "long" descriptions.

Each reflection object in `Zend_Reflection` overrides the `getDocblock()` method to return an instance of `Zend_Reflection_Docblock`. This class provides introspection into the docblocks and annotation tags.

`Zend_Reflection_File` is a new reflection class that allows introspection of PHP files. With it, you can retrieve the classes, functions, and global PHP code contained in the file.

Finally, the various methods that return other reflection objects allow a second parameter, the name of the reflection class to use for the returned reflection object.

Zend_Reflection_Docblock

`Zend_Reflection_Docblock` is the heart of `Zend_Reflection`'s value-add over PHP's Reflection API. It provides the following methods:

- `getContents()`: returns the full contents of the docblock.

- `getStartLine()`: returns the starting position of the docblock within the defining file.

- `getEndLine()`: get last line of docblock within the defining file.

- `getShortDescription()`: get the short, one-line description (usually the first line of the docblock).

- `getLongDescription()`: get the long description from the docblock.

- `hasTag($name)`: determine if the docblock has the given annotation tag.

- `getTag($name)`: Retrieve the given annotation tag reflection object, or a boolean `false` if it's not present.

- `getTags($filter)`: Retrieve all tags, or all tags matching the given `$filter` string. The tags returned will be an array of `Zend_Reflection_Docblock_Tag` objects.

Zend_Reflection_Docblock_Tag

`Zend_Reflection_Docblock_Tag` provides reflection for individual annotation tags. Most tags consist of only a name and a description. In the case of some special tags, the class provides a factory method for retrieving an instance of the appropriate class.

The following methods are defined for `Zend_Reflection_Docblock_Tag`:

- `factory($tagDocblockLine)`: instantiate the appropriate tag reflection class and return it.

- `getName()`: return the annotation tag name.

- `getDescription()`: return the annotation description.

Zend_Reflection_Docblock_Tag_Param

`Zend_Reflection_Docblock_Tag_Param` is a specialized version of `Zend_Reflection_Docblock_Tag`. The `@param` annotation tag description consists of the parameter type, variable name, and variable description. It adds the following methods to `Zend_Reflection_Docblock_Tag`:

* `getType()`: return the parameter variable type.

* `getVariableName()`: return the parameter variable name.

Zend_Reflection_Docblock_Tag_Return

Like `Zend_Reflection_Docblock_Tag_Param`, `Zend_Reflection_Docblock_Tag_Return` is a specialized version of `Zend_Reflection_Docblock_Tag`. The `@return` annotation tag description consists of the return type and variable description. It adds the following method to `Zend_Reflection_Docblock_Tag`:

* `getType()`: return the return type.

Zend_Reflection_File

`Zend_Reflection_File` provides introspection into PHP files. With it, you can introspect the classes, functions, and bare PHP code defined in a file. It defines the following methods:

* `getFileName()`: retrieve the filename of the file being reflected.

* `getStartLine()`: retrieve the starting line of the file (always "1").

* `getEndLine()` retrieve the last line / number of lines in the file.

* `getDocComment($reflectionClass = 'Zend_Reflection_Docblock')`: retrive the file-level docblock reflection object.

* `getClasses($reflectionClass = 'Zend_Reflection_Class')`: retrieve an array of reflection objects, one for each class defined in the file.

* `getFunctions($reflectionClass = 'Zend_Reflection_Function')`: retrieve an array of reflection objects, one for each function defined in the file.

* `getClass($name = null, $reflectionClass = 'Zend_Reflection_Class')`: retrieve the reflection object for a single class.

* `getContents()`: retrieve the full contents of the file.

Zend_Reflection_Class

`Zend_Reflection_Class` extends `ReflectionClass`, and follows its API. It adds one additional method, `getDeclaringFile()`, which may be used to retrieve the `Zend_Reflection_File` reflection object for the defining file.

Additionally, the following methods add an additional argument for specifying the reflection class to use when fetching a reflection object:

* `getDeclaringFile($reflectionClass = 'Zend_Reflection_File')`

* `getDocblock($reflectionClass = 'Zend_Reflection_Docblock')`

* `getInterfaces($reflectionClass = 'Zend_Reflection_Class')`

- `getMethod($reflectionClass = 'Zend_Reflection_Method')`

- `getMethods($filter = -1, $reflectionClass = 'Zend_Reflection_Method')`

- `getParentClass($reflectionClass = 'Zend_Reflection_Class')`

- `getProperty($name, $reflectionClass = 'Zend_Reflection_Property')`

- `getProperties($filter = -1, $reflectionClass = 'Zend_Reflection_Property')`

Zend_Reflection_Extension

`Zend_Reflection_Extension` extends `ReflectionExtension`, and follows its API. It overrides the following methods to add an additional argument for specifying the reflection class to use when fetching a reflection object:

- `getFunctions($reflectionClass = 'Zend_Reflection_Function')`: retrieve an array of reflection objects representing the functions defined by the extension.

- `getClasses($reflectionClass = 'Zend_Reflection_Class')`: retrieve an array of reflection objects representing the classes defined by the extension.

Zend_Reflection_Function

`Zend_Reflection_Function` adds a method for retrieving the function return type, as well as overrides several methods to allow specifying the reflection class to use for returned reflection objects.

- `getDocblock($reflectionClass = 'Zend_Reflection_Docblock')`: retrieve the function docblock reflection object.

- `getParameters($reflectionClass = 'Zend_Reflection_Parameter')`: retrieve an array of all function parameter reflection objects.

- `getReturn()`: retrieve the return type reflection object.

Zend_Reflection_Method

`Zend_Reflection_Method` mirrors `Zend_Reflection_Function`, and only overrides one additional method:

- `getParentClass($reflectionClass = 'Zend_Reflection_Class')`: retrieve the parent class reflection object.

Zend_Reflection_Parameter

`Zend_Reflection_Parameter` adds a method for retrieving the parameter type, as well as overrides methods to allow specifying the reflection class to use on returned reflection objects.

- `getDeclaringClass($reflectionClass = 'Zend_Reflection_Class')`: get the declaring class of the parameter as a reflection object (if available).

- `getClass($reflectionClass = 'Zend_Reflection_Class')`: get the class of the parameter as a reflection object (if available).

- `getDeclaringFunction($reflectionClass = 'Zend_Reflection_Function')`: get the function of the parameter as a reflection object (if available).

- `getType()`: get the parameter type.

Zend_Reflection_Property

`Zend_Reflection_Property` overrides a single method in order to allow specifying the returned reflection object class:

- `getDeclaringClass($reflectionClass = 'Zend_Reflection_Class')`: retrieve the declaring class of the property as a reflection object.

Chapter 18. Zend_Registry

Using the Registry

A registry is a container for storing objects and values in the application space. By storing the value in a registry, the same object is always available throughout your application. This mechanism is an alternative to using global storage.

The typical method to use registries with Zend Framework is through static methods in the Zend_Registry class. Alternatively, the registry can be used as an array object, so you can access elements stored within it with a convenient array-like interface.

Setting Values in the Registry

Use the static method set() to store an entry in the registry, .

Example 18.1. Example of set() Method Usage

```
Zend_Registry::set('index', $value);
```

The value returned can be an object, an array, or a scalar. You can change the value stored in a specific entry of the registry by calling the set() method to set the entry to a new value.

The index can be a scalar (null, string, or number), like an ordinary array.

Getting Values from the Registry

To retrieve an entry from the registry, use the static get() method.

Example 18.2. Example of get() Method Usage

```
$value = Zend_Registry::get('index');
```

The getInstance() method returns the singleton registry object. This registry object is iterable, making all values stored in the registry easily accessible.

Example 18.3. Example of Iterating over the Registry

```
$registry = Zend_Registry::getInstance();

foreach ($registry as $index => $value) {
    echo "Registry index $index contains:\n";
    var_dump($value);
}
```

Constructing a Registry Object

In addition to accessing the static registry via static methods, you can create an instance directly and use it as an object.

The registry instance you access through the static methods is simply one such instance. It is for convenience that it is stored statically, so that it is accessible from anywhere in an application.

Use the traditional new operator to instantiate Zend_Registry. Instantiating Zend_Registry using its constructor also makes initializing the entries in the registry simple by taking an associative array as an argument.

Example 18.4. Example of Constructing a Registry

```
$registry = new Zend_Registry(array('index' => $value));
```

Once such a Zend_Registry object is instantiated, you can use it by calling any array object method or by setting it as the singleton instance for Zend_Registry with the static method setInstance().

Example 18.5. Example of Initializing the Singleton Registry

```
$registry = new Zend_Registry(array('index' => $value));

Zend_Registry::setInstance($registry);
```

The setInstance() method throws a Zend_Exception if the static registry has already been initialized.

Accessing the Registry as an Array

If you have several values to get or set, you may find it convenient to access the registry with array notation.

Example 18.6. Example of Array Access

```
$registry = Zend_Registry::getInstance();

$registry['index'] = $value;

var_dump( $registry['index'] );
```

Accessing the Registry as an Object

You may also find it convenient to access the registry in an object-oriented fashion by using index names as object properties. You must specifically construct the registry object using the ArrayObject::ARRAY_AS_PROPS option and initialize the static instance to enable this functionality.

Note

You must set the `ArrayObject::ARRAY_AS_PROPS` option *before* the static registry has been accessed for the first time.

Known Issues with the ArrayObject::ARRAY_AS_PROPS Option

Some versions of PHP have proven very buggy when using the registry with the `ArrayObject::ARRAY_AS_PROPS` option.

Example 18.7. Example of Object Access

```
// in your application bootstrap:
$registry = new Zend_Registry(array(), ArrayObject::ARRAY_AS_PROPS)
Zend_Registry::setInstance($registry);
$registry->tree = 'apple';

  .
  .
  .

// in a different function, elsewhere in your application:
$registry = Zend_Registry::getInstance();

echo $registry->tree; // echo's "apple"

$registry->index = $value;

var_dump($registry->index);
```

Querying if an Index Exists

To find out if a particular index in the registry has been set, use the static method `isRegistered()`.

Example 18.8. Example of isRegistered() Method Usage

```
if (Zend_Registry::isRegistered($index)) {
    $value = Zend_Registry::get($index);
}
```

To find out if a particular index in a registry array or object has a value, use the `isset()` function as you would with an ordinary array.

Example 18.9. Example of isset() Method Usage

```
$registry = Zend_Registry::getInstance();

// using array access syntax
```

```
if (isset($registry['index'])) {
    var_dump( $registry['index'] );
}

// using object access syntax
if (isset($registry->index)) {
    var_dump( $registry->index );
}
```

Extending the Registry

The static registry is an instance of the class Zend_Registry. If you want to add functionality to the registry, you should create a class that extends Zend_Registry and specify this class to instantiate for the singleton in the static registry. Use the static method setClassName() to specify the class.

Note

The class must be a subclass of Zend_Registry.

Example 18.10. Example of Specifying the Singleton Registry's Class Name

```
Zend_Registry::setClassName('My_Registry');

Zend_Registry::set('index', $value);
```

The registry throws a Zend_Exception if you attempt to set the classname after the registry has been accessed for the first time. It is therefore recommended that you specify the class name for your static registry in your application bootstrap.

Unsetting the Static Registry

Although it is not normally necessary, you can unset the singleton instance of the registry, if desired. Use the static method _unsetInstance() to do so.

Data Loss Risk

When you use _unsetInstance(), all data in the static registry are discarded and cannot be recovered.

You might use this method, for example, if you want to use setInstance() or setClassName() after the singleton registry object has been initialized. Unsetting the singleton instance allows you to use these methods even after the singleton registry object has been set. Using Zend_Registry in this manner is not recommended for typical applications and environments.

Example 18.11. Example of _unsetInstance() Method Usage

```
Zend_Registry::set('index', $value);

Zend_Registry::_unsetInstance();

// change the class
Zend_Registry::setClassName('My_Registry');

Zend_Registry::set('index', $value);
```

Chapter 19. Zend_Rest

Introduction

REST Web Services use service-specific XML formats. These ad-hoc standards mean that the manner for accessing a REST web service is different for each service. REST web services typically use URL parameters (GET data) or path information for requesting data and POST data for sending data.

Zend Framework provides both Client and Server capabilities, which, when used together allow for a much more "local" interface experience via virtual object property access. The Server component features automatic exposition of functions and classes using a meaningful and simple XML format. When accessing these services using the Client, it is possible to easily retrieve the return data from the remote call. Should you wish to use the client with a non-Zend_Rest_Server based service, it will still provide easier data access.

Zend_Rest_Client

Introduction

Using the `Zend_Rest_Client` is very similar to using `SoapClient` objects (SOAP web service extension [http://www.php.net/soap]). You can simply call the REST service procedures as `Zend_Rest_Client` methods. Specify the service's full address in the `Zend_Rest_Client` constructor.

Example 19.1. A basic REST request

```
/**
 * Connect to framework.zend.com server and retrieve a greeting
 */
$client = new Zend_Rest_Client('http://framework.zend.com/rest');

echo $client->sayHello('Davey', 'Day')->get(); // "Hello Davey, Good Day"
```

Differences in calling

`Zend_Rest_Client` attempts to make remote methods look as much like native methods as possible, the only difference being that you must follow the method call with one of either `get()`, `post()`, `put()` or `delete()`. This call may be made via method chaining or in separate method calls:

```
$client->sayHello('Davey', 'Day');
echo $client->get();
```

Responses

All requests made using `Zend_Rest_Client` return a `Zend_Rest_Client_Response` object. This object has many properties that make it easier to access the results.

When the service is based on `Zend_Rest_Server`, `Zend_Rest_Client` can make several assumptions about the response, including response status (success or failure) and return type.

Example 19.2. Response Status

```
$result = $client->sayHello('Davey', 'Day')->get();

if ($result->isSuccess()) {
    echo $result; // "Hello Davey, Good Day"
}
```

In the example above, you can see that we use the request result as an object, to call isSuccess(), and then because of __toString(), we can simply echo the object to get the result. Zend_Rest_Client_Response will allow you to echo any scalar value. For complex types, you can use either array or object notation.

If however, you wish to query a service not using Zend_Rest_Server the Zend_Rest_Client_Response object will behave more like a SimpleXMLElement. However, to make things easier, it will automatically query the XML using XPath if the property is not a direct descendant of the document root element. Additionally, if you access a property as a method, you will receive the PHP value for the object, or an array of PHP value results.

Example 19.3. Using Technorati's Rest Service

```
$technorati = new Zend_Rest_Client('http://api.technorati.com/bloginfo');
$technorati->key($key);
$technorati->url('http://pixelated-dreams.com');
$result = $technorati->get();
echo $result->firstname() .' '. $result->lastname();
```

Example 19.4. Example Technorati Response

```
<?xml version="1.0" encoding="utf-8"?>
<!-- generator="Technorati API version 1.0 /bloginfo" -->
<!DOCTYPE tapi PUBLIC "-//Technorati, Inc.//DTD TAPI 0.02//EN"
                    "http://api.technorati.com/dtd/tapi-002.xml">
<tapi version="1.0">
    <document>
        <result>
            <url>http://pixelated-dreams.com</url>
            <weblog>
                <name>Pixelated Dreams</name>
                <url>http://pixelated-dreams.com</url>
                <author>
                    <username>DShafik</username>
                    <firstname>Davey</firstname>
                    <lastname>Shafik</lastname>
                </author>
                <rssurl>
                    http://pixelated-dreams.com/feeds/index.rss2
                </rssurl>
                <atomurl>
                    http://pixelated-dreams.com/feeds/atom.xml
                </atomurl>
```

```
            <inboundblogs>44</inboundblogs>
            <inboundlinks>218</inboundlinks>
            <lastupdate>2006-04-26 04:36:36 GMT</lastupdate>
            <rank>60635</rank>
        </weblog>
        <inboundblogs>44</inboundblogs>
        <inboundlinks>218</inboundlinks>
    </result>
  </document>
</tapi>
```

Here we are accessing the `firstname` and `lastname` properties. Even though these are not top-level elements, they are automatically returned when accessed by name.

Multiple items

If multiple items are found when accessing a value by name, an array of SimpleXMLElements will be returned; accessing via method notation will return an array of PHP values.

Request Arguments

Unless you are making a request to a Zend_Rest_Server based service, chances are you will need to send multiple arguments with your request. This is done by calling a method with the name of the argument, passing in the value as the first (and only) argument. Each of these method calls returns the object itself, allowing for chaining, or "fluent" usage. The first call, or the first argument if you pass in more than one argument, is always assumed to be the method when calling a Zend_Rest_Server service.

Example 19.5. Setting Request Arguments

```
$client = new Zend_Rest_Client('http://example.org/rest');

$client->arg('value1');
$client->arg2('value2');
$client->get();

// or

$client->arg('value1')->arg2('value2')->get();
```

Both of the methods in the example above, will result in the following get args: `?method=arg&arg1=value1&arg=value1&arg2=value2`

You will notice that the first call of `$client->arg('value1');` resulted in both `method=arg&arg1=value1` and `arg=value1`; this is so that `Zend_Rest_Server` can understand the request properly, rather than requiring pre-existing knowledge of the service.

Strictness of Zend_Rest_Client

Any REST service that is strict about the arguments it receives will likely fail using `Zend_Rest_Client`, because of the behavior described above. This is not a common practice and should not cause problems.

Zend_Rest_Server

Introduction

Zend_Rest_Server is intended as a fully-featured REST server.

REST Server Usage

Example 19.6. Basic Zend_Rest_Server Usage - Classes

```
$server = new Zend_Rest_Server();
$server->setClass('My_Service_Class');
$server->handle();
```

Example 19.7. Basic Zend_Rest_Server Usage - Functions

```
/**
 * Say Hello
 *
 * @param string $who
 * @param string $when
 * @return string
 */
function sayHello($who, $when)
{
    return "Hello $who, Good $when";
}

$server = new Zend_Rest_Server();
$server->addFunction('sayHello');
$server->handle();
```

Calling a Zend_Rest_Server Service

To call a Zend_Rest_Server service, you must supply a GET/POST method argument with a value that is the method you wish to call. You can then follow that up with any number of arguments using either the name of the argument (i.e. "who") or using arg following by the numeric position of the argument (i.e. "arg1").

Numeric index

Numeric arguments use a 1-based index.

To call sayHello from the example above, you can use either:

?method=sayHello&who=Davey&when=Day

or:

?method=sayHello&arg1=Davey&arg2=Day

Sending A Custom Status

When returning values, to return a custom status, you may return an array with a `status` key.

Example 19.8. Returning Custom Status

```
/**
 * Say Hello
 *
 * @param string $who
 * @param string $when
 * @return array
 */
function sayHello($who, $when)
{
    return array('msg' => "An Error Occurred", 'status' => false);
}

$server = new Zend_Rest_Server();
$server->addFunction('sayHello');
$server->handle();
```

Returning Custom XML Responses

If you wish to return custom XML, simply return a DOMDocument, DOMElement or SimpleXMLElement object.

Example 19.9. Return Custom XML

```
/**
 * Say Hello
 *
 * @param string $who
 * @param string $when
 * @return SimpleXMLElement
 */
function sayHello($who, $when)
{
    $xml ='<?xml version="1.0" encoding="ISO-8859-1"?>
<mysite>
    <value>Hey $who! Hope you\'re having a good $when</value>
    <code>200</code>
</mysite>';

    $xml = simplexml_load_string($xml);
    return $xml;
}

$server = new Zend_Rest_Server();
$server->addFunction('sayHello');

$server->handle();
```

The response from the service will be returned without modification to the client.

Chapter 20. Zend_Search_Lucene

Overview

Introduction

Zend_Search_Lucene is a general purpose text search engine written entirely in PHP 5. Since it stores its index on the filesystem and does not require a database server, it can add search capabilities to almost any PHP-driven website. Zend_Search_Lucene supports the following features:

- Ranked searching - best results returned first

- Many powerful query types: phrase queries, boolean queries, wildcard queries, proximity queries, range queries and many others.

- Search by specific field (e.g., title, author, contents)
Zend_Search_Lucene was derived from the Apache Lucene project. The currently (starting from ZF 1.6) supported Lucene index format versions are 1.4 - 2.3. For more information on Lucene, visit http://lucene.apache.org/java/docs/.

> Previous Zend_Search_Lucene implementations support the Lucene 1.4 (1.9) - 2.1 index formats.

> Starting from ZF 1.5 any index created using pre-2.1 index format is automatically upgraded to Lucene 2.1 format after the Zend_Search_Lucene update and will not be compatible with Zend_Search_Lucene implementations included into ZF 1.0.x.

Document and Field Objects

Zend_Search_Lucene operates with documents as atomic objects for indexing. A document is divided into named fields, and fields have content that can be searched.

A document is represented by the Zend_Search_Lucene_Document class, and this objects of this class contain instances of Zend_Search_Lucene_Field that represent the fields on the document.

It is important to note that any information can be added to the index. Application-specific information or metadata can be stored in the document fields, and later retrieved with the document during search.

It is the responsibility of your application to control the indexer. This means that data can be indexed from any source that is accessible by your application. For example, this could be the filesystem, a database, an HTML form, etc.

Zend_Search_Lucene_Field class provides several static methods to create fields with different characteristics:

```
$doc = new Zend_Search_Lucene_Document();

// Field is not tokenized, but is indexed and stored within the index.
// Stored fields can be retrived from the index.
$doc->addField(Zend_Search_Lucene_Field::Keyword('doctype',
                                                  'autogenerated'));

// Field is not tokenized nor indexed, but is stored in the index.
$doc->addField(Zend_Search_Lucene_Field::UnIndexed('created',
                                                   time()));

// Binary String valued Field that is not tokenized nor indexed,
```

```
// but is stored in the index.
$doc->addField(Zend_Search_Lucene_Field::Binary('icon',
                                                 $iconData));

// Field is tokenized and indexed, and is stored in the index.
$doc->addField(Zend_Search_Lucene_Field::Text('annotation',
                                               'Document annotation text'));

// Field is tokenized and indexed, but is not stored in the index.
$doc->addField(Zend_Search_Lucene_Field::UnStored('contents',
                                                  'My document content'));
```

Each of these methods (excluding the Zend_Search_Lucene_Field::Binary() method) has an optional $encoding parameter for specifying input data encoding.

Encoding may differ for different documents as well as for different fields within one document:

```
$doc = new Zend_Search_Lucene_Document();
$doc->addField(Zend_Search_Lucene_Field::Text('title',
                                              $title,
                                              'iso-8859-1'));
$doc->addField(Zend_Search_Lucene_Field::UnStored('contents',
                                                  $contents,
                                                  'utf-8'));
```

If encoding parameter is omitted, then the current locale is used at processing time. For example:

```
setlocale(LC_ALL, 'de_DE.iso-8859-1');
...
$doc->addField(Zend_Search_Lucene_Field::UnStored('contents', $contents));
```

Fields are always stored and returned from the index in UTF-8 encoding. Any required conversion to UTF-8 happens automatically.

Text analyzers (see below) may also convert text to some other encodings. Actually, the default analyzer converts text to 'ASCII//TRANSLIT' encoding. Be careful, however; this translation may depend on current locale.

Fields' names are defined at your discretion in the addField() method.

Java Lucene uses the 'contents' field as a default field to search. Zend_Search_Lucene searches through all fields by default, but the behavior is configurable. See the "Default search field" chapter for details.

Understanding Field Types

- Keyword fields are stored and indexed, meaning that they can be searched as well as displayed in search results. They are not split up into separate words by tokenization. Enumerated database fields usually translate well to Keyword fields in Zend_Search_Lucene.

- UnIndexed fields are not searchable, but they are returned with search hits. Database timestamps, primary keys, file system paths, and other external identifiers are good candidates for UnIndexed fields.

- Binary fields are not tokenized or indexed, but are stored for retrieval with search hits. They can be used to store any data encoded as a binary string, such as an image icon.

- Text fields are stored, indexed, and tokenized. Text fields are appropriate for storing information like subjects and titles that need to be searchable as well as returned with search results.

- UnStored fields are tokenized and indexed, but not stored in the index. Large amounts of text are best indexed using this type of field. Storing data creates a larger index on disk, so if you need to search but not redisplay the data, use an UnStored field. UnStored fields are practical when using a Zend_Search_Lucene index in combination with a relational database. You can index large data fields with UnStored fields for searching, and retrieve them from your relational database by using a separate field as an identifier.

Table 20.1. Zend_Search_Lucene_Field Types

Field Type	Stored	Indexed	Tokenized	Binary
Keyword	Yes	Yes	No	No
UnIndexed	Yes	No	No	No
Binary	Yes	No	No	Yes
Text	Yes	Yes	Yes	No
UnStored	No	Yes	Yes	No

HTML documents

Zend_Search_Lucene offers a HTML parsing feature. Documents can be created directly from a HTML file or string:

```
$doc = Zend_Search_Lucene_Document_Html::loadHTMLFile($filename);
$index->addDocument($doc);
...
$doc = Zend_Search_Lucene_Document_Html::loadHTML($htmlString);
$index->addDocument($doc);
```

Zend_Search_Lucene_Document_Html class uses the DOMDocument::loadHTML() and DOMDocument::loadHTMLFile() methods to parse the source HTML, so it doesn't need HTML to be well formed or to be XHTML. On the other hand, it's sensitive to the encoding specified by the "meta http-equiv" header tag.

Zend_Search_Lucene_Document_Html class recognizes document title, body and document header meta tags.

The 'title' field is actually the /html/head/title value. It's stored within the index, tokenized and available for search.

The 'body' field is the actual body content of the HTML file or string. It doesn't include scripts, comments or attributes.

The loadHTML() and loadHTMLFile() methods of Zend_Search_Lucene_Document_Html class also have second optional argument. If it's set to true, then body content is also stored within index and can be retrieved from the index. By default, the body is tokenized and indexed, but not stored.

The third parameter of loadHTML() and loadHTMLFile() methods optionally specifies source HTML document encoding. It's used if encoding is not specified using Content-type HTTP-EQUIV meta tag.

Other document header meta tags produce additional document fields. The field 'name' is taken from 'name' attribute, and the 'content' attribute populates the field 'value'. Both are tokenized, indexed and stored, so documents may be searched by their meta tags (for example, by keywords).

Parsed documents may be augmented by the programmer with any other field:

```
$doc = Zend_Search_Lucene_Document_Html::loadHTML($htmlString);
$doc->addField(Zend_Search_Lucene_Field::UnIndexed('created',
                                                   time()));
$doc->addField(Zend_Search_Lucene_Field::UnIndexed('updated',
                                                   time()));
$doc->addField(Zend_Search_Lucene_Field::Text('annotation',
                                       'Document annotation text'));
$index->addDocument($doc);
```

Document links are not included in the generated document, but may be retrieved with the Zend_Search_Lucene_Document_Html::getLinks() and Zend_Search_Lucene_Document_Html::getHeaderLinks() methods:

```
$doc = Zend_Search_Lucene_Document_Html::loadHTML($htmlString);
$linksArray = $doc->getLinks();
$headerLinksArray = $doc->getHeaderLinks();
```

Starting from ZF 1.6 it's also possible to exclude links with rel attribute set to 'nofollow'. Use Zend_Search_Lucene_Document_Html::setExcludeNoFollowLinks($true) to turn on this option.

Zend_Search_Lucene_Document_Html::getExcludeNoFollowLinks() method returns current state of "Exclude nofollow links" flag.

Word 2007 documents

Zend_Search_Lucene offers a Word 2007 parsing feature. Documents can be created directly from a Word 2007 file:

```
$doc = Zend_Search_Lucene_Document_Docx::loadDocxFile($filename);
$index->addDocument($doc);
```

Zend_Search_Lucene_Document_Docx class uses the ZipArchive class and simplexml methods to parse the source document. If the ZipArchive class (from module php_zip) is not available, the Zend_Search_Lucene_Document_Docx will also not be available for use with Zend Framework.

Zend_Search_Lucene_Document_Docx class recognizes document meta data and document text. Meta data consists, depending on document contents, of filename, title, subject, creator, keywords, description, lastModifiedBy, revision, modified, created.

The 'filename' field is the actual Word 2007 file name.

The 'title' field is the actual document title.

The 'subject' field is the actual document subject.

The 'creator' field is the actual document creator.

The 'keywords' field contains the actual document keywords.

The 'description' field is the actual document description.

The 'lastModifiedBy' field is the username who has last modified the actual document.

The 'revision' field is the actual document revision number.

The 'modified' field is the actual document last modified date / time.

The 'created' field is the actual document creation date / time.

The 'body' field is the actual body content of the Word 2007 document. It only includes normal text, comments and revisions are not included.

The loadDocxFile() methods of Zend_Search_Lucene_Document_Docx class also have second optional argument. If it's set to true, then body content is also stored within index and can be retrieved from the index. By default, the body is tokenized and indexed, but not stored.

Parsed documents may be augmented by the programmer with any other field:

```
$doc = Zend_Search_Lucene_Document_Docx::loadDocxFile($filename);
$doc->addField(Zend_Search_Lucene_Field::UnIndexed(
    'indexTime',
    time())
);
$doc->addField(Zend_Search_Lucene_Field::Text(
    'annotation',
    'Document annotation text')
);
$index->addDocument($doc);
```

Powerpoint 2007 documents

Zend_Search_Lucene offers a Powerpoint 2007 parsing feature. Documents can be created directly from a Powerpoint 2007 file:

```
$doc = Zend_Search_Lucene_Document_Pptx::loadPptxFile($filename);
$index->addDocument($doc);
```

Zend_Search_Lucene_Document_Pptx class uses the ZipArchive class and simplexml methods to parse the source document. If the ZipArchive class (from module php_zip) is not available, the Zend_Search_Lucene_Document_Pptx will also not be available for use with Zend Framework.

Zend_Search_Lucene_Document_Pptx class recognizes document meta data and document text. Meta data consists, depending on document contents, of filename, title, subject, creator, keywords, description, lastModifiedBy, revision, modified, created.

The 'filename' field is the actual Powerpoint 2007 file name.

The 'title' field is the actual document title.

The 'subject' field is the actual document subject.

The 'creator' field is the actual document creator.

The 'keywords' field contains the actual document keywords.

The 'description' field is the actual document description.

The 'lastModifiedBy' field is the username who has last modified the actual document.

The 'revision' field is the actual document revision number.

The 'modified' field is the actual document last modified date / time.

The 'created' field is the actual document creation date / time.

The 'body' field is the actual content of all slides and slide notes in the Powerpoint 2007 document.

The loadPptxFile() methods of Zend_Search_Lucene_Document_Pptx class also have second optional argument. If it's set to true, then body content is also stored within index and can be retrieved from the index. By default, the body is tokenized and indexed, but not stored.

Parsed documents may be augmented by the programmer with any other field:

```
$doc = Zend_Search_Lucene_Document_Pptx::loadPptxFile($filename);
$doc->addField(Zend_Search_Lucene_Field::UnIndexed(
    'indexTime',
    time()));
$doc->addField(Zend_Search_Lucene_Field::Text(
    'annotation',
    'Document annotation text'));
$index->addDocument($doc);
```

Excel 2007 documents

Zend_Search_Lucene offers a Excel 2007 parsing feature. Documents can be created directly from a Excel 2007 file:

```
$doc = Zend_Search_Lucene_Document_Xlsx::loadXlsxFile($filename);
$index->addDocument($doc);
```

Zend_Search_Lucene_Document_Xlsx class uses the ZipArchive class and simplexml methods to parse the source document. If the ZipArchive class (from module php_zip) is not available, the Zend_Search_Lucene_Document_Xlsx will also not be available for use with Zend Framework.

Zend_Search_Lucene_Document_Xlsx class recognizes document meta data and document text. Meta data consists, depending on document contents, of filename, title, subject, creator, keywords, description, lastModifiedBy, revision, modified, created.

The 'filename' field is the actual Excel 2007 file name.

The 'title' field is the actual document title.

The 'subject' field is the actual document subject.

The 'creator' field is the actual document creator.

The 'keywords' field contains the actual document keywords.

The 'description' field is the actual document description.

The 'lastModifiedBy' field is the username who has last modified the actual document.

The 'revision' field is the actual document revision number.

The 'modified' field is the actual document last modified date / time.

The 'created' field is the actual document creation date / time.

The 'body' field is the actual content of all cells in all worksheets of the Excel 2007 document.

The loadXlsxFile() methods of Zend_Search_Lucene_Document_Xlsx class also have second optional argument. If it's set to true, then body content is also stored within index and can be retrieved from the index. By default, the body is tokenized and indexed, but not stored.

Parsed documents may be augmented by the programmer with any other field:

```
$doc = Zend_Search_Lucene_Document_Xlsx::loadXlsxFile($filename);
$doc->addField(Zend_Search_Lucene_Field::UnIndexed(
    'indexTime',
    time()));
$doc->addField(Zend_Search_Lucene_Field::Text(
    'annotation',
```

```
                  'Document annotation text'));
$index->addDocument($doc);
```

Building Indexes

Creating a New Index

Index creation and updating capabilities are implemented within the Zend_Search_Lucene component, as well as the Java Lucene project. You can use either of these options to create indexes that Zend_Search_Lucene can search.

The PHP code listing below provides an example of how to index a file using Zend_Search_Lucene indexing API:

```
// Create index
$index = Zend_Search_Lucene::create('/data/my-index');

$doc = new Zend_Search_Lucene_Document();

// Store document URL to identify it in the search results
$doc->addField(Zend_Search_Lucene_Field::Text('url', $docUrl));

// Index document contents
$doc->addField(Zend_Search_Lucene_Field::UnStored('contents', $docContent));

// Add document to the index
$index->addDocument($doc);
```

Newly added documents are immediately searchable in the index.

Updating Index

The same procedure is used to update an existing index. The only difference is that the open() method is called instead of the create() method:

```
// Open existing index
$index = Zend_Search_Lucene::open('/data/my-index');

$doc = new Zend_Search_Lucene_Document();
// Store document URL to identify it in search result.
$doc->addField(Zend_Search_Lucene_Field::Text('url', $docUrl));
// Index document content
$doc->addField(Zend_Search_Lucene_Field::UnStored('contents',
                                                  $docContent));

// Add document to the index.
$index->addDocument($doc);
```

Updating Documents

The Lucene index file format doesn't support document updating. Documents should be removed and re-added to the index to effectively update them.

Zend_Search_Lucene::delete() method operates with an internal index document id. It can be retrieved from a query hit by 'id' property:

```
$removePath = ...;
$hits = $index->find('path:' . $removePath);
foreach ($hits as $hit) {
    $index->delete($hit->id);
}
```

Retrieving Index Size

There are two methods to retrieve the size of an index in Zend_Search_Lucene.

Zend_Search_Lucene::maxDoc() returns one greater than the largest possible document number. It's actually the overall number of the documents in the index including deleted documents, so it has a synonym: Zend_Search_Lucene::count().

Zend_Search_Lucene::numDocs() returns the total number of non-deleted documents.

```
$indexSize = $index->count();
$documents = $index->numDocs();
```

Zend_Search_Lucene::isDeleted($id) method may be used to check if a document is deleted.

```
for ($count = 0; $count < $index->maxDoc(); $count++) {
    if ($index->isDeleted($count)) {
        echo "Document #$id is deleted.\n";
    }
}
```

Index optimization removes deleted documents and squeezes documents' IDs in to a smaller range. A document's internal id may therefore change during index optimization.

Index optimization

A Lucene index consists of many segments. Each segment is a completely independent set of data.

Lucene index segment files can't be updated by design. A segment update needs full segment reorganization. See Lucene index file formats for details (http://lucene.apache.org/java/docs/fileformats.html)[*] . New documents are added to the index by creating new segment.

Increasing number of segments reduces quality of the index, but index optimization restores it. Optimization essentially merges several segments into a new one. This process also doesn't update segments. It generates one new large segment and updates segment list ('segments' file).

Full index optimization can be trigger by calling the Zend_Search_Lucene::optimize() method. It merges all index segments into one new segment:

```
// Open existing index
$index = Zend_Search_Lucene::open('/data/my-index');

// Optimize index.
$index->optimize();
```

Automatic index optimization is performed to keep indexes in a consistent state.

Automatic optimization is an iterative process managed by several index options. It merges very small segments into larger ones, then merges these larger segments into even larger segments and so on.

---

[*]The currently supported Lucene index file format is version 2.3 (starting from ZF 1.6).

MaxBufferedDocs auto-optimization option

MaxBufferedDocs is a minimal number of documents required before the buffered in-memory documents are written into a new segment.

MaxBufferedDocs can be retrieved or set by `$index->getMaxBufferedDocs()` or `$index->setMaxBufferedDocs($maxBufferedDocs)` calls.

Default value is 10.

MaxMergeDocs auto-optimization option

MaxMergeDocs is a largest number of documents ever merged by addDocument(). Small values (e.g., less than 10.000) are best for interactive indexing, as this limits the length of pauses while indexing to a few seconds. Larger values are best for batched indexing and speedier searches.

MaxMergeDocs can be retrieved or set by `$index->getMaxMergeDocs()` or `$index->setMaxMergeDocs($maxMergeDocs)` calls.

Default value is PHP_INT_MAX.

MergeFactor auto-optimization option

MergeFactor determines how often segment indices are merged by addDocument(). With smaller values, less RAM is used while indexing, and searches on unoptimized indices are faster, but indexing speed is slower. With larger values, more RAM is used during indexing, and while searches on unoptimized indices are slower, indexing is faster. Thus larger values (> 10) are best for batch index creation, and smaller values (< 10) for indices that are interactively maintained.

MergeFactor is a good estimation for average number of segments merged by one auto-optimization pass. Too large values produce large number of segments while they are not merged into new one. It may be a cause of "failed to open stream: Too many open files" error message. This limitation is system dependent.

MergeFactor can be retrieved or set by `$index->getMergeFactor()` or `$index->setMergeFactor($mergeFactor)` calls.

Default value is 10.

Lucene Java and Luke (Lucene Index Toolbox - http://www.getopt.org/luke/) can also be used to optimize an index. Latest Luke release (v0.8) is based on Lucene v2.3 and compatible with current implementation of `Zend_Search_Lucene` component (ZF 1.6). Earlier versions of `Zend_Search_Lucene` implementations need another versions of Java Lucene tools to be compatible:

- ZF 1.5 - Java Lucene 2.1 (Luke tool v0.7.1 - http://www.getopt.org/luke/luke-0.7.1/)

- ZF 1.0 - Java Lucene 1.4 - 2.1 (Luke tool v0.6 - http://www.getopt.org/luke/luke-0.6/)

Permissions

By default, index files are available for reading and writing by everyone.

It's possible to override this with the `Zend_Search_Lucene_Storage_Directory_Filesystem::setDefaultFilePermissions()` method:

```
// Get current default file permissions
$currentPermissions =
    Zend_Search_Lucene_Storage_Directory_Filesystem::getDefaultFile
      Permissions();
```

```
// Give read-writing permissions only for current user and group
Zend_Search_Lucene_Storage_Directory_Filesystem::setDefaultFile
    Permissions(0660);
```

Limitations

Index size

Index size is limited by 2GB for 32-bit platforms.

Use 64-bit platforms for larger indices.

Supported Filesystems

Zend_Search_Lucene uses flock() to provide concurrent searching, index updating and optimization.

According to the PHP documentation [http://www.php.net/manual/en/function.flock.php], "flock() will not work on NFS and many other networked file systems".

Do not use networked file systems with Zend_Search_Lucene.

Searching an Index

Building Queries

There are two ways to search the index. The first method uses query parser to construct a query from a string. The second is to programmatically create your own queries through the Zend_Search_Lucene API.

Before choosing to use the provided query parser, please consider the following:

1. If you are programmatically creating a query string and then parsing it with the query parser then you should consider building your queries directly with the query API. Generally speaking, the query parser is designed for human-entered text, not for program-generated text.

2. Untokenized fields are best added directly to queries and not through the query parser. If a field's values are generated programmatically by the application, then the query clauses for this field should also be constructed programmatically. An analyzer, which the query parser uses, is designed to convert human-entered text to terms. Program-generated values, like dates, keywords, etc., should be added with the query API.

3. In a query form, fields that are general text should use the query parser. All others, such as date ranges, keywords, etc., are better added directly through the query API. A field with a limited set of values that can be specified with a pull-down menu should not be added to a query string that is subsequently parsed but instead should be added as a TermQuery clause.

4. Boolean queries allow the programmer to logically combine two or more queries into new one. Thus it's the best way to add additional criteria to a search defined by a query string.

Both ways use the same API method to search through the index:

```
$index = Zend_Search_Lucene::open('/data/my_index');

$index->find($query);
```

The Zend_Search_Lucene::find() method determines the input type automatically and uses the query parser to construct an appropriate Zend_Search_Lucene_Search_Query object from an input of type string.

It is important to note that the query parser uses the standard analyzer to tokenize separate parts of query string. Thus all transformations which are applied to indexed text are also applied to query strings.

The standard analyzer may transform the query string to lower case for case-insensitivity, remove stop-words, and stem among other transformations.

The API method doesn't transform or filter input terms in any way. It's therefore more suitable for computer generated or untokenized fields.

Query Parsing

`Zend_Search_Lucene_Search_QueryParser::parse()` method may be used to parse query strings into query objects.

This query object may be used in query construction API methods to combine user entered queries with programmatically generated queries.

Actually, in some cases it's the only way to search for values within untokenized fields:

```
$userQuery = Zend_Search_Lucene_Search_QueryParser::parse($queryStr);

$pathTerm  = new Zend_Search_Lucene_Index_Term(
                    '/data/doc_dir/' . $filename, 'path'
            );
$pathQuery = new Zend_Search_Lucene_Search_Query_Term($pathTerm);

$query = new Zend_Search_Lucene_Search_Query_Boolean();
$query->addSubquery($userQuery, true /* required */);
$query->addSubquery($pathQuery, true /* required */);

$hits = $index->find($query);
```

`Zend_Search_Lucene_Search_QueryParser::parse()` method also takes an optional encoding parameter, which can specify query string encoding:

```
$userQuery = Zend_Search_Lucene_Search_QueryParser::parse($queryStr,
                                                   'iso-8859-5');
```

If the encoding parameter is omitted, then current locale is used.

It's also possible to specify the default query string encoding with `Zend_Search_Lucene_Search_QueryParser::setDefaultEncoding()` method:

```
Zend_Search_Lucene_Search_QueryParser::setDefaultEncoding('iso-8859-5');
...
$userQuery = Zend_Search_Lucene_Search_QueryParser::parse($queryStr);
```

`Zend_Search_Lucene_Search_QueryParser::getDefaultEncoding()` returns the current default query string encoding (the empty string means "current locale").

Search Results

The search result is an array of `Zend_Search_Lucene_Search_QueryHit` objects. Each of these has two properties: `$hit->document` is a document number within the index and `$hit->score` is a score of the hit in a search result. The results are ordered by score (descending from highest score).

The `Zend_Search_Lucene_Search_QueryHit` object also exposes each field of the `Zend_Search_Lucene_Document` found in the search as a property of the hit. In the following example, a hit is returned with two fields from the corresponding document: title and author.

```
$index = Zend_Search_Lucene::open('/data/my_index');

$hits = $index->find($query);

foreach ($hits as $hit) {
    echo $hit->score;
    echo $hit->title;
    echo $hit->author;
}
```

Stored fields are always returned in UTF-8 encoding.

Optionally, the original Zend_Search_Lucene_Document object can be returned from the Zend_Search_Lucene_Search_QueryHit. You can retrieve stored parts of the document by using the getDocument() method of the index object and then get them by getFieldValue() method:

```
$index = Zend_Search_Lucene::open('/data/my_index');

$hits = $index->find($query);
foreach ($hits as $hit) {
    // return Zend_Search_Lucene_Document object for this hit
    echo $document = $hit->getDocument();

    // return a Zend_Search_Lucene_Field object
    // from the Zend_Search_Lucene_Document
    echo $document->getField('title');

    // return the string value of the Zend_Search_Lucene_Field object
    echo $document->getFieldValue('title');

    // same as getFieldValue()
    echo $document->title;
}
```

The fields available from the Zend_Search_Lucene_Document object are determined at the time of indexing. The document fields are either indexed, or index and stored, in the document by the indexing application (e.g. LuceneIndexCreation.jar).

Note that the document identity ('path' in our example) is also stored in the index and must be retrieved from it.

Limiting the Result Set

The most computationally expensive part of searching is score calculation. It may take several seconds for large result sets (tens of thousands of hits).

Zend_Search_Lucene gives the possibility to limit result set size with getResultSetLimit() and setResultSetLimit() methods:

```
$currentResultSetLimit = Zend_Search_Lucene::getResultSetLimit();

Zend_Search_Lucene::setResultSetLimit($newLimit);
```

The default value of 0 means 'no limit'.

It doesn't give the 'best N' results, but only the 'first N'[§] .

[§]Returned hits are still ordered by score or by the the specified order, if given.

Results Scoring

Zend_Search_Lucene uses the same scoring algorithms as Java Lucene. All hits in the search result are ordered by score by default. Hits with greater score come first, and documents having higher scores should match the query more precisely than documents having lower scores.

Roughly speaking, search hits that contain the searched term or phrase more frequently will have a higher score.

A hit's score can be retrieved by accessing the score property of the hit:

```
$hits = $index->find($query);

foreach ($hits as $hit) {
    echo $hit->id;
    echo $hit->score;
}
```

The Zend_Search_Lucene_Search_Similarity class is used to calculate the score for each hit. See Extensibility. Scoring Algorithms section for details.

Search Result Sorting

By default, the search results are ordered by score. The programmer can change this behavior by setting a sort field (or a list of fields), sort type and sort order parameters.

$index->find() call may take several optional parameters:

```
$index->find($query [, $sortField [, $sortType [, $sortOrder]]]
                    [, $sortField2 [, $sortType [, $sortOrder]]]
                ...);
```

A name of stored field by which to sort result should be passed as the $sortField parameter.

$sortType may be omitted or take the following enumerated values: SORT_REGULAR (compare items normally- default value), SORT_NUMERIC (compare items numerically), SORT_STRING (compare items as strings).

$sortOrder may be omitted or take the following enumerated values: SORT_ASC (sort in ascending order- default value), SORT_DESC (sort in descending order).

Examples:

```
$index->find($query, 'quantity', SORT_NUMERIC, SORT_DESC);
```

```
$index->find($query, 'fname', SORT_STRING, 'lname', SORT_STRING);
```

```
$index->find($query, 'name', SORT_STRING, 'quantity', SORT_NUMERIC, SORT_DESC);
```

Please use caution when using a non-default search order; the query needs to retrieve documents completely from an index, which may dramatically reduce search performance.

Search Results Highlighting

Zend_Search_Lucene provides two options for search results highlighting.

The first one is utilizing `Zend_Search_Lucene_Document_Html` class (see HTML documents section for details) using the following methods:

```
/**
 * Highlight text with specified color
 *
 * @param string|array $words
 * @param string $colour
 * @return string
 */
public function highlight($words, $colour = '#66ffff');
```

```
/**
 * Highlight text using specified View helper or callback function.
 *
 * @param string|array $words  Words to highlight. Words could be
 *        organized using the array or string.
 * @param callback $callback   Callback method, used to transform
 *        (highlighting) text.
 * @param array    $params     Array of additionall callback
 *        parameters passed through into it
 *                             (first non-optional parameter is an HTML
 *                                  fragment for highlighting)
 * @return string
 * @throws Zend_Search_Lucene_Exception
 */
public function highlightExtended($words, $callback, $params = array())
```

To customize highlighting behavior use `highlightExtended()` method with specified callback, which takes one or more parameters [†], or extend `Zend_Search_Lucene_Document_Html` class and redefine `applyColour($stringToHighlight, $colour)` method used as a default highlighting callback. [‡]

View helpers also can be used as callbacks in context of view script:

```
$doc->highlightExtended('word1 word2 word3...', array($this,
    'myViewHelper'));
```

The result of highlighting operation is retrieved by `Zend_Search_Lucene_Document_Html->getHTML()` method.

Note

Highlighting is performed in terms of current analyzer. So all forms of the word(s) recognized by analyzer are highlighted.

E.g. if current analyzer is case insensitive and we request to highlight 'text' word, then 'text', 'Text', 'TEXT' and other case combinations will be highlighted.

In the same way, if current analyzer supports stemming and we request to highlight 'indexed', then 'index', 'indexing', 'indices' and other word forms will be highlighted.

On the other hand, if word is skipped by corrent analyzer (e.g. if short words filter is applied to the analyzer), then nothing will be highlighted.

The second option is to use `Zend_Search_Lucene_Search_Query->highlightMatches`

[†] The first is an HTML fragment for highlighting and others are callback behavior dependent. Returned value is a highlighted HTML fragment.
[‡] In both cases returned HTML is automatically transformed into valid XHTML.

```
(string $inputHTML[, $defaultEncoding = 'UTF-8'[, Zend_Search_Lucene
_Search_Highlighter_Interface $highlighter]]) method:
```

```
$query = Zend_Search_Lucene_Search_QueryParser::parse($queryStr);
$highlightedHTML = $query->highlightMatches($sourceHTML);
```

Optional second parameter is a default HTML document encoding. It's used if encoding is not specified using Content-type HTTP-EQUIV meta tag.

Optional third parameter is a highlighter object which has to implement `Zend_Search_Lucene_Search_Highlighter_Interface` interface:

```
interface Zend_Search_Lucene_Search_Highlighter_Interface
{
    /**
     * Set document for highlighting.
     *
     * @param Zend_Search_Lucene_Document_Html $document
     */
    public function setDocument(Zend_Search_Lucene_Document_Html $document);

    /**
     * Get document for highlighting.
     *
     * @return Zend_Search_Lucene_Document_Html $document
     */
    public function getDocument();

    /**
     * Highlight specified words (method is invoked once per subquery)
     *
     * @param string|array $words  Words to highlight. They could be
     *        organized using the array or string.
     */
    public function highlight($words);
}
```

Where `Zend_Search_Lucene_Document_Html` object is an object constructed from the source HTML provided to the `Zend_Search_Lucene_Search_Query->highlightMatches()` method.

If `$highlighter` parameter is omitted, then `Zend_Search_Lucene_Search_Highlighter_Default` object is instantiated and used.

Highlighter `highlight()` method is invoked once per subquery, so it has an ability to differentiate highlighting for them.

Actually, default highlighter does this walking through predefined color table. So you can implement your own highlighter or just extend the default and redefine color table.

`Zend_Search_Lucene_Search_Query->htmlFragmentHighlightMatches()` has similar behavior. The only differenece is that it takes as an input and returns HTML fragment without <>HTML>, <HEAD>, <BODY> tags. Nevertheless, fragment is automatically transformed to valid XHTML.

Query Language

Java Lucene and `Zend_Search_Lucene` provide quite powerful query languages.

These languages are mostly the same with some minor differences, which are mentioned below.

Full Java Lucene query language syntax documentation can be found here [http://lucene.apache.org /java/docs/queryparsersyntax.html].

Terms

A query is broken up into terms and operators. There are three types of terms: Single Terms, Phrases, and Subqueries.

A Single Term is a single word such as "test" or "hello".

A Phrase is a group of words surrounded by double quotes such as "hello dolly".

A Subquery is a query surrounded by parentheses such as "(hello dolly)".

Multiple terms can be combined together with boolean operators to form complex queries (see below).

Fields

Lucene supports fields of data. When performing a search you can either specify a field, or use the default field. The field names depend on indexed data and default field is defined by current settings.

The first and most significant difference from Java Lucene is that terms are searched through *all fields* by default.

There are two static methods in the Zend_Search_Lucene class which allow the developer to configure these settings:

```
$defaultSearchField = Zend_Search_Lucene::getDefaultSearchField();
...
Zend_Search_Lucene::setDefaultSearchField('contents');
```

The null value indicated that the search is performed across all fields. It's the default setting.

You can search specific fields by typing the field name followed by a colon ":" followed by the term you are looking for.

As an example, let's assume a Lucene index contains two fields- title and text- with text as the default field. If you want to find the document entitled "The Right Way" which contains the text "don't go this way", you can enter:

```
title:"The Right Way" AND text:go
```

or

```
title:"Do it right" AND go
```

Because "text" is the default field, the field indicator is not required.

Note: The field is only valid for the term, phrase or subquery that it directly precedes, so the query

```
title:Do it right
```

Will only find "Do" in the title field. It will find "it" and "right" in the default field (if the default field is set) or in all indexed fields (if the default field is set to null).

Wildcards

Lucene supports single and multiple character wildcard searches within single terms (but not within phrase queries).

To perform a single character wildcard search use the "?" symbol.

To perform a multiple character wildcard search use the "*" symbol.

The single character wildcard search looks for string that match the term with the "?" replaced by any single character. For example, to search for "text" or "test" you can use the search:

```
te?t
```

Multiple character wildcard searches look for 0 or more characters when matching strings against terms. For example, to search for test, tests or tester, you can use the search:

```
test*
```

You can use "?", "*" or both at any place of the term:

```
*wr?t*
```

It searches for "write", "wrote", "written", "rewrite", "rewrote" and so on.

Starting from ZF 1.7.7 wildcard patterns need some non-wildcard prefix. Default prefix length is 3 (like in Java Lucene). So "*", "te?t", "*wr?t*" terms will cause an exception [*].

It can be altered using `Zend_Search_Lucene_Search_Query_Wildcard::getMinPrefixLength()` and `Zend_Search_Lucene_Search_Query_Wildcard::setMinPrefixLength()` methods.

Term Modifiers

Lucene supports modifying query terms to provide a wide range of searching options.

"~" modifier can be used to specify proximity search for phrases or fuzzy search for individual terms.

Range Searches

Range queries allow the developer or user to match documents whose field(s) values are between the lower and upper bound specified by the range query. Range Queries can be inclusive or exclusive of the upper and lower bounds. Sorting is performed lexicographically.

```
mod_date:[20020101 TO 20030101]
```

This will find documents whose mod_date fields have values between 20020101 and 20030101, inclusive. Note that Range Queries are not reserved for date fields. You could also use range queries with non-date fields:

```
title:{Aida TO Carmen}
```

This will find all documents whose titles would be sorted between Aida and Carmen, but not including Aida and Carmen.

Inclusive range queries are denoted by square brackets. Exclusive range queries are denoted by curly brackets.

If field is not specified then `Zend_Search_Lucene` searches for specified interval through all fields by default.

```
{Aida TO Carmen}
```

---

[*] Please note, that it's not a `Zend_Search_Lucene_Search_QueryParserException`, but a `Zend_Search_Lucene_Exception`. It's thrown during query rewrite (execution) operation.

Fuzzy Searches

Zend_Search_Lucene as well as Java Lucene supports fuzzy searches based on the Levenshtein Distance, or Edit Distance algorithm. To do a fuzzy search use the tilde, "~", symbol at the end of a Single word Term. For example to search for a term similar in spelling to "roam" use the fuzzy search:

```
roam~
```

This search will find terms like foam and roams. Additional (optional) parameter can specify the required similarity. The value is between 0 and 1, with a value closer to 1 only terms with a higher similarity will be matched. For example:

```
roam~0.8
```

The default that is used if the parameter is not given is 0.5.

Matched terms limitation.

Wildcard, range and fuzzy search queries may match too many terms. It may cause incredible search performance downgrade.

So Zend_Search_Lucene sets a limit of matching terms per query (subquery). This limit can be retrieved and set using Zend_Search_Lucene::getTermsPerQueryLimit()/Zend_Search _Lucene::setTermsPerQueryLimit($limit) methods.

Default matched terms per query limit is 1024.

Proximity Searches

Lucene supports finding words from a phrase that are within a specified word distance in a string. To do a proximity search use the tilde, "~", symbol at the end of the phrase. For example to search for a "Zend" and "Framework" within 10 words of each other in a document use the search:

```
"Zend Framework"~10
```

Boosting a Term

Java Lucene and Zend_Search_Lucene provide the relevance level of matching documents based on the terms found. To boost the relevance of a term use the caret, "^", symbol with a boost factor (a number) at the end of the term you are searching. The higher the boost factor, the more relevant the term will be.

Boosting allows you to control the relevance of a document by boosting individual terms. For example, if you are searching for

```
PHP framework
```

and you want the term "PHP" to be more relevant boost it using the ^ symbol along with the boost factor next to the term. You would type:

```
PHP^4 framework
```

This will make documents with the term PHP appear more relevant. You can also boost phrase terms and subqueries as in the example:

```
"PHP framework"^4 "Zend Framework"
```

By default, the boost factor is 1. Although the boost factor must be positive, it may be less than 1 (e.g. 0.2).

Boolean Operators

Boolean operators allow terms to be combined through logic operators. Lucene supports AND, "+", OR, NOT and "-" as Boolean operators. Java Lucene requires boolean operators to be ALL CAPS. Zend_Search_Lucene does not.

AND, OR, and NOT operators and "+", "-" defines two different styles to construct boolean queries. Unlike Java Lucene, Zend_Search_Lucene doesn't allow these two styles to be mixed.

If the AND/OR/NOT style is used, then an AND or OR operator must be present between all query terms. Each term may also be preceded by NOT operator. The AND operator has higher precedence than the OR operator. This differs from Java Lucene behavior.

AND

The AND operator means that all terms in the "AND group" must match some part of the searched field(s).

To search for documents that contain "PHP framework" and "Zend Framework" use the query:

```
"PHP framework" AND "Zend Framework"
```

OR

The OR operator divides the query into several optional terms.

To search for documents that contain "PHP framework" or "Zend Framework" use the query:

```
"PHP framework" OR "Zend Framework"
```

NOT

The NOT operator excludes documents that contain the term after NOT. But an "AND group" which contains only terms with the NOT operator gives an empty result set instead of a full set of indexed documents.

To search for documents that contain "PHP framework" but not "Zend Framework" use the query:

```
"PHP framework" AND NOT "Zend Framework"
```

&&, ||, and ! operators

&&, ||, and ! may be used instead of AND, OR, and NOT notation.

+

The "+" or required operator stipulates that the term after the "+" symbol must match the document.

To search for documents that must contain "Zend" and may contain "Framework" use the query:

```
+Zend Framework
```

-

The "-" or prohibit operator excludes documents that match the term after the "-" symbol.

To search for documents that contain "PHP framework" but not "Zend Framework" use the query:

```
"PHP framework" -"Zend Framework"
```

No Operator

If no operator is used, then the search behavior is defined by the "default boolean operator".

This is set to OR by default.

That implies each term is optional by default. It may or may not be present within document, but documents with this term will receive a higher score.

To search for documents that requires "PHP framework" and may contain "Zend Framework" use the query:

```
+"PHP framework" "Zend Framework"
```

The default boolean operator may be set or retrieved with the Zend_Search_Lucene_Search_QueryParser::setDefaultOperator($operator) and Zend_Search_Lucene_Search_QueryParser::getDefaultOperator() methods, respectively.

These methods operate with the Zend_Search_Lucene_Search_QueryParser::B_AND and Zend_Search_Lucene_Search_QueryParser::B_OR constants.

Grouping

Java Lucene and Zend_Search_Lucene support using parentheses to group clauses to form sub queries. This can be useful if you want to control the precedence of boolean logic operators for a query or mix different boolean query styles:

```
+(framework OR library) +php
```

Zend_Search_Lucene supports subqueries nested to any level.

Field Grouping

Lucene also supports using parentheses to group multiple clauses to a single field.

To search for a title that contains both the word "return" and the phrase "pink panther" use the query:

```
title:(+return +"pink panther")
```

Escaping Special Characters

Lucene supports escaping special characters that are used in query syntax. The current list of special characters is:

+ - && || ! ( ) { } [ ] ^ " ~ * ? : \

+ and - inside single terms are automatically treated as common characters.

For other instances of these characters use the \ before each special character you'd like to escape. For example to search for (1+1):2 use the query:

```
\(1\+1\)\:2
```

Query Construction API

In addition to parsing a string query automatically it's also possible to construct them with the query API.

User queries can be combined with queries created through the query API. Simply use the query parser to construct a query from a string:

```
$query = Zend_Search_Lucene_Search_QueryParser::parse($queryString);
```

Query Parser Exceptions

The query parser may generate two types of exceptions:

- `Zend_Search_Lucene_Exception` is thrown if something goes wrong in the query parser itself.

- `Zend_Search_Lucene_Search_QueryParserException` is thrown when there is an error in the query syntax.

It's a good idea to catch `Zend_Search_Lucene_Search_QueryParserExceptions` and handle them appropriately:

```
try {
    $query = Zend_Search_Lucene_Search_QueryParser::parse($queryString);
} catch (Zend_Search_Lucene_Search_QueryParserException $e) {
    echo "Query syntax error: " . $e->getMessage() . "\n";
}
```

The same technique should be used for the find() method of a `Zend_Search_Lucene` object.

Starting in 1.5, query parsing exceptions are suppressed by default. If query doesn't conform query language, then it's tokenized using current default analyzer and all tokenized terms are used for searching. Use `Zend_Search_Lucene_Search_QueryParser::dontSuppressQueryParsingExceptions()` method to turn exceptions on. `Zend_Search_Lucene_Search_QueryParser::suppressQueryParsingExceptions()` and `Zend_Search_Lucene_Search_QueryParser::queryParsingExceptionsSuppressed()` methods are also intended to manage exceptions handling behavior.

Term Query

Term queries can be used for searching with a single term.

Query string:

```
word1
```

or

Query construction by API:

```
$term  = new Zend_Search_Lucene_Index_Term('word1', 'field1');
$query = new Zend_Search_Lucene_Search_Query_Term($term);
```

```
$hits  = $index->find($query);
```

The term field is optional. Zend_Search_Lucene searches through all indexed fields in each document if the field is not specified:

```
// Search for 'word1' in all indexed fields
$term  = new Zend_Search_Lucene_Index_Term('word1');
$query = new Zend_Search_Lucene_Search_Query_Term($term);
$hits  = $index->find($query);
```

Multi-Term Query

Multi-term queries can be used for searching with a set of terms.

Each term in a set can be defined as *required*, *prohibited*, or *neither*.

- *required* means that documents not matching this term will not match the query;

- *prohibited* means that documents matching this term will not match the query;

- *neither*, in which case matched documents are neither prohibited from, nor required to, match the term. A document must match at least 1 term, however, to match the query.

If optional terms are added to a query with required terms, both queries will have the same result set but the optional terms may affect the score of the matched documents.

Both search methods can be used for multi-term queries.

Query string:

```
+word1 author:word2 -word3
```

- '+' is used to define a required term.

- '-' is used to define a prohibited term.

- 'field:' prefix is used to indicate a document field for a search. If it's omitted, then all fields are searched.

or

Query construction by API:

```
$query = new Zend_Search_Lucene_Search_Query_MultiTerm();

$query->addTerm(new Zend_Search_Lucene_Index_Term('word1'), true);
$query->addTerm(new Zend_Search_Lucene_Index_Term('word2', 'author'),
                null);
$query->addTerm(new Zend_Search_Lucene_Index_Term('word3'), false);

$hits  = $index->find($query);
```

It's also possible to specify terms list within MultiTerm query constructor:

```
$terms = array(new Zend_Search_Lucene_Index_Term('word1'),
               new Zend_Search_Lucene_Index_Term('word2', 'author'),
               new Zend_Search_Lucene_Index_Term('word3'));
$signs = array(true, null, false);
```

```
$query = new Zend_Search_Lucene_Search_Query_MultiTerm($terms, $signs);

$hits   = $index->find($query);
```

The $signs array contains information about the term type:

- true is used to define required term.

- false is used to define prohibited term.

- null is used to define a term that is neither required nor prohibited.

Boolean Query

Boolean queries allow to construct query using other queries and boolean operators.

Each subquery in a set can be defined as *required*, *prohibited*, or *optional*.

- *required* means that documents not matching this subquery will not match the query;

- *prohibited* means that documents matching this subquery will not match the query;

- *optional*, in which case matched documents are neither prohibited from, nor required to, match the subquery. A document must match at least 1 subquery, however, to match the query.

If optional subqueries are added to a query with required subqueries, both queries will have the same result set but the optional subqueries may affect the score of the matched documents.

Both search methods can be used for boolean queries.

Query string:

```
+(word1 word2 word3) author:(word4 word5) -word6
```

- '+' is used to define a required subquery.

- '-' is used to define a prohibited subquery.

- 'field:' prefix is used to indicate a document field for a search. If it's omitted, then all fields are searched.

or

Query construction by API:

```
$query = new Zend_Search_Lucene_Search_Query_Boolean();

$subquery1 = new Zend_Search_Lucene_Search_Query_MultiTerm();
$subquery1->addTerm(new Zend_Search_Lucene_Index_Term('word1'));
$subquery1->addTerm(new Zend_Search_Lucene_Index_Term('word2'));
$subquery1->addTerm(new Zend_Search_Lucene_Index_Term('word3'));

$subquery2 = new Zend_Search_Lucene_Search_Query_MultiTerm();
$subquery2->addTerm(new Zend_Search_Lucene_Index_Term('word4', 'author'));
$subquery2->addTerm(new Zend_Search_Lucene_Index_Term('word5', 'author'));

$term6 = new Zend_Search_Lucene_Index_Term('word6');
$subquery3 = new Zend_Search_Lucene_Search_Query_Term($term6);

$query->addSubquery($subquery1, true  /* required */);
```

```
$query->addSubquery($subquery2, null   /* optional */);
$query->addSubquery($subquery3, false /* prohibited */);

$hits  = $index->find($query);
```

It's also possible to specify subqueries list within Boolean query constructor:

```
...
$subqueries = array($subquery1, $subquery2, $subquery3);
$signs = array(true, null, false);

$query = new Zend_Search_Lucene_Search_Query_Boolean($subqueries, $signs);

$hits  = $index->find($query);
```

The $signs array contains information about the subquery type:

- true is used to define required subquery.

- false is used to define prohibited subquery.

- null is used to define a subquery that is neither required nor prohibited.

Each query which uses boolean operators can be rewritten using signs notation and constructed using API. For example:

```
word1 AND (word2 AND word3 AND NOT word4) OR word5
```

is equivalent to

```
(+(word1) +(+word2 +word3 -word4)) (word5)
```

Wildcard Query

Wildcard queries can be used to search for documents containing strings matching specified patterns.

The '?' symbol is used as a single character wildcard.

The '*' symbol is used as a multiple character wildcard.

Query string:

```
field1:test*
```

or

Query construction by API:

```
$pattern = new Zend_Search_Lucene_Index_Term('test*', 'field1');
$query = new Zend_Search_Lucene_Search_Query_Wildcard($pattern);
$hits  = $index->find($query);
```

The term field is optional. Zend_Search_Lucene searches through all fields on each document if a field is not specified:

```
$pattern = new Zend_Search_Lucene_Index_Term('test*');
```

```
$query = new Zend_Search_Lucene_Search_Query_Wildcard($pattern);
$hits  = $index->find($query);
```

Fuzzy Query

Fuzzy queries can be used to search for documents containing strings matching terms similar to specified term.

Query string:

```
field1:test~
```

This query matches documents containing 'test' 'text' 'best' words and others.

or

Query construction by API:

```
$term = new Zend_Search_Lucene_Index_Term('test', 'field1');
$query = new Zend_Search_Lucene_Search_Query_Fuzzy($term);
$hits  = $index->find($query);
```

Optional similarity can be specified after "~" sign.

Query string:

```
field1:test~0.4
```

or

Query construction by API:

```
$term = new Zend_Search_Lucene_Index_Term('test', 'field1');
$query = new Zend_Search_Lucene_Search_Query_Fuzzy($term, 0.4);
$hits  = $index->find($query);
```

The term field is optional. Zend_Search_Lucene searches through all fields on each document if a field is not specified:

```
$term = new Zend_Search_Lucene_Index_Term('test');
$query = new Zend_Search_Lucene_Search_Query_Fuzzy($term);
$hits  = $index->find($query);
```

Phrase Query

Phrase Queries can be used to search for a phrase within documents.

Phrase Queries are very flexible and allow the user or developer to search for exact phrases as well as 'sloppy' phrases.

Phrases can also contain gaps or terms in the same places; they can be generated by the analyzer for different purposes. For example, a term can be duplicated to increase the term its weight, or several synonyms can be placed into a single position.

```
$query1 = new Zend_Search_Lucene_Search_Query_Phrase();

// Add 'word1' at 0 relative position.
$query1->addTerm(new Zend_Search_Lucene_Index_Term('word1'));

// Add 'word2' at 1 relative position.
$query1->addTerm(new Zend_Search_Lucene_Index_Term('word2'));

// Add 'word3' at 3 relative position.
$query1->addTerm(new Zend_Search_Lucene_Index_Term('word3'), 3);

...

$query2 = new Zend_Search_Lucene_Search_Query_Phrase(
            array('word1', 'word2', 'word3'), array(0,1,3));

...

// Query without a gap.
$query3 = new Zend_Search_Lucene_Search_Query_Phrase(
            array('word1', 'word2', 'word3'));

...

$query4 = new Zend_Search_Lucene_Search_Query_Phrase(
            array('word1', 'word2'), array(0,1), 'annotation');
```

A phrase query can be constructed in one step with a class constructor or step by step with
Zend_Search_Lucene_Search_Query_Phrase::addTerm() method calls.

Zend_Search_Lucene_Search_Query_Phrase class constructor takes three optional
arguments:

```
Zend_Search_Lucene_Search_Query_Phrase(
    [array $terms[, array $offsets[, string $field]]]
);
```

The $terms parameter is an array of strings that contains a set of phrase terms. If it's omitted or equal
to null, then an empty query is constructed.

The $offsets parameter is an array of integers that contains offsets of terms in a phrase. If it's omitted
or equal to null, then the terms' positions are assumed to be sequential with no gaps.

The $field parameter is a string that indicates the document field to search. If it's omitted or equal to
null, then the default field is searched.

Thus:

```
$query =
    new Zend_Search_Lucene_Search_Query_Phrase(array('zend', 'framework'));
```

will search for the phrase 'zend framework' in all fields.

```
$query = new Zend_Search_Lucene_Search_Query_Phrase(
            array('zend', 'download'), array(0, 2)
        );
```

will search for the phrase 'zend ????? download' and match 'zend platform download', 'zend studio
download', 'zend core download', 'zend framework download', and so on.

```
$query = new Zend_Search_Lucene_Search_Query_Phrase(
            array('zend', 'framework'), null, 'title'
          );
```

will search for the phrase 'zend framework' in the 'title' field.

`Zend_Search_Lucene_Search_Query_Phrase::addTerm()` takes two arguments, a required `Zend_Search_Lucene_Index_Term` object and an optional position:

```
Zend_Search_Lucene_Search_Query_Phrase::addTerm(
    Zend_Search_Lucene_Index_Term $term[, integer $position]
);
```

The `$term` parameter describes the next term in the phrase. It must indicate the same field as previous terms, or an exception will be thrown.

The `$position` parameter indicates the term position in the phrase.

Thus:

```
$query = new Zend_Search_Lucene_Search_Query_Phrase();
$query->addTerm(new Zend_Search_Lucene_Index_Term('zend'));
$query->addTerm(new Zend_Search_Lucene_Index_Term('framework'));
```

will search for the phrase 'zend framework'.

```
$query = new Zend_Search_Lucene_Search_Query_Phrase();
$query->addTerm(new Zend_Search_Lucene_Index_Term('zend'), 0);
$query->addTerm(new Zend_Search_Lucene_Index_Term('framework'), 2);
```

will search for the phrase 'zend ????? download' and match 'zend platform download', 'zend studio download', 'zend core download', 'zend framework download', and so on.

```
$query = new Zend_Search_Lucene_Search_Query_Phrase();
$query->addTerm(new Zend_Search_Lucene_Index_Term('zend', 'title'));
$query->addTerm(new Zend_Search_Lucene_Index_Term('framework', 'title'));
```

will search for the phrase 'zend framework' in the 'title' field.

The slop factor sets the number of other words permitted between specified words in the query phrase. If set to zero, then the corresponding query is an exact phrase search. For larger values this works like the WITHIN or NEAR operators.

The slop factor is in fact an edit distance, where the edits correspond to moving terms in the query phrase. For example, to switch the order of two words requires two moves (the first move places the words atop one another), so to permit re-orderings of phrases, the slop factor must be at least two.

More exact matches are scored higher than sloppier matches; thus, search results are sorted by exactness. The slop is zero by default, requiring exact matches.

The slop factor can be assigned after query creation:

```
// Query without a gap.
$query =
    new Zend_Search_Lucene_Search_Query_Phrase(array('word1', 'word2'));

// Search for 'word1 word2', 'word1 ... word2'
```

```
$query->setSlop(1);
$hits1 = $index->find($query);

// Search for 'word1 word2', 'word1 ... word2',
// 'word1 ... ... word2', 'word2 word1'
$query->setSlop(2);
$hits2 = $index->find($query);
```

Range Query

Range queries are intended for searching terms within specified interval.

Query string:

```
mod_date:[20020101 TO 20030101]
title:{Aida TO Carmen}
```

or

Query construction by API:

```
$from = new Zend_Search_Lucene_Index_Term('20020101', 'mod_date');
$to   = new Zend_Search_Lucene_Index_Term('20030101', 'mod_date');
$query = new Zend_Search_Lucene_Search_Query_Range(
                $from, $to, true // inclusive
            );
$hits  = $index->find($query);
```

Term fields are optional. Zend_Search_Lucene searches through all fields if the field is not specified:

```
$from = new Zend_Search_Lucene_Index_Term('Aida');
$to   = new Zend_Search_Lucene_Index_Term('Carmen');
$query = new Zend_Search_Lucene_Search_Query_Range(
                $from, $to, false // non-inclusive
            );
$hits  = $index->find($query);
```

Either (but not both) of the boundary terms may be set to null. Zend_Search_Lucene searches from the beginning or up to the end of the dictionary for the specified field(s) in this case:

```
// searches for ['20020101' TO ...]
$from = new Zend_Search_Lucene_Index_Term('20020101', 'mod_date');
$query = new Zend_Search_Lucene_Search_Query_Range(
                $from, null, true // inclusive
            );
$hits  = $index->find($query);
```

Character Set

UTF-8 and single-byte character set support

Zend_Search_Lucene works with the UTF-8 charset internally. Index files store unicode data in Java's "modified UTF-8 encoding". Zend_Search_Lucene core completely supports this encoding with one exception. [6]

Actual input data encoding may be specified through `Zend_Search_Lucene` API. Data will be automatically converted into UTF-8 encoding.

Default text analyzer

However, the default text analyzer (which is also used within query parser) uses ctype_alpha() for tokenizing text and queries.

ctype_alpha() is not UTF-8 compatible, so the analyzer converts text to 'ASCII//TRANSLIT' encoding before indexing. The same processing is transparently performed during query parsing. [7]

> Default analyzer doesn't treats numbers as parts of terms. Use corresponding 'Num' analyzer if you don't want words to be broken by numbers.

UTF-8 compatible text analyzers

`Zend_Search_Lucene` also contains a set of UTF-8 compatible analyzers:
`Zend_Search_Lucene_Analysis_Analyzer_Common_Utf8`,
`Zend_Search_Lucene_Analysis_Analyzer_Common_Utf8Num`,
`Zend_Search_Lucene_Analysis_Analyzer_Common_Utf8_CaseInsensitive`,
`Zend_Search_Lucene_Analysis_Analyzer_Common_Utf8Num_CaseInsensitive`.

Any of this analyzers can be enabled with the code like this:

```
Zend_Search_Lucene_Analysis_Analyzer::setDefault(
    new Zend_Search_Lucene_Analysis_Analyzer_Common_Utf8());
```

> UTF-8 compatible analyzers were improved in ZF 1.5. Early versions of analyzers assumed all non-ascii characters are letters. New analyzers implementation has more accurate behavior.
>
> This may need you to re-build index to have data and search queries tokenized in the same way, otherwise search engine may return wrong result sets.

All of these analyzers need PCRE (Perl-compatible regular expressions) library to be compiled with UTF-8 support turned on. PCRE UTF-8 support is turned on for the PCRE library sources bundled with PHP source code distribution, but if shared library is used instead of bundled with PHP sources, then UTF-8 support state may depend on you operating system.

Use the following code to check, if PCRE UTF-8 support is enabled:

```
if (@preg_match('/\pL/u', 'a') == 1) {
    echo "PCRE unicode support is turned on.\n";
} else {
    echo "PCRE unicode support is turned off.\n";
}
```

Case insensitive versions of UTF-8 compatible analyzers also need mbstring [http://www.php.net/manual/en/ref.mbstring.php] extension to be enabled.

If you don't want mbstring extension to be turned on, but need case insensitive search, you may use the

---

[6] `Zend_Search_Lucene` supports only Basic Multilingual Plane (BMP) characters (from 0x0000 to 0xFFFF) and doesn't support "supplementary characters" (characters whose code points are greater than 0xFFFF)

Java 2 represents these characters as a pair of char (16-bit) values, the first from the high-surrogates range (0xD800-0xDBFF), the second from the low-surrogates range (0xDC00-0xDFFF). Then they are encoded as usual UTF-8 characters in six bytes. Standard UTF-8 representation uses four bytes for supplementary characters.

[7] Conversion to 'ASCII//TRANSLIT' may depend on current locale and OS.

following approach: normalize source data before indexing and query string before searching by converting them to lowercase:

```
// Indexing
setlocale(LC_CTYPE, 'de_DE.iso-8859-1');

...

Zend_Search_Lucene_Analysis_Analyzer::setDefault(
    new Zend_Search_Lucene_Analysis_Analyzer_Common_Utf8());

...

$doc = new Zend_Search_Lucene_Document();

$doc->addField(Zend_Search_Lucene_Field::UnStored('contents',
                                                  strtolower($contents)));

// Title field for search through (indexed, unstored)
$doc->addField(Zend_Search_Lucene_Field::UnStored('title',
                                                  strtolower($title)));

// Title field for retrieving (unindexed, stored)
$doc->addField(Zend_Search_Lucene_Field::UnIndexed('_title', $title));


// Searching
setlocale(LC_CTYPE, 'de_DE.iso-8859-1');

...

Zend_Search_Lucene_Analysis_Analyzer::setDefault(
    new Zend_Search_Lucene_Analysis_Analyzer_Common_Utf8());

...

$hits = $index->find(strtolower($query));
```

Extensibility

Text Analysis

The `Zend_Search_Lucene_Analysis_Analyzer` class is used by the indexer to tokenize document text fields.

The `Zend_Search_Lucene_Analysis_Analyzer::getDefault()` and `Zend_Search_Lucene_Analysis_Analyzer::setDefault()` methods are used to get and set the default analyzer.

You can assign your own text analyzer or choose it from the set of predefined analyzers: `Zend_Search_Lucene_Analysis_Analyzer_Common_Text` and `Zend_Search_Lucene_Analysis_Analyzer_Common_Text_CaseInsensitive` (default). Both of them interpret tokens as sequences of letters. `Zend_Search_Lucene_Analysis_Analyzer_Common_Text_CaseInsensitive` converts all tokens to lower case.

To switch between analyzers:

```
Zend_Search_Lucene_Analysis_Analyzer::setDefault(
    new Zend_Search_Lucene_Analysis_Analyzer_Common_Text());
...
$index->addDocument($doc);
```

The Zend_Search_Lucene_Analysis_Analyzer_Common class is designed to be an ancestor of all user defined analyzers. User should only define the reset() and nextToken() methods, which takes its string from the $_input member and returns tokens one by one (a null value indicates the end of the stream).

The nextToken() method should call the normalize() method on each token. This will allow you to use token filters with your analyzer.

Here is an example of a custom analyzer, which accepts words with digits as terms:

Example 20.1. Custom text Analyzer.

```
/**
 * Here is a custom text analyser, which treats words with digits as
 * one term
 */

class My_Analyzer extends Zend_Search_Lucene_Analysis_Analyzer_Common
{
    private $_position;

    /**
     * Reset token stream
     */
    public function reset()
    {
        $this->_position = 0;
    }

    /**
     * Tokenization stream API
     * Get next token
     * Returns null at the end of stream
     *
     * @return Zend_Search_Lucene_Analysis_Token|null
     */
    public function nextToken()
    {
        if ($this->_input === null) {
            return null;
        }

        while ($this->_position < strlen($this->_input)) {
            // skip white space
            while ($this->_position < strlen($this->_input) &&
                    !ctype_alnum( $this->_input[$this->_position] )) {
                $this->_position++;
            }

            $termStartPosition = $this->_position;

            // read token
            while ($this->_position < strlen($this->_input) &&
                    ctype_alnum( $this->_input[$this->_position] )) {
                $this->_position++;
            }
```

```
                    // Empty token, end of stream.
                    if ($this->_position == $termStartPosition) {
                        return null;
                    }

                    $token = new Zend_Search_Lucene_Analysis_Token(
                                        substr($this->_input,
                                               $termStartPosition,
                                               $this->_position -
                                               $termStartPosition),
                                        $termStartPosition,
                                        $this->_position);
                    $token = $this->normalize($token);
                    if ($token !== null) {
                        return $token;
                    }
                    // Continue if token is skipped
                }

                return null;
            }
        }

        Zend_Search_Lucene_Analysis_Analyzer::setDefault(
            new My_Analyzer());
```

Tokens Filtering

The `Zend_Search_Lucene_Analysis_Analyzer_Common` analyzer also offers a token filtering mechanism.

The `Zend_Search_Lucene_Analysis_TokenFilter` class provides an abstract interface for such filters. Your own filters should extend this class either directly or indirectly.

Any custom filter must implement the `normalize()` method which may transform input token or signal that the current token should be skipped.

There are three filters already defined in the analysis subpackage:

- `Zend_Search_Lucene_Analysis_TokenFilter_LowerCase`

- `Zend_Search_Lucene_Analysis_TokenFilter_ShortWords`

- `Zend_Search_Lucene_Analysis_TokenFilter_StopWords`

The `LowerCase` filter is already used for `Zend_Search_Lucene_Analysis_Analyzer_Common_Text_CaseInsensitive` analyzer by default.

The `ShortWords` and `StopWords` filters may be used with pre-defined or custom analyzers like this:

```
$stopWords = array('a', 'an', 'at', 'the', 'and', 'or', 'is', 'am');
$stopWordsFilter =
    new Zend_Search_Lucene_Analysis_TokenFilter_StopWords($stopWords);

$analyzer =
    new Zend_Search_Lucene_Analysis_Analyzer_Common_TextNum_CaseInsensitive()
$analyzer->addFilter($stopWordsFilter);

Zend_Search_Lucene_Analysis_Analyzer::setDefault($analyzer);
```

```
$shortWordsFilter = new Zend_Search_Lucene_Analysis_TokenFilter_ShortWords();

$analyzer =
    new Zend_Search_Lucene_Analysis_Analyzer_Common_TextNum_CaseInsensitive();
$analyzer->addFilter($shortWordsFilter);

Zend_Search_Lucene_Analysis_Analyzer::setDefault($analyzer);
```

The `Zend_Search_Lucene_Analysis_TokenFilter_StopWords` constructor takes an array of stop-words as an input. But stop-words may be also loaded from a file:

```
$stopWordsFilter = new Zend_Search_Lucene_Analysis_TokenFilter_StopWords();
$stopWordsFilter->loadFromFile($my_stopwords_file);

$analyzer =
    new Zend_Search_Lucene_Analysis_Analyzer_Common_TextNum_CaseInsensitive();
$analyzer->addFilter($stopWordsFilter);

Zend_Search_Lucene_Analysis_Analyzer::setDefault($analyzer);
```

This file should be a common text file with one word in each line. The '#' character marks a line as a comment.

The `Zend_Search_Lucene_Analysis_TokenFilter_ShortWords` constructor has one optional argument. This is the word length limit, set by default to 2.

Scoring Algorithms

The score of a document d for a query q is defined as follows:

```
score(q,d) = sum( tf(t in d) * idf(t) * getBoost(t.field in d) *
lengthNorm(t.field in d) ) * coord(q,d) * queryNorm(q)
```

tf(t in d) - `Zend_Search_Lucene_Search_Similarity::tf($freq)` - a score factor based on the frequency of a term or phrase in a document.

idf(t) - `Zend_Search_Lucene_Search_Similarity::tf($term, $reader)` - a score factor for a simple term with the specified index.

getBoost(t.field in d) - the boost factor for the term field.

lengthNorm($term) - the normalization value for a field given the total number of terms contained in a field. This value is stored within the index. These values, together with field boosts, are stored in an index and multiplied into scores for hits on each field by the search code.

Matches in longer fields are less precise, so implementations of this method usually return smaller values when numTokens is large, and larger values when numTokens is small.

coord(q,d) - `Zend_Search_Lucene_Search_Similarity::coord($overlap, $maxOverlap)` - a score factor based on the fraction of all query terms that a document contains.

The presence of a large portion of the query terms indicates a better match with the query, so implementations of this method usually return larger values when the ratio between these parameters is large and smaller values when the ratio between them is small.

queryNorm(q) - the normalization value for a query given the sum of the squared weights of each of the query terms. This value is then multiplied into the weight of each query term.

This does not affect ranking, but rather just attempts to make scores from different queries comparable.

The scoring algorithm can be customized by defining your own Similarity class. To do this extend the `Zend_Search_Lucene_Search_Similarity` class as defined below, then use the

Zend_Search_Lucene_Search_Similarity::setDefault($similarity); method to set it as default.

```
class MySimilarity extends Zend_Search_Lucene_Search_Similarity {
    public function lengthNorm($fieldName, $numTerms) {
        return 1.0/sqrt($numTerms);
    }

    public function queryNorm($sumOfSquaredWeights) {
        return 1.0/sqrt($sumOfSquaredWeights);
    }

    public function tf($freq) {
        return sqrt($freq);
    }

    /**
     * It's not used now. Computes the amount of a sloppy phrase match,
     * based on an edit distance.
     */
    public function sloppyFreq($distance) {
        return 1.0;
    }

    public function idfFreq($docFreq, $numDocs) {
        return log($numDocs/(float)($docFreq+1)) + 1.0;
    }

    public function coord($overlap, $maxOverlap) {
        return $overlap/(float)$maxOverlap;
    }
}

$mySimilarity = new MySimilarity();
Zend_Search_Lucene_Search_Similarity::setDefault($mySimilarity);
```

Storage Containers

The abstract class Zend_Search_Lucene_Storage_Directory defines directory functionality.

The Zend_Search_Lucene constructor uses either a string or a Zend_Search_Lucene_Storage_Directory object as an input.

The Zend_Search_Lucene_Storage_Directory_Filesystem class implements directory functionality for a file system.

If a string is used as an input for the Zend_Search_Lucene constructor, then the index reader (Zend_Search_Lucene object) treats it as a file system path and instantiates the Zend_Search_Lucene_Storage_Directory_Filesystem object.

You can define your own directory implementation by extending the Zend_Search_Lucene_Storage_Directory class.

Zend_Search_Lucene_Storage_Directory methods:

```
abstract class Zend_Search_Lucene_Storage_Directory {
/**
 * Closes the store.
 *
 * @return void
 */
abstract function close();
```

```
/**
 * Creates a new, empty file in the directory with the given $filename.
 *
 * @param string $name
 * @return void
 */
abstract function createFile($filename);

/**
 * Removes an existing $filename in the directory.
 *
 * @param string $filename
 * @return void
 */
abstract function deleteFile($filename);

/**
 * Returns true if a file with the given $filename exists.
 *
 * @param string $filename
 * @return boolean
 */
abstract function fileExists($filename);

/**
 * Returns the length of a $filename in the directory.
 *
 * @param string $filename
 * @return integer
 */
abstract function fileLength($filename);

/**
 * Returns the UNIX timestamp $filename was last modified.
 *
 * @param string $filename
 * @return integer
 */
abstract function fileModified($filename);

/**
 * Renames an existing file in the directory.
 *
 * @param string $from
 * @param string $to
 * @return void
 */
abstract function renameFile($from, $to);

/**
 * Sets the modified time of $filename to now.
 *
 * @param string $filename
 * @return void
 */
abstract function touchFile($filename);

/**
 * Returns a Zend_Search_Lucene_Storage_File object for a given
 * $filename in the directory.
 *
 * @param string $filename
 * @return Zend_Search_Lucene_Storage_File
```

```
 */
abstract function getFileObject($filename);

}
```

The   getFileObject($filename)   method   of   a
Zend_Search_Lucene_Storage_Directory   instance   returns   a
Zend_Search_Lucene_Storage_File object.

The Zend_Search_Lucene_Storage_File abstract class implements file abstraction and index file reading primitives.

You must also extend Zend_Search_Lucene_Storage_File for your directory implementation.

Only two methods of Zend_Search_Lucene_Storage_File must be overridden in your implementation:

```
class MyFile extends Zend_Search_Lucene_Storage_File {
    /**
     * Sets the file position indicator and advances the file pointer.
     * The new position, measured in bytes from the beginning of the file,
     * is obtained by adding offset to the position specified by whence,
     * whose values are defined as follows:
     * SEEK_SET - Set position equal to offset bytes.
     * SEEK_CUR - Set position to current location plus offset.
     * SEEK_END - Set position to end-of-file plus offset. (To move to
     * a position before the end-of-file, you need to pass a negative value
     * in offset.)
     * Upon success, returns 0; otherwise, returns -1
     *
     * @param integer $offset
     * @param integer $whence
     * @return integer
     */
    public function seek($offset, $whence=SEEK_SET) {
        ...
    }

    /**
     * Read a $length bytes from the file and advance the file pointer.
     *
     * @param integer $length
     * @return string
     */
    protected function _fread($length=1) {
        ...
    }
}
```

Interoperating with Java Lucene

File Formats

Zend_Search_Lucene index file formats are binary compatible with Java Lucene version 1.4 and greater.

A   detailed   description   of   this   format   is   available   here:
http://lucene.apache.org/java/docs/fileformats.html [8] .

---

[8]The currently supported Lucene index file format version is 2.3 (starting from ZF 1.6).

Index Directory

After index creation, the index directory will contain several files:

- The segments file is a list of index segments.

- The *.cfs files contain index segments. Note! An optimized index always has only one segment.

- The deletable file is a list of files that are no longer used by the index, but which could not be deleted.

Java Source Code

The Java program listing below provides an example of how to index a file using Java Lucene:

```
/**
 * Index creation:
 */
import org.apache.lucene.index.IndexWriter;
import org.apache.lucene.document.*;

import java.io.*

...

IndexWriter indexWriter = new IndexWriter("/data/my_index",
                                    new SimpleAnalyzer(), true);

...

String filename = "/path/to/file-to-index.txt"
File f = new File(filename);

Document doc = new Document();
doc.add(Field.Text("path", filename));
doc.add(Field.Keyword("modified",DateField.timeToString(f.lastModified())));
doc.add(Field.Text("author", "unknown"));
FileInputStream is = new FileInputStream(f);
Reader reader = new BufferedReader(new InputStreamReader(is));
doc.add(Field.Text("contents", reader));

indexWriter.addDocument(doc);
```

Advanced

Starting from 1.6, handling index format transformations.

Zend_Search_Lucene component works with Java Lucene 1.4-1.9, 2.1 and 2.3 index formats.

Current index format may be requested using $index->getFormatVersion() call. It returns one of the following values:

- Zend_Search_Lucene::FORMAT_PRE_2_1 for Java Lucene 1.4-1.9 index format.

- Zend_Search_Lucene::FORMAT_2_1 for Java Lucene 2.1 index format (also used for Lucene 2.2).

- Zend_Search_Lucene::FORMAT_2_3 for Java Lucene 2.3 index format.

Index modifications are performed *only* if any index update is done. That happens if a new document is added to an index or index optimization is started manually by $index->optimize() call.

In a such case Zend_Search_Lucene may convert index to the higher format version. That *always* happens for the indices in Zend_Search_Lucene::FORMAT_PRE_2_1 format, which are automatically converted to 2.1 format.

You may manage conversion process and assign target index format by $index->setFormatVersion() which takes Zend_Search_Lucene::FORMAT_2_1 or Zend_Search_Lucene::FORMAT_2_3 constant as a parameter:

- Zend_Search_Lucene::FORMAT_2_1 actually does nothing since pre-2.1 indices are automatically converted to 2.1 format.

- Zend_Search_Lucene::FORMAT_2_3 forces conversion to the 2.3 format.

Backward conversions are not supported.

Important!

Once index is converted to upper version it can't be converted back. So make a backup of your index when you plan migration to upper version, but want to have possibility to go back.

Using the index as static property

The Zend_Search_Lucene object uses the destructor method to commit changes and clean up resources.

It stores added documents in memory and dumps new index segment to disk depending on MaxBufferedDocs parameter.

If MaxBufferedDocs limit is not reached then there are some "unsaved" documents which are saved as a new segment in the object's destructor method. The index auto-optimization procedure is invoked if necessary depending on the values of the MaxBufferedDocs, MaxMergeDocs and MergeFactor parameters.

Static object properties (see below) are destroyed *after* the last line of the executed script.

```
class Searcher {
    private static $_index;

    public static function initIndex() {
        self::$_index = Zend_Search_Lucene::open('path/to/index');
    }
}

Searcher::initIndex();
```

All the same, the destructor for static properties is correctly invoked at this point in the program's execution.

One potential problem is exception handling. Exceptions thrown by destructors of static objects don't have context, because the destructor is executed after the script has already completed.

You might see a "Fatal error: Exception thrown without a stack frame in Unknown on line 0" error message instead of exception description in such cases.

Zend_Search_Lucene provides a workaround to this problem with the commit() method. It saves all unsaved changes and frees memory used for storing new segments. You are free to use the commit operation any time- or even several times- during script execution. You can still use the Zend_Search_Lucene object for searching, adding or deleting document after the commit operation. But the commit() call guarantees that if there are no document added or deleted after the call to commit(), then the Zend_Search_Lucene destructor has nothing to do and will not throw exception:

```
class Searcher {
    private static $_index;

    public static function initIndex() {
        self::$_index = Zend_Search_Lucene::open('path/to/index');
    }

    ...

    public static function commit() {
        self::$_index->commit();
    }
}

Searcher::initIndex();

...

// Script shutdown routine
...
Searcher::commit();
...
```

Best Practices

Field names

There are no limitations for field names in Zend_Search_Lucene.

Nevertheless it's a good idea not to use '*id*' and '*score*' names to avoid ambiguity in QueryHit properties names.

The Zend_Search_Lucene_Search_QueryHit id and score properties always refer to internal Lucene document id and hit score. If the indexed document has the same stored fields, you have to use the getDocument() method to access them:

```
$hits = $index->find($query);

foreach ($hits as $hit) {
    // Get 'title' document field
    $title = $hit->title;

    // Get 'contents' document field
    $contents = $hit->contents;

    // Get internal Lucene document id
    $id = $hit->id;

    // Get query hit score
    $score = $hit->score;

    // Get 'id' document field
    $docId = $hit->getDocument()->id;

    // Get 'score' document field
    $docId = $hit->getDocument()->score;
```

```
        // Another way to get 'title' document field
        $title = $hit->getDocument()->title;
}
```

Indexing performance

Indexing performance is a compromise between used resources, indexing time and index quality.

Index quality is completely determined by number of index segments.

Each index segment is entirely independent portion of data. So indexes containing more segments need more memory and time for searching.

Index optimization is a process of merging several segments into a new one. A fully optimized index contains only one segment.

Full index optimization may be performed with the optimize() method:

```
$index = Zend_Search_Lucene::open($indexPath);

$index->optimize();
```

Index optimization works with data streams and doesn't take a lot of memory but does require processor resources and time.

Lucene index segments are not updatable by their nature (the update operation requires the segment file to be completely rewritten). So adding new document(s) to an index always generates a new segment. This, in turn, decreases index quality.

An index auto-optimization process is performed after each segment generation and consists of merging partial segments.

There are three options to control the behavior of auto-optimization (see Index optimization section):

- *MaxBufferedDocs* is the number of documents that can be buffered in memory before a new segment is generated and written to the hard drive.

- *MaxMergeDocs* is the maximum number of documents merged by auto-optimization process into a new segment.

- *MergeFactor* determines how often auto-optimization is performed.

Note

All these options are Zend_Search_Lucene object properties- not index properties. They affect only current Zend_Search_Lucene object behavior and may vary for different scripts.

MaxBufferedDocs doesn't have any effect if you index only one document per script execution. On the other hand, it's very important for batch indexing. Greater values increase indexing performance, but also require more memory.

There is simply no way to calculate the best value for the *MaxBufferedDocs* parameter because it depends on average document size, the analyzer in use and allowed memory.

A good way to find the right value is to perform several tests with the largest document you expect to be added to the index [9]. It's a best practice not to use more than a half of the allowed memory.

---

[9] memory_get_usage() and memory_get_peak_usage() may be used to control memory usage.

MaxMergeDocs limits the segment size (in terms of documents). It therefore also limits auto-optimization time by guaranteeing that the `addDocument()` method is not executed more than a certain number of times. This is very important for interactive applications.

Lowering the *MaxMergeDocs* parameter also may improve batch indexing performance. Index auto-optimization is an iterative process and is performed from bottom up. Small segments are merged into larger segment, which are in turn merged into even larger segments and so on. Full index optimization is achieved when only one large segment file remains.

Small segments generally decrease index quality. Many small segments may also trigger the "Too many open files" error determined by OS limitations [10].

in general, background index optimization should be performed for interactive indexing mode and *MaxMergeDocs* shouldn't be too low for batch indexing.

MergeFactor affects auto-optimization frequency. Lower values increase the quality of unoptimized indexes. Larger values increase indexing performance, but also increase the number of merged segments. This again may trigger the "Too many open files" error.

MergeFactor groups index segments by their size:

1. Not greater than *MaxBufferedDocs*.

2. Greater than *MaxBufferedDocs*, but not greater than *MaxBufferedDocs*MergeFactor*.

3. Greater   than   *MaxBufferedDocs*MergeFactor*,   but   not   greater   than *MaxBufferedDocs*MergeFactor*MergeFactor*.

4. ...

`Zend_Search_Lucene` checks during each `addDocument()` call to see if merging any segments may move the newly created segment into the next group. If yes, then merging is performed.

So an index with N groups may contain *MaxBufferedDocs* + (N-1)*MergeFactor segments and contains at least *MaxBufferedDocs*MergeFactor* $^{(N-1)}$ documents.

This gives good approximation for the number of segments in the index:

NumberOfSegments   <=   *MaxBufferedDocs*   +   *MergeFactor**log $_{MergeFactor}$ (*NumberOfDocuments/MaxBufferedDocs*)

MaxBufferedDocs is determined by allowed memory. This allows for the appropriate merge factor to get a reasonable number of segments.

Tuning the *MergeFactor* parameter is more effective for batch indexing performance than *MaxMergeDocs*. But it's also more course-grained. So use the estimation above for tuning *MergeFactor*, then play with *MaxMergeDocs* to get best batch indexing performance.

Index during Shut Down

The `Zend_Search_Lucene` instance performs some work at exit time if any documents were added to the index but not written to a new segment.

It also may trigger an auto-optimization process.

The index object is automatically closed when it, and all returned QueryHit objects, go out of scope.

If index object is stored in global variable than it's closed only at the end of script execution [11].

PHP exception processing is also shut down at this moment.

---

[10] `Zend_Search_Lucene` keeps each segment file opened to improve search performance.

[11] This also may occur if the index or QueryHit instances are referred to in some cyclical data structures, because PHP garbage collects objects with cyclic references only at the end of script execution.

It doesn't prevent normal index shutdown process, but may prevent accurate error diagnostic if any error occurs during shutdown.

There are two ways with which you may avoid this problem.

The first is to force going out of scope:

```
$index = Zend_Search_Lucene::open($indexPath);

...

unset($index);
```

And the second is to perform a commit operation before the end of script execution:

```
$index = Zend_Search_Lucene::open($indexPath);

$index->commit();
```

This possibility is also described in the "Advanced. Using index as static property" section.

Retrieving documents by unique id

It's a common practice to store some unique document id in the index. Examples include url, path, or database id.

Zend_Search_Lucene provides a termDocs() method for retrieving documents containing specified terms.

This is more efficient than using the find() method:

```
// Retrieving documents with find() method using a query string
$query = $idFieldName . ':' . $docId;
$hits  = $index->find($query);
foreach ($hits as $hit) {
    $title    = $hit->title;
    $contents = $hit->contents;
    ...
}
...

// Retrieving documents with find() method using the query API
$term = new Zend_Search_Lucene_Index_Term($docId, idFieldName);
$query = new Zend_Search_Lucene_Search_Query_Term($term);
$hits  = $index->find($query);
foreach ($hits as $hit) {
    $title    = $hit->title;
    $contents = $hit->contents;
    ...
}

...

// Retrieving documents with termDocs() method
$term = new Zend_Search_Lucene_Index_Term($docId, idFieldName);
$docIds  = $index->termDocs($term);
foreach ($docIds as $id) {
    $doc = $index->getDocument($id);
    $title    = $doc->title;
    $contents = $doc->contents;
    ...
}
```

Memory Usage

Zend_Search_Lucene is a relatively memory-intensive module.

It uses memory to cache some information and optimize searching and indexing performance.

The memory required differs for different modes.

The terms dictionary index is loaded during the search. It's actually each 128th [12] term of the full dictionary.

Thus memory usage is increased if you have a high number of unique terms. This may happen if you use untokenized phrases as a field values or index a large volume of non-text information.

An unoptimized index consists of several segments. It also increases memory usage. Segments are independent, so each segment contains its own terms dictionary and terms dictionary index. If an index consists of N segments it may increase memory usage by N times in worst case. Perform index optimization to merge all segments into one to avoid such memory consumption.

Indexing uses the same memory as searching plus memory for buffering documents. The amount of memory used may be managed with *MaxBufferedDocs* parameter.

Index optimization (full or partial) uses stream-style data processing and doesn't require a lot of memory.

Encoding

Zend_Search_Lucene works with UTF-8 strings internally. So all strings returned by Zend_Search_Lucene are UTF-8 encoded.

You shouldn't be concerned with encoding if you work with pure ASCII data, but you should be careful if this is not the case.

Wrong encoding may cause error notices at the encoding conversion time or loss of data.

Zend_Search_Lucene offers a wide range of encoding possibilities for indexed documents and parsed queries.

Encoding may be explicitly specified as an optional parameter of field creation methods:

```
$doc = new Zend_Search_Lucene_Document();
$doc->addField(Zend_Search_Lucene_Field::Text('title',
                                              $title,
                                              'iso-8859-1'));
$doc->addField(Zend_Search_Lucene_Field::UnStored('contents',
                                                  $contents,
                                                  'utf-8'));
```

This is the best way to avoid ambiguity in the encoding used.

If optional encoding parameter is omitted, then the current locale is used. The current locale may contain character encoding data in addition to the language specification:

```
setlocale(LC_ALL, 'fr_FR');
...

setlocale(LC_ALL, 'de_DE.iso-8859-1');
...
```

---

[12] The Lucene file format allows you to configure this number, but Zend_Search_Lucene doesn't expose this in its API. Nevertheless you still have the ability to configure this value if the index is prepared with another Lucene implementation.

```
setlocale(LC_ALL, 'ru_RU.UTF-8');
...
```

The same approach is used to set query string encoding.

If encoding is not specified, then the current locale is used to determine the encoding.

Encoding may be passed as an optional parameter, if the query is parsed explicitly before search:

```
$query =
    Zend_Search_Lucene_Search_QueryParser::parse($queryStr, 'iso-8859-5');
$hits = $index->find($query);
...
```

The default encoding may also be specified with setDefaultEncoding() method:

```
Zend_Search_Lucene_Search_QueryParser::setDefaultEncoding('iso-8859-1');
$hits = $index->find($queryStr);
...
```

The empty string implies 'current locale'.

If the correct encoding is specified it can be correctly processed by analyzer. The actual behavior depends on which analyzer is used. See the Character Set documentation section for details.

Index maintenance

It should be clear that Zend_Search_Lucene as well as any other Lucene implementation does not comprise a "database".

Indexes should not be used for data storage. They do not provide partial backup/restore functionality, journaling, logging, transactions and many other features associated with database management systems.

Nevertheless, Zend_Search_Lucene attempts to keep indexes in a consistent state at all times.

Index backup and restoration should be performed by copying the contents of the index folder.

If index corruption occurs for any reason, the corrupted index should be restored or completely rebuilt.

So it's a good idea to backup large indexes and store changelogs to perform manual restoration and roll-forward operations if necessary. This practice dramatically reduces index restoration time.

Chapter 21. Zend_Server

Introduction

The Zend_Server family of classes provides functionality for the various server classes, including Zend_XmlRpc_Server, Zend_Rest_Server, Zend_Json_Server and Zend_Soap_Wsdl. Zend_Server_Interface provides an interface that mimics PHP 5's SoapServer class; all server classes should implement this interface in order to provide a standard server API.

The Zend_Server_Reflection tree provides a standard mechanism for performing function and class introspection for use as callbacks with the server classes, and provides data suitable for use with Zend_Server_Interface's getFunctions() and loadFunctions() methods.

Zend_Server_Reflection

Introduction

Zend_Server_Reflection provides a standard mechanism for performing function and class introspection for use with server classes. It is based on PHP 5's Reflection API, augmenting it with methods for retrieving parameter and return value types and descriptions, a full list of function and method prototypes (i.e., all possible valid calling combinations), and function/method descriptions.

Typically, this functionality will only be used by developers of server classes for the framework.

Usage

Basic usage is simple:

```
$class    = Zend_Server_Reflection::reflectClass('My_Class');
$function = Zend_Server_Reflection::reflectFunction('my_function');

// Get prototypes
$prototypes = $reflection->getPrototypes();

// Loop through each prototype for the function
foreach ($prototypes as $prototype) {

    // Get prototype return type
    echo "Return type: ", $prototype->getReturnType(), "\n";

    // Get prototype parameters
    $parameters = $prototype->getParameters();

    echo "Parameters: \n";
    foreach ($parameters as $parameter) {
        // Get parameter type
        echo "    ", $parameter->getType(), "\n";
    }
}

// Get namespace for a class, function, or method.
// Namespaces may be set at instantiation time (second argument), or using
// setNamespace()
$reflection->getNamespace();
```

reflectFunction() returns a Zend_Server_Reflection_Function object; reflectClass returns a Zend_Server_Reflection_Class object. Please refer to the API documentation to see what methods are available to each.

Chapter 22. Zend_Service

Introduction

`Zend_Service` is an abstract class which serves as a foundation for web service implementations, such as SOAP or REST.

If you need support for generic, XML-based REST services, you may want to look at `Zend_Rest_Client`.

In addition to being able to extend the `Zend_Service` and use `Zend_Rest_Client` for REST-based web services, Zend also provides support for popular web services. See the following sections for specific information on each supported web service.

- Akismet

- Amazon

- Audioscrobbler

- Del.icio.us

- Flickr

- Simpy

- SlideShare

- StrikeIron

- Yahoo!

Additional services are coming in the future.

Zend_Service_Akismet

Introduction

`Zend_Service_Akismet` provides a client for the Akismet API [http://akismet.com/development/api/]. The Akismet service is used to determine if incoming data is potentially spam; it also exposes methods for submitting data as known spam or as false positives (ham). Originally intended to help categorize and identify spam for Wordpress, it can be used for any type of data.

Akismet requires an API key for usage. You may get one for signing up for a WordPress.com [http://wordpress.com/] account. You do not need to activate a blog; simply acquiring the account will provide you with the API key.

Additionally, Akismet requires that all requests contain a URL to the resource for which data is being filtered, and, because of Akismet's origins in WordPress, this resource is called the blog url. This value should be passed as the second argument to the constructor, but may be reset at any time using the `setBlogUrl()` accessor, or overridden by specifying a 'blog' key in the various method calls.

Verify an API key

`Zend_Service_Akismet::verifyKey($key)` is used to verify that an Akismet API key is valid. In most cases, you will not need to check, but if you need a sanity check, or to determine if a newly acquired key is active, you may do so with this method.

```
// Instantiate with the API key and a URL to the application or
// resource being used
$akismet = new Zend_Service_Akismet($apiKey,
                                    'http://framework.zend.com/wiki/');
if ($akismet->verifyKey($apiKey) {
    echo "Key is valid.\n";
} else {
    echo "Key is not valid\n";
}
```

If called with no arguments, verifyKey() uses the API key provided to the constructor.

verifyKey() implements Akismet's verify-key REST method.

Check for spam

Zend_Service_Akismet::isSpam($data) is used to determine if the data provided is considered spam by Akismet. It accepts an associative array as the sole argument. That array requires the following keys be set:

- user_ip, the IP address of the user submitting the data (not your IP address, but that of a user on your site).

- user_agent, the reported UserAgent string (browser and version) of the user submitting the data.

The following keys are also recognized specifically by the API:

- blog, the fully qualified URL to the resource or application. If not specified, the URL provided to the constructor will be used.

- referrer, the content of the HTTP_REFERER header at the time of submission. (Note spelling; it does not follow the header name.)

- permalink, the permalink location, if any, of the entry the data was submitted to.

- comment_type, the type of data provided. Values specifically specified in the API include 'comment', 'trackback', 'pingback', and an empty string (''), but it may be any value.

- comment_author, name of the person submitting the data.

- comment_author_email, email of the person submitting the data.

- comment_author_url, URL or home page of the person submitting the data.

- comment_content, actual data content submitted.

You may also submit any other environmental variables you feel might be a factor in determining if data is spam. Akismet suggests the contents of the entire $_SERVER array.

The isSpam() method will return either true or false, and throw an exception if the API key is invalid.

Example 22.1. isSpam() Usage

```
$data = array(
    'user_ip'              => '111.222.111.222',
    'user_agent'           => 'Mozilla/5.0 ' . (Windows; U; Windows NT ' .
                              '5.2; en-GB; rv:1.8.1) Gecko/20061010 ' .
                              'Firefox/2.0',
    'comment_type'         => 'contact',
    'comment_author'       => 'John Doe',
```

```
      'comment_author_email' => 'nospam@myhaus.net',
      'comment_content'       => "I'm not a spammer, honest!"
);
if ($akismet->isSpam($data)) {
    echo "Sorry, but we think you're a spammer.";
} else {
    echo "Welcome to our site!";
}
```

isSpam() implements the comment-check Akismet API method.

Submitting known spam

Occasionally spam data will get through the filter. If in your review of incoming data you discover spam that you feel should have been caught, you can submit it to Akismet to help improve their filter.

Zend_Service_Akismet::submitSpam() takes the same data array as passed to isSpam(), but does not return a value. An exception will be raised if the API key used is invalid.

Example 22.2. submitSpam() Usage

```
$data = array(
    'user_ip'                => '111.222.111.222',
    'user_agent'             => 'Mozilla/5.0 (Windows; U; Windows NT 5.2;' .
                                'en-GB; rv:1.8.1) Gecko/20061010 Firefox/2.0',
    'comment_type'           => 'contact',
    'comment_author'         => 'John Doe',
    'comment_author_email'   => 'nospam@myhaus.net',
    'comment_content'        => "I'm not a spammer, honest!"
);
$akismet->submitSpam($data));
```

submitSpam() implements the submit-spam Akismet API method.

Submitting false positives (ham)

Occasionally data will be trapped erroneously as spam by Akismet. For this reason, you should probably keep a log of all data trapped as spam by Akismet and review it periodically. If you find such occurrences, you can submit the data to Akismet as "ham", or a false positive (ham is good, spam is not).

Zend_Service_Akismet::submitHam() takes the same data array as passed to isSpam() or submitSpam(), and, like submitSpam(), does not return a value. An exception will be raised if the API key used is invalid.

Example 22.3. submitHam() Usage

```
$data = array(
    'user_ip'                => '111.222.111.222',
    'user_agent'             => 'Mozilla/5.0 (Windows; U; Windows NT 5.2;' .
                                'en-GB; rv:1.8.1) Gecko/20061010 Firefox/2.0',
    'comment_type'           => 'contact',
    'comment_author'         => 'John Doe',
```

```
        'comment_author_email' => 'nospam@myhaus.net',
        'comment_content'       => "I'm not a spammer, honest!"
);
$akismet->submitHam($data));
```

submitHam() implements the submit-ham Akismet API method.

Zend-specific Accessor Methods

While the Akismet API only specifies four methods, Zend_Service_Akismet has several additional accessors that may be used for modifying internal properties.

- getBlogUrl() and setBlogUrl() allow you to retrieve and modify the blog URL used in requests.

- getApiKey() and setApiKey() allow you to retrieve and modify the API key used in requests.

- getCharset() and setCharset() allow you to retrieve and modify the character set used to make the request.

- getPort() and setPort() allow you to retrieve and modify the TCP port used to make the request.

- getUserAgent() and setUserAgent() allow you to retrieve and modify the HTTP user agent used to make the request. Note: this is not the user_agent used in data submitted to the service, but rather the value provided in the HTTP User-Agent header when making a request to the service.

  The value used to set the user agent should be of the form some user agent/version | Akismet/version. The default is Zend Framework/ZF-VERSION | Akismet/1.11, where ZF-VERSION is the current Zend Framework version as stored in the Zend_Framework::VERSION constant.

Zend_Service_Amazon

Introduction

Zend_Service_Amazon is a simple API for using Amazon web services. Zend_Service_Amazon has two APIs: a more traditional one that follows Amazon's own API, and a simpler "Query API" for constructing even complex search queries easily.

Zend_Service_Amazon enables developers to retrieve information appearing throughout Amazon.com web sites directly through the Amazon Web Services API. Examples include:

- Store item information, such as images, descriptions, pricing, and more

- Customer and editorial reviews

- Similar products and accessories

- Amazon.com offers

- ListMania lists

In order to use Zend_Service_Amazon, you should already have an Amazon developer API key. To get a key and for more information, please visit the Amazon Web Services [http://www.amazon.com/gp/aws/landing.html] web site.

Attention

Your Amazon developer API key is linked to your Amazon identity, so take appropriate measures to keep your API key private.

Example 22.4. Search Amazon Using the Traditional API

In this example, we search for PHP books at Amazon and loop through the results, printing them.

```
$amazon = new Zend_Service_Amazon('AMAZON_API_KEY');
$results = $amazon->itemSearch(array('SearchIndex' => 'Books',
                                     'Keywords' => 'php'));
foreach ($results as $result) {
    echo $result->Title . '<br />';
}
```

Example 22.5. Search Amazon Using the Query API

Here, we also search for PHP books at Amazon, but we instead use the Query API, which resembles the Fluent Interface design pattern.

```
$query = new Zend_Service_Amazon_Query('AMAZON_API_KEY');
$query->category('Books')->Keywords('PHP');
$results = $query->search();
foreach ($results as $result) {
    echo $result->Title . '<br />';
}
```

Country Codes

By default, Zend_Service_Amazon connects to the United States ("US") Amazon web service. To connect from a different country, simply specify the appropriate country code string as the second parameter to the constructor:

Example 22.6. Choosing an Amazon Web Service Country

```
// Connect to Amazon in Japan
$amazon = new Zend_Service_Amazon('AMAZON_API_KEY', 'JP');
```

Country codes

Valid country codes are: CA, DE, FR, JP, UK, and US.

Looking up a Specific Amazon Item by ASIN

The itemLookup() method provides the ability to fetch a particular Amazon item when the ASIN is known.

Example 22.7. Looking up a Specific Amazon Item by ASIN

```
$amazon = new Zend_Service_Amazon('AMAZON_API_KEY');
$item = $amazon->itemLookup('B0000A432X');
```

The itemLookup() method also accepts an optional second parameter for handling search options. For full details, including a list of available options, please see the relevant Amazon documentation [http://www.amazon.com/gp/aws/sdk/main.html/103-9285448-4703844?s=AWSEcommerceService&v= 2005-10-05&p=ApiReference/ItemLookupOperation].

Image information

To retrieve images information for your search results, you must set ResponseGroup option to Medium or Large.

Performing Amazon Item Searches

Searching for items based on any of various available criteria are made simple using the itemSearch() method, as in the following example:

Example 22.8. Performing Amazon Item Searches

```
$amazon = new Zend_Service_Amazon('AMAZON_API_KEY');
$results = $amazon->itemSearch(array('SearchIndex' => 'Books',
                                     'Keywords' => 'php'));
foreach ($results as $result) {
    echo $result->Title . '<br />';
}
```

Example 22.9. Using the ResponseGroup Option

The ResponseGroup option is used to control the specific information that will be returned in the response.

```
$amazon = new Zend_Service_Amazon('AMAZON_API_KEY');
$results = $amazon->itemSearch(array(
    'SearchIndex'   => 'Books',
    'Keywords'      => 'php',
    'ResponseGroup' => 'Small,ItemAttributes,Images,SalesRank,Reviews,' .
                       'EditorialReview,Similarities,ListmaniaLists'
    ));
foreach ($results as $result) {
    echo $result->Title . '<br />';
}
```

The itemSearch() method accepts a single array parameter for handling search options. For full details, including a list of available options, please see the relevant Amazon documentation [http://www.amazon.com/gp/aws/sdk/main.html/103-9285448-4703844?s=AWSEcommerceService&v= 2005-10-05&p=ApiReference/ItemSearchOperation]

Tip

The `Zend_Service_Amazon_Query` class is an easy to use wrapper around this method.

Using the Alternative Query API

Introduction

`Zend_Service_Amazon_Query` provides an alternative API for using the Amazon Web Service. The alternative API uses the Fluent Interface pattern. That is, all calls can be made using chained method calls. (e.g., `$obj->method()->method2($arg)`)

The `Zend_Service_Amazon_Query` API uses overloading to easily set up an item search and then allows you to search based upon the criteria specified. Each of the options is provided as a method call, and each method's argument corresponds to the named option's value:

Example 22.10. Search Amazon Using the Alternative Query API

In this example, the alternative query API is used as a fluent interface to specify options and their respective values:

```
$query = new Zend_Service_Amazon_Query('MY_API_KEY');
$query->Category('Books')->Keywords('PHP');
$results = $query->search();
foreach ($results as $result) {
    echo $result->Title . '<br />';
}
```

This sets the option `Category` to "Books" and `Keywords` to "PHP".

For more information on the available options, please refer to the relevant Amazon documentation [http://www.amazon.com/gp/aws/sdk/main.html/102-9041115-9057709?s=AWSEcommerceService&v=2005-10-05&p=ApiReference/ItemSearchOperation].

Zend_Service_Amazon Classes

The following classes are all returned by `Zend_Service_Amazon::itemLookup()` and `Zend_Service_Amazon::itemSearch()`:

* `Zend_Service_Amazon_Item`

* `Zend_Service_Amazon_Image`

* `Zend_Service_Amazon_ResultSet`

* `Zend_Service_Amazon_OfferSet`

* `Zend_Service_Amazon_Offer`

* `Zend_Service_Amazon_SimilarProduct`

* `Zend_Service_Amazon_Accessories`

* `Zend_Service_Amazon_CustomerReview`

* `Zend_Service_Amazon_EditorialReview`

* `Zend_Service_Amazon_ListMania`

Zend_Service_Amazon_Item

Zend_Service_Amazon_Item is the class type used to represent an Amazon item returned by the web service. It encompasses all of the items attributes, including title, description, reviews, etc.

Zend_Service_Amazon_Item::asXML()

```
string asXML();
```

Return the original XML for the item

Properties

Zend_Service_Amazon_Item has a number of properties directly related to their standard Amazon API counterparts.

Table 22.1. Zend_Service_Amazon_Item Properties

Name	Type	Description
ASIN	string	Amazon Item ID
DetailPageURL	string	URL to the Items Details Page
SalesRank	int	Sales Rank for the Item
SmallImage	Zend_Service_Amazon_Image	Small Image of the Item
MediumImage	Zend_Service_Amazon_Image	Medium Image of the Item
LargeImage	Zend_Service_Amazon_Image	Large Image of the Item
Subjects	array	Item Subjects
Offers	Zend_Service_Amazon_OfferSet	Offer Summary and Offers for the Item
CustomerReviews	array	Customer reviews represented as an array of Zend_Service_Amazon_CustomerReview objects
EditorialReviews	array	Editorial reviews represented as an array of Zend_Service_Amazon_EditorialReview objects
SimilarProducts	array	Similar Products represented as an array of Zend_Service_Amazon_SimilarProduct objects
Accessories	array	Accessories for the item represented as an array of Zend_Service_Amazon_Accessories objects
Tracks	array	An array of track numbers and names for Music CDs and DVDs
ListmaniaLists	array	Item related Listmania Lists as an array of Zend_Service_Amazon_ListmainList objects

Name	Type	Description
PromotionalTag	string	Item Promotional Tag

Back to Class List

Zend_Service_Amazon_Image

`Zend_Service_Amazon_Image` represents a remote Image for a product.

Properties

Table 22.2. Zend_Service_Amazon_Image Properties

Name	Type	Description
Url	Zend_Uri	Remote URL for the Image
Height	int	The Height of the image in pixels
Width	int	The Width of the image in pixels

Back to Class List

Zend_Service_Amazon_ResultSet

`Zend_Service_Amazon_ResultSet` objects are returned by Zend_Service_Amazon::itemSearch() and allow you to easily handle the multiple results returned.

SeekableIterator

Implements the `SeekableIterator` for easy iteration (e.g. using `foreach`), as well as direct access to a specific result using `seek()`.

Zend_Service_Amazon_ResultSet::totalResults()

```
int totalResults();
```

Returns the total number of results returned by the search

Back to Class List

Zend_Service_Amazon_OfferSet

Each result returned by Zend_Service_Amazon::itemSearch() and Zend_Service_Amazon::itemLookup() contains a `Zend_Service_Amazon_OfferSet` object through which pricing information for the item can be retrieved.

Properties

Table 22.3. Zend_Service_Amazon_OfferSet Properties

Name	Type	Description
LowestNewPrice	int	Lowest Price for the item in "New" condition
LowestNewPriceCurrency	string	The currency for the `LowestNewPrice`

Name	Type	Description
LowestOldPrice	int	Lowest Price for the item in "Used" condition
LowestOldPriceCurrency	string	The currency for the `LowestOldPrice`
TotalNew	int	Total number of "new" condition available for the item
TotalUsed	int	Total number of "used" condition available for the item
TotalCollectible	int	Total number of "collectible" condition available for the item
TotalRefurbished	int	Total number of "refurbished" condition available for the item
Offers	array	An array of `Zend_Service_Amazon_Offer` objects.

Back to Class List

Zend_Service_Amazon_Offer

Each offer for an item is returned as an `Zend_Service_Amazon_Offer` object.

Zend_Service_Amazon_Offer Properties

Table 22.4. Properties

Name	Type	Description
MerchantId	string	Merchants Amazon ID
GlancePage	string	URL for a page with a summary of the Merchant
Condition	string	Condition of the item
OfferListingId	string	ID of the Offer Listing
Price	int	Price for the item
CurrencyCode	string	Currency Code for the price of the item
Availability	string	Availability of the item
IsEligibleForSuperSaverShipping	boolean	Whether the item is eligible for Super Saver Shipping or not

Back to Class List

Zend_Service_Amazon_SimilarProduct

When searching for items, Amazon also returns a list of similar products that the searcher may find to their liking. Each of these is returned as a `Zend_Service_Amazon_SimilarProduct` object.

Each object contains the information to allow you to make sub-sequent requests to get the full information on the item.

Properties

Table 22.5. Zend_Service_Amazon_SimilarProduct Properties

Name	Type	Description
ASIN	string	Products Amazon Unique ID (ASIN)
Title	string	Products Title

Back to Class List

Zend_Service_Amazon_Accessories

Accessories for the returned item are represented as `Zend_Service_Amazon_Accessories` objects

Properties

Table 22.6. Zend_Service_Amazon_Accessories Properties

Name	Type	Description
ASIN	string	Products Amazon Unique ID (ASIN)
Title	string	Products Title

Back to Class List

Zend_Service_Amazon_CustomerReview

Each Customer Review is returned as a `Zend_Service_Amazon_CustomerReview` object.

Properties

Table 22.7. Zend_Service_Amazon_CustomerReview Properties

Name	Type	Description
Rating	string	Item Rating
HelpfulVotes	string	Votes on how helpful the review is
CustomerId	string	Customer ID
TotalVotes	string	Total Votes
Date	string	Date of the Review
Summary	string	Review Summary
Content	string	Review Content

Back to Class List

Zend_Service_Amazon_EditorialReview

Each items Editorial Reviews are returned as a `Zend_Service_Amazon_EditorialReview` object

Properties

Table 22.8. Zend_Service_Amazon_EditorialReview Properties

Name	Type	Description
Source	string	Source of the Editorial Review
Content	string	Review Content

Back to Class List

Zend_Service_Amazon_Listmania

Each results List Mania List items are returned as `Zend_Service_Amazon_Listmania` objects.

Properties

Table 22.9. Zend_Service_Amazon_Listmania Properties

Name	Type	Description
ListId	string	List ID
ListName	string	List Name

Back to Class List

Zend_Service_Amazon_Ec2

Introduction

`Zend_Service_Amazon_Ec2` provides an interface to Amazon Elastic Cloud Computing (EC2).

What is Amazon Ec2?

Amazon EC2 is a web service that enables you to launch and manage server instances in Amazon's data centers using APIs or available tools and utilities. You can use Amazon EC2 server instances at any time, for as long as you need, and for any legal purpose.

Zend_Service_Amazon_Ec2: Instances

Instance Types

Amazon EC2 instances are grouped into two families: standard and High-CPU. Standard instances have memory to CPU ratios suitable for most general purpose applications; High-CPU instances have proportionally more CPU resources than memory (RAM) and are well suited for compute-intensive applications. When selecting instance types, you might want to use less powerful instance types for your web server instances and more powerful instance types for your database instances. Additionally, you might want to run CPU instance types for CPU-intensive data processing tasks.

One of the advantages of EC2 is that you pay by the instance hour, which makes it convenient and inexpensive to test the performance of your application on different instance families and types. One good way to determine the most appropriate instance family and instance type is to launch test instances and benchmark your application.

Instance Types

The instance types are defined as constants in the code. Column eight in the table is the defined constant name

Table 22.10. Available Instance Types

Type	CPU	Memory	Storage	Platform	I/O	Name	Constant Name
Small	1 EC2 Compute Unit (1 virtual core with 1 EC2 Compute Unit)	1.7 GB	160 GB instance storage (150 GB plus 10 GB root partition)	32-bit	Moderate	m1.small	Zend _Service _Amazon _Ec2_ Instance ::SMALL
Large	4 EC2 Compute Units (2 virtual cores with 2 EC2 Compute Units each)	7.5 GB	850 GB instance storage (2 x 420 GB plus 10 GB root partition)	64-bit	High	m1.large	Zend _Service _Amazon _Ec2_ Instance ::LARGE
Extra Large	8 EC2 Compute Units (4 virtual cores with 2 EC2 Compute Units each)	15 GB	1,690 GB instance storage (4 x 420 GB plus 10 GB root partition)	64-bit	High	m1.xlarge	Zend _Service _Amazon _Ec2_ Instance ::XLARGE
High-CPU Medium	5 EC2 Compute Units (2 virtual cores with 2.5 EC2 Compute Units each)	1.7 GB	350 GB instance storage (340 GB plus 10 GB root partition)	32-bit	Moderate	c1.medium	Zend _Service _Amazon _Ec2_ Instance ::HCPU _MEDIUM
High-CPU Extra Large	20 EC2 Compute Units (8 virtual cores with 2.5 EC2 Compute	7 GB	1,690 GB instance storage (4 x 420 GB plus 10 GB root partition)	64-bit	High	c1.xlarge	Zend _Service _Amazon _Ec2_ Instance ::HCPU _XLARGE

Type	CPU	Memory	Storage	Platform	I/O	Name	Constant Name
	Units each)						

Running Amazon EC2 Instances

This section describes the operation methods for maintaining Amazon EC2 Instances.

Example 22.11. Starting New Ec2 Instances

run will launch a specified number of EC2 Instances. run takes an array of parameters to start, below is a table containing the valid values.

Table 22.11. Valid Run Options

Name	Description	Required
imageId	ID of the AMI with which to launch instances.	Yes
minCount	Minimum number of instances to launch. Default: 1	No
maxCount	Maximum number of instances to launch. Default: 1	No
keyName	Name of the key pair with which to launch instances. If you do not provide a key, all instances will be inaccessible.	No
securityGroup	Names of the security groups with which to associate the instances.	No
userData	The user data available to the launched instances. This should not be Base64 encoded.	No
instanceType	Specifies the instance type. Default: m1.small	No
placement	Specifies the availability zone in which to launch the instance(s). By default, Amazon EC2 selects an availability zone for you.	No
kernelId	The ID of the kernel with which to launch the instance.	No
ramdiskId	The ID of the RAM disk with which to launch the instance.	No
blockDeviceVirtualName	Specifies the virtual name to map to the corresponding device name. For example: instancestore0	No
blockDeviceName	Specifies the device to which you are mapping a virtual name. For example: sdb	No

Name	Description	Required

run will return information about each instance that is starting up.

```
$ec2_instance = new Zend_Service_Amazon_Ec2_Instance('aws_key',
                                                     'aws_secret_key');
$return = $ec2_instance->run(array('imageId' => 'ami-509320',
                                   'keyName' => 'myKey',
                                   'securityGroup' => array('web',
                                                            'default')));
```

Example 22.12. Rebooting an Ec2 Instances

reboot will reboot one or more instances.

This operation is asynchronous; it only queues a request to reboot the specified instance(s). The operation will succeed if the instances are valid and belong to the user. Requests to reboot terminated instances are ignored.

reboot returns boolean true or false

```
$ec2_instance = new Zend_Service_Amazon_Ec2_Instance('aws_key',
                                                     'aws_secret_key');
$return = $ec2_instance->reboot('instanceId');
```

Example 22.13. Terminating an Ec2 Instances

terminate shuts down one or more instances. This operation is idempotent; if you terminate an instance more than once, each call will succeed.

terminate returns boolean true or false

```
$ec2_instance = new Zend_Service_Amazon_Ec2_Instance('aws_key',
                                                     'aws_secret_key');
$return = $ec2_instance->terminate('instanceId');
```

Terminated Instances

Terminated instances will remain visible after termination (approximately one hour).

Amazon Instance Utilities

In this section you will find out how to retreive information, the console output and see if an instance contains a product code.

Example 22.14. Describing Instances

describe returns information about instances that you own.

If you specify one or more instance IDs, Amazon EC2 returns information for those instances. If you do not specify instance IDs, Amazon EC2 returns information for all relevant instances. If you specify an invalid instance ID, a fault is returned. If you specify an instance that you do not own, it will not be included in the returned results.

describe will return an array containing information on the instance.

```
$ec2_instance = new Zend_Service_Amazon_Ec2_Instance('aws_key',
                                                     'aws_secret_key');
$return = $ec2_instance->describe('instanceId');
```

Terminated Instances

Recently terminated instances might appear in the returned results. This interval is usually less than one hour. If you do not want terminated instances to be returned, pass in a second variable of boolean true to describe and the terminated instances will be ignored.

Example 22.15. Describing Instances By Image Id

describeByImageId is functionally the same as describe but it will only return the instances that are using the provided imageId.

describeByImageId will return an array containing information on the instances thare were started by the passed in imageId

```
$ec2_instance = new Zend_Service_Amazon_Ec2_Instance('aws_key',
                                                     'aws_secret_key');
$return = $ec2_instance->describeByImageId('imageId');
```

Terminated Instances

Recently terminated instances might appear in the returned results. This interval is usually less than one hour. If you do not want terminated instances to be returned, pass in a second variable of boolean true to describe and the terminated instances will be ignored.

Example 22.16. Retreiving Console Output

consoleOutput retrieves console output for the specified instance.

Instance console output is buffered and posted shortly after instance boot, reboot, and termination. Amazon EC2 preserves the most recent 64 KB output which will be available for at least one hour after the most recent post.

consoleOutput returns an array containing the instanceId, timestamp from the last output and the output from the console.

```
$ec2_instance = new Zend_Service_Amazon_Ec2_Instance('aws_key',
                                                     'aws_secret_key');
$return = $ec2_instance->consoleOutput('instanceId');
```

Example 22.17. Confirm Product Code on an Instance

`confirmProduct` returns true if the specified product code is attached to the specified instance. The operation returns false if the product code is not attached to the instance.

The `confirmProduct` operation can only be executed by the owner of the AMI. This feature is useful when an AMI owner is providing support and wants to verify whether a user's instance is eligible.

```
$ec2_instance = new Zend_Service_Amazon_Ec2_Instance('aws_key',
                                                     'aws_secret_key');
$return = $ec2_instance->terminate('productCode', 'instanceId');
```

Zend_Service_Amazon_Ec2: Amazon Machine Images (AMI)

Amazon Machine Images (AMIs) are preconfigured with an ever-growing list of operating systems.

AMI Information Utilities

Example 22.18. Register an AMI with EC2

`register` Each AMI is associated with an unique ID which is provided by the Amazon EC2 service through the RegisterImage operation. During registration, Amazon EC2 retrieves the specified image manifest from Amazon S3 and verifies that the image is owned by the user registering the image.

`register` returns the imageId for the registered Image.

```
$ec2_img = new Zend_Service_Amazon_Ec2_Image('aws_key','aws_secret_key');
$ip = $ec2_img->register('imageLocation');
```

Example 22.19. Deregister an AMI with EC2

`deregister`, Deregisters an AMI. Once deregistered, instances of the AMI can no longer be launched.

`deregister` returns boolean true or false.

```
$ec2_img = new Zend_Service_Amazon_Ec2_Image('aws_key','aws_secret_key');
$ip = $ec2_img->deregister('imageId');
```

Example 22.20. Describe an AMI

`describe` Returns information about AMIs, AKIs, and ARIs available to the user. Information returned includes image type, product codes, architecture, and kernel and RAM disk IDs. Images available to the user include public images available for any user to launch, private images owned by the user making the request, and private images owned by other users for which the user has explicit launch permissions.

Table 22.12. Launch permissions fall into three categories

Name	Description
public	The owner of the AMI granted launch permissions for the AMI to the all group. All users have launch permissions for these AMIs.
explicit	The owner of the AMI granted launch permissions to a specific user.
implicit	A user has implicit launch permissions for all AMIs he or she owns.

The list of AMIs returned can be modified by specifying AMI IDs, AMI owners, or users with launch permissions. If no options are specified, Amazon EC2 returns all AMIs for which the user has launch permissions.

If you specify one or more AMI IDs, only AMIs that have the specified IDs are returned. If you specify an invalid AMI ID, a fault is returned. If you specify an AMI ID for which you do not have access, it will not be included in the returned results.

If you specify one or more AMI owners, only AMIs from the specified owners and for which you have access are returned. The results can include the account IDs of the specified owners, amazon for AMIs owned by Amazon or self for AMIs that you own.

If you specify a list of executable users, only users that have launch permissions for the AMIs are returned. You can specify account IDs (if you own the AMI(s)), self for AMIs for which you own or have explicit permissions, or all for public AMIs.

describe returns an array for all the images that match the critera that was passed in. The array contains the imageId, imageLocation, imageState, imageOwnerId, isPublic, architecture, imageType, kernelId, ramdiskId and platform.

```
$ec2_img = new Zend_Service_Amazon_Ec2_Image('aws_key','aws_secret_key');
$ip = $ec2_img->describe();
```

AMI Attribute Utilities

Example 22.21. Modify Image Attributes

Modifies an attribute of an AMI

Table 22.13. Valid Attributes

Name	Description
launchPermission	Controls who has permission to launch the AMI. Launch permissions can be granted to specific users by adding userIds. To make the AMI public, add the all group.

Name	Description
productCodes	Associates a product code with AMIs. This allows developers to charge users for using AMIs. The user must be signed up for the product before they can launch the AMI. *This is a write once attribute; after it is set, it cannot be changed or removed.*

modifyAttribute returns boolean true or false.

```
$ec2_img = new Zend_Service_Amazon_Ec2_Image('aws_key','aws_secret_key');
// modify the launchPermission of an AMI
$return = $ec2_img->modifyAttribute('imageId',
                                    'launchPermission',
                                    'add',
                                    'userId',
                                    'userGroup');

// set the product code of the AMI.
$return = $ec2_img->modifyAttribute('imageId',
                                    'productCodes',
                                    'add',
                                    null,
                                    null,
                                    'productCode');
```

Example 22.22. Reset an AMI Attribute

resetAttribute will reset the attribute of an AMI to its default value. *The productCodes attribute cannot be reset.*

```
$ec2_img = new Zend_Service_Amazon_Ec2_Image('aws_key','aws_secret_key');
$return = $ec2_img->resetAttribute('imageId', 'launchPermission');
```

Example 22.23. Describe AMI Attribute

describeAttribute returns information about an attribute of an AMI. Only one attribute can be specified per call. Currently only launchPermission and productCodes are supported.

describeAttribute returns an array with the value of the attribute that was requested.

```
$ec2_img = new Zend_Service_Amazon_Ec2_Image('aws_key','aws_secret_key');
$return = $ec2_img->describeAttribute('imageId', 'launchPermission');
```

Zend_Service_Amazon_Ec2: Elastic Block Stroage (EBS)

Amazon Elastic Block Store (Amazon EBS) is a new type of storage designed specifically for Amazon EC2 instances. Amazon EBS allows you to create volumes that can be mounted as devices by Amazon

EC2 instances. Amazon EBS volumes behave like raw unformatted external block devices. They have user supplied device names and provide a block device interface. You can load a file system on top of Amazon EBS volumes, or use them just as you would use a block device.

You can create up to twenty Amazon EBS volumes of any size (from one GiB up to one TiB). Each Amazon EBS volume can be attached to any Amazon EC2 instance in the same Availability Zone or can be left unattached.

Amazon EBS provides the ability to create snapshots of your Amazon EBS volumes to Amazon S3. You can use these snapshots as the starting point for new Amazon EBS volumes and can protect your data for long term durability.

Create EBS Volumes and Snapshots

Example 22.24. Create a new EBS Volume

Creating a brand new EBS Volume requires the size and which zone you want the EBS Volume to be in.

createNewVolume will return an array containing information about the new Volume which includes the volumeId, size, zone, status and createTime.

```
$ec2_ebs = new Zend_Service_Amazon_Ec2_Ebs('aws_key','aws_secret_key');
$return = $ec2_ebs->createNewVolume(40, 'us-east-1a');
```

Example 22.25. Create an EBS Volume from a Snapshot

Creating an EBS Volume from a snapshot requires the snapshot_id and which zone you want the EBS Volume to be in.

createVolumeFromSnapshot will return an array containing information about the new Volume which includes the volumeId, size, zone, status, createTime and snapshotId.

```
$ec2_ebs = new Zend_Service_Amazon_Ec2_Ebs('aws_key','aws_secret_key');
$return = $ec2_ebs->createVolumeFromSnapshot('snap-78a54011', 'us-east-1a');
```

Example 22.26. Create a Snapshot of an EBS Volume

Creating a Snapshot of an EBS Volume requires the volumeId of the EBS Volume.

createSnapshot will return an array containing information about the new Volume Snapshot which includes the snapshotId, volumeId, status, startTime and progress.

```
$ec2_ebs = new Zend_Service_Amazon_Ec2_Ebs('aws_key','aws_secret_key');
$return = $ec2_ebs->createSnapshot('volumeId');
```

Describing EBS Volumes and Snapshots

Example 22.27. Describing an EBS Volume

describeVolume allows you to get information on an EBS Volume or a set of EBS Volumes. If nothing is passed in then it will return all EBS Volumes. If only one EBS Volume needs to be described a string can be passed in while an array of EBS Volume Id's can be passed in to describe them.

describeVolume will return an array with information about each Volume which includes the volumeId, size, status and createTime. If the volume is attached to an instance, an addition value of attachmentSet will be returned. The attachment set contains information about the instance that the EBS Volume is attached to, which includes volumeId, instanceId, device, status and attachTime.

```
$ec2_ebs = new Zend_Service_Amazon_Ec2_Ebs('aws_key','aws_secret_key');
$return = $ec2_ebs->describeVolume('volumeId');
```

Example 22.28. Describe Attached Volumes

To return a list of EBS Volumes currently attached to a running instance you can call this method. It will only return EBS Volumes attached to the instance with the passed in instanceId.

describeAttachedVolumes returns the same information as the describeVolume but only for the EBS Volumes that are currently attached to the specified instanceId.

```
$ec2_ebs = new Zend_Service_Amazon_Ec2_Ebs('aws_key','aws_secret_key');
$return = $ec2_ebs->describeAttachedVolumes('instanceId');
```

Example 22.29. Describe an EBS Volume Snapshot

describeSnapshot allows you to get information on an EBS Volume Snapshot or a set of EBS Volume Snapshots. If nothing is passed in then it will return information about all EBS Volume Snapshots. If only one EBS Volume Snapshot needs to be described its snapshotId can be passed in while an array of EBS Volume Snapshot Id's can be passed in to describe them.

describeSnapshot will return an array containing information about each EBS Volume Snapshot which includes the snapshotId, volumeId, status, startTime and progress.

```
$ec2_ebs = new Zend_Service_Amazon_Ec2_Ebs('aws_key','aws_secret_key');
$return = $ec2_ebs->describeSnapshot('volumeId');
```

Attach and Detaching Volumes from Instances

Example 22.30. Attaching an EBS Volume

attachVolume will attach an EBS Volume to a running Instance. To attach a volume you need to specify the volumeId, the instanceId and the device (ex: /dev/sdh).

attachVolume will return an array with information about the attach status which contains volumeId, instanceId, device, status and attachTime

```
$ec2_ebs = new Zend_Service_Amazon_Ec2_Ebs('aws_key','aws_secret_key');
$return = $ec2_ebs->attachVolume('volumeId', 'instanceid', '/dev/sdh');
```

Example 22.31. Detaching an EBS Volume

detachVolume will detach an EBS Volume from a running Instance. detachVolume requires that you specify the volumeId with the optional instanceId and device name that was passed when attaching the volume. If you need to force the detachment you can set the forth parameter to be true and it will force the volume to detach.

detachVolume returns an array containing status information about the EBS Volume which includes volumeId, instanceId, device, status and attachTime.

```
$ec2_ebs = new Zend_Service_Amazon_Ec2_Ebs('aws_key','aws_secret_key');
$return = $ec2_ebs->detachVolume('volumeId');
```

Forced Detach

You should only force a detach if the previous detachment attempt did not occur cleanly (logging into an instance, unmounting the volume, and detaching normally). This option can lead to data loss or a corrupted file system. Use this option only as a last resort to detach a volume from a failed instance. The instance will not have an opportunity to flush file system caches or file system meta data. If you use this option, you must perform file system check and repair procedures.

Deleting EBS Volumes and Snapshots

Example 22.32. Deleting an EBS Volume

deleteVolume will delete an unattached EBS Volume.

deleteVolume will return boolean true or false.

```
$ec2_ebs = new Zend_Service_Amazon_Ec2_Ebs('aws_key','aws_secret_key');
$return = $ec2_ebs->deleteVolume('volumeId');
```

Example 22.33. Deleting an EBS Volume Snapshot

deleteSnapshot will delete an EBS Volume Snapshot.

deleteSnapshot returns booleen true or false.

```
$ec2_ebs = new Zend_Service_Amazon_Ec2_Ebs('aws_key','aws_secret_key');
$return = $ec2_ebs->deleteSnapshot('snapshotId');
```

Zend_Service_Amazon_Ec2: Elastic IP Addresses

By default, all Amazon EC2 instances are assigned two IP addresses at launch: a private (RFC 1918) address and a public address that is mapped to the private IP address through Network Address Translation (NAT).

If you use dynamic DNS to map an existing DNS name to a new instance's public IP address, it might take up to 24 hours for the IP address to propagate through the Internet. As a result, new instances might not receive traffic while terminated instances continue to receive requests.

To solve this problem, Amazon EC2 provides elastic IP addresses. Elastic IP addresses are static IP addresses designed for dynamic cloud computing. Elastic IP addresses are associated with your account, not specific instances. Any elastic IP addresses that you associate with your account remain associated with your account until you explicitly release them. Unlike traditional static IP addresses, however, elastic IP addresses allow you to mask instance or Availability Zone failures by rapidly remapping your public IP addresses to any instance in your account.

Example 22.34. Allocating a new Elastic IP

`allocate` will assign your account a new Elastic IP Address.

`allocate` returns the newly allocated ip.

```
$ec2_eip = new Zend_Service_Amazon_Ec2_Elasticip('aws_key','aws_secret_key');
$ip = $ec2_eip->allocate();

// print out your newly allocated elastic ip address;
print $ip;
```

Example 22.35. Describing Allocated Elastic IP Addresses

`describe` has an optional paramater to describe all of your allocated Elastic IP addresses or just some of your allocated addresses.

`describe` returns an array that contains information on each Elastic IP Address which contains the publicIp and the instanceId if it is assocated.

```
$ec2_eip = new Zend_Service_Amazon_Ec2_Elasticip('aws_key','aws_secret_key');
// describe all
$ips = $ec2_eip->describe();

// describe a subset
$ips = $ec2_eip->describe(array('ip1', 'ip2', 'ip3'));

// describe a single ip address
$ip = $ec2_eip->describe('ip1');
```

Example 22.36. Releasing Elastic IP

`release` will release an Elastic IP to Amazon.

Returns a boolean true or false.

```
$ec2_eip = new Zend_Service_Amazon_Ec2_Elasticip('aws_key','aws_secret_key')
$ec2_eip->release('ipaddress');
```

Example 22.37. Associates an Elastic IP to an Instance

associate will assign an Elastic IP to an already running instance.

Returns a boolean true or false.

```
$ec2_eip = new Zend_Service_Amazon_Ec2_Elasticip('aws_key','aws_secret_key')
$ec2_eip->associate('instance_id', 'ipaddress');
```

Example 22.38. Disassociate an Elastic IP from an instance

disassociate will disassociate an Elastic IP from an instance. If you terminate an Instance it will automaticly disassociate the Elastic IP address for you.

Returns a boolean true or false.

```
$ec2_eip = new Zend_Service_Amazon_Ec2_Elasticip('aws_key','aws_secret_key')
$ec2_eip->disassociate('ipaddress');
```

Zend_Service_Amazon_Ec2: Keypairs

Keypairs are used to access instances.

Example 22.39. Creating a new Amazon Keypair

create, creates a new 2048 bit RSA key pair and returns a unique ID that can be used to reference this key pair when launching new instances.

create returns an array which contains the keyName, keyFingerprint and keyMaterial.

```
$ec2_kp = new Zend_Service_Amazon_Ec2_Keypair('aws_key','aws_secret_key');
$return = $ec2_kp->create('my-new-key');
```

Example 22.40. Deleting an Amazon Keypair

delete, will delete the key pair. This will only prevent it from being used with new instances. Instances currently running with the keypair will still allow you to access them.

delete returns boolean true or false

```
$ec2_kp = new Zend_Service_Amazon_Ec2_Keypair('aws_key','aws_secret_key');
$return = $ec2_kp->delete('my-new-key');
```

Example 22.41. Describe an Amazon Keypair

describe returns information about key pairs available to you. If you specify key pairs, information about those key pairs is returned. Otherwise, information for all registered key pairs is returned.

describe returns an array which contains keyName and keyFingerprint

```
$ec2_kp = new Zend_Service_Amazon_Ec2_Keypair('aws_key','aws_secret_key');
$return = $ec2_kp->describe('my-new-key');
```

Zend_Service_Amazon_Ec2: Regions and Availability Zones

Amazon EC2 provides the ability to place instances in different regions and Availability Zones. Regions are dispersed in separate geographic areas or countries. Availability Zones are located within regions and are engineered to be insulated from failures in other Availability Zones and provide inexpensive low latency network connectivity to other Availability Zones in the same region. By launching instances in separate Availability Zones, you can protect your applications from the failure of a single Availability Zone.

Amazon EC2 Regions

Amazon EC2 provides multiple regions so you can launch Amazon EC2 instances in locations that meet your requirements. For example, you might want to launch instances in Europe to be closer to your European customers or to meet legal requirements.

Each Amazon EC2 region is designed to be completely isolated from the other Amazon EC2 regions. This achieves the greatest possible failure independence and stability, and it makes the locality of each EC2 resource unambiguous.

Example 22.42. Viewing the available regions

describe is used to find out which regions your accout has access to.

describe will return an array containing information about which regions are available. Each array will contain regionName and regionUrl.

```
$ec2_region = new Zend_Service_Amazon_Ec2_Region('aws_key','aws_secret_key');
$regions = $ec2_region->describe();

foreach($regions as $region) {
    print $region['regionName'] . ' -- ' . $region['regionUrl'] . '<br />';
}
```

Amazon EC2 Availability Zones

When you launch an instance, you can optionally specify an Availability Zone. If you do not specify an Availability Zone, Amazon EC2 selects one for you in the region that you are using. When launching your initial instances, we recommend accepting the default Availability Zone, which allows Amazon EC2 to select the best Availability Zone for you based on system health and available capacity. Even if you have other instances running, you might consider not specifying an Availability Zone if your new instances do not need to be close to, or separated from, your existing instances.

Example 22.43. Viewing the available zones

describe is used to find out which what the status is of each availability zone.

describe will return an array containing information about which zones are available. Each array will contain zoneName and zoneState.

```
$ec2_zones = new Zend_Service_Amazon_Ec2_Availabilityzones('aws_key',
                                                             'aws_secret_key')
$zones = $ec2_zones->describe();

foreach($zones as $zone) {
    print $zone['zoneName'] . ' -- ' . $zone['zoneState'] . '<br />';
}
```

Zend_Service_Amazon_Ec2: Security Groups

A security group is a named collection of access rules. These access rules specify which ingress (i.e., incoming) network traffic should be delivered to your instance. All other ingress traffic will be discarded.

You can modify rules for a group at any time. The new rules are automatically enforced for all running instances and instances launched in the future.

Maximum Security Groups

You can create up to 100 security groups.

Security Group Maintenance

Example 22.44. Create a new Security Group

create a new security group. Every instance is launched in a security group. If no security group is specified during launch, the instances are launched in the default security group. Instances within the same security group have unrestricted network access to each other. Instances will reject network access attempts from other instances in a different security group.

create returns boolean true or false

```
$ec2_sg = new Zend_Service_Amazon_Ec2_Securitygroups('aws_key',
                                                       'aws_secret_key');
$return = $ec2_sg->create('mygroup', 'my group description');
```

Example 22.45. Describe a Security Group

describe returns information about security groups that you own.

If you specify security group names, information about those security groups is returned. Otherwise, information for all security groups is returned. If you specify a group that does not exist, a fault is returned.

describe will return an array containing information about security groups which includes the ownerId, groupName, groupDescription and an array containing all the rules for that security group.

```
$ec2_sg = new Zend_Service_Amazon_Ec2_Securitygroups('aws_key',
                                                     'aws_secret_key');
$return = $ec2_sg->describe('mygroup');
```

Example 22.46. Delete a Security Group

delete will remove the security group. If you attempt to delete a security group that contains instances, a fault is returned. If you attempt to delete a security group that is referenced by another security group, a fault is returned. For example, if security group B has a rule that allows access from security group A, security group A cannot be deleted until the allow rule is removed.

delete returns boolean true or false.

```
$ec2_sg = new Zend_Service_Amazon_Ec2_Securitygroups('aws_key',
                                                     'aws_secret_key');
$return = $ec2_sg->delete('mygroup');
```

Authorizing Access

Example 22.47. Authorizing by IP

authorizeIp Adds permissions to a security group based on an IP address, protocol type and port range.

Permissions are specified by the IP protocol (TCP, UDP or ICMP), the source of the request (by IP range or an Amazon EC2 user-group pair), the source and destination port ranges (for TCP and UDP), and the ICMP codes and types (for ICMP). When authorizing ICMP, -1 can be used as a wildcard in the type and code fields.

Permission changes are propagated to instances within the security group as quickly as possible. However, depending on the number of instances, a small delay might occur.

authorizeIp returns boolean true or false

```
$ec2_sg = new Zend_Service_Amazon_Ec2_Securitygroups('aws_key',
                                                     'aws_secret_key');
$return = $ec2_sg->authorizeIp('mygroup',
                               'protocol',
                               'fromPort',
                               'toPort',
                               'ipRange');
```

Example 22.48. Authorize By Group

authorizeGroup Adds permissions to a security group.

Permission changes are propagated to instances within the security group as quickly as possible.

However, depending on the number of instances, a small delay might occur.

`authorizeGroup` returns boolean true or false.

```
$ec2_sg = new Zend_Service_Amazon_Ec2_Securitygroups('aws_key',
                                          'aws_secret_key');
$return = $ec2_sg->authorizeGroup('mygroup', 'securityGroupName', 'ownerId')
```

Revoking Access

Example 22.49. Revoke by IP

`revokeIp` Revokes permissions to a security group based on an IP address, protocol type and port range. The permissions used to revoke must be specified using the same values used to grant the permissions.

Permissions are specified by the IP protocol (TCP, UDP or ICMP), the source of the request (by IP range or an Amazon EC2 user-group pair), the source and destination port ranges (for TCP and UDP), and the ICMP codes and types (for ICMP). When authorizing ICMP, -1 can be used as a wildcard in the type and code fields.

Permission changes are propagated to instances within the security group as quickly as possible. However, depending on the number of instances, a small delay might occur.

`revokeIp` returns boolean true or false

```
$ec2_sg = new Zend_Service_Amazon_Ec2_Securitygroups('aws_key',
                                          'aws_secret_key');
$return = $ec2_sg->revokeIp('mygroup',
                            'protocol',
                            'fromPort',
                            'toPort',
                            'ipRange');
```

Example 22.50. Revoke By Group

`revokeGroup` Adds permissions to a security group. The permissions to revoke must be specified using the same values used to grant the permissions.

Permission changes are propagated to instances within the security group as quickly as possible. However, depending on the number of instances, a small delay might occur.

`revokeGroup` returns boolean true or false.

```
$ec2_sg = new Zend_Service_Amazon_Ec2_Securitygroups('aws_key',
                                          'aws_secret_key');
$return = $ec2_sg->revokeGroup('mygroup', 'securityGroupName', 'ownerId');
```

Zend_Service_Amazon_S3

Introduction

Amazon S3 provides a simple web services interface that can be used to store and retrieve any amount of data, at any time, from anywhere on the web. It gives any developer access to the same highly scalable, reliable, fast, inexpensive data storage infrastructure that Amazon uses to run its own global network of web sites. The service aims to maximize benefits of scale and to pass those benefits on to developers.

Registering with Amazon S3

Before you can get started with `Zend_Service_Amazon_S3`, you must first register for an account. Please see the S3 FAQ [http://aws.amazon.com/s3/faqs/] page on the Amazon website for more information.

After registering, you will receive an application key and a secret key. You will need both to access the S3 service.

API Documentation

The `Zend_Service_Amazon_S3` class provides the PHP wrapper to the Amazon S3 REST interface. Please consult the Amazon S3 documentation [http://developer.amazonwebservices.com/connect/kbcategory.jspa?categoryID=48] for detailed description of the service. You will need to be familiar with basic concepts in order to use this service.

Features

`Zend_Service_Amazon_S3` provides the following functionality:

- A single point for configuring your amazon.s3 authentication credentials that can be used across the amazon.s3 namespaces.

- A proxy object that is more convenient to use than an HTTP client alone, mostly removing the need to manually construct HTTP POST requests to access the REST service.

- A response wrapper that parses each response body and throws an exception if an error occurred, alleviating the need to repeatedly check the success of many commands.

- Additional convenience methods for some of the more common operations.

Getting Started

Once you have registered with Amazon S3, you're ready to store your first data object on the S3. The objects on S3 are stored in containers, called "buckets". Bucket names are unique on S3, and each user can have no more than 100 buckets simultaneously. Each bucket can contain unlimited amount of objects, identified by name.

The following example demonstrates creating a bucket, storing and retrieving the data.

Example 22.51. Zend_Service_Amazon_S3 Usage Example

```php
<?php
require_once 'Zend/Service/Amazon/S3.php';
```

```
$s3 = new Zend_Service_Amazon_S3($my_aws_key, $my_aws_secret_key);

$s3->createBucket("my-own-bucket");

$s3->putObject("my-own-bucket/myobject", "somedata");

echo $s3->getObject("my-own-bucket/myobject");
```

Since Zend_Service_Amazon_S3 service requires authentication, you should pass your credentials (AWS key and secret key) to the constructor. If you only use one account, you can set default credentials for the service:

```
<?php
require_once 'Zend/Service/Amazon/S3.php';

Zend_Service_Amazon_S3::setKeys($my_aws_key, $my_aws_secret_key);
$s3 = new Zend_Service_Amazon_S3();
```

Bucket operations

All objects in S3 system are stored in buckets. Bucket has to be created before any storage operation. Bucket name is unique in the system, so you can not have bucket named the same as someone else's bucket.

Bucket name can contain lowercase letters, digits, periods (.), underscores (_), and dashes (-). No other symbols allowed. Bucket name should start with letter or digit, and be 3 to 255 characters long. Names looking like an IP address (e.g. "192.168.16.255") are not allowed.

- createBucket() creates a new bucket.

- cleanBucket() removes all objects that are contained in a bucket.

- removeBucket() removes the bucket from the system. The bucket should be empty to be removed.

Example 22.52. Zend_Service_Amazon_S3 Bucket Removal Example

```
<?php
require_once 'Zend/Service/Amazon/S3.php';

$s3 = new Zend_Service_Amazon_S3($my_aws_key, $my_aws_secret_key);

$s3->cleanBucket("my-own-bucket");
$s3->removeBucket("my-own-bucket");
```

- getBuckets() returns the list of the names of all buckets belonging to the user.

Example 22.53. Zend_Service_Amazon_S3 Bucket Listing Example

```
<?php
require_once 'Zend/Service/Amazon/S3.php';

$s3 = new Zend_Service_Amazon_S3($my_aws_key, $my_aws_secret_key);

$list = $s3->getBuckets();
```

```
foreach($list as $bucket) {
    echo "I have bucket $bucket\n";
}
```

- `isBucketAvailable()` check if the bucket exists and returns true if it does.

Object operations

The object is the basic storage unit in S3. Object stores unstructured data, which can be any size up to 4 gigabytes. There's no limit on how many objects can be stored on the system.

The object are contained in buckets. Object is identified by name, which can be any utf-8 string. It is common to use hierarchical names (such as `Pictures/Myself/CodingInPHP.jpg`) to organise object names. Object name is prefixed with bucket name when using object functions, so for object "mydata" in bucket "my-own-bucket" the name would be `my-own-bucket/mydata`.

Objects can be replaced (by rewriting new data with the same key) or deleted, but not modified, appended, etc. Object is always stored whole.

By default, all objects are private and can be accessed only by their owner. However, it is possible to specify object with public access, in which case it will be available through the URL: `http://s3.amazonaws.com/[bucket-name]/[object-name]`.

- `putObject($object, $data, $meta)` created an object with name `$object` (should contain the bucket name as prefix!) having `$data` as its content.

  Optional `$meta` parameter is the array of metadata, which currently supports the following parameters as keys:

`S3_CONTENT_TYPE_HEADER`	MIME content type of the data. If not specified, the type will be guessed according to the file extension of the object name.
`S3_ACL_HEADER`	The access to the item. Following access constants can be used:

`S3_ACL_PRIVATE`	Only the owner has access to the item.
`S3_ACL_PUBLIC_READ`	Anybody can read the object, but only owner can write. This is setting may be used to store publicly accessible content.
`S3_ACL_PUBLIC_WRITE`	Anybody can read or write the object. This policy is rarely useful.
`S3_ACL_AUTH_READ`	Only the owner has write access to the item, and other authenticated S3 users have read access. This is useful for sharing data between S3 accounts without exposing them to the public.

  By default, all the items are private.

Example 22.54. Zend_Service_Amazon_S3 Public Object Example

```php
<?php
require_once 'Zend/Service/Amazon/S3.php';
```

```
$s3 = new Zend_Service_Amazon_S3($my_aws_key, $my_aws_secret_key);

$s3->putObject("my-own-bucket/Pictures/Me.png", file_get_contents("me.png
    array(Zend_Service_Amazon_S3::S3_ACL_HEADER =>
        Zend_Service_Amazon_S3::S3_ACL_PUBLIC_READ));
// or:
$s3->putFile("me.png", "my-own-bucket/Pictures/Me.png",
    array(Zend_Service_Amazon_S3::S3_ACL_HEADER =>
        Zend_Service_Amazon_S3::S3_ACL_PUBLIC_READ));
echo "Go to http://s3.amazonaws.com/my-own-bucket/Pictures/Me.png
    to see me!\n";
```

- getObject($object) retrieves object data from the storage by name.

- removeObject($object) removes the object from the storage.

- getInfo($object) retrieves the metadata information about the object. The function will return array with metadata information. Some of the useful keys are:

type   The MIME type of the item.

size   The size of the object data.

mtime   UNIX-type timestamp of the last modification for the object.

etag   The ETag of the data, which is the MD5 hash of the data, surrounded by quotes (").
The function will return false if the key does not correspond to any existing object.

- getObjectsByBucket($bucket) returns the list of the object keys, contained in the bucket.

Example 22.55. Zend_Service_Amazon_S3 Object Listing Example

```
<?php
require_once 'Zend/Service/Amazon/S3.php';

$s3 = new Zend_Service_Amazon_S3($my_aws_key, $my_aws_secret_key);

$list = $s3->getObjectsByBucket("my-own-bucket");
foreach($list as $name) {
  echo "I have $name key:\n";
  $data = $s3->getObject("my-own-bucket/$name");
  echo "with data: $data\n";
}
```

- isObjectAvailable($object) checks if the object with given name exists.

- putFile($path, $object, $meta) puts the content of the file in $path into the object named $object.

The optional $meta argument is the same as for putObject. If the content type is omitted, it will be guessed basing on the source file name.

Stream wrapper

In addition to the interfaces described above, Zend_Service_Amazon_S3 also supports operating as a stream wrapper. For this, you need to register the client object as the stream wrapper:

Example 22.56. Zend_Service_Amazon_S3 Streams Example

```php
<?php
require_once 'Zend/Service/Amazon/S3.php';

$s3 = new Zend_Service_Amazon_S3($my_aws_key, $my_aws_secret_key);

$s3->registerStreamWrapper("s3");

mkdir("s3://my-own-bucket");
file_put_contents("s3://my-own-bucket/testdata", "mydata");

echo file_get_contents("s3://my-own-bucket/testdata");
```

Directory operations (mkdir, rmdir, opendir, etc.) will operate on buckets and thus their arguments should be of the form of s3://bucketname. File operations operate on objects. Object creation, reading, writing, deletion, stat and directory listing is supported.

Zend_Service_Audioscrobbler

Introduction

Zend_Service_Audioscrobbler is a simple API for using the Audioscrobbler REST Web Service. The Audioscrobbler Web Service provides access to its database of Users, Artists, Albums, Tracks, Tags, Groups, and Forums. The methods of the Zend_Service_Audioscrobbler class begin with one of these terms. The syntax and namespaces of the Audioscrobbler Web Service are mirrored in Zend_Service_Audioscrobbler. For more information about the Audioscrobbler REST Web Service, please visit the Audioscrobbler Web Service site [http://www.audioscrobbler.net/data/webservices/].

Users

In order to retrieve information for a specific user, the setUser() method is first used to select the user for which data are to be retrieved. Zend_Service_Audioscrobbler provides several methods for retrieving data specific to a single user:

- userGetProfileInformation(): Returns a SimpleXML object containing the current user's profile information.

- userGetTopArtists(): Returns a SimpleXML object containing a list of the current user's most listened to artists.

- userGetTopAlbums(): Returns a SimpleXML object containing a list of the current user's most listened to albums.

- userGetTopTracks(): Returns a SimpleXML object containing a list of the current user's most listened to tracks.

- userGetTopTags(): Returns a SimpleXML object containing a list of tags most applied by the current user.

- userGetTopTagsForArtist(): Requires that an artist be set via setArtist(). Returns a SimpleXML object containing the tags most applied to the current artist by the current user.

- userGetTopTagsForAlbum(): Requires that an album be set via setAlbum(). Returns a SimpleXML object containing the tags most applied to the current album by the current user.

- `userGetTopTagsForTrack()`: Requires that a track be set via `setTrack()`. Returns a SimpleXML object containing the tags most applied to the current track by the current user.

- `userGetFriends()`: Returns a SimpleXML object containing the user names of the current user's friends.

- `userGetNeighbours()`: Returns a SimpleXML object containing the user names of people with similar listening habits to the current user.

- `userGetRecentTracks()`: Returns a SimpleXML object containing the 10 tracks most recently played by the current user.

- `userGetRecentBannedTracks()`: Returns a SimpleXML object containing a list of the 10 tracks most recently banned by the current user.

- `userGetRecentLovedTracks()`: Returns a SimpleXML object containing a list of the 10 tracks most recently loved by the current user.

- `userGetRecentJournals()`: Returns a SimpleXML object containing a list of the current user's most recent journal entries.

- `userGetWeeklyChartList()`: Returns a SimpleXML object containing a list of weeks for which there exist Weekly Charts for the current user.

- `userGetRecentWeeklyArtistChart()`: Returns a SimpleXML object containing the most recent Weekly Artist Chart for the current user.

- `userGetRecentWeeklyAlbumChart()`: Returns a SimpleXML object containing the most recent Weekly Album Chart for the current user.

- `userGetRecentWeeklyTrackChart()`: Returns a SimpleXML object containing the most recent Weekly Track Chart for the current user.

- `userGetPreviousWeeklyArtistChart($fromDate,      $toDate)`:   Returns   a SimpleXML object containing the Weekly Artist Chart from `$fromDate` to `$toDate` for the current user.

- `userGetPreviousWeeklyAlbumChart($fromDate, $toDate)`: Returns a SimpleXML object containing the Weekly Album Chart from `$fromDate` to `$toDate` for the current user.

- `userGetPreviousWeeklyTrackChart($fromDate, $toDate)`: Returns a SimpleXML object containing the Weekly Track Chart from `$fromDate` to `$toDate` for the current user.

Example 22.57. Retrieving User Profile Information

In this example, we use the `setUser()` and `userGetProfileInformation()` methods to retrieve a specific user's profile information:

```
$as = new Zend_Service_Audioscrobbler();
// Set the user whose profile information we want to retrieve
$as->setUser('BigDaddy71');
// Retrieve BigDaddy71's profile information
$profileInfo = $as->userGetProfileInformation();
// Display some of it
print "Information for $profileInfo->realname "
    . "can be found at $profileInfo->url";
```

Example 22.58. Retrieving a User's Weekly Artist Chart

```
$as = new Zend_Service_Audioscrobbler();
// Set the user whose profile weekly artist chart we want to retrieve
$as->setUser('lo_fye');
// Retrieves a list of previous weeks for which there are chart data
$weeks = $as->userGetWeeklyChartList();
if (count($weeks) < 1) {
    echo 'No data available';
}
sort($weeks); // Order the list of weeks

$as->setFromDate($weeks[0]); // Set the starting date
$as->setToDate($weeks[0]); // Set the ending date

$previousWeeklyArtists = $as->userGetPreviousWeeklyArtistChart();

echo 'Artist Chart For Week Of '
    . date('Y-m-d h:i:s', $as->from_date)
    . '<br />';

foreach ($previousWeeklyArtists as $artist) {
    // Display the artists' names with links to their profiles
    print '<a href="' . $artist->url . '">' . $artist->name . '</a><br />';
}
```

Artists

Zend_Service_Audioscrobbler provides several methods for retrieving data about a specific artist, specified via the setArtist() method:

- artistGetRelatedArtists(): Returns a SimpleXML object containing a list of Artists similar to the current Artist.

- artistGetTopFans(): Returns a SimpleXML object containing a list of Users who listen most to the current Artist.

- artistGetTopTracks(): Returns a SimpleXML object containing a list of the current Artist's top-rated Tracks.

- artistGetTopAlbums(): Returns a SimpleXML object containing a list of the current Artist's top-rated Albums.

- artistGetTopTags(): Returns a SimpleXML object containing a list of the Tags most frequently applied to current Artist.

Example 22.59. Retrieving Related Artists

```
$as = new Zend_Service_Audioscrobbler();
// Set the artist for whom you would like to retrieve related artists
$as->setArtist('LCD Soundsystem');
// Retrieve the related artists
$relatedArtists = $as->artistGetRelatedArtists();
foreach ($relatedArtists as $artist) {
    // Display the related artists
    print '<a href="' . $artist->url . '">' . $artist->name . '</a><br />';
}
```

Tracks

`Zend_Service_Audioscrobbler` provides two methods for retrieving data specific to a single track, specified via the `setTrack()` method:

- `trackGetTopFans()`: Returns a SimpleXML object containing a list of Users who listen most to the current Track.

- `trackGetTopTags()`: Returns a SimpleXML object containing a list of the Tags most frequently applied to the current Track.

Tags

`Zend_Service_Audioscrobbler` provides several methods for retrieving data specific to a single tag, specified via the `setTag()` method:

- `tagGetOverallTopTags()`: Returns a SimpleXML object containing a list of Tags most frequently used on Audioscrobbler.

- `tagGetTopArtists()`: Returns a SimpleXML object containing a list of Artists to whom the current Tag was most frequently applied.

- `tagGetTopAlbums()`: Returns a SimpleXML object containing a list of Albums to which the current Tag was most frequently applied.

- `tagGetTopTracks()`: Returns a SimpleXML object containing a list of Tracks to which the current Tag was most frequently applied.

Groups

`Zend_Service_Audioscrobbler` provides several methods for retrieving data specific to a single group, specified via the `setGroup()` method:

- `groupGetRecentJournals()`: Returns a SimpleXML object containing a list of recent journal posts by Users in the current Group.

- `groupGetWeeklyChart()`: Returns a SimpleXML object containing a list of weeks for which there exist Weekly Charts for the current Group.

- `groupGetRecentWeeklyArtistChart()`: Returns a SimpleXML object containing the most recent Weekly Artist Chart for the current Group.

- `groupGetRecentWeeklyAlbumChart()`: Returns a SimpleXML object containing the most recent Weekly Album Chart for the current Group.

- `groupGetRecentWeeklyTrackChart()`: Returns a SimpleXML object containing the most recent Weekly Track Chart for the current Group.

- `groupGetPreviousWeeklyArtistChart($fromDate, $toDate)`: Requires `setFromDate()` and `setToDate()`. Returns a SimpleXML object containing the Weekly Artist Chart from the current fromDate to the current toDate for the current Group.

- `groupGetPreviousWeeklyAlbumChart($fromDate, $toDate)`: Requires `setFromDate()` and `setToDate()`. Returns a SimpleXML object containing the Weekly Album Chart from the current fromDate to the current toDate for the current Group.

- `groupGetPreviousWeeklyTrackChart($fromDate, $toDate)`: Returns a SimpleXML object containing the Weekly Track Chart from the current fromDate to the current toDate for the current Group.

Forums

`Zend_Service_Audioscrobbler` provides a method for retrieving data specific to a single forum, specified via the `setForum()` method:

- `forumGetRecentPosts()`: Returns a SimpleXML object containing a list of recent posts in the current forum.

Zend_Service_Delicious

Introduction

`Zend_Service_Delicious` is simple API for using del.icio.us [http://del.icio.us] XML and JSON web services. This component gives you read-write access to posts at del.icio.us if you provide credentials. It also allows read-only access to public data of all users.

Example 22.60. Get all posts

```
$delicious = new Zend_Service_Delicious('username', 'password');
$posts = $delicious->getAllPosts();

foreach ($posts as $post) {
    echo "--\n";
    echo "Title: {$post->getTitle()}\n";
    echo "Url: {$post->getUrl()}\n";
}
```

Retrieving posts

`Zend_Service_Delicious` provides three methods for retrieving posts: `getPosts()`, `getRecentPosts()` and `getAllPosts()`. All of these methods return an instance of `Zend_Service_Delicious_PostList`, which holds all retrieved posts.

```
/**
 * Get posts matching the arguments. If no date or url is given,
 * most recent date will be used.
 *
 * @param string $tag Optional filtering by tag
 * @param Zend_Date $dt Optional filtering by date
 * @param string $url Optional filtering by url
 * @return Zend_Service_Delicious_PostList
 */
public function getPosts($tag = null, $dt = null, $url = null);

/**
 * Get recent posts
 *
 * @param string $tag    Optional filtering by tag
 * @param string $count Maximal number of posts to be returned
 *                         (default 15)
 * @return Zend_Service_Delicious_PostList
 */
public function getRecentPosts($tag = null, $count = 15);
```

```
/**
 * Get all posts
 *
 * @param string $tag Optional filtering by tag
 * @return Zend_Service_Delicious_PostList
 */
public function getAllPosts($tag = null);
```

Zend_Service_Delicious_PostList

Instances of this class are returned by the `getPosts()`, `getAllPosts()`, `getRecentPosts()`, and `getUserPosts()` methods of `Zend_Service_Delicious`.

For easier data access this class implements the `Countable`, `Iterator`, and `ArrayAccess` interfaces.

Example 22.61. Accessing post lists

```
$delicious = new Zend_Service_Delicious('username', 'password');
$posts = $delicious->getAllPosts();

// count posts
echo count($posts);

// iterate over posts
foreach ($posts as $post) {
    echo "--\n";
    echo "Title: {$post->getTitle()}\n";
    echo "Url: {$post->getUrl()}\n";
}

// get post using array access
echo $posts[0]->getTitle();
```

Note

The `ArrayAccess::offsetSet()` and `ArrayAccess::offsetUnset()` methods throw exceptions in this implementation. Thus, code like `unset($posts[0]);` and `$posts[0] = 'A';` will throw exceptions because these properties are read-only.

Post list objects have two built-in filtering capabilities. Post lists may be filtered by tags and by URL.

Example 22.62. Filtering a Post List with Specific Tags

Posts may be filtered by specific tags using `withTags()`. As a convenience, `withTag()` is also provided for when only a single tag needs to be specified.

```
$delicious = new Zend_Service_Delicious('username', 'password');
$posts = $delicious->getAllPosts();

// Print posts having "php" and "zend" tags
foreach ($posts->withTags(array('php', 'zend')) as $post) {
    echo "Title: {$post->getTitle()}\n";
    echo "Url: {$post->getUrl()}\n";
}
```

Example 22.63. Filtering a Post List by URL

Posts may be filtered by URL matching a specified regular expression using the withUrl() method:

```
$delicious = new Zend_Service_Delicious('username', 'password');
$posts = $delicious->getAllPosts();

// Print posts having "help" in the URL
foreach ($posts->withUrl('/help/') as $post) {
    echo "Title: {$post->getTitle()}\n";
    echo "Url: {$post->getUrl()}\n";
}
```

Editing posts

Example 22.64. Post editing

```
$delicious = new Zend_Service_Delicious('username', 'password');
$posts = $delicious->getPosts();

// set title
$posts[0]->setTitle('New title');
// save changes
$posts[0]->save();
```

Example 22.65. Method call chaining

Every setter method returns the post object so that you can chain method calls using a fluent interface.

```
$delicious = new Zend_Service_Delicious('username', 'password');
$posts = $delicious->getPosts();

$posts[0]->setTitle('New title')
         ->setNotes('New notes')
         ->save();
```

Deleting posts

There are two ways to delete a post, by specifying the post URL or by calling the delete() method upon a post object.

Example 22.66. Deleting posts

```
$delicious = new Zend_Service_Delicious('username', 'password');

// by specifying URL
$delicious->deletePost('http://framework.zend.com');

// or by calling the method upon a post object
$posts = $delicious->getPosts();
$posts[0]->delete();

// another way of using deletePost()
$delicious->deletePost($posts[0]->getUrl());
```

Adding new posts

To add a post you first need to call the createNewPost() method, which returns a Zend_Service_Delicious_Post object. When you edit the post, you need to save it to the del.icio.us database by calling the save() method.

Example 22.67. Adding a post

```
$delicious = new Zend_Service_Delicious('username', 'password');

// create a new post and save it (with method call chaining)
$delicious->createNewPost('Zend Framework', 'http://framework.zend.com')
        ->setNotes('Zend Framework Homepage')
        ->save();

// create a new post and save it  (without method call chaining)
$newPost = $delicious->createNewPost('Zend Framework',
                                      'http://framework.zend.com');
$newPost->setNotes('Zend Framework Homepage');
$newPost->save();
```

Tags

Example 22.68. Tags

```
$delicious = new Zend_Service_Delicious('username', 'password');

// get all tags
print_r($delicious->getTags());

// rename tag ZF to zendFramework
$delicious->renameTag('ZF', 'zendFramework');
```

Bundles

Example 22.69. Bundles

```
$delicious = new Zend_Service_Delicious('username', 'password');

// get all bundles
print_r($delicious->getBundles());

// delete bundle someBundle
$delicious->deleteBundle('someBundle');

// add bundle
$delicious->addBundle('newBundle', array('tag1', 'tag2'));
```

Public data

The del.icio.us web API allows access to the public data of all users.

Table 22.14. Methods for retrieving public data

Name	Description	Return type
getUserFans()	Retrieves fans of a user	Array
getUserNetwork()	Retrieves network of a user	Array
getUserPosts()	Retrieves posts of a user	Zend_Service_Delicious_PostList
getUserTags()	Retrieves tags of a user	Array

Note

When using only these methods, a username and password combination is not required when constructing a new Zend_Service_Delicious object.

Example 22.70. Retrieving public data

```
// username and password are not required
$delicious = new Zend_Service_Delicious();

// get fans of user someUser
print_r($delicious->getUserFans('someUser'));

// get network of user someUser
print_r($delicious->getUserNetwork('someUser'));

// get tags of user someUser
print_r($delicious->getUserTags('someUser'));
```

Public posts

When retrieving public posts with the `getUserPosts()` method, a `Zend_Service_Delicious_PostList` object is returned, and it contains `Zend_Service_Delicious_SimplePost` objects, which contain basic information about the posts, including URL, title, notes, and tags.

Table 22.15. Methods of the Zend_Service_Delicious_SimplePost class

Name	Description	Return type
`getNotes()`	Returns notes of a post	String
`getTags()`	Returns tags of a post	Array
`getTitle()`	Returns title of a post	String
`getUrl()`	Returns URL of a post	String

HTTP client

`Zend_Service_Delicious` uses `Zend_Rest_Client` for making HTTP requests to the del.icio.us web service. To change which HTTP client `Zend_Service_Delicious` uses, you need to change the HTTP client of `Zend_Rest_Client`.

Example 22.71. Changing the HTTP client of Zend_Rest_Client

```
$myHttpClient = new My_Http_Client();
Zend_Rest_Client::setHttpClient($myHttpClient);
```

When you are making more than one request with `Zend_Service_Delicious` to speed your requests, it's better to configure your HTTP client to keep connections alive.

Example 22.72. Configuring your HTTP client to keep connections alive

```
Zend_Rest_Client::getHttpClient()->setConfig(array(
        'keepalive' => true
));
```

Note

When a `Zend_Service_Delicious` object is constructed, the SSL transport of `Zend_Rest_Client` is set to `'ssl'` rather than the default of `'ssl2'`. This is because del.icio.us has some problems with `'ssl2'`, such as requests taking a long time to complete (around 2 seconds).

Zend_Service_Flickr

Introduction

`Zend_Service_Flickr` is a simple API for using the Flickr REST Web Service. In order to use the Flickr web services, you must have an API key. To obtain a key and for more information about the Flickr REST Web Service, please visit the Flickr API Documentation [http://www.flickr.com/services/api/].

In the following example, we use the `tagSearch()` method to search for photos having "php" in the tags.

Example 22.73. Simple Flickr Photo Search

```
$flickr = new Zend_Service_Flickr('MY_API_KEY');

$results = $flickr->tagSearch("php");

foreach ($results as $result) {
    echo $result->title . '<br />';
}
```

Optional parameter

`tagSearch()` accepts an optional second parameter as an array of options.

Finding Flickr Users' Photos and Information

`Zend_Service_Flickr` provides several ways to get information about Flickr users:

- `userSearch()`: Accepts a string query of space-delimited tags and an optional second parameter as an array of search options, and returns a set of photos as a `Zend_Service_Flickr_ResultSet` object.

- `getIdByUsername()`: Returns a string user ID associated with the given username string.

- `getIdByEmail()`: Returns a string user ID associated with the given email address string.

Example 22.74. Finding a Flickr User's Public Photos by E-Mail Address

In this example, we have a Flickr user's e-mail address, and we search for the user's public photos by using the `userSearch()` method:

```
$flickr = new Zend_Service_Flickr('MY_API_KEY');

$results = $flickr->userSearch($userEmail);

foreach ($results as $result) {
    echo $result->title . '<br />';
}
```

Finding photos From a Group Pool

`Zend_Service_Flickr` allows to retrieve a group's pool photos based on the group ID. Use the `groupPoolGetPhotos()` method:

Example 22.75. Retrieving a Group's Pool Photos by Group ID

```
$flickr = new Zend_Service_Flickr('MY_API_KEY');

    $results = $flickr->groupPoolGetPhotos($groupId);
```

```
foreach ($results as $result) {
    echo $result->title . '<br />';
}
```

Optional parameter

`groupPoolGetPhotos()` accepts an optional second parameter as an array of options.

Retrieving Flickr Image Details

`Zend_Service_Flickr` makes it quick and easy to get an image's details based on a given image ID. Just use the `getImageDetails()` method, as in the following example:

Example 22.76. Retrieving Flickr Image Details

Once you have a Flickr image ID, it is a simple matter to fetch information about the image:

```
$flickr = new Zend_Service_Flickr('MY_API_KEY');

$image = $flickr->getImageDetails($imageId);

echo "Image ID $imageId is $image->width x $image->height pixels.<br />\n";
echo "<a href=\"$image->clickUri\">Click for Image</a>\n";
```

Zend_Service_Flickr Result Classes

The following classes are all returned by `tagSearch()` and `userSearch()`:

*   `Zend_Service_Flickr_ResultSet`

*   `Zend_Service_Flickr_Result`

*   `Zend_Service_Flickr_Image`

Zend_Service_Flickr_ResultSet

Represents a set of Results from a Flickr search.

Note

Implements the `SeekableIterator` interface for easy iteration (e.g., using `foreach`), as well as direct access to a specific result using `seek()`.

Properties

Table 22.16. Zend_Service_Flickr_ResultSet Properties

Name	Type	Description
totalResultsAvailable	int	Total Number of Results available
totalResultsReturned	int	Total Number of Results returned

Name	Type	Description
firstResultPosition	int	The offset in the total result set of this result set

Zend_Service_Flickr_ResultSet::totalResults()

```
int totalResults();
```

Returns the total number of results in this result set.

Back to Class List

Zend_Service_Flickr_Result

A single Image result from a Flickr query

Properties

Table 22.17. Zend_Service_Flickr_Result Properties

Name	Type	Description
id	string	Image ID
owner	string	The photo owner's NSID.
secret	string	A key used in url construction.
server	string	The servername to use for URL construction.
title	string	The photo's title.
ispublic	string	The photo is public.
isfriend	string	The photo is visible to you because you are a friend of the owner.
isfamily	string	The photo is visible to you because you are family of the owner.
license	string	The license the photo is available under.
dateupload	string	The date the photo was uploaded.
datetaken	string	The date the photo was taken.
ownername	string	The screenname of the owner.
iconserver	string	The server used in assembling icon URLs.
Square	Zend_Service_Flickr_Image	A 75x75 thumbnail of the image.
Thumbnail	Zend_Service_Flickr_Image	A 100 pixel thumbnail of the image.
Small	Zend_Service_Flickr_Image	A 240 pixel version of the image.
Medium	Zend_Service_Flickr_Image	A 500 pixel version of the image.
Large	Zend_Service_Flickr_Image	A 640 pixel version of the image.
Original	Zend_Service_Flickr_Image	The original image.

Back to Class List

Zend_Service_Flickr_Image

Represents an Image returned by a Flickr search.

Properties

Table 22.18. Zend_Service_Flickr_Image Properties

Name	Type	Description
uri	string	URI for the original image
clickUri	string	Clickable URI (i.e. the Flickr page) for the image
width	int	Width of the Image
height	int	Height of the Image

Back to Class List

Zend_Service_Nirvanix

Introduction

Nirvanix provides an Internet Media File System (IMFS), an Internet storage service that allows applications to upload, store and organize files and subsequently access them using a standard Web Services interface. An IMFS is distributed clustered file system, accessed over the Internet, and optimized for dealing with media files (audio, video, etc). The goal of an IMFS is to provide massive scalability to deal with the challenges of media storage growth, with guaranteed access and availability regardless of time and location. Finally, an IMFS gives applications the ability to access data securely, without the large fixed costs associated with acquiring and maintaining physical storage assets.

Registering with Nirvanix

Before you can get started with Zend_Service_Nirvanix, you must first register for an account. Please see the Getting Started [http://www.nirvanix.com/gettingStarted.aspx] page on the Nirvanix website for more information.

After registering, you will receive a Username, Password, and Application Key. All three are required to use Zend_Service_Nirvanix.

API Documentation

Access to the Nirvanix IMFS is available through both SOAP and a faster REST service. Zend_Service_Nirvanix provides a relatively thin PHP 5 wrapper around the REST service.

Zend_Service_Nirvanix aims to make using the Nirvanix REST service easier but understanding the service itself is still essential to be successful with Nirvanix.

The Nirvanix API Documentation [http://developer.nirvanix.com/sitefiles/1000/API.html] provides an overview as well as detailed information using the service. Please familiarize yourself with this document and refer back to it as you use Zend_Service_Nirvanix.

Features

Nirvanix's REST service can be used effectively with PHP using the SimpleXML [http://www.php.net/simplexml] extension and Zend_Http_Client alone. However, using it this way is somewhat inconvenient due to repetitive operations like passing the session token on every request and repeatedly checking the response body for error codes.

`Zend_Service_Nirvanix` provides the following functionality:

- A single point for configuring your Nirvanix authentication credentials that can be used across the Nirvanix namespaces.

- A proxy object that is more convenient to use than an HTTP client alone, mostly removing the need to manually construct HTTP POST requests to access the REST service.

- A response wrapper that parses each response body and throws an exception if an error occurred, alleviating the need to repeatedly check the success of many commands.

- Additional convenience methods for some of the more common operations.

Getting Started

Once you have registered with Nirvanix, you're ready to store your first file on the IMFS. The most common operations that you will need to do on the IMFS are creating a new file, downloading an existing file, and deleting a file. `Zend_Service_Nirvanix` provides convenience methods for these three operations.

```
$auth = array('username' => 'your-username',
              'password' => 'your-password',
              'appKey'   => 'your-app-key');

$nirvanix = new Zend_Service_Nirvanix($auth);
$imfs = $nirvanix->getService('IMFS');

$imfs->putContents('/foo.txt', 'contents to store');

echo $imfs->getContents('/foo.txt');

$imfs->unlink('/foo.txt');
```

The first step to using `Zend_Service_Nirvanix` is always to authenticate against the service. This is done by passing your credentials to the `Zend_Service_Nirvanix` constructor above. The associative array is passed directly to Nirvanix as POST parameters.

Nirvanix divides its web services into namespaces [http://developer.nirvanix.com/sitefiles/1000/API.html#_Toc175999879]. Each namespace encapsulates a group of related operations. After getting an instance of `Zend_Service_Nirvanix`, call the `getService()` method to create a proxy for the namespace you want to use. Above, a proxy for the IMFS namespace is created.

After you have a proxy for the namespace you want to use, call methods on it. The proxy will allow you to use any command available on the REST API. The proxy may also make convenience methods available, which wrap web service commands. The example above shows using the IMFS convenience methods to create a new file, retrieve and display that file, and finally delete the file.

Understanding the Proxy

In the previous example, we used the `getService()` method to return a proxy object to the IMFS namespace. The proxy object allows you to use the Nirvanix REST service in a way that's closer to making a normal PHP method call, as opposed to constructing your own HTTP request objects.

A proxy object may provide convenience methods. These are methods that the `Zend_Service_Nirvanix` provides to simplify the use of the Nirvanix web services. In the previous example, the methods `putContents()`, `getContents()`, and `unlink()` do not have direct equivalents in the REST API. They are convenience methods provided by `Zend_Service_Nirvanix` that abstract more complicated operations on the REST API.

For all other method calls to the proxy object, the proxy will dynamically convert the method call to the equivalent HTTP POST request to the REST API. It does this by using the method name as the API command, and an associative array in the first argument as the POST parameters.

Let's say you want to call the REST API method RenameFile [http://developer.nirvanix.com/sitefiles/1000/API.html#_Toc175999923], which does not have a convenience method in Zend_Service_Nirvanix:

```
$auth = array('username' => 'your-username',
              'password' => 'your-password',
              'appKey'   => 'your-app-key');

$nirvanix = new Zend_Service_Nirvanix($auth);
$imfs = $nirvanix->getService('IMFS');

$result = $imfs->renameFile(array('filePath' => '/path/to/foo.txt',
                                  'newFileName' => 'bar.txt'));
```

Above, a proxy for the IMFS namespace is created. A method, renameFile(), is then called on the proxy. This method does not exist as a convenience method in the PHP code, so it is trapped by __call() and converted into a POST request to the REST API where the associative array is used as the POST parameters.

Notice in the Nirvanix API documentation that sessionToken is required for this method but we did not give it to the proxy object. It is added automatically for your convenience.

The result of this operation will either be a Zend_Service_Nirvanix_Response object wrapping the XML returned by Nirvanix, or a Zend_Service_Nirvanix_Exception if an error occurred.

Examining Results

The Nirvanix REST API always returns its results in XML. Zend_Service_Nirvanix parses this XML with the SimpleXML extension and then decorates the resulting SimpleXMLElement with a Zend_Service_Nirvanix_Response object.

The simplest way to examine a result from the service is to use the built-in PHP functions like print_r():

```
<?php
$auth = array('username' => 'your-username',
              'password' => 'your-password',
              'appKey'   => 'your-app-key');

$nirvanix = new Zend_Service_Nirvanix($auth);
$imfs = $nirvanix->getService('IMFS');

$result = $imfs->putContents('/foo.txt', 'fourteen bytes');
print_r($result);
?>

Zend_Service_Nirvanix_Response Object
(
    [_sxml:protected] => SimpleXMLElement Object
        (
            [ResponseCode] => 0
            [FilesUploaded] => 1
            [BytesUploaded] => 14
        )
)
```

You can access any property or method of the decorated `SimpleXMLElement`. In the above example, `$result->BytesUploaded` could be used to see the number of bytes received. Should you want to access the `SimpleXMLElement` directly, just use `$result->getSxml()`.

The most common response from Nirvanix is success (`ResponseCode` of zero). It is not normally necessary to check `ResponseCode` because any non-zero result will throw a `Zend_Service_Nirvanix_Exception`. See the next section on handling errors.

Handling Errors

When using Nirvanix, it's important to anticipate errors that can be returned by the service and handle them appropriately.

All operations against the REST service result in an XML return payload that contains a `ResponseCode` element, such as the following example:

```
<Response>
    <ResponseCode>0</ResponseCode>
</Response>
```

When the `ResponseCode` is zero such as in the example above, the operation was successful. When the operation is not successful, the `ResponseCode` is non-zero and an `ErrorMessage` element should be present.

To alleviate the need to repeatedly check if the `ResponseCode` is non-zero, `Zend_Service_Nirvanix` automatically checks each response returned by Nirvanix. If the `ResponseCode` indicates an error, a `Zend_Service_Nirvanix_Exception` will be thrown.

```
$auth = array('username' => 'your-username',
              'password' => 'your-password',
              'appKey'   => 'your-app-key');
$nirvanix = new Zend_Service_Nirvanix($auth);

try {

  $imfs = $nirvanix->getService('IMFS');
  $imfs->unlink('/a-nonexistant-path');

} catch (Zend_Service_Nirvanix_Exception $e) {
  echo $e->getMessage() . "\n";
  echo $e->getCode();
}
```

In the example above, `unlink()` is a convenience method that wraps the `DeleteFiles` command on the REST API. The `filePath` parameter required by the `DeleteFiles` [http://developer.nirvanix.com/sitefiles/1000/API.html#_Toc175999918] command contains a path that does not exist. This will result in a `Zend_Service_Nirvanix` exception being thrown with the message "Invalid path" and code 70005.

The Nirvanix API Documentation [http://developer.nirvanix.com/sitefiles/1000/API.html] describes the errors associated with each command. Depending on your needs, you may wrap each command in a `try` block or wrap many commands in the same `try` block for convenience.

Zend_Service_ReCaptcha

Introduction

`Zend_Service_ReCaptcha` provides a client for the reCAPTCHA Web Service [http://recaptcha.net/]. Per the reCAPTCHA site, "reCAPTCHA is a free CAPTCHA service that helps to digitize books." Each reCAPTCHA requires the user to input two words, the first of which is the actual captcha, and the second of which is a word from some scanned text that Optical Character Recognition (OCR) software has been unable to identify. The assumption is that if a user correctly provides the first word, the second is likely correctly entered as well, and can be used to improve OCR software for digitizing books.

In order to use the reCAPTCHA service, you will need to sign up for an account [http://recaptcha.net/whyrecaptcha.html] and register one or more domains with the service in order to generate public and private keys.

Simplest use

Instantiate a `Zend_Service_ReCaptcha` object, passing it your public and private keys:

```
$recaptcha = new Zend_Service_ReCaptcha($pubKey, $privKey);
```

To render the reCAPTCHA, simply call the `getHTML()` method:

```
echo $recaptcha->getHTML();
```

When the form is submitted, you should receive two fields, 'recaptcha_challenge_field' and 'recaptcha_response_field'. Pass these to the ReCaptcha object's `verify()` method:

```
$result = $recaptcha->verify(
    $_POST['recaptcha_challenge_field'],
    $_POST['recaptcha_response_field']
);
```

Once you have the result, test against it to see if it is valid. The result is a `Zend_Service_ReCaptcha_Response` object, which provides an `isValid()` method.

```
if (!$result->isValid()) {
    // Failed validation
}
```

Even simpler is to use the ReCaptcha `Zend_Captcha` adapter, or to use that adapter as a backend for the Captcha form element. In each case, the details of rendering and validating the reCAPTCHA are automated for you.

Zend_Service_Simpy

Introduction

`Zend_Service_Simpy` is a lightweight wrapper for the free REST API available for the Simpy social bookmarking service.

In order to use `Zend_Service_Simpy`, you should already have a Simpy account. To get an account, visit the Simpy web site [http://simpy.com]. For more information on the Simpy REST API, refer to the Simpy REST API documentation [http://www.simpy.com/doc/api/rest].

The Simpy REST API allows developers to interact with specific aspects of the service that the Simpy web site offers. The sections following will outline the use of `Zend_Service_Simpy` for each of these areas.

- Links: Create, Retrieve, Update, Delete

- Tags: Retrieve, Delete, Rename, Merge, Split

- Notes: Create, Retrieve, Update, Delete

- Watchlists: Get, Get All

Links

When querying links, results are returned in descending order by date added. Links can be searched by title, nickname, tags, note, or even the content of the web page associated with the link. Simpy offers searching by any or all of these fields with phrases, boolean operators, and wildcards. See the search syntax [http://www.simpy.com/faq#searchSyntax] and search fields [http://www.simpy.com/faq#searchFieldsLinks] sections of the Simpy FAQ for more information.

Example 22.77. Querying Links

```
$simpy = new Zend_Service_Simpy('yourusername', 'yourpassword');

/* Search for the 10 links added most recently */
$linkQuery = new Zend_Service_Simpy_LinkQuery();
$linkQuery->setLimit(10);

/* Get and display the links */
$linkSet = $simpy->getLinks($linkQuery);
foreach ($linkSet as $link) {
    echo '<a href="';
    echo $link->getUrl();
    echo '">';
    echo $link->getTitle();
    echo '</a><br />';
}

/* Search for the 5 links added most recently with 'PHP' in
the title */
$linkQuery->setQueryString('title:PHP');
$linkQuery->setLimit(5);

/* Search for all links with 'French' in the title and
'language' in the tags */
$linkQuery->setQueryString('+title:French +tags:language');

/* Search for all links with 'French' in the title and without
'travel' in the tags */
$linkQuery->setQueryString('+title:French -tags:travel');

/* Search for all links added on 12/9/06 */
$linkQuery->setDate('2006-12-09');

/* Search for all links added after 12/9/06 (excluding that
date) */
$linkQuery->setAfterDate('2006-12-09');

/* Search for all links added before 12/9/06 (excluding that
date) */
$linkQuery->setBeforeDate('2006-12-09');

/* Search for all links added between 12/1/06 and 12/9/06
(excluding those two dates) */
$linkQuery->setBeforeDate('2006-12-01');
$linkQuery->setAfterDate('2006-12-09');
```

Links are represented uniquely by their URLs. In other words, if an attempt is made to save a link that has the same URL as an existing link, data for the existing link will be overwritten with the data specified in the save attempt.

Example 22.78. Modifying Links

```
$simpy = new Zend_Service_Simpy('yourusername', 'yourpassword');

/* Save a link */
$simpy->saveLink(
    'Zend Framework' // Title
    'http://framework.zend.com', // URL
    Zend_Service_Simpy_Link::ACCESSTYPE_PUBLIC, // Access Type
    'zend, framework, php' // Tags
    'Zend Framework home page' // Alternative title
    'This site rocks!' // Note
);

/* Overwrite the existing link with new data */
$simpy->saveLink(
    'Zend Framework'
    'http://framework.zend.com',
    Zend_Service_Simpy_Link::ACCESSTYPE_PRIVATE, // Access Type has changed
    'php, zend, framework' // Tags have changed order
    'Zend Framework' // Alternative title has changed
    'This site REALLY rocks!' // Note has changed
);

/* Delete the link */
$simpy->deleteLink('http://framework.zend.com');

/* A really easy way to do spring cleaning on your links ;) */
$linkSet = $this->_simpy->getLinks();
foreach ($linkSet as $link) {
    $this->_simpy->deleteLink($link->getUrl());
}
```

Tags

When retrieved, tags are sorted in decreasing order (i.e. highest first) by the number of links that use the tag.

Example 22.79. Working With Tags

```
$simpy = new Zend_Service_Simpy('yourusername', 'yourpassword');

/* Save a link with tags */
$simpy->saveLink(
    'Zend Framework' // Title
    'http://framework.zend.com', // URL
    Zend_Service_Simpy_Link::ACCESSTYPE_PUBLIC, // Access Type
    'zend, framework, php' // Tags
);
```

```
/* Get a list of all tags in use by links and notes */
$tagSet = $simpy->getTags();

/* Display each tag with the number of links using it */
foreach ($tagSet as $tag) {
    echo $tag->getTag();
    echo ' - ';
    echo $tag->getCount();
    echo '<br />';
}

/* Remove the 'zend' tag from all links using it */
$simpy->removeTag('zend');

/* Rename the 'framework' tag to 'frameworks' */
$simpy->renameTag('framework', 'frameworks');

/* Split the 'frameworks' tag into 'framework' and
'development', which will remove the 'frameworks' tag for
all links that use it and add the tags 'framework' and
'development' to all of those links */
$simpy->splitTag('frameworks', 'framework', 'development');

/* Merge the 'framework' and 'development' tags back into
'frameworks', basically doing the opposite of splitting them */
$simpy->mergeTags('framework', 'development', 'frameworks');
```

Notes

Notes can be saved, retrieved, and deleted. They are uniquely identified by a numeric ID value.

Example 22.80. Working With Notes

```
$simpy = new Zend_Service_Simpy('yourusername', 'yourpassword');

/* Save a note */
$simpy->saveNote(
    'Test Note', // Title
    'test,note', // Tags
    'This is a test note.' // Description
);

/* Overwrite an existing note */
$simpy->saveNote(
    'Updated Test Note', // Title
    'test,note,updated', // Tags
    'This is an updated test note.', // Description
    $note->getId() // Unique identifier
);

/* Search for the 10 most recently added notes */
$noteSet = $simpy->getNotes(null, 10);

/* Display the notes */
foreach ($noteSet as $note) {
    echo '<p>';
    echo $note->getTitle();
    echo '<br />';
    echo $note->getDescription();
```

```
        echo '<br >';
        echo $note->getTags();
        echo '</p>';
}

/* Search for all notes with 'PHP' in the title */
$noteSet = $simpy->getNotes('title:PHP');

/* Search for all notes with 'PHP' in the title and
without 'framework' in the description */
$noteSet = $simpy->getNotes('+title:PHP -description:framework');

/* Delete a note */
$simpy->deleteNote($note->getId());
```

Watchlists

Watchlists cannot be created or removed using the API, only retrieved. Thus, you must set up a watchlist via the Simpy web site prior to attempting to access it using the API.

Example 22.81. Retrieving Watchlists

```
$simpy = new Zend_Service_Simpy('yourusername', 'yourpassword');

/* Get a list of all watchlists */
$watchlistSet = $simpy->getWatchlists();

/* Display data for each watchlist */
foreach ($watchlistSet as $watchlist) {
    echo $watchlist->getId();
    echo '<br />';
    echo $watchlist->getName();
    echo '<br />';
    echo $watchlist->getDescription();
    echo '<br />';
    echo $watchlist->getAddDate();
    echo '<br />';
    echo $watchlist->getNewLinks();
    echo '<br />';

    foreach ($watchlist->getUsers() as $user) {
        echo $user;
        echo '<br />';
    }

    foreach ($watchlist->getFilters() as $filter) {
        echo $filter->getName();
        echo '<br />';
        echo $filter->getQuery();
        echo '<br />';
    }
}

/* Get an individual watchlist by its identifier */
$watchlist = $simpy->getWatchlist($watchlist->getId());
$watchlist = $simpy->getWatchlist(1);
```

Introduction

The Zend_Service_SlideShare component is used to interact with the slideshare.net [http://www.slideshare.net/] web services for hosting slide shows online. With this component, you can embed slide shows which are hosted on this web site within a web site and even upload new slide shows to your account.

Getting Started with Zend_Service_SlideShare

In order to use the Zend_Service_SlideShare component you must first create an account on the slideshare.net servers (more information can be found here [http://www.slideshare.net/developers/]) in order to receive an API key, username, password and shared secret value -- all of which are needed in order to use the Zend_Service_SlideShare component.

Once you have setup an account, you can begin using the Zend_Service_SlideShare component by creating a new instance of the Zend_Service_SlideShare object and providing these values as shown below:

```
// Create a new instance of the component
$ss = new Zend_Service_SlideShare('APIKEY',
                                  'SHAREDSECRET',
                                  'USERNAME',
                                  'PASSWORD');
```

The SlideShow object

All slide shows in the Zend_Service_SlideShare component are represented using the Zend_Service_SlideShare_SlideShow object (both when retrieving and uploading new slide shows). For your reference a pseudo-code version of this class is provided below.

```
class Zend_Service_SlideShare_SlideShow {

    /**
     * Retrieves the location of the slide show
     */
    public function getLocation() {
        return $this->_location;
    }

    /**
     * Gets the transcript for this slide show
     */
    public function getTranscript() {
        return $this->_transcript;
    }

    /**
     * Adds a tag to the slide show
     */
    public function addTag($tag) {
        $this->_tags[] = (string)$tag;
        return $this;
    }

    /**
     * Sets the tags for the slide show
     */
    public function setTags(Array $tags) {
```

```
        $this->_tags = $tags;
        return $this;
    }

    /**
     * Gets all of the tags associated with the slide show
     */
    public function getTags() {
        return $this->_tags;
    }

    /**
     * Sets the filename on the local filesystem of the slide show
     * (for uploading a new slide show)
     */
    public function setFilename($file) {
        $this->_slideShowFilename = (string)$file;
        return $this;
    }

    /**
     * Retrieves the filename on the local filesystem of the slide show
     * which will be uploaded
     */
    public function getFilename() {
        return $this->_slideShowFilename;
    }

    /**
     * Gets the ID for the slide show
     */
    public function getId() {
        return $this->_slideShowId;
    }

    /**
     * Retrieves the HTML embed code for the slide show
     */
    public function getEmbedCode() {
        return $this->_embedCode;
    }

    /**
     * Retrieves the Thumbnail URi for the slide show
     */
    public function getThumbnailUrl() {
        return $this->_thumbnailUrl;
    }

    /**
     * Sets the title for the Slide show
     */
    public function setTitle($title) {
        $this->_title = (string)$title;
        return $this;
    }

    /**
     * Retrieves the Slide show title
     */
    public function getTitle() {
        return $this->_title;
    }
```

```
/**
 * Sets the description for the Slide show
 */
public function setDescription($desc) {
    $this->_description = (string)$desc;
    return $this;
}

/**
 * Gets the description of the slide show
 */
public function getDescription() {
    return $this->_description;
}

/**
 * Gets the numeric status of the slide show on the server
 */
public function getStatus() {
    return $this->_status;
}

/**
 * Gets the textual description of the status of the slide show on
 * the server
 */
public function getStatusDescription() {
    return $this->_statusDescription;
}

/**
 * Gets the permanent link of the slide show
 */
public function getPermaLink() {
    return $this->_permalink;
}

/**
 * Gets the number of views the slide show has received
 */
public function getNumViews() {
    return $this->_numViews;
}
}
```

Note

The above pseudo-class only shows those methods which should be used by end-user developers. Other available methods are internal to the component.

When using the Zend_Service_SlideShare component, this data class will be used frequently to browse or add new slide shows to or from the web service.

Retrieving a single slide show

The simplest usage of the Zend_Service_SlideShare component is the retrieval of a single slide show by slide show ID provided by the slideshare.net application and is done by calling the getSlideShow() method of a Zend_Service_SlideShare object and using the resulting Zend_Service_SlideShare_SlideShow object as shown.

```
// Create a new instance of the component
```

```
$ss = new Zend_Service_SlideShare('APIKEY',
                                  'SHAREDSECRET',
                                  'USERNAME',
                                  'PASSWORD');

$slideshow = $ss->getSlideShow(123456);

print "Slide Show Title: {$slideshow->getTitle()}<br/>\n";
print "Number of views: {$slideshow->getNumViews()}<br/>\n";
```

Retrieving Groups of Slide Shows

If you do not know the specific ID of a slide show you are interested in retrieving, you can retrieving groups of slide shows by using one of three methods:

- *Slide shows from a specific account*

  You can retrieve slide shows from a specific account by using the getSlideShowsByUsername() method and providing the username from which the slide shows should be retrieved

- *Slide shows which contain specific tags*

  You can retrieve slide shows which contain one or more specific tags by using the getSlideShowsByTag method and providing one or more tags which the slide show must have assigned to it in order to be retrieved

- *Slide shows by group*

  You can retrieve slide shows which are a member of a specific group using the getSlideShowsByGroup method and providing the name of the group which the slide show must belong to in order to be retrieved

Each of the above methods of retrieving multiple slide shows a similar approach is used. An example of using each method is shown below:

```
// Create a new instance of the component
$ss = new Zend_Service_SlideShare('APIKEY',
                                  'SHAREDSECRET',
                                  'USERNAME',
                                  'PASSWORD');

$starting_offset = 0;
$limit = 10;

// Retrieve the first 10 of each type
$ss_user = $ss->getSlideShowsByUser('username', $starting_offset, $limit);
$ss_tags = $ss->getSlideShowsByTag('zend', $starting_offset, $limit);
$ss_group = $ss->getSlideShowsByGroup('mygroup', $starting_offset, $limit);

// Iterate over the slide shows
foreach($ss_user as $slideshow) {
    print "Slide Show Title: {$slideshow->getTitle}<br/>\n";
}
```

Zend_Service_SlideShare Caching policies

By default, Zend_Service_SlideShare will cache any request against the web service automatically to the filesystem (default path /tmp) for 12 hours. If you desire to change this behavior, you must provide your own Chapter 6, *Zend_Cache* object using the setCacheObject method as shown:

```
$frontendOptions = array(
                    'lifetime' => 7200,
                    'automatic_serialization' => true);
$backendOptions  = array(
                    'cache_dir' => '/webtmp/');

$cache = Zend_Cache::factory('Core',
                    'File',
                    $frontendOptions,
                    $backendOptions);

$ss = new Zend_Service_SlideShare('APIKEY',
                    'SHAREDSECRET',
                    'USERNAME',
                    'PASSWORD');
$ss->setCacheObject($cache);

$ss_user = $ss->getSlideShowsByUser('username', $starting_offset, $limit);
```

Changing the behavior of the HTTP Client

If for whatever reason you would like to change the behavior of the HTTP client when making the web service request, you can do so by creating your own instance of the Zend_Http_Client object (see Chapter 25, *Zend_Http*). This is useful for instance when it is desirable to set the timeout for the connection to something other then default as shown:

```
$client = new Zend_Http_Client();
$client->setConfig(array('timeout' => 5));

$ss = new Zend_Service_SlideShare('APIKEY',
                    'SHAREDSECRET',
                    'USERNAME',
                    'PASSWORD');
$ss->setHttpClient($client);
$ss_user = $ss->getSlideShowsByUser('username', $starting_offset, $limit);
```

Zend_Service_StrikeIron

Zend_Service_StrikeIron provides a PHP 5 client to StrikeIron web services. See the following sections:

- the section called "Zend_Service_StrikeIron"

- the section called "Zend_Service_StrikeIron: Bundled Services"

- the section called "Zend_Service_StrikeIron: Advanced Uses"

Overview

StrikeIron [http://www.strikeiron.com] offers hundreds of commercial data services ("Data as a Service") such as Online Sales Tax, Currency Rates, Stock Quotes, Geocodes, Global Address Verification, Yellow/White Pages, MapQuest Driving Directions, Dun & Bradstreet Business Credit Checks, and much, much more.

Each StrikeIron web service service shares a standard SOAP (and REST) API, making it easy to integrate and manage multiple services. StrikeIron also manages customer billing for all services in a single account, making it perfect for solution providers. Get started with free web services at http://www.strikeiron.com/sdp.

StrikeIron's services may be used through the PHP 5 SOAP extension [http://us.php.net/soap] alone. However, using StrikeIron this way does not give an ideal PHP-like interface. The `Zend_Service_StrikeIron` component provides a lightweight layer on top of the SOAP extension for working with StrikeIron services in a more convenient, PHP-like manner.

Note

The PHP 5 SOAP extension must be installed and enabled to use `Zend_Service_StrikeIron`.

The `Zend_Service_StrikeIron` component provides:

- A single point for configuring your StrikeIron authentication credentials that can be used across many StrikeIron services.

- A standard way of retrieving your StrikeIron subscription information such as license status and the number of hits remaining to a service.

- The ability to use any StrikeIron service from its WSDL without creating a PHP wrapper class, and the option of creating a wrapper for a more convenient interface.

- Wrappers for three popular StrikeIron services.

Registering with StrikeIron

Before you can get started with `Zend_Service_StrikeIron`, you must first register [http://strikeiron.com/Register.aspx] for a StrikeIron developer account.

After registering, you will receive a StrikeIron username and password. These will be used when connecting to StrikeIron using `Zend_Service_StrikeIron`.

You will also need to sign up [http://www.strikeiron.com/ProductDetail.aspx?p=257] for StrikeIron's Super Data Pack Web Service.

Both registration steps are free and can be done relatively quickly through the StrikeIron website.

Getting Started

Once you have registered [http://strikeiron.com/Register.aspx] for a StrikeIron account and signed up for the Super Data Pack [http://www.strikeiron.com/ProductDetail.aspx?p=257], you're ready to start using `Zend_Service_StrikeIron`.

StrikeIron consists of hundreds of different web services. `Zend_Service_StrikeIron` can be used with many of these services but provides supported wrappers for three of them:

- ZIP Code Information

- US Address Verification

- Sales & Use Tax Basic

The class `Zend_Service_StrikeIron` provides a simple way of specifying your StrikeIron account information and other options in its constructor. It also has a factory method that will return clients for StrikeIron services:

```
$strikeIron = new Zend_Service_StrikeIron(array('username' =>
            'your-username', 'password' => 'your-password'));
```

```
$taxBasic = $strikeIron->getService(array('class' => 'SalesUseTaxBasic'));
```

The `getService()` method will return a client for any StrikeIron service by the name of its PHP wrapper class. In this case, the name `SalesUseTaxBasic` refers to the wrapper class `Zend_Service_StrikeIron_SalesUseTaxBasic`. Wrappers are included for three services and described in Bundled Services.

The `getService()` method can also return a client for a StrikeIron service that does not yet have a PHP wrapper. This is explained in Using Services by WSDL.

Making Your First Query

Once you have used the `getService()` method to get a client for a particular StrikeIron service, you can utilize that client by calling methods on it just like any other PHP object.

```
$strikeIron = new Zend_Service_StrikeIron(array('username' =>
            'your-username', 'password' => 'your-password'));

// Get a client for the Sales & Use Tax Basic service
$taxBasic = $strikeIron->getService(array('class' => 'SalesUseTaxBasic'));

// Query tax rate for Ontario, Canada
$rateInfo = $taxBasic->getTaxRateCanada(array('province' => 'ontario'));
echo $rateInfo->province;
echo $rateInfo->abbreviation;
echo $rateInfo->GST;
```

In the example above, the `getService()` method is used to return a client to the Sales & Use Tax Basic service. The client object is stored in `$taxBasic`.

The `getTaxRateCanada()` method is then called on the service. An associative array is used to supply keyword parameters to the method. This is the way that all StrikeIron methods are called.

The result from `getTaxRateCanada()` is stored in `$rateInfo` and has properties like `province` and `GST`.

Many of the StrikeIron services are as simple to use as the example above. See Bundled Services for detailed information on three StrikeIron services.

Examining Results

When learning or debugging the StrikeIron services, it's often useful to dump the result returned from a method call. The result will always be an object that is an instance of `Zend_Service_StrikeIron_Decorator`. This is a small decorator [http://en.wikipedia.org/wiki/Decorator_pattern] object that wraps the results from the method call.

The simplest way to examine a result from the service is to use the built-in PHP functions like print_r() [http://www.php.net/print_r]:

```
<?php
$strikeIron = new Zend_Service_StrikeIron(array('username' =>
            'your-username', 'password' => 'your-password'));

$taxBasic = $strikeIron->getService(array('class' => 'SalesUseTaxBasic'));

$rateInfo = $taxBasic->getTaxRateCanada(array('province' => 'ontario'));
print_r($rateInfo);
?>

Zend_Service_StrikeIron_Decorator Object
```

```
(
    [_name:protected] => GetTaxRateCanadaResult
    [_object:protected] => stdClass Object
        (
            [abbreviation] => ON
            [province] => ONTARIO
            [GST] => 0.06
            [PST] => 0.08
            [total] => 0.14
            [HST] => Y
        )
)
```

In the output above, we see that the decorator ($rateInfo) wraps an object named GetTaxRateCanadaResult, the result of the call to getTaxRateCanada().

This means that $rateInfo has public properties like abbreviation, province, and GST. These are accessed like $rateInfo->province.

Tip

StrikeIron result properties sometimes start with an uppercase letter such as Foo or Bar where most PHP object properties normally start with a lowercase letter as in foo or bar. The decorator will automatically do this inflection so you may read a property Foo as foo.

If you ever need to get the original object or its name out of the decorator, use the respective methods getDecoratedObject() and getDecoratedObjectName().

Handling Errors

The previous examples are naive, i.e. no error handling was shown. It's possible that StrikeIron will return a fault during a method call. Events like bad account credentials or an expired subscription can cause StrikeIron to raise a fault.

An exception will be thrown when such a fault occurs. You should anticipate and catch these exceptions when making method calls to the service:

```
$strikeIron = new Zend_Service_StrikeIron(array('username' =>
                'your-username', 'password' => 'your-password'));

$taxBasic = $strikeIron->getService(array('class' => 'SalesUseTaxBasic'));

try {

  $taxBasic->getTaxRateCanada(array('province' => 'ontario'));

} catch (Zend_Service_StrikeIron_Exception $e) {

  // error handling for events like connection
  // problems or subscription errors

}
```

The exceptions thrown will always be Zend_Service_StrikeIron_Exception.

It's important to understand the difference between exceptions and normal failed method calls. Exceptions occur for *exceptional* conditions, such as the network going down or your subscription expiring. Failed method calls that are a common occurrence, such as getTaxRateCanada() not finding the province you supplied, will not result an in exception.

Note

Every time you make a method call to a StrikeIron service, you should check the response object for validity and also be prepared to catch an exception.

Checking Your Subscription

StrikeIron provides many different services. Some of these are free, some are available on a trial basis, and some are pay subscription only. When using StrikeIron, it's important to be aware of your subscription status for the services you are using and check it regularly.

Each StrikeIron client returned by the `getService` method has the ability to check the subscription status for that service using the `getSubscriptionInfo()` method of the client:

```
// Get a client for the Sales & Use Tax Basic service
$strikeIron = new Zend_Service_StrikeIron(array('username' =>
               'your-username', 'password' => 'your-password'));

$taxBasic = $strikeIron->getService(array('class => 'SalesUseTaxBasic'));

// Check remaining hits for the Sales & Use Tax Basic service
$subscription = $taxBasic->getSubscriptionInfo();
echo $subscription->remainingHits;
```

The `getSubscriptionInfo()` method will return an object that typically has a `remainingHits` property. It's important to check the status on each service that you are using. If a method call is made to StrikeIron after the remaining hits have been used up, an exception will occur.

Checking your subscription to a service does not use any remaining hits to the service. Each time any method call to the service is made, the number of hits remaining will be cached and this cached value will be returned by `getSubscriptionInfo()` without connecting to the service again. To force `getSubscriptionInfo()` to override its cache and query the subscription information again, use `getSubscriptionInfo(true)`.

Zend_Service_StrikeIron: Bundled Services

`Zend_Service_StrikeIron` comes with wrapper classes for three popular StrikeIron services.

ZIP Code Information

`Zend_Service_StrikeIron_ZipCodeInfo` provides a client for StrikeIron's Zip Code Information Service. For more information on this service, visit these StrikeIron resources:

- Zip Code Information Service Page [http://www.strikeiron.com/ProductDetail.aspx?p=267]

- Zip   Code   Information   Service   WSDL
  [http://sdpws.strikeiron.com/zf1.StrikeIron/sdpZIPCodeInfo?WSDL]

The service contains a `getZipCode()` method that will retrieve information about a United States ZIP code or Canadian postal code:

```
$strikeIron = new Zend_Service_StrikeIron(array('username' =>
               'your-username', 'password' => 'your-password'));

// Get a client for the Zip Code Information service
$zipInfo = $strikeIron->getService(array('class' => 'ZipCodeInfo'));

// Get the Zip information for 95014
```

```
$response = $zipInfo->getZipCode(array('ZipCode' => 95014));
$zips = $response->serviceResult;

// Display the results
if ($zips->count == 0) {
    echo 'No results found';
} else {
    // a result with one single zip code is returned as an object,
    // not an array with one element as one might expect.
    if (! is_array($zips->zipCodes)) {
        $zips->zipCodes = array($zips->zipCodes);
    }

    // print all of the possible results
    foreach ($zips->zipCodes as $z) {
        $info = $z->zipCodeInfo;

        // show all properties
        print_r($info);

        // or just the city name
        echo $info->preferredCityName;
    }
}

// Detailed status information
// http://www.strikeiron.com/exampledata/StrikeIronZipCodeInformation_v3.pdf
$status = $response->serviceStatus;
```

U.S. Address Verification

Zend_Service_StrikeIron_USAddressVerification provides a client for StrikeIron's U.S. Address Verification Service. For more information on this service, visit these StrikeIron resources:

- U.S. Address Verification Service Page [http://www.strikeiron.com/ProductDetail.aspx?p=198]

- U.S. Address Verification Service WSDL [http://ws.strikeiron.com/zf1.StrikeIron/USAddressVerification4_0?WSDL]

The service contains a verifyAddressUSA() method that will verify an address in the United States:

```
$strikeIron = new Zend_Service_StrikeIron(array('username' =>
                'your-username', 'password' => 'your-password'));

// Get a client for the Zip Code Information service
$verifier = $strikeIron->getService(array('class' => 'USAddress
                Verification'));

// Address to verify. Not all fields are required but
// supply as many as possible for the best results.
$address = array('firm'           => 'Zend Technologies',
                'addressLine1'    => '19200 Stevens Creek Blvd',
                'addressLine2'    => '',
                'city_state_zip'  => 'Cupertino CA 95014');

// Verify the address
$result = $verifier->verifyAddressUSA($address);

// Display the results
if ($result->addressErrorNumber != 0) {
    echo $result->addressErrorNumber;
```

```
    echo $result->addressErrorMessage;
} else {
    // show all properties
    print_r($result);

    // or just the firm name
    echo $result->firm;

    // valid address?
    $valid = ($result->valid == 'VALID');
}
```

Sales & Use Tax Basic

Zend_Service_StrikeIron_SalesUseTaxBasic provides a client for StrikeIron's Sales & Use Tax Basic service. For more information on this service, visit these StrikeIron resources:

- Sales & Use Tax Basic Service Page [http://www.strikeiron.com/ProductDetail.aspx?p=351]

- Sales & Use Tax Basic Service WSDL [http://ws.strikeiron.com/zf1.StrikeIron/taxdatabasic4?WSDL]

The service contains two methods, getTaxRateUSA() and getTaxRateCanada(), that will retrieve sales and use tax data for the United States and Canada, respectively.

```
$strikeIron = new Zend_Service_StrikeIron(array('username' =>
                'your-username', 'password' => 'your-password'));

// Get a client for the Sales & Use Tax Basic service
$taxBasic = $strikeIron->getService(array('class' => 'SalesUseTaxBasic'));

// Query tax rate for Ontario, Canada
$rateInfo = $taxBasic->getTaxRateCanada(array('province' => 'foo'));
print_r($rateInfo);              // show all properties
echo $rateInfo->GST;             // or just the GST (Goods & Services Tax)

// Query tax rate for Cupertino, CA USA
$rateInfo = $taxBasic->getTaxRateUS(array('zip_code' => 95014));
print_r($rateInfo);              // show all properties
echo $rateInfo->state_sales_tax; // or just the state sales tax
```

Zend_Service_StrikeIron: Advanced Uses

This section describes the more advanced uses of Zend_Service_StrikeIron.

Using Services by WSDL

Some StrikeIron services may have a PHP wrapper class available, such as those described in Bundled Services. However, StrikeIron offers hundreds of services and many of these may be usable even without creating a special wrapper class.

To try a StrikeIron service that does not have a wrapper class available, give the wsdl option to getService() instead of the class option:

```
$strikeIron = new Zend_Service_StrikeIron(array('username' =>
                'your-username', 'password' => 'your-password'));

// Get a generic client to the Reverse Phone Lookup service
```

```
$phone = $strikeIron->getService(
    array('wsdl' => 'http://ws.strikeiron.com/ReversePhoneLookup?WSDL')
);

$result = $phone->lookup(array('Number' => '(408) 253-8800'));
echo $result->listingName;

// Zend Technologies USA Inc
```

Using StrikeIron services from the WSDL will require at least some understanding of the WSDL files. StrikeIron has many resources on its site to help with this. Also, Jan Schneider [http://janschneider.de] from the Horde project [http://horde.org] has written a small PHP routine [http://janschneider.de/news/25/268] that will format a WSDL file into more readable HTML.

Please note that only the services described in the Bundled Services section are officially supported.

Viewing SOAP Transactions

All communication with StrikeIron is done using the SOAP extension. It is sometimes useful to view the XML exchanged with StrikeIron for debug purposes.

Every StrikeIron client (subclass of `Zend_Service_StrikeIron_Base`) contains a `getSoapClient()` method to return the underlying instance of `SOAPClient` used to communicate with StrikeIron.

PHP's SOAPClient [http://www.php.net/manual/en/function.soap-soapclient-construct.php] has a `trace` option that causes it to remember the XML exchanged during the last transaction. `Zend_Service_StrikeIron` does not enable the `trace` option by default but this can easily by changed by specifying the options that will be passed to the `SOAPClient` constructor.

To view a SOAP transaction, call the `getSoapClient()` method to get the `SOAPClient` instance and then call the appropriate methods like `__getLastRequest()` [http://www.php.net/manual/en/function.soap-soapclient-getlastrequest.php] and `__getLastRequest()` [http://www.php.net/manual/en/function.soap-soapclient-getlastresponse.php]:

```
$strikeIron =
    new Zend_Service_StrikeIron(array('username' => 'your-username',
                                      'password' => 'your-password',
                                      'options'  => array('trace' => true)));

// Get a client for the Sales & Use Tax Basic service
$taxBasic = $strikeIron->getService(array('class' => 'SalesUseTaxBasic'));

// Perform a method call
$taxBasic->getTaxRateCanada(array('province' => 'ontario'));

// Get SOAPClient instance and view XML
$soapClient = $taxBasic->getSoapClient();
echo $soapClient->__getLastRequest();
echo $soapClient->__getLastResponse();
```

Zend_Service_Technorati

Introduction

`Zend_Service_Technorati` provides an easy, intuitive and object-oriented interface for using the Technorati API. It provides access to all available Technorati API queries [http://technorati.com/developers/api/] and returns the original XML response as a friendly PHP object.

Technorati [http://technorati.com/] is one of the most popular blog search engines. The API interface enables developers to retrieve information about a specific blog, search blogs matching a single tag or phrase and get information about a specific author (blogger). For a full list of available queries please see the Technorati API documentation [http://technorati.com/developers/api/] or the Available Technorati queries section of this document.

Getting Started

Technorati requires a valid API key for usage. To get your own API Key you first need to create a new Technorati account [http://technorati.com/signup/], then visit the API Key section [http://technorati.com/developers/apikey.html].

API Key limits

You can make up to 500 Technorati API calls per day, at no charge. Other usage limitations may apply, depending on the current Technorati API license.

Once you have a valid API key, you're ready to start using Zend_Service_Technorati.

Making Your First Query

In order to run a query, first you need a Zend_Service_Technorati instance with a valid API key. Then choose one of the available query methods, and call it providing required arguments.

Example 22.82. Sending your first query

```
// create a new Zend_Service_Technorati
// with a valid API_KEY
$technorati = new Zend_Service_Technorati('VALID_API_KEY');

// search Technorati for PHP keyword
$resultSet = $technorati->search('PHP');
```

Each query method accepts an array of optional parameters that can be used to refine your query.

Example 22.83. Refining your query

```
// create a new Zend_Service_Technorati
// with a valid API_KEY
$technorati = new Zend_Service_Technorati('VALID_API_KEY');

// filter your query including only results
// with some authority (Results from blogs with a handful of links)
$options = array('authority' => 'a4');

// search Technorati for PHP keyword
$resultSet = $technorati->search('PHP', $options);
```

A Zend_Service_Technorati instance is not a single-use object. That is, you don't need to create a new instance for each query call; simply use your current Zend_Service_Technorati object as long as you need it.

Example 22.84. Sending multiple queries with the same Zend_Service_Technorati instance

```
// create a new Zend_Service_Technorati
// with a valid API_KEY
$technorati = new Zend_Service_Technorati('VALID_API_KEY');

// search Technorati for PHP keyword
$search = $technorati->search('PHP');

// get top tags indexed by Technorati
$topTags = $technorati->topTags();
```

Consuming Results

You can get one of two types of result object in response to a query.

The first group is represented by Zend_Service_Technorati_*ResultSet objects. A result set object is basically a collection of result objects. It extends the basic Zend_Service_Technorati_ResultSet class and implements the SeekableIterator PHP interface. The best way to consume a result set object is to loop over it with the PHP foreach statement.

Example 22.85. Consuming a result set object

```
// create a new Zend_Service_Technorati
// with a valid API_KEY
$technorati = new Zend_Service_Technorati('VALID_API_KEY');

// search Technorati for PHP keyword
// $resultSet is an instance of Zend_Service_Technorati_SearchResultSet
$resultSet = $technorati->search('PHP');

// loop over all result objects
foreach ($resultSet as $result) {
    // $result is an instance of Zend_Service_Technorati_SearchResult
}
```

Because Zend_Service_Technorati_ResultSet implements the SeekableIterator interface, you can seek a specific result object using its position in the result collection.

Example 22.86. Seeking a specific result set object

```
// create a new Zend_Service_Technorati
// with a valid API_KEY
$technorati = new Zend_Service_Technorati('VALID_API_KEY');

// search Technorati for PHP keyword
// $resultSet is an instance of Zend_Service_Technorati_SearchResultSet
$resultSet = $technorati->search('PHP');

// $result is an instance of Zend_Service_Technorati_SearchResult
```

```
$resultSet->seek(1);
$result = $resultSet->current();
```

Note

SeekableIterator works as an array and counts positions starting from index 0. Fetching position number 1 means getting the second result in the collection.

The second group is represented by special standalone result objects. Zend_Service_Technorati_GetInfoResult, Zend_Service_Technorati_BlogInfoResult and Zend_Service_Technorati_KeyInfoResult act as wrappers for additional objects, such as Zend_Service_Technorati_Author and Zend_Service_Technorati_Weblog.

Example 22.87. Consuming a standalone result object

```
// create a new Zend_Service_Technorati
// with a valid API_KEY
$technorati = new Zend_Service_Technorati('VALID_API_KEY');

// get info about weppos author
$result = $technorati->getInfo('weppos');

$author = $result->getAuthor();
echo '<h2>Blogs authored by ' . $author->getFirstName() . " " .
        $author->getLastName() . '</h2>';
echo '<ol>';
foreach ($result->getWeblogs() as $weblog) {
    echo '<li>' . $weblog->getName() . '</li>';
}
echo "</ol>";
```

Please read the Zend_Service_Technorati Classes section for further details about response classes.

Handling Errors

Each Zend_Service_Technorati query method throws a Zend_Service_Technorati_Exception exception on failure with a meaningful error message.

There are several reasons that may cause a Zend_Service_Technorati query to fail. Zend_Service_Technorati validates all parameters for any query request. If a parameter is invalid or it contains an invalid value, a new Zend_Service_Technorati_Exception exception is thrown. Additionally, the Technorati API interface could be temporally unavailable, or it could return a response that is not well formed.

You should always wrap a Technorati query with a try...catch block.

Example 22.88. Handling a Query Exception

```
$technorati = new Zend_Service_Technorati('VALID_API_KEY');
try {
    $resultSet = $technorati->search('PHP');
} catch(Zend_Service_Technorati_Exception $e) {
    echo "An error occurred: " $e->getMessage();
}
```

Checking Your API Key Daily Usage

From time to time you probably will want to check your API key daily usage. By default Technorati limits your API usage to 500 calls per day, and an exception is returned by Zend_Service_Technorati if you try to use it beyond this limit. You can get information about your API key usage using the Zend_Service_Technorati::keyInfo() method.

Zend_Service_Technorati::keyInfo() returns a Zend_Service_Technorati_KeyInfoResult object. For full details please see the API reference guide [http://framework.zend.com/apidoc/core/].

Example 22.89. Getting API key daily usage information

```
$technorati = new Zend_Service_Technorati('VALID_API_KEY');
$key = $technorati->keyInfo();

echo "API Key: " . $key->getApiKey() . "<br />";
echo "Daily Usage: " . $key->getApiQueries() . "/" .
    $key->getMaxQueries() . "<br />";
```

Available Technorati Queries

Zend_Service_Technorati provides support for the following queries:

*   Cosmos

*   Search

*   Tag

*   DailyCounts

*   TopTags

*   BlogInfo

*   BlogPostTags

*   GetInfo

Technorati Cosmos

Cosmos [http://technorati.com/developers/api/cosmos.html] query lets you see what blogs are linking to a given URL. It returns a Zend_Service_Technorati_CosmosResultSet object. For full details please see Zend_Service_Technorati::cosmos() in the API reference guide [http://framework.zend.com/apidoc/core/].

Example 22.90. Cosmos Query

```
$technorati = new Zend_Service_Technorati('VALID_API_KEY');
$resultSet = $technorati->cosmos('http://devzone.zend.com/');
```

```
echo "<p>Reading " . $resultSet->totalResults() .
    " of " . $resultSet->totalResultsAvailable() .
    " available results</p>";
echo "<ol>";
foreach ($resultSet as $result) {
    echo "<li>" . $result->getWeblog()->getName() . "</li>";
}
echo "</ol>";
```

Technorati Search

The Search [http://technorati.com/developers/api/search.html] query lets you see what blogs contain a given search string. It returns a Zend_Service_Technorati_SearchResultSet object. For full details please see Zend_Service_Technorati::search() in the API reference guide [http://framework.zend.com/apidoc/core/].

Example 22.91. Search Query

```
$technorati = new Zend_Service_Technorati('VALID_API_KEY');
$resultSet = $technorati->search('zend framework');

echo "<p>Reading " . $resultSet->totalResults() .
    " of " . $resultSet->totalResultsAvailable() .
    " available results</p>";
echo "<ol>";
foreach ($resultSet as $result) {
    echo "<li>" . $result->getWeblog()->getName() . "</li>";
}
echo "</ol>";
```

Technorati Tag

The Tag [http://technorati.com/developers/api/tag.html] query lets you see what posts are associated with a given tag. It returns a Zend_Service_Technorati_TagResultSet object. For full details please see Zend_Service_Technorati::tag() in the API reference guide [http://framework.zend.com/apidoc/core/].

Example 22.92. Tag Query

```
$technorati = new Zend_Service_Technorati('VALID_API_KEY');
$resultSet = $technorati->tag('php');

echo "<p>Reading " . $resultSet->totalResults() .
    " of " . $resultSet->totalResultsAvailable() .
    " available results</p>";
echo "<ol>";
foreach ($resultSet as $result) {
    echo "<li>" . $result->getWeblog()->getName() . "</li>";
}
echo "</ol>";
```

Technorati DailyCounts

The DailyCounts [http://technorati.com/developers/api/dailycounts.html] query provides daily counts of posts containing the queried keyword. It returns a `Zend_Service_Technorati_DailyCountsResultSet` object. For full details please see `Zend_Service_Technorati::dailyCounts()` in the API reference guide [http://framework.zend.com/apidoc/core/].

Example 22.93. DailyCounts Query

```
$technorati = new Zend_Service_Technorati('VALID_API_KEY');
$resultSet = $technorati->dailyCounts('php');

foreach ($resultSet as $result) {
    echo "<li>" . $result->getDate() .
         "(" . $result->getCount() . ")</li>";
}
echo "</ol>";
```

Technorati TopTags

The TopTags [http://technorati.com/developers/api/toptags.html] query provides information on top tags indexed by Technorati. It returns a `Zend_Service_Technorati_TagsResultSet` object. For full details please see `Zend_Service_Technorati::topTags()` in the API reference guide [http://framework.zend.com/apidoc/core/].

Example 22.94. TopTags Query

```
$technorati = new Zend_Service_Technorati('VALID_API_KEY');
$resultSet = $technorati->topTags();

echo "<p>Reading " . $resultSet->totalResults() .
     " of " . $resultSet->totalResultsAvailable() .
     " available results</p>";
echo "<ol>";
foreach ($resultSet as $result) {
    echo "<li>" . $result->getTag() . "</li>";
}
echo "</ol>";
```

Technorati BlogInfo

The BlogInfo [http://technorati.com/developers/api/bloginfo.html] query provides information on what blog, if any, is associated with a given URL. It returns a `Zend_Service_Technorati_BlogInfoResult` object. For full details please see `Zend_Service_Technorati::blogInfo()` in the API reference guide [http://framework.zend.com/apidoc/core/].

Example 22.95. BlogInfo Query

```
$technorati = new Zend_Service_Technorati('VALID_API_KEY');
$result = $technorati->blogInfo('http://devzone.zend.com/');

echo '<h2><a href="' . (string) $result->getWeblog()->getUrl() . '">' .
    $result->getWeblog()->getName() . '</a></h2>';
```

Technorati BlogPostTags

The BlogPostTags [http://technorati.com/developers/api/blogposttags.html] query provides information on the top tags used by a specific blog. It returns a Zend_Service_Technorati_TagsResultSet object. For full details please see Zend_Service_Technorati::blogPostTags() in the API reference guide [http://framework.zend.com/apidoc/core/].

Example 22.96. BlogPostTags Query

```
$technorati = new Zend_Service_Technorati('VALID_API_KEY');
$resultSet = $technorati->blogPostTags('http://devzone.zend.com/');

echo "<p>Reading " . $resultSet->totalResults() .
    " of " . $resultSet->totalResultsAvailable() .
    " available results</p>";
echo "<ol>";
foreach ($resultSet as $result) {
    echo "<li>" . $result->getTag() . "</li>";
}
echo "</ol>";
```

Technorati GetInfo

The GetInfo [http://technorati.com/developers/api/getinfo.html] query tells you things that Technorati knows about a member. It returns a Zend_Service_Technorati_GetInfoResult object. For full details please see Zend_Service_Technorati::getInfo() in the API reference guide [http://framework.zend.com/apidoc/core/].

Example 22.97. GetInfo Query

```
$technorati = new Zend_Service_Technorati('VALID_API_KEY');
$result = $technorati->getInfo('weppos');

$author = $result->getAuthor();
echo "<h2>Blogs authored by " . $author->getFirstName() . " " .
    $author->getLastName() . "</h2>";
echo "<ol>";
foreach ($result->getWeblogs() as $weblog) {
    echo "<li>" . $weblog->getName() . "</li>";
}
echo "</ol>";
```

Technorati KeyInfo

The KeyInfo query provides information on daily usage of an API key. It returns a `Zend_Service_Technorati_KeyInfoResult` object. For full details please see `Zend_Service_Technorati::keyInfo()` in the API reference guide [http://framework.zend.com/apidoc/core/].

Zend_Service_Technorati Classes

The following classes are returned by the various Technorati queries. Each `Zend_Service_Technorati_*ResultSet` class holds a type-specific result set which can be easily iterated, with each result being contained in a type result object. All result set classes extend `Zend_Service_Technorati_ResultSet` class and implement the `SeekableIterator` interface, allowing for easy iteration and seeking to a specific result.

- `Zend_Service_Technorati_ResultSet`

- `Zend_Service_Technorati_CosmosResultSet`

- `Zend_Service_Technorati_SearchResultSet`

- `Zend_Service_Technorati_TagResultSet`

- `Zend_Service_Technorati_DailyCountsResultSet`

- `Zend_Service_Technorati_TagsResultSet`

- `Zend_Service_Technorati_Result`

- `Zend_Service_Technorati_CosmosResult`

- `Zend_Service_Technorati_SearchResult`

- `Zend_Service_Technorati_TagResult`

- `Zend_Service_Technorati_DailyCountsResult`

- `Zend_Service_Technorati_TagsResult`

- `Zend_Service_Technorati_GetInfoResult`

- `Zend_Service_Technorati_BlogInfoResult`

- `Zend_Service_Technorati_KeyInfoResult`

Note

`Zend_Service_Technorati_GetInfoResult`, `Zend_Service_Technorati_BlogInfoResult` and `Zend_Service_Technorati_KeyInfoResult` represent exceptions to the above because they don't belong to a result set and they don't implement any interface. They represent a single response object and they act as a wrapper for additional `Zend_Service_Technorati` objects, such as `Zend_Service_Technorati_Author` and `Zend_Service_Technorati_Weblog`.

The `Zend_Service_Technorati` library includes additional convenient classes representing specific response objects. `Zend_Service_Technorati_Author` represents a single Technorati account, also known as a blog author or blogger. `Zend_Service_Technorati_Weblog` represents a single weblog object, along with all specific weblog properties such as feed URLs or blog name. For full details please see Zend_Service_Technorati in the API reference guide [http://framework.zend.com/apidoc/core/].

Zend_Service_Technorati_ResultSet

Zend_Service_Technorati_ResultSet is the most essential result set. The scope of this class is to be extended by a query-specific child result set class, and it should never be used to initialize a standalone object. Each of the specific result sets represents a collection of query-specific Zend_Service_Technorati_Result objects.

Zend_Service_Technorati_ResultSet implements the PHP SeekableIterator interface, and you can iterate all result objects via the PHP foreach statement.

Example 22.98. Iterating result objects from a resultset collection

```
// run a simple query
$technorati = new Zend_Service_Technorati('VALID_API_KEY');
$resultSet = $technorati->search('php');

// $resultSet is now an instance of
// Zend_Service_Technorati_SearchResultSet
// it extends Zend_Service_Technorati_ResultSet
foreach ($resultSet as $result) {
    // do something with your
    // Zend_Service_Technorati_SearchResult object
}
```

Zend_Service_Technorati_CosmosResultSet

Zend_Service_Technorati_CosmosResultSet represents a Technorati Cosmos query result set.

Note

Zend_Service_Technorati_CosmosResultSet extends Zend_Service_Technorati_ResultSet.

Zend_Service_Technorati_SearchResultSet

Zend_Service_Technorati_SearchResultSet represents a Technorati Search query result set.

Note

Zend_Service_Technorati_SearchResultSet extends Zend_Service_Technorati_ResultSet.

Zend_Service_Technorati_TagResultSet

Zend_Service_Technorati_TagResultSet represents a Technorati Tag query result set.

Note

Zend_Service_Technorati_TagResultSet extends Zend_Service_Technorati_ResultSet.

Zend_Service_Technorati_DailyCountsResultSet

`Zend_Service_Technorati_DailyCountsResultSet` represents a Technorati DailyCounts query result set.

Note

`Zend_Service_Technorati_DailyCountsResultSet` extends Zend_Service_Technorati_ResultSet.

Zend_Service_Technorati_TagsResultSet

`Zend_Service_Technorati_TagsResultSet` represents a Technorati TopTags or BlogPostTags queries result set.

Note

`Zend_Service_Technorati_TagsResultSet` extends Zend_Service_Technorati_ResultSet.

Zend_Service_Technorati_Result

`Zend_Service_Technorati_Result` is the most essential result object. The scope of this class is to be extended by a query specific child result class, and it should never be used to initialize a standalone object.

Zend_Service_Technorati_CosmosResult

`Zend_Service_Technorati_CosmosResult` represents a single Technorati Cosmos query result object. It is never returned as a standalone object, but it always belongs to a valid Zend_Service_Technorati_CosmosResultSet object.

Note

`Zend_Service_Technorati_CosmosResult` extends Zend_Service_Technorati_Result.

Zend_Service_Technorati_SearchResult

`Zend_Service_Technorati_SearchResult` represents a single Technorati Search query result object. It is never returned as a standalone object, but it always belongs to a valid Zend_Service_Technorati_SearchResultSet object.

Note

`Zend_Service_Technorati_SearchResult` extends Zend_Service_Technorati_Result.

Zend_Service_Technorati_TagResult

`Zend_Service_Technorati_TagResult` represents a single Technorati Tag query result object. It is never returned as a standalone object, but it always belongs to a valid Zend_Service_Technorati_TagResultSet object.

Note

`Zend_Service_Technorati_TagResult` extends Zend_Service_Technorati_Result.

Zend_Service_Technorati_DailyCountsResult

`Zend_Service_Technorati_DailyCountsResult` represents a single Technorati DailyCounts query result object. It is never returned as a standalone object, but it always belongs to a valid Zend_Service_Technorati_DailyCountsResultSet object.

Note

`Zend_Service_Technorati_DailyCountsResult` extends Zend_Service_Technorati_Result.

Zend_Service_Technorati_TagsResult

`Zend_Service_Technorati_TagsResult` represents a single Technorati TopTags or BlogPostTags query result object. It is never returned as a standalone object, but it always belongs to a valid Zend_Service_Technorati_TagsResultSet object.

Note

`Zend_Service_Technorati_TagsResult` extends Zend_Service_Technorati_Result.

Zend_Service_Technorati_GetInfoResult

`Zend_Service_Technorati_GetInfoResult` represents a single Technorati GetInfo query result object.

Zend_Service_Technorati_BlogInfoResult

`Zend_Service_Technorati_BlogInfoResult` represents a single Technorati BlogInfo query result object.

Zend_Service_Technorati_KeyInfoResult

`Zend_Service_Technorati_KeyInfoResult` represents a single Technorati KeyInfo query result object. It provides information about your Technorati API Key daily usage.

Zend_Service_Twitter

Introduction

`Zend_Service_Twitter` provides a client for the Twitter REST API [http://apiwiki.twitter.com/REST+API+Documentation]. `Zend_Service_Twitter` will allow you to query the public timeline and if you provide a username and password for Twitter it will allow you to get and update your status, reply to friends, direct message friends, mark tweets as favorite and much more.

`Zend_Service_Twitter` is implementing a REST service and all methods return an instance of `Zend_Rest_Client_Result`.

`Zend_Service_Twitter` is broken up into subsections so you can easily identify which type of call is being requested.

- `account`, make sure that your account credentials are valid, check your api rate limit and end the current session for the authenticated user.

- `status`, retrieves the public and user timelines and allows you to show, update, destroy and retrieve replies for the authenticated user.

- user, retrieves the friends, followers for the authenticated user. With the show method you can return extended information about the passed in user.

- directMessage, retrieves the authenticated users received direct message and allows you to send and delete new direct message.

- friendship, create or remove a friendship for the authenticated user.

- favorite, list, create or remove a favorite tweet.

Authentication

With the exception of fetching the public timeline Zend_Service_Twitter requires authentication to work. Twitter currently uses HTTP Basic Authentication [http://en.wikipedia.org/wiki/Basic_authentication_scheme]. You can pass in your username or registered email along with your password for twitter to login.

Example 22.99. Creating the Twitter Class

The following code sample is how you create the Twitter Service and pass in your username and password and then verify that they are correct.

```
$twitter = new Zend_Service_Twitter('myusername', 'mysecretpassword');
// verify your credentials with twitter
$response = $twitter->account->verifyCredentials();
```

Account Methods

- verifyCredentials, Use this method to test if supplied user credentials are valid with minimal overhead.

Example 22.100. Verifying credentials

```
$twitter = new Zend_Service_Twitter('myusername', 'mysecretpassword');
$response = $twitter->account->verifyCredentials();
```

- endSession, Use this method to sign users out of client-facing applications.

Example 22.101. Sessions ending

```
$twitter = new Zend_Service_Twitter('myusername', 'mysecretpassword');
$response = $twitter->account->endSession();
```

- rateLimitStatus, Returns the remaining number of API requests available to the authenticating user before the API limit is reached for the current hour.

Example 22.102. Rating limit status

```
$twitter = new Zend_Service_Twitter('myusername', 'mysecretpassword');
$response = $twitter->account->rateLimitStatus();
```

Status Methods

- publicTimeline, Returns the 20 most recent statuses from non-protected users with a custom user icon. The public timeline is cached by twitter for 60 seconds.

Example 22.103. Retrieving public timeline

```
$twitter = new Zend_Service_Twitter('myusername', 'mysecretpassword');
$response = $twitter->status->publicTimeline();
```

- friendsTimeline, Returns the 20 most recent statuses posted by the authenticating user and that user's friends.

Example 22.104. Retrieving friends timeline

```
$twitter = new Zend_Service_Twitter('myusername', 'mysecretpassword');
$response = $twitter->status->friendsTimeline();
```

The friendsTimeline method accepts an array of optional parameters to modify the query.

- since, Narrows the returned results to just those statuses created after the specified date/time (up to 24 hours old).

- page, Which page you want to return.

- userTimeline, Returns the 20 most recent statuses posted from the authenticating user.

Example 22.105. Retrieving user timeline

```
$twitter = new Zend_Service_Twitter('myusername', 'mysecretpassword');
$response = $twitter->status->userTimeline();
```

The userTimeline method accepts an array of optional parameters to modify the query.

- id, Specifies the ID or screen name of the user for whom to return the friends_timeline.

- since, Narrows the returned results to just those statuses created after the specified date/time (up to 24 hours old).

- page, Which page you want to return.

- count, Specifies the number of statuses to retrieve. May not be greater than 200.

- show, Returns a single status, specified by the id parameter below. The status's author will be returned inline. This method required a tweet id to be passed in.

Example 22.106. Showing user status

```
$twitter = new Zend_Service_Twitter('myusername', 'mysecretpassword');
$response = $twitter->status->show(1234);
```

- update, Updates the authenticating user's status. This method requires that you pass in the status update that you want to post to twitter. A second optional parameter is the id of the tweet that you are replying to.

Example 22.107. Updating user status

```
$twitter = new Zend_Service_Twitter('myusername', 'mysecretpassword');
$response = $twitter->status->update('My Great Tweet');
```

The update method accepts a second additional parameter.

- in_reply_to_status_id, The ID of an existing status that the status to be posted is in reply to.

- replies, Returns the 20 most recent @replies (status updates prefixed with @username) for the authenticating user.

Example 22.108. Showing user replies

```
$twitter = new Zend_Service_Twitter('myusername', 'mysecretpassword');
$response = $twitter->status->replies();
```

The replies method accepts an array of optional parameters to modify the query.

- since, Narrows the returned results to just those statuses created after the specified date/time (up to 24 hours old).

- page, Which page you want to return.

- since_id, Returns only statuses with an ID greater than (that is, more recent than) the specified ID.

- destroy, Destroys the status specified by the required ID parameter.

Example 22.109. Deleting user status

```
$twitter = new Zend_Service_Twitter('myusername', 'mysecretpassword');
$response = $twitter->status->destroy(12345);
```

User Methods

- `friends`, Returns up to 100 of the authenticating user's friends who have most recently updated, each with current status inline.

Example 22.110. Retrieving user friends

```
$twitter = new Zend_Service_Twitter('myusername', 'mysecretpassword');
$response = $twitter->user->friends();
```

The `friends` method accepts an array of optional parameters to modify the query.

- `id`, Specifies the ID or screen name of the user for whom to return a list of friends.
- `since`, Narrows the returned results to just those statuses created after the specified date/time (up to 24 hours old).
- `page`, Which page you want to return.
- `followers`, Returns the authenticating user's followers, each with current status inline.

Example 22.111. Retrieving user followers

```
$twitter = new Zend_Service_Twitter('myusername', 'mysecretpassword');
$response = $twitter->user->followers();
```

The `followers` method accepts an array of optional parameters to modify the query.

- `id`, Specifies the ID or screen name of the user for whom to return a list of followers.
- `page`, Which page you want to return.
- `show`, Returns extended information of a given user, specified by ID or screen name as per the required id parameter below

Example 22.112. Showing user informations

```
$twitter = new Zend_Service_Twitter('myusername', 'mysecretpassword');
$response = $twitter->user->show('myfriend');
```

Direct Message Methods

- `messages`, Returns a list of the 20 most recent direct messages sent to the authenticating user.

Example 22.113. Retrieving recent direct messages received

```
$twitter = new Zend_Service_Twitter('myusername', 'mysecretpassword');
$response = $twitter->directMessage->messages();
```

The `message` method accepts an array of optional parameters to modify the query.

- `since_id`, Returns only direct messages with an ID greater than (that is, more recent than) the specified ID.

- `since`, Narrows the returned results to just those statuses created after the specified date/time (up to 24 hours old).

- `page`, Which page you want to return.

- `sent`, Returns a list of the 20 most recent direct messages sent by the authenticating user.

Example 22.114. Retrieving recent direct messages sent

```
$twitter = new Zend_Service_Twitter('myusername', 'mysecretpassword');
$response = $twitter->directMessage->sent();
```

The `sent` method accepts an array of optional parameters to modify the query.

- `since_id`, Returns only direct messages with an ID greater than (that is, more recent than) the specified ID.

- `since`, Narrows the returned results to just those statuses created after the specified date/time (up to 24 hours old).

- `page`, Which page you want to return.

- `new`, Sends a new direct message to the specified user from the authenticating user. Requires both the user and text parameters below.

Example 22.115. Sending direct message

```
$twitter = new Zend_Service_Twitter('myusername', 'mysecretpassword');
$response = $twitter->directMessage->new('myfriend', 'mymessage');
```

- `destroy`, Destroys the direct message specified in the required ID parameter. The authenticating user must be the recipient of the specified direct message.

Example 22.116. Deleting direct message

```
$twitter = new Zend_Service_Twitter('myusername', 'mysecretpassword');
$response = $twitter->directMessage->destroy(123548);
```

Friendship Methods

- create, Befriends the user specified in the ID parameter as the authenticating user.

Example 22.117. Creating friend

```
$twitter = new Zend_Service_Twitter('myusername', 'mysecretpassword');
$response = $twitter->friendship->create('mynewfriend');
```

- destroy, Discontinues friendship with the user specified in the ID parameter as the authenticating user.

Example 22.118. Deleting friend

```
$twitter = new Zend_Service_Twitter('myusername', 'mysecretpassword');
$response = $twitter->friendship->destroy('myoldfriend');
```

- exists, Tests if a friendship exists between the authenticated user and the passed in user.

Example 22.119. Checking friend existence

```
$twitter = new Zend_Service_Twitter('myusername', 'mysecretpassword');
$response = $twitter->friendship->exists('myfriend');
```

Favorite Methods

- favorites, Returns the 20 most recent favorite statuses for the authenticating user or user specified by the ID parameter

Example 22.120. Retrieving favorites

```
$twitter = new Zend_Service_Twitter('myusername', 'mysecretpassword');
$response = $twitter->favorite->favorites();
```

- id, The ID or screen name of the user for whom to request a list of favorite statuses.

- page, Which page you want to return.

- create, Favorites the status specified in the ID parameter as the authenticating user..

Example 22.121. Creating favorites

```
$twitter = new Zend_Service_Twitter('myusername', 'mysecretpassword');
$response = $twitter->favorite->create(12351);
```

- destroy, Un-favorites the status specified in the ID parameter as the authenticating user.

Example 22.122. Deleting favorites

```
$twitter = new Zend_Service_Twitter('myusername', 'mysecretpassword');
$response = $twitter->favorite->destroy(12351);
```

Zend_Service_Twitter_Search

Introduction

Zend_Service_Twitter_Search provides a client for the Twitter Search API [http://apiwiki.twitter.com/Search+API+Documentation]. The Twitter Search service is use to search Twitter. Currently it only returns data in Atom or JSON format but a full REST service is in the future which will support XML responses.

Twitter Trends

Returns the top ten queries that are currently trending on Twitter. The response includes the time of the request, the name of each trending topic, and the url to the Twitter Search results page for that topic. Currently the search API for trends only supports a JSON return so the function returns an array.

```
$twitter_search = new Zend_Service_Twitter_Search();
$twitter_trends = $twitter_search->trends();

foreach($twitter_trends as $trend) {
    print $trend['name'] . ' - ' . $trend['url'] . PHP_EOL
}
```

The return array has two values in it:

- name, the name of trend.

- url, the url to see the tweets for that trend.

Searching Twitter

Using the search method returns tweets that match a specific query. There are a number of Search Operators [http://search.twitter.com/operators] that you can use to query with.

The search method can accept six different optional URL parameters passed in as an array:

- `lang`, restricts the tweets to a given language, lang must be given by an ISO 639-1 code [http://en.wikipedia.org/wiki/ISO_639-1].

- `rpp`, the number of tweets to return per page, up to a max of 100.

- `page`, the page number to return, up to a max of roughly 1500 results (based on rpp * page)

- `since_id`, returns tweets with status ids greater than the given id.

- `show_user`, when "true", adds ">user<:" to the beginning of the tweet. This is useful for readers that do not display Atom's author field. The default is "false"

- `geocode`, returns tweets by users located within a given radius of the given latitude/longitude, where the user's location is taken from their Twitter profile. The parameter value is specified by "latitude,longitude,radius", where radius units must be specified as either "mi" (miles) or "km" (kilometers).

Example 22.123. JSON Search Example

The following code sample will return an array with the values search results

```
$twitter_search = new Zend_Service_Twitter_Search('json');
$search_results = $twitter_search->search('zend', array('lang' => 'en'));
```

Example 22.124. ATOM Search Example

The following code sample will return a `Zend_Feed_Atom` object.

```
$twitter_search = new Zend_Service_Twitter_Search('atom');
$search_results = $twitter_search->search('zend', array('lang' => 'en'));
```

Zend-specific Accessor Methods

While the Twitter Search API only specifies two methods, `Zend_Service_Twitter_Search` has additional accessors that may be used for modifying internal properties.

- `getResponseType()` and `setResponseType()` allow you to retrieve and modify the response type of the search between JSON and ATOM.

Zend_Service_Yahoo

Introduction

`Zend_Service_Yahoo` is a simple API for using many of the Yahoo! REST APIs. `Zend_Service_Yahoo` allows you to search Yahoo! Web search, Yahoo! News, Yahoo! Local, Yahoo! Images. In order to use the Yahoo! REST API, you must have a Yahoo! Application ID. To obtain an Application ID, please complete and submit the Application ID Request Form [http://developer.yahoo.com/wsregapp/].

Searching the Web with Yahoo!

Zend_Service_Yahoo enables you to search the Web with Yahoo! using the webSearch() method, which accepts a string query parameter and an optional second parameter as an array of search options. For full details and an option list, please visit the Yahoo! Web Search Documentation [http://developer.yahoo.com/search/web/V1/webSearch.html]. The webSearch() method returns a Zend_Service_Yahoo_WebResultSet object.

Example 22.125. Searching the Web with Yahoo!

```
$yahoo = new Zend_Service_Yahoo("YAHOO_APPLICATION_ID");
$results = $yahoo->webSearch('PHP');
foreach ($results as $result) {
    echo $result->Title .'<br />';
}
```

Finding Images with Yahoo!

You can search for Images with Yahoo using Zend_Service_Yahoo's imageSearch() method. This method accepts a string query parameter and an optional array of search options, as for the webSearch() method. For full details and an option list, please visit the Yahoo! Image Search Documentation [http://developer.yahoo.com/search/image/V1/imageSearch.html].

Example 22.126. Finding Images with Yahoo!

```
$yahoo = new Zend_Service_Yahoo("YAHOO_APPLICATION_ID");
$results = $yahoo->imageSearch('PHP');
foreach ($results as $result) {
    echo $result->Title .'<br />';
}
```

Finding videos with Yahoo!

You can search for videos with Yahoo using Zend_Service_Yahoo's videoSearch() method. For full details and an option list, please visit the Yahoo! Video Search Documentation [http://developer.yahoo.com/search/video/V1/videoSearch.html].

Example 22.127. Finding videos with Yahoo!

```
$yahoo = new Zend_Service_Yahoo("YAHOO_APPLICATION_ID");
$results = $yahoo->videoSearch('PHP');
foreach ($results as $result) {
    echo $result->Title .'<br />';
}
```

Finding Local Businesses and Services with Yahoo!

You can search for local businesses and services with Yahoo! by using the `localSearch()` method. For full details, please see the Yahoo! Local Search Documentation [http://developer.yahoo.com/search/local/V1/localSearch.html].

Example 22.128. Finding Local Businesses and Services with Yahoo!

```
$yahoo = new Zend_Service_Yahoo("YAHOO_APPLICATION_ID");
$results = $yahoo->localSearch('Apple Computers', array('zip' => '95014'));
foreach ($results as $result) {
    echo $result->Title .'<br />';
}
```

Searching Yahoo! News

Searching Yahoo! News is simple; just use the `newsSearch()` method, as in the following example. For full details, please see the Yahoo! News Search Documentation [http://developer.yahoo.com/search/news/V1/newsSearch.html].

Example 22.129. Searching Yahoo! News

```
$yahoo = new Zend_Service_Yahoo("YAHOO_APPLICATION_ID");
$results = $yahoo->newsSearch('PHP');
foreach ($results as $result) {
    echo $result->Title .'<br />';
}
```

Searching Yahoo! Site Explorer Inbound Links

Searching Yahoo! Site Explorer Inbound Links is simple; just use the `inlinkDataSearch()` method, as in the following example. For full details, please see the Yahoo! Site Explorer Inbound Links Documentation [http://developer.yahoo.com/search/siteexplorer/V1/inlinkData.html].

Example 22.130. Searching Yahoo! Site Explorer Inbound Links

```
$yahoo = new Zend_Service_Yahoo("YAHOO_APPLICATION_ID");
$results = $yahoo->inlinkDataSearch('http://framework.zend.com/');
foreach ($results as $result) {
    echo $result->Title .'<br />';
}
```

Searching Yahoo! Site Explorer's PageData

Searching Yahoo! Site Explorer's PageData is simple; just use the `pageDataSearch()` method, as in the following example. For full details, please see the Yahoo! Site Explorer PageData Documentation [http://developer.yahoo.com/search/siteexplorer/V1/pageData.html].

Example 22.131. Searching Yahoo! Site Explorer's PageData

```
$yahoo = new Zend_Service_Yahoo("YAHOO_APPLICATION_ID");
$results = $yahoo->pageDataSearch('http://framework.zend.com/');
foreach ($results as $result) {
    echo $result->Title .'<br />';
}
```

Zend_Service_Yahoo Classes

The following classes are all returned by the various Yahoo! searches. Each search type returns a type-specific result set which can be easily iterated, with each result being contained in a type result object. All result set classes implement the `SeekableIterator` interface, allowing for easy iteration and seeking to a specific result.

- `Zend_Service_Yahoo_ResultSet`

- `Zend_Service_Yahoo_WebResultSet`

- `Zend_Service_Yahoo_ImageResultSet`

- `Zend_Service_Yahoo_VideoResultSet`

- `Zend_Service_Yahoo_LocalResultSet`

- `Zend_Service_Yahoo_NewsResultSet`

- `Zend_Service_Yahoo_InlinkDataResultSet`

- `Zend_Service_Yahoo_PageDataResultSet`

- `Zend_Service_Yahoo_Result`

- `Zend_Service_Yahoo_WebResult`

- `Zend_Service_Yahoo_ImageResult`

- `Zend_Service_Yahoo_VideoResult`

- `Zend_Service_Yahoo_LocalResult`

- `Zend_Service_Yahoo_NewsResult`

- `Zend_Service_Yahoo_InlinkDataResult`

- `Zend_Service_Yahoo_PageDataResult`

- `Zend_Service_Yahoo_Image`

Zend_Service_Yahoo_ResultSet

Each of the search specific result sets is extended from this base class.

Each of the specific result sets returns a search specific Zend_Service_Yahoo_Result objects.

Zend_Service_Yahoo_ResultSet::totalResults()

```
int totalResults();
```

Returns the number of results returned for the search.

Properties

Table 22.19. Zend_Service_Yahoo_ResultSet

Name	Type	Description
totalResultsAvailable	int	Total number of results found.
totalResultsReturned	int	Number of results in the current result set
firstResultPosition	int	Position of the first result in this set relative to the total number of results.

Back to Class List

Zend_Service_Yahoo_WebResultSet

Zend_Service_Yahoo_WebResultSet represents a Yahoo! Web Search result set.

Note

Zend_Service_Yahoo_WebResultSet extends Zend_Service_Yahoo_ResultSet

Back to Class List

Zend_Service_Yahoo_ImageResultSet

Zend_Service_Yahoo_ImageResultSet represents a Yahoo! Image Search result set.

Note

Zend_Service_Yahoo_ImageResultSet extends Zend_Service_Yahoo_ResultSet

Back to Class List

Zend_Service_Yahoo_VideoResultSet

Zend_Service_Yahoo_VideoResultSet represents a Yahoo! Video Search result set.

Note

Zend_Service_Yahoo_VideoResultSet extends Zend_Service_Yahoo_ResultSet

Back to Class List

Zend_Service_Yahoo_LocalResultSet

Zend_Service_Yahoo_LocalResultSet represents a Yahoo! Local Search result set.

Table 22.20. Zend_Service_Yahoo_LocalResultSet Properties

Name	Type	Description
resultSetMapURL	string	The URL of a webpage containing a map graphic with all returned results plotted on it.

Note

`Zend_Service_Yahoo_LocalResultSet` extends Zend_Service_Yahoo_ResultSet

Back to Class List

Zend_Service_Yahoo_NewsResultSet

`Zend_Service_Yahoo_NewsResultSet` represents a Yahoo! News Search result set.

Note

`Zend_Service_Yahoo_NewsResultSet` extends Zend_Service_Yahoo_ResultSet

Back to Class List

Zend_Service_Yahoo_InlinkDataResultSet

`Zend_Service_Yahoo_InlinkDataResultSet` represents a Yahoo! Inbound Link Search result set.

Note

`Zend_Service_Yahoo_InlinkDataResultSet`   extends Zend_Service_Yahoo_ResultSet

Back to Class List

Zend_Service_Yahoo_PageDataResultSet

`Zend_Service_Yahoo_PageDataResultSet` represents a Yahoo! PageData Search result set.

Note

`Zend_Service_Yahoo_PageDataResultSet` extends Zend_Service_Yahoo_ResultSet

Back to Class List

Zend_Service_Yahoo_Result

Each of the search specific results is extended from this base class.

Properties

Table 22.21. Zend_Service_Yahoo_Result Properties

Name	Type	Description
Title	string	Title of the Result item
Url	string	The URL of the result item
ClickUrl	string	The URL for linking to the result item

Back to Class List

Zend_Service_Yahoo_WebResult

Each Web Search result is returned as a `Zend_Service_Yahoo_WebResult` object.

Properties

Table 22.22. Zend_Service_Yahoo_WebResult Properties

Name	Type	Description
Summary	string	Result summary
MimeType	string	Result MIME type
ModificationDate	string	The last modification date of the result as a UNIX timestamp.
CacheUrl	string	Yahoo! web cache URL for the result, if it exists.
CacheSize	int	The size of the Cache entry

Back to Class List

Zend_Service_Yahoo_ImageResult

Each Image Search result is returned as a `Zend_Service_Yahoo_ImageResult` object.

Properties

Table 22.23. Zend_Service_Yahoo_ImageResult Properties

Name	Type	Description
Summary	string	Result summary
RefererUrl	string	The URL of the page which contains the image
FileSize	int	The size of the image file in bytes
FileFormat	string	The format of the image (bmp, gif, jpeg, png, etc.)
Height	int	The height of the image
Width	int	The width of the image
Thumbnail	Zend_Service_Yahoo_Image	Image thumbnail

Back to Class List

Zend_Service_Yahoo_VideoResult

Each Video Search result is returned as a `Zend_Service_Yahoo_VideoResult` object.

Properties

Table 22.24. Zend_Service_Yahoo_VideoResult Properties

Name	Type	Description
Summary	string	Result summary
RefererUrl	string	The URL of the page which contains the video
FileSize	int	The size of the video file in bytes
FileFormat	string	The format of the video (avi, flash, mpeg, msmedia, quicktime, realmedia, etc.)
Height	int	The height of the video in pixels
Width	int	The width of the video in pixels
Duration	int	The length of the video in seconds
Channels	int	Number of audio channels in the video
Streaming	boolean	Whether the video is streaming or not
Thumbnail	Zend_Service_Yahoo_Image	Image thumbnail

Back to Class List

Zend_Service_Yahoo_LocalResult

Each Local Search result is returned as a `Zend_Service_Yahoo_LocalResult` object.

Properties

Table 22.25. Zend_Service_Yahoo_LocalResult Properties

Name	Type	Description
Address	string	Street Address of the result
City	string	City in which the result resides in
State	string	State in which the result resides in
Phone	string	Phone number for the result
Rating	int	User submitted rating for the result
Distance	float	The distance to the result from your specified location
MapUrl	string	A URL of a map for the result
BusinessUrl	string	The URL for the business website, if known
BusinessClickUrl	string	The URL for linking to the business website, if known

Back to Class List

Zend_Service_Yahoo_NewsResult

Each News Search result is returned as a `Zend_Service_Yahoo_NewsResult` object.

Properties

Table 22.26. Zend_Service_Yahoo_NewsResult Properties

Name	Type	Description
Summary	string	Result summary
NewsSource	string	The company who distributed the article
NewsSourceUrl	string	The URL for the company who distributed the article
Language	string	The language the article is in
PublishDate	string	The date the article was published as a UNIX timestamp
ModificationDate	string	The date the article was last modified as a UNIX timestamp
Thumbnail	Zend_Service_Yahoo_Image	Image Thumbnail for the article, if it exists

Back to Class List

Zend_Service_Yahoo_InlinkDataResult

Each Inbound Link Search result is returned as a `Zend_Service_Yahoo_InlinkDatabResult` object.

Back to Class List

Zend_Service_Yahoo_PageDataResult

Each Page Data Search result is returned as a `Zend_Service_Yahoo_PageDatabResult` object.

Back to Class List

Zend_Service_Yahoo_Image

All images returned either by the Yahoo! Image Search or the Yahoo! News Search are represented by `Zend_Service_Yahoo_Image` objects

Properties

Table 22.27. Zend_Service_Yahoo_Image Properties

Name	Type	Description
Url	string	Image URL
Width	int	Image Width
Height	int	Image Height

Back to Class List

Chapter 23. Zend_Session

Introduction

The Zend Framework Auth team greatly appreciates your feedback and contributions on our email list: fw-auth@lists.zend.com [mailto:fw-auth@lists.zend.com]

With web applications written using PHP, a **session** represents a logical, one-to-one connection between server-side, persistent state data and a particular user agent client (e.g., web browser). Zend_Session helps manage and preserve session data, a logical complement of cookie data, across multiple page requests by the same client. Unlike cookie data, session data are not stored on the client side and are only shared with the client when server-side source code voluntarily makes the data available in response to a client request. For the purposes of this component and documentation, the term "session data" refers to the server-side data stored in $_SESSION [http://www.php.net/manual/en/reserved.variables.php#reserved.variables.session], managed by Zend_Session, and individually manipulated by Zend_Session_Namespace accessor objects. **Session namespaces** provide access to session data using classic namespaces [http://en.wikipedia.org/wiki/Namespace_%28computer_science%29] implemented logically as named groups of associative arrays, keyed by strings (similar to normal PHP arrays).

Zend_Session_Namespace instances are accessor objects for namespaced slices of $_SESSION. The Zend_Session component wraps the existing PHP ext/session with an administration and management interface, as well as providing an API for Zend_Session_Namespace to persist session namespaces. Zend_Session_Namespace provides a standardized, object-oriented interface for working with namespaces persisted inside PHP's standard session mechanism. Support exists for both anonymous and authenticated (e.g., "login") session namespaces. Zend_Auth, the authentication component of Zend Framework, uses Zend_Session_Namespace to store some information associated with authenticated users. Since Zend_Session uses the normal PHP ext/session functions internally, all the familiar configuration options and settings apply (see http://www.php.net/session), with such bonuses as the convenience of an object-oriented interface and default behavior that provides both best practices and smooth integration with Zend Framework. Thus, a standard PHP session identifier, whether conveyed by cookie or within URLs, maintains the association between a client and session state data.

The default ext/session save handler [http://www.php.net/manual/en/function.session-set -save-handler.php] does not maintain this association for server clusters under certain conditions because session data are stored to the filesystem of the server that responded to the request. If a request may be processed by a different server than the one where the session data are located, then the responding server has no access to the session data (if they are not available from a networked filesystem). A list of additional, appropriate save handlers will be provided, when available. Community members are encouraged to suggest and submit save handlers to the fw-auth@lists.zend.com [mailto:fw-auth@lists.zend.com] list. A Zend_Db compatible save handler has been posted to the list.

Basic Usage

Zend_Session_Namespace instances provide the primary API for manipulating session data in the Zend Framework. Namespaces are used to segregate all session data, although a default namespace exists for those who only want one namespace for all their session data. Zend_Session utilizes ext/session and its special $_SESSION superglobal as the storage mechanism for session state data. While $_SESSION is still available in PHP's global namespace, developers should refrain from directly accessing it, so that Zend_Session and Zend_Session_Namespace can most effectively and securely provide its suite of session related functionality.

Each instance of Zend_Session_Namespace corresponds to an entry of the $_SESSION superglobal array, where the namespace is used as the key.

```
$myNamespace = new Zend_Session_Namespace('myNamespace');

// $myNamespace corresponds to $_SESSION['myNamespace']
```

It is possible to use Zend_Session in conjunction with other code that uses $_SESSION directly. To avoid problems, however, it is highly recommended that such code only uses parts of $_SESSION that do not correspond to instances of Zend_Session_Namespace.

Tutorial Examples

If no namespace is specified when instantiating Zend_Session_Namespace, all data will be transparently stored in a namespace called "Default". Zend_Session is not intended to work directly on the contents of session namespace containers. Instead, we use Zend_Session_Namespace. The example below demonstrates use of this default namespace, showing how to count the number of client requests during a session:

Example 23.1. Counting Page Views

```
$defaultNamespace = new Zend_Session_Namespace('Default');

if (isset($defaultNamespace->numberOfPageRequests)) {
    // this will increment for each page load.
    $defaultNamespace->numberOfPageRequests++;
} else {
    $defaultNamespace->numberOfPageRequests = 1; // first time
}

echo "Page requests this session: ",
    $defaultNamespace->numberOfPageRequests;
```

When multiple modules use instances of Zend_Session_Namespace having different namespaces, each module obtains data encapsulation for its session data. The Zend_Session_Namespace constructor can be passed an optional $namespace argument, which allows developers to partition session data into separate namespaces. Namespacing provides an effective and popular way to secure session state data against changes due to accidental naming collisions.

Namespace names are restricted to character sequences represented as non-empty PHP strings that do not begin with an underscore ("_") character. Only core components included in Zend Framework should use namespace names starting with "Zend".

Example 23.2. New Way: Namespaces Avoid Collisions

```
// in the Zend_Auth component
$authNamespace = new Zend_Session_Namespace('Zend_Auth');
$authNamespace->user = "myusername";

// in a web services component
$webServiceNamespace = new Zend_Session_Namespace('Some_Web_Service');
$webServiceNamespace->user = "mywebusername";
```

The example above achieves the same effect as the code below, except that the session objects above preserve encapsulation of session data within their respective namespaces.

Example 23.3. Old Way: PHP Session Access

```
$_SESSION['Zend_Auth']['user'] = "myusername";
$_SESSION['Some_Web_Service']['user'] = "mywebusername";
```

Iterating Over Session Namespaces

Zend_Session_Namespace provides the full IteratorAggregate interface [http://www.php.net/~helly/php/ext/spl/interfaceIteratorAggregate.html], including support for the foreach statement:

Example 23.4. Session Iteration

```
$aNamespace =
    new Zend_Session_Namespace('some_namespace_with_data_present');

foreach ($aNamespace as $index => $value) {
    echo "aNamespace->$index = '$value';\n";
}
```

Accessors for Session Namespaces

Zend_Session_Namespace implements the __get(), __set(), __isset(), and __unset() magic methods [http://www.php.net/manual/en/language.oop5.overloading.php], which should not be invoked directly, except from within a subclass. Instead, the normal operators automatically invoke these methods, such as in the following example:

Example 23.5. Accessing Session Data

```
$namespace = new Zend_Session_Namespace(); // default namespace

$namespace->foo = 100;

echo "\$namespace->foo = $namespace->foo\n";

if (!isset($namespace->bar)) {
    echo "\$namespace->bar not set\n";
}

unset($namespace->foo);
```

Advanced Usage

While the basic usage examples are a perfectly acceptable way to utilize Zend Framework sessions, there are some best practices to consider. This section discusses the finer details of session handling and illustrates more advanced usage of the Zend_Session component.

Starting a Session

If you want all requests to have a session facilitated by Zend_Session, then start the session in the bootstrap file:

Example 23.6. Starting the Global Session

```
Zend_Session::start();
```

By starting the session in the bootstrap file, you avoid the possibility that your session might be started after headers have been sent to the browser, which results in an exception, and possibly a broken page for website viewers. Various advanced features require Zend_Session::start() first. (More on advanced features later.)

There are four ways to start a session, when using Zend_Session. Two are wrong.

1. Wrong: Do not enable PHP's session.auto_start setting [http://www.php.net/manual/en/ref.session.php#ini.session.auto-start]. If you do not have the ability to disable this setting in php.ini, you are using mod_php (or equivalent), and the setting is already enabled in php.ini, then add the following to your .htaccess file (usually in your HTML document root directory):

    ```
    php_value session.auto_start 0
    ```

2. Wrong: Do not use PHP's session_start() [http://www.php.net/session_start] function directly. If you use session_start() directly, and then start using Zend_Session_Namespace, an exception will be thrown by Zend_Session::start() ("session has already been started"). If you call session_start() after using Zend_Session_Namespace or calling Zend_Session::start(), an error of level E_NOTICE will be generated, and the call will be ignored.

3. Correct: Use Zend_Session::start(). If you want all requests to have and use sessions, then place this function call early and unconditionally in your bootstrap code. Sessions have some overhead. If some requests need sessions, but other requests will not need to use sessions, then:

    *   Unconditionally set the strict option to true using Zend_Session::setOptions() in your bootstrap.

    *   Call Zend_Session::start() only for requests that need to use sessions and before any Zend_Session_Namespace objects are instantiated.

    *   Use "new Zend_Session_Namespace()" normally, where needed, but make sure Zend_Session::start() has been called previously.

    The strict option prevents new Zend_Session_Namespace() from automatically starting the session using Zend_Session::start(). Thus, this option helps application developers enforce a design decision to avoid using sessions for certain requests, since it causes an exception to be thrown when Zend_Session_Namespace is instantiated before Zend_Session::start() is called. Developers should carefully consider the impact of using Zend_Session::setOptions(), since these options have global effect, owing to their correspondence to the underlying options for ext/session.

4. Correct: Just instantiate Zend_Session_Namespace whenever needed, and the underlying PHP session will be automatically started. This offers extremely simple usage that works well in most situations. However, you then become responsible for ensuring that the first new

Zend_Session_Namespace() happens *before* any output (e.g., HTTP headers [http://www.php.net/headers_sent]) has been sent by PHP to the client, if you are using the default, cookie-based sessions (strongly recommended). See the section called "Error: Headers Already Sent" for more information.

Locking Session Namespaces

Session namespaces can be locked, to prevent further alterations to the data in that namespace. Use lock() to make a specific namespace read-only, unLock() to make a read-only namespace read-write, and isLocked() to test if a namespace has been previously locked. Locks are transient and do not persist from one request to the next. Locking the namespace has no effect on setter methods of objects stored in the namespace, but does prevent the use of the namespace's setter method to remove or replace objects stored directly in the namespace. Similarly, locking Zend_Session_Namespace instances does not prevent the use of symbol table aliases to the same data (see PHP references [http://www.php.net/references]).

Example 23.7. Locking Session Namespaces

```
$userProfileNamespace = new Zend_Session_Namespace('userProfileNamespace');

// marking session as read only locked
$userProfileNamespace->lock();

// unlocking read-only lock
if ($userProfileNamespace->isLocked()) {
    $userProfileNamespace->unLock();
}
```

Namespace Expiration

Limits can be placed on the longevity of both namespaces and individual keys in namespaces. Common use cases include passing temporary information between requests, and reducing exposure to certain security risks by removing access to potentially sensitive information some time after authentication occurred. Expiration can be based on either elapsed seconds or the number of "hops", where a hop occurs for each successive request.

Example 23.8. Expiration Examples

```
$s = new Zend_Session_Namespace('expireAll');
$s->a = 'apple';
$s->p = 'pear';
$s->o = 'orange';

$s->setExpirationSeconds(5, 'a'); // expire only the key "a" in 5 seconds

// expire entire namespace in 5 "hops"
$s->setExpirationHops(5);

$s->setExpirationSeconds(60);
// The "expireAll" namespace will be marked "expired" on
// the first request received after 60 seconds have elapsed,
// or in 5 hops, whichever happens first.
```

When working with data expiring from the session in the current request, care should be used when retrieving them. Although the data are returned by reference, modifying the data will not make expiring data persist past the current request. In order to "reset" the expiration time, fetch the data into temporary variables, use the namespace to unset them, and then set the appropriate keys again.

Session Encapsulation and Controllers

Namespaces can also be used to separate session access by controllers to protect variables from contamination. For example, an authentication controller might keep its session state data separate from all other controllers for meeting security requirements.

Example 23.9. Namespaced Sessions for Controllers with Automatic Expiration

The following code, as part of a controller that displays a test question, initiates a boolean variable to represent whether or not a submitted answer to the test question should be accepted. In this case, the application user is given 300 seconds to answer the displayed question.

```
// ...
// in the question view controller
$testSpace = new Zend_Session_Namespace('testSpace');
// expire only this variable
$testSpace->setExpirationSeconds(300, 'accept_answer');
$testSpace->accept_answer = true;
//...
```

Below, the controller that processes the answers to test questions determines whether or not to accept an answer based on whether the user submitted the answer within the allotted time:

```
// ...
// in the answer processing controller
$testSpace = new Zend_Session_Namespace('testSpace');
if ($testSpace->accept_answer === true) {
    // within time
}
else {
    // not within time
}
// ...
```

Preventing Multiple Instances per Namespace

Although session locking provides a good degree of protection against unintended use of namespaced session data, Zend_Session_Namespace also features the ability to prevent the creation of multiple instances corresponding to a single namespace.

To enable this behavior, pass true to the second constructor argument when creating the last allowed instance of Zend_Session_Namespace. Any subsequent attempt to instantiate the same namespace would result in a thrown exception.

Example 23.10. Limiting Session Namespace Access to a Single Instance

```
// create an instance of a namespace
$authSpaceAccessor1 = new Zend_Session_Namespace('Zend_Auth');
```

```
// create another instance of the same namespace, but disallow any
// new instances
$authSpaceAccessor2 = new Zend_Session_Namespace('Zend_Auth', true);

// making a reference is still possible
$authSpaceAccessor3 = $authSpaceAccessor2;

$authSpaceAccessor1->foo = 'bar';

assert($authSpaceAccessor2->foo, 'bar');

try {
    $aNamespaceObject = new Zend_Session_Namespace('Zend_Auth');
} catch (Zend_Session_Exception $e) {
    echo 'Cannot instantiate this namespace since ' .
        '$authSpaceAccessor2 was created\n';
}
```

The second parameter in the constructor above tells Zend_Session_Namespace that any future instances with the "Zend_Auth" namespace are not allowed. Attempting to create such an instance causes an exception to be thrown by the constructor. The developer therefore becomes responsible for storing a reference to an instance object ($authSpaceAccessor1, $authSpaceAccessor2, or $authSpaceAccessor3 in the example above) somewhere, if access to the session namespace is needed at a later time during the same request. For example, a developer may store the reference in a static variable, add the reference to a registry [http://www.martinfowler.com/eaaCatalog/registry.html] (see Chapter 43, *Zend_Registry*), or otherwise make it available to other methods that may need access to the session namespace.

Working with Arrays

Due to the implementation history of PHP magic methods, modifying an array inside a namespace may not work under PHP versions before 5.2.1. If you will only be working with PHP 5.2.1 or later, then you may skip to the next section.

Example 23.11. Modifying Array Data with a Session Namespace

The following illustrates how the problem may be reproduced:

```
$sessionNamespace = new Zend_Session_Namespace();
$sessionNamespace->array = array();

// may not work as expected before PHP 5.2.1
$sessionNamespace->array['testKey'] = 1;
echo $sessionNamespace->array['testKey'];
```

Example 23.12. Building Arrays Prior to Session Storage

If possible, avoid the problem altogether by storing arrays into a session namespace only after all desired array values have been set.

```
$sessionNamespace = new Zend_Session_Namespace('Foo');
$sessionNamespace->array = array('a', 'b', 'c');
```

If you are using an affected version of PHP and need to modify the array after assigning it to a session namespace key, you may use either or both of the following workarounds.

Example 23.13. Workaround: Reassign a Modified Array

In the code that follows, a copy of the stored array is created, modified, and reassigned to the location from which the copy was created, overwriting the original array.

```
$sessionNamespace = new Zend_Session_Namespace();

// assign the initial array
$sessionNamespace->array = array('tree' => 'apple');

// make a copy of the array
$tmp = $sessionNamespace->array;

// modfiy the array copy
$tmp['fruit'] = 'peach';

// assign a copy of the array back to the session namespace
$sessionNamespace->array = $tmp;

echo $sessionNamespace->array['fruit']; // prints "peach"
```

Example 23.14. Workaround: store array containing reference

Alternatively, store an array containing a reference to the desired array, and then access it indirectly.

```
$myNamespace = new Zend_Session_Namespace('myNamespace');
$a = array(1, 2, 3);
$myNamespace->someArray = array( &$a );
$a['foo'] = 'bar';
echo $myNamespace->someArray['foo']; // prints "bar"
```

Using Sessions with Objects

If you plan to persist objects in the PHP session, know that they will be serialized [http://www.php.net/manual/en/language.oop.serialization.php] for storage. Thus, any object persisted with the PHP session must be unserialized upon retrieval from storage. The implication is that the developer must ensure that the classes for the persisted objects must have been defined before the object is unserialized from session storage. If an unserialized object's class is not defined, then it becomes an instance of stdClass.

Using Sessions with Unit Tests

Zend Framework relies on PHPUnit to facilitate testing of itself. Many developers extend the existing suite of unit tests to cover the code in their applications. The exception "*Zend_Session is currently marked as read-only*" is thrown while performing unit tests, if any write-related methods are used after ending the session. However, unit tests using Zend_Session require extra attention, because closing (Zend_Session::writeClose()), or destroying a session (Zend_Session::destroy()) prevents any further setting or unsetting of keys in any instance of Zend_Session_Namespace. This behavior is a direct result of the underlying ext/session mechanism and PHP's session_destroy() and session_write_close(), which have no "undo" mechanism to facilitate setup/teardown with unit tests.

To work around this, see the unit test testSetExpirationSeconds() in SessionTest.php and SessionTestHelper.php, both located in tests/Zend/Session, which make use of PHP's exec() to launch a separate process. The new process more accurately simulates a second, successive request from a browser. The separate process begins with a "clean" session, just like any PHP script execution for a web request. Also, any changes to $_SESSION made in the calling process become available to the child process, provided the parent closed the session before using exec().

Example 23.15. PHPUnit Testing Code Dependent on Zend_Session

```
// testing setExpirationSeconds()
$script = 'SessionTestHelper.php';
$s = new Zend_Session_Namespace('space');
$s->a = 'apple';
$s->o = 'orange';
$s->setExpirationSeconds(5);

Zend_Session::regenerateId();
$id = Zend_Session::getId();
session_write_close(); // release session so process below can use it
sleep(4); // not long enough for things to expire
exec($script . "expireAll $id expireAll", $result);
$result = $this->sortResult($result);
$expect = ';a === apple;o === orange;p === pear';
$this->assertTrue($result === $expect,
    "iteration over default Zend_Session namespace failed; " .
    "expecting result === '$expect', but got '$result'");

sleep(2); // long enough for things to expire (total of 6 seconds
          // waiting, but expires in 5)
exec($script . "expireAll $id expireAll", $result);
$result = array_pop($result);
$this->assertTrue($result === '',
    "iteration over default Zend_Session namespace failed; " .
    "expecting result === '', but got '$result')");
session_start(); // resume artificially suspended session

// We could split this into a separate test, but actually, if anything
// leftover from above contaminates the tests below, that is also a
// bug that we want to know about.
$s = new Zend_Session_Namespace('expireGuava');
$s->setExpirationSeconds(5, 'g'); // now try to expire only 1 of the
                                  // keys in the namespace

$s->g = 'guava';
$s->p = 'peach';
$s->p = 'plum';

session_write_close(); // release session so process below can use it
sleep(6); // not long enough for things to expire
exec($script . "expireAll $id expireGuava", $result);
$result = $this->sortResult($result);
session_start(); // resume artificially suspended session
$this->assertTrue($result === ';p === plum',
    "iteration over named Zend_Session namespace failed (result=$result)");
```

Global Session Management

The default behavior of sessions can be modified using the static methods of Zend_Session. All management and manipulation of global session management occurs using Zend_Session, including configuration of the usual options provided by ext/session [http://www.php.net/session#session.configuration], using Zend_Session::setOptions(). For example, failure to insure the use of a safe save_path or a unique cookie name by ext/session using Zend_Session::setOptions() may result in security issues.

Configuration Options

When the first session namespace is requested, Zend_Session will automatically start the PHP session, unless already started with Zend_Session::start() . The underlying PHP session will use defaults from Zend_Session, unless modified first by Zend_Session::setOptions().

To set a session configuration option, include the basename (the part of the name after "session.") as a key of an array passed to Zend_Session::setOptions(). The corresponding value in the array is used to set the session option value. If no options are set by the developer, Zend_Session will utilize recommended default options first, then the default php.ini settings. Community feedback about best practices for these options should be sent to fw-auth@lists.zend.com [mailto:fw-auth@lists.zend.com].

Example 23.16. Using Zend_Config to Configure Zend_Session

To configure this component using Zend_Config_Ini , first add the configuration options to the INI file:

```
; Accept defaults for production
[production]
; bug_compat_42
; bug_compat_warn
; cache_expire
; cache_limiter
; cookie_domain
; cookie_lifetime
; cookie_path
; cookie_secure
; entropy_file
; entropy_length
; gc_divisor
; gc_maxlifetime
; gc_probability
; hash_bits_per_character
; hash_function
; name should be unique for each PHP application sharing the same
; domain name
name = UNIQUE_NAME
; referer_check
; save_handler
; save_path
; serialize_handler
; use_cookies
; use_only_cookies
; use_trans_sid

; remember_me_seconds = <integer seconds>
; strict = on|off

; Development inherits configuration from production, but overrides
; several values
[development : production]
; Don't forget to create this directory and make it rwx (readable and
; modifiable) by PHP.
save_path = /home/myaccount/zend_sessions/myapp
use_only_cookies = on
; When persisting session id cookies, request a TTL of 10 days
remember_me_seconds = 864000
```

Next, load the configuration file and pass its array representation to
`Zend_Session::setOptions()`:

```
$config = new Zend_Config_Ini('myapp.ini', 'development');

Zend_Session::setOptions($config->toArray());
```

Most options shown above need no explanation beyond that found in the standard PHP documentation, but those of particular interest are noted below.

- boolean `strict` - disables automatic starting of `Zend_Session` when using new `Zend_Session_Namespace()`.

- integer `remember_me_seconds` - how long should session id cookie persist, after user agent has ended (e.g., browser application terminated).

- string `save_path` - The correct value is system dependent, and should be provided by the developer using an *absolute path* to a directory readable and writable by the PHP process. If a writable path is not supplied, then `Zend_Session` will throw an exception when started (i.e., when `start()` is called).

Security Risk

If the path is readable by other applications, then session hijacking might be possible. If the path is writable by other applications, then session poisoning [http://en.wikipedia.org/wiki/Session_poisoning] might be possible. If this path is shared with other users or other PHP applications, various security issues might occur, including theft of session content, hijacking of sessions, and collision of garbage collection (e.g., another user's application might cause PHP to delete your application's session files).

For example, an attacker can visit the victim's website to obtain a session cookie. Then, he edits the cookie path to his own domain on the same server, before visiting his own website to execute `var_dump($_SESSION)`. Armed with detailed knowledge of the victim's use of data in their sessions, the attacker can then modify the session state (poisoning the session), alter the cookie path back to the victim's website, and then make requests from the victim's website using the poisoned session. Even if two applications on the same server do not have read/write access to the other application's `save_path`, if the `save_path` is guessable, and the attacker has control over one of these two websites, the attacker could alter their website's `save_path` to use the other's save_path, and thus accomplish session poisoning, under some common configurations of PHP. Thus, the value for `save_path` should not be made public knowledge and should be altered to a secure location unique to each application.

- string `name` - The correct value is system dependent and should be provided by the developer using a value *unique* to the application.

Security Risk

If the `php.ini` setting for `session.name` is the same (e.g., the default "PHPSESSID"), and there are two or more PHP applications accessible through the same domain name then they will share the same session data for visitors to both websites. Additionally, possible corruption of session data may result.

- boolean `use_only_cookies` - In order to avoid introducing additional security risks, do not alter the default value of this option.

Security Risk

If this setting is not enabled, an attacker can easily fix victim's session ids, using links on the attacker's website, such as `http://www.example.com/index.php?PHPSESSID=fixed_session_id`. The fixation works, if the victim does not already have a session id cookie for example.com. Once a victim is using a known session id, the attacker can then attempt to hijack the session by pretending to be the victim, and emulating the victim's user agent.

Error: Headers Already Sent

If you see the error message, "Cannot modify header information - headers already sent", or, "You must call ... before any output has been sent to the browser; output started in ...", then carefully examine the immediate cause (function or method) associated with the message. Any actions that require sending HTTP headers, such as sending a cookie, must be done before sending normal output (unbuffered output), except when using PHP's output buffering.

- Using output buffering [http://php.net/outcontrol] often is sufficient to prevent this issue, and may help improve performance. For example, in `php.ini`, "`output_buffering = 65535`" enables output buffering with a 64K buffer. Even though output buffering might be a good tactic on production servers to increase performance, relying only on buffering to resolve the "headers already sent" problem is not sufficient. The application must not exceed the buffer size, or the problem will occur whenever the output sent (prior to the HTTP headers) exceeds the buffer size.

- Alternatively, try rearranging the application logic so that actions manipulating headers are performed prior to sending any output whatsoever.

- If a Zend_Session method is involved in causing the error message, examine the method carefully, and make sure its use really is needed in the application. For example, the default usage of `destroy()` also sends an HTTP header to expire the client-side session cookie. If this is not needed, then use `destroy(false)`, since the instructions to set cookies are sent with HTTP headers.

- Alternatively, try rearranging the application logic so that all actions manipulating headers are performed prior to sending any output whatsoever.

- Remove any closing "`?>`" tags, if they occur at the end of a PHP source file. They are not needed, and newlines and other nearly invisible whitespace following the closing tag can trigger output to the client.

Session Identifiers

Introduction: Best practice in relation to using sessions with ZF calls for using a browser cookie (i.e. a normal cookie stored in your web browser), instead of embedding a unique session identifier in URLs as a means to track individual users. By default this component uses only cookies to maintain session identifiers. The cookie's value is the unique identifier of your browser's session. PHP's ext/session uses this identifier to maintain a unique one-to-one relationship between website visitors, and persistent session data storage unique to each visitor. Zend_Session* wraps this storage mechanism (`$_SESSION`) with an object-oriented interface. Unfortunately, if an attacker gains access to the value of the cookie (the session id), an attacker might be able to hijack a visitor's session. This problem is not unique to PHP, or Zend Framework. The `regenerateId()` method allows an application to change the session id (stored in the visitor's cookie) to a new, random, unpredictable value. Note: Although not the same, to make this section easier to read, we use the terms "user agent" and "web browser" interchangeably.

Why?: If an attacker obtains a valid session identifier, an attacker might be able to impersonate a valid user (the victim), and then obtain access to confidential information or otherwise manipulate the victim's data managed by your application. Changing session ids helps protect against session hijacking. If the session id is changed, and an attacker does not know the new value, the attacker can not use the new session id in their attempts to hijack the visitor's session. Even if an attacker gains access to an old session id, `regenerateId()` also moves the session data from the old session id "handle" to the new one, so no data remains accessible via the old session id.

When to use regenerateId(): Adding `Zend_Session::regenerateId()` to your Zend Framework bootstrap yields one of the safest and most secure ways to regenerate session id's in user agent cookies. If there is no conditional logic to determine when to regenerate the session id, then there are no flaws in that logic. Although regenerating on every request prevents several possible avenues of attack, not everyone wants the associated small performance and bandwidth cost. Thus, applications commonly try to dynamically determine situations of greater risk, and only regenerate the session ids in those situations. Whenever a website visitor's session's privileges are "escalated" (e.g. a visitor re-authenticates their identity before editing their personal "profile"), or whenever a security "sensitive" session parameter change occurs, consider using `regenerateId()` to create a new session id. If you call the `rememberMe()` function, then don't use `regenerateId()`, since the former calls the latter. If a user has successfully logged into your website, use `rememberMe()` instead of `regenerateId()`.

Session Hijacking and Fixation

Avoiding cross-site script (XSS) vulnerabilities [http://en.wikipedia.org/wiki/Cross_site_scripting] helps preventing session hijacking. According to Secunia's [http://secunia.com/] statistics XSS problems occur frequently, regardless of the languages used to create web applications. Rather than expecting to never have a XSS problem with an application, plan for it by following best practices to help minimize damage, if it occurs. With XSS, an attacker does not need direct access to a victim's network traffic. If the victim already has a session cookie, Javascript XSS might allow an attacker to read the cookie and steal the session. For victims with no session cookies, using XSS to inject Javascript, an attacker could create a session id cookie on the victim's browser with a known value, then set an identical cookie on the attacker's system, in order to hijack the victim's session. If the victim visited an attacker's website, then the attacker can also emulate most other identifiable characteristics of the victim's user agent. If your website has an XSS vulnerability, the attacker might be able to insert an AJAX Javascript that secretly "visits" the attacker's website, so that the attacker knows the victim's browser characteristics and becomes aware of a compromised session at the victim website. However, the attacker can not arbitrarily alter the server-side state of PHP sessions, provided the developer has correctly set the value for the `save_path` option.

By itself, calling `Zend_Session::regenerateId()` when the user's session is first used, does not prevent session fixation attacks, unless you can distinguish between a session originated by an attacker emulating the victim. At first, this might sound contradictory to the previous statement above, until we consider an attacker who first initiates a real session on your website. The session is "first used" by the attacker, who then knows the result of the initialization (`regenerateId()`). The attacker then uses the new session id in combination with an XSS vulnerability, or injects the session id via a link on the attacker's website (works if `use_only_cookies = off`).

If you can distinguish between an attacker and victim using the same session id, then session hijacking can be dealt with directly. However, such distinctions usually involve some form of usability tradeoffs, because the methods of distinction are often imprecise. For example, if a request is received from an IP in a different country than the IP of the request when the session was created, then the new request probably belongs to an attacker. Under the following conditions, there might not be any way for a website application to distinguish between a victim and an attacker:

- attacker first initiates a session on your website to obtain a valid session id

- attacker uses XSS vulnerability on your website to create a cookie on the victim's browser with the same, valid session id (i.e. session fixation)

- both the victim and attacker originate from the same proxy farm (e.g. both are behind the same firewall at a large company, like AOL)

The sample code below makes it much harder for an attacker to know the current victim's session id, unless the attacker has already performed the first two steps above.

Example 23.17. Session Fixation

```
$defaultNamespace = new Zend_Session_Namespace();

if (!isset($defaultNamespace->initialized)) {
    Zend_Session::regenerateId();
    $defaultNamespace->initialized = true;
}
```

rememberMe(integer $seconds)

Ordinarily, sessions end when the user agent terminates, such as when an end user exits a web browser program. However, your application may provide the ability to extend user sessions beyond the lifetime of the client program through the use of persistent cookies. Use Zend_Session::rememberMe() before a session is started to control the length of time before a persisted session cookie expires. If you do not specify a number of seconds, then the session cookie lifetime defaults to remember_me_seconds, which may be set using Zend_Session::setOptions(). To help thwart session fixation/hijacking, use this function when a user successfully authenticates with your application (e.g., from a "login" form).

forgetMe()

This function complements rememberMe() by writing a session cookie that has a lifetime ending when the user agent terminates.

sessionExists()

Use this method to determine if a session already exists for the current user agent/request. It may be used before starting a session, and independently of all other Zend_Session and Zend_Session_Namespace methods.

destroy(bool $remove_cookie = true, bool $readonly = true)

Zend_Session::destroy() destroys all of the persistent data associated with the current session. However, no variables in PHP are affected, so your namespaced sessions (instances of Zend_Session_Namespace) remain readable. To complete a "logout", set the optional parameter to true (the default) to also delete the user agent's session id cookie. The optional $readonly parameter removes the ability to create new Zend_Session_Namespace instances and for Zend_Session methods to write to the session data store.

If you see the error message, "Cannot modify header information - headers already sent", then either avoid using true as the value for the first argument (requesting removal of the session cookie), or see the section called "Error: Headers Already Sent". Thus, Zend_Session::destroy(true) must either be called before PHP has sent HTTP headers, or output buffering must be enabled. Also, the total output sent must not exceed the set buffer size, in order to prevent triggering sending the output before the call to destroy().

Throws

By default, $readonly is enabled and further actions involving writing to the session data store will throw an exception.

stop()

This method does absolutely nothing more than toggle a flag in Zend_Session to prevent further writing to the session data store. We are specifically requesting feedback on this feature. Potential uses/abuses might include temporarily disabling the use of Zend_Session_Namespace instances or Zend_Session methods to write to the session data store, while execution is transferred to view-related code. Attempts to perform actions involving writes via these instances or methods will throw an exception.

writeClose($readonly = true)

Shutdown the session, close writing and detach $_SESSION from the back-end storage mechanism. This will complete the internal data transformation on this request. The optional $readonly boolean parameter can remove write access by throwing an exception upon any attempt to write to the session via Zend_Session or Zend_Session_Namespace.

Throws

By default, $readonly is enabled and further actions involving writing to the session data store will throw an exception. However, some legacy application might expect $_SESSION to remain writable after ending the session via session_write_close(). Although not considered "best practice", the $readonly option is available for those who need it.

expireSessionCookie()

This method sends an expired session id cookie, causing the client to delete the session cookie. Sometimes this technique is used to perform a client-side logout.

setSaveHandler(Zend_Session_SaveHandler_Interface $interface)

Most developers will find the default save handler sufficient. This method provides an object-oriented wrapper for session_set_save_handler() [http://php.net/session_set_save_handler].

namespaceIsset($namespace)

Use this method to determine if a session namespace exists, or if a particular index exists in a particular namespace.

Throws

An exception will be thrown if Zend_Session is not marked as readable (e.g., before Zend_Session has been started).

namespaceUnset($namespace)

Use Zend_Session::namespaceUnset($namespace) to efficiently remove an entire namespace and its contents. As with all arrays in PHP, if a variable containing an array is unset, and the array contains other objects, those objects will remain available, if they were also stored by reference in other array/objects that remain accessible via other variables. So namespaceUnset() does not perform a "deep" unsetting/deleting of the contents of the entries in the namespace. For a more detailed explanation, please see References Explained [http://php.net/references] in the PHP manual.

Throws

An exception will be thrown if the namespace is not writable (e.g., after `destroy()`).

namespaceGet($namespace)

DEPRECATED: Use `getIterator()` in `Zend_Session_Namespace`. This method returns an array of the contents of `$namespace`. If you have logical reasons to keep this method publicly accessible, please provide feedback to the fw-auth@lists.zend.com [mailto:fw-auth@lists.zend.com] mail list. Actually, all participation on any relevant topic is welcome :)

Throws

An exception will be thrown if `Zend_Session` is not marked as readable (e.g., before `Zend_Session` has been started).

getIterator()

Use `getIterator()` to obtain an array containing the names of all namespaces.

Throws
in PHP

An exception will be thrown if `Zend_Session` is not marked as readable (e.g., before `Zend_Session` has been started).

Zend_Session_SaveHandler_DbTable

The basic setup for Zend_Session_SaveHandler_DbTable must at least have four columns, denoted in the config array/Zend_Config object: primary, which is the primary key and defaults to just the session id which by default is a string of length 32; modified, which is the unix timestamp of the last modified date; lifetime, which is the lifetime of the session (modified + lifetime > time()); and data, which is the serialized data stored in the session

Example 23.18. Basic Setup

```
CREATE TABLE `session` (
  `id` char(32),
  `modified` int,
  `lifetime` int,
  `data` text,
  PRIMARY KEY (`id`)
);


//get your database connection ready
$db = Zend_Db::factory('Pdo_Mysql', array(
    'host'        =>'example.com',
    'username'    => 'dbuser',
    'password'    => '******',
    'dbname'      => 'dbname'
));

//you can either set the Zend_Db_Table default adapter
//or you can pass the db connection straight to the save handler $config
```

```
Zend_Db_Table_Abstract::setDefaultAdapter($db);
$config = array(
    'name'            => 'session',
    'primary'         => 'id',
    'modifiedColumn'  => 'modified',
    'dataColumn'      => 'data',
    'lifetimeColumn'  => 'lifetime'
);

//create your Zend_Session_SaveHandler_DbTable and
//set the save handler for Zend_Session
Zend_Session::setSaveHandler(new Zend_Session_SaveHandler_DbTable($config));

//start your session!
Zend_Session::start();

//now you can use Zend_Session like any other time
```

You can also use Multiple Columns in your primary key for Zend_Session_SaveHandler_DbTable.

Example 23.19. Using a Multi-Column Primary Key

```
CREATE TABLE `session` (
    `session_id` char(32) NOT NULL,
    `save_path` varchar(32) NOT NULL,
    `name` varchar(32) NOT NULL DEFAULT '',
    `modified` int,
    `lifetime` int,
    `session_data` text,
    PRIMARY KEY (`Session_ID`, `save_path`, `name`)
);


//setup your DB connection like before
//NOTE: this config is also passed to Zend_Db_Table so anything specific
//to the table can be put in the config as well
$config = array(
    'name'            => 'session', //table name as per Zend_Db_Table
    'primary'         => array(
        'session_id',   //the sessionID given by PHP
        'save_path',    //session.save_path
        'name',         //session name
    ),
    'primaryAssignment' => array(
        //you must tell the save handler which columns you
        //are using as the primary key. ORDER IS IMPORTANT
        'sessionId', //first column of the primary key is of the
                     sessionID
        'sessionSavePath', //second column of the primary key is the
                          save path
        'sessionName', //third column of the primary key is the session name
    ),
    'modifiedColumn'   => 'modified',     //time the session should
                                          expire
    'dataColumn'       => 'session_data', //serialized data
    'lifetimeColumn'   => 'lifetime',     //end of life for a specific
                                          record
);
```

```
//Tell Zend_Session to use your Save Handler
Zend_Session::setSaveHandler(new Zend_Session_SaveHandler_DbTable($config));

//start your session
Zend_Session::start();

//use Zend_Session as normal
```

Chapter 24. Zend_Soap

Zend_Soap_Server

`Zend_Soap_Server` class is intended to simplify Web Services server part development for PHP programmers.

It may be used in WSDL or non-WSDL mode, and using classes or functions to define Web Service API.

When Zend_Soap_Server component works in the WSDL mode, it uses already prepared WSDL document to define server object behavior and transport layer options.

WSDL document may be auto-generated with functionality provided by Zend_Soap_AutoDiscovery component or should be constructed manually using `Zend_Soap_Wsdl` class or any other XML generating tool.

If the non-WSDL mode is used, then all protocol options have to be set using options mechanism.

Zend_Soap_Server constructor.

`Zend_Soap_Server` constructor should be used a bit differently for WSDL and non-WSDL modes.

Zend_Soap_Server constructor for the WSDL mode.

`Zend_Soap_Server` constructor takes two optional parameters when it works in WSDL mode:

1. `$wsdl`, which is an URI of a WSDL file [*].

2. `$options` - options to create SOAP server object [§].

    The following options are recognized in the WSDL mode:

    *   'soap_version' ('soapVersion') - soap version to use (SOAP_1_1 or SOAP_1_2).

    *   'actor' - the actor URI for the server.

    *   'classmap' ('classMap') which can be used to map some WSDL types to PHP classes.
        The option must be an array with WSDL types as keys and names of PHP classes as values.

    *   'encoding' - internal character encoding (UTF-8 is always used as an external encoding).

    *   'wsdl' which is equivalent to `setWsdl($wsdlValue)` call.

Zend_Soap_Server constructor for the non-WSDL mode.

The first constructor parameter *must* be set to `null` if you plan to use `Zend_Soap_Server` functionality in non-WSDL mode.

You also have to set 'uri' option in this case (see below).

The second constructor parameter (`$options`) is an array with options to create SOAP server object [†].

The following options are recognized in the non-WSDL mode:

*   'soap_version' ('soapVersion') - soap version to use (SOAP_1_1 or SOAP_1_2).

*   'actor' - the actor URI for the server.

*   'classmap' ('classMap') which can be used to map some WSDL types to PHP classes.

---

[*] May be set later using `setWsdl($wsdl)` method.
[§] Options may be set later using `setOptions($options)` method.
[†] Options may be set later using `setOptions($options)` method.

The option must be an array with WSDL types as keys and names of PHP classes as values.

- 'encoding' - internal character encoding (UTF-8 is always used as an external encoding).

- 'uri' (required) - URI namespace for SOAP server.

Methods to define Web Service API.

There are two ways to define Web Service API when your want to give access to your PHP code through SOAP.

The first one is to attach some class to the `Zend_Soap_Server` object which has to completely describe Web Service API:

```
...
class MyClass {
    /**
     * This method takes ...
     *
     * @param integer $inputParam
     * @return string
     */
    public function method1($inputParam) {
        ...
    }

    /**
     * This method takes ...
     *
     * @param integer $inputParam1
     * @param string  $inputParam2
     * @return float
     */
    public function method2($inputParam1, $inputParam2) {
        ...
    }

    ...
}
...
$server = new Zend_Soap_Server(null, $options);
// Bind Class to Soap Server
$server->setClass('MyClass');
// Bind already initialized object to Soap Server
$server->setObject(new MyClass());
...
$server->handle();
```

Important!

You should completely describe each method using method docblock if you plan to use autodiscover functionality to prepare corresponding Web Service WSDL.

The second method of defining Web Service API is using set of functions and `addFunction()` or `loadFunctions()` methods:

```
...
/**
 * This function ...
 *
```

```
 * @param integer $inputParam
 * @return string
 */
function function1($inputParam) {
    ...
}

/**
 * This function ...
 *
 * @param integer $inputParam1
 * @param string  $inputParam2
 * @return float
 */
function function2($inputParam1, $inputParam2) {
    ...
}
...
$server = new Zend_Soap_Server(null, $options);
$server->addFunction('function1');
$server->addFunction('function2');
...
$server->handle();
```

Request and response objects handling.

Advanced

This section describes advanced request/response processing options and may be skipped.

Zend_Soap_Server component performs request/response processing automatically, but allows to catch it and do some pre- and post-processing.

Request processing.

Zend_Soap_Server::handle() method takes request from the standard input stream ('php://input'). It may be overridden either by supplying optional parameter to the handle() method or by setting request using setRequest() method:

```
...
$server = new Zend_Soap_Server(...);
...
// Set request using optional $request parameter
$server->handle($request);
...
// Set request using setRequest() method
$server->setRequest();
$server->handle();
```

Request object may be represented using any of the following:

- DOMDocument (casted to XML)

- DOMNode (owner document is grabbed and casted to XML)

- SimpleXMLElement (casted to XML)

- stdClass (__toString() is called and verified to be valid XML)

- string (verified to be valid XML)

Last processed request may be retrieved using `getLastRequest()` method as an XML string:

```
...
$server = new Zend_Soap_Server(...);
...
$server->handle();
$request = $server->getLastRequest();
```

Response pre-processing.

`Zend_Soap_Server::handle()` method automatically emits generated response to the output stream. It may be blocked using `setReturnResponse()` with `true` or `false` as a parameter [‡]. Generated response is returned by `handle()` method in this case.

```
...
$server = new Zend_Soap_Server(...);
...
// Get a response as a return value of handle() method
// instead of emitting it to the standard output
$server->setReturnResponse(true);
...
$response = $server->handle();
...
```

Last response may be also retrieved by `getLastResponse()` method for some post-processing:

```
...
$server = new Zend_Soap_Server(...);
...
$server->handle();
$response = $server->getLastResponse();
...
```

Zend_Soap_Client

The `Zend_Soap_Client` class simplifies SOAP client development for PHP programmers.

It may be used in WSDL or non-WSDL mode.

Under the WSDL mode, the Zend_Soap_Client component uses a WSDL document to define transport layer options.

The WSDL description is usually provided by the web service the client will access. If the WSDL description is not made available, you may want to use Zend_Soap_Client in non-WSDL mode. Under this mode, all SOAP protocol options have to be set explicitly on the Zend_Soap_Client class.

Zend_Soap_Client Constructor

The `Zend_Soap_Client` constructor takes two parameters:

- `$wsdl` - the URI of a WSDL file.

- `$options` - options to create SOAP client object.

Both of these parameters may be set later using `setWsdl($wsdl)` and `setOptions($options)` methods respectively.

[‡] Current state of the Return Response flag may be requested with `setReturnResponse()` method.

Important!

If you use Zend_Soap_Client component in non-WSDL mode, you *must* set the 'location' and 'uri' options.

The following options are recognized:

- 'soap_version' ('soapVersion') - soap version to use (SOAP_1_1 or SOAP_1_2).

- 'classmap' ('classMap') - can be used to map some WSDL types to PHP classes.

  The option must be an array with WSDL types as keys and names of PHP classes as values.

- 'encoding' - internal character encoding (UTF-8 is always used as an external encoding).

- 'wsdl' which is equivalent to setWsdl($wsdlValue) call.

  Changing this option may switch Zend_Soap_Client object to or from WSDL mode.

- 'uri' - target namespace for the SOAP service (required for non-WSDL-mode, doesn't work for WSDL mode).

- 'location' - the URL to request (required for non-WSDL-mode, doesn't work for WSDL mode).

- 'style' - request style (doesn't work for WSDL mode): SOAP_RPC or SOAP_DOCUMENT.

- 'use' - method to encode messages (doesn't work for WSDL mode): SOAP_ENCODED or SOAP_LITERAL.

- 'login' and 'password' - login and password for an HTTP authentication.

- 'proxy_host', 'proxy_port', 'proxy_login', and 'proxy_password' - an HTTP connection through a proxy server.

- 'local_cert' and 'passphrase' - HTTPS client certificate authentication options.

- 'compression' - compression options; it's a combination of SOAP_COMPRESSION_ACCEPT, SOAP_COMPRESSION_GZIP and SOAP_COMPRESSION_DEFLATE options which may be used like this:

```
// Accept response compression
$client = new Zend_Soap_Client("some.wsdl",
  array('compression' => SOAP_COMPRESSION_ACCEPT));
...

// Compress requests using gzip with compression level 5
$client = new Zend_Soap_Client("some.wsdl",
  array('compression' => SOAP_COMPRESSION_ACCEPT | SOAP_COMPRESSION
    _GZIP | 5));
...

// Compress requests using deflate compression
$client = new Zend_Soap_Client("some.wsdl",
  array('compression' => SOAP_COMPRESSION_ACCEPT | SOAP_COMPRESSION
    _DEFLATE));
```

Performing SOAP Requests

After we've created a Zend_Soap_Client object we are ready to perform SOAP requests.

Each web service method is mapped to the virtual Zend_Soap_Client object method which takes parameters with common PHP types.

Use it like in the following example:

```
//**********************************************************
//                 Server code
//**********************************************************
// class MyClass {
//     /**
//        * This method takes ...
//        *
//        * @param integer $inputParam
//        * @return string
//        */
//     public function method1($inputParam) {
//          ...
//     }
//
//     /**
//        * This method takes ...
//        *
//        * @param integer $inputParam1
//        * @param string  $inputParam2
//        * @return float
//        */
//     public function method2($inputParam1, $inputParam2) {
//          ...
//     }
//
//      ...
// }
// ...
// $server = new Zend_Soap_Server(null, $options);
// $server->setClass('MyClass');
// ...
// $server->handle();
//
//**********************************************************
//                 End of server code
//**********************************************************

$client = new Zend_Soap_Client("MyService.wsdl");
...

// $result1 is a string
$result1 = $client->method1(10);
...

// $result2 is a float
$result2 = $client->method2(22, 'some string');
```

WSDL Accessor

Note

Zend_Soap_Wsdl class is used by Zend_Soap_Server component internally to operate with WSDL documents. Nevertheless, you could also use functionality provided by this class for your own needs. The Zend_Soap_Wsdl package contains both a parser and a builder of WSDL documents.

If you don't plan to do this, you can skip this documentation section.

Zend_Soap_Wsdl constructor.

`Zend_Soap_Wsdl` constructor takes three parameters:

1. `$name` - name of the Web Service being described.

2. `$uri` - URI where the WSDL will be available (could also be a reference to the file in the filesystem.)

3. `$strategy` - optional flag used to identify the strategy for complex types (objects) detection. This was a boolean `$extractComplexTypes` before version 1.7 and can still be set as a boolean for backwards compatibility. By default the 1.6 detection behaviour is set. To read more on complex type detection strategies go to the section: the section called "Adding complex type information.".

addMessage() method.

`addMessage($name, $parts)` method adds new message description to the WSDL document (/definitions/message element).

Each message correspond to methods in terms of `Zend_Soap_Server` and `Zend_Soap_Client` functionality.

`$name` parameter represents message name.

`$parts` parameter is an array of message parts which describe SOAP call parameters. It's an associative array: 'part name' (SOAP call parameter name) => 'part type'.

Type mapping management is performed using `addTypes()`, `addTypes()` and `addComplexType()` methods (see below).

Note

Messages parts can use either 'element' or 'type' attribute for typing (see http://www.w3.org/TR/wsdl#_messages).

'element' attribute must refer to a corresponding element of data type definition. 'type' attribute refers to a corresponding complexType entry.

All standard XSD types have both 'element' and 'complexType' definitions (see http://schemas.xmlsoap.org/soap/encoding/).

All non-standard types, which may be added using `Zend_Soap_Wsdl::addComplexType()` method, are described using 'complexType' node of '/definitions/types/schema/' section of WSDL document.

So `addMessage()` method always uses 'type' attribute to describe types.

addPortType() method.

`addPortType($name)` method adds new port type to the WSDL document (/definitions/portType) with the specified port type name.

It joins a set of Web Service methods defined in terms of Zend_Soap_Server implementation.

See http://www.w3.org/TR/wsdl#_porttypes for the details.

addPortOperation() method.

`addPortOperation($portType, $name, $input = false, $output = false, $fault = false)` method adds new port operation to the specified port type of the WSDL document (/definitions/portType/operation).

Each port operation corresponds to a class method (if Web Service is based on a class) or function (if Web Service is based on a set of methods) in terms of Zend_Soap_Server implementation.

It also adds corresponding port operation messages depending on specified $input, $output and $fault parameters.

Note

Zend_Soap_Server component generates two messages for each port operation while describing service based on Zend_Soap_Server class:

- input message with name $methodName . 'Request'.

- output message with name $methodName . 'Response'.

See http://www.w3.org/TR/wsdl#_request-response for the details.

addBinding() method.

addBinding($name, $portType) method adds new binding to the WSDL document (/definitions/binding).

'binding' WSDL document node defines message format and protocol details for operations and messages defined by a particular portType (see http://www.w3.org/TR/wsdl#_bindings).

The method creates binding node and returns it. Then it may be used to fill with actual data.

Zend_Soap_Server implementation uses $serviceName . 'Binding' name for 'binding' element of WSDL document.

addBindingOperation() method.

addBindingOperation($binding, $name, $input = false, $output = false, $fault = false) method adds an operation to a binding element (/definitions/binding/operation) with the specified name.

It takes XML_Tree_Node object returned by addBinding() as an input ($binding parameter) to add 'operation' element with input/output/false entries depending on specified parameters

Zend_Soap_Server implementation adds corresponding binding entry for each Web Service method with input and output entries defining 'soap:body' element as '<soap:body use="encoded" encodingStyle="http://schemas.xmlsoap.org/soap/encoding/"/>

See http://www.w3.org/TR/wsdl#_bindings for the details.

addSoapBinding() method.

addSoapBinding($binding, $style = 'document', $transport = 'http://schemas.xmlsoap.org/soap/http') method adds SOAP binding ('soap:binding') entry to the binding element (which is already linked to some port type) with the specified style and transport (Zend_Soap_Server implementation uses RPC style over HTTP).

'/definitions/binding/soap:binding' element is used to signify that the binding is bound to the SOAP protocol format.

See http://www.w3.org/TR/wsdl#_bindings for the details.

addSoapOperation() method.

addSoapOperation($binding, $soap_action) method adds SOAP operation ('soap:operation') entry to the binding element with the specified action. 'style' attribute of the 'soap:operation' element is not used since programming model (RPC-oriented or document-oriented) may be st using `addSoapBinding()` method

'soapAction' attribute of '/definitions/binding/soap:operation' element specifies the value of the SOAPAction header for this operation. This attribute is required for SOAP over HTTP and *must not* be specified for other transports.

Zend_Soap_Server implementation uses `$serviceUri . '#' . $methodName` for SOAP operation action name.

See http://www.w3.org/TR/wsdl#_soap:operation for the details.

addService() method.

`addService($name, $port_name, $binding, $location)` method adds '/definitions/service' element to the WSDL document with the specified Wed Service name, port name, binding, and location.

WSDL 1.1 allows to have several port types (sets of operations) per service. This ability is not used by Zend_Soap_Server implementation and not supported by `Zend_Soap_Wsdl` class.

Zend_Soap_Server implementation uses:

- `$name . 'Service'` as a Web Service name,

- `$name . 'Port'` as a port type name,

- `'tns:' . $name . 'Binding'` [*] as binding name,

- script URI [6] as a service URI for Web Service definition using classes.
where $name is a class name for the Web Service definition mode using class and script name for the Web Service definition mode using set of functions.

See http://www.w3.org/TR/wsdl#_services for the details.

Type mapping.

Zend_Soap WSDL accessor implementation uses the following type mapping between PHP and SOAP types:

- PHP strings <-> `xsd:string`.

- PHP integers <-> `xsd:int`.

- PHP floats and doubles <-> `xsd:float`.

- PHP booleans <-> `xsd:boolean`.

- PHP arrays <-> `soap-enc:Array`.

- PHP object <-> `xsd:struct`.

---

[*] `'tns:'` namespace is defined as script URI (`'http://' .$_SERVER['HTTP_HOST'] . $_SERVER['SCRIPT_NAME']`).
[6] `'http://' .$_SERVER['HTTP_HOST'] . $_SERVER['SCRIPT_NAME']`

- PHP class <-> based on complex type strategy (See: the section called "Adding complex type information.") [7] .

- PHP void <-> empty type.

- If type is not matched to any of these types by some reason, then xsd:anyType is used. Where xsd: is "http://www.w3.org/2001/XMLSchema" namespace, soap-enc: is a "http://schemas.xmlsoap.org/soap/encoding/" namespace, tns: is a "target namespace" for a service.

Retrieving type information.

getType($type) method may be used to get mapping for a specified PHP type:

```
...
$wsdl = new Zend_Soap_Wsdl('My_Web_Service', $myWebServiceUri);

...
$soapIntType = $wsdl->getType('int');

...
class MyClass {
    ...
}
...
$soapMyClassType = $wsdl->getType('MyClass');
```

Adding complex type information.

addComplexType($type) method is used to add complex types (PHP classes) to a WSDL document.

It's automatically used by getType() method to add corresponding complex types of method parameters or return types.

Its detection and building algorithm is based on the currently active detection strategy for complex types. You can set the detection strategy either by specifying the class name as string or instance of a Zend_Soap_Wsdl_Strategy_Interface implementation as the third parameter of the constructor or using the setComplexTypeStrategy($strategy) function of Zend_Soap_Wsdl. The following detection strategies currently exist:

- Class Zend_Soap_Wsdl_Strategy_DefaultComplexType: Enabled by default (when no third constructor parameter is set). Iterates over the public attributes of a class type and registers them as subtypes of the complex object type.

- Class Zend_Soap_Wsdl_Strategy_AnyType: Casts all complex types into the simple XSD type xsd:anyType. Be careful this shortcut for complex type detection can probably only be handled successfully by weakly typed languages such as PHP.

- Class Zend_Soap_Wsdl_Strategy_ArrayOfTypeSequence: This strategy allows to specify return parameters of the type: int[] or string[]. It can only handle simple PHP types such as int, string, boolean, float and so on, but allows to specify nested arrays of arrays of type.

---

[7] By default Zend_Soap_Wsdl will be created with the Zend_Soap_Wsdl_Strategy_DefaultComplexType class as detection algorithm for complex types. The first parameter of the AutoDiscover constructor takes any complex type strategy implementing Zend_Soap_Wsdl_Strategy_Interface or a string with the name of the class. For backwards compatibility with $extractComplexType boolean variables are parsed the following way: If true, Zend_Soap_Wsdl_Strategy_DefaultComplexType, if false Zend_Soap_Wsdl_Strategy_AnyType.

- Class `Zend_Soap_Wsdl_Strategy_ArrayOfTypeComplex`: This strategy allows to detect very complex arrays of objects. Objects types are detected based on the `Zend_Soap_Wsdl_Strategy_DefaultComplexType` and an array is wrapped around that definition.

- Class `Zend_Soap_Wsdl_Strategy_Composite`: This strategy can combine all strategies by connecting PHP Complex types (Classnames) to the desired strategy via the `connectTypeToStrategy($type, $strategy)` method. A complete typemap can be given to the constructor as an array with `$type -> $strategy` pairs. The second parameter specifies the default strategy that will be used if an unknown type is requested for adding. This parameter defaults to the `Zend_Soap_Wsdl_Strategy_DefaultComplexType` strategy.

`addComplexType()` method creates '/definitions/types/xsd:schema/xsd:complexType' element for each described complex type with name of the specified PHP class.

Class property *MUST* have docblock section with the described PHP type to have property included into WSDL description.

`addComplexType()` checks if type is already described within types section of the WSDL document.

It prevents duplications if this method is called two or more times and recursion in the types definition section.

See http://www.w3.org/TR/wsdl#_types for the details.

addDocumentation() method.

`addDocumentation($input_node, $documentation)` method adds human readable documentation using optional 'wsdl:document' element.

'/definitions/binding/soap:binding' element is used to signify that the binding is bound to the SOAP protocol format.

See http://www.w3.org/TR/wsdl#_documentation for the details.

Get finalized WSDL document.

`toXML()`, `toDomDocument()` and `dump($filename = false)` methods may be used to get WSDL document as an XML, DOM structure or a file.

Parsing WSDL documents

Zend_Soap_Wsdl also contains a parser for WSDL documents that has its main application in unit-testing and code-generation for SOAP Webservices (Client and Server). The following example will show how the Parser can be used:

```
// Load WSDL into DOMDocument
$dom = new DOMDocument();
$dom->loadXML($wsdlString);

// Create parser
$parser = Zend_Soap_Wsdl_Parser::factory($dom);
$result = $parser->parse();

// Webservice Name
echo $result->getName();

// Access Ports and inner elements
foreach($result->ports AS $port) {
    echo $port->getName();
```

```
    foreach($port->bindings AS $binding) {
        echo $binding->getName();

        foreach($binding->operations AS $operation) {
            echo $operation->getName();
            echo $operation->inputMessage->getName();
            echo $operation->outputMessage->getName();
        }
    }
}
// You can access bindings, messages and operations
// and other elements directly too
foreach($result->operations AS $operation) {
    // do stuff
}
foreach($result->bindings AS $binding {
    // do stuff
}
foreach($result->messages AS $message) {
    // do stuff
}
foreach($result->services AS $service) {
    // do stuff
}
foreach($result->types AS $type) {
    // do stuff
}
```

All elements implement the interface Zend_Soap_Wsdl_Element_Interface that proxies a getName() and a getDocumentation() function with the unique identifier of the element and its documentation respectivly. All the elements have public properties that describe its state in more detail and also contain their nested dependencies for easy iteratable access.

AutoDiscovery

AutoDiscovery Introduction

SOAP functionality implemented within Zend Framework is intended to make all steps required for SOAP communications more simple.

SOAP is language independent protocol. So it may be used not only for PHP-to-PHP communications.

There are three configurations for SOAP applications where Zend Framework may be utilized:

1. SOAP server PHP application <---> SOAP client PHP application

2. SOAP server non-PHP application <---> SOAP client PHP application

3. SOAP server PHP application <---> SOAP client non-PHP application

We always have to know, which functionality is provided by SOAP server to operate with it. WSDL [http://www.w3.org/TR/wsdl] is used to describe network service API in details.

WSDL language is complex enough (see http://www.w3.org/TR/wsdl for the details). So it's difficult to prepare correct WSDL description.

Another problem is synchronizing changes in network service API with already existing WSDL.

Both these problem may be solved by WSDL autogeneration. A prerequisite for this is a SOAP server autodiscovery. It constructs object similar to object used in SOAP server application, extracts necessary information and generates correct WSDL using this information.

There are two ways for using Zend Framework for SOAP server application:

- Use separated class.

- Use set of functions

Both methods are supported by Zend Framework Autodiscovery functionality.

TheZend_Soap_AutoDiscover class also supports datatypes mapping from PHP to XSD types [http://www.w3.org/TR/xmlschema-2/].

Here is an example of common usage of the autodiscovery functionality. The handle() function generates the WSDL file and posts it to the browser.

```
class My_SoapServer_Class {
...
}

$autodiscover = new Zend_Soap_AutoDiscover();
$autodiscover->setClass('My_SoapServer_Class');
$autodiscover->handle();
```

If you need access to the generated WSDL file either to save it to a file or as an XML string you can use the dump($filename) or toXml() functions the AutoDiscover class provides.

Zend_Soap_Autodiscover is not a Soap Server

It is very important to note, that the class Zend_Soap_AutoDiscover does not act as a SOAP Server on its own. It only generates the WSDL and serves it to anyone accessing the url it is listening on.

As the SOAP Endpoint Uri is uses the default 'http://' .$_SERVER['HTTP_HOST'] . $_SERVER['SCRIPT_NAME'], but this can be changed with the setUri() function or the Constructor parameter of Zend_Soap_AutoDiscover class. The endpoint has to provide a Zend_Soap_Server that listens to requests.

```
if(isset($_GET['wsdl'])) {
    $autodiscover = new Zend_Soap_AutoDiscover();
    $autodiscover->setClass('HelloWorldService');
    $autodiscover->handle();
} else {
    // pointing to the current file here
    $soap = new Zend_Soap_Server("http://example.com/soap.php?wsdl");
    $soap->setClass('HelloWorldService');
    $soap->handle();
}
```

Class autodiscovering

If class is used to provide SOAP server functionality, then the same class should be provided to Zend_Soap_AutoDiscover for WSDL generation:

```
$autodiscover = new Zend_Soap_AutoDiscover();
$autodiscover->setClass('My_SoapServer_Class');
$autodiscover->handle();
```

The following rules are used while WSDL generation:

- Generated WSDL describes an RPC style Web Service.

- Class name is used as a name of the Web Service being described.

- `'http://' .$_SERVER['HTTP_HOST'] . $_SERVER['SCRIPT_NAME']` is used as an URI where the WSDL is available by default but can be overwritten via `setUri()` method.

  It's also used as a target namespace for all service related names (including described complex types).

- Class methods are joined into one Port Type [http://www.w3.org/TR/wsdl#_porttypes].

  `$className . 'Port'` is used as Port Type name.

- Each class method is registered as a corresponding port operation.

- Each method prototype generates corresponding Request/Response messages.

  Method may have several prototypes if some method parameters are optional.

Important!

WSDL autodiscovery utilizes the PHP docblocks provided by the developer to determine the parameter and return types. In fact, for scalar types, this is the only way to determine the parameter types, and for return types, this is the only way to determine them.

That means, providing correct and fully detailed docblocks is not only best practice, but is required for discovered class.

Functions autodiscovering

If set of functions are used to provide SOAP server functionality, then the same set should be provided to `Zend_Soap_AutoDiscovery` for WSDL generation:

```
$autodiscover = new Zend_Soap_AutoDiscover();
$autodiscover->addFunction('function1');
$autodiscover->addFunction('function2');
$autodiscover->addFunction('function3');
...
$autodiscover->handle();
```

The following rules are used while WSDL generation:

- Generated WSDL describes an RPC style Web Service.

- Current script name is used as a name of the Web Service being described.

- `'http://' .$_SERVER['HTTP_HOST'] . $_SERVER['SCRIPT_NAME']` is used as an URI where the WSDL is available.

  It's also used as a target namespace for all service related names (including described complex types).

- Functions are joined into one Port Type [http://www.w3.org/TR/wsdl#_porttypes].

  `$functionName . 'Port'` is used as Port Type name.

- Each function is registered as a corresponding port operation.

- Each function prototype generates corresponding Request/Response messages.

  Function may have several prototypes if some method parameters are optional.

Important!

WSDL autodiscovery utilizes the PHP docblocks provided by the developer to determine the parameter and return types. In fact, for scalar types, this is the only way to determine the parameter types, and for return types, this is the only way to determine them.

That means, providing correct and fully detailed docblocks is not only best practice, but is required for discovered class.

Autodiscovering Datatypes

Input/output datatypes are converted into network service types using the following mapping:

- PHP strings <-> xsd:string.

- PHP integers <-> xsd:int.

- PHP floats and doubles <-> xsd:float.

- PHP booleans <-> xsd:boolean.

- PHP arrays <-> soap-enc:Array.

- PHP object <-> xsd:struct.

- PHP class <-> based on complex type strategy (See: the section called "Adding complex type information.") [8] .

- type[] or object[] (ie. int[]) <-> based on complex type strategy

- PHP void <-> empty type.

- If type is not matched to any of these types by some reason, then xsd:anyType is used.
Where xsd: is "http://www.w3.org/2001/XMLSchema" namespace, soap-enc: is a "http://schemas.xmlsoap.org/soap/encoding/" namespace, tns: is a "target namespace" for a service.

WSDL Binding Styles

WSDL offers different transport mechanisms and styles. This affects the soap:binding and soap:body tags within the Binding section of WSDL. Different clients have different requirements as to what options really work. Therefore you can set the styles before you call any setClass or addFunction method on the AutoDiscover class.

```
$autodiscover = new Zend_Soap_AutoDiscover();
// Default is 'use' => 'encoded' and
// 'encodingStyle' => 'http://schemas.xmlsoap.org/soap/encoding/'
$autodiscover->setOperationBodyStyle(
                array('use' => 'literal',
                      'namespace' => 'http://framework.zend.com')
            );

// Default is 'style' => 'rpc' and
// 'transport' => 'http://schemas.xmlsoap.org/soap/http'
$autodiscover->setBindingStyle(
                array('style' => 'document',
                      'transport' => 'http://framework.zend.com')
            );
...
$autodiscover->addFunction('myfunc1');
$autodiscover->handle();
```

---

[8] Zend_Soap_AutoDiscover will be created with the Zend_Soap_Wsdl_Strategy_DefaultComplexType class as detection algorithm for complex types. The first parameter of the AutoDiscover constructor takes any complex type strategy implementing Zend_Soap_Wsdl_Strategy_Interface or a string with the name of the class. For backwards compatibility with $extractComplexType boolean variables are parsed exactly like in Zend_Soap_Wsdl. See the Zend_Soap_Wsdl manual on adding complex types for more information.

Chapter 25. Zend_Tag

Introduction

Zend_Tag is a component suite which provides a facility to work with taggable Items. As its base, it provides two classes to work with Tags, Zend_Tag_Item and Zend_Tag_ItemList. Additionally, it comes with the interface Zend_Tag_Taggable, which allows you to use any of your models as a taggable item in conjunction with Zend_Tag.

Zend_Tag_Item is a basic taggable item implementation which comes with the essential functionallity required to work with the Zend_Tag suite. A taggable item always consists of a title and a relative weight (e.g. number of occurences). It also stores parameters which are used by the different sub-components of Zend_Tag.

To group multiple items together, Zend_Tag_ItemList exists as an array iterator and provides additional functionallity to calculate absolute weight values based on on the given relative weights of each item in it.

Example 25.1. Using Zend_Tag

This example illustrates how to create a list of tags and spread absolute weight values on them.

```
// Create the item list
$list = new Zend_Tag_ItemList();

// Assign tags to it
$list[] = new Zend_Tag_Item(array('title' => 'Code', 'weight' => 50));
$list[] = new Zend_Tag_Item(array('title' => 'Zend Framework', 'weight'=>
          1));
$list[] = new Zend_Tag_Item(array('title' => 'PHP', 'weight' => 5));

// Spread absolute values on the items
$list->spreadWeightValues(array(1, 2, 3, 4, 5, 6, 7, 8, 9, 10));

// Output the items with their absolute values
foreach ($list as $item) {
    printf("%s: %d\n", $item->getTitle(), $item->getParam('weightValue'));
}
```

This will output the three items Code, Zend Framework and PHP with the absolute values 10, 1 and 2.

Zend_Tag_Cloud

Zend_Tag_Cloud is the rendering part of Zend_Tag. By default it comes with with a set of HTML decorators, which allow you to create tag clouds for a website, but also supplies you with two abstract classes to create your own decorators, to create tag clouds in PDF documents for example.

You can instantiate and configure Zend_Tag_Cloud either programatically or completly via an array or an instance of Zend_Config. The available options are:

- cloudDecorator: defines the decorator for the cloud. Can either be the name of the class which should be loaded by the pluginloader, an instance of Zend_Tag_Cloud_Decorator_Cloud or an array containing the string decorator and optionally an array options, which will be passed to the decorators constructor.

- tagDecorator: defines the decorator for individual tags. This can either be the name of the class which should be loaded by the pluginloader, an instance of Zend_Tag_Cloud_Decorator_Tag or an array containing the string decorator and optionally an array options, which will be passed to the decorators constructor.

- pluginLoader: a different plugin loader to use. Must be an instance of Zend_Loader_PluginLoader_Interface.

- prefixPath: prefix paths to add to the plugin loader. Must be an array containing the keys prefix and path or multiple arrays containing the keys prefix and path. Invalid elements will be skipped.

- itemList: a different item list to use. Must be an instance of Zend_Tag_ItemList.

- tags: a list of tags to assign to the cloud. Each tag must either implement Zend_Tag_Taggable or be an array which can be used to instantiate Zend_Tag_Item.

Example 25.2. Using Zend_Tag_Cloud

This example illustrates a basic example of how to create a tag cloud, add multiple tags to it and finally render it.

```
// Create the cloud and assign static tags to it
$cloud = new Zend_Tag_Cloud(array(
    'tags' => array(
        array('title' => 'Code', 'weight' => 50,
              'params' => array('url' => '/tag/code')),
        array('title' => 'Zend Framework', 'weight' => 1,
              'params' => array('url' => '/tag/zend-framework')),
        array('title' => 'PHP', 'weight' => 5,
              'params' => array('url' => '/tag/php')),
    )
));

// Render the cloud
echo $cloud;
```

This will output the tag cloud with the three tags, spread with the default font-sizes.

Decorators

Zend_Tag_Cloud requires two types of decorators to be able to render a tag cloud. This includes a decorator which renders the single tags as well as a decorator which renders the surounding cloud. Zend_Tag_Cloud ships a default decorator set for formatting a tag cloud in HTML. This set will by default create a tag cloud as ul/li-list, spread with different font-sizes according to the weight values of the tags assigned to them.

HTML Tag decorator

The HTML tag decorator will by default render every tag in an anchor element, surounded by a li element. The anchor itself is fixed and cannot be changed, but the surounding element(s) can.

URL parameter

As the HTML tag decorator always surounds the tag title with an anchor, you should define an URL parameter for every tag used in it.

The tag decorator can either spread different font-sizes over the anchors or a defined list of classnames. When setting options for one of those possibilities, the corespondening one will automatically be enabled. The following configuration options are available:

- fontSizeUnit: defines the font-size unit used for all font-sizes. The possible values are: em, ex, px, in, cm, mm, pt, pc and %.

- minFontSize: the minimum font-size distributed through the tags (must be an integer).

- maxFontSize: the maximum font-size distributed through the tags (must be an integer).

- classList: an arry of classes distributed through the tags.

- htmlTags: an array of HTML tags surounding the anchor. Each element can either be a string, which is used as element type then, or an array containing an attribute list for the element, defined as key/value pair. In this case, the array key is used as element type.

HTML Cloud decorator

The HTML cloud decorator will suround the HTML tags with an ul-element by default and add no separation. Like in the tag decorator, you can define multiple surounding HTML tags and additionally define a separator. The available options are:

- separator: defines the separator which is placed between all tags.

- htmlTags: an array of HTML tags surrounding all tags. Each element can either be a string, which is used as element type then, or an array containing an attribute list for the element, defined as key/value pair. In this case, the array key is used as element type.

Chapter 26. Zend_Test

Introduction

Zend_Test provides tools to facilitate unit testing of your Zend Framework applications. At this time, we offer facilities to enable testing of your Zend Framework MVC applications

Zend_Test_PHPUnit

Zend_Test_PHPUnit provides a TestCase for MVC applications that contains assertions for testing against a variety of responsibilities. Probably the easiest way to understand what it can do is to see an example.

Example 26.1. Application Login TestCase example

The following is a simple test case for a UserController to verify several things:

- The login form should be displayed to non-authenticated users.

- When a user logs in, they should be redirected to their profile page, and that profile page should show relevant information.

This particular example assumes a few things. First, we're moving most of our bootstrapping to a plugin. This simplifies setup of the test case as it allows us to specify our environment succinctly, and also allows us to bootstrap the application in a single line. Also, our particular example is assuming that autoloading is setup so we do not need to worry about requiring the appropriate classes (such as the correct controller, plugin, etc).

```
class UserControllerTest extends Zend_Test_PHPUnit_ControllerTestCase
{
    public function setUp()
    {
        $this->bootstrap = array($this, 'appBootstrap');
        parent::setUp();
    }

    public function appBootstrap()
    {
        $this->frontController
            ->registerPlugin(new Bugapp_Plugin_Initialize('development'));
    }

    public function testCallWithoutActionShouldPullFromIndexAction()
    {
        $this->dispatch('/user');
        $this->assertController('user');
        $this->assertAction('index');
    }

    public function testIndexActionShouldContainLoginForm()
    {
        $this->dispatch('/user');
        $this->assertAction('index');
        $this->assertQueryCount('form#loginForm', 1);
    }
```

```
public function testValidLoginShouldGoToProfilePage()
{
    $this->request->setMethod('POST')
        ->setPost(array(
            'username' => 'foobar',
            'password' => 'foobar'
        ));
    $this->dispatch('/user/login');
    $this->assertRedirectTo('/user/view');

    $this->resetRequest()
        ->resetResponse();

    $this->request->setMethod('GET')
        ->setPost(array());
    $this->dispatch('/user/view');
    $this->assertRoute('default');
    $this->assertModule('default');
    $this->assertController('user');
    $this->assertAction('view');
    $this->assertNotRedirect();
    $this->assertQuery('dl');
    $this->assertQueryContentContains('h2', 'User: foobar');
}
}
```

This example could be written somewhat simpler -- not all the assertions shown are necessary, and are provided for illustration purposes only. Hopefully, it shows how simple it can be to test your applications.

Bootstrapping your TestCase

As noted in the Login example, all MVC test cases should extend Zend_Test_PHPUnit_ControllerTestCase. This class in turn extends PHPUnit_Framework_TestCase, and gives you all the structure and assertions you'd expect from PHPUnit -- as well as some scaffolding and assertions specific to Zend Framework's MVC implementation.

In order to test your MVC application, you will need to bootstrap it. There are several ways to do this, all of which hinge on the public $bootstrap property.

First, you can set this property to point to a file. If you do this, the file should *not* dispatch the front controller, but merely setup the front controller and any application specific needs.

```
class UserControllerTest extends Zend_Test_PHPUnit_ControllerTestCase
{
    public $bootstrap = '/path/to/bootstrap/file.php'

    // ...
}
```

Second, you can provide a PHP callback to execute in order to bootstrap your application. This method is seen in the Login example. If the callback is a function or static method, this could be set at the class level:

```
class UserControllerTest extends Zend_Test_PHPUnit_ControllerTestCase
{
    public $bootstrap = array('App', 'bootstrap');
```

```
    // ...
}
```

In cases where an object instance is necessary, we recommend performing this in your setUp() method:

```
class UserControllerTest extends Zend_Test_PHPUnit_ControllerTestCase
{
    public function setUp()
    {
        // Use the 'start' method of a Bootstrap object instance:
        $bootstrap = new Bootstrap('test');
        $this->bootstrap = array($bootstrap, 'start');
        parent::setUp();
    }
}
```

Note the call to parent::setUp(); this is necessary, as the setUp() method of Zend_Test_PHPUnit_Controller_TestCase will perform the remainder of the bootstrapping process (which includes calling the callback).

During normal operation, the setUp() method will bootstrap the application. This process first will include cleaning up the environment to a clean request state, resetting any plugins and helpers, resetting the front controller instance, and creating new request and response objects. Once this is done, it will then either include the file specified in $bootstrap, or call the callback specified.

Bootstrapping should be as close as possible to how the application will be bootstrapped. However, there are several caveats:

- Do not provide alternate implementations of the Request and Response objects; they will not be used. Zend_Test_PHPUnit_Controller_TestCase uses custom request and response objects, Zend_Controller_Request_HttpTestCase and Zend_Controller_Response_HttpTestCase, respectively. These objects provide methods for setting up the request environment in targeted ways, and pulling response artifacts in specific ways.

- Do not expect to test server specifics. In other words, the tests are not a guarantee that the code will run on a specific server configuration, but merely that the application should run as expected should the router be able to route the given request. To this end, do not set server-specific headers in the request object.

Once the application is bootstrapped, you can then start creating your tests.

Testing your Controllers and MVC Applications

Once you have your bootstrap in place, you can begin testing. Testing is basically as you would expect in an PHPUnit test suite, with a few minor differences.

First, you will need to dispatch a URL to test, using the dispatch() method of the TestCase:

```
class IndexControllerTest extends Zend_Test_PHPUnit_Controller_TestCase
{
    // ...

    public function testHomePage()
    {
        $this->dispatch('/');
        // ...
    }
}
```

There will be times, however, that you need to provide extra information -- GET and POST variables, COOKIE information, etc. You can populate the request with that information:

```
class FooControllerTest extends Zend_Test_PHPUnit_Controller_TestCase
{
    // ...

    public function testBarActionShouldReceiveAllParameters()
    {
        // Set GET variables:
        $this->request->setQuery(array(
            'foo' => 'bar',
            'bar' => 'baz',
        ));

        // Set POST variables:
        $this->request->setPost(array(
            'baz'  => 'bat',
            'lame' => 'bogus',
        ));

        // Set a cookie value:
        $this->request->setCookie('user', 'matthew');
        // or many:
        $this->request->setCookies(array(
            'timestamp' => time(),
            'host'      => 'foobar',
        ));

        // Set headers, even:
        $this->request->setHeader('X-Requested-With', 'XmlHttpRequest');

        // Set the request method:
        $this->request->setMethod('POST');

        // Dispatch:
        $this->dispatch('/foo/bar');

        // ...
    }
}
```

Now that the request is made, it's time to start making assertions against it.

Assertions

Assertions are at the heart of Unit Testing; you use them to verify that the results are what you expect. To this end, Zend_Test_PHPUnit_ControllerTestCase provides a number of assertions to make testing your MVC apps and controllers simpler.

CSS Selector Assertions

CSS selectors are an easy way to verify that certain artifacts are present in the response content. They also make it trivial to ensure that items necessary for Javascript UIs and/or AJAX integration will be present; most JS toolkits provide some mechanism for pulling DOM elements based on CSS selectors, so the syntax would be the same.

This functionality is provided via Zend_Dom_Query, and integrated into a set of 'Query' assertions. Each of these assertions takes as their first argument a CSS selector, with optionally additional arguments and/or an error message, based on the assertion type. You can find the rules for writing the

CSS selectors in the Zend_Dom_Query theory of operation chapter. Query assertions include:

- `assertQuery($path, $message = '')`: assert that one or more DOM elements matching the given CSS selector are present. If a `$message` is present, it will be prepended to any failed assertion message.

- `assertQueryContentContains($path, $match, $message = '')`: assert that one or more DOM elements matching the given CSS selector are present, and that at least one contains the content provided in `$match`. If a `$message` is present, it will be prepended to any failed assertion message.

- `assertQueryContentRegex($path, $pattern, $message = '')`: assert that one or more DOM elements matching the given CSS selector are present, and that at least one matches the regular expression provided in `$pattern`. If a `$message` is present, it will be prepended to any failed assertion message.

- `assertQueryCount($path, $count, $message = '')`: assert that there are exactly `$count` DOM elements matching the given CSS selector present. If a `$message` is present, it will be prepended to any failed assertion message.

- `assertQueryCountMin($path, $count, $message = '')`: assert that there are at least `$count` DOM elements matching the given CSS selector present. If a `$message` is present, it will be prepended to any failed assertion message. *Note:* specifying a value of 1 for `$count` is the same as simply using `assertQuery()`.

- `assertQueryCountMax($path, $count, $message = '')`: assert that there are no more than `$count` DOM elements matching the given CSS selector present. If a `$message` is present, it will be prepended to any failed assertion message. *Note:* specifying a value of 1 for `$count` is the same as simply using `assertQuery()`.

Additionally, each of the above has a 'Not' variant that provides a negative assertion: `assertNotQuery()`, `assertNotQueryContentContains()`, `assertNotQueryContentRegex()`, and `assertNotQueryCount()`. (Note that the min and max counts do not have these variants, for what should be obvious reasons.)

XPath Assertions

Some developers are more familiar with XPath than with CSS selectors, and thus XPath variants of all the Query assertions are also provided. These are:

- `assertXpath($path, $message = '')`

- `assertNotXpath($path, $message = '')`

- `assertXpathContentContains($path, $match, $message = '')`

- `assertNotXpathContentContains($path, $match, $message = '')`

- `assertXpathContentRegex($path, $pattern, $message = '')`

- `assertNotXpathContentRegex($path, $pattern, $message = '')`

- `assertXpathCount($path, $count, $message = '')`

- `assertNotXpathCount($path, $count, $message = '')`

- `assertXpathCountMin($path, $count, $message = '')`

- `assertNotXpathCountMax($path, $count, $message = '')`

Redirect Assertions

Often an action will redirect. Instead of following the redirect, `Zend_Test_PHPUnit_ControllerTestCase` allows you to test for redirects with a handful of assertions.

- `assertRedirect($message = '')`: assert simply that a redirect has occurred.

- `assertNotRedirect($message = '')`: assert that no redirect has occurred.

- `assertRedirectTo($url, $message = '')`: assert that a redirect has occurred, and that the value of the Location header is the `$url` provided.

- `assertNotRedirectTo($url, $message = '')`: assert that a redirect has either NOT occurred, or that the value of the Location header is NOT the `$url` provided.

- `assertRedirectRegex($pattern, $message = '')`: assert that a redirect has occurred, and that the value of the Location header matches the regular expression provided by `$pattern`.

- `assertNotRedirectRegex($pattern, $message = '')`: assert that a redirect has either NOT occurred, or that the value of the Location header does NOT match the regular expression provided by `$pattern`.

Response Header Assertions

In addition to checking for redirect headers, you will often need to check for specific HTTP response codes and headers -- for instance, to determine whether an action results in a 404 or 500 response, or to ensure that JSON responses contain the appropriate Content-Type header. The following assertions are available.

- `assertResponseCode($code, $message = '')`: assert that the response resulted in the given HTTP response code.

- `assertHeader($header, $message = '')`: assert that the response contains the given header.

- `assertHeaderContains($header, $match, $message = '')`: assert that the response contains the given header and that its content contains the given string.

- `assertHeaderRegex($header, $pattern, $message = '')`: assert that the response contains the given header and that its content matches the given regex.

Additionally, each of the above assertions have a 'Not' variant for negative assertions.

Request Assertions

It's often useful to assert against the last run action, controller, and module; additionally, you may want to assert against the route that was matched. The following assertions can help you in this regard:

- `assertModule($module, $message = '')`: Assert that the given module was used in the last dispatched action.

- `assertController($controller, $message = '')`: Assert that the given controller was selected in the last dispatched action.

- `assertAction($action, $message = '')`: Assert that the given action was last dispatched.

- `assertRoute($route, $message = '')`: Assert that the given named route was matched by the router.

Each also has a 'Not' variant for negative assertions.

Examples

Knowing how to setup your testing infrastructure and how to make assertions is only half the battle; now it's time to start looking at some actual testing scenarios to see how you can leverage them.

Example 26.2. Testing a UserController

Let's consider a standard task for a website: authenticating and registering users. In our example, we'll define a UserController for handling this, and have the following requirements:

- If a user is not authenticated, they will always be redirected to the login page of the controller, regardless of the action specified.

- The login form page will show both the login form and the registration form.

- Providing invalid credentials should result in returning to the login form.

- Valid credentials should result in redirecting to the user profile page.

- The profile page should be customized to contain the user's username.

- Authenticated users who visit the login page should be redirected to their profile page.

- On logout, a user should be redirected to the login page.

- With invalid data, registration should fail.

We could, and should define further tests, but these will do for now.

For our application, we will define a plugin, 'Initialize', that runs at `routeStartup()`. This allows us to encapsulate our bootstrap in an OOP interface, which also provides an easy way to provide a callback. Let's look at the basics of this class first:

```
class Bugapp_Plugin_Initialize extends Zend_Controller_Plugin_Abstract
{
    /**
     * @var Zend_Config
     */
    protected static $_config;

    /**
     * @var string Current environment
     */
    protected $_env;

    /**
     * @var Zend_Controller_Front
     */
    protected $_front;

    /**
     * @var string Path to application root
     */
    protected $_root;

    /**
     * Constructor
     *
     * Initialize environment, root path, and configuration.
     *
     * @param  string $env
```

```
 * @param  string|null $root
 * @return void
 */
public function __construct($env, $root = null)
{
    $this->_setEnv($env);
    if (null === $root) {
        $root = realpath(dirname(__FILE__) . '/../../../');
    }
    $this->_root = $root;

    $this->initPhpConfig();

    $this->_front = Zend_Controller_Front::getInstance();
}

/**
 * Route startup
 *
 * @return void
 */
public function routeStartup(Zend_Controller_Request_Abstract $request)
{
    $this->initDb();
    $this->initHelpers();
    $this->initView();
    $this->initPlugins();
    $this->initRoutes();
    $this->initControllers();
}

// definition of methods would follow...
}
```

This allows us to create a bootstrap callback like the following:

```
class UserControllerTest extends Zend_Test_PHPUnit_ControllerTestCase
{
    public function appBootstrap()
    {
        $controller = $this->getFrontController();
        $controller->registerPlugin(
            new Bugapp_Plugin_Initialize('development')
        );
    }

    public function setUp()
    {
        $this->bootstrap = array($this, 'appBootstrap');
        parent::setUp();
    }

    // ...
}
```

Once we have that in place, we can write our tests. However, what about those tests that require a user is logged in? The easy solution is to use our application logic to do so... and fudge a little by using the resetRequest() and resetResponse() methods, which will allow us to dispatch another request.

```
class UserControllerTest extends Zend_Test_PHPUnit_ControllerTestCase
{
    // ...

    public function loginUser($user, $password)
    {
        $this->request->setMethod('POST')
                      ->setPost(array(
                          'username' => $user,
                          'password' => $password,
                      ));
        $this->dispatch('/user/login');
        $this->assertRedirectTo('/user/view');

        $this->resetRequest()
             ->resetResponse();

        $this->request->setPost(array());

        // ...
    }

    // ...
}
```

Now let's write tests:

```
class UserControllerTest extends Zend_Test_PHPUnit_ControllerTestCase
{
    // ...

    public function testCallWithoutActionShouldPullFromIndexAction()
    {
        $this->dispatch('/user');
        $this->assertController('user');
        $this->assertAction('index');
    }

    public function testLoginFormShouldContainLoginAndRegistrationForms()
    {
        $this->dispatch('/user');
        $this->assertQueryCount('form', 2);
    }

    public function testInvalidCredentialsShouldResultInRedisplayOfLoginForm()
    {
        $request = $this->getRequest();
        $request->setMethod('POST')
                ->setPost(array(
                    'username' => 'bogus',
                    'password' => 'reallyReallyBogus',
                ));
        $this->dispatch('/user/login');
        $this->assertNotRedirect();
        $this->assertQuery('form');
    }

    public function testValidLoginShouldRedirectToProfilePage()
    {
        $this->loginUser('foobar', 'foobar');
    }
```

```
public function testAuthenticatedUserShouldHaveCustomizedProfilePage()
{
    $this->loginUser('foobar', 'foobar');
    $this->request->setMethod('GET');
    $this->dispatch('/user/view');
    $this->assertNotRedirect();
    $this->assertQueryContentContains('h2', 'foobar');
}

public function
    testAuthenticatedUsersShouldBeRedirectedToProfileWhenVisitingLogin()
{
    $this->loginUser('foobar', 'foobar');
    $this->request->setMethod('GET');
    $this->dispatch('/user');
    $this->assertRedirectTo('/user/view');
}

public function testUserShouldRedirectToLoginPageOnLogout()
{
    $this->loginUser('foobar', 'foobar');
    $this->request->setMethod('GET');
    $this->dispatch('/user/logout');
    $this->assertRedirectTo('/user');
}

public function testRegistrationShouldFailWithInvalidData()
{
    $data = array(
        'username' => 'This will not work',
        'email'    => 'this is an invalid email',
        'password' => 'Th1s!s!nv@l1d',
        'passwordVerification' => 'wrong!',
    );
    $request = $this->getRequest();
    $request->setMethod('POST')
            ->setPost($data);
    $this->dispatch('/user/register');
    $this->assertNotRedirect();
    $this->assertQuery('form .errors');
}
}
```

Notice that these are terse, and, for the most part, don't look for actual content. Instead, they look for artifacts within the response -- response codes and headers, and DOM nodes. This allows you to verify that the structure is as expected -- preventing your tests from choking every time new content is added to the site.

Also notice that we use the structure of the document in our tests. For instance, in the final test, we look for a form that has a node with the class of "errors"; this allows us to test merely for the presence of form validation errors, and not worry about what specific errors might have been thrown.

This application *may* utilize a database. If so, you will probably need some scaffolding to ensure that the database is in a pristine, testable configuration at the beginning of each test. PHPUnit already provides functionality for doing so; read about it in the PHPUnit documentation [http://www.phpunit.de/pocket_guide/3.3/en/database.html]. We recommend using a separate database for testing versus production, and in particular recommend using either a SQLite file or in-memory database, as both options perform very well, do not require a separate server, and can utilize most SQL syntax.

Chapter 27. Zend_Text

Zend_Text_Figlet

`Zend_Text_Figlet` is a component which enables developers to create a so called FIGlet text. A FIGlet text is a string, which is represented as ASCII art. FIGlets use a special font format, called FLT (FigLet Font). By default, one standard font is shipped with `Zend_Text_Figlet`, but you can download additional fonts at http://www.figlet.org [http://www.figlet.org/fontdb.cgi].

Compressed fonts

`Zend_Text_Figlet` supports gzipped fonts. This means that you can take an `.flf` file and gzip it. To allow `Zend_Text_Figlet` to recognize this, the gzipped font must have the extension `.gz`. Further, to be able to use gzipped fonts, you have to have enabled the GZIP extension of PHP.

Encoding

`Zend_Text_Figlet` expects your strings to be UTF-8 encoded by default. If this is not the case, you can supply the character encoding as second parameter to the `render()` method.

You can define multiple options for a FIGlet. When instantiating `Zend_Text_Figlet`, you can supply an array or an instance of `Zend_Config`.

- `font` - Defines the font which should be used for rendering. If not defines, the built-in font will be used.

- `outputWidth` - Defines the maximum width of the output string. This is used for word-wrap as well as justification. Beware of too small values, they may result in an undefined behaviour. The default value is 80.

- `handleParagraphs` - A boolean which indicates, how new lines are handled. When set to true, single new lines are ignored and instead treated as single spaces. Only multiple new lines will be handled as such. The default value is `false`.

- `justification` - May be one of the values of `Zend_Text_Figlet::JUSTIFICATION_*`. There is `JUSTIFICATION_LEFT`, `JUSTIFICATION_CENTER` and `JUSTIFICATION_RIGHT` The default justification is defined by the `rightToLeft` value.

- `rightToLeft` - Defines in which direction the text is written. May be either `Zend_Text_Figlet::DIRECTION_LEFT_TO_RIGHT` or `Zend_Text_Figlet::DIRECTION_RIGHT_TO_LEFT`. By default the setting of the font file is used. When justification is not defined, a text written from right-to-left is automatically right-aligned.

- `smushMode` - An integer bitfield which defines, how the single characters are smushed together. Can be the sum of multiple values from `Zend_Text_Figlet::SM_*`. There are the following smush modes: SM_EQUAL, SM_LOWLINE, SM_HIERARCHY, SM_PAIR, SM_BIGX, SM_HARDBLANK, SM_KERN and SM_SMUSH. A value of 0 doesn't disable the entire smushing, but forces SM_KERN to be applied, while a value of -1 disables it. An explanation of the different smush modes can be found here [http://www.jave.de/figlet/figfont.txt]. By default the setting of the font file is used. The smush mode option is normally used only by font designers testing the various layoutmodes with a new font.

Example 27.1. Using Zend_Text_Figlet

This example illustrates the basic use of `Zend_Text_Figlet` to create a simple FIGlet text:

```
$figlet = new Zend_Text_Figlet();
echo $figlet->render('Zend');
```

Assuming you are using a monospace font, this would look as follows:

Zend_Text_Table

`Zend_Text_Table` is a component to create text based tables on the fly with different decorators. This can be helpful, if you either want to send structured data in text emails, which are used to have mono-spaced fonts, or to display table information in a CLI application. `Zend_Text_Table` supports multi-line columns, colspan and align as well.

Encoding

`Zend_Text_Table` expects your strings to be UTF-8 encoded by default. If this is not the case, you can either supply the character encoding as a parameter to the `constructor` or the `setContent` method of `Zend_Text_Table_Column`. Alternatively if you have a different encoding in the entire process, you can define the standard input charset with `Zend_Text_Table::setInputCharset($charset)`. In case you need another output charset for the table, you can set this with `Zend_Text_Table::setOutputCharset($charset)`.

A `Zend_Text_Table` object consists of rows, which contain columns, represented by `Zend_Text_Table_Row` and `Zend_Text_Table_Column`. When creating a table, you can supply an array with options for the table. Those are:

- `columnWidths` (required): An array defining all columns width their widths in characters.

- `decorator`: The decorator to use for the table borders. The default is `unicode`, but you may also specify `ascii` or give an instance of a custom decorator object.

- `padding`: The left and right padding withing the columns in characters. The default padding is zero.

- `AutoSeparate`: The way how the rows are separated with horizontal lines. The default is a separation between all rows. This is defined as a bitmask containing one ore more of the following constants of `Zend_Text_Table`:

  - `Zend_Text_Table::AUTO_SEPARATE_NONE`

  - `Zend_Text_Table::AUTO_SEPARATE_HEADER`

  - `Zend_Text_Table::AUTO_SEPARATE_FOOTER`

  - `Zend_Text_Table::AUTO_SEPARATE_ALL`

Where header is always the first row, and the footer is always the last row.

Rows are simply added to the table by creating a new instance of Zend_Text_Table_Row, and appending it to the table via the appendRow method. Rows themselves have no options. You can also give an array to directly to the appendRow method, which then will automatically converted to a row object, containing multiple column objects.

The same way you can add columns to the rows. Create a new instance of Zend_Text_Table_Column and then either set the column options in the constructor or later with the set* methods. The first parameter is the content of the column which may have multiple lines, which in the best case are separated by just the \n character. The second parameter defines the align, which is left by default and can be one of the class constants of Zend_Text_Table_Column:

- ALIGN_LEFT

- ALIGN_CENTER

- ALIGN_RIGHT

The third parameter is the colspan of the column. For example, when you choose "2" as colspan, the column will span over two columns of the table. The last parameter defines the encoding of the content, which should be supplied, if the content is neither ASCII nor UTF-8. To append the column to the row, you simply call appendColumn in your row object with the column object as parameter. Alternatively you can directly give a string to the appendColumn method.

To finally render the table, you can either use the render method of the table, or use the magic method __toString by doing echo $table; or $tableString = (string) $table.

Example 27.2. Using Zend_Text_Table

This example illustrates the basic use of Zend_Text_Table to create a simple table:

```
$table = new Zend_Text_Table(array('columnWidths' => array(10, 20)));

// Either simple
$table->appendRow(array('Zend', 'Framework'));

// Or verbose
$row = new Zend_Text_Table_Row();

$row->appendColumn(new Zend_Text_Table_Column('Zend'));
$row->appendColumn(new Zend_Text_Table_Column('Framework'));

$table->appendRow($row);

echo $table;
```

This will result in the following output:

```
##############################
#Zend      #Framework        #
##############################
```

Chapter 28. Zend_TimeSync

Introduction

Zend_TimeSync is able to receive internet or network time from a time server using the *NTP* or *SNTP* protocol. With Zend_TimeSync, Zend Framework is able to act independently from the time settings of the server where it is running.

To be independent from the actual time of the server, Zend_TimeSync works with the difference of the real time which is sent through NTP or SNTP and the internal server's time.

Background

Zend_TimeSync is not able to change the server's time, but it will return a Zend_Date instance from which the difference from the server's time can be worked with.

Why Zend_TimeSync ?

So why would someone use Zend_TimeSync ?

Normally every server within a multi-server farm will have a service running which synchronizes its own time with a time server. So within a standard environment it should not be necessary to use Zend_TimeSync. But it can become handy if there is no service available and if you don't have the right to install such a service.

Here are some example use cases, for which Zend_TimeSync is perfect suited:

* *Server without time service*

    If your application is running on a server and this server does not have any time service running, it may make sense to use Zend_TimeSync in your application.

* *Separate database server*

    If your database is running on a different server and this server is not connected with *NTP* or *SNTP* to the application server, you might have problems using storing and using time stamp data.

* *Multiple servers*

    If your application is running on more than one server and these servers' time bases are not syncronized, you can expect problems within your application when part of the application is coming from one server and another part from another server.

* *Batch processing*

    If you want to work with a time service within a batch file or within a command line application, Zend_TimeSync may be of use.

Zend_TimeSync may provide a good solution solution in all of these cases and can be used if you are unable to run any services on your server.

What is NTP ?

The Network Time Protocol (*NTP*) is a protocol for synchronizing multiple systems' clocks over packet-switched, variable-latency data networks. NTP uses UDP port 123 as its transport layer. See the wikipedia article [http://en.wikipedia.org/wiki/Network_Time_Protocol] for details about this protocol.

What is SNTP?

The `Simple Network Time Protocol` (*SNTP*) is a protocol synchronizing multiple systems' clocks over packet-switched, variable-latency data networks. SNTP uses UDP port 37 as its transport layer. It is closely related to the Network Time Protocol, but simpler.

Problematic usage

Be warned that when you are using `Zend_TimeSync` you will have to think about some details related to the structure of time sync and the internet itself. Correct usage and best practices will be described here. Read carefully before you begin using `Zend_TimeSync`.

Decide which server to use

You should select the time server that you want to use very carefully according to the following criteria:

- Distance

  The distance from your application server to the time server. If your server is in Europe, it would make little sense to select a time server in Tahiti. Always select a server which is not far away. This reduces the request time and overall network load.

- Speed

  How long it takes to receive the request is also relevant. Try different servers to get the best result. If you are requesting a server which is never accessible, you will always have an unnecessary delay.

- Splitting

  Do not always use the same server. All time servers will lock out requests from servers that are flooding the server. If your application requires heavy use of time servers, you should consider one of the pools described later.

So where can you find a time server? Generally you can use any timeserver you can connect to. This can be a time server within your LAN or any public time server you have access to. If you decide to use a public time server, you should consider using a server pool. Server pools are public addresses from which you will get a random, pooled time server by requesting the time. This way you will not have to split your requests. There are public server pools available for many regions which you may use to avoid problems mentioned above.

See pool.ntp.org [http://www.pool.ntp.org] to find your nearest server pool. For example, if your server is located within Germany you can connect to `0.europe.pool.ntp.org`.

Working with Zend_TimeSync

`Zend_TimeSync` can return the actual time from any given *NTP* or *SNTP* time server. It can automatically handle multiple servers and provides a simple interface.

Note

All examples in this chapter use a public, generic time server: *0.europe.pool.ntp.org*. You should use a public, generic time server which is close to your application server. See http://www.pool.ntp.org for information.

Generic Time Server Request

Requesting the time from a time server is simple. First, you provide the time server from which you want to request the time.

```
$server = new Zend_TimeSync('0.pool.ntp.org');

print $server->getDate()->getIso();
```

So what is happening in the background of Zend_TimeSync? First the syntax of the time server is checked. In our example, '0.pool.ntp.org' is checked and recognised as a possible address for a time server. Then when calling getDate() the actual set time server is requested and it will return its own time. Zend_TimeSync then calculates the difference to the actual time of the server running the script and returns a Zend_Date object with the correct time.

For details about Zend_Date and its methods see the Zend_Date documentation.

Multiple Time Servers

Not all time servers are always available to return their time. Servers may be unavailable during maintenance, for example. When the time cannot be requested from the time server, you will get an exception.

Zend_TimeSync is a simple solution that can handle multiple time servers and supports an automatic fallback mechanism. There are two supported ways; you can either specify an array of time servers when creating the instance, or you can add additional time servers to the instance using the addServer() method.

```
$server = new Zend_TimeSync(array('0.pool.ntp.org',
                                  '1.pool.ntp.org',
                                  '2.pool.ntp.org'));
$server->addServer('3.pool.ntp.org');

print $server->getDate()->getIso();
```

There is no limit to the number of time servers you can add. When a time server can not be reached, Zend_TimeSync will fallback and try to connect to the next time server.

When you supply more than one time server- which is considered a best practice for Zend_TimeSync- you should name each server. You can name your servers with array keys, with the second parameter at instantiation, or with the second parameter when adding another time server.

```
$server = new Zend_TimeSync(array('generic'  => '0.pool.ntp.org',
                                  'fallback' => '1.pool.ntp.org',
                                  'reserve'  => '2.pool.ntp.org'));
$server->addServer('3.pool.ntp.org', 'additional');

print $server->getDate()->getIso();
```

Naming the time servers allows you to request a specific time server as we will see later in this chapter.

Protocols of Time Servers

There are different types of time servers. Most public time servers use the *NTP* protocol. But there are other time synchronization protocols available.

You set the proper protocol in the address of the time server. There are two protocols which are supported by Zend_TimeSync: *NTP* and *SNTP*. The default protocol is *NTP*. If you are using *NTP*, you can omit the protocol in the address as demonstrated in the previous examples.

```
$server = new Zend_TimeSync(array('generic'  => 'ntp:\\0.pool.ntp.org',
                                  'fallback' => 'ntp:\\1.pool.ntp.org',
```

```
                                      'reserve'  => 'ntp:\\2.pool.ntp.org'));
$server->addServer('sntp:\\internal.myserver.com', 'additional');

print $server->getDate()->getIso();
```

Zend_TimeSync can handle mixed time servers. So you are not restricted to only one protocol; you can add any server independently from its protocol.

Using Ports for Time Servers

As with every protocol within the world wide web, the *NTP* and *SNTP* protocols use standard ports. NTP uses port *123* and SNTP uses port *37*.

But sometimes the port that the protocols use differs from the standard one. You can define the port which has to be used for each server within the address. Just add the number of the port after the address. If no port is defined, then Zend_TimeSync will use the standard port.

```
$server = new Zend_TimeSync(array('generic'  => 'ntp:\\0.pool.ntp.org:200',
                                   'fallback' => 'ntp:\\1.pool.ntp.org'));
$server->addServer('sntp:\\internal.myserver.com:399', 'additional');

print $server->getDate()->getIso();
```

Time Servers Options

There is only one option within Zend_TimeSync which will be used internally: *timeout*. You can set any self-defined option you are in need of and request it, however.

The option *timeout* defines the number of seconds after which a connection is detected as broken when there was no response. The default value is *1*, which means that Zend_TimeSync will fallback to the next time server if the requested time server does not respond in one second.

With the setOptions() method, you can set any option. This function accepts an array where the key is the option to set and the value is the value of that option. Any previously set option will be overwritten by the new value. If you want to know which options are set, use the getOptions() method. It accepts either a key which returns the given option if specified, or, if no key is set, it will return all set options.

```
Zend_TimeSync::setOptions(array('timeout' => 3, 'myoption' => 'timesync'));
$server = new Zend_TimeSync(array('generic'  => 'ntp:\\0.pool.ntp.org',
                                   'fallback' => 'ntp:\\1.pool.ntp.org'));
$server->addServer('sntp:\\internal.myserver.com', 'additional');

print $server->getDate()->getIso();
print_r(Zend_TimeSync::getOptions();
print "Timeout = " . Zend_TimeSync::getOptions('timeout');
```

As you can see, the options for Zend_TimeSync are static. Each instance of Zend_TimeSync will use the same options.

Using Different Time Servers

Zend_TimeSync's default behavior for requesting a time is to request it from the first given server. But sometimes it is useful to set a different time server from which to request the time. This can be done with the setServer() method. To define the used time server set the alias as a parameter within the method. To get the actual used time server call the getServer() method. It accepts an alias as a parameter which defines the time server to be returned. If no parameter is given, the current time server will be returned.

```
$server = new Zend_TimeSync(array('generic'  => 'ntp:\\0.pool.ntp.org',
                                  'fallback' => 'ntp:\\1.pool.ntp.org'));
$server->addServer('sntp:\\internal.myserver.com', 'additional');

$actual = $server->getServer();
$server = $server->setServer('additional');
```

Information from Time Servers

Time servers not only offer the time itself, but also additional information. You can get this information with the getInfo() method.

```
$server = new Zend_TimeSync(array('generic'  => 'ntp:\\0.pool.ntp.org',
                                  'fallback' => 'ntp:\\1.pool.ntp.org'));

print_r ($server->getInfo());
```

The returned information differs with the protocol used and can also differ with the server used.

Handling Exceptions

Exceptions are collected for all time servers and returned as an array. So you can iterate through all thrown exceptions as shown in the following example:

```
$serverlist = array(
        // invalid servers
        'invalid_a'  => 'ntp://a.foo.bar.org',
        'invalid_b'  => 'sntp://b.foo.bar.org',
);

$server = new Zend_TimeSync($serverlist);

try {
    $result = $server->getDate();
    echo $result->getIso();
} catch (Zend_TimeSync_Exception $e) {

    $exceptions = $e->get();

    foreach ($exceptions as $key => $myException) {
        echo $myException->getMessage();
        echo '<br />';
    }
}
```

Chapter 29. Zend_Tool_Framework

Introduction

Zend_Tool_Framework is a framework for exposing common functionalities such as the creation of project scaffolds, code generation, search index generation, and much more. Functionality may be written and exposed via PHP classes dropped into the PHP include_path, providing incredible flexibility of implementation. The functionality may then be consumed by writing implementation and/or protocol-specific clients -- such as console clients, XML-RPC, SOAP, and much more.

Zend_Tool_Framework provides the following:

- Common interfaces and abstracts that allow developers to create functionality and capabilities that are dispatchable by tooling clients.

- *Base client functionality* and a concrete console implementation that connect external tools and interfaces to the Zend_Tool_Framework. The Console client may be used in CLI environments such as unix shells and the Windows console.

- *"Provider" and "Manifest" interfaces* that can be utilized by the tooling system. "Providers" represent the functional aspect of the framework, and define the actions that tooling clients may call. "Manifests" act as metadata registries that provide additional context for the various defined providers.

- *An introspective loading system* that will scan the environment for providers and determine what is required to dispatch them.

- *A standard set of system providers"* that allow the system to report what the full capabilities of the system are as well as provide useful feedback. This also includes a comprehensive "Help System".

Definitions that you should be aware of through this manual with respect to Zend_Tool_Framework include:

- Zend_Tool_Framework - The framework which exposes tooling capabilities.

- *Tooling Client* - A developer tool that connects to and consumes Zend_Tool_Framework.

- *Client* - The subsystem of Zend_Tool_Framework that exposes an interface such that tooling clients can connect, query and execute commands.

- *Console Client / Command Line Interface / zf.php* - The tooling client for the command line.

- *Provider* - A subsystem and a collection of built-in functionality that the framework exports.

- *Manifest* - A subsystem for defining, organizing, and disseminating provider requirement data.

- Zend_Tool_Project Provider - A set of providers specifically for creating and maintaining Zend Framework-based projects.

Using the CLI Tool

The CLI, or command line tool (internally known as the console tool), is currently the primary interface for dispatching Zend_Tool requests. With the CLI tool, developers can issue tooling requests inside a the "command line windows", also commonly known as a "terminal" window. This environment is predominant in the *nix environment, but also has a common implementation in windows with the cmd.exe, console2 and also with the Cygwin project.

Setting up the CLI tool

To issue tooling requests via the command line client, you first need to setup the client so that your system can handle the "zf" command. The command line client, for all intents and purposes, is the `.sh` or `.bat` file that is provided with your Zend Framework distribution. In trunk, it can be found here: http://framework.zend.com/svn/framework/standard/trunk/bin/

As you can see, there are 3 files in the `bin/` directory: a `zf.php`, `zf.sh`, and `zf.bat`. The `zf.sh` and the `zf.bat` are the operating system specific client wrappers: `zf.sh` for the *nix environment, and zf.bat for the Win32 environment. These client wrappers are responsible for finding the proper `php.exe`, finding the `zf.php`, and passing on the client request. The `zf.php` is the responsible for handling understanding your environment, constructing the proper include_path, and passing what is provided on the command line to the proper library component for dispatching.

Ultimately, you want to ensure two things to make everything work regardless of the operating system you are on:

1. `zf.sh/zf.bat` is reachable from your system path. This is the ability to call `zf` from anywhere on your command line, regardless of what your current working directory is.

2. ZendFramework/library is in your `include_path`.

Note: while the above are the most ideal requirements, you can simply download Zend Framework and expect it to work as `./path/to/zf.php` some command.

Setting up the CLI tool on Unix-like Systems

The most common setup in the *nix environment, is to copy the `zf.sh` and `zf.php` into the same directory as your PHP binary. This can generally be found in one of the following places:

```
/usr/bin
/usr/local/bin
/usr/local/ZendServer/bin/
/Applications/ZendServer/bin/
```

To find out the location of your PHP binary, you can execute 'which php' on the command line. This will return the location of the php binary you will be using to run php scripts in this environment.

The next order of business is to ensure that the Zend Framework library is setup correctly inside of the system PHP `include_path`. To find out where your `include_path` is located, you can execute 'php -i' and look for the `include_path` variable, or more succinctly, execute 'php -i | grep include_path'. Once you have found where your `include_path` is located (this will generally be something like /usr/lib/php, /usr/share/php, /usr/local/lib/php, or similar), ensure that the contents of the library/ directory are put inside your `include_path` specified directory.

Once you have done those two things, you should be able to issue a command and get back the proper response like this:

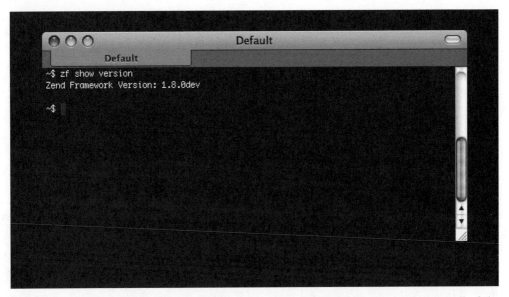

If you do not see this type of output, go back and check your setup to ensure you have all of the necessary peices in the proper place.

There are a couple of alternative setups you might want to employ depending on your servers configuration, your level of access, or for other reasons.

ALTERNATIVE SETUP involves keeping the Zend Framework download together as is, and creating a link from a PATH location to the zf.sh. What this means is you can place the contents of the ZendFramework download into a location such as /usr/local/share/ZendFramework, or more locally like /home/username/lib/ZendFramework, and creating a symbolic link to the zf.sh.

Assuming you want to put the link inside /usr/local/bin (this could also work for placing the link inside /home/username/bin/ for example) you would issue a command similar to this:

```
ln -s /usr/local/share/ZendFramework/bin/zf.sh /usr/local/bin/zf

# OR (for example)
ln -s /home/username/lib/ZendFramework/bin/zf.sh /home/username/bin/zf
```

This will create a link which you should be able to access globally on the command line.

Setting up the CLI tool on Windows

The most common setup in the Windows Win32 environment, is to copy the zf.sh and zf.php into the same directory as your PHP binary. This can generally be found in one of the following places:

```
C:\PHP
C:\Program Files\ZendServer\bin\
C:\WAMP\PHP\bin
```

You should be able to run php.exe on the command line. If you are not able to, first check the documentation that came with your PHP distribution, or ensure that the path to php.exe is in your windows PATH environment variable.

The next order of business is to ensure that the Zend Framework library is setup correctly inside of the system PHP include_path. To find out where your include_path is located, you can type 'php -i' and look for the include_path variable, or more succinctly execute 'php -i | grep include_path' if you have Cygwin setup with grep available. Once you have found where your include_path is located (this will generally be something like C:\PHP\pear, C:\PHP\share, C:\Program Files\ZendServer\share or similar), ensure that the contents of the library/ directory are put inside your include_path specified directory.

Once you have done those two things, you should be able to issue a command and get back the proper response like this:

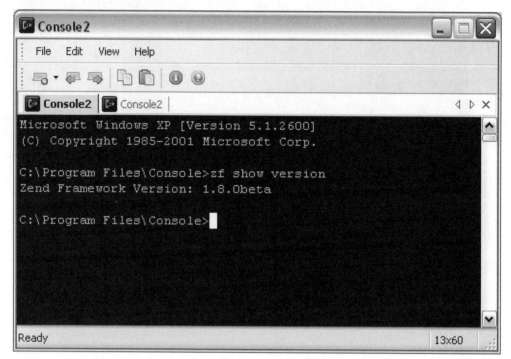

If you do not see this type of output, go back and check your setup to ensure you have all of the necessary pieces in the proper place.

There are a couple of alternative setups you might want to employ depending on your server's configuration, your level of access, or for other reasons.

ALTERNATIVE SETUP involves keeping the Zend Framework download together as is, and altering both your system PATH as well as the php.ini file. In your user's environment, make sure to add C:\Path\To\ZendFramework\bin, so that your zf.bat file is executable. Also, alter the php.ini file to ensure that C:\Path\To\ZendFramework\library is in your include_path.

Other Setup Considerations

If for some reason you do not want the Zend Framework library inside your include_path, there is another option. There are two special environment variables that zf.php will utilize to determine the location of your Zend Framework installation.

The first is ZEND_TOOL_INCLUDE_PATH_PREPEND, which will prepend the value of this environment variable to the system (php.ini) include_path before loading the client.

Alternatively, you might want to use ZEND_TOOL_INCLUDE_PATH to completely *replace* the system include_path for one that makes sense specifically for the zf command line tool.

Where To Go Next?

At this point, your should be setup to start initiating some more "interesting" commands. To get going, you can issue the `zf --help` command to see what is available to you.

```
~/tmp/scratch$ php ~/Projects/ScratchPHP/scripts/test-cli-prototyper.php
~/temp$ zf --help
Usage:
    zf [--global-options] action-name [--action-options] provider-name [--provider-options] [provider parameters ...]
    Note: You may use "?" in any place of the above usage string to ask for more specific help information.
    Example: "zf ? project" will provide all available actions for the project provider.

Providers and their actions:
  Model
    zf create model [model name]

  Version
    zf show version

  Profile
    zf show profile

  Phpinfo
    zf show phpinfo [section name]

  Project
    zf create project [project path] [alternate profile]

  Controller
    zf create controller [controller name] [view included]

  View
    zf create view [controller name] [action or script name]

  Action
    zf create action [controller name] [view included]

  DbAdapter
    zf configure db-adapter [adapter type] [parameters]
    zf test db-adapter.connection
```

Continue on to the `Zend_Tool_Project` "Create Project" section to understand how to use the `zf` script for project creation.

Architecture

Registry

Because providers and manifests may come from anywhere in the `include_path`, a registry is provided to simplify access to the various pieces of the toolchain. This registry is injected into registry-aware components, which may then pull dependencies from them as necessary. Most dependencies registered with the registry will be sub-component-specific repositories.

The interface for the registry consists of the following definition:

```
interface Zend_Tool_Framework_Registry_Interface
{
    public function setClient(Zend_Tool_Framework_Client_Abstract $client);
    public function getClient();
    public function setLoader(Zend_Tool_Framework_Loader_Abstract $loader);
    public function getLoader();
    public function setActionRepository(
        Zend_Tool_Framework_Action_Repository $actionRepository
    );
    public function getActionRepository();
    public function setProviderRepository(
        Zend_Tool_Framework_Provider_Repository $providerRepository
    );
```

```
    public function getProviderRepository();
    public function setManifestRepository(
        Zend_Tool_Framework_Manifest_Repository $manifestRepository
    );
    public function getManifestRepository();
    public function setRequest(Zend_Tool_Framework_Client_Request
        $request);
    public function getRequest();
    public function setResponse(Zend_Tool_Framework_Client_Response
        $response);
    public function getResponse();
}
```

The various objects the registry manages will be discussed in their appropriate sections.

Classes that should be registry-aware should implement Zend_Tool_Framework _Registry_EnabledInterface. This interface merely allows initialization of the registry in the target class.

```
interface Zend_Tool_Framework_Registry_EnabledInterface
{
    public function setRegistry(
        Zend_Tool_Framework_Registry_Interface $registry
    );
}
```

Providers

Zend_Tool_Framework_Provider represents the functional or "capability" aspect of the framework. Fundamentally, Zend_Tool_Framework_Provider will provide the interfaces necessary to produce "providers", or bits of tooling functionality that can be called and used inside the Zend_Tool_Framework toolchain. The simplistic nature of implementing this provider interface allows the developer a "one-stop-shop" of adding functionality/capabilities to Zend_Tool_Framework.

The provider interface is an empty interface and enforces no methods (this is the Marker Interface pattern):

```
interface Zend_Tool_Framework_Provider_Interface
{}
```

Or, if you wish, you can implement the base (or abstract) Provider which will give you access to the Zend_Tool_Framework_Registry:

```
abstract class Zend_Tool_Framework_Provider_Abstract
    implements Zend_Tool_Framework_Provider_Interface,
               Zend_Tool_Registry_EnabledInterface
{
    protected $_registry;
    public function setRegistry(
        Zend_Tool_Framework_Registry_Interface $registry
    );
}
```

Loaders

The purpose of a Loader is to find Providers and Manifest files that contain classes which implement either `Zend_Tool_Framework_Provider_Interface` or `Zend_Tool_Framework_Manifest_Interface`. Once these files are found by a loader, providers are loaded into the Provider Repository and manifest metadata is loaded into the Manifest Repository.

To implement a loader, one must extend the following abstract class:

```
abstract class Zend_Tool_Framework_Loader_Abstract
{

    abstract protected function _getFiles();

    public function load()
    {
        /** ... */
    }
}
```

The `_getFiles()` method should return an array of files (absolute paths). The built-in loader supplied with ZF is called the IncludePath loader. By default, the Tooling framework will use an include_path based loader to find files that might include Providers or Manifest Metadata objects. `Zend_Tool_Framework_Loader_IncludePathLoader`, without any other options, will search for files inside the include path that end in `Mainfest.php`, `Tool.php` or `Provider.php`. Once found, they will be tested (by the `load()` method of the `Zend_Tool_Framework_Loader_Abstract`) to determine if they implement any of the supported interfaces. If they do, an instance of the found class is instantiated, and it is appended to the proper repository.

```
class Zend_Tool_Framework_Loader_IncludePathLoader
    extends Zend_Tool_Framework_Loader_Abstract
{

    protected $_filterDenyDirectoryPattern = '.*(/|\\\\).svn';
    protected $_filterAcceptFilePattern = '.*(?:Manifest|Provider)\.php$';

    protected function _getFiles()
    {
        /** ... */
    }
}
```

As you can see, the IncludePath loader will search all include_paths for the files that match the `$_filterAcceptFilePattern` and NOT match the `$_filterDenyDirectoryPattern`.

Manifests

In short, the Manifest shall contain specific or arbitrary metadata that is useful to any provider or client, as well as be responsible for loading any additional providers into the provider repository.

To introduce metadata into the manifest repository, all one must do is implement the empty `Zend_Tool_Framework_Manifest_Interface`, and provide a `getMetadata()` method which shall return an array of objects that implement `Zend_Tool_Framework_Manifest_Metadata`.

```
interface Zend_Tool_Framework_Manifest_Interface
```

```
{
    public function getMetadata();
}
```

Metadata objects are loaded (by a loader defined below) into the Manfiest Repository (Zend_Tool_Framework_Manifest_Repository). Manifests will be processed after all Providers have been found a loaded into the provider repository. This shall allow Manifests to created Metadata objects based on what is currently inside the provider repository.

There are a few different metadata classes that can be used to describe metadata. The Zend_Tool_Framework_Manifest_Metadata is the base metadata object. As you can see by the following code snippet, the base metadata class is fairly lightweight and abstract in nature:

```
class Zend_Tool_Framework_Metadata_Basic
{

    protected $_type       = 'Global';
    protected $_name       = null;
    protected $_value      = null;
    protected $_reference  = null;

    public function getType();
    public function getName();
    public function getValue();
    public function getReference();
    /** ... */
}
```

There are other built in metadata classes as well for describing more specialized metadata: ActionMetadata and ProviderMetadata. These classes will help you describe in more detail metadata that is specific to either actions or providers, and the reference is expected to be a reference to an action or a provider respectively. These classes are described in the follow code snippet.

```
class Zend_Tool_Framework_Manifest_ActionMetadata
    extends Zend_Tool_Framework_Manifest_Metadata
{

    protected $_type = 'Action';
    protected $_actionName = null;

    public function getActionName();
    /** ... */
}

class Zend_Tool_Framework_Manifest_ProviderMetadata
    extends Zend_Tool_Framework_Manifest_Metadata
{

    protected $_type = 'Provider';
    protected $_providerName  = null;
    protected $_actionName    = null;
    protected $_specialtyName = null;

    public function getProviderName();
    public function getActionName();
    public function getSpecialtyName();
    /** ... */
}
```

'Type' in these classes is used to describe the type of metadata the object is responsible for. In the cases of the ActionMetadata, the type would be 'Action', and conversely in the case of the

ProviderMetadata the type is 'Provider'. These metadata types will also include additional structured information about both the "thing" they are describing as well as the object (the ->getReference()) they are referencing with this new metadata.

In order to create your own metadata type, all one must do is extend the base Zend_Tool_Framework_Manifest_Metadata class and return these new metadata objects via a local Manifest class/object. These user based classes will live in the Manifest Repository

Once these metadata objects are in the repository there are then two different methods that can be used in order to search for them in the repository.

```
class Zend_Tool_Framework_Manifest_Repository
{
    /**
     * To use this method to search, $searchProperties should contain
     * the names and values of the key/value pairs you would like to
     * match within the manifest.
     *
     * For Example:
     *     $manifestRepository->findMetadatas(array(
     *         'action' => 'Foo',
     *         'name'   => 'cliActionName'
     *         ));
     *
     * Will find any metadata objects that have a key with name 'action'
     * value of 'Foo', AND a key named 'name' value of 'cliActionName'
     *
     * Note: to either exclude or include name/value pairs that exist
     * in the search critera but do not appear in the object, pass a
     * bool value to
     * $includeNonExistentProperties
     */
    public function findMetadatas(Array $searchProperties = array(),
                                  $includeNonExistentProperties = true);

    /**
     * The following will return exactly one of the matching search
     * criteria, regardless of how many have been returned. First
     * one in the manifest is what will be returned.
     */
    public function findMetadata(Array $searchProperties = array(),
                                 $includeNonExistentProperties = true)
    {
        $metadatas = $this->getMetadatas($searchProperties,
                                         $includeNonExistentProperties);
        return array_shift($metadatas);
    }
}
```

Looking at the search methods above, the signatures allow for extremely flexible searching. In order to find a metadata object, simply pass in an array of matching constraints via an array. If the data is accessible through the Property accessor (the getSomething() methods implemented on the metadata object), then it will be passed back to the user as a "found" metadata object.

Clients

Clients are the interface which bridges a user or external tool into the Zend_Tool_Framework system. Clients can come in all shapes and sizes: RPC endpoints, Command Line Interface, or even a web interface. Zend_Tool has implemented the command line interface as the default interface for interacting with the Zend_Tool_Framework system.

To implement a client, one would need to extend the following abstract class:

```
abstract class Zend_Tool_Framework_Client_Abstract
{
    /**
     * This method should be implemented by the client implementation to
     * construct and set custom loaders, request and response objects.
     *
     * (not required, but suggested)
     */
    protected function _preInit();

    /**
     * This method should be implemented by the client implementation
     * to parse out and setup the request objects action, provider
     * and parameter information.
     */
    abstract protected function _preDispatch();

    /**
     * This method should be implemented by the client implementation
     * to take the output of the response object and return it (in an
     * client specific way) back to the Tooling Client.
     *
     * (not required, but suggested)
     */
    abstract protected function _postDispatch();
}
```

As you can see, there 1 method required to fulfill the needs of a client (two others suggested), the initialization, prehandling and post handling. For a more in depth study of how the command line client works, please see the source code [http://framework.zend.com/svn/framework/standard /branches/release-1.8/library/Zend/Tool/Framework/Client/Console.php].

Creating Providers to use with Zend_Tool_Framework

In general, a provider, on its own, is nothing more than the shell for a developer to bundle up some capabilities they wish to dispatch with the command line (or other) clients. It is an analogue to what a "controller" is inside of your MVC application.

Basic Instructions for Creating Providers

As an example, if a developer wants to add the capability of showing the version of a datafile that his 3rd party component is working from, there is only one class the developer would need to implement. Assuming the component is called My_Component, he would create a class named My_Component_HelloProvider in a file named HelloProvider.php somewhere on the include_path. This class would implement Zend_Tool_Framework_Provider _Interface, and the body of this file would only have to look like the following:

```
class My_Component_HelloProvider
    implements Zend_Tool_Framework_Provider_Interface
{
    public function say()
    {
        echo 'Hello from my provider!';
    }
}
```

Given that code above, and assuming the developer wishes to access this functionality through the console client, the call would look like this:

```
% zf say hello
Hello from my provider!
```

Advanced Development Information

The above "Hello World" example is great for simple commands, but what about something more advanced? As your scripting and tooling needs grow, you might find that you need the ability to accept variables. Much like function signatures have parameters, your tooling requests can also accept parameters.

Just as each tooling request can be isolated to a method within a class, the parameters of a tooling request can also be isolated in a very well known place. Parameters of the action methods of a provider can include the same parameters you want your client to utilize when calling that provider and action combination. For example, if you wanted to accept a name in the above example, you would probably do this in OO code:

```
class My_Component_HelloProvider
    implements Zend_Tool_Framework_Provider_Interface
{
    public function say($name = 'Ralph')
    {
        echo 'Hello' . $name . ', from my provider!';
    }
}
```

The above example can then be called via the command line `zf say hello Joe`. "Joe" will be supplied to the provider as a parameter of the method call. Also note, as you see that the parameter is optional, that means it is also optional on the command line, so that `zf say hello` will still work, and default to the name "Ralph".

Another interesting feature you might wish to implement is *pretendability*. Pretendabilty is the ability for your provider to "pretend" as if it is doing the requested action and provider combination and give the user as much information about what it *would* do without actually doing it. This might be an important notion when doing heavy database or filesystem modifications that the user might not otherwise want to do.

Pretendability is easy to implement. There are two parts to this feature: 1) marking the provider as having the ability to "pretend", and 2) checking the request to ensure the current request was indeed asked to be "pretended". This feature is demonstrated in the code sample below.

```
class My_Component_HelloProvider
    extends    Zend_Tool_Framework_Provider_Abstract
    implements Zend_Tool_Framework_Provider_Pretendable
{
    public function say($name = 'Ralph')
    {
        if ($this->_registry->getRequest()->isPretend()) {
            echo 'I would say hello to ' . $name . '.';
        } else {
            echo 'Hello' . $name . ', from my provider!';
        }
    }
}
```

Shipped System Providers

In addition to the more useful project based providers that come shipped with Zend_Tool_Project, there are also some more basic, but interesting providers that come built into Zend_Tool_Framework. Some of these exist for the purpose of providing a means via the command line to extract information, such as the version, while others are intended to aid the developer when creating additional providers.

The Version Provider

The Version provider is included so that you may determine which version of the framework that the zf or Zend_Tool is currently set to work with.

Through the command line, simply run zf show version.

The Manifest Provider

The Manifest provider is included so that you may determine what kind of "manifest" information is available during the Zend_Tool runtime. Manifest data is information that is attached to specific objects during Zend_Tool's runtime. Inside the manifest you will find the console specific namings that you are expected to use when calling certain commands. Data found in the manifest can be used by any provider or client on an as-needed basis.

Through the command line, simply run zf show manifest.

Chapter 30. Zend_Tool_Project

Zend_Tool_Project Introduction

Zend_Tool_Project builds on and extends the capabilities of Zend_Tool_Framework to that of managing a "project". In general, a "project" is a planned endeavor or an initiative. In the computer world, projects generally are a collection of resources. These resources can be files, directories, databases, schemas, images, styles, and more.

This same concept applies to Zend Framework projects. In ZF projects, you have controllers, actions, views, models, databases and so on and so forth. In terms of Zend_Tool, we need a way to track these types of resources - thus Zend_Tool_Project.

Zend_Tool_Project is capable of tracking project resources throughout the development of a project. So, for example, if in one command you created a controller, and in the next command you wish to create an action within that controller, Zend_Tool_Project is gonna have to *know* about the controller file you created so that you can (in the next action), be able to append that action to it. This is what keeps our projects up to date and *stateful*.

Another important point to understand about projects is that typically, resources are organized in a hierarchical fashion. With that in mind, Zend_Tool_Project is capable of serializing the current project into a internal representation that allows it to keep track of not only *what* resources are part of a project at any given time, but also *where* they are in relation to one another.

Create A Project

Note: the following examples will assume you have the command line interface of Zend_Tool_Framework available to you.

Note: to issue any of the commands for Zend_Tool_Project with CLI, you must be in the directory where the project was initially created.

To get started with Zend_Tool_Project, you simply need to create a project. Creating a project is simple: go to a place on your filesystem, create a directory, change to that directory, then issue the following command:

```
/tmp/project$ zf create project
```

Optionally, you can create a directory anywhere by the following:

```
$ zf create project /path/to/non-existent-dir
```

The following table will describe the capabilities of providers that are available to you. As you can see in this table, there is a "Project" provider. The Project provider has a couple of actions associated to it, and with those actions a number of options that can be used to modify the behavior of the action and provider.

Table 30.1. Project Provider Options

Provider Name	Available Actions	Parameters	CLI Usage
Project	Create Show	create - [path=null, profile='default']	zf create project some/path

---

Zend Tool Project Providers

Below is a table of all of the providers shipped with Zend Tool Project.

Table 30.2. Project Provider Options

Provider Name	Available Actions	Parameters	CLI Usage
Controller	Create	create - [name, indexActionIncluded =true]	zf create controller foo
Action	Create	create - [name, controllerName=index, viewIncluded=true]	zf create action bar foo (OR zf create action --name bar --controlller-name=foo)
Controller	Create	create - [name, indexActionIncluded =true]	zf create controller foo
Profile	Show	show - []	zf show profile
View	Create	create - [controllerName,action NameOrSimpleName]	zf create view foo bar (or zf create view -c foo -a bar)
Test	Create Enable Disable	create - [libraryClassName]	zf create test My_Foo_Baz zf disable test zf enable test

Chapter 31. Zend_Translate

Introduction

Zend_Translate is Zend Framework's solution for multilingual applications.

In multilingual applications, the content must be translated into several languages and display content depending on the user's language. PHP offers already several ways to handle such problems, however the PHP solution has some problems:

- *Inconsistent API:* There is no single API for the different source formats. The usage of gettext for example is very complicated.

- *PHP supports only gettext and native array:* PHP itself offers only support for array or gettext. All other source formats have to be coded manually, because there is no native support.

- *No detection of the default language:* The default language of the user cannot be detected without deeper knowledge of the backgrounds for the different web browsers.

- *Gettext is not thread-safe:* PHP's gettext library is not thread safe, and it should not be used in a multithreaded environment. This is due to problems with gettext itself, not PHP, but it is an existing problem.

Zend_Translate does not have the above problems. This is why we recommend using Zend_Translate instead of PHP's native functions. The benefits of Zend_Translate are:

- *Supports multiple source formats:* Zend_Translate supports several source formats, including those supported by PHP, and other formats including TMX and CSV files.

- *Thread-safe gettext:* The gettext reader of Zend_Translate is thread-safe. There are no problems using it in multi-threaded environments.

- *Easy and generic API:* The API of Zend_Translate is very simple and requires only a handful of functions. So it's easy to learn and easy to maintain. All source formats are handled the same way, so if the format of your source files change from Gettext to TMX, you only need to change one line of code to specify the storage adapter.

- *Detection of the user's standard language:* The preferred language of the user accessing the site can be detected and used by Zend_Translate.

- *Automatic source detection:* Zend_Translate is capable of detecting and integrating multiple source files and additionally detect the locale to be used depending on directory or filenames.

Starting multi-lingual

So let's get started with multi-lingual business. What we want to do is translate our string output so the view produces the translated output. Otherwise we would have to write one view for each language, and no one would like to do this. Generally, multi-lingual sites are very simple in their design. There are only four steps you would have to do:

1. Decide which adapter you want to use;

2. Create your view and integrate Zend_Translate in your code;

3. Create the source file from your code;

4. Translate your source file to the desired language.

The following sections guide you through all four steps. Read through the next few pages to create your own multi-lingual web application.

Adapters for Zend_Translate

Zend_Translate can handle different adapters for translation. Each adapter has its own advantages and disadvantages. Below is a comprehensive list of all supported adapters for translation source files.

Table 31.1. Adapters for Zend_Translate

Adapter	Description	Usage
Array	Use PHP arrays	Small pages; simplest usage; only for programmers
Csv	Use comma seperated (*.csv/*.txt) files	Simple text file format; fast; possible problems with unicode characters
Gettext	Use binary gettext (*.mo) files	GNU standard for linux; thread-safe; needs tools for translation
Ini	Use simple ini (*.ini) files	Simple text file format; fast; possible problems with unicode characters
Tbx	Use termbase exchange (*.tbx/*.xml) files	Industry standard for inter application terminology strings; XML format
Tmx	Use tmx (*.tmx/*.xml) files	Industry standard for inter application translation; XML format; human readable
Qt	Use qt linguist (*.ts) files	Cross platform application framework; XML format; human readable
Xliff	Use xliff (*.xliff/*.xml) files	A simpler format as TMX but related to it; XML format; human readable
XmlTm	Use xmltm (*.xml) files	Industry standard for XML document translation memory; XML format; human readable
Others	*.sql	Different other adapters may be implemented in the future

How to decide which translation adapter to use

You should decide which Adapter you want to use for Zend_Translate. Frequently, external criteria such as a project requirement or a customer requirement determines this for you, but if you are in the position to do this yourself, the following hints may simplify your decision.

Note

When deciding your adapter you should also be aware of the used encoding. Even if Zend Framework declares UTF-8 as default encoding you will sometimes be in the need of other encoding. Zend_Translate will not change any encoding which is defined within the source file which means that if your Gettext source is build upon ISO-8859-1 it will also return strings in this encoding without converting them. There is only one restriction:

When you use a xml based source format like TMX or XLIFF you must define the encoding within the xml files header because xml files without defined encoding will be treated as UTF-8 by any xml parser by default. You should also be aware that actually the encoding of xml files is limited to the encodings supported by PHP which are UTF-8, ISO-8859-1 and US-ASCII.

Zend_Translate_Adapter_Array

The Array Adapter is the Adapter which is simplest to use for programmers. But when you have numerous translation strings or many languages you should think about another Adapter. For example, if you have 5000 translation strings, the Array Adapter is possibly not the best choice for you.

You should only use this Adapter for small sites with a handful of languages, and if you or your programmer team creates the translations yourselves.

Zend_Translate_Adapter_Csv

The Csv Adapter is the Adapter which is simplest to use for customers. CSV files are readable by standard text editors, but text editors often do not support utf8 character sets.

You should only use this Adapter if your customer wants to do translations himself.

Note

Beware that the Csv Adapter has problems when your Csv files are encoded differently than the locale setting of your environment. This is due to a Bug of PHP itself which will not be fixed before PHP 6.0 (http://bugs.php.net/bug.php?id=38471). So you should be aware that the Csv Adapter due to PHP restrictions is not locale aware.

Zend_Translate_Adapter_Gettext

The Gettext Adapter is the Adapter which is used most frequently. Gettext is a translation source format which was introduced by GNU, and is now used worldwide. It is not human readable, but there are several freeware tools (for instance, POEdit [http://sourceforge.net/projects/poedit/]), which are very helpful. The Zend_Translate Gettext Adapter is not implemented using PHP's gettext extension. You can use the Gettext Adapter even if you do not have the PHP gettext extension installed. Also the Adapter is thread-safe and the PHP gettext extension is currently not thread-safe.

Most people will use this adapter. With the available tools, professional translation is very simple. But gettext data are is stored in a machine-readable format, which is not readable without tools.

Zend_Translate_Adapter_Ini

The Ini Adapter is a very simple Adapter which can even be used directly by customers. INI files are readable by standard text editors, but text editors often do not support utf8 character sets.

You should only use this Adapter when your customer wants to do translations himself. Do not use this adapter as generic translation source.

Zend_Translate_Adapter_Tbx

The Tbx Adapter is an Adapter which will be used by customers which already use the TBX format for their internal translation system. Tbx is no standard translation format but more a collection of already translated and pre translated source strings. When you use this adapter you have to be sure that all your needed source string are translated. TBX is a XML file based format and a completly new format. XML files are human-readable, but the parsing is not as fast as with gettext files.

This adapter is perfect for companies when pre translated source files already exist. The files are human readable and system-independent.

Zend_Translate_Adapter_Tmx

The Tmx Adapter is the Adapter which will be used by most customers which have multiple systems which use the same translation source, or when the translation source must be system-independent. TMX is a XML file based format, which is announced to be the next industry standard. XML files are human-readable, but the parsing is not as fast as with gettext files.

Most medium to large companies use this adapter. The files are human readable and system-independent.

Zend_Translate_Adapter_Qt

The Qt Adapter is for all customers which have TS files as their translation source which are made by QtLinguist. QT is a XML file based format. XML files are human-readable, but the parsing is not as fast as with gettext files.

Several big players have build software upon the QT framework. The files are human readable and system-independent.

Zend_Translate_Adapter_Xliff

The Xliff Adapter is the Adapter which will be used by most customers which want to have XML files but do not have tools for TMX. XLIFF is a XML file based format, which is related to TMX but simpler as it does not support all possibilities of it. XML files are human-readable, but the parsing is not as fast as with gettext files.

Most medium companies use this adapter. The files are human readable and system-independent.

Zend_Translate_Adapter_XmlTm

The XmlTm Adapter is the Adapter which will be used by customers which do their layout themself. XmlTm is a format which allows the complete html source to be included in the translation source, so the translation is coupled with the layout. XLIFF is a XML file based format, which is related to XLIFF but its not as simple to read.

This adapter should only be used when source files already exist. The files are human readable and system-independent.

Integrate self written Adapters

Zend_Translate allows you to integrate and use self written Adapter classes. They can be used like the standard Adapter classes which are already included within Zend_Translate.

Any adapter class you want to use with Zend_Translate must be a subclass of Zend_Translate_Adapter. Zend_Translate_Adapter is an abstract class which already defines all what is needed for translation. What has to be done by you, is the definition of the reader for translation datas.

The usage of the prefix "Zend" should be limited to Zend Framework. If you extend Zend_Translate with your own adapter, you should name it like "Company_Translate_Adapter_MyFormat". The following code shows an example of how a self written adapter class could be implemented:

```
try {
    $translate = new Zend_Translate('Company_Translate_Adapter_MyFormat',
                                    '/path/to/translate.xx',
                                    'en',
                                    array('myoption' => 'myvalue'));
} catch (Exception $e) {
```

```
        // File not found, no adapter class...
        // General failure
}
```

Speedup all Adapters

Zend_Translate allows you use internally Zend_Cache to fasten the loading of translation sources. This comes very handy if you use many translation sources or extensive source formats like XML based files.

To use caching you will just have to give a cache object to the Zend_Translate::setCache() method. It takes a instance of Zend_Cache as only parameter. Also if you use any adapter direct you can use the setCache() method. For convenience there are also the static methods getCache(), hasCache(), clearCache() and removeCache().

```
$cache = Zend_Cache::factory('Core',
                            'File',
                            $frontendOptions,
                            $backendOptions);
Zend_Translate::setCache($cache);
$translate = new Zend_Translate('gettext',
                                '/path/to/translate.mo',
                                'en');
```

Note

You must set the cache *before* you use or initiate any adapter or instance of Zend_Translate. Otherwise your translation source will not be cached until you add a new source with the addTranslation() method.

Using Translation Adapters

The next step is to use the adapter within your code.

Example 31.1. Example of single-language PHP code

```
print "Example\n";
print "=======\n";
print "Here is line one\n";
print "Today is the " . date("d.m.Y") . "\n";
print "\n";
print "Here is line two\n";
```

The example above shows some output with no support for translation. You probably write your code in your native language. Generally you need to translate not only the output, but also error and log messages.

The next step is to integrate Zend Translate into your existing code. Of course it is much easier if you had already written your code with translation in mind, than changing your code afterwards.

Example 31.2. Example of multi-lingual PHP code

```
$translate = new Zend_Translate('gettext', '/my/path/source-de.mo', 'de');
$translate->addTranslation('/path/to/translation/fr-source.mo', 'fr');

print $translate->_("Example") . "\n";
print "=======\n";
print $translate->_("Here is line one") . "\n";
printf($translate->_("Today is the %1\$s") . "\n", date('d.m.Y'));
print "\n";

$translate->setLocale('fr');
print $translate->_("Here is line two") . "\n";
```

Now let's take a deeper look into what has been done and how to integrate Zend_Translate into your own code.

Create a new Zend_Translate object and define the base adapter:

```
$translate = new Zend_Translate
    'gettext',
    '/path/to/translation/source-de.mo',
    'de'
);
```

In this example we chose the **Gettext Adapter**. We place our file **source-de.mo** into the directory **/path/to/translation**. The gettext file will have German translation included, and we also added another language source for French.

The next step is to wrap all strings which are to be translated. The simplest approach is to have only simple strings or sentences like this:

```
print $translate->_("Example") . "\n";
print "=======\n";
print $translate->_("Here is line one") . "\n";
```

Some strings do not needed to be translated. The separating line is always a separating line, even in other languages.

Having data values integrated into a translation string is also supported through the use of embedded parameters.

```
printf($translate->_("Today is the %1\$s") . "\n", date("d.m.Y"));
```

Instead of print(), use the printf() function and replace all parameters with %1\$s parts. The first is %1\$s, the second is %2\$s, and so on. This way a translation can be done without knowing the exact value. In our example, the date is always the actual day, but the string can be translated without the knowledge of the actual day.

Each string is identified in the translation storage by a message ID. You can use message IDs instead of strings in your code, like this:

```
print $translate->_(1) . "\n";
print "=======\n";
print $translate->_(2) . "\n";
```

But doing this has several disadvantages:

You can not see what your code should output just by viewing your code.

Also you will have problems if some strings are not translated. You must always keep in mind how translation works. First `Zend_Translate` checks whether the specified language has a translation for the given message ID or string. If no translation string has been found it refers to the next lower level language as defined within `Zend_Locale`. So "**de_AT**" becomes "**de**" only. If there is no translation found for "**de**" either, then the original message is returned. This way you always have an output, even in case the message translation does not exist in your message storage. `Zend_Translate` never throws an error or exception when translating strings.

Translation Source Structures

Your next step is to create the translation sources for the languages you want to translate. Every adapter is created its own way as described here, but there are common features applicable for all adapters.

You have to decide where to store your translation source files. Using `Zend_Translate` you are not restricted in any way. The following structures are preferable:

- Single structured source

```
/application/
/languages/
/languages/lang.en
/languages/lang.de
/library/
```

Positive: all source files for every languages are stored in one directory. No splitting of related files.

- Language structured source

```
/application/
/languages/
/languages/en/
/languages/en/first.en
/languages/en/second.en
/languages/de/
/languages/de/first.de
/languages/de/second.de
/library
```

Positive: Every language is stored in their own directories. Easy translation, as every language team has to translate only one directory. Also the usage of multiple files is transparent.

- Application structured source

```
/application/
/application/languages/
/application/languages/first.en
/application/languages/first.de
/application/languages/second.en
/application/languages/second.de
/library/
```

Positive: all source files for every language are stored in one directory. No splitting of related files.

Negative: having multiple files for the same language can be problematic.

- Gettext structured source

```
/application/
/languages/
/languages/de/
/languages/de/LC_MESSAGES/
/languages/de/LC_MESSAGES/first.mo
/languages/de/LC_MESSAGES/second.mo
/languages/en/
/languages/en/LC_MESSAGES/
/languages/en/LC_MESSAGES/first.mo
/languages/en/LC_MESSAGES/second.mo
/library/
```

Positive: existing gettext sources can be used without changing structure.

Negative: having sub-sub directories may be confusing for people who have not used gettext before.

- File structured source

```
/application/
/application/models/
/application/models/MyModel.php
/application/models/MyModel.de
/application/models/MyModel.en
/application/controllers/
/application/controllers/MyController.php
/application/controllers/MyController.de
/application/controllers/MyController.en
/library/
```

Positive: translation files are localted near their source.

Negative: too many and also small translation files result in being tendious to translate. Also every file has to be added as translation source.

Single structured and language structured source files are most usable for Zend_Translate.

So now, that we know which structure we want to have, we should create our translation source files.

Creating Array source files

Array source files are plain arrays. But you have to define them manually since there is no tool to aid this. But because they are so simple, it's the fastest way to look up messages if your code works as expected. It's generally the best adapter to get started with translation business.

```
$english = array(
    'message1' => 'message1',
    'message2' => 'message2',
    'message3' => 'message3');

$german = array(
    'message1' => 'Nachricht1',
    'message2' => 'Nachricht2',
    'message3' => 'Nachricht3');

$translate = new Zend_Translate('array', $english, 'en');
$translate->addTranslation($deutsch, 'de');
```

Since release 1.5 it is also supported to have arrays included within an external file. You just have to provide the filename and Zend_Translate will automatically include it and look for the array. See the following example for details:

```
// myarray.php
return array(
    'message1' => 'Nachricht1',
    'message2' => 'Nachricht2',
    'message3' => 'Nachricht3');

// controller
$translate = new Zend_Translate('array', '/path/to/myarray.php', 'de');
```

Note

Files which do not return an array will fail to be included. Also any output within this file will be ignored and suppressed.

Creating Gettext source files

Gettext source files are created by GNU's gettext library. There are several free tools available that can parse your code files and create the needed gettext source files. These have the extension ***.mo** and they are binary files. An open source tool for creating the files is poEdit [http://sourceforge.net/projects/poedit/]. This tool also supports you during the translation process itself.

```
// We accume that we have created the mo files and translated them
$translate = new Zend_Translate('gettext', '/path/to/english.mo', 'en');
$translate->addTranslation('/path/to/german.mo', 'de');
```

As you can see the adapters are used exactly the same way, with one small difference: change **array** to **gettext**. All other usages are exactly the same as with all other adapters. With the gettext adapter you no longer have to be aware of gettext's standard directory structure, bindtextdomain and textdomain. Just give the path and filename to the adapter.

Note

You should always use UTF-8 as source encoding. Otherwise you will have problems when using two different source encodings. E.g. one of your source files is encoded with ISO-8815-11 and another one with CP815. You can set only one encoding for your source file, so one of your languages probably will not display correctly.

UTF-8 is a portable format which supports all languages. When using UTF-8 for all languages, you will eliminate the problem of incompatible encodings.

Many gettext editors add adapter informations as empty translation string. This is the reason why empty strings are not translated when using the gettext adapter. Instead they are erased from the translation table and provided by the getAdapterInfo() method. It will return the adapter informations for all added gettext files as array using the filename as key.

```
// Getting the adapter informations
$translate = new Zend_Translate('gettext', '/path/to/english.mo', 'en');
print_r($translate->getAdapterInfo());
```

Creating TMX source files

TMX source files are a new industry standard. They have the advantage of being XML files and so they are readable by every editor and of course by humans. You can either create TMX files manually with a text editor, or you can use a special tool. But most tools currently available for creating TMX source files are not freely available.

Example 31.3. Example TMX file

```
<?xml version="1.0" ?>
<!DOCTYPE tmx SYSTEM "tmx14.dtd">
<tmx version="1.4">
 <header creationtoolversion="1.0.0" datatype="winres" segtype="sentence"
         adminlang="en-us" srclang="de-at" o-tmf="abc"
         creationtool="XYZTool" >
 </header>
 <body>
  <tu tuid='message1'>
   <tuv xml:lang="de"><seg>Nachricht1</seg></tuv>
   <tuv xml:lang="en"><seg>message1</seg></tuv>
  </tu>
  <tu tuid='message2'>
   <tuv xml:lang="en"><seg>message2</seg></tuv>
   <tuv xml:lang="de"><seg>Nachricht2</seg></tuv>
  </tu>
```

```
$translate = new Zend_Translate('tmx', 'path/to/mytranslation.tmx', 'en');
```

TMX files can have several languages within the same file. All other included languages are added automatically, so you do not have to call addLanguage().

If you want to have only specified languages from the source translated you can set the option 'defined_language' to true. With this option you can add the wished languages explicitly with addLanguage(). The default value for this option is to add all languages.

Creating CSV source files

CSV source files are small and human readable. If your customers want to translate their own, you will probably use the CSV adapter.

Example 31.4. Example CSV file

```
 #Example csv file
message1;Nachricht1
message2;Nachricht2
```

```
$translate = new Zend_Translate('csv', '/path/to/mytranslation.csv', 'de');
$translate->addTranslation('path/to/other.csv', 'fr');
```

There are three different options for the CSV adapter. You can set 'delimiter', 'limit' and 'enclosure'.

The default delimiter for CSV string is ';', but with the option 'delimiter' you can decide to use another one.

The default limit for a line within a CSV file is '0'. This means that the end of a CSV line is searched automatically. If you set 'limit' to any value, then the CSV file will be read faster, but any line exceeding this limit will be truncated.

The default enclosure to use for CSV files is '"'. You can set a different one using the option 'enclosure'.

Example 31.5. Second CSV file example

```
 # Example CSV file
"message,1",Nachricht1
message2,"Nachricht,2"
"message3,",Nachricht3


$translate = new Zend_Translate(
    'csv',
    '/path/to/mytranslation.csv',
    'de',
    array('delimiter' => ','));

$translate->addTranslation('/path/to/other.csv', 'fr');
```

Creating INI source files

INI source files are human readable but normally not very small as they also include other data beside translations. If you have data which shall be editable by your customers you can use the INI adapter.

Example 31.6. Example INI file

```
[Test]
;TestPage Comment
Message_1="Nachricht 1 (de)"
Message_2="Nachricht 2 (de)"
Message_3="Nachricht :3 (de)"


$translate = new Zend_Translate('ini', '/path/to/mytranslation.ini', 'de');
$translate->addTranslation('/path/to/other.ini', 'it');
```

INI files have several restrictions. If a value in the ini file contains any non-alphanumeric characters it needs to be enclosed in double-quotes ("). There are also reserved words which must not be used as keys for ini files. These include: null, yes, no, true, and false. Values null, no and false results in "", yes and true results in 1. Characters { } | &~ ! [() " must not be used anywhere in the key and have a special meaning in the value. Do not use them as it will produce unexpected behaviour.

Options for adapters

Options can be used with all adapters. Of course the options are different for all adapters. You can set options when you create the adapter. Actually there is one option which is available to all adapters: 'clear' sets if translation data should be added to existing one or not. Standard behaviour is to add new translation data to existing one. But the translation data is only cleared for the selected language. So other languages remain untouched.

You can set options temporarily when using addTranslation($data, $locale, array $options = array()) as third and optional parameter. And you can use the method setOptions() to set the options permanently.

Example 31.7. Using translation options

```
// define ':' as separator for the translation source files
$options = array('delimiter' => ':');
$translate = new Zend_Translate(
    'csv',
    '/path/to/mytranslation.csv',
    'de',
    $options);

...

// clear the defined language and use new translation data
$options = array('clear' => true);
$translate->addTranslation('/path/to/new.csv', 'fr', $options);
```

Here you can find all available options for the different adapters with a description of their usage:

Table 31.2. Options for translation adapters

Option	Adapter	Description	Default value
clear	all	If set to true, the already read translations will be cleared. This can be used instead of creating a new instance when reading new translation data	**false**
disableNotices	all	If set to true, all notices regarding not available translations will be disabled. You should set this option to true in production environment	**false**
ignore	all	All directories and files beginning with this prefix will be ignored when searching for files. This value defaults to '.' which leads to the behavior that all hidden files will be ignored. Setting this value to 'tmp' would mean that directories and files like 'tmpImages' and 'tmpFiles' would be ignored as well as all subsequent directories	.

Option	Adapter	Description	Default value
log	all	An instance of Zend_Log where untranslated messages and notices will be written to	**null**
logMessage	all	The message which will be written into the log	**Untranslated message within '%locale%': %message%**
logUntranslated	all	When this option is set to true, all message IDs which can not be translated will be written into the attached log	**false**
scan	all	If set to null, no scanning of the directory structure will be done. If set to Zend_Translate:: LOCALE_DIRECTORY the locale will be detected within the directory. If set to Zend_Translate:: LOCALE_FILENAME the locale will be detected within the filename. See the section called "Automatic source detection" for details	**null**
delimiter	Csv	Defines which sign is used as delimiter for separating source and translation	**;**
enclosure	Csv	Defines the enclosure character to be used. Defaults to a doublequote	**"**
length	Csv	Defines the maximum length of a csv line. When set to 0 it will be detected automatically	**0**

When you want to have self defined options, you are also able to use them within all adapters. The setOptions() method can be used to define your option. setOptions() needs an array with the options you want to set. If an given option exists it will be signed over. You can define as much options as needed as they will not be checked by the adapter. Just make sure not to overwrite any existing option which is used by an adapter.

To return the option you can use the getOptions() method. When getOptions() is called without a parameter it will return all options set. When the optional parameter is given you will only get the specified option.

Handling languages

When working with different languages there are a few methods which will be useful.

The getLocale() method can be used to get the currently set language. It can either hold an instance of Zend_Locale or the identifier of a locale.

The setLocale() method sets a new standard language for translation. This prevents the need of setting the optional language parameter more than once to the translate() method. If the given language does not exist, or no translation data is available for the language, setLocale() tries to downgrade to the language without the region if any was given. A language of en_US would be downgraded to en. When even the downgraded language can not be found an exception will be thrown.

The isAvailable() method checks if a given language is already available. It returns true if data for the given language exist.

And finally the getList() method can be used to get all currently set languages for an adapter returned as array.

Example 31.8. Handling languages with adapters

```
// returns the currently set language
$actual = $translate->getLocale();

// you can use the optional parameter while translating
echo $translate->_("my_text", "fr");
// or set a new language
$translate->setLocale("fr");
echo $translate->_("my_text");
// refer to the base language
// fr_CH will be downgraded to fr
$translate->setLocale("fr_CH");
echo $translate->_("my_text");

// check if this language exist
if ($translate->isAvailable("fr")) {
    // language exists
}
```

Automatical handling of languages

Note that as long as you only add new translation sources with the addTranslation() method Zend_Translate will automatically set the best fitting language for your environment when you use one of the automatic locales which are 'auto' or 'browser'. So normally you will not need to call setLocale(). This should only be used in conjunction with automatic source detection.

The algorithm will search for the best fitting locale depending on the user's browser and your environment. See the following example for details:

Example 31.9. Automatically language detection

```
// Let's expect the browser returns these language settings:
// HTTP_ACCEPT_LANGUAGE = "de_AT=1;fr=1;en_US=0.8";

// Example 1:
// When no fitting language is found, the message ID is returned
```

```
$translate = new Zend_Translate(
    'gettext',
    'my_it.mo',
    'auto',
    array('scan' => Zend_Translate::LOCALE_FILENAME));

// Example 2:
// Best found fitting language is 'fr'
$translate = new Zend_Translate(
    'gettext',
    'my_fr.mo',
    'auto',
    array('scan' => Zend_Translate::LOCALE_FILENAME));

// Example 3:
// Best found fitting language is 'de' ('de_AT' will be degraded)
$translate = new Zend_Translate(
    'gettext',
    'my_de.mo',
    'auto',
    array('scan' => Zend_Translate::LOCALE_FILENAME));

// Example 4:
// Returns 'it' as translation source and overrides the automatic settings
$translate = new Zend_Translate(
    'gettext',
    'my_it.mo',
    'auto',
    array('scan' => Zend_Translate::LOCALE_FILENAME));

$translate->addTranslation('my_ru.mo', 'ru');
$translate->setLocale('it_IT');
```

After setting a language manually with the setLocale() method the automatic detection will be switched off and overridden.

If you want to use it again, you can set the language **auto** with setLocale() which will reactivate the automatic detection for Zend_Translate.

Since Zend Framework 1.7.0 Zend_Translate also recognises an application wide locale. You can simply set a Zend_Locale instance to the registry like shown below. With this notation you can forget about setting the locale manually with each instance when you want to use the same locale multiple times.

```
// in your bootstrap file
$locale = new Zend_Locale();
Zend_Registry::set('Zend_Locale', $locale);

// default language when requested language is not available
$defaultlanguage = 'en';

// somewhere in your application
$translate = new Zend_Translate('gettext', 'my_de.mo');

if (!$translate->isAvailable($locale->getLanguage())) {
    // not available languages are rerouted to another language
    $translate->setLocale($defaultlanguage);
}

$translate->getLocale();
```

Automatic source detection

Zend_Translate can detect translation sources automatically. So you don't have to declare each source file manually. You can let Zend_Translate do this job and scan the complete directory structure for source files.

Note

Automatic source detection is available since Zend Framework version 1.5 .

The usage is quite the same as initiating a single translation source with one difference. You must give a directory which has to be scanned instead a file.

Example 31.10. Scanning a directory structure for sources

```
// assuming we have the following structure
//   /language/
//   /language/login/login.tmx
//   /language/logout/logout.tmx
//   /language/error/loginerror.tmx
//   /language/error/logouterror.tmx

$translate = new Zend_Translate('tmx', '/language');
```

So Zend_Translate does not only search the given directory, but also all subdirectories for translation source files. This makes the usage quite simple. But Zend_Translate will ignore all files which are not sources or which produce failures while reading the translation data. So you have to make sure that all of your translation sources are correct and readable because you will not get any failure if a file is bogus or can not be read.

Note

Depending on how deep your directory structure is and how much files are within this structure it can take a long time for Zend_Translate to complete.

In our example we have used the TMX format which includes the language to be used within the source. But many of the other source formats are not able to include the language within the file. Even this sources can be used with automatic scanning if you do some pre-requisits as described below:

Language through naming directories

One way to include automatic language detection is to name the directories related to the language which is used for the sources within this directory. This is the easiest way and is used for example within standard gettext implementations.

Zend_Translate needs the 'scan' option to know that it should search the names of all directories for languages. See the following example for details:

Example 31.11. Directory scanning for languages

```
// assuming we have the following structure
//   /language/
//   /language/de/login/login.mo
```

```
//  /language/de/error/loginerror.mo
//  /language/en/login/login.mo
//  /language/en/error/loginerror.mo

$translate = new Zend_Translate(
    'gettext',
    '/language',
    null,
    array('scan' => Zend_Translate::LOCALE_DIRECTORY));
```

Note

This works only for adapters which do not include the language within the source file. Using this option for example with TMX will be ignored. Also language definitions within the filename will be ignored when using this option.

Note

You should be aware if you have several subdirectories under the same structure. Assuming we have a structure like /language/module/de/en/file.mo. In this case the path contains multiple strings which would be detected as locale. It could be either de or en. In such a case the behaviour is undefined and it is recommended to use file detection in such situations.

Language through filenames

Another way to detect the language automatically is to use special filenames. You can either name the complete file or parts of a file after the used language. To use this way of detection you will have to set the 'scan' option at initiation. There are several ways of naming the sourcefiles which are described below:

Example 31.12. Filename scanning for languages

```
// assuming we have the following structure
//  /language/
//  /language/login/login_en.mo
//  /language/login/login_de.mo
//  /language/error/loginerror_en.mo
//  /language/error/loginerror_de.mo

$translate = new Zend_Translate(
    'gettext',
    '/language',
    null,
    array('scan' => Zend_Translate::LOCALE_FILENAME));
```

Complete filename

Having the whole file named after the language is the simplest way but only viable if you have only one file per language.

```
/languages/
/languages/en.mo
/languages/de.mo
/languages/es.mo
```

Extension of the file

Another simple way to use the extension of the file for language detection. But this may be confusing since you will no longer have an idea which extension the file originally had.

```
/languages/
/languages/view.en
/languages/view.de
/languages/view.es
```

Filename tokens

Zend_Translate is also capable of detecting the language if it is included within the filename. But if you go this way you will have to separate the language with a token. There are three supported tokens which can be used: a dot '.', an underscore '_', or a hyphen '-'.

```
/languages/
/languages/view_en.mo -> detects english
/languages/view_de.mo -> detects german
/languages/view_it.mo -> detects italian
```

The first found string delimited by a token which can be interpreted as a locale will be used. See the following example for details.

```
/languages/
/languages/view_en_de.mo -> detects english
/languages/view_en_es.mo -> detects english and overwrites the first file
/languages/view_it_it.mo -> detects italian
```

All three tokens are used to detect the locale. When the filename contains multiple tokens, the first found token depends on the order of the tokens which are used. See the following example for details.

```
/languages/
/languages/view_en-it.mo -> detects english because '_' will be used
    before '-'
/languages/view-en_it.mo -> detects italian because '_' will be used
    before '-'
/languages/view_en.it.mo -> detects italian because '.' will be used
    before '_'
```

Checking for translations

Normally text will be translated without any computation. But sometimes it is necessary to know if a text is translated or not, therefor the isTranslated() method can be used.

isTranslated($messageId, $original = false, $locale = null) takes the text you want to check as its first parameter, and as optional third parameter the locale for which you want to do the check. The optional second parameter declares whether translation is fixed to the declared language or a lower set of translations can be used. If you have a text which can be returned for 'en' but not for 'en_US' you will normally get the translation returned, but by setting $original to true, isTranslated() will return false.

Example 31.13. Checking if a text is translatable

```
$english = array(
    'message1' => 'Nachricht 1',
    'message2' => 'Nachricht 2',
    'message3' => 'Nachricht 3');

$translate = new Zend_Translate('array', $english, 'de_AT');

if ($translate->isTranslated('message1')) {
    print "'message1' can be translated";
}

if (!($translate->isTranslated('message1', true, 'de'))) {
    print "'message1' can not be translated to 'de'"
        . " as it's available only in 'de_AT'";
}

if ($translate->isTranslated('message1', false, 'de')) {
    print "'message1' can be translated in 'de_AT' as it falls back
        to 'de'";
}
```

How to log not found translations

When you have a bigger site or you are creating the translation files manually, you often have the problem that some messages are not translated. But there is an easy solution for you when you are using Zend_Translate.

You have to follow two or three simple steps. First, you have to create an instance of Zend_Log. Then you have to attach this instance to Zend_Translate. See the following example:

Example 31.14. Log translations

```
$translate = new Zend_Translate('gettext', $path, 'de');

// Create a log instance
$writer = new Zend_Log_Writer_Stream('/path/to/file.log');
$log    = new Zend_Log($writer);

// Attach it to the translation instance
$translate->setOptions(array(
    'log'             => $log,
    'logUntranslated' => true));

$translate->translate('unknown string');
```

Now you will have a new notice in the log: Untranslated message within 'de': unknown string.

Note

You should note that any translation which can not be found will be logged. This means all translations when a user requests a language which is not supported. Also every request for a message which can not be translated will be logged. Be aware, that 100 people requesting the same translation, will result 100 logged notices.

This feature can not only be used to log messages but also to attach this untranslated messages into an empty translation file. To do so you will have to write your own log writer which writes the format you want to have and strips the prepending "Untranslated message".

You can also set the 'logMessage' option when you want to have your own log message. Use the '%message%' token for placing the messageId within your log message, and the '%locale%' token for the requested locale. See the following example for a self defined log message:

Example 31.15. Self defined log messages

```
$translate = new Zend_Translate('gettext', $path, 'de');

// Create a log instance
$writer = new Zend_Log_Writer_Stream('/path/to/file.log');
$log    = new Zend_Log($writer);

// Attach it to the translation instance
$translate->setOptions(array(
    'log'              => $log,
    'logMessage'       => "Missing '%message%' within locale '%locale%'",
    'logUntranslated' => true));

$translate->translate('unknown string');
```

Accessing source data

Sometimes it is useful to have access to the translation source data. Therefor the following two functions are provided.

The getMessageIds($locale = null) method returns all known message IDs as array.

The getMessages($locale = null) method returns the complete translation source as an array. The message ID is used as key and the translation data as value.

Both methods accept an optional parameter $locale which, if set, returns the translation data for the specified language. If this parameter is not given, the actual set language will be used. Keep in mind that normally all translations should be available in all languages. Which means that in a normal situation you will not have to set this parameter.

Additionally the getMessages() method can be used to return the complete translation dictionary using the pseudo-locale 'all'. This will return all available translation data for each added locale.

Note

Attention: the returned array can be **very big**, depending on the number of added locales and the amount of translation data.

Example 31.16. Handling languages with adapters

```
// returns all known message IDs
$messageIds = $translate->getMessageIds();
print_r($messageIds);

// or just for the specified language
$messageIds = $translate->getMessageIds('en_US');
```

```
print_r($messageIds);

// returns all the complete translation data
$source = $translate->getMessages();
print_r($source);
```

Migrating from previous versions

The API of Zend_Translate has changed from time to time. If you started to use Zend_Translate and its subcomponents in earlier versions follow the guidelines below to migrate your scripts to use the new API.

Migrating from 1.6 to 1.7 or newer

Setting languages

When using automatic detection of languages, or setting languages manually to Zend_Translate you may have mentioned that from time to time a notice is thrown about not added or empty translations. In some previous release also an exception was raised in some cases.

The reason is, that when a user requests a non existing language, you have no simple way to detect what's going wrong. So we added those notices which show up in your log and tell you that the user requested a language which you do not support. Note that the code, even when we trigger such an notice, keeps working without problems.

But when you use a own error or exception handler, like xdebug, you will get all notices returned, even if this was not your intention. This is due to the fact that these handlers override all settings from within PHP.

To get rid of these notices you can simply set the new option 'disableNotices' to true. It defaults to false.

Example 31.17. Setting languages without getting notices

Let's assume that we have 'en' available and our user requests 'fr' which is not in our portfolio of translated languages.

```
$language = new Zend_Translate('gettext',
                               '/path/to/translations',
                               'auto');
```

In this case we will get an notice about a not available language 'fr'. Simply add the option and the notices will be disabled.

```
$language = new Zend_Translate('gettext',
                               '/path/to/translations',
                               'auto',
                               array('disableNotices' => true));
```

Chapter 32. Zend_Uri

Zend_Uri

Overview

Zend_Uri is a component that aids in manipulating and validating Uniform Resource Identifiers [http://www.w3.org/Addressing/] (URIs). Zend_Uri exists primarily to service other components such as Zend_Http_Client but is also useful as a standalone utility.

URIs always begin with a scheme, followed by a colon. The construction of the many different schemes varies significantly. The Zend_Uri class provides a factory that returns a subclass of itself which specializes in each scheme. The subclass will be named Zend_Uri_<scheme>, where <scheme> is the scheme lowercased with the first letter capitalized. An exception to this rule is HTTPS, which is also handled by Zend_Uri_Http.

Creating a New URI

Zend_Uri will build a new URI from scratch if only a scheme is passed to Zend_Uri::factory().

Example 32.1. Creating a New URI with Zend_Uri::factory()

```
// To create a new URI from scratch, pass only the scheme.
$uri = Zend_Uri::factory('http');

// $uri instanceof Zend_Uri_Http
```

To create a new URI from scratch, pass only the scheme to Zend_Uri::factory() [*]. If an unsupported scheme is passed, a Zend_Uri_Exception will be thrown.

If the scheme or URI passed is supported, Zend_Uri::factory() will return a subclass of itself that specializes in the scheme to be created.

Manipulating an Existing URI

To manipulate an existing URI, pass the entire URI to Zend_Uri::factory().

Example 32.2. Manipulating an Existing URI with Zend_Uri::factory()

```
// To manipulate an existing URI, pass it in.
$uri = Zend_Uri::factory('http://www.zend.com');

// $uri instanceof Zend_Uri_Http
```

The URI will be parsed and validated. If it is found to be invalid, a Zend_Uri_Exception will be thrown immediately. Otherwise, Zend_Uri::factory() will return a subclass of itself that specializes in the scheme to be manipulated.

---

[*] At the time of writing, Zend_Uri only supports the HTTP and HTTPS schemes.

URI Validation

The `Zend_Uri::check()` function can be used if only validation of an existing URI is needed.

Example 32.3. URI Validation with Zend_Uri::check()

```
// Validate whether a given URI is well formed
$valid = Zend_Uri::check('http://uri.in.question');

// $valid is TRUE for a valid URI, or FALSE otherwise.
```

`Zend_Uri::check()` returns a boolean, which is more convenient than using `Zend_Uri::factory()` and catching the exception.

Allowing "Unwise" characters in URIs

By default, Zend_Uri will not accept the following characters, defined by the RFC as "unwise" and invalid: `"{"`, `"}"`, `"|"`, `"\"`, `"^"`, `"`"`. However, many implementations do accept these characters as valid.

Zend_Uri can be set to accept these "unwise" characters by setting the 'allow_unwise' option to boolean TRUE using the Zend_Uri::setConfig() method:

Example 32.4. Allowing special characters in URIs

```
// Contains '|' symbol
// Normally, this would return false:
$valid = Zend_Uri::check('http://example.com/?q=this|that');

// However, you can allow "unwise" characters
Zend_Uri::setConfig(array('allow_unwise' => true));
// will return 'true'
$valid = Zend_Uri::check('http://example.com/?q=this|that');

// Reset the 'allow_unwise' value to the default FALSE
Zend_Uri::setConfig(array('allow_unwise' => false));
```

Note

`Zend_Uri::setConfig()` sets configuration options globally. It is recommended to reset the 'allow_unwise' option to 'false' like in the example above, unless you are certain you want to always allow unwise characters globally.

Common Instance Methods

Every instance of a `Zend_Uri` subclass (e.g. `Zend_Uri_Http`) has several instance methods that are useful for working with any kind of URI.

Getting the Scheme of the URI

The scheme of the URI is the part of the URI that precedes the colon. For example, the scheme of `http://www.zend.com` is `http`.

Example 32.5. Getting the Scheme from a Zend_Uri_* Object

```
$uri = Zend_Uri::factory('http://www.zend.com');

$scheme = $uri->getScheme();   // "http"
```

The getScheme() instance method returns only the scheme part of the URI object.

Getting the Entire URI

Example 32.6. Getting the Entire URI from a Zend_Uri_* Object

```
$uri = Zend_Uri::factory('http://www.zend.com');

echo $uri->getUri();   // "http://www.zend.com"
```

The getUri() method returns the string representation of the entire URI.

Validating the URI

Zend_Uri::factory() will always validate any URI passed to it and will not instantiate a new Zend_Uri subclass if the given URI is found to be invalid. However, after the Zend_Uri subclass is instantiated for a new URI or a valid existing one, it is possible that the URI can then later become invalid after it is manipulated.

Example 32.7. Validating a Zend_Uri_* Object

```
$uri = Zend_Uri::factory('http://www.zend.com');

$isValid = $uri->valid();   // TRUE
```

The valid() instance method provides a means to check that the URI object is still valid.

Chapter 33. Zend_Validate

Introduction

The Zend_Validate component provides a set of commonly needed validators. It also provides a simple validator chaining mechanism by which multiple validators may be applied to a single datum in a user-defined order.

What is a validator?

A validator examines its input with respect to some requirements and produces a boolean result - whether the input successfully validates against the requirements. If the input does not meet the requirements, a validator may additionally provide information about which requirement(s) the input does not meet.

For example, a web application might require that a username be between six and twelve characters in length and may only contain alphanumeric characters. A validator can be used for ensuring that usernames meet these requirements. If a chosen username does not meet one or both of the requirements, it would be useful to know which of the requirements the username fails to meet.

Basic usage of validators

Having defined validation in this way provides the foundation for Zend_Validate_Interface, which defines two methods, isValid() and getMessages(). The isValid() method performs validation upon the provided value, returning true if and only if the value passes against the validation criteria.

If isValid() returns false, the getMessages() returns an array of messages explaining the reason(s) for validation failure. The array keys are short strings that identify the reasons for validation failure, and the array values are the corresponding human-readable string messages. The keys and values are class-dependent; each validation class defines its own set of validation failure messages and the unique keys that identify them. Each class also has a const definition that matches each identifier for a validation failure cause.

Note

The getMessages() methods return validation failure information only for the most recent isValid() call. Each call to isValid() clears any messages and errors caused by a previous isValid() call, because it's likely that each call to isValid() is made for a different input value.

The following example illustrates validation of an e-mail address:

```
$validator = new Zend_Validate_EmailAddress();

if ($validator->isValid($email)) {
    // email appears to be valid
} else {
    // email is invalid; print the reasons
    foreach ($validator->getMessages() as $messageId => $message) {
        echo "Validation failure '$messageId': $message\n";
    }
}
```

Customizing messages

Validate classes provide a `setMessage()` method with which you can specify the format of a message returned by `getMessages()` in case of validation failure. The first argument of this method is a string containing the error message. You can include tokens in this string which will be substituted with data relevant to the validator. The token `%value%` is supported by all validators; this is substituted with the value you passed to `isValid()`. Other tokens may be supported on a case-by-case basis in each validation class. For example, `%max%` is a token supported by Zend_Validate_LessThan. The `getMessageVariables()` method returns an array of variable tokens supported by the validator.

The second optional argument is a string that identifies the validation failure message template to be set, which is useful when a validation class defines more than one cause for failure. If you omit the second argument, `setMessage()` assumes the message you specify should be used for the first message template declared in the validation class. Many validation classes only have one error message template defined, so there is no need to specify which message template you are changing.

```
$validator = new Zend_Validate_StringLength(8);

$validator->setMessage(
    'The string \'%value%\' is too short; it must be at least %min% ' .
    'characters',
    Zend_Validate_StringLength::TOO_SHORT);

if (!$validator->isValid('word')) {
    $messages = $validator->getMessages();
    echo current($messages);

    // "The string 'word' is too short; it must be at least 8 characters"
}
```

You can set multiple messages using the `setMessages()` method. Its argument is an array containing key/message pairs.

```
$validator = new Zend_Validate_StringLength(8, 12);

$validator->setMessages( array(
    Zend_Validate_StringLength::TOO_SHORT =>
        'The string \'%value%\' is too short',
    Zend_Validate_StringLength::TOO_LONG  =>
        'The string \'%value%\' is too long'
));
```

If your application requires even greater flexibility with which it reports validation failures, you can access properties by the same name as the message tokens supported by a given validation class. The value property is always available in a validator; it is the value you specified as the argument of `isValid()`. Other properties may be supported on a case-by-case basis in each validation class.

```
$validator = new Zend_Validate_StringLength(8, 12);

if (!validator->isValid('word')) {
    echo 'Word failed: '
        . $validator->value
        . '; its length is not between '
        . $validator->min
        . ' and '
        . $validator->max
        . "\n";
}
```

Using the static is() method

If it's inconvenient to load a given validation class and create an instance of the validator, you can use the static method `Zend_Validate::is()` as an alternative invocation style. The first argument of this method is a data input value, that you would pass to the `isValid()` method. The second argument is a string, which corresponds to the basename of the validation class, relative to the `Zend_Validate` namespace. The `is()` method automatically loads the class, creates an instance, and applies the `isValid()` method to the data input.

```
if (Zend_Validate::is($email, 'EmailAddress')) {
    // Yes, email appears to be valid
}
```

You can also pass an array of constructor arguments, if they are needed for the validator.

```
if (Zend_Validate::is($value, 'Between', array(1, 12))) {
    // Yes, $value is between 1 and 12
}
```

The `is()` method returns a boolean value, the same as the `isValid()` method. When using the static `is()` method, validation failure messages are not available.

The static usage can be convenient for invoking a validator ad hoc, but if you have the need to run a validator for multiple inputs, it's more efficient to use the non-static usage, creating an instance of the validator object and calling its `isValid()` method.

Also, the `Zend_Filter_Input` class allows you to instantiate and run multiple filter and validator classes on demand to process sets of input data. See the section called "Zend_Filter_Input".

Translating messages

Validate classes provide a `setTranslator()` method with which you can specify a instance of `Zend_Translate` which will translate the messages in case of a validation failure. The `getTranslator()` method returns the set translator instance.

```
$validator = new Zend_Validate_StringLength(8, 12);
$translate = new Zend_Translate(
    'array',
    array(Zend_Validate_StringLength::TOO_SHORT => 'Translated \'%value%\''),
    'en'
);

$validator->setTranslator($translate);
```

With the static `setDefaultTranslator()` method you can set a instance of `Zend_Translate` which will be used for all validation classes, and can be retrieved with `getDefaultTranslator()`. This prevents you from setting a translator manually for all validator classes, and simplifies your code.

```
$translate = new Zend_Translate(
    'array',
    array(Zend_Validate_StringLength::TOO_SHORT => 'Translated \'%value%\''),
    'en'
);
Zend_Validate::setDefaultTranslator($translate);
```

Note

When you have set an application wide locale within your registry, then this locale will be used as default translator.

Sometimes it is necessary to disable the translator within a validator. To archive this you can use the `setDisableTranslator()` method, which accepts a boolean parameter, and `translatorIsDisabled()` to get the set value.

```
$validator = new Zend_Validate_StringLength(8, 12);
if (!$validator->isTranslatorDisabled()) {
    $validator->setDisableTranslator();
}
```

It is also possible to use a translator instead of setting own messages with `setMessage()`. But doing so, you should keep in mind, that the translator works also on messages you set your own.

Standard Validation Classes

Zend Framework comes with a standard set of validation classes, which are ready for you to use.

Alnum

Returns `true` if and only if `$value` contains only alphabetic and digit characters. This validator includes an option to also consider white space characters as valid.

Note

The alphabetic characters mean characters that makes up words in each language. However, the English alphabet is treated as the alphabetic characters in following languages: Chinese, Japanese, Korean. The language is specified by Zend_Locale.

Alpha

Returns `true` if and only if `$value` contains only alphabetic characters. This validator includes an option to also consider white space characters as valid.

Barcode

This validator is instantiated with a barcode type against which you wish to validate a barcode value. It currently supports "UPC-A" (Universal Product Code) and "EAN-13" (European Article Number) barcode types, and the `isValid()` method returns true if and only if the input successfully validates against the barcode validation algorithm. You should remove all characters other than the digits zero through nine (0-9) from the input value before passing it on to the validator.

Between

Returns `true` if and only if `$value` is between the minimum and maximum boundary values. The comparison is inclusive by default (`$value` may equal a boundary value), though this may be overridden in order to do a strict comparison, where `$value` must be strictly greater than the minimum and strictly less than the maximum.

Ccnum

Returns `true` if and only if `$value` follows the Luhn algorithm (mod-10 checksum) for credit card numbers.

Date

Returns true if $value is a valid date of the format YYYY-MM-DD. If the optional locale option is set then the date will be validated according to the set locale. And if the optional format option is set this format is used for the validation. For details about the optional parameters see Zend_Date::isDate().

Db_RecordExists and Db_NoRecordExists

Zend_Validate_Db_RecordExists and Zend_Validate_Db_NoRecordExists provide a means to test whether a record exists in a given table of a database, with a given value.

Basic usage

An example of basic usage of the validators:

```
//Check that the email address exists in the database
$validator = new Zend_Validate_Db_RecordExists('users', 'emailaddress');
if ($validator->isValid($emailaddress)) {
    // email address appears to be valid
} else {
    // email address is invalid; print the reasons
    foreach ($validator->getMessages() as $message) {
        echo "$message\n";
    }
}
```

The above will test that a given email address is in the database table. If no record is found containing the value of $emailaddress in the specified column, then an error message is displayed.

```
//Check that the username is not present in the database
$validator = new Zend_Validate_Db_NoRecordExists('users', 'username');
if ($validator->isValid($username)) {
    // username appears to be valid
} else {
    // username is invalid; print the reason
    $messages = $validator->getMessages();
    foreach ($messages as $message) {
        echo "$message\n";
    }
}
```

The above will test that a given username is not in the database table. If a record is found containing the value of $username in the specified column, then an error message is displayed.

Excluding records

Zend_Validate_Db_RecordExists and Zend_Validate_Db_NoRecordExists also provide a means to test the database, excluding a part of the table, either by providing a where clause as a string, or an array with the keys "field" and "value".

When providing an array for the exclude clause, the != operator is used, so you can check the rest of a table for a value before altering a record (for example on a user profile form)

```
//Check no other users have the username
$user_id  = $user->getId();
$validator = new Zend_Validate_Db_NoRecordExists(
    'users',
    'username',
```

```
    array(
        'field' => 'id',
        'value' => $user_id
    )
);

if ($validator->isValid($username)) {
    // username appears to be valid
} else {
    // username is invalid; print the reason
    $messages = $validator->getMessages();
    foreach ($messages as $message) {
        echo "$message\n";
    }
}
```

The above example will check the table to ensure no records other than the one where id =
$user_id contains the value $username.

You can also provide a string to the exclude clause so you can use an operator other than ! =. This can
be useful for testing against composite keys.

```
$post_id   = $post->getId();
$clause    = $db->quoteInto('post_id = ?', $category_id);
$validator = new Zend_Validate_Db_RecordExists(
    'posts_categories',
    'post_id',
    $clause
);

if ($validator->isValid($username)) {
    // username appears to be valid
} else {
    // username is invalid; print the reason
    $messages = $validator->getMessages();
    foreach ($messages as $message) {
        echo "$message\n";
    }
}
```

The above example will check the posts_categories table to ensure that a record with the
post_id has a value matching $category_id

Database Adapters

You can also specify an adapter, as the fourth parameter when instantiating your validator, this will
allow you to work with applications using multiple database adapters, or where you have not set a
default adapter. As in the example below:

```
$validator = new Zend_Validate_Db_RecordExists('users', 'id', null,
    $dbAdapter);
```

Digits

Returns true if and only if $value only contains digit characters.

EmailAddress

Zend_Validate_EmailAddress allows you to validate an email address. The validator first splits
the email address on local-part @ hostname and attempts to match these against known specifications
for email addresses and hostnames.

Basic usage

A basic example of usage is below:

```
$validator = new Zend_Validate_EmailAddress();
if ($validator->isValid($email)) {
    // email appears to be valid
} else {
    // email is invalid; print the reasons
    foreach ($validator->getMessages() as $message) {
        echo "$message\n";
    }
}
```

This will match the email address $email and on failure populate $validator->getMessages() with useful error messages.

Complex local parts

Zend_Validate_EmailAddress will match any valid email address according to RFC2822. For example, valid emails include bob@domain.com, bob+jones@domain.us, "bob@jones"@domain.com and "bob jones"@domain.com

Some obsolete email formats will not currently validate (e.g. carriage returns or a "\" character in an email address).

Validating different types of hostnames

The hostname part of an email address is validated against Zend_Validate_Hostname. By default only DNS hostnames of the form domain.com are accepted, though if you wish you can accept IP addresses and Local hostnames too.

To do this you need to instantiate Zend_Validate_EmailAddress passing a parameter to indicate the type of hostnames you want to accept. More details are included in Zend_Validate_Hostname, though an example of how to accept both DNS and Local hostnames appears below:

```
$validator = new Zend_Validate_EmailAddress(
                Zend_Validate_Hostname::ALLOW_DNS |
                Zend_Validate_Hostname::ALLOW_LOCAL);
if ($validator->isValid($email)) {
    // email appears to be valid
} else {
    // email is invalid; print the reasons
    foreach ($validator->getMessages() as $message) {
        echo "$message\n";
    }
}
```

Checking if the hostname actually accepts email

Just because an email address is in the correct format, it doesn't necessarily mean that email address actually exists. To help solve this problem, you can use MX validation to check whether an MX (email) entry exists in the DNS record for the email's hostname. This tells you that the hostname accepts email, but doesn't tell you the exact email address itself is valid.

MX checking is not enabled by default and at this time is only supported by UNIX platforms. To enable MX checking you can pass a second parameter to the Zend_Validate_EmailAddress constructor.

```
$validator = new Zend_Validate_EmailAddress(Zend_Validate_Hostname::ALLOW_DNS,
                                            true);
```

Alternatively you can either pass `true` or `false` to `$validator->setValidateMx()` to enable or disable MX validation.

By enabling this setting network functions will be used to check for the presence of an MX record on the hostname of the email address you wish to validate. Please be aware this will likely slow your script down.

Validating International Domains Names

`Zend_Validate_EmailAddress` will also match international characters that exist in some domains. This is known as International Domain Name (IDN) support. This is enabled by default, though you can disable this by changing the setting via the internal `Zend_Validate_Hostname` object that exists within `Zend_Validate_EmailAddress`.

```
$validator->hostnameValidator->setValidateIdn(false);
```

More information on the usage of `setValidateIdn()` appears in the `Zend_Validate_Hostname` documentation.

Please note IDNs are only validated if you allow DNS hostnames to be validated.

Validating Top Level Domains

By default a hostname will be checked against a list of known TLDs. This is enabled by default, though you can disable this by changing the setting via the internal `Zend_Validate_Hostname` object that exists within `Zend_Validate_EmailAddress`.

```
$validator->hostnameValidator->setValidateTld(false);
```

More information on the usage of `setValidateTld()` appears in the `Zend_Validate_Hostname` documentation.

Please note TLDs are only validated if you allow DNS hostnames to be validated.

Float

Returns `true` if and only if `$value` is a floating-point value. Since Zend Framework 1.8 this validator takes into account the actual locale from browser, environment or application wide set locale. You can of course use the get/setLocale accessors to change the used locale or give it while creating a instance of this validator.

GreaterThan

Returns `true` if and only if `$value` is greater than the minimum boundary.

Hex

Returns `true` if and only if `$value` contains only hexadecimal digit characters.

Hostname

Zend_Validate_Hostname allows you to validate a hostname against a set of known specifications. It is possible to check for three different types of hostnames: a DNS Hostname (i.e. domain.com), IP address (i.e. 1.2.3.4), and Local hostnames (i.e. localhost). By default only DNS hostnames are matched.

Basic usage

A basic example of usage is below:

```
$validator = new Zend_Validate_Hostname();
```

```
if ($validator->isValid($hostname)) {
    // hostname appears to be valid
} else {
    // hostname is invalid; print the reasons
    foreach ($validator->getMessages() as $message) {
        echo "$message\n";
    }
}
```

This will match the hostname $hostname and on failure populate $validator->getMessages() with useful error messages.

Validating different types of hostnames

You may find you also want to match IP addresses, Local hostnames, or a combination of all allowed types. This can be done by passing a parameter to Zend_Validate_Hostname when you instantiate it. The parameter should be an integer which determines what types of hostnames are allowed. You are encouraged to use the Zend_Validate_Hostname constants to do this.

The Zend_Validate_Hostname constants are: ALLOW_DNS to allow only DNS hostnames, ALLOW_IP to allow IP addresses, ALLOW_LOCAL to allow local network names, and ALLOW_ALL to allow all three types. To just check for IP addresses you can use the example below:

```
$validator = new Zend_Validate_Hostname(Zend_Validate_Hostname::ALLOW_IP);
if ($validator->isValid($hostname)) {
    // hostname appears to be valid
} else {
    // hostname is invalid; print the reasons
    foreach ($validator->getMessages() as $message) {
        echo "$message\n";
    }
}
```

As well as using ALLOW_ALL to accept all hostnames types you can combine these types to allow for combinations. For example, to accept DNS and Local hostnames instantiate your Zend_Validate_Hostname object as so:

```
$validator = new Zend_Validate_Hostname(Zend_Validate_Hostname::ALLOW_DNS |
                                        Zend_Validate_Hostname::ALLOW_IP);
```

Validating International Domains Names

Some Country Code Top Level Domains (ccTLDs), such as 'de' (Germany), support international characters in domain names. These are known as International Domain Names (IDN). These domains can be matched by Zend_Validate_Hostname via extended characters that are used in the validation process.

At present the list of supported ccTLDs include:

- at (Austria)

- ch (Switzerland)

- li (Liechtenstein)

- de (Germany)

- fi (Finland)

- hu (Hungary)

- no (Norway)

- se (Sweden)

To match an IDN domain it's as simple as just using the standard Hostname validator since IDN matching is enabled by default. If you wish to disable IDN validation this can be done by by either passing a parameter to the Zend_Validate_Hostname constructor or via the `$validator->setValidateIdn()` method.

You can disable IDN validation by passing a second parameter to the Zend_Validate_Hostname constructor in the following way.

```
$validator =
    new Zend_Validate_Hostname(Zend_Validate_Hostname::ALLOW_DNS, false);
```

Alternatively you can either pass TRUE or FALSE to `$validator->setValidateIdn()` to enable or disable IDN validation. If you are trying to match an IDN hostname which isn't currently supported it is likely it will fail validation if it has any international characters in it. Where a ccTLD file doesn't exist in Zend/Validate/Hostname specifying the additional characters a normal hostname validation is performed.

Please note IDNs are only validated if you allow DNS hostnames to be validated.

Validating Top Level Domains

By default a hostname will be checked against a list of known TLDs. If this functionality is not required it can be disabled in much the same way as disabling IDN support. You can disable TLD validation by passing a third parameter to the Zend_Validate_Hostname constructor. In the example below we are supporting IDN validation via the second parameter.

```
$validator =
    new Zend_Validate_Hostname(Zend_Validate_Hostname::ALLOW_DNS,
                               true,
                               false);
```

Alternatively you can either pass TRUE or FALSE to `$validator->setValidateTld()` to enable or disable TLD validation.

Please note TLDs are only validated if you allow DNS hostnames to be validated.

Iban

Returns `true` if and only if `$value` contains a valid IBAN (International Bank Account Number). IBAN numbers are validated against the country where they are used and by a checksum.

There are two ways to validate IBAN numbers. As first way you can give a locale which represents a country. Any given IBAN number will then be validated against this country.

```
$validator = new Zend_Validate_Iban('de_AT');
$iban = 'AT611904300234573201';
if ($validator->isValid($iban)) {
    // IBAN appears to be valid
} else {
    // IBAN is invalid
    foreach ($validator->getMessages() as $message) {
        echo "$message\n";
    }
}
```

This should be done when you want to validate IBAN numbers for a single countries. The simpler way of validation is not to give a locale like shown in the next example.

```
$validator = new Zend_Validate_Iban();
```

```
$iban = 'AT611904300234573201';
if ($validator->isValid($iban)) {
    // IBAN appears to be valid
} else {
    // IBAN is invalid
}
```

But this shows one big problem: When you have to accept only IBAN numbers from one single country, for example france, then IBAN numbers from other countries would also be valid. Therefor just remember: When you have to validate a IBAN number against a defined country you should give the locale. And when you accept all IBAN numbers regardless of any country omit the locale for simplicity.

InArray

Returns `true` if and only if a "needle" `$value` is contained in a "haystack" array. If the strict option is `true`, then the type of `$value` is also checked.

Int

Returns `true` if and only if `$value` is a valid integer. Since Zend Framework 1.8 this validator takes into account the actual locale from browser, environment or application wide set locale. You can of course use the get/setLocale accessors to change the used locale or give it while creating a instance of this validator.

Ip

Returns `true` if and only if `$value` is a valid IP address.

LessThan

Returns `true` if and only if `$value` is less than the maximum boundary.

NotEmpty

Returns `true` if and only if `$value` is not an empty value.

Regex

Returns `true` if and only if `$value` matches against a regular expression pattern.

Sitemap Validators

The following validators conform to the Sitemap XML protocol [http://www.sitemaps.org/protocol.php].

Sitemap_Changefreq

Validates whether a string is valid for using as a 'changefreq' element in a Sitemap XML document. Valid values are: 'always', 'hourly', 'daily', 'weekly', 'monthly', 'yearly', or 'never'.

Returns `true` if and only if the value is a string and is equal to one of the frequencies specified above.

Sitemap_Lastmod

Validates whether a string is valid for using as a 'lastmod' element in a Sitemap XML document. The lastmod element should contain a W3C date string, optionally discarding information about time.

Returns `true` if and only if the given value is a string and is valid according to the protocol.

Example 33.1. Sitemap Lastmod Validator

```
$validator = new Zend_Validate_Sitemap_Lastmod();

$validator->isValid('1999-11-11T22:23:52-02:00'); // true
$validator->isValid('2008-05-12T00:42:52+02:00'); // true
$validator->isValid('1999-11-11'); // true
$validator->isValid('2008-05-12'); // true

$validator->isValid('1999-11-11t22:23:52-02:00'); // false
$validator->isValid('2008-05-12T00:42:60+02:00'); // false
$validator->isValid('1999-13-11'); // false
$validator->isValid('2008-05-32'); // false
$validator->isValid('yesterday'); // false
```

Sitemap_Loc

Validates whether a string is valid for using as a 'loc' element in a Sitemap XML document. This uses Zend_Form::check() internally. Read more at URI Validation.

Sitemap_Priority

Validates whether a value is valid for using as a 'priority' element in a Sitemap XML document. The value should be be a decimal between 0.0 and 1.0. This validator accepts both numeric values and string values.

Example 33.2. Sitemap Priority Validator

```
$validator = new Zend_Validate_Sitemap_Priority();

$validator->isValid('0.1'); // true
$validator->isValid('0.789'); // true
$validator->isValid(0.8); // true
$validator->isValid(1.0); // true

$validator->isValid('1.1'); // false
$validator->isValid('-0.4'); // false
$validator->isValid(1.00001); // false
$validator->isValid(0xFF); // false
$validator->isValid('foo'); // false
```

StringLength

Returns true if and only if the string length of $value is at least a minimum and no greater than a maximum (when the max option is not null). The setMin() method throws an exception if the minimum length is set to a value greater than the set maximum length, and the setMax() method throws an exception if the maximum length is set to a value less than than the set minimum length. This class supports UTF-8 and other character encodings, based on the current value of iconv.internal_encoding [http://www.php.net/manual/en/ref.iconv.php#iconv.configuration]. If you need a different encoding you can set it with the accessor methods getEncoding and setEncoding.

Validator Chains

Often multiple validations should be applied to some value in a particular order. The following code demonstrates a way to solve the example from the introduction, where a username must be between 6 and 12 alphanumeric characters:

```
// Create a validator chain and add validators to it
$validatorChain = new Zend_Validate();
$validatorChain->addValidator(new Zend_Validate_StringLength(6, 12))
               ->addValidator(new Zend_Validate_Alnum());

// Validate the username
if ($validatorChain->isValid($username)) {
    // username passed validation
} else {
    // username failed validation; print reasons
    foreach ($validatorChain->getMessages() as $message) {
        echo "$message\n";
    }
}
```

Validators are run in the order they were added to Zend_Validate. In the above example, the username is first checked to ensure that its length is between 6 and 12 characters, and then it is checked to ensure that it contains only alphanumeric characters. The second validation, for alphanumeric characters, is performed regardless of whether the first validation, for length between 6 and 12 characters, succeeds. This means that if both validations fail, getMessages() will return failure messages from both validators.

In some cases it makes sense to have a validator break the chain if its validation process fails. Zend_Validate supports such use cases with the second parameter to the addValidator() method. By setting $breakChainOnFailure to true, the added validator will break the chain execution upon failure, which avoids running any other validations that are determined to be unnecessary or inappropriate for the situation. If the above example were written as follows, then the alphanumeric validation would not occur if the string length validation fails:

```
$validatorChain->addValidator(new Zend_Validate_StringLength(6, 12), true)
               ->addValidator(new Zend_Validate_Alnum());
```

Any object that implements Zend_Validate_Interface may be used in a validator chain.

Writing Validators

Zend_Validate supplies a set of commonly needed validators, but inevitably, developers will wish to write custom validators for their particular needs. The task of writing a custom validator is described in this section.

Zend_Validate_Interface defines three methods, isValid(), getMessages(), and getErrors(), that may be implemented by user classes in order to create custom validation objects. An object that implements Zend_Validate_Interface interface may be added to a validator chain with Zend_Validate::addValidator(). Such objects may also be used with Zend_Filter_Input.

As you may already have inferred from the above description of Zend_Validate_Interface, validation classes provided with Zend Framework return a boolean value for whether or not a value validates successfully. They also provide information about **why** a value failed validation. The availability of the reasons for validation failures may be valuable to an application for various purposes, such as providing statistics for usability analysis.

Basic validation failure message functionality is implemented in `Zend_Validate_Abstract`. To include this functionality when creating a validation class, simply extend `Zend_Validate_Abstract`. In the extending class you would implement the `isValid()` method logic and define the message variables and message templates that correspond to the types of validation failures that can occur. If a value fails your validation tests, then `isValid()` should return `false`. If the value passes your validation tests, then `isValid()` should return `true`.

In general, the `isValid()` method should not throw any exceptions, except where it is impossible to determine whether or not the input value is valid. A few examples of reasonable cases for throwing an exception might be if a file cannot be opened, an LDAP server could not be contacted, or a database connection is unavailable, where such a thing may be required for validation success or failure to be determined.

Example 33.3. Creating a Simple Validation Class

The following example demonstrates how a very simple custom validator might be written. In this case the validation rules are simply that the input value must be a floating point value.

```
class MyValid_Float extends Zend_Validate_Abstract
{
    const FLOAT = 'float';

    protected $_messageTemplates = array(
        self::FLOAT => "'%value%' is not a floating point value"
    );

    public function isValid($value)
    {
        $this->_setValue($value);

        if (!is_float($value)) {
            $this->_error();
            return false;
        }

        return true;
    }
}
```

The class defines a template for its single validation failure message, which includes the built-in magic parameter, `%value%`. The call to `_setValue()` prepares the object to insert the tested value into the failure message automatically, should the value fail validation. The call to `_error()` tracks a reason for validation failure. Since this class only defines one failure message, it is not necessary to provide `_error()` with the name of the failure message template.

Example 33.4. Writing a Validation Class having Dependent Conditions

The following example demonstrates a more complex set of validation rules, where it is required that the input value be numeric and within the range of minimum and maximum boundary values. An input value would fail validation for exactly one of the following reasons:

• The input value is not numeric.

• The input value is less than the minimum allowed value.

• The input value is more than the maximum allowed value.

These validation failure reasons are then translated to definitions in the class:

```
class MyValid_NumericBetween extends Zend_Validate_Abstract
{
    const MSG_NUMERIC = 'msgNumeric';
    const MSG_MINIMUM = 'msgMinimum';
    const MSG_MAXIMUM = 'msgMaximum';

    public $minimum = 0;
    public $maximum = 100;

    protected $_messageVariables = array(
        'min' => 'minimum',
        'max' => 'maximum'
    );

    protected $_messageTemplates = array(
        self::MSG_NUMERIC => "'%value%' is not numeric",
        self::MSG_MINIMUM => "'%value%' must be at least '%min%'",
        self::MSG_MAXIMUM => "'%value%' must be no more than '%max%'"
    );

    public function isValid($value)
    {
        $this->_setValue($value);

        if (!is_numeric($value)) {
            $this->_error(self::MSG_NUMERIC);
            return false;
        }

        if ($value < $this->minimum) {
            $this->_error(self::MSG_MINIMUM);
            return false;
        }

        if ($value > $this->maximum) {
            $this->_error(self::MSG_MAXIMUM);
            return false;
        }

        return true;
    }
}
```

The public properties $minimum and $maximum have been established to provide the minimum and maximum boundaries, respectively, for a value to successfully validate. The class also defines two message variables that correspond to the public properties and allow min and max to be used in message templates as magic parameters, just as with value.

Note that if any one of the validation checks in isValid() fails, an appropriate failure message is prepared, and the method immediately returns false. These validation rules are therefore sequentially dependent. That is, if one test should fail, there is no need to test any subsequent validation rules. This need not be the case, however. The following example illustrates how to write a class having independent validation rules, where the validation object may return multiple reasons why a particular validation attempt failed.

Example 33.5. Validation with Independent Conditions, Multiple Reasons for Failure

Consider writing a validation class for password strength enforcement - when a user is required to choose a password that meets certain criteria for helping secure user accounts. Let us assume that the password security criteria enforce that the password:

- is at least 8 characters in length,

- contains at least one uppercase letter,

- contains at least one lowercase letter,

- and contains at least one digit character.

The following class implements these validation criteria:

```php
class MyValid_PasswordStrength extends Zend_Validate_Abstract
{
    const LENGTH = 'length';
    const UPPER  = 'upper';
    const LOWER  = 'lower';
    const DIGIT  = 'digit';

    protected $_messageTemplates = array(
        self::LENGTH => "'%value%' must be at least 8 characters in length",
        self::UPPER  => "'%value%' must contain at least one uppercase letter",
        self::LOWER  => "'%value%' must contain at least one lowercase letter",
        self::DIGIT  => "'%value%' must contain at least one digit character"
    );

    public function isValid($value)
    {
        $this->_setValue($value);

        $isValid = true;

        if (strlen($value) < 8) {
            $this->_error(self::LENGTH);
            $isValid = false;
        }

        if (!preg_match('/[A-Z]/', $value)) {
            $this->_error(self::UPPER);
            $isValid = false;
        }

        if (!preg_match('/[a-z]/', $value)) {
            $this->_error(self::LOWER);
            $isValid = false;
        }

        if (!preg_match('/\d/', $value)) {
            $this->_error(self::DIGIT);
            $isValid = false;
        }

        return $isValid;
    }
}
```

Note that the four criteria tests in `isValid()` do not immediately return `false`. This allows the validation class to provide **all** of the reasons that the input password failed to meet the validation requirements. If, for example, a user were to input the string "#$%" as a password, `isValid()` would cause all four validation failure messages to be returned by a subsequent call to `getMessages()`.

Validation Messages

Each validator which is based on `Zend_Validate` provides one or multiple messages in the case of a failed validation. You can use this information for setting own messages or when you have to translate the messages a validator can return. The following table lists all available messages which are returned by each validator.

Table 33.1. Available Validation Messages

Validator	Constant	Message	
Alnum	NOT_ALNUM	'%value%' has not only alphabetic and digit characters	
	STRING_EMPTY	'%value%' is an empty string	
Alpha	NOT_ALPHA	'%value%' has not only alphabetic characters	
	STRING_EMPTY	'%value%' is an empty string	
Barcode	---	messages are thrown by a subclass	
Barcode_Ean13	INVALID	'%value%' is an invalid EAN-13 barcode	
	INVALID_LENGTH	'%value%' should be 13 characters	
	NOT_NUMERIC	'%value%' should contain only numeric characters	
Barcode_UpcA	INVALID	'%value%' is an invalid UPC-A barcode	
	INVALID_LENGTH	'%value%' should be 12 characters	
Between	NOT_BETWEEN	'%value%' is not between '%min%' and '%max%', inclusively	
	NOT_BETWEEN_STRICT	'%value%' is not strictly between '%min%' and '%max%'	
Ccnum	LENGTH	'%value%' must contain between 13 and 19 digits	
	CHECKSUM	Luhn algorithm (mod-10 checksum) failed on '%value%'	

Validator	Constant	Message	
Date	FALSEFORMAT	'%value%' does not fit given date format	
	INVALID	'%value%' does not appear to be a valid date	
	NOT_YYYY_MM_DD	'%value%' is not of the format YYYY-MM-DD	
Digits	NOT_DIGITS	'%value%' contains not only digit characters	
	STRING_EMPTY	'%value%' is an empty string	
EmailAddress	INVALID	'%value%' is not a valid email address in the basic format local-part@hostname	
	INVALID_HOSTNAME	'%hostname%' is not a valid hostname for email address '%value%'	
	INVALID_MX _RECORD	'%hostname%' does not appear to have a valid MX record for the email address '%value%'	
	DOT_ATOM	'%localPart%' not matched against dot-atom format	
	QUOTED_STRING	'%localPart%' not matched against quoted-string format	
	INVALID_LOCAL _PART	'%localPart%' is not a valid local part for email address '%value%'	
	LENGTH_EXCEEDED	'%value%' exceeds the allowed length	
File_Count	TOO_MUCH	Too much files, maximum '%max%' are allowed but '%count%' are given	
	TOO_LESS	Too less files, minimum '%min%' are expected but '%count%' are given	
File_Crc32	DOES_NOT_MATCH	The file '%value%' does not match the given crc32 hashes	
	NOT_DETECTED	There was no crc32 hash detected for the given file	
	NOT_FOUND	The file '%value%' could not be found	

Validator	Constant	Message	
File_ExcludeExtension	FALSE_EXTENSION	The file '%value%' has a false extension	
	NOT_FOUND	The file '%value%' was not found	
File_ExcludeMimeType	FALSE_TYPE	The file '%value%' has a false mimetype of '%type%'	
	NOT_DETECTED	The mimetype of file '%value%' could not been detected	
	NOT_READABLE	The file '%value%' can not be read	
File_Exists	DOES_NOT_EXIST	The file '%value%' does not exist	
	File_Extension	FALSE_EXTENSION	The file '%value%' has a false extension
		NOT_FOUND	The file '%value%' was not found
File_FilesSize	TOO_BIG	All files in sum should have a maximum size of '%max%' but '%size%' were detected	
	TOO_SMALL	All files in sum should have a minimum size of '%min%' but '%size%' were detected	
	NOT_READABLE	One or more files can not be read	
File_Hash	DOES_NOT_MATCH	The file '%value%' does not match the given hashes	
	NOT_DETECTED	There was no hash detected for the given file	
	NOT_FOUND	The file '%value%' could not be found	

Validator	Constant	Message	
File_ImageSize	WIDTH_TOO_BIG	Maximum allowed width for image '%value%' should be '%maxwidth%' but '%width%' detected	
	WIDTH_TOO_SMALL	Minimum expected width for image '%value%' should be '%minwidth%' but '%width%' detected	
	HEIGHT_TOO_BIG	Maximum allowed height for image '%value%' should be '%maxheight%' but '%height%' detected	
	HEIGHT_TOO_SMALL	Minimum expected height for image '%value%' should be '%minheight%' but '%height%' detected	
	NOT_DETECTED	The size of image '%value%' could not be detected	
	NOT_READABLE	The image '%value%' can not be read	
File_IsCompressed	FALSE_TYPE	The file '%value%' is not compressed, '%type%' detected	
	NOT_DETECTED	The mimetype of file '%value%' could not been detected	
	NOT_READABLE	The file '%value%' can not be read	
File_IsImage	FALSE_TYPE	The file '%value%' is no image, '%type%' detected	
	NOT_DETECTED	The mimetype of file '%value%' could not been detected	
	NOT_READABLE	The file '%value%' can not be read	
File_Md5	DOES_NOT_MATCH	The file '%value%' does not match the given md5 hashes	
	NOT_DETECTED	There was no md5 hash detected for the given file	
	NOT_FOUND	The file '%value%' could not be found	
File_MimeType	FALSE_TYPE	The file '%value%' has a false mimetype of	

Validator	Constant	Message	
		'%type%'	
	NOT_DETECTED	The mimetype of file '%value%' could not been detected	
	NOT_READABLE	The file '%value%' can not be read	
File_NotExists	DOES_EXIST	The file '%value%' does exist	
File_Sha1	DOES_NOT_MATCH	The file '%value%' does not match the given sha1 hashes	
	NOT_DETECTED	There was no sha1 hash detected for the given file	
	NOT_FOUND	The file '%value%' could not be found	
File_Size	TOO_BIG	Maximum allowed size for file '%value%' is '%max%' but '%size%' detected	
	TOO_SMALL	Minimum expected size for file '%value%' is '%min%' but '%size%' detected	
	NOT_FOUND	The file '%value%' could not be found	

Validator	Constant	Message	
File_Upload	INI_SIZE	The file '%value%' exceeds the defined ini size	
	FORM_SIZE	The file '%value%' exceeds the defined form size	
	PARTIAL	The file '%value%' was only partially uploaded	
	NO_FILE	The file '%value%' was not uploaded	
	NO_TMP_DIR	No temporary directory was found for the file '%value%'	
	CANT_WRITE	The file '%value%' can't be written	
	EXTENSION	The extension returned an error while uploading the file '%value%'	
	ATTACK	The file '%value%' was illegal uploaded, possible attack	
	FILE_NOT_FOUND	The file '%value%' was not found	
	UNKNOWN	Unknown error while uploading the file '%value%'	
File_WordCount	TOO_MUCH	Too much words, maximum '%max%' are allowed but '%count%' were counted	
	TOO_LESS	Too less words, minimum '%min%' are expected but '%count%' were counted	
	NOT_FOUND	The file '%value%' could not be found	
Float	NOT_FLOAT	'%value%' does not appear to be a float	
GreaterThan	NOT_GREATER	'%value%' is not greater than '%min%'	
Hex	NOT_HEX	'%value%' has not only hexadecimal digit characters	

Validator	Constant	Message	
Hostname	IP_ADDRESS_NOT _ALLOWED	'%value%' appears to be an IP address, but IP addresses are not allowed	
	UNKNOWN_TLD	'%value%' appears to be a DNS hostname but cannot match TLD against known list	
	INVALID_DASH	'%value%' appears to be a DNS hostname but contains a dash (-) in an invalid position	
	INVALID_HOSTNAME _SCHEMA	'%value%' appears to be a DNS hostname but cannot match against hostname schema for TLD '%tld%'	
	UNDECIPHERABLE _TLD	'%value%' appears to be a DNS hostname but cannot extract TLD part	
	INVALID_HOSTNAME	'%value%' does not match the expected structure for a DNS hostname	
	INVALID_LOCAL _NAME	'%value%' does not appear to be a valid local network name	
	LOCAL_NAME_NOT _ALLOWED	'%value%' appears to be a local network name but local network names are not allowed	
Iban	NOTSUPPORTED	'%value%' does not have IBAN	
	FALSEFORMAT	'%value%' has a false format	
	CHECKFAILED	'%value%' has failed the IBAN check	
Identical	NOT_SAME	Tokens do not match	
	MISSING_TOKEN	No token was provided to match against	
InArray	NOT_IN_ARRAY	'%value%' was not found in the haystack	
Int	NOT_INT	'%value%' does not appear to be an integer	
Ip	NOT_IP_ADDRESS	'%value%' does not appear to be a valid IP address	
LessThan	NOT_LESS	'%value%' is not less than '%max%'	
NotEmpty	IS_EMPTY	Value is required and	

Validator	Constant	Message	
		can't be empty	
Regex	NOT_MATCH	'%value%' does not match against pattern '%pattern%'	
StringLength	TOO_SHORT	'%value%' is less than %min% characters long	
	TOO_LONG	'%value%' is greater than %max% characters long	

Additionally you can retrieve all message templates of a validator with the method getMessageTemplates(). It returns you an array with the messages a validator could return in the case of a failed validation.

```
$validator = new Zend_Validate_Alnum();
$messages  = $validator->getMessageTemplates();
```

Chapter 34. Zend_Version

Getting the Zend Framework Version

Zend_Version provides a class constant Zend_Version::VERSION that contains a string identifying the version number of your Zend Framework installation. Zend_Version::VERSION might contain "1.7.4", for example.

The static method Zend_Version::compareVersion($version) is based on the PHP function version_compare() [http://php.net/version_compare]. This method returns -1 if the specified version is older than the installed Zend Framework version, 0 if they are the same and +1 if the specified version is newer than the version of the Zend Framework installation.

Example 34.1. Example of the compareVersion() Method

```
// returns -1, 0 or 1
$cmp = Zend_Version::compareVersion('2.0.0');
```

Chapter 35. Zend_View

Introduction

Zend_View is a class for working with the "view" portion of the model-view-controller pattern. That is, it exists to help keep the view script separate from the model and controller scripts. It provides a system of helpers, output filters, and variable escaping.

Zend_View is template system agnostic; you may use PHP as your template language, or create instances of other template systems and manipulate them within your view script.

Essentially, using Zend_View happens in two major steps: 1. Your controller script creates an instance of Zend_View and assigns variables to that instance. 2. The controller tells the Zend_View to render a particular view, thereby handing control over to the view script, which generates the view output.

Controller Script

As a simple example, let us say your controller has a list of book data that it wants to have rendered by a view. The controller script might look something like this:

```
// use a model to get the data for book authors and titles.
$data = array(
    array(
        'author' => 'Hernando de Soto',
        'title' => 'The Mystery of Capitalism'
    ),
    array(
        'author' => 'Henry Hazlitt',
        'title' => 'Economics in One Lesson'
    ),
    array(
        'author' => 'Milton Friedman',
        'title' => 'Free to Choose'
    )
);

// now assign the book data to a Zend_View instance
Zend_Loader::loadClass('Zend_View');
$view = new Zend_View();
$view->books = $data;

// and render a view script called "booklist.php"
echo $view->render('booklist.php');
```

View Script

Now we need the associated view script, "booklist.php". This is a PHP script like any other, with one exception: it executes inside the scope of the Zend_View instance, which means that references to $this point to the Zend_View instance properties and methods. (Variables assigned to the instance by the controller are public properties of the Zend_View instance.) Thus, a very basic view script could look like this:

```
if ($this->books): ?>

    <!-- A table of some books. -->
    <table>
```

```
        <tr>
            <th>Author</th>
            <th>Title</th>
        </tr>

        <?php foreach ($this->books as $key => $val): ?>
        <tr>
            <td><?php echo $this->escape($val['author']) ?></td>
            <td><?php echo $this->escape($val['title']) ?></td>
        </tr>
        <?php endforeach; ?>

    </table>

<?php else: ?>

    <p>There are no books to display.</p>

<?php endif;?>
```

Note how we use the "escape()" method to apply output escaping to variables.

Options

Zend_View has several options that may be set to configure the behaviour of your view scripts.

- basePath: indicate a base path from which to set the script, helper, and filter path. It assumes a directory structure of:

```
base/path/
    helpers/
    filters/
    scripts/
```

  This may be set via setBasePath(), addBasePath(), or the basePath option to the constructor.

- encoding: indicate the character encoding to use with htmlentities(), htmlspecialchars(), and other operations. Defaults to ISO-8859-1 (latin1). May be set via setEncoding() or the encoding option to the constructor.

- escape: indicate a callback to be used by escape(). May be set via setEscape() or the escape option to the constructor.

- filter: indicate a filter to use after rendering a view script. May be set via setFilter(), addFilter(), or the filter option to the constructor.

- strictVars: force Zend_View to emit notices and warnings when uninitialized view variables are accessed. This may be set by calling strictVars(true) or passing the strictVars option to the constructor.

Short Tags with View Scripts

In our examples and documentation, we make use of PHP short tags: <? and <?=. In addition, we typically use the alternate syntax for control structures [http://us.php.net/manual/en/control-structures.alternative-syntax.php]. These are convenient shorthands to use when writing view scripts, as they make the constructs more terse, and keep statements on single lines.

That said, many developers prefer to use full tags for purposes of validation or portability. For instance, short_open_tag is disabled in the php.ini.recommended file, and if you template XML in view scripts, short open tags will cause the templates to fail validation.

Additionally, if you use short tags when the setting is off, then the view scripts will either cause errors or simply echo code to the user.

For this latter case, where you wish to use short tags but they are disabled, you have two options:

- Turn on short tags in your .htaccess file:

```
php_value "short_open_tag" "on"
```

This will only be possible if you are allowed to create and utilize .htaccess files. This directive can also be added to your httpd.conf file.

- Enable an optional stream wrapper to convert short tags to long tags on the fly:

```
$view->setUseStreamWrapper(true);
```

This registers Zend_View_Stream as a stream wrapper for view scripts, and will ensure that your code continues to work as if short tags were enabled.

View Stream Wrapper Degrades Performance

Usage of the stream wrapper *will* degrade performance of your application, though actual benchmarks are unavailable to quantify the amount of degradation. We recommend that you either enable short tags, convert your scripts to use full tags, or have a good partial and/or full page content caching strategy in place.

Utility Accessors

Typically, you'll only ever need to call on assign(), render(), or one of the methods for setting/adding filter, helper, and script paths. However, if you wish to extend Zend_View yourself, or need access to some of its internals, a number of accessors exist:

- getVars() will return all assigned variables.

- clearVars() will clear all assigned variables; useful when you wish to re-use a view object, but want to control what variables are available.

- getScriptPath($script) will retrieve the resolved path to a given view script.

- getScriptPaths() will retrieve all registered script paths.

- getHelperPath($helper) will retrieve the resolved path to the named helper class.

- getHelperPaths() will retrieve all registered helper paths.

- getFilterPath($filter) will retrieve the resolved path to the named filter class.

- getFilterPaths() will retrieve all registered filter paths.

Controller Scripts

The controller is where you instantiate and configure Zend_View. You then assign variables to the view, and tell the view to render output using a particular script.

Assigning Variables

Your controller script should assign necessary variables to the view before it hands over control to the view script. Normally, you can do assignments one at a time by assigning to property names of the view instance:

```
$view = new Zend_View();
$view->a = "Hay";
$view->b = "Bee";
$view->c = "Sea";
```

However, this can be tedious when you have already collected the values to be assigned into an array or object.

The assign() method lets you assign from an array or object "in bulk." The following examples have the same effect as the above one-by-one property assignments.

```
$view = new Zend_View();

// assign an array of key-value pairs, where the
// key is the variable name, and the value is
// the assigned value.
$array = array(
    'a' => "Hay",
    'b' => "Bee",
    'c' => "Sea",
);
$view->assign($array);

// do the same with an object's public properties;
// note how we cast it to an array when assigning.
$obj = new StdClass;
$obj->a = "Hay";
$obj->b = "Bee";
$obj->c = "Sea";
$view->assign((array) $obj);
```

Alternatively, you can use the assign method to assign one-by-one by passing a string variable name, and then the variable value.

```
$view = new Zend_View();
$view->assign('a', "Hay");
$view->assign('b', "Bee");
$view->assign('c', "Sea");
```

Rendering a View Script

Once you have assigned all needed variables, the controller should tell Zend_View to render a particular view script. Do so by calling the render() method. Note that the method will return the rendered view, not print it, so you need to print or echo it yourself at the appropriate time.

```
$view = new Zend_View();
$view->a = "Hay";
$view->b = "Bee";
$view->c = "Sea";
echo $view->render('someView.php');
```

View Script Paths

By default, `Zend_View` expects your view scripts to be relative to your calling script. For example, if your controller script is at "/path/to/app/controllers" and it calls $view->render('someView.php'), `Zend_View` will look for "/path/to/app/controllers/someView.php".

Obviously, your view scripts are probably located elsewhere. To tell `Zend_View` where it should look for view scripts, use the setScriptPath() method.

```
$view = new Zend_View();
$view->setScriptPath('/path/to/app/views');
```

Now when you call $view->render('someView.php'), it will look for "/path/to/app/views/someView.php".

In fact, you can "stack" paths using the addScriptPath() method. As you add paths to the stack, `Zend_View` will look at the most-recently-added path for the requested view script. This allows you override default views with custom views so that you may create custom "themes" or "skins" for some views, while leaving others alone.

```
$view = new Zend_View();
$view->addScriptPath('/path/to/app/views');
$view->addScriptPath('/path/to/custom/');

// now when you call $view->render('booklist.php'), Zend_View will
// look first for "/path/to/custom/booklist.php", then for
// "/path/to/app/views/booklist.php", and finally in the current
// directory for "booklist.php".
```

Never use user input to set script paths

`Zend_View` uses script paths to lookup and render view scripts. As such, these directories should be known before-hand, and under your control. *Never* set view script paths based on user input, as you can potentially open yourself up to Local File Inclusion vulnerability if the specified path includes parent directory traversals. For example, the following input could trigger the issue:

```
// $_GET['foo'] == '../../../etc'
$view->addScriptPath($_GET['foo']);
$view->render('passwd');
```

While this example is contrived, it does clearly show the potential issue. If you *must* rely on user input to set your script path, properly filter the input and check to ensure it exists under paths controlled by your application.

View Scripts

Once your controller has assigned variables and called `render()`, `Zend_View` then includes the requested view script and executes it "inside" the scope of the `Zend_View` instance. Therefore, in your view scripts, references to $this actually point to the `Zend_View` instance itself.

Variables assigned to the view from the controller are referred to as instance properties. For example, if the controller were to assign a variable 'something', you would refer to it as $this->something in the view script. (This allows you to keep track of which values were assigned to the script, and which are internal to the script itself.)

By way of reminder, here is the example view script from the `Zend_View` introduction.

```php
<?php if ($this->books): ?>

    <!-- A table of some books. -->
    <table>
        <tr>
            <th>Author</th>
            <th>Title</th>
        </tr>

        <?php foreach ($this->books as $key => $val): ?>
        <tr>
            <td><?php echo $this->escape($val['author']) ?></td>
            <td><?php echo $this->escape($val['title']) ?></td>
        </tr>
        <?php endforeach; ?>

    </table>

<?php else: ?>

    <p>There are no books to display.</p>

<?php endif;?>
```

Escaping Output

One of the most important tasks to perform in a view script is to make sure that output is escaped properly; among other things, this helps to avoid cross-site scripting attacks. Unless you are using a function, method, or helper that does escaping on its own, you should always escape variables when you output them.

Zend_View comes with a method called escape() that does such escaping for you.

```php
// bad view-script practice:
echo $this->variable;

// good view-script practice:
echo $this->escape($this->variable);
```

By default, the escape() method uses the PHP htmlspecialchars() function for escaping. However, depending on your environment, you may wish for escaping to occur in a different way. Use the setEscape() method at the controller level to tell Zend_View what escaping callback to use.

```php
// create a Zend_View instance
$view = new Zend_View();

// tell it to use htmlentities as the escaping callback
$view->setEscape('htmlentities');

// or tell it to use a static class method as the callback
$view->setEscape(array('SomeClass', 'methodName'));

// or even an instance method
$obj = new SomeClass();
$view->setEscape(array($obj, 'methodName'));

// and then render your view
echo $view->render(...);
```

The callback function or method should take the value to be escaped as its first parameter, and all other parameters should be optional.

Using Alternate Template Systems

Although PHP is itself a powerful template system, many developers feel it is too powerful or complex for their template designers and will want to use an alternate template engine. Zend_View provides two mechanisms for doing so, the first through view scripts, the second by implementing Zend_View_Interface.

Template Systems Using View Scripts

A view script may be used to instantiate and manipulate a separate template object, such as a PHPLIB-style template. The view script for that kind of activity might look something like this:

```
include_once 'template.inc';
$tpl = new Template();

if ($this->books) {
    $tpl->setFile(array(
        "booklist" => "booklist.tpl",
        "eachbook" => "eachbook.tpl",
    ));

    foreach ($this->books as $key => $val) {
        $tpl->set_var('author', $this->escape($val['author']));
        $tpl->set_var('title', $this->escape($val['title']));
        $tpl->parse("books", "eachbook", true);
    }

    $tpl->pparse("output", "booklist");
} else {
    $tpl->setFile("nobooks", "nobooks.tpl")
    $tpl->pparse("output", "nobooks");
}
```

These would be the related template files:

```
<!-- booklist.tpl -->
<table>
    <tr>
        <th>Author</th>
        <th>Title</th>
    </tr>
    {books}
</table>

<!-- eachbook.tpl -->
    <tr>
        <td>{author}</td>
        <td>{title}</td>
    </tr>

<!-- nobooks.tpl -->
<p>There are no books to display.</p>
```

Template Systems Using Zend_View_Interface

Some may find it easier to simply provide a Zend_View-compatible template engine. Zend_View_Interface defines the minimum interface needed for compatability:

```
/**
 * Return the actual template engine object
 */
public function getEngine();

/**
 * Set the path to view scripts/templates
 */
public function setScriptPath($path);

/**
 * Set a base path to all view resources
 */
public function setBasePath($path, $prefix = 'Zend_View');

/**
 * Add an additional base path to view resources
 */
public function addBasePath($path, $prefix = 'Zend_View');

/**
 * Retrieve the current script paths
 */
public function getScriptPaths();

/**
 * Overloading methods for assigning template variables as object
 * properties
 */
public function __set($key, $value);
public function __isset($key);
public function __unset($key);

/**
 * Manual assignment of template variables, or ability to assign
 * multiple variables en masse.
 */
public function assign($spec, $value = null);

/**
 * Unset all assigned template variables
 */
public function clearVars();

/**
 * Render the template named $name
 */
public function render($name);
```

Using this interface, it becomes relatively easy to wrap a third-party template engine as a Zend_View-compatible class. As an example, the following is one potential wrapper for Smarty:

```
class Zend_View_Smarty implements Zend_View_Interface
{
    /**
     * Smarty object
```

```
 * @var Smarty
 */
protected $_smarty;

/**
 * Constructor
 *
 * @param string $tmplPath
 * @param array $extraParams
 * @return void
 */
public function __construct($tmplPath = null, $extraParams = array())
{
    $this->_smarty = new Smarty;

    if (null !== $tmplPath) {
        $this->setScriptPath($tmplPath);
    }

    foreach ($extraParams as $key => $value) {
        $this->_smarty->$key = $value;
    }
}

/**
 * Return the template engine object
 *
 * @return Smarty
 */
public function getEngine()
{
    return $this->_smarty;
}

/**
 * Set the path to the templates
 *
 * @param string $path The directory to set as the path.
 * @return void
 */
public function setScriptPath($path)
{
    if (is_readable($path)) {
        $this->_smarty->template_dir = $path;
        return;
    }

    throw new Exception('Invalid path provided');
}

/**
 * Retrieve the current template directory
 *
 * @return string
 */
public function getScriptPaths()
{
    return array($this->_smarty->template_dir);
}

/**
 * Alias for setScriptPath
 *
 * @param string $path
```

```
 * @param string $prefix Unused
 * @return void
 */
public function setBasePath($path, $prefix = 'Zend_View')
{
    return $this->setScriptPath($path);
}

/**
 * Alias for setScriptPath
 *
 * @param string $path
 * @param string $prefix Unused
 * @return void
 */
public function addBasePath($path, $prefix = 'Zend_View')
{
    return $this->setScriptPath($path);
}

/**
 * Assign a variable to the template
 *
 * @param string $key The variable name.
 * @param mixed $val The variable value.
 * @return void
 */
public function __set($key, $val)
{
    $this->_smarty->assign($key, $val);
}

/**
 * Allows testing with empty() and isset() to work
 *
 * @param string $key
 * @return boolean
 */
public function __isset($key)
{
    return (null !== $this->_smarty->get_template_vars($key));
}

/**
 * Allows unset() on object properties to work
 *
 * @param string $key
 * @return void
 */
public function __unset($key)
{
    $this->_smarty->clear_assign($key);
}

/**
 * Assign variables to the template
 *
 * Allows setting a specific key to the specified value, OR passing
 * an array of key => value pairs to set en masse.
 *
 * @see __set()
 * @param string|array $spec The assignment strategy to use (key or
 * array of key => value pairs)
 * @param mixed $value (Optional) If assigning a named variable,
```

```
 *     use this as the value.
 * @return void
 */
public function assign($spec, $value = null)
{
    if (is_array($spec)) {
        $this->_smarty->assign($spec);
        return;
    }

    $this->_smarty->assign($spec, $value);
}

/**
 * Clear all assigned variables
 *
 * Clears all variables assigned to Zend_View either via
 * {@link assign()} or property overloading
 * ({@link __get()}/{@link __set()}).
 *
 * @return void
 */
public function clearVars()
{
    $this->_smarty->clear_all_assign();
}

/**
 * Processes a template and returns the output.
 *
 * @param string $name The template to process.
 * @return string The output.
 */
public function render($name)
{
    return $this->_smarty->fetch($name);
}
}
```

In this example, you would instantiate the Zend_View_Smarty class instead of Zend_View, and then use it in roughly the same fashion as Zend_View:

```
//Example 1. In initView() of initializer.
$view = new Zend_View_Smarty('/path/to/templates');
$viewRenderer =
    new Zend_Controller_Action_HelperBroker::getStaticHelper('ViewRenderer');
$viewRenderer->setView($view)
            ->setViewBasePathSpec($view->_smarty->template_dir)
            ->setViewScriptPathSpec(':controller/:action.:suffix')
            ->setViewScriptPathNoControllerSpec(':action.:suffix')
            ->setViewSuffix('tpl');

//Example 2. Usage in action controller remains the same...
class FooController extends Zend_Controller_Action
{
    public function barAction()
    {
        $this->view->book   = 'Zend PHP 5 Certification Study Guide';
        $this->view->author = 'Davey Shafik and Ben Ramsey'
    }
}

//Example 3. Initializing view in action controller
```

```
class FooController extends Zend_Controller_Action
{
    public function init()
    {
        $this->view    = new Zend_View_Smarty('/path/to/templates');
        $viewRenderer = $this->_helper->getHelper('viewRenderer');
        $viewRenderer->setView($this->view)
                     ->setViewBasePathSpec($view->_smarty->template_dir)
                     ->setViewScriptPathSpec(':controller/:action.:suffix')
                     ->setViewScriptPathNoControllerSpec(':action.:suffix')
                     ->setViewSuffix('tpl');
    }
}
```

View Helpers

In your view scripts, often it is necessary to perform certain complex functions over and over: e.g., formatting a date, generating form elements, or displaying action links. You can use helper classes to perform these behaviors for you.

A helper is simply a class. Let's say we want a helper named 'fooBar'. By default, the class is prefixed with 'Zend_View_Helper_' (you can specify a custom prefix when setting a helper path), and the last segment of the class name is the helper name; this segment should be TitleCapped; the full class name is then: Zend_View_Helper_FooBar. This class should contain at the minimum a single method, named after the helper, and camelCased: fooBar().

Watch the Case

Helper names are always camelCased, i.e., they never begin with an uppercase character. The class name itself is MixedCased, but the method that is actually executed is camelCased.

Default Helper Path

The default helper path always points to the Zend Framework view helpers, i.e., 'Zend/View/Helper/'. Even if you call setHelperPath() to overwrite the existing paths, this path will be set to ensure the default helpers work.

To use a helper in your view script, call it using $this->helperName(). Behind the scenes, Zend_View will load the Zend_View_Helper_HelperName class, create an object instance of it, and call its helperName() method. The object instance is persistent within the Zend_View instance, and is reused for all future calls to $this->helperName().

Initial Helpers

Zend_View comes with an initial set of helper classes, most of which relate to form element generation and perform the appropriate output escaping automatically. In addition, there are helpers for creating route-based URLs and HTML lists, as well as declaring variables. The currently shipped helpers include:

- declareVars(): Primarily for use when using strictVars(), this helper can be used to declare template variables that may or may not already be set in the view object, as well as to set default values. Arrays passed as arguments to the method will be used to set default values; otherwise, if the variable does not exist, it is set to an empty string.

- fieldset($name, $content, $attribs): Creates an XHTML fieldset. If $attribs contains a 'legend' key, that value will be used for the fieldset legend. The fieldset will surround the $content as provided to the helper.

- form($name, $attribs, $content): Generates an XHTML form. All $attribs are escaped and rendered as XHTML attributes of the form tag. If $content is present and not a boolean false, then that content is rendered within the start and close form tags; if `$content` is a boolean false (the default), only the opening form tag is generated.

- `formButton($name, $value, $attribs)`: Creates an <button /> element.

- `formCheckbox($name, $value, $attribs, $options)`: Creates an <input type="checkbox" /> element.

  By default, when no $value is provided and no $options are present, '0' is assumed to be the unchecked value, and '1' the checked value. If a $value is passed, but no $options are present, the checked value is assumed to be the value passed.

  $options should be an array. If the array is indexed, the first value is the checked value, and the second the unchecked value; all other values are ignored. You may also pass an associative array with the keys 'checked' and 'unChecked'.

  If $options has been passed, if $value matches the checked value, then the element will be marked as checked. You may also mark the element as checked or unchecked by passing a boolean value for the attribute 'checked'.

  The above is probably best summed up with some examples:

```
// '1' and '0' as checked/unchecked options; not checked
echo $this->formCheckbox('foo');

// '1' and '0' as checked/unchecked options; checked
echo $this->formCheckbox('foo', null, array('checked' => true));

// 'bar' and '0' as checked/unchecked options; not checked
echo $this->formCheckbox('foo', 'bar');

// 'bar' and '0' as checked/unchecked options; checked
echo $this->formCheckbox('foo', 'bar', array('checked' => true));

// 'bar' and 'baz' as checked/unchecked options; unchecked
echo $this->formCheckbox('foo', null, null, array('bar', 'baz');

// 'bar' and 'baz' as checked/unchecked options; unchecked
echo $this->formCheckbox('foo', null, null, array(
    'checked' => 'bar',
    'unChecked' => 'baz'
));

// 'bar' and 'baz' as checked/unchecked options; checked
echo $this->formCheckbox('foo', 'bar', null, array('bar', 'baz');
echo $this->formCheckbox('foo',
                         null,
                         array('checked' => true),
                         array('bar', 'baz');

// 'bar' and 'baz' as checked/unchecked options; unchecked
echo $this->formCheckbox('foo', 'baz', null, array('bar', 'baz');
echo $this->formCheckbox('foo',
                         null,
                         array('checked' => false),
                         array('bar', 'baz');
```

  In all cases, the markup prepends a hidden element with the unchecked value; this way, if the value is unchecked, you will still get a valid value returned to your form.

- `formErrors($errors, $options)`: Generates an XHTML unordered list to show errors. `$errors` should be a string or an array of strings; `$options` should be any attributes you want placed in the opening list tag.

You can specify alternate opening, closing, and separator content when rendering the errors by calling several methods on the helper:

- `setElementStart($string)`; default is `'<ul class="errors"%s"><li>'`, where %s is replaced with the attributes as specified in `$options`.

- `setElementSeparator($string)`; default is `'</li><li>'`.

- `setElementEnd($string)`; default is `'</li></ul>'`.

- `formFile($name, $attribs)`: Creates an <input type="file" /> element.

- `formHidden($name, $value, $attribs)`: Creates an <input type="hidden" /> element.

- `formLabel($name, $value, $attribs)`: Creates a <label> element, setting the `for` attribute to `$name`, and the actual label text to `$value`. If `disable` is passed in `attribs`, nothing will be returned.

- `formMultiCheckbox($name, $value, $attribs, $options, $listsep)`: Creates a list of checkboxes. `$options` should be an associative array, and may be arbitrarily deep. `$value` may be a single value or an array of selected values that match the keys in the `$options` array. `$listsep` is an HTML break ("<br />") by default. By default, this element is treated as an array; all checkboxes share the same name, and are submitted as an array.

- `formPassword($name, $value, $attribs)`: Creates an <input type="password" /> element.

- `formRadio($name, $value, $attribs, $options)`: Creates a series of <input type="radio" /> elements, one for each of the $options elements. In the $options array, the element key is the radio value, and the element value is the radio label. The $value radio will be preselected for you.

- `formReset($name, $value, $attribs)`: Creates an <input type="reset" /> element.

- `formSelect($name, $value, $attribs, $options)`: Creates a <select>...</select> block, with one <option>one for each of the $options elements. In the $options array, the element key is the option value, and the element value is the option label. The $value option(s) will be preselected for you.

- `formSubmit($name, $value, $attribs)`: Creates an <input type="submit" /> element.

- `formText($name, $value, $attribs)`: Creates an <input type="text" /> element.

- `formTextarea($name, $value, $attribs)`: Creates a <textarea>...</textarea> block.

- `url($urlOptions, $name, $reset)`: Creates a URL string based on a named route. `$urlOptions` should be an associative array of key/value pairs used by the particular route.

- `htmlList($items, $ordered, $attribs, $escape)`: generates unordered and ordered lists based on the $items passed to it. If $items is a multidimensional array, a nested list will be built. If the $escape flag is true (default), individual items will be escaped using the view objects registered escaping mechanisms; pass a false value if you want to allow markup in your lists.

Using these in your view scripts is very easy, here is an example. Note that you all you need to do is call them; they will load and instantiate themselves as they are needed.

```
// inside your view script, $this refers to the Zend_View instance.
//
// say that you have already assigned a series of select options under
// the name $countries as array('us' => 'United States', 'il' =>
// 'Israel', 'de' => 'Germany').
?>
```

```
<form action="action.php" method="post">
    <p><label>Your Email:
<?php echo $this->formText('email', 'you@example.com', array('size' =>
    32)) ?>
    </label></p>
    <p><label>Your Country:
<?php echo $this->formSelect('country', 'us', null, $this->countries) ?>
    </label></p>
    <p><label>Would you like to opt in?
<?php echo $this->formCheckbox('opt_in', 'yes', null, array('yes', 'no')) ?>
    </label></p>
</form>
```

The resulting output from the view script will look something like this:

```
<form action="action.php" method="post">
    <p><label>Your Email:
        <input type="text" name="email" value="you@example.com" size="32" />
    </label></p>
    <p><label>Your Country:
        <select name="country">
            <option value="us" selected="selected">United States</option>
            <option value="il">Israel</option>
            <option value="de">Germany</option>
        </select>
    </label></p>
    <p><label>Would you like to opt in?
        <input type="hidden" name="opt_in" value="no" />
        <input type="checkbox" name="opt_in" value="yes" checked="checked" />
    </label></p>
</form>
```

Action View Helper

The Action view helper enables view scripts to dispatch a given controller action; the result of the response object following the dispatch is then returned. These can be used when a particular action could generate re-usable content or "widget-ized" content.

Actions that result in a _forward() or redirect are considered invalid, and will return an empty string.

The API for the Action view helper follows that of most MVC components that invoke controller actions: action($action, $controller, $module = null, array $params = array()). $action and $controller are required; if no module is specified, the default module is assumed.

Example 35.1. Basic Usage of Action View Helper

As an example, you may have a CommentController with a listAction() method you wish to invoke in order to pull a list of comments for the current request:

```
<div id="sidebar right">
    <div class="item">
        <?php echo $this->action('list',
                                 'comment',
                                 null,
                                 array('count' => 10)); ?>
    </div>
</div>
```

Cycle Helper

The `Cycle` helper is used to alternate a set of values.

Example 35.2. Cycle Helper Basic Usage

To add elements to cycle just specify them in constructor or use `assign(array $data)` function

```
<?php foreach ($this->books as $book):?>
  <tr style="background-color:<?php echo $this->cycle(array("#F0F0F0",
                                                            "#FFFFFF"))
                                      ->next()?>">
  <td><?php echo $this->escape($book['author']) ?></td>
</tr>
<?php endforeach;?>

// Moving in backwards order and assign function
$this->cycle()->assign(array("#F0F0F0","#FFFFFF"));
$this->cycle()->prev();
?>
```

The output

```
<tr style="background-color:'#F0F0F0'">
    <td>First</td>
</tr>
<tr style="background-color:'#FFFFFF'">
    <td>Second</td>
</tr>
```

Example 35.3. Working with two or more cycles

To use two cycles you have to specify the names of cycles. Just set second parameter in cycle method. `$this->cycle(array("#F0F0F0","#FFFFFF"),'cycle2')`. You can also use setName($name) function.

```
<?php foreach ($this->books as $book):?>
  <tr style="background-color:<?php echo $this->cycle(array("#F0F0F0",
                                                            "#FFFFFF"))
                                      ->next()?>">
  <td><?php echo $this->cycle(array(1,2,3),'number')->next()?></td>
  <td><?php echo $this->escape($book['author'])?></td>
</tr>
<?php endforeach;?>
```

Partial Helper

The `Partial` view helper is used to render a specified template within its own variable scope. The primary use is for reusable template fragments with which you do not need to worry about variable name clashes. Additionally, they allow you to specify partial view scripts from specific modules.

A sibling to the `Partial`, the `PartialLoop` view helper allows you to pass iterable data, and render a partial for each item.

PartialLoop Counter

The `PartialLoop` view helper assigns a variable to the view named `partialCounter` which passes the current position of the array to the view script. This provides an easy way to have alternating colors on table rows for example.

Example 35.4. Basic Usage of Partials

Basic usage of partials is to render a template fragment in its own view scope. Consider the following partial script:

```
<?php // partial.phtml ?>
<ul>
    <li>From: <?php echo $this->escape($this->from) ?></li>
    <li>Subject: <?php echo $this->escape($this->subject) ?></li>
</ul>
```

You would then call it from your view script using the following:

```
<?php echo $this->partial('partial.phtml', array(
    'from' => 'Team Framework',
    'subject' => 'view partials')); ?>
```

Which would then render:

```
<ul>
    <li>From: Team Framework</li>
    <li>Subject: view partials</li>
</ul>
```

What is a model?

A model used with the `Partial` view helper can be one of the following:

- *Array*. If an array is passed, it should be associative, as its key/value pairs are assigned to the view with keys as view variables.

- *Object implementing toArray() method*. If an object is passed an has a `toArray()` method, the results of `toArray()` will be assigned to the view object as view variables.

- *Standard object*. Any other object will assign the results of `object_get_vars()` (essentially all public properties of the object) to the view object.

If your model is an object, you may want to have it passed *as an object* to the partial script, instead of serializing it to an array of variables. You can do this by setting the 'objectKey' property of the appropriate helper:

```
// Tell partial to pass objects as 'model' variable
$view->partial()->setObjectKey('model');

// Tell partial to pass objects from partialLoop as 'model' variable
// in final partial view script:
$view->partialLoop()->setObjectKey('model');
```

This technique is particularly useful when passing Zend_Db_Table_Rowsets to partialLoop(), as you then have full access to your row objects within the view scripts, allowing you to call methods on them (such as retrieving values from parent or dependent rows).

Example 35.5. Using PartialLoop to Render Iterable Models

Typically, you'll want to use partials in a loop, to render the same content fragment many times; this way you can put large blocks of repeated content or complex display logic into a single location. However this has a performance impact, as the partial helper needs to be invoked once for each iteration.

The PartialLoop view helper helps solve this issue. It allows you to pass an iterable item (array or object implementing Iterator) as the model. It then iterates over this, passing, the items to the partial script as the model. Items in the iterator may be any model the Partial view helper allows.

Let's assume the following partial view script:

```php
<?php // partialLoop.phtml ?>
    <dt><?php echo $this->key ?></dt>
    <dd><?php echo $this->value ?></dd>
```

And the following "model":

```php
$model = array(
    array('key' => 'Mammal', 'value' => 'Camel'),
    array('key' => 'Bird', 'value' => 'Penguin'),
    array('key' => 'Reptile', 'value' => 'Asp'),
    array('key' => 'Fish', 'value' => 'Flounder'),
);
```

In your view script, you could then invoke the PartialLoop helper:

```php
<dl>
<?php echo $this->partialLoop('partialLoop.phtml', $model) ?>
</dl>
```

```html
<dl>
    <dt>Mammal</dt>
    <dd>Camel</dd>

    <dt>Bird</dt>
    <dd>Penguin</dd>

    <dt>Reptile</dt>
    <dd>Asp</dd>

    <dt>Fish</dt>
    <dd>Flounder</dd>
</dl>
```

Example 35.6. Rendering Partials in Other Modules

Sometime a partial will exist in a different module. If you know the name of the module, you can pass it as the second argument to either `partial()` or `partialLoop()`, moving the $model argument to third position.

For instance, if there's a pager partial you wish to use that's in the 'list' module, you could grab it as follows:

```
<?php echo $this->partial('pager.phtml', 'list', $pagerData) ?>
```

In this way, you can re-use partials created specifically for other modules. That said, it's likely a better practice to put re-usable partials in shared view script paths.

Placeholder Helper

The `Placeholder` view helper is used to persist content between view scripts and view instances. It also offers some useful features such as aggregating content, capturing view script content for later use, and adding pre- and post-text to content (and custom separators for aggregated content).

Example 35.7. Basic Usage of Placeholders

Basic usage of placeholders is to persist view data. Each invocation of the `Placeholder` helper expects a placeholder name; the helper then returns a placeholder container object that you can either manipulate or simply echo out.

```
<?php $this->placeholder('foo')->set("Some text for later") ?>

<?php
    echo $this->placeholder('foo');
    // outputs "Some text for later"
?>
```

Example 35.8. Using Placeholders to Aggregate Content

Aggregating content via placeholders can be useful at times as well. For instance, your view script may have a variable array from which you wish to retrieve messages to display later; a later view script can then determine how those will be rendered.

The `Placeholder` view helper uses containers that extend `ArrayObject`, providing a rich featureset for manipulating arrays. In addition, it offers a variety of methods for formatting the content stored in the container:

- `setPrefix($prefix)` sets text with which to prefix the content. Use `getPrefix()` at any time to determine what the current setting is.

- `setPostfix($prefix)` sets text with which to append the content. Use `getPostfix()` at any time to determine what the current setting is.

- `setSeparator($prefix)` sets text with which to separate aggregated content. Use `getSeparator()` at any time to determine what the current setting is.

- setIndent($prefix) can be used to set an indentation value for content. If an integer is passed, that number of spaces will be used; if a string is passed, the string will be used. Use getIndent() at any time to determine what the current setting is.

```
<!-- first view script -->
<?php $this->placeholder('foo')->exchangeArray($this->data) ?>


<!-- later view script -->
<?php
$this->placeholder('foo')->setPrefix("<ul>\n    <li>")
                         ->setSeparator("</li><li>\n")
                         ->setIndent(4)
                         ->setPostfix("</li></ul>\n");
?>

<?php
    echo $this->placeholder('foo');
    // outputs as unordered list with pretty indentation
?>
```

Because the Placeholder container objects extend ArrayObject, you can also assign content to a specific key in the container easily, instead of simply pushing it into the container. Keys may be accessed either as object properties or as array keys.

```
<?php $this->placeholder('foo')->bar = $this->data ?>
<?php echo $this->placeholder('foo')->bar ?>

<?php
$foo = $this->placeholder('foo');
echo $foo['bar'];
?>
```

Example 35.9. Using Placeholders to Capture Content

Occasionally you may have content for a placeholder in a view script that is easiest to template; the Placeholder view helper allows you to capture arbitrary content for later rendering using the following API.

- captureStart($type, $key) begins capturing content.

  $type should be one of the Placeholder constants APPEND or SET. If APPEND, captured content is appended to the list of current content in the placeholder; if SET, captured content is used as the sole value of the placeholder (potentially replacing any previous content). By default, $type is APPEND.

  $key can be used to specify a specific key in the placeholder container to which you want content captured.

  captureStart() locks capturing until captureEnd() is called; you cannot nest capturing with the same placeholder container. Doing so will raise an exception.

- captureEnd() stops capturing content, and places it in the container object according to how captureStart() was called.

```
<!-- Default capture: append -->
<?php $this->placeholder('foo')->captureStart();
foreach ($this->data as $datum): ?>
<div class="foo">
    <h2><?php echo $datum->title ?></h2>
    <p><?php echo $datum->content ?></p>
</div>
<?php endforeach; ?>
<?php $this->placeholder('foo')->captureEnd() ?>

<?php echo $this->placeholder('foo') ?>


<!-- Capture to key -->
<?php $this->placeholder('foo')->captureStart('SET', 'data');
foreach ($this->data as $datum): ?>
<div class="foo">
    <h2><?php echo $datum->title ?></h2>
    <p><?php echo $datum->content ?></p>
</div>
 <?php endforeach; ?>
<?php $this->placeholder('foo')->captureEnd() ?>

<?php echo $this->placeholder('foo')->data ?>
```

Concrete Placeholder Implementations

Zend Framework ships with a number of "concrete" placeholder implementations. These are for commonly used placeholders: doctype, page title, and various <head> elements. In all cases, calling the placeholder with no arguments returns the element itself.

Documentation for each element is covered separately, as linked below:

- Doctype

- HeadLink

- HeadMeta

- HeadScript

- HeadStyle

- HeadTitle

- InlineScript

Doctype Helper

Valid HTML and XHTML documents should include a DOCTYPE declaration. Besides being difficult to remember, these can also affect how certain elements in your document should be rendered (for instance, CDATA escaping in <script> and <style> elements.

The Doctype helper allows you to specify one of the following types:

- XHTML11

- XHTML1_STRICT

- XHTML1_TRANSITIONAL

- XHTML1_FRAMESET

- XHTML_BASIC1

- HTML4_STRICT

- HTML4_LOOSE

- HTML4_FRAMESET

- HTML5

You can also specify a custom doctype as long as it is well-formed.

The Doctype helper is a concrete implementation of the Placeholder helper.

Example 35.10. Doctype Helper Basic Usage

You may specify the doctype at any time. However, helpers that depend on the doctype for their output will recognize it only after you have set it, so the easiest approach is to specify it in your bootstrap:

```
$doctypeHelper = new Zend_View_Helper_Doctype();
$doctypeHelper->doctype('XHTML1_STRICT');
```

And then print it out on top of your layout script:

```
<?php echo $this->doctype() ?>
```

Example 35.11. Retrieving the Doctype

If you need to know the doctype, you can do so by calling getDoctype() on the object, which is returned by invoking the helper.

```
$doctype = $view->doctype()->getDoctype();
```

Typically, you'll simply want to know if the doctype is XHTML or not; for this, the isXhtml() method will suffice:

```
if ($view->doctype()->isXhtml()) {
    // do something differently
}
```

HeadLink Helper

The HTML <link> element is increasingly used for linking a variety of resources for your site: stylesheets, feeds, favicons, trackbacks, and more. The HeadLink helper provides a simple interface for creating and aggregating these elements for later retrieval and output in your layout script.

The HeadLink helper has special methods for adding stylesheet links to its stack:

- appendStylesheet($href, $media, $conditionalStylesheet, $extras)

- offsetSetStylesheet($index, $href, $media, $conditionalStylesheet, $extras)

- prependStylesheet($href, $media, $conditionalStylesheet, $extras)

- setStylesheet($href, $media, $conditionalStylesheet, $extras)

The $media value defaults to 'screen', but may be any valid media value. $conditionalStylesheet is a string or boolean false, and will be used at rendering time to determine if special comments should be included to prevent loading of the stylesheet on certain platforms. $extras is an array of any extra values that you want to be added to the tag.

Additionally, the HeadLink helper has special methods for adding 'alternate' links to its stack:

- appendAlternate($href, $type, $title, $extras)

- offsetSetAlternate($index, $href, $type, $title, $extras)

- prependAlternate($href, $type, $title, $extras)

- setAlternate($href, $type, $title, $extras)

The headLink() helper method allows specifying all attributes necessary for a <link> element, and allows you to also specify placement -- whether the new element replaces all others, prepends (top of stack), or appends (end of stack).

The HeadLink helper is a concrete implementation of the Placeholder helper.

Example 35.12. HeadLink Helper Basic Usage

You may specify a headLink at any time. Typically, you will specify global links in your layout script, and application specific links in your application view scripts. In your layout script, in the <head> section, you will then echo the helper to output it.

```php
<?php // setting links in a view script:
$this->headLink()->appendStylesheet('/styles/basic.css')
                ->headLink(array('rel' => 'favicon',
                                 'href' => '/img/favicon.ico'),
                           'PREPEND')
                ->prependStylesheet('/styles/moz.css',
                                    'screen',
                                    true,
                                    array('id' => 'my_stylesheet'));
?>
<?php // rendering the links: ?>
<?php echo $this->headLink() ?>
```

HeadMeta Helper

The HTML <meta> element is used to provide meta information about your HTML document -- typically keywords, document character set, caching pragmas, etc. Meta tags may be either of the 'http-equiv' or 'name' types, must contain a 'content' attribute, and can also have either of the 'lang' or 'scheme' modifier attributes.

The HeadMeta helper supports the following methods for setting and adding meta tags:

- appendName($keyValue, $content, $conditionalName)

- offsetSetName($index, $keyValue, $content, $conditionalName)

- prependName($keyValue, $content, $conditionalName)

- setName($keyValue, $content, $modifiers)

- appendHttpEquiv($keyValue, $content, $conditionalHttpEquiv)

- offsetSetHttpEquiv($index, $keyValue, $content, $conditionalHttpEquiv)

- prependHttpEquiv($keyValue, $content, $conditionalHttpEquiv)

- setHttpEquiv($keyValue, $content, $modifiers)

The $keyValue item is used to define a value for the 'name' or 'http-equiv' key; $content is the value for the 'content' key, and $modifiers is an optional associative array that can contain keys for 'lang' and/or 'scheme'.

You may also set meta tags using the headMeta() helper method, which has the following signature: headMeta($content, $keyValue, $keyType = 'name', $modifiers = array(), $placement = 'APPEND'). $keyValue is the content for the key specified in $keyType, which should be either 'name' or 'http-equiv'. $placement can be either 'SET' (overwrites all previously stored values), 'APPEND' (added to end of stack), or 'PREPEND' (added to top of stack).

HeadMeta overrides each of append(), offsetSet(), prepend(), and set() to enforce usage of the special methods as listed above. Internally, it stores each item as a stdClass token, which it later serializes using the itemToString() method. This allows you to perform checks on the items in the stack, and optionally modify these items by simply modifying the object returned.

The HeadMeta helper is a concrete implementation of the Placeholder helper.

Example 35.13. HeadMeta Helper Basic Usage

You may specify a new meta tag at any time. Typically, you will specify client-side caching rules or SEO keywords.

For instance, if you wish to specify SEO keywords, you'd be creating a meta name tag with the name 'keywords' and the content the keywords you wish to associate with your page:

```
// setting meta keywords
$this->headMeta()->appendName('keywords', 'framework php productivity');
```

If you wished to set some client-side caching rules, you'd set http-equiv tags with the rules you wish to enforce:

```
// disabling client-side cache
$this->headMeta()->appendHttpEquiv('expires',
                                    'Wed, 26 Feb 1997 08:21:57 GMT')
            ->appendHttpEquiv('pragma', 'no-cache')
            ->appendHttpEquiv('Cache-Control', 'no-cache');
```

Another popular use for meta tags is setting the content type, character set, and language:

```
// setting content type and character set
$this->headMeta()->appendHttpEquiv('Content-Type',
                                    'text/html; charset=UTF-8')
            ->appendHttpEquiv('Content-Language', 'en-US');
```

As a final example, an easy way to display a transitional message before a redirect is using a "meta refresh":

```
// setting a meta refresh for 3 seconds to a new url:
$this->headMeta()->appendHttpEquiv('Refresh',
                                    '3;URL=http://www.some.org/some.html');
```

When you're ready to place your meta tags in the layout, simply echo the helper:

```
<?php echo $this->headMeta() ?>
```

HeadScript Helper

The HTML `<script>` element is used to either provide inline client-side scripting elements or link to a remote resource containing client-side scripting code. The `HeadScript` helper allows you to manage both.

The `HeadScript` helper supports the following methods for setting and adding scripts:

- `appendFile($src, $type = 'text/javascript', $attrs = array())`

- `offsetSetFile($index, $src, $type = 'text/javascript', $attrs = array())`

- `prependFile($src, $type = 'text/javascript', $attrs = array())`

- `setFile($src, $type = 'text/javascript', $attrs = array())`

- `appendScript($script, $type = 'text/javascript', $attrs = array())`

- `offsetSetScript($index, $script, $type = 'text/javascript', $attrs = array())`

- `prependScript($script, $type = 'text/javascript', $attrs = array())`

- `setScript($script, $type = 'text/javascript', $attrs = array())`

In the case of the `*File()` methods, `$src` is the remote location of the script to load; this is usually in the form of a URL or a path. For the `*Script()` methods, `$script` is the client-side scripting directives you wish to use in the element.

Setting Conditional Comments

`HeadScript` allows you to wrap the script tag in conditional comments, which allows you to hide it from specific browsers. To add the conditional tags, pass the conditional value as part of the `$attrs` parameter in the method calls.

Example 35.14. Headscript With Conditional Comments

```
// adding scripts
$this->headScript()->appendFile(
    '/js/prototype.js',
    'text/javascript',
    array('conditional' => 'lt IE 7')
);
```

`HeadScript` also allows capturing scripts; this can be useful if you want to create the client-side script programmatically, and then place it elsewhere. The usage for this will be showed in an example below.

Finally, you can also use the `headScript()` method to quickly add script elements; the signature for this is `headScript($mode = 'FILE', $spec, $placement = 'APPEND')`. The `$mode` is either 'FILE' or 'SCRIPT', depending on if you're linking a script or defining one. `$spec` is either the script file to link or the script source itself. $placement should be either 'APPEND', 'PREPEND', or 'SET'.

HeadScript overrides each of append(), offsetSet(), prepend(), and set() to enforce usage of the special methods as listed above. Internally, it stores each item as a stdClass token, which it later serializes using the itemToString() method. This allows you to perform checks on the items in the stack, and optionally modify these items by simply modifying the object returned.

The HeadScript helper is a concrete implementation of the Placeholder helper.

Use InlineScript for HTML Body Scripts

HeadScript's sibling helper, InlineScript, should be used when you wish to include scripts inline in the HTML body. Placing scripts at the end of your document is a good practice for speeding up delivery of your page, particularly when using 3rd party analytics scripts.

Arbitrary Attributes are Disabled by Default

By default, HeadScript only will render <script> attributes that are blessed by the W3C. These include 'type', 'charset', 'defer', 'language', and 'src'. However, some javascript frameworks, notably Dojo [http://www.dojotoolkit.org/], utilize custom attributes in order to modify behavior. To allow such attributes, you can enable them via the setAllowArbitraryAttributes() method:

```
$this->headScript()->setAllowArbitraryAttributes(true);
```

Example 35.15. HeadScript Helper Basic Usage

You may specify a new script tag at any time. As noted above, these may be links to outside resource files or scripts themselves.

```
// adding scripts
$this->headScript()->appendFile('/js/prototype.js')
                   ->appendScript($onloadScript);
```

Order is often important with client-side scripting; you may need to ensure that libraries are loaded in a specific order due to dependencies each have; use the various append, prepend, and offsetSet directives to aid in this task:

```
// Putting scripts in order

// place at a particular offset to ensure loaded last
$this->headScript()->offsetSetFile(100, '/js/myfuncs.js');

// use scriptaculous effects (append uses next index, 101)
$this->headScript()->appendFile('/js/scriptaculous.js');

// but always have base prototype script load first:
$this->headScript()->prependFile('/js/prototype.js');
```

When you're finally ready to output all scripts in your layout script, simply echo the helper:

```
<?php echo $this->headScript() ?>
```

Example 35.16. Capturing Scripts Using the HeadScript Helper

Sometimes you need to generate client-side scripts programmatically. While you could use string concatenation, heredocs, and the like, often it's easier just to do so by creating the script and sprinkling in PHP tags. HeadScript lets you do just that, capturing it to the stack:

```
<?php $this->headScript()->captureStart() ?>
var action = '<?php echo $this->baseUrl ?>';
$('foo_form').action = action;
<?php $this->headScript()->captureEnd() ?>
```

The following assumptions are made:

- The script will be appended to the stack. If you wish for it to replace the stack or be added to the top, you will need to pass 'SET' or 'PREPEND', respectively, as the first argument to captureStart().

- The script MIME type is assumed to be 'text/javascript'; if you wish to specify a different type, you will need to pass it as the second argument to captureStart().

- If you wish to specify any additional attributes for the <script> tag, pass them in an array as the third argument to captureStart().

HeadStyle Helper

The HTML <style> element is used to include CSS stylesheets inline in the HTML <head> element.

Use HeadLink to link CSS files

HeadLink should be used to create <link> elements for including external stylesheets. HeadScript is used when you wish to define your stylesheets inline.

The HeadStyle helper supports the following methods for setting and adding stylesheet declarations:

- appendStyle($content, $attributes = array())

- offsetSetStyle($index, $content, $attributes = array())

- prependStyle($content, $attributes = array())

- setStyle($content, $attributes = array())

In all cases, $content is the actual CSS declarations. $attributes are any additional attributes you wish to provide to the style tag: lang, title, media, or dir are all permissible.

Setting Conditional Comments

HeadStyle allows you to wrap the style tag in conditional comments, which allows you to hide it from specific browsers. To add the conditional tags, pass the conditional value as part of the $attributes parameter in the method calls.

Example 35.17. Headstyle With Conditional Comments

```
// adding scripts
$this->headStyle()->appendStyle($styles, array('conditional' => 'lt IE 7')
```

HeadStyle also allows capturing style declarations; this can be useful if you want to create the declarations programmatically, and then place them elsewhere. The usage for this will be showed in an example below.

Finally, you can also use the headStyle() method to quickly add declarations elements; the signature for this is headStyle($content$placement = 'APPEND', $attributes = array()). $placement should be either 'APPEND', 'PREPEND', or 'SET'.

HeadStyle overrides each of append(), offsetSet(), prepend(), and set() to enforce usage of the special methods as listed above. Internally, it stores each item as a stdClass token, which it later serializes using the itemToString() method. This allows you to perform checks on the items in the stack, and optionally modify these items by simply modifying the object returned.

The HeadStyle helper is a concrete implementation of the Placeholder helper.

Example 35.18. HeadStyle Helper Basic Usage

You may specify a new style tag at any time:

```
// adding styles
$this->headStyle()->appendStyle($styles);
```

Order is very important with CSS; you may need to ensure that declarations are loaded in a specific order due to the order of the cascade; use the various append, prepend, and offsetSet directives to aid in this task:

```
// Putting styles in order

// place at a particular offset:
$this->headStyle()->offsetSetStyle(100, $customStyles);

// place at end:
$this->headStyle()->appendStyle($finalStyles);

// place at beginning
$this->headStyle()->prependStyle($firstStyles);
```

When you're finally ready to output all style declarations in your layout script, simply echo the helper:

```
<?php echo $this->headStyle() ?>
```

Example 35.19. Capturing Style Declarations Using the HeadStyle Helper

Sometimes you need to generate CSS style declarations programmatically. While you could use string concatenation, heredocs, and the like, often it's easier just to do so by creating the styles and sprinkling in PHP tags. `HeadStyle` lets you do just that, capturing it to the stack:

```
<?php $this->headStyle()->captureStart() ?>
body {
    background-color: <?php echo $this->bgColor ?>;
}
<?php $this->headStyle()->captureEnd() ?>
```

The following assumptions are made:

- The style declarations will be appended to the stack. If you wish for them to replace the stack or be added to the top, you will need to pass 'SET' or 'PREPEND', respectively, as the first argument to `captureStart()`.

- If you wish to specify any additional attributes for the `<style>` tag, pass them in an array as the second argument to `captureStart()`.

HeadTitle Helper

The HTML `<title>` element is used to provide a title for an HTML document. The `HeadTitle` helper allows you to programmatically create and store the title for later retrieval and output.

The `HeadTitle` helper is a concrete implementation of the Placeholder helper. It overrides the `toString()` method to enforce generating a `<title>` element, and adds a `headTitle()` method for quick and easy setting and aggregation of title elements. The signature for that method is `headTitle($title, $setType = 'APPEND')`; by default, the value is appended to the stack (aggregating title segments), but you may also specify either 'PREPEND' (place at top of stack) or 'SET' (overwrite stack).

Example 35.20. HeadTitle Helper Basic Usage

You may specify a title tag at any time. A typical usage would have you setting title segments for each level of depth in your application: site, controller, action, and potentially resource.

```
// setting the controller and action name as title segments:
$request = Zend_Controller_Front::getInstance()->getRequest();
$this->headTitle($request->getActionName())
    ->headTitle($request->getControllerName());

// setting the site in the title; possibly in the layout script:
$this->headTitle('Zend Framework');

// setting a separator string for segments:
$this->headTitle()->setSeparator(' / ');
```

When you're finally ready to render the title in your layout script, simply echo the helper:

```
<!-- renders <action> / <controller> / Zend Framework -->
<?php echo $this->headTitle() ?>
```

HTML Object Helpers

The HTML `<object>` element is used for embedding media like Flash or QuickTime in web pages. The object view helpers take care of embedding media with minimum effort.

There are four initial Object helpers:

- `formFlash` Generates markup for embedding Flash files.

- `formObject` Generates markup for embedding a custom Object.

- `formPage` Generates markup for embedding other (X)HTML pages.

- `formQuicktime` Generates markup for embedding QuickTime files.

All of these helpers share a similar interface. For this reason, this documentation will only contain examples of two of these helpers.

Example 35.21. Flash helper

Embedding Flash in your page using the helper is pretty straight-forward. The only required argument is the resource URI.

```php
<?php echo $this->htmlFlash('/path/to/flash.swf'); ?>
```

This outputs the following HTML:

```
<object data="/path/to/flash.swf"
        type="application/x-shockwave-flash"
        classid="clsid:D27CDB6E-AE6D-11cf-96B8-444553540000"
        codebase="http://download.macromedia.com/pub/shockwave/cabs/flash
                  /swflash.cab">
</object>
```

Additionally you can specify attributes, parameters and content that can be rendered along with the `<object>`. This will be demonstrated using the `htmlObject` helper.

Example 35.22. Customizing the object by passing additional arguments

The first argument in the object helpers is always required. It is the URI to the resource you want to embed. The second argument is only required in the `htmlObject` helper. The other helpers already contain the correct value for this argument. The third argument is used for passing along attributes to the object element. It only accepts an array with key-value pairs. The `classid` and `codebase` are examples of such attributes. The fourth argument also only takes a key-value array and uses them to create `<param>` elements. You will see an example of this shortly. Lastly, there is the option of providing additional content to the object. Now for an example which utilizes all arguments.

```php
echo $this->htmlObject(
    '/path/to/file.ext',
    'mime/type',
    array(
        'attr1' => 'aval1',
        'attr2' => 'aval2'
    ),
    array(
        'param1' => 'pval1',
        'param2' => 'pval2'
    ),
    'some content'
);
```

```
/*
This would output:

<object data="/path/to/file.ext" type="mime/type"
    attr1="aval1" attr2="aval2">
    <param name="param1" value="pval1" />
    <param name="param2" value="pval2" />
    some content
</object>
*/
```

InlineScript Helper

The HTML `<script>` element is used to either provide inline client-side scripting elements or link to a remote resource containing client-side scripting code. The `InlineScript` helper allows you to manage both. It is derived from HeadScript, and any method of that helper is available; however, use the `inlineScript()` method in place of `headScript()`.

Use InlineScript for HTML Body Scripts

`InlineScript`, should be used when you wish to include scripts inline in the HTML body. Placing scripts at the end of your document is a good practice for speeding up delivery of your page, particularly when using 3rd party analytics scripts.

Some JS libraries need to be included in the HTML `head`; use HeadScript for those scripts.

JSON Helper

When creating views that return JSON, it's important to also set the appropriate response header. The JSON view helper does exactly that. In addition, by default, it disables layouts (if currently enabled), as layouts generally aren't used with JSON responses.

The JSON helper sets the following header:

```
Content-Type: application/json
```

Most AJAX libraries look for this header when parsing responses to determine how to handle the content.

Usage of the JSON helper is very straightforward:

```
<?php echo $this->json($this->data) ?>
```

Keeping layouts and enabling encoding using Zend_Json_Expr

Each method in the JSON helper accepts a second, optional argument. This second argument can be a boolean flag to enable or disable layouts, or an array of options that will be passed to `Zend_Json::encode()` and used internally to encode data.

To keep layouts, the second parameter needs to be boolean `true`. When the second parameter is an array, keeping layouts can be achieved by including a `keepLayouts` key with a value of a boolean `true`.

```
// Boolean true as second argument enables layouts:
echo $this->json($this->data, true);
```

```
// Or boolean true as "keepLayouts" key:
echo $this->json($this->data, array('keepLayouts' => true));
```

Zend_Json::encode allows the encoding of native JSON expressions using Zend_Json_Expr objects. This option is disabled by default. To enable this option, pass a boolean true to the enableJsonExprFinder key of the options array:

```
<?php echo $this->json($this->data, array(
    'enableJsonExprFinder' => true,
    'keepLayouts'          => true,
)) ?>
```

Navigation Helpers

The navigation helpers are used for rendering navigational elements from Zend_Navigation_Container instances.

There are 5 built-in helpers:

- Breadcrumbs, used for rendering the path to the currently active page.

- Links, used for rendering navigational head links (e.g. <link rel="next" href="..." />)

- Menu, used for rendering menus.

- Sitemap, used for rendering sitemaps conforming to the Sitemaps XML format [http://www.sitemaps.org/protocol.php].

- Navigation, used for proxying calls to other navigational helpers.
All built-in helpers extend Zend_View_Helper_Navigation_HelperAbstract, which adds integration with ACL and translation. The abstract class implements the interface Zend_View_Helper_Navigation_Helper, which defines the following methods:

- {get|set}Container() gets/sets the navigation container the helper should operate on by default, and hasContainer() checks if the helper has container registered.

- {get|set}Translator() gets/sets the translator used for translating labels and titles, and {get|set}UseTranslator() controls whether the translator should be enabled. The method hasTranslator() checks if the helper has a translator registered.

- {get|set}Acl(), {get|set}Role(), gets/sets ACL (Zend_Acl) instance and role (string or Zend_Acl_Role_Interface) used for filtering out pages when rendering, and {get|set}UseAcl() controls whether ACL should be enabled. The methods hasAcl() and hasRole() checks if the helper has an ACL instance or a role registered.

- __toString(), magic method to ensure that helpers can be rendered by echoing the helper instance directly.

- render(), must be implemented by concrete helpers to do the actual rendering.
In addition to the method stubs from the interface, the abstract class also implements the following methods:

- {get|set}Indent() gets/set indentation. The setter accepts a string or an int. In the case of an int, the helper will use the given number of spaces for indentation. I.e., setIndent(4) means 4 initial spaces of indentation. Indentation can be specified for all helpers except the Sitemap helper.

- {get|set}MinDepth() gets/set the minimum depth a page must have to be included by the helper. Setting null means no minimum depth.

- {get|set}MaxDepth() gets/set the maximum depth a page can have to be included by the helper. Setting `null` means no maximum depth.

- `__call()` is used for proxying calls to the container registered in the helper, which means you can call methods on a helper as if it was a container. See example below.

- `findActive($container, $minDepth, $maxDepth)` is used for finding the deepest active page in the given container. If depths are not given, the method will use the values retrieved from `getMinDepth()` and `getMaxDepth()`. The deepest active page must be between `$minDepth` and `$axnDepth` inclusively. Returns an array containing a reference to the found page instance and the depth at which the page was found.

- `htmlify()` renders an a HTML element from a `Zend_Navigation_Page` instance.

- `accept()` is used for determining if a page should be accepted when iterating containers. This method checks for page visibility and verifies that the helper's role is allowed access to the page's resource/privilege.

- `static setDefaultAcl()` is used for setting a defualt ACL object that will be used by helpers.

- `static setDefaultRole()` is used for setting a default ACL that will be used by helpers

If a navigation container is not explicitly set in a helper using `$helper->setContainer($nav)`, the helper will look for a container instance with the key `Zend_Navigation` in the registry. If a container is not explicitly set or found in the registry, the helper will create an empty `Zend_Navigation` container when calling `$helper->getContainer()`.

Example 35.23. Proxying calls to the navigation container

Navigation view helpers use the magic method `__call()` to proxy method calls to the navigation container that is registered in the view helper.

```
$this->navigation()->addPage(array(
    'type' => 'uri',
    'label' => 'New page'));
```

The call above will add a page to the container in the `Navigation` helper.

Translation of labels and titles

The navigation helpers support translation of page labels and titles. You can set a translator of type `Zend_Translate` or `Zend_Translate_Adapter` in the helper using `$helper->setTranslator($translator)`, or like with other I18n-enabled components; by adding the translator to the registry by using the key `Zend_Translate`.

If you want to disable translation, use `$helper->setUseTranslator(false)`.

The proxy helper will inject its own translator to the helper it proxies to if the proxied helper doesn't already have a translator.

Note

There is no translation in the sitemap helper, since there are no page labels or titles involved in an XML sitemap.

Integration with ACL

All navigational view helpers support ACL inherently from the class `Zend_View_Helper_Navigation_HelperAbstract`. A `Zend_Acl` object can be assigned to a helper instance with `$helper->setAcl($acl)`, and role with `$helper->setRole('member')` or `$helper->setRole(new Zend_Acl_Role('member'))`. If ACL is used in the helper, the role in the helper must be allowed by the ACL to access a page's `resource` and/or have the page's `privilege` for the page to be included when rendering.

If a page is not accepted by ACL, any descendant page will also be excluded from rendering.

The proxy helper will inject its own ACL and role to the helper it proxies to if the proxied helper doesn't already have any.

The examples below all show how ACL affects rendering.

Navigation setup used in examples

This example shows the setup of a navigation container for a fictional software company.

Notes on the setup:

- The domain for the site is `www.example.com`.

- Interesting page properties are marked with a comment.

- Unless otherwise is stated in other examples, the user is requesting the URL `http://www.example.com/products/server/faq/`, which translates to the page labeled FAQ under Foo Server.

- The assumed ACL and router setup is shown below the container setup.

```
/*
 * Navigation container (config/array)

 * Each element in the array will be passed to
 * Zend_Navigation_Page::factory() when constructing
 * the navigation container below.
 */
$pages = array(
    array(
        'label'      => 'Home',
        'title'      => 'Go Home',
        'module'     => 'default',
        'controller' => 'index',
        'action'     => 'index',
        'order'      => -100 // make sure home is the first page
    ),
    array(
        'label'      => 'Special offer this week only!',
        'module'     => 'store',
        'controller' => 'offer',
        'action'     => 'amazing',
        'visible'    => false // not visible
    ),
    array(
        'label'      => 'Products',
        'module'     => 'products',
        'controller' => 'index',
        'action'     => 'index',
        'pages'      => array(
            array(
```

```
                'label'     => 'Foo Server',
                'module'    => 'products',
                'controller' => 'server',
                'action'    => 'index',
                'pages'     => array(
                    array(
                        'label'     => 'FAQ',
                        'module'    => 'products',
                        'controller' => 'server',
                        'action'    => 'faq',
                        'rel'       => array(
                            'canonical' => 'http://www.example.com/?page=faq',
                            'alternate' => array(
                                'module'    => 'products',
                                'controller' => 'server',
                                'action'    => 'faq',
                                'params'    => array('format' => 'xml')
                            )
                        )
                    ),
                    array(
                        'label'     => 'Editions',
                        'module'    => 'products',
                        'controller' => 'server',
                        'action'    => 'editions'
                    ),
                    array(
                        'label'     => 'System Requirements',
                        'module'    => 'products',
                        'controller' => 'server',
                        'action'    => 'requirements'
                    )
                )
            ),
            array(
                'label'     => 'Foo Studio',
                'module'    => 'products',
                'controller' => 'studio',
                'action'    => 'index',
                'pages'     => array(
                    array(
                        'label'     => 'Customer Stories',
                        'module'    => 'products',
                        'controller' => 'studio',
                        'action'    => 'customers'
                    ),
                    array(
                        'label'     => 'Support',
                        'module'    => 'prodcts',
                        'controller' => 'studio',
                        'action'    => 'support'
                    )
                )
            )
        )
    ),
    array(
        'label'     => 'Company',
        'title'     => 'About us',
        'module'    => 'company',
        'controller' => 'about',
        'action'    => 'index',
        'pages'     => array(
            array(
```

```
                    'label'       => 'Investor Relations',
                    'module'      => 'company',
                    'controller' => 'about',
                    'action'      => 'investors'
                ),
            array(
                    'label'       => 'News',
                    'class'       => 'rss', // class
                    'module'      => 'company',
                    'controller' => 'news',
                    'action'      => 'index',
                    'pages'       => array(
                        array(
                            'label'       => 'Press Releases',
                            'module'      => 'company',
                            'controller' => 'news',
                            'action'      => 'press'
                        ),
                        array(
                            'label'       => 'Archive',
                            'route'       => 'archive', // route
                            'module'      => 'company',
                            'controller' => 'news',
                            'action'      => 'archive'
                        )
                    )
                )
            )
        ),
    array(
        'label'       => 'Community',
        'module'      => 'community',
        'controller' => 'index',
        'action'      => 'index',
        'pages'       => array(
            array(
                'label'       => 'My Account',
                'module'      => 'community',
                'controller' => 'account',
                'action'      => 'index',
                'resource'    => 'mvc:community.account' // resource
            ),
            array(
                'label' => 'Forums',
                'uri'   => 'http://forums.example.com/',
                'class' => 'external' // class
            )
        )
    ),
    array(
        'label'       => 'Administration',
        'module'      => 'admin',
        'controller' => 'index',
        'action'      => 'index',
        'resource'    => 'mvc:admin', // resource
        'pages'       => array(
            array(
                'label'       => 'Write new article',
                'module'      => 'admin',
                'controller' => 'post',
                'aciton'      => 'write'
            )
        )
    )
)
```

```
);

// Create container from array
$container = new Zend_Navigation($pages);

// Store the container in the proxy helper:
$view->getHelper('navigation')->setContainer($container);

// ...or simply:
$view->navigation($container);

// ...or store it in the reigstry:
Zend_Registry::set('Zend_Navigation', $container);
```

In addition to the container above, the following setup is assumed:

```
// Setup router (default routes and 'archive' route):
$front = Zend_Controller_Front::getInstance();
$router = $front->getRouter();
$router->addDefaultRoutes();
$router->addRoute(
    'archive',
    new Zend_Controller_Router_Route(
        '/archive/:year',
        array(
            'module'     => 'company',
            'controller' => 'news',
            'action'     => 'archive',
            'year'       => (int) date('Y') - 1
        ),
        array('year' => '\d+')
    )
);

// Setup ACL:
$acl = new Zend_Acl();
$acl->addRole(new Zend_Acl_Role('member'));
$acl->addRole(new Zend_Acl_Role('admin'));
$acl->add(new Zend_Acl_Resource('mvc:admin'));
$acl->add(new Zend_Acl_Resource('mvc:community.account'));
$acl->allow('member', 'mvc:community.account');
$acl->allow('admin', null);

// Store ACL and role in the proxy helper:
$view->navigation()->setAcl($acl)->setRole('member');

// ...or set default ACL and role statically:
Zend_View_Helper_Navigation_HelperAbstract::setDefaultAcl($acl);
Zend_View_Helper_Navigation_HelperAbstract::setDefaultRole('member');
```

Breadcrumbs Helper

Breadcrumbs are used for indicating where in a sitemap a user is currently browsing, and are typically rendered like this: "You are here: Home > Products > FantasticProduct 1.0". The breadcrumbs helper follows the guidelines from Breadcrumbs Pattern - Yahoo! Design Pattern Library [http://developer.yahoo.com/ypatterns/pattern.php?pattern=breadcrumbs], and allows simple customization (minimum/maximum depth, indentation, separator, and whether the last element should be linked), or rendering using a partial view script.

The Breadcrumbs helper works like this; it finds the deepest active page in a navigation container, and renders an upwards path to the root. For MVC pages, the "activeness" of a page is determined by inspecting the request object, as stated in the section on Zend_Navigation_Page_Mvc.

The helper sets the `minDepth` property to 1 by default, meaning breadcrumbs will not be rendered if the deepest active page is a root page. If `maxDepth` is specified, the helper will stop rendering when at the specified depth (e.g. stop at level 2 even if the deepest active page is on level 3).

Methods in the breadcrumbs helper:

- `{get|set}Separator()` gets/sets separator string that is used between breadcrumbs. Defualt is `' &gt; '`.

- `{get|set}LinkLast()` gets/sets whether the last breadcrumb should be rendered as an anchor or not. Default is `false`.

- `{get|set}Partial()` gets/sets a partial view script that should be used for rendering breadcrumbs. If a partial view script is set, the helper's `render()` method will use the `renderPartial()` method. If no partial is set, the `renderStraight()` method is used. The helper expects the partial to be a `string` or an `array` with two elements. If the partial is a `string`, it denotes the name of the partial script to use. If it is an `array`, the first element will be used as the name of the partial view script, and the second element is the module where the script is found.

- `renderStraight()` is the default render method.

- `renderPartial()` is used for rendering using a partial view script.

Example 35.24. Rendering breadcrumbs

This example shows how to render breadcrumbs with default settings.

```
In a view script or layout:
<?php echo $this->navigation()->breadcrumbs(); ?>

or if short tags are enabled:
<?= $this->navigation()->breadcrumbs(); ?>

The two calls above take advantage of the magic __toString() method,
and are equivalent to:
<?php echo $this->navigation()->breadcrumbs()->render(); ?>

Output:
<a href="/products">Products</a> &gt; <a href="/products/server">Foo
    Server</a> &gt; FAQ
```

Example 35.25. Specifying indentation

This example shows how to render breadcrumbs with initial indentation.

```
Rendering with 8 spaces indentation:
<?php echo $this->navigation()->breadcrumbs()->setIndent(8);?>

Output:
        <a href="/products">Products</a> &gt; <a href="/products/server">Foo
            Server</a> &gt; FAQ
```

Example 35.26. Customize breadcrums output

This example shows how to customze breadcrumbs output by specifying various options.

In a view script or layout:

```php
<?php
echo $this->navigation()
          ->breadcrumbs()
          ->setLinkLast(true)                       // link last page
          ->setMaxDepth(1)                          // stop at level 1
          ->setSeparator(' &#9654;' . PHP_EOL); // cool separator with
                                                              newline
?>
```

Output:

```
<a href="/products">Products</a> &#9654;
<a href="/products/server">Foo Server</a>
```

//

Setting minimum depth required to render breadcrumbs:

```php
<?php
$this->navigation()->breadcrumbs()->setMinDepth(10);
echo $this->navigation()->breadcrumbs();
?>
```

Output:
Nothing, because the deepest active page is not at level 10 or deeper.

Example 35.27. Rendering breadcrumbs using a partial view script

This example shows how to render customized breadcrumbs using a partial vew script. By calling setPartial(), you can specify a partial view script that will be used when calling render(). When a partial is specified, the renderPartial() method will be called. This method will find the deepest active page and pass an array of pages that leads to the active page to the partial view script.

In a layout:

```php
$partial = ;
echo $this->navigation()->breadcrumbs()
                        ->setPartial(array('breadcrumbs.phtml', 'default'));
```

Contents of application/modules/default/views/breadcrumbs.phtml:

```php
echo implode(', ', array_map(
        create_function('$a', 'return $a->getLabel();'),
        $this->pages));
```

Output:

```
Products, Foo Server, FAQ
```

Links Helper

The links helper is used for rendering HTML LINK elements. Links are used for describing document relationships of the currently active page. Read more about links and link types at Document relationships: the LINK element (HTML4 W3C Rec.) [http://www.w3.org/TR/html4/struct/links.html#h-12.3] and Link types (HTML4 W3C Rec.) [http://www.w3.org/TR/html4/types.html#h-6.12] in the HTML4 W3C Recommendation.

There are two types of relations; forward and reverse, indicated by the keords 'rel' and 'rev'. Most methods in the helper will take a $rel param, which must be either 'rel' or 'rev'. Most methods also take a $type param, which is used for specifying the link type (e.g. alternate, start, next, prev, chapter, etc).

Relationships can be added to page objects manually, or found by traversing the container registered in the helper. The method findRelation($page, $rel, $type) will first try to find the given $rel of $type from the $page by calling $page->findRel($type) or $page->findRel($type). If the $page has a relation that can be converted to a page instance, that relation will be used. If the $page instance doesn't have the specified $type, the helper will look for a method in the helper named searchreltype (e.g. searchRelNext() or searchRevAlternate()). If such a method exists, it will be used for determining the $page's relation by traversing the container.

Not all relations can be determined by traversing the container. These are the relations that will be found by searching:

- searchRelStart(), forward 'start' relation: the first page in the container.

- searchRelNext(), forward 'next' relation; finds the next page in the container, i.e. the page after the active page.

- searchRelPrev(), forward 'prev' relation; finds the previous page, i.e. the page before the active page.

- searchRelChapter(), forward 'chapter' relations; finds all pages on level 0 except the 'start' relation or the active page if it's on level 0.

- searchRelSection(), forward 'section' relations; finds all child pages of the active page if the active page is on level 0 (a 'chapter').

- searchRelSubsection(), forward 'subsection' relations; finds all child pages of the active page if the active pages is on level 1 (a 'section').

- searchRevSection(), reverse 'section' relation; finds the parent of the active page if the active page is on level 1 (a 'section').

- searchRevSubsection(), reverse 'subsection' relation; finds the parent of the active page if the active page is on level 2 (a 'subsection').

Note

When looking for relations in the the page instance ($page->getRel($type) or $page->getRev($type)), the helper accepts the values of type string, array, Zend_Config, or Zend_Navigation_Page. If a string is found, it will be converted to a Zend_Navigation_Page_Uri. If an array or a config is found, it will be converted to one or several page instances. If the first key of the array/config is numeric, it will be considered to contain several pages, and each element will be passed to the page factory. If the first key is not numeric, the array/config will be passed to the page factory directly, and a single page will be returned.

The helper also supports magic methods for finding relations. E.g. to find forward alternate relations, call $helper->findRelAlternate($page), and to find reverse section relations, call

```
$helper->findRevSection($page).      Those     calls    correspond      to
$helper->findRelation($page,      'rel',      'alternate');      and
$helper->findRelation($page, 'rev', 'section'); respectively.
```

To customize which relations should be rendered, the helper uses a render flag. The render flag is an integer value, and will be used in a bitwse and (&) operation [http://php.net/manual/en/language.operators.bitwise.php] against the helper's render constants to determine if the relation that belongs to the render constant should be rendered.

See the example below for more information.

- `Zend_View_Helper_Navigation_Link::RENDER_ALTERNATE`

- `Zend_View_Helper_Navigation_Link::RENDER_STYLESHEET`

- `Zend_View_Helper_Navigation_Link::RENDER_START`

- `Zend_View_Helper_Navigation_Link::RENDER_NEXT`

- `Zend_View_Helper_Navigation_Link::RENDER_PREV`

- `Zend_View_Helper_Navigation_Link::RENDER_CONTENTS`

- `Zend_View_Helper_Navigation_Link::RENDER_INDEX`

- `Zend_View_Helper_Navigation_Link::RENDER_GLOSSARY`

- `Zend_View_Helper_Navigation_Link::RENDER_COPYRIGHT`

- `Zend_View_Helper_Navigation_Link::RENDER_CHAPTER`

- `Zend_View_Helper_Navigation_Link::RENDER_SECTION`

- `Zend_View_Helper_Navigation_Link::RENDER_SUBSECTION`

- `Zend_View_Helper_Navigation_Link::RENDER_APPENDIX`

- `Zend_View_Helper_Navigation_Link::RENDER_HELP`

- `Zend_View_Helper_Navigation_Link::RENDER_BOOKMARK`

- `Zend_View_Helper_Navigation_Link::RENDER_CUSTOM`

- `Zend_View_Helper_Navigation_Link::RENDER_ALL`

The constants from RENDER_ALTERNATE to RENDER_BOOKMARK denote standard HTML link types. RENDER_CUSTOM denotes non-standard relations that specified in pages. RENDER_ALL denotes standard and non-standard relations.

Methods in the links helper:

- `{get|set}RenderFlag()` gets/sets the render flag. Default is RENDER_ALL. See examples below on how to set the render flag.

- `findAllRelations()` finds all relations of all types for a given page.

- `findRelation()` finds all relations of a given type from a given page.

- `searchRel{Start|Next|Prev|Chapter|Section|Subsection}()` traverses a container to find forward relations to the start page, the next page, the previous page, chapters, sections, and subsections.

- `searchRev{Section|Subsection}()` traverses a container to find reverse relations to sections or subsections.

- renderLink() renders a single link element.

Example 35.28. Specify relations in pages

This example shows how to specify relations in pages.

```
$container = new Zend_Navigation(array(
    array(
        'label' => 'Relations using strings',
        'rel'   => array(
            'alternate' => 'http://www.example.org/'
        ),
        'rev'   => array(
            'alternate' => 'http://www.example.net/'
        )
    ),
    array(
        'label' => 'Relations using arrays',
        'rel'   => array(
            'alternate' => array(
                'label' => 'Example.org',
                'uri'   => 'http://www.example.org/'
            )
        )
    ),
    array(
        'label' => 'Relations using configs',
        'rel'   => array(
            'alternate' => new Zend_Config(array(
                'label' => 'Example.org',
                'uri'   => 'http://www.example.org/'
            ))
        )
    ),
    array(
        'label' => 'Relations using pages instance',
        'rel'   => array(
            'alternate' => Zend_Navigation_Page::factory(array(
                'label' => 'Example.org',
                'uri'   => 'http://www.example.org/'
            ))
        )
    )
));
```

Example 35.29. Default rendering of links

This example shows how to render a menu from a container registered/found in the view helper.

```
In a view script or layout:
<?php echo $this->view->navigation()->links(); ?>

Output:
<link rel="alternate" href="/products/server/faq/format/xml">
<link rel="start" href="/" title="Home">
<link rel="next" href="/products/server/editions" title="Editions">
<link rel="prev" href="/products/server" title="Foo Server">
```

```
<link rel="chapter" href="/products" title="Products">
<link rel="chapter" href="/company/about" title="Company">
<link rel="chapter" href="/community" title="Community">
<link rel="canonical" href="http://www.example.com/?page=server-faq">
<link rev="subsection" href="/products/server" title="Foo Server">
```

Example 35.30. Specify which relations to render

This example shows how to specify which relations to find and render.

```
Render only start, next, and prev:
$helper->setRenderFlag(Zend_View_Helper_Navigation_Links::RENDER_START |
                       Zend_View_Helper_Navigation_Links::RENDER_NEXT |
                       Zend_View_Helper_Navigation_Links::RENDER_PREV);

Output:
<link rel="start" href="/" title="Home">
<link rel="next" href="/products/server/editions" title="Editions">
<link rel="prev" href="/products/server" title="Foo Server">
```

```
Render only native link types:
$helper->setRenderFlag(Zend_View_Helper_Navigation_Links::RENDER_ALL ^
                       Zend_View_Helper_Navigation_Links::RENDER_CUSTOM);

Output:
<link rel="alternate" href="/products/server/faq/format/xml">
<link rel="start" href="/" title="Home">
<link rel="next" href="/products/server/editions" title="Editions">
<link rel="prev" href="/products/server" title="Foo Server">
<link rel="chapter" href="/products" title="Products">
<link rel="chapter" href="/company/about" title="Company">
<link rel="chapter" href="/community" title="Community">
<link rev="subsection" href="/products/server" title="Foo Server">
```

```
Render all but chapter:
$helper->setRenderFlag(Zend_View_Helper_Navigation_Links::RENDER_ALL ^
                       Zend_View_Helper_Navigation_Links::RENDER_CHAPTER);

Output:
<link rel="alternate" href="/products/server/faq/format/xml">
<link rel="start" href="/" title="Home">
<link rel="next" href="/products/server/editions" title="Editions">
<link rel="prev" href="/products/server" title="Foo Server">
<link rel="canonical" href="http://www.example.com/?page=server-faq">
<link rev="subsection" href="/products/server" title="Foo Server">
```

Menu Helper

The Menu helper is used for rendering menus from navigation containers. By default, the menu will be rendered using HTML UL and LI tags, but the helper also allows using a partial view script.

Methods in the Menu helper:

- {get|set}UlClass() gets/sets the CSS class used in renderMenu().

- {get|set}OnlyActiveBranch() gets/sets a flag specifying whether only the active branch of a container should be rendered.

- {get|set}RenderParents() gets/sets a flag specifying whether parents should be rendered when only rendering active branch of a container. If set to false, only the deepest active menu will be rendered.

- {get|set}Partial() gets/sets a partial view script that should be used for rendering menu. If a partial view script is set, the helper's render() method will use the renderPartial() method. If no partial is set, the renderMenu() method is used. The helper expects the partial to be a string or an array with two elements. If the partial is a string, it denotes the name of the partial script to use. If it is an array, the first element will be used as the name of the partial view script, and the second element is the module where the script is found.

- htmlify() overrides the method from the abstract class to return span elements if the page has no href.

- renderMenu($container = null, $options = array()) is the default render method, and will render a container as a HTML UL list.

  If $container is not given, the container registered in the helper will be rendered.

  $options is used for overriding options specified temporarily without rsetting the values in the helper instance. It is an associative array where each key corresponds to an option in the helper.

  Recognized options:

  - indent; indentation. Expects a string or an int value.

  - minDepth; minimum depth. Expcects an int or null (no minimum depth).

  - maxDepth; maximum depth. Expcects an int or null (no maximum depth).

  - ulClass; CSS class for ul element. Expects a string.

  - onlyActiveBranch; whether only active branch should be rendered. Expects a boolean value.

  - renderParents; whether parents should be rendered if only rendering active branch. Expects a boolean value.

  If an option is not given, the value set in the helper will be used.

- renderPartial() is used for rendering the menu using a partial view script.

- renderSubMenu() renders the deepest menu level of a container's active branch.

Example 35.31. Rendering a menu

This example shows how to render a menu from a container registered/found in the view helper. Notice how pages are filtered out based on visibility and ACL.

```
In a view script or layout:
<?php echo $this->navigation()->menu()->render() ?>

Or simply:
<?php echo $this->navigation()->menu() ?>

Or if short tags are enabled:
<?= $this->navigation()->menu() ?>

Output:
```

```
<ul class="navigation">
    <li>
        <a title="Go Home" href="/">Home</a>
    </li>
    <li class="active">
        <a href="/products">Products</a>
        <ul>
            <li class="active">
                <a href="/products/server">Foo Server</a>
                <ul>
                    <li class="active">
                        <a href="/products/server/faq">FAQ</a>
                    </li>
                    <li>
                        <a href="/products/server/editions">Editions</a>
                    </li>
                    <li>
                        <a href="/products/server/requirements">System
                            Requirements</a>
                    </li>
                </ul>
            </li>
            <li>
                <a href="/products/studio">Foo Studio</a>
                <ul>
                    <li>
                        <a href="/products/studio/customers">Customer
                            Stories</a>
                    </li>
                    <li>
                        <a href="/prodcts/studio/support">Support</a>
                    </li>
                </ul>
            </li>
        </ul>
    </li>
    <li>
        <a title="About us" href="/company/about">Company</a>
        <ul>
            <li>
                <a href="/company/about/investors">Investor Relations</a>
            </li>
            <li>
                <a class="rss" href="/company/news">News</a>
                <ul>
                    <li>
                        <a href="/company/news/press">Press Releases</a>
                    </li>
                    <li>
                        <a href="/archive">Archive</a>
                    </li>
                </ul>
            </li>
        </ul>
    </li>
    <li>
        <a href="/community">Community</a>
        <ul>
            <li>
                <a href="/community/account">My Account</a>
            </li>
            <li>
                <a class="external" href="http://forums.example
                    .com/">Forums</a>
```

```
                    </li>
                </ul>
            </li>
        </ul>
```

Example 35.32. Calling renderMenu() directly

This example shows how to render a menu that is not registered in the view helper by calling the
renderMenu() directly and specifying a few options.

```php
<?php
// render only the 'Community' menu
$community = $this->navigation()->findOneByLabel('Community');
$options = array(
    'indent'  => 16,
    'ulClass' => 'community'
);
echo $this->navigation()
        ->menu()
        ->renderMenu($community, $options);
?>
Output:
                <ul class="community">
                    <li>
                        <a href="/community/account">My Account</a>
                    </li>
                    <li>
                        <a class="external" href="http://forums.example.com/'
                            Forums</a>
                    </li>
                </ul>
```

Example 35.33. Rendering the deepest active menu

This example shows how the renderSubMenu() will render the deepest sub menu of the active
branch.

Calling renderSubMenu($container, $ulClass, $indent) is equivalent to calling
renderMenu($container, $options) with the following options: array('ulClass' =>
$ulClass, 'indent' => $indent, 'minDepth' => null, 'maxDepth' => null,
'onlyActiveBranch' => true, 'renderParents' => false)

```php
<?php
echo $this->navigation()
        ->menu()
        ->renderSubMenu(null, 'sidebar', 4);
?>
```

```
The output will be the same if 'FAQ' or 'Foo Server' is active:
    <ul class="sidebar">
        <li class="active">
            <a href="/products/server/faq">FAQ</a>
        </li>
        <li>
            <a href="/products/server/editions">Editions</a>
```

```
            </li>
            <li>
                <a href="/products/server/requirements">System
                        Requirements</a>
            </li>
        </ul>
```

Example 35.34. Rendering a menu with maximum depth

```php
<?php
echo $this->navigation()
            ->menu()
            ->setMaxDepth(1);
?>
```

```
Output:
<ul class="navigation">
    <li>
        <a title="Go Home" href="/">Home</a>
    </li>
    <li class="active">
        <a href="/products">Products</a>
        <ul>
            <li class="active">
                <a href="/products/server">Foo Server</a>
            </li>
            <li>
                <a href="/products/studio">Foo Studio</a>
            </li>
        </ul>
    </li>
    <li>
        <a title="About us" href="/company/about">Company</a>
        <ul>
            <li>
                <a href="/company/about/investors">Investor Relations</a>
            </li>
            <li>
                <a class="rss" href="/company/news">News</a>
            </li>
        </ul>
    </li>
    <li>
        <a href="/community">Community</a>
        <ul>
            <li>
                <a href="/community/account">My Account</a>
            </li>
            <li>
                <a class="external" href="http://forums.example.com/">
                        Forums</a>
            </li>
        </ul>
    </li>
</ul>
```

Example 35.35. Rendering a menu with minimum depth

```php
<?php
echo $this->navigation()
        ->menu()
        ->setMinDepth(1);
?>
```

```
Output:
<ul class="navigation">
    <li class="active">
        <a href="/products/server">Foo Server</a>
        <ul>
            <li class="active">
                <a href="/products/server/faq">FAQ</a>
            </li>
            <li>
                <a href="/products/server/editions">Editions</a>
            </li>
            <li>
                <a href="/products/server/requirements">System
                    Requirements</a>
            </li>
        </ul>
    </li>
    <li>
        <a href="/products/studio">Foo Studio</a>
        <ul>
            <li>
                <a href="/products/studio/customers">Customer Stories</a>
            </li>
            <li>
                <a href="/prodcts/studio/support">Support</a>
            </li>
        </ul>
    </li>
    <li>
        <a href="/company/about/investors">Investor Relations</a>
    </li>
    <li>
        <a class="rss" href="/company/news">News</a>
        <ul>
            <li>
                <a href="/company/news/press">Press Releases</a>
            </li>
            <li>
                <a href="/archive">Archive</a>
            </li>
        </ul>
    </li>
    <li>
        <a href="/community/account">My Account</a>
    </li>
    <li>
        <a class="external" href="http://forums.example.com/">Forums</a>
    </li>
</ul>
```

Example 35.36. Rendering only the active branch of a menu

```
<?php
echo $this->navigation()
        ->menu()
        ->setOnlyActiveBranch(true);
?>

Output:
<ul class="navigation">
    <li class="active">
        <a href="/products">Products</a>
        <ul>
            <li class="active">
                <a href="/products/server">Foo Server</a>
                <ul>
                    <li class="active">
                        <a href="/products/server/faq">FAQ</a>
                    </li>
                    <li>
                        <a href="/products/server/editions">Editions</a>
                    </li>
                    <li>
                        <a href="/products/server/requirements">System
                            Requirements</a>
                    </li>
                </ul>
            </li>
        </ul>
    </li>
</ul>
```

Example 35.37. Rendering only the active branch of a menu with minimum depth

```
<?php
echo $this->navigation()
        ->menu()
        ->setOnlyActiveBranch(true)
        ->setMinDepth(1);
?>

Output:
<ul class="navigation">
    <li class="active">
        <a href="/products/server">Foo Server</a>
        <ul>
            <li class="active">
                <a href="/products/server/faq">FAQ</a>
            </li>
            <li>
                <a href="/products/server/editions">Editions</a>
            </li>
            <li>
                <a href="/products/server/requirements">System
                    Requirements</a>
            </li>
```

```
        </ul>
      </li>
</ul>
```

Example 35.38. Rendering only the active branch of a menu with maximum depth

```php
<?php
echo $this->navigation()
          ->menu()
          ->setOnlyActiveBranch(true)
          ->setMaxDepth(1);
?>

Output:
<ul class="navigation">
    <li class="active">
        <a href="/products">Products</a>
        <ul>
            <li class="active">
                <a href="/products/server">Foo Server</a>
            </li>
            <li>
                <a href="/products/studio">Foo Studio</a>
            </li>
        </ul>
    </li>
</ul>
```

Example 35.39. Rendering only the active branch of a menu with maximum depth and no parents

```php
<?php
echo $this->navigation()
          ->menu()
          ->setOnlyActiveBranch(true)
          ->setRenderParents(false)
          ->setMaxDepth(1);
?>

Output:
<ul class="navigation">
    <li class="active">
        <a href="/products/server">Foo Server</a>
    </li>
    <li>
        <a href="/products/studio">Foo Studio</a>
    </li>
</ul>
```

Example 35.40. Rendering a custom menu using a partial view script

This example shows how to render a custom menu using a partial vew script. By calling `setPartial()`, you can specify a partial view script that will be used when calling `render()`. When a partial is specified, the `renderPartial()` method will be called. This method will assign the container to the view with the key `container`.

In a layout:

```
$partial = array('menu.phtml', 'default');
$this->navigation()->menu()->setPartial($partial);
echo $this->navigation()->menu()->render();
```

In application/modules/default/views/menu.phtml:

```
foreach ($this->container as $page) {
    echo $this->menu()->htmlify($page), PHP_EOL;
}
```

Output:

```
<a title="Go Home" href="/">Home</a>
<a href="/products">Products</a>
<a title="About us" href="/company/about">Company</a>
<a href="/community">Community</a>
```

Sitemap Helper

The Sitemap helper is used for generating XML sitemaps, as defined by the Sitemaps XML format [http://www.sitemaps.org/protocol.php]. Read more about Sitemaps on Wikpedia [http://en.wikipedia.org/wiki/Sitemaps].

By default, the sitemap helper uses sitemap validators to validate each element that is rendered. This can be disabled by calling `$helper->setUseSitemapValidators(false)`.

Note

If you disable sitemap validators, the custom properties (see table) are not validated at all.

The sitemap helper also supports Sitemap XSD Schema [http://www.sitemaps.org/schemas/sitemap/0.9/sitemap.xsd] validation of the generated sitemap. This is disabled by default, since it will require a request to the Schema file. It can be enabled with `$helper->setUseSchemaValidation(true)`.

Table 35.1. Sitemap XML elements

Element	Description
loc	Absolute URL to page. An absolute URL will be generated by the helper.
lastmod	The date of last modification of the file, in W3C Datetime [http://www.w3.org/TR/NOTE-datetime] format. This time portion can be omitted if desired, and only use YYYY-MM-DD.

Element	Description
	The helper will try to retrieve the `lastmod` value from the page's custom property `lastmod` if it is set in the page. If the value is not a valid date, it is ignored.
changefreq	How frequently the page is likely to change. This value provides general information to search engines and may not correlate exactly to how often they crawl the page. Valid values are: • always • hourly • daily • weekly • monthly • yearly • never The helper will try to retrieve the `changefreq` value from the page's custom property `changefreq` if it is set in the page. If the value is not valid, it is ignored.
priority	The priority of this URL relative to other URLs on your site. Valid values range from 0.0 to 1.0. The helper will try to retrieve the `priority` value from the page's custom property `priority` if it is set in the page. If the value is not valid, it is ignored.

Methods in the sitemap helper:

- `{get|set}FormatOutput()` gets/sets a flag indicating whether XML output should be formatted. This corresponds to the `formatOutput` property of the native `DOMDocument` class. Read more at PHP: DOMDocument - Manual [http://php.net/domdocument]. Default is `false`.

- `{get|set}UseXmlDeclaration()` gets/sets a flag indicating whether the XML declaration should be included when rendering. Default is `true`.

- `{get|set}UseSitemapValidators()` gets/sets a flag indicating whether sitemap validators should be used when generating the DOM sitemap. Default is `true`.

- `{get|set}UseSchemaValidation()` gets/sets a flag indicating whether the helper should use XML Schema validation when generating the DOM sitemap. Default is `false`. If `true`.

- `{get|set}ServerUrl()` gets/sets server URL that will be prepended to non-absolute URLs in the `url()` method. If no server URL is specified, it will be determined by the helper.

- `url()` is used to generate absolute URLs to pages.

- `getDomSitemap()` generates a DOMDocument from a given container.

Example 35.41. Rendering an XML sitemap

This example shows how to render an XML sitemap based on the setup we did further up.

```
// In a view script or layout:

// format output
$this->navigation()
        ->sitemap()
        ->setFormatOutput(true); // default is false

// other possible methods:
// ->setUseXmlDeclaration(false); // default is true
// ->setServerUrl('http://my.otherhost.com');
// default is to detect automatically

// print sitemap
echo $this->navigation()->sitemap();
```

Notice how pages that are invisible or pages with ACL roles incompatible with the view helper are filtered out:

```
<urlset xmlns="http://www.sitemaps.org/schemas/sitemap/0.9">
  <url>
    <loc>http://www.example.com/</loc>
  </url>
  <url>
    <loc>http://www.example.com/products</loc>
  </url>
  <url>
    <loc>http://www.example.com/products/server</loc>
  </url>
  <url>
    <loc>http://www.example.com/products/server/faq</loc>
  </url>
  <url>
    <loc>http://www.example.com/products/server/editions</loc>
  </url>
  <url>
    <loc>http://www.example.com/products/server/requirements</loc>
  </url>
  <url>
    <loc>http://www.example.com/products/studio</loc>
  </url>
  <url>
    <loc>http://www.example.com/products/studio/customers</loc>
  </url>
  <url>
    <loc>http://www.example.com/prodcts/studio/support</loc>
  </url>
  <url>
    <loc>http://www.example.com/company/about</loc>
  </url>
  <url>
    <loc>http://www.example.com/company/about/investors</loc>
  </url>
  <url>
    <loc>http://www.example.com/company/news</loc>
  </url>
  <url>
    <loc>http://www.example.com/company/news/press</loc>
```

```
    </url>
    <url>
      <loc>http://www.example.com/archive</loc>
    </url>
    <url>
      <loc>http://www.example.com/community</loc>
    </url>
    <url>
      <loc>http://www.example.com/community/account</loc>
    </url>
    <url>
      <loc>http://forums.example.com/</loc>
    </url>
</urlset>
```

Render the sitemap using no ACL role (should filter out /community/account):

```
echo $this->navigation()
          ->sitemap()
          ->setFormatOutput(true)
          ->setRole();
```

```
<urlset xmlns="http://www.sitemaps.org/schemas/sitemap/0.9">
  <url>
    <loc>http://www.example.com/</loc>
  </url>
  <url>
    <loc>http://www.example.com/products</loc>
  </url>
  <url>
    <loc>http://www.example.com/products/server</loc>
  </url>
  <url>
    <loc>http://www.example.com/products/server/faq</loc>
  </url>
  <url>
    <loc>http://www.example.com/products/server/editions</loc>
  </url>
  <url>
    <loc>http://www.example.com/products/server/requirements</loc>
  </url>
  <url>
    <loc>http://www.example.com/products/studio</loc>
  </url>
  <url>
    <loc>http://www.example.com/products/studio/customers</loc>
  </url>
  <url>
    <loc>http://www.example.com/prodcts/studio/support</loc>
  </url>
  <url>
    <loc>http://www.example.com/company/about</loc>
  </url>
  <url>
    <loc>http://www.example.com/company/about/investors</loc>
  </url>
  <url>
    <loc>http://www.example.com/company/news</loc>
  </url>
  <url>
    <loc>http://www.example.com/company/news/press</loc>
  </url>
```

```
  <url>
    <loc>http://www.example.com/archive</loc>
  </url>
  <url>
    <loc>http://www.example.com/community</loc>
  </url>
  <url>
    <loc>http://forums.example.com/</loc>
  </url>
</urlset>
```

Render the sitemap using a maximum depth of 1.

```
echo $this->navigation()
          ->sitemap()
          ->setFormatOutput(true)
          ->setMaxDepth(1);
```

```
<urlset xmlns="http://www.sitemaps.org/schemas/sitemap/0.9">
  <url>
    <loc>http://www.example.com/</loc>
  </url>
  <url>
    <loc>http://www.example.com/products</loc>
  </url>
  <url>
    <loc>http://www.example.com/products/server</loc>
  </url>
  <url>
    <loc>http://www.example.com/products/studio</loc>
  </url>
  <url>
    <loc>http://www.example.com/company/about</loc>
  </url>
  <url>
    <loc>http://www.example.com/company/about/investors</loc>
  </url>
  <url>
    <loc>http://www.example.com/company/news</loc>
  </url>
  <url>
    <loc>http://www.example.com/community</loc>
  </url>
  <url>
    <loc>http://www.example.com/community/account</loc>
  </url>
  <url>
    <loc>http://forums.example.com/</loc>
  </url>
</urlset>
```

Navigation Helper

The Navigation helper is a proxy helper that relays calls to other navigational helpers. It can be considered an entry point to all navigation-related view tasks. The aforementioned navigational helpers are in the namespace Zend_View_Helper_Navigation, and would thus require the path Zend/View/Helper/Navigation to be added as a helper path to the view. With the proxy helper residing in the Zend_View_Helper namespace, it will always be available, without the need to add any helper paths to the view.

The Navigation helper finds other helpers that implement the `Zend_View_Helper_Navigation_Helper` interface, which means custom view helpers can also be proxied. This would, however, require that the custom helper path is added to the view.

When proxying to other helpers, the Navigation helper can inject its container, ACL/role, and translator. This means that you won't have to explicitly set all three in all navigational helpers, nor resort to injecting by means of `Zend_Registry` or static methods.

- `findHelper()` finds the given helper, verifies that it is a navigational helper, and injects container, ACL/role and translator.

- `{get|set}InjectContainer()` gets/sets a flag indicating whether the container should be injected to proxied helpers. Default is `true`.

- `{get|set}InjectAcl()` gets/sets a flag indicating whether the ACL/role should be injected to proxied helpers. Default is `true`.

- `{get|set}InjectTranslator()` gets/sets a flag indicating whether the translator should be injected to proxied helpers. Default is `true`.

- `{get|set}DefaultProxy()` gets/sets the default proxy. Default is `'menu'`.

- `render()` proxies to the render method of the default proxy.

Translate Helper

Often web sites are available in several languages. To translate the content of a site you should simply use Zend Translate and to integrate `Zend Translate` within your view you should use the `Translate` View Helper.

In all following examples we are using the simple Array Translation Adapter. Of course you can also use any instance of `Zend_Translate` and also any subclasses of `Zend_Translate_Adapter`. There are several ways to initiate the `Translate` View Helper:

- Registered, through a previously registered instance in `Zend_Registry`

- Afterwards, through the fluent interface

- Directly, through initiating the class

A registered instance of `Zend_Translate` is the preferred usage for this helper. You can also select the locale to be used simply before you add the adapter to the registry.

Note

We are speaking of locales instead of languages because a language also may contain a region. For example English is spoken in different dialects. There may be a translation for British and one for American English. Therefore, we say "locale" instead of "language."

Example 35.42. Registered instance

To use a registered instance just create an instance of `Zend_Translate` or `Zend_Translate_Adapter` and register it within `Zend_Registry` using `Zend_Translate` as its key.

```
// our example adapter
$adapter = new Zend_Translate('array', array('simple' => 'einfach'), 'de');
Zend_Registry::set('Zend_Translate', $adapter);

// within your view
```

```
echo $this->translate('simple');
// this returns 'einfach'
```

If you are more familiar with the fluent interface, then you can also create an instance within your view and initiate the helper afterwards.

Example 35.43. Within the view

To use the fluent interface, create an instance of `Zend_Translate` or `Zend_Translate_Adapter`, call the helper without a parameter, and call the `setTranslator()` method.

```
// within your view
$adapter = new Zend_Translate('array', array('simple' => 'einfach'), 'de');
$this->translate()->setTranslator($adapter)->translate('simple');
// this returns 'einfach'
```

If you are using the helper without `Zend_View` then you can also use it directly.

Example 35.44. Direct usage

```
// our example adapter
$adapter = new Zend_Translate('array', array('simple' => 'einfach'), 'de');

// initiate the adapter
$translate = new Zend_View_Helper_Translate($adapter);
print $translate->translate('simple'); // this returns 'einfach'
```

You would use this way if you are not working with `Zend_View` and need to create translated output.

As already seen, the `translate()` method is used to return the translation. Just call it with the needed messageid of your translation adapter. But it can also replace parameters within the translation string. Therefore, it accepts variable parameters in two ways: either as a list of parameters, or as an array of parameters. As examples:

Example 35.45. Single parameter

To use a single parameter just add it to the method.

```
// within your view
$date = "Monday";
$this->translate("Today is %1\$s", $date);
// could return 'Heute ist Monday'
```

Note

Keep in mind that if you are using parameters which are also text, you may also need to translate these parameters.

Example 35.46. List of parameters

Or use a list of parameters and add it to the method.

```
// within your view
$date = "Monday";
$month = "April";
$time = "11:20:55";
$this->translate("Today is %1\$s in %2\$s. Actual time: %3\$s",
                 $date,
                 $month,
                 $time);
// Could return 'Heute ist Monday in April. Aktuelle Zeit: 11:20:55'
```

Example 35.47. Array of parameters

Or use an array of parameters and add it to the method.

```
// within your view
$date = array("Monday", "April", "11:20:55");
$this->translate("Today is %1\$s in %2\$s. Actual time: %3\$s", $date);
// Could return 'Heute ist Monday in April. Aktuelle Zeit: 11:20:55'
```

Sometimes it is necessary to change the locale of the translation. This can be done either dynamically per translation or statically for all following translations. And you can use it with both a parameter list and an array of parameters. In both cases the locale must be given as the last single parameter.

Example 35.48. Change locale dynamically

```
// within your view
$date = array("Monday", "April", "11:20:55");
$this->translate("Today is %1\$s in %2\$s. Actual time: %3\$s", $date, 'it');
```

This example returns the Italian translation for the messageid. But it will only be used once. The next translation will use the locale from the adapter. Normally you will set the desired locale within the translation adapter before you add it to the registry. But you can also set the locale from within the helper:

Example 35.49. Change locale statically

```
// within your view
$date = array("Monday", "April", "11:20:55");
$this->translate()->setLocale('it');
$this->translate("Today is %1\$s in %2\$s. Actual time: %3\$s", $date);
```

The above example sets 'it' as the new default locale which will be used for all further translations.

Of course there is also a getLocale() method to get the currently set locale.

Example 35.50. Get the currently set locale

```
// within your view
$date = array("Monday", "April", "11:20:55");

// returns 'de' as set default locale from our above examples
$this->translate()->getLocale();

$this->translate()->setLocale('it');
$this->translate("Today is %1\$s in %2\$s. Actual time: %3\$s", $date);

// returns 'it' as new set default locale
$this->translate()->getLocale();
```

Helper Paths

As with view scripts, your controller can specify a stack of paths for Zend_View to search for helper classes. By default, Zend_View looks in "Zend/View/Helper/*" for helper classes. You can tell Zend_View to look in other locations using the setHelperPath() and addHelperPath() methods. Additionally, you can indicate a class prefix to use for helpers in the path provided, to allow namespacing your helper classes. By default, if no class prefix is provided, 'Zend_View_Helper_' is assumed.

```
$view = new Zend_View();

// Set path to /path/to/more/helpers, with prefix 'My_View_Helper'
$view->setHelperPath('/path/to/more/helpers', 'My_View_Helper');
```

In fact, you can "stack" paths using the addHelperPath() method. As you add paths to the stack, Zend_View will look at the most-recently-added path for the requested helper class. This allows you to add to (or even override) the initial distribution of helpers with your own custom helpers.

```
$view = new Zend_View();
// Add /path/to/some/helpers with class prefix 'My_View_Helper'
$view->addHelperPath('/path/to/some/helpers', 'My_View_Helper');
// Add /other/path/to/helpers with class prefix 'Your_View_Helper'
$view->addHelperPath('/other/path/to/helpers', 'Your_View_Helper');

// now when you call $this->helperName(), Zend_View will look first for
// "/path/to/some/helpers/HelperName" using class name
// "Your_View_Helper_HelperName", then for
// "/other/path/to/helpers/HelperName.php" using class name
// "My_View_Helper_HelperName", and finally for
// "Zend/View/Helper/HelperName.php" using class name
// "Zend_View_Helper_HelperName".
```

Writing Custom Helpers

Writing custom helpers is easy; just follow these rules:

- While not strictly necessary, we recommend either implementing Zend_View_Helper_Interface or extending Zend_View_Helper_Abstract when creating your helpers. Introduced in 1.6.0, these simply define a setView() method; however, in upcoming releases, we plan to implement a strategy pattern that will simplify much of the naming schema detailed below. Building off these now will help you future-proof your code.

- The class name must, at the very minimum, end with the helper name itself, using MixedCaps. E.g., if you were writing a helper called "specialPurpose", the class name would minimally need to be "SpecialPurpose". You may, and should, give the class name a prefix, and it is recommended that you use 'View_Helper' as part of that prefix: "My_View_Helper_SpecialPurpose". (You will need to pass in the prefix, with or without the trailing underscore, to addHelperPath() or setHelperPath()).

- The class must have a public method that matches the helper name; this is the method that will be called when your template calls "$this->specialPurpose()". In our "specialPurpose" helper example, the required method declaration would be "public function specialPurpose()".

- In general, the class should not echo or print or otherwise generate output. Instead, it should return values to be printed or echoed. The returned values should be escaped appropriately.

- The class must be in a file named after the helper class. Again using our "specialPurpose" helper example, the file has to be named "SpecialPurpose.php".

Place the helper class file somewhere in your helper path stack, and Zend_View will automatically load, instantiate, persist, and execute it for you.

Here is an example of our SpecialPurpose helper code:

```
class My_View_Helper_SpecialPurpose extends Zend_View_Helper_Abstract
{
    protected $_count = 0;
    public function specialPurpose()
    {
        $this->_count++;
        $output = "I have seen 'The Jerk' {$this->_count} time(s).";
        return htmlspecialchars($output);
    }
}
```

Then in a view script, you can call the SpecialPurpose helper as many times as you like; it will be instantiated once, and then it persists for the life of that Zend_View instance.

```
// remember, in a view script, $this refers to the Zend_View instance.
echo $this->specialPurpose();
echo $this->specialPurpose();
echo $this->specialPurpose();
```

The output would look something like this:

```
I have seen 'The Jerk' 1 time(s).
I have seen 'The Jerk' 2 time(s).
I have seen 'The Jerk' 3 time(s).
```

Sometimes you will need access to the calling Zend_View object -- for instance, if you need to use the registered encoding, or want to render another view script as part of your helper. To get access to the view object, your helper class should have a setView($view) method, like the following:

```
class My_View_Helper_ScriptPath
{
    public $view;

    public function setView(Zend_View_Interface $view)
    {
        $this->view = $view;
```

```
    }

    public function scriptPath($script)
    {
        return $this->view->getScriptPath($script);
    }
}
```

If your helper class has a `setView()` method, it will be called when the helper class is first instantiated, and passed the current view object. It is up to you to persist the object in your class, as well as determine how it should be accessed.

If you are extending `Zend_View_Helper_Abstract`, you do not need to define this method, as it is defined for you.

Zend_View_Abstract

`Zend_View_Abstract` is the base class on which `Zend_View` is built; `Zend_View` itself simply extends it and declares a concrete implementation of the `_run()` method (which is invoked by `render()`).

Many developers find that they want to extend `Zend_View_Abstract` to add custom functionality, and inevitably run into issues with its design, which includes a number of private members. This document aims to explain the decision behind the design.

`Zend_View` is something of an anti-templating engine in that it uses PHP natively for its templating. As a result, all of PHP is available, and view scripts inherit the scope of their calling object.

It is this latter point that is salient to the design decisions. Internally, `Zend_View::_run()` does the following:

```
protected function _run()
{
    include func_get_arg(0);
}
```

As such, the view scripts have access to the current object (`$this`), *and any methods or members of that object*. Since many operations depend on members with limited visibility, this poses a problem: the view scripts could potentially make calls to such methods or modify critical properties directly. Imagine a script overwriting `$_path` or `$_file` inadvertently -- any further calls to `render()` or view helpers would break!

Fortunately, PHP 5 has an answer to this with its visibility declarations: private members are not accessible by objects extending a given class. This led to the current design: since `Zend_View` *extends* `Zend_View_Abstract`, view scripts are thus limited to only protected or public methods and members of `Zend_View_Abstract` -- effectively limiting the actions it can perform, and allowing us to secure critical areas from abuse by view scripts.

Migrating from Previous Versions

This chapter documents primarily backwards compatibility breaks made in Zend_View, and should serve to aid in migration from previous versions.

Migrating from versions prior to 1.7.5

Prior to the 1.7.5 release, the Zend Framework team was notified of a potential Local File Inclusion (LFI) vulnerability in the `Zend_View::render()` method. Prior to 1.7.5, the method allowed, by default, the ability to specify view scripts that included parent directory notation (e.g., "../" or "..\"). This opens the possibility for an LFI attack if unfiltered user input is passed to the `render()` method:

```
// Where $_GET['foobar'] = '../../../../etc/passwd'
echo $view->render($_GET['foobar']); // LFI inclusion
```

`Zend_View` now by default raises an exception when such a view script is requested.

Disabling LFI protection for the render() method

Since a number of developers reported that they were using such notation within their applications that was *not* the result of user input, a special flag was created to allow disabling the default protection. You have two methods for doing so: by passing the 'lfiProtectionOn' key to the constructor options, or by explicitly calling the `setLfiProtection()` method.

```
// Disabling via constructor
$view = new Zend_View(array('lfiProtectionOn' => false));

// Disabling via exlicit method call:
$view = new Zend_View();
$view->setLfiProtection(false);
```

Chapter 36. Zend_Wildfire

Zend_Wildfire

`Zend_Wildfire` is a component that facilitates communication between PHP code and Wildfire [http://www.wildfirehq.org/] client components.

The purpose of the Wildfire Project is to develop standardized communication channels between a large variety of components and a dynamic and scriptable plugin architecture. At this time the primary focus is to provide a system to allow server-side PHP code to inject logging messages into the Firebug [http://www.getfirebug.com/] Console [http://getfirebug.com/logging.html].

For the purpose of logging to Firebug the `Zend_Log_Writer_Firebug` component is provided and a communication protocol has been developed that uses HTTP request and response headers to send data between the server and client components. It is great for logging intelligence data, generated during script execution, to the browser without interfering with the page content. Debugging AJAX requests that require clean JSON and XML responses is possible with this approach.

There is also a `Zend_Db_Profiler_Firebug` component to log database profiling information to Firebug.

Chapter 37. Zend_XmlRpc

Introduction

From its home page [http://www.xmlrpc.com/], XML-RPC is described as a "...remote procedure calling using HTTP as the transport and XML as the encoding. XML-RPC is designed to be as simple as possible, while allowing complex data structures to be transmitted, processed and returned."

Zend Framework provides support for both consuming remote XML-RPC services and building new XML-RPC servers.

Zend_XmlRpc_Client

Introduction

Zend Framework provides support for consuming remote XML-RPC services as a client in the `Zend_XmlRpc_Client` package. Its major features include automatic type conversion between PHP and XML-RPC, a server proxy object, and access to server introspection capabilities.

Method Calls

The constructor of `Zend_XmlRpc_Client` receives the URL of the remote XML-RPC server endpoint as its first parameter. The new instance returned may be used to call any number of remote methods at that endpoint.

To call a remote method with the XML-RPC client, instantiate it and use the `call()` instance method. The code sample below uses a demonstration XML-RPC server on the Zend Framework website. You can use it for testing or exploring the `Zend_XmlRpc` components.

Example 37.1. XML-RPC Method Call

```
$client = new Zend_XmlRpc_Client('http://framework.zend.com/xmlrpc');

echo $client->call('test.sayHello');

// hello
```

The XML-RPC value returned from the remote method call will be automatically unmarshaled and cast to the equivalent PHP native type. In the example above, a PHP `string` is returned and is immediately ready to be used.

The first parameter of the `call()` method receives the name of the remote method to call. If the remote method requires any parameters, these can be sent by supplying a second, optional parameter to `call()` with an `array` of values to pass to the remote method:

Example 37.2. XML-RPC Method Call with Parameters

```
$client = new Zend_XmlRpc_Client('http://framework.zend.com/xmlrpc');

$arg1 = 1.1;
$arg2 = 'foo';
```

```
$result = $client->call('test.sayHello', array($arg1, $arg2));

// $result is a native PHP type
```

If the remote method doesn't require parameters, this optional parameter may either be left out or an empty `array()` passed to it. The array of parameters for the remote method can contain native PHP types, Zend_XmlRpc_Value objects, or a mix of each.

The `call()` method will automatically convert the XML-RPC response and return its equivalent PHP native type. A Zend_XmlRpc_Response object for the return value will also be available by calling the `getLastResponse()` method after the call.

Types and Conversions

Some remote method calls require parameters. These are given to the `call()` method of Zend_XmlRpc_Client as an array in the second parameter. Each parameter may be given as either a native PHP type which will be automatically converted, or as an object representing a specific XML-RPC type (one of the Zend_XmlRpc_Value objects).

PHP Native Types as Parameters

Parameters may be passed to `call()` as native PHP variables, meaning as a `string`, `integer`, `float`, `boolean`, `array`, or an `object`. In this case, each PHP native type will be auto-detected and converted into one of the XML-RPC types according to this table:

Table 37.1. PHP and XML-RPC Type Conversions

PHP Native Type	XML-RPC Type
integer	int
double	double
boolean	boolean
string	string
array	array
associative array	struct
object	array

What type do empty arrays get cast to?

Passing an empty array to an XML-RPC method is problematic, as it could represent either an array or a struct. Zend_XmlRpc_Client detects such conditions and makes a request to the server's system.methodSignature method to determine the appropriate XML-RPC type to cast to.

However, this in itself can lead to issues. First off, servers that do not support system.methodSignature will log failed requests, and Zend_XmlRpc_Client will resort to casting the value to an XML-RPC array type. Additionally, this means that any call with array arguments will result in an additional call to the remote server.

To disable the lookup entirely, you can call the setSkipSystemLookup() method prior to making your XML-RPC call:

```
$client->setSkipSystemLookup(true);
$result = $client->call('foo.bar', array(array()));
```

Zend_XmlRpc_Value Objects as Parameters

Parameters may also be created as `Zend_XmlRpc_Value` instances to specify an exact XML-RPC type. The primary reasons for doing this are:

- When you want to make sure the correct parameter type is passed to the procedure (i.e. the procedure requires an integer and you may get it from a database as a string)

- When the procedure requires `base64` or `dateTime.iso8601` type (which doesn't exists as a PHP native type)

- When auto-conversion may fail (i.e. you want to pass an empty XML-RPC struct as a parameter. Empty structs are represented as empty arrays in PHP but, if you give an empty array as a parameter it will be auto-converted to an XML-RPC array since it's not an associative array)

There are two ways to create a `Zend_XmlRpc_Value` object: instantiate one of the `Zend_XmlRpc_Value` subclasses directly, or use the static factory method `Zend_XmlRpc_Value::getXmlRpcValue()`.

Table 37.2. Zend_XmlRpc_Value Objects for XML-RPC Types

XML-RPC Type	Zend_XmlRpc_Value Constant	Zend_XmlRpc_Value Object
int	Zend_XmlRpc_Value ::XMLRPC_TYPE_INTEGER	Zend_XmlRpc_Value _Integer
double	Zend_XmlRpc_Value ::XMLRPC_TYPE_DOUBLE	Zend_XmlRpc_Value _Double
boolean	Zend_XmlRpc_Value ::XMLRPC_TYPE_BOOLEAN	Zend_XmlRpc_Value _Boolean
string	Zend_XmlRpc_Value ::XMLRPC_TYPE_STRING	Zend_XmlRpc_Value _String
base64	Zend_XmlRpc_Value ::XMLRPC_TYPE_BASE64	Zend_XmlRpc_Value _Base64
dateTime.iso8601	Zend_XmlRpc_Value ::XMLRPC_TYPE_DATETIME	Zend_XmlRpc_Value _DateTime
array	Zend_XmlRpc_Value ::XMLRPC_TYPE_ARRAY	Zend_XmlRpc_Value _Array
struct	Zend_XmlRpc_Value ::XMLRPC_TYPE_STRUCT	Zend_XmlRpc_Value _Struct

Automatic Conversion

When building a new `Zend_XmlRpc_Value` object, its value is set by a PHP type. The PHP type will be converted to the specified type using PHP casting. For example, if a string is given as a value to the `Zend_XmlRpc_Value_Integer` object, it will be converted using `(int)$value`.

Server Proxy Object

Another way to call remote methods with the XML-RPC client is to use the server proxy. This is a PHP object that proxies a remote XML-RPC namespace, making it work as close to a native PHP object as possible.

To instantiate a server proxy, call the getProxy() instance method of Zend_XmlRpc_Client. This will return an instance of Zend_XmlRpc_Client_ServerProxy. Any method call on the server proxy object will be forwarded to the remote, and parameters may be passed like any other PHP method.

Example 37.3. Proxy the Default Namespace

```
$client = new Zend_XmlRpc_Client('http://framework.zend.com/xmlrpc');

$server = $client->getProxy();              // Proxy the default namespace

$hello = $server->test->sayHello(1, 2);  // test.Hello(1, 2) returns "hello"
```

The getProxy() method receives an optional argument specifying which namespace of the remote server to proxy. If it does not receive a namespace, the default namespace will be proxied. In the next example, the test namespace will be proxied:

Example 37.4. Proxy Any Namespace

```
$client = new Zend_XmlRpc_Client('http://framework.zend.com/xmlrpc');

$test  = $client->getProxy('test');      // Proxy the "test" namespace

$hello = $test->sayHello(1, 2);          // test.Hello(1,2) returns "hello"
```

If the remote server supports nested namespaces of any depth, these can also be used through the server proxy. For example, if the server in the example above had a method test.foo.bar(), it could be called as $test->foo->bar().

Error Handling

Two kinds of errors can occur during an XML-RPC method call: HTTP errors and XML-RPC faults. The Zend_XmlRpc_Client recognizes each and provides the ability to detect and trap them independently.

HTTP Errors

If any HTTP error occurs, such as the remote HTTP server returns a 404 Not Found, a Zend_XmlRpc_Client_HttpException will be thrown.

Example 37.5. Handling HTTP Errors

```
$client = new Zend_XmlRpc_Client('http://foo/404');

try {

    $client->call('bar', array($arg1, $arg2));

} catch (Zend_XmlRpc_Client_HttpException $e) {
```

```
    // $e->getCode() returns 404
    // $e->getMessage() returns "Not Found"

}
```

Regardless of how the XML-RPC client is used, the `Zend_XmlRpc_Client_HttpException` will be thrown whenever an HTTP error occurs.

XML-RPC Faults

An XML-RPC fault is analogous to a PHP exception. It is a special type returned from an XML-RPC method call that has both an error code and an error message. XML-RPC faults are handled differently depending on the context of how the `Zend_XmlRpc_Client` is used.

When the `call()` method or the server proxy object is used, an XML-RPC fault will result in a `Zend_XmlRpc_Client_FaultException` being thrown. The code and message of the exception will map directly to their respective values in the original XML-RPC fault response.

Example 37.6. Handling XML-RPC Faults

```
$client = new Zend_XmlRpc_Client('http://framework.zend.com/xmlrpc');

try {

    $client->call('badMethod');

} catch (Zend_XmlRpc_Client_FaultException $e) {

    // $e->getCode() returns 1
    // $e->getMessage() returns "Unknown method"

}
```

When the `call()` method is used to make the request, the `Zend_XmlRpc_Client_FaultException` will be thrown on fault. A `Zend_XmlRpc_Response` object containing the fault will also be available by calling `getLastResponse()`.

When the `doRequest()` method is used to make the request, it will not throw the exception. Instead, it will return a `Zend_XmlRpc_Response` object returned will containing the fault. This can be checked with `isFault()` instance method of `Zend_XmlRpc_Response`.

Server Introspection

Some XML-RPC servers support the de facto introspection methods under the XML-RPC `system.` namespace. `Zend_XmlRpc_Client` provides special support for servers with these capabilities.

A `Zend_XmlRpc_Client_ServerIntrospection` instance may be retrieved by calling the `getIntrospector()` method of `Zend_XmlRpcClient`. It can then be used to perform introspection operations on the server.

From Request to Response

Under the hood, the `call()` instance method of `Zend_XmlRpc_Client` builds a request object (`Zend_XmlRpc_Request`) and sends it to another method, `doRequest()`, that returns a response object (`Zend_XmlRpc_Response`).

The `doRequest()` method is also available for use directly:

Example 37.7. Processing Request to Response

```
$client = new Zend_XmlRpc_Client('http://framework.zend.com/xmlrpc');

$request = new Zend_XmlRpc_Request();
$request->setMethod('test.sayHello');
$request->setParams(array('foo', 'bar'));

$client->doRequest($request);

// $server->getLastRequest() returns instanceof Zend_XmlRpc_Request
// $server->getLastResponse() returns instanceof Zend_XmlRpc_Response
```

Whenever an XML-RPC method call is made by the client through any means, either the `call()` method, `doRequest()` method, or server proxy, the last request object and its resultant response object will always be available through the methods `getLastRequest()` and `getLastResponse()` respectively.

HTTP Client and Testing

In all of the prior examples, an HTTP client was never specified. When this is the case, a new instance of `Zend_Http_Client` will be created with its default options and used by `Zend_XmlRpc_Client` automatically.

The HTTP client can be retrieved at any time with the `getHttpClient()` method. For most cases, the default HTTP client will be sufficient. However, the `setHttpClient()` method allows for a different HTTP client instance to be injected.

The `setHttpClient()` is particularly useful for unit testing. When combined with the `Zend_Http_Client_Adapter_Test`, remote services can be mocked out for testing. See the unit tests for `Zend_XmlRpc_Client` for examples of how to do this.

Zend_XmlRpc_Server

Introduction

`Zend_XmlRpc_Server` is intended as a fully-featured XML-RPC server, following the specifications outlined at www.xmlrpc.com [http://www.xmlrpc.com/spec]. Additionally, it implements the system.multicall() method, allowing boxcarring of requests.

Basic Usage

An example of the most basic use case:

```
$server = new Zend_XmlRpc_Server();
$server->setClass('My_Service_Class');
echo $server->handle();
```

Server Structure

Zend_XmlRpc_Server is composed of a variety of components, ranging from the server itself to request, response, and fault objects.

To bootstrap Zend_XmlRpc_Server, the developer must attach one or more classes or functions to the server, via the setClass() and addFunction() methods.

Once done, you may either pass a Zend_XmlRpc_Request object to Zend_XmlRpc_Server::handle(), or it will instantiate a Zend_XmlRpc_Request_Http object if none is provided -- thus grabbing the request from php://input.

Zend_XmlRpc_Server::handle() then attempts to dispatch to the appropriate handler based on the method requested. It then returns either a Zend_XmlRpc_Response-based object or a Zend_XmlRpc_Server_Faultobject. These objects both have __toString() methods that create valid XML-RPC XML responses, allowing them to be directly echoed.

Conventions

Zend_XmlRpc_Server allows the developer to attach functions and class method calls as dispatchable XML-RPC methods. Via Zend_Server_Reflection, it does introspection on all attached methods, using the function and method docblocks to determine the method help text and method signatures.

XML-RPC types do not necessarily map one-to-one to PHP types. However, the code will do its best to guess the appropriate type based on the values listed in @param and @return lines. Some XML-RPC types have no immediate PHP equivalent, however, and should be hinted using the XML-RPC type in the PHPDoc. These include:

- dateTime.iso8601, a string formatted as YYYYMMDDTHH:mm:ss

- base64, base64 encoded data

- struct, any associative array

An example of how to hint follows:

```
/**
 * This is a sample function
 *
 * @param base64 $val1 Base64-encoded data
 * @param dateTime.iso8601 $val2 An ISO date
 * @param struct $val3 An associative array
 * @return struct
 */
function myFunc($val1, $val2, $val3)
{

}
```

PhpDocumentor does no validation of the types specified for params or return values, so this will have no impact on your API documentation. Providing the hinting is necessary, however, when the server is validating the parameters provided to the method call.

It is perfectly valid to specify multiple types for both params and return values; the XML-RPC specification even suggests that system.methodSignature should return an array of all possible method signatures (i.e., all possible combinations of param and return values). You may do so just as you normally would with PhpDocumentor, using the '|' operator:

```
/**
* This is a sample function
*
* @param string|base64 $val1 String or base64-encoded data
* @param string|dateTime.iso8601 $val2 String or an ISO date
* @param array|struct $val3 Normal indexed array or an associative array
* @return boolean|struct
*/
function myFunc($val1, $val2, $val3)
{

}
```

One note, however: allowing multiple signatures can lead to confusion for developers using the services; generally speaking, an XML-RPC method should only have a single signature.

Utilizing Namespaces

XML-RPC has a concept of namespacing; basically, it allows grouping XML-RPC methods by dot-delimited namespaces. This helps prevent naming collisions between methods served by different classes. As an example, the XML-RPC server is expected to server several methods in the 'system' namespace:

- system.listMethods

- system.methodHelp

- system.methodSignature

Internally, these map to the methods of the same name in Zend_XmlRpc_Server.

If you want to add namespaces to the methods you serve, simply provide a namespace to the appropriate method when attaching a function or class:

```
// All public methods in My_Service_Class will be accessible as
// myservice.METHODNAME
$server->setClass('My_Service_Class', 'myservice');

// Function 'somefunc' will be accessible as funcs.somefunc
$server->addFunction('somefunc', 'funcs');
```

Custom Request Objects

Most of the time, you'll simply use the default request type included with Zend_XmlRpc_Server, Zend_XmlRpc_Request_Http. However, there may be times when you need XML-RPC to be available via the CLI, a GUI, or other environment, or want to log incoming requests. To do so, you may create a custom request object that extends Zend_XmlRpc_Request. The most important thing to remember is to ensure that the getMethod() and getParams() methods are implemented so that the XML-RPC server can retrieve that information in order to dispatch the request.

Custom Responses

Similar to request objects, Zend_XmlRpc_Server can return custom response objects; by default, a Zend_XmlRpc_Response_Http object is returned, which sends an appropriate Content-Type HTTP header for use with XML-RPC. Possible uses of a custom object would be to log responses, or to send responses back to STDOUT.

To use a custom response class, use Zend_XmlRpc_Server::setResponseClass() prior to calling handle().

Handling Exceptions via Faults

Zend_XmlRpc_Server catches Exceptions generated by a dispatched method, and generates an XML-RPC fault response when such an exception is caught. By default, however, the exception messages and codes are not used in a fault response. This is an intentional decision to protect your code; many exceptions expose more information about the code or environment than a developer would necessarily intend (a prime example includes database abstraction or access layer exceptions).

Exception classes can be whitelisted to be used as fault responses, however. To do so, simply utilize Zend_XmlRpc_Server_Fault::attachFaultException() to pass an exception class to whitelist:

```
Zend_XmlRpc_Server_Fault::attachFaultException('My_Project_Exception');
```

If you utilize an exception class that your other project exceptions inherit, you can then whitelist a whole family of exceptions at a time. Zend_XmlRpc_Server_Exceptions are always whitelisted, to allow reporting specific internal errors (undefined methods, etc.).

Any exception not specifically whitelisted will generate a fault response with a code of '404' and a message of 'Unknown error'.

Caching Server Definitions Between Requests

Attaching many classes to an XML-RPC server instance can utilize a lot of resources; each class must introspect using the Reflection API (via Zend_Server_Reflection), which in turn generates a list of all possible method signatures to provide to the server class.

To reduce this performance hit somewhat, Zend_XmlRpc_Server_Cache can be used to cache the server definition between requests. When combined with __autoload(), this can greatly increase performance.

An sample usage follows:

```
function __autoload($class)
{
    Zend_Loader::loadClass($class);
}

$cacheFile = dirname(__FILE__) . '/xmlrpc.cache';
$server = new Zend_XmlRpc_Server();

if (!Zend_XmlRpc_Server_Cache::get($cacheFile, $server)) {
    require_once 'My/Services/Glue.php';
    require_once 'My/Services/Paste.php';
    require_once 'My/Services/Tape.php';

    $server->setClass('My_Services_Glue', 'glue');    // glue. namespace
    $server->setClass('My_Services_Paste', 'paste');  // paste. namespace
    $server->setClass('My_Services_Tape', 'tape');    // tape. namespace

    Zend_XmlRpc_Server_Cache::save($cacheFile, $server);
}

echo $server->handle();
```

The above example attempts to retrieve a server definition from xmlrpc.cache in the same directory as the script. If unsuccessful, it loads the service classes it needs, attaches them to the server instance, and then attempts to create a new cache file with the server definition.

Usage Examples

Below are several usage examples, showing the full spectrum of options available to developers. Usage examples will each build on the previous example provided.

Basic Usage

The example below attaches a function as a dispatchable XML-RPC method and handles incoming calls.

```
/**
 * Return the MD5 sum of a value
 *
 * @param string $value Value to md5sum
 * @return string MD5 sum of value
 */
function md5Value($value)
{
    return md5($value);
}

$server = new Zend_XmlRpc_Server();
$server->addFunction('md5Value');
echo $server->handle();
```

Attaching a class

The example below illustrates attaching a class' public methods as dispatchable XML-RPC methods.

```
require_once 'Services/Comb.php';

$server = new Zend_XmlRpc_Server();
$server->setClass('Services_Comb');
echo $server->handle();
```

Attaching several classes using namespaces

The example below illustrates attaching several classes, each with their own namespace.

```
require_once 'Services/Comb.php';
require_once 'Services/Brush.php';
require_once 'Services/Pick.php';

$server = new Zend_XmlRpc_Server();
$server->setClass('Services_Comb', 'comb');    // methods called as comb.*
$server->setClass('Services_Brush', 'brush');  // methods called as brush.*
$server->setClass('Services_Pick', 'pick');    // methods called as pick.*
echo $server->handle();
```

Specifying exceptions to use as valid fault responses

The example below allows any Services_Exception-derived class to report its code and message in the fault response.

```
require_once 'Services/Exception.php';
require_once 'Services/Comb.php';
require_once 'Services/Brush.php';
```

```
require_once 'Services/Pick.php';

// Allow Services_Exceptions to report as fault responses
Zend_XmlRpc_Server_Fault::attachFaultException('Services_Exception');

$server = new Zend_XmlRpc_Server();
$server->setClass('Services_Comb', 'comb');    // methods called as comb.*
$server->setClass('Services_Brush', 'brush'); // methods called as brush.*
$server->setClass('Services_Pick', 'pick');    // methods called as pick.*
echo $server->handle();
```

Utilizing a custom request object

The example below instantiates a custom request object and passes it to the server to handle.

```
require_once 'Services/Request.php';
require_once 'Services/Exception.php';
require_once 'Services/Comb.php';
require_once 'Services/Brush.php';
require_once 'Services/Pick.php';

// Allow Services_Exceptions to report as fault responses
Zend_XmlRpc_Server_Fault::attachFaultException('Services_Exception');

$server = new Zend_XmlRpc_Server();
$server->setClass('Services_Comb', 'comb');    // methods called as comb.*
$server->setClass('Services_Brush', 'brush'); // methods called as brush.*
$server->setClass('Services_Pick', 'pick');    // methods called as pick.*

// Create a request object
$request = new Services_Request();

echo $server->handle($request);
```

Utilizing a custom response object

The example below illustrates specifying a custom response class for the returned response.

```
require_once 'Services/Request.php';
require_once 'Services/Response.php';
require_once 'Services/Exception.php';
require_once 'Services/Comb.php';
require_once 'Services/Brush.php';
require_once 'Services/Pick.php';

// Allow Services_Exceptions to report as fault responses
Zend_XmlRpc_Server_Fault::attachFaultException('Services_Exception');

$server = new Zend_XmlRpc_Server();
$server->setClass('Services_Comb', 'comb');    // methods called as comb.*
$server->setClass('Services_Brush', 'brush'); // methods called as brush.*
$server->setClass('Services_Pick', 'pick');    // methods called as pick.*

// Create a request object
$request = new Services_Request();

// Utilize a custom response
$server->setResponseClass('Services_Response');

echo $server->handle($request);
```

Cache server definitions between requests

The example below illustrates caching server definitions between requests.

```
// Specify a cache file
$cacheFile = dirname(__FILE__) . '/xmlrpc.cache';

// Allow Services_Exceptions to report as fault responses
Zend_XmlRpc_Server_Fault::attachFaultException('Services_Exception');

$server = new Zend_XmlRpc_Server();

// Attempt to retrieve server definition from cache
if (!Zend_XmlRpc_Server_Cache::get($cacheFile, $server)) {
    $server->setClass('Services_Comb', 'comb');   // methods called as comb.*
    $server->setClass('Services_Brush', 'brush'); // methods called as brush.
    $server->setClass('Services_Pick', 'pick');   // methods called as pick.*

    // Save cache
    Zend_XmlRpc_Server_Cache::save($cacheFile, $server);
}

// Create a request object
$request = new Services_Request();

// Utilize a custom response
$server->setResponseClass('Services_Response');

echo $server->handle($request);
```

Appendix A. Zend Framework Requirements

Introduction

Zend Framework requires a PHP 5 interpreter with a web server configured to handle PHP scripts correctly. Some features require additional extensions or web server features; in most cases the framework can be used without them, although performance may suffer or ancillary features may not be fully functional. An example of such a dependency is mod_rewrite in an Apache environment, which can be used to implement "pretty URL's" like "http://www.example.com/user/edit". If mod_rewrite is not enabled, ZF can be configured to support URL's such as "http://www.example.com?controller=user&action=edit". Pretty URL's may be used to shorten URL's for textual representation or search engine optimization (SEO), but they do not directly affect the functionality of the application.

PHP Version

Zend recommends the most current release of PHP for critical security and performance enhancements, and currently supports PHP 5.2.4 or later.

Zend Framework has an extensive collection of unit tests, which you can run using PHPUnit 3.3.0 or later.

PHP Extensions

You will find a table listing all extensions typically found in PHP and how they are used in Zend Framework below. You should verify that the extensions on which ZF components you'll be using in your application are available in your PHP environments. Many applications will not require every extension listed below.

A dependency of type "hard" indicates that the components or classes cannot function properly if the respective extension is not available, while a dependency of type "soft" indicates that the component may use the extension if it is available but will function properly if it is not. Many components will automatically use certain extensions if they are available to optimize performance but will execute code with similar functionality in the component itself if the extensions are unavailable.

Table A.1. PHP Extensions Used in Zend Framework by Component

Extension	Dependency Type	Used by Zend Framework Components
apc	Hard	Zend_Cache_Backend_Apc
	Soft	Zend_File_Transfer
bcmath	Soft	Zend_Locale
bitset	Soft	Zend_Search_Lucene
bz2	---	---
calendar	---	---
com_dotnet	---	---

Extension	Dependency Type	Used by Zend Framework Components
ctype	Hard	Zend_Auth_Adapter_Http
		Zend_Gdata
		Zend_Http_Client
		Zend_Pdf
		Zend_Rest_Client
		Zend_Rest_Server
		Zend_Search_Lucene
		Zend_Uri
		Zend_Validate
curl	Hard	Zend_Http_Client _Adapter_Curl
date	Soft	Zend_Amf
dba	---	---
dbase	---	---
dom	Hard	Zend_Amf
		Zend_Dom
		Zend_Feed
		Zend_Gdata
		Zend_Log_Formatter_Xml
		Zend_Rest_Server
		Zend_Soap
		Zend_Search_Lucene
		Zend_Service_Amazon
		Zend_Service_Delicious
		Zend_Service_Flickr
		Zend_Service_Simpy
		Zend_Service_Yahoo
		Zend_XmlRpc
exif	---	---
fbsql	---	---
fdf	---	---
filter	---	---
ftp	---	---
gd	Hard	Zend_Captcha
		Zend_Pdf
gettext	---	---
gmp	---	---
hash	Hard	Zend_Auth_Adapter_Http
ibm_db2	Hard	Zend_Db_Adapter_Db2

Extension	Dependency Type	Used by Zend Framework Components
iconv	Hard	Zend_Currency
		Zend_Locale_Format
		Zend_Mime
		Zend_Pdf
		Zend_Search_Lucene
		Zend_Service_Audio scrobbler
		Zend_Service_Flickr
		Zend_XmlRpc_Client
imap	---	---
informix	---	---
interbase	Hard	Zend_Db_Adapter_Firebird
json	Soft	Zend_Json
ldap	Hard	Zend_Ldap
libxml	---	---
mbstring	Hard	Zend_Feed
mcrypt	Hard	Zend_Service_ReCaptcha
memcache	Hard	Zend_Cache_Backend _Memcached
mhash	---	---
mime_magic	Hard	Zend_Http_Client
ming	---	---
msql	---	---
mssql	---	---
mysql	---	---
mysqli	Hard	Zend_Db_Adapter_Mysqli
ncurses	---	---
oci8	Hard	Zend_Db_Adapter_Oracle
odbc	---	---
openssl	---	---
pcntl	---	---
pcre	Hard	Virtually all components
pdo	Hard	All PDO database adapters
pdo_dblib	---	---
pdo_firebird	---	---
pdo_mssql	Hard	Zend_Db_Adapter_Pdo _Mssql
pdo_mysql	Hard	Zend_Db_Adapter_Pdo _Mysql
pdo_oci	Hard	Zend_Db_Adapter_Pdo _Oci
pdo_pgsql	Hard	Zend_Db_Adapter_Pdo

Extension	Dependency Type	Used by Zend Framework Components
		_Pgsql
pdo_sqlite	Hard	Zend_Db_Adapter_Pdo_Sqlite
pgsql	---	---
posix	Soft	Zend_Mail
pspell	---	---
readline	---	---
recode	---	---
Reflection	Hard	Zend_Controller
		Zend_Filter
		Zend_Filter_Input
		Zend_Json
		Zend_Log
		Zend_Rest_Server
		Zend_Server_Reflection
		Zend_Validate
		Zend_View
		Zend_XmlRpc_Server
session	Hard	Zend_Controller_Action_Helper_Redirector
		Zend_Session
shmop	---	
SimpleXML	Hard	Zend_Config_Xml
		Zend_Feed
		Zend_Rest_Client
		Zend_Service_Audio_scrobbler
		Zend_Soap
		Zend_XmlRpc
	Soft	Zend_Amf
soap	Hard	Zend_Service_StrikeIron
		Zend_Soap
sockets	---	---
SPL	Hard	Virtually all components
SQLite	Hard	Zend_Cache_Backend_Sqlite
standard	Hard	Virtually all components
sybase	---	---
sysvmsg	---	---
sysvsem	---	--
sysvshm	---	---
tidy	---	---

Extension	Dependency Type	Used by Zend Framework Components
tokenizer	---	---
wddx	---	---
xml	Hard	Zend_Translate_Adapter_Qt
		Zend_Translate_Adapter_Tmx
		Zend_Translate_Adapter_Xliff
XMLReader	---	---
xmlrpc	---	---
XMLWriter	---	---
xsl	---	---
zip	---	---
zlib	Hard	Zend_Pdf

Zend Framework Components

Below is a table that lists all available Zend Framework Components and which PHP extension they need. This can help guide you to know which extensions are required for your application. Not all extensions used by Zend Framework are required for every application.

A dependency of type "hard" indicates that the components or classes cannot function properly if the respective extension is not available, while a dependency of type "soft" indicates that the component may use the extension if it is available but will function properly if it is not. Many components will automatically use certain extensions if they are available to optimize performance but will execute code with similar functionality in the component itself if the extensions are unavailable.

Table A.2. Zend Framework Components and the PHP Extensions they use

Zend Framework Components	Dependency Type	PHP Extension
All Components	Hard	pcre
		SPL
		standard
Zend_Acl	---	---
Zend_Amf	Hard	date
	Soft	dom
		SimpleXML
Zend_Auth	Hard	ctype
		hash
Zend_Cache	Hard	apc
		memcache
		sqlite
		zlib
Zend_Captcha	Hard	gd

Zend Framework Components	Dependency Type	PHP Extension
Zend_Config	Hard	libxml
		SimpleXML
Zend_Console_Getopt	---	---
Zend_Controller	Hard	Reflection
		session
Zend_Currency	Hard	iconv
Zend_Date	---	---
Zend_Db	Hard	ibm_db2
		mysqli
		oci8
		pdo
		pdo_mssql
		pdo_mysql
		pdo_oci
		pdo_pgsql
		pdo_sqlite
Zend_Debug	---	---
Zend_Dojo	---	---
Zend_Dom	Hard	dom
Zend_Exception	---	---
Zend_Feed	Hard	dom
		libxml
		mbstring
		SimpleXML
Zend_File_Transfer	Soft	apc
		upload_extension
Zend_Filter	Hard	Reflection
Zend_Form	---	---
Zend_Gdata	Hard	ctype
		dom
		libxml
Zend_Http	Hard	ctype
		curl
		mime_magic
Zend_InfoCard	---	---
Zend_Json	Soft	json
	Hard	Reflection
Zend_Layout	---	---
Zend_Ldap	---	ldap
Zend_Loader	---	---

Zend Framework Components	Dependency Type	PHP Extension
Zend_Locale	Soft	bcmath
	Hard	iconv
Zend_Log	Hard	dom
		libxml
		Reflection
Zend_Mail	Soft	posix
Zend_Measure	---	---
Zend_Memory	---	---
Zend_Mime	Hard	iconv
Zend_OpenId	---	---
Zend_Paginator	---	---
Zend_Pdf	Hard	ctype
		gd
		iconv
		zlib
Zend_ProgressBar	---	---
Zend_Registry	---	---
Zend_Request	---	---
Zend_Rest	Hard	ctype
		dom
		libxml
		Reflection
		SimpleXML
Zend_Search_Lucene	Soft	bitset
	Hard	ctype
		dom
		iconv
		libxml
Zend_Server_Reflection	Hard	Reflection
Zend_Service_Akismet	---	---
Zend_Service_Amazon	Hard	dom
		libxml
Zend_Service_Audioscrobbler	Hard	iconv
		libxml
		SimpleXML
Zend_Service_Delicious	Hard	dom
		libxml
Zend_Service_Flickr	Hard	dom
		iconv
		libxml
Zend_Service_Nirvanix	---	---

Zend Framework Components	Dependency Type	PHP Extension
Zend_Service_ReCaptcha	Hard	mcrypt
Zend_Service_Simpy	Hard	dom
		libxml
Zend_Service_SlideShare	---	---
Zend_Service_StrikeIron	Hard	soap
Zend_Service_Technorati	---	---
Zend_Service_Twitter	---	---
Zend_Service_Yahoo	Hard	dom
		libxml
Zend_Session	Hard	session
Zend_Soap	Hard	dom
		SimpleXML
		soap
Zend_Test	---	---
Zend_Text	---	---
Zend_TimeSync	---	---
Zend_Translate	Hard	xml
Zend_Uri	Hard	ctype
Zend_Validate	Hard	ctype
		Reflection
Zend_Version	---	---
Zend_Validate	Hard	Reflection
Zend_Wildfire	---	---
Zend_XmlRpc	Hard	dom
		iconv
		libxml
		Reflection
		SimpleXML

Zend Framework Dependencies

Below you can find a table listing Zend Framework Components and their dependencies to other Zend Framework Components. This can help you if you need to have only single components instead of the complete Zend Framework.

A dependency of type "hard" indicates that the components or classes cannot function properly if the respective dependent component is not available, while a dependency of type "soft" indicates that the component may need the dependent component in special situations or with special adapters. At last a dependency of type "fix" indicated that this components or classes are in any case used by subcomponents, and a dependency of type "sub" indicates that these components can be used by subcomponents in special situations or with special adapters.

Note

Even if it's possible to seperate single components for usage from the complete Zend Framework you should keep in mind that this can lead to problems when files are missed or components are used dynamically.

Table A.3. Zend Framework Components and their dependency to other Zend Framework Components

Zend Framework Component	Dependency Type	Dependent Zend Framework Component
Zend_Acl	Hard	Zend_Exception
Zend_Amf	Hard	Zend_Exception
		Zend_Server
	Soft	Zend_Date
		Zend_Loader
	Sub	Zend_Locale
		Zend_Registry

Zend Framework Component	Dependency Type	Dependent Zend Framework Component
Zend_Auth	Hard	Zend_Exception
	Soft	Zend_Db
		Zend_InfoCard
		Zend_Ldap
		Zend_OpenId
		Zend_Session
	Fix	Zend_Controller
		Zend_Http
		Zend_Loader
		Zend_Locale
		Zend_Uri
		Zend_View
	Sub	Zend_Captcha
		Zend_Config
		Zend_Date
		Zend_Dojo
		Zend_Filter
		Zend_Form
		Zend_Json
		Zend_Layout
		Zend_Registry
		Zend_Server
		Zend_Service_ReCaptcha
		Zend_Text
		Zend_Validate
		Zend_Wildfire

Zend Framework Component	Dependency Type	Dependent Zend Framework Component
Zend_Cache	Hard	Zend_Exception
	Soft	Zend_Log
	Sub	Zend_Captcha
		Zend_Config
		Zend_Controller
		Zend_Date
		Zend_Db
		Zend_Dojo
		Zend_Filter
		Zend_Form
		Zend_Http
		Zend_Json
		Zend_Layout
		Zend_Loader
		Zend_Locale
		Zend_Registry
		Zend_Server
		Zend_Service_ReCaptcha
		Zend_Session
		Zend_Text
		Zend_Uri
		Zend_Validate
		Zend_View
		Zend_Wildfire
Zend_Captcha	Hard	Zend_Exception
		Zend_Service_ReCaptcha
		Zend_Text
		Zend_Validate
	Fix	Zend_Http
		Zend_Json
		Zend_Loader
		Zend_Locale
		Zend_Server
		Zend_Uri
	Sub	Zend_Date
		Zend_Filter
		Zend_ReLoader
Zend_Config	Hard	Zend_Exception

Zend Framework Component	Dependency Type	Dependent Zend Framework Component
Zend_Console_Getopt	Hard	Zend_Exception
	Soft	Zend_Json
	Sub	Zend_Loader
		Zend_Server
Zend_Controller	Hard	Zend_Config
		Zend_Exception
		Zend_Loader
		Zend_Registry
		Zend_Uri
		Zend_View
	Soft	Zend_Dojo
		Zend_Filter
		Zend_Json
		Zend_Layout
	Fix	Zend_Locale
		Zend_Validate
	Sub	Zend_Captcha
		Zend_Date
		Zend_Db
		Zend_Form
		Zend_Http
		Zend_Server
		Zend_Service_ReCaptcha
		Zend_Session
		Zend_Text
		Zend_Wildfire
Zend_Currency	Hard	Zend_Exception
		Zend_Locale
	Sub	Zend_Loader
		Zend_Registry
Zend_Date	Hard	Zend_Exception
		Zend_Locale
	Sub	Zend_Loader
		Zend_Registry

Zend Framework Component	Dependency Type	Dependent Zend Framework Component
Zend_Db	Hard	Zend_Exception
		Zend_Loader
	Soft	Zend_Registry
		Zend_Wildfire
	Sub	Zend_Captcha
		Zend_Config
		Zend_Controller
		Zend_Date
		Zend_Db
		Zend_Dojo
		Zend_Filter
		Zend_Form
		Zend_Http
		Zend_Json
		Zend_Layout
		Zend_Server
		Zend_Service_ReCaptcha
		Zend_Session
		Zend_Text
		Zend_Uri
		Zend_Validate
		Zend_View
Zend_Debug	---	---

Zend Framework Component	Dependency Type	Dependent Zend Framework Component
Zend_Dojo	Hard	Zend_Exception
		Zend_Form
		Zend_Json
		Zend_Registry
		Zend_View
	Soft	Zend_Filter
	Fix	Zend_Config
		Zend_Loader
		Zend_Locale
		Zend_Uri
		Zend_Validate
	Sub	Zend_Captcha
		Zend_Controller
		Zend_Date
		Zend_Db
		Zend_Dojo
		Zend_Http
		Zend_Layout
		Zend_Server
		Zend_Service_ReCaptcha
		Zend_Session
		Zend_Text
		Zend_Wildfire
Zend_Dom	Hard	Zend_Exception
Zend_Exception	---	---
Zend_Feed	Hard	Zend_Exception
		Zend_Loader
		Zend_Uri
	Fix	Zend_Locale
		Zend_Validate
	Sub	Zend_Date
		Zend_Filter
		Zend_Http
		Zend_Registry
Zend_File_Transfer	Hard	Zend_Exception
	Soft	Zend_Loader

Zend Framework Component	Dependency Type	Dependent Zend Framework Component
Zend_Filter	Hard	Zend_Exception
		Zend_Loader
		Zend_Validate
	Soft	Zend_Locale
	Sub	Zend_Date
		Zend_Registry
Zend_Form	Hard	Zend_Exception
		Zend_Filter
		Zend_Validate
	Soft	Zend_Captcha
		Zend_Controller
		Zend_Json
		Zend_Loader
		Zend_Registry
		Zend_Session
	Fix	Zend_Config
		Zend_Http
		Zend_Locale
		Zend_Server
		Zend_Service_ReCaptcha
		Zend_Text
		Zend_Uri
		Zend_View
	Sub	Zend_Date
		Zend_Db
		Zend_Dojo
		Zend_Form
		Zend_Layout
		Zend_Wildfire
Zend_Gdata	Hard	Zend_Exception
		Zend_Http
		Zend_Mime
		Zend_Version
	Soft	Zend_Loader
	Fix	Zend_Locale
		Zend_Uri
		Zend_Validate
	Sub	Zend_Date
		Zend_Filter
		Zend_Registry

Zend Framework Component	Dependency Type	Dependent Zend Framework Component
Zend_Http	Hard	Zend_Exception
		Zend_Loader
		Zend_Uri
	Fix	Zend_Locale
		Zend_Validate
	Sub	Zend_Date
		Zend_Filter
		Zend_Registry
Zend_InfoCard	Hard	Zend_Exception
		Zend_Loader
Zend_Json	Hard	Zend_Exception
		Zend_Loader
		Zend_Server
Zend_Layout	Hard	Zend_Exception
	Soft	Zend_Controller
		Zend_Filter
		Zend_Loader
		Zend_View
	Fix	Zend_Config
		Zend_Layout
		Zend_Registry
		Zend_Uri
		Zend_Validate
	Sub	Zend_Captcha
		Zend_Date
		Zend_Db
		Zend_Dojo
		Zend_Form
		Zend_Http
		Zend_Json
		Zend_Locale
		Zend_Server
		Zend_Service_ReCaptcha
		Zend_Session
		Zend_Text
		Zend_Wildfire
Zend_Ldap	Hard	Zend_Exception
Zend_Loader	Hard	Zend_Exception
Zend_Locale	Hard	Zend_Exception
	Soft	Zend_Registry
	Sub	Zend_Loader

Zend Framework Component	Dependency Type	Dependent Zend Framework Component
Zend_Log	Hard	Zend_Exception
	Soft	Zend_Wildfire
	Sub	Zend_Captcha
		Zend_Config
		Zend_Controller
		Zend_Date
		Zend_Db
		Zend_Dojo
		Zend_Filter
		Zend_Form
		Zend_Http
		Zend_Json
		Zend_Layout
		Zend_Loader
		Zend_Registry
		Zend_Server
		Zend_Service_ReCaptcha
		Zend_Session
		Zend_Text
		Zend_Uri
		Zend_Validate
		Zend_View
Zend_Mail	Hard	Zend_Exception
		Zend_Loader
		Zend_Mime
		Zend_Validate
	Fix	Zend_Locale
	Sub	Zend_Date
		Zend_Filter
		Zend_Registry
Zend_Measure	Hard	Zend_Exception
		Zend_Locale
		Zend_Registry
	Sub	Zend_Loader

Zend Framework Component	Dependency Type	Dependent Zend Framework Component
Zend_Memory	Hard	Zend_Cache
		Zend_Exception
	Sub	Zend_Captcha
		Zend_Config
		Zend_Controller
		Zend_Date
		Zend_Db
		Zend_Dojo
		Zend_Filter
		Zend_Form
		Zend_Http
		Zend_Json
		Zend_Layout
		Zend_Loader
		Zend_Locale
		Zend_Log
		Zend_Registry
		Zend_Server
		Zend_Service_ReCaptcha
		Zend_Session
		Zend_Text
		Zend_Uri
		Zend_Validate
		Zend_View
		Zend_Wildfire
Zend_Mime	Hard	Zend_Exception

Zend Framework Component	Dependency Type	Dependent Zend Framework Component
Zend_OpenId	Hard	Zend_Controller
		Zend_Exception
		Zend_Http
		Zend_Session
	Fix	Zend_Config
		Zend_Dojo
		Zend_Loader
		Zend_Locale
		Zend_Registry
		Zend_Uri
		Zend_Validate
		Zend_View
	Sub	Zend_Captcha
		Zend_Date
		Zend_Db
		Zend_Filter
		Zend_Form
		Zend_Json
		Zend_Layout
		Zend_Server
		Zend_Service_ReCaptcha
		Zend_Text
		Zend_Wildfire

Zend Framework Component	Dependency Type	Dependent Zend Framework Component
Zend_Paginator	Hard	Zend_Exception
		Zend_Json
		Zend_Loader
	Soft	Zend_Controller
		Zend_Db
		Zend_View
	Fix	Zend_Server
	Sub	Zend_Captcha
		Zend_Config
		Zend_Date
		Zend_Dojo
		Zend_Filter
		Zend_Form
		Zend_Http
		Zend_Layout
		Zend_Locale
		Zend_Registry
		Zend_Service_ReCaptcha
		Zend_Session
		Zend_Text
		Zend_Uri
		Zend_Validate
		Zend_Wildfire

Zend Framework Component	Dependency Type	Dependent Zend Framework Component
Zend_Pdf	Hard	Zend_Exception
		Zend_Log
		Zend_Memory
	Fix	Zend_Cache
	Sub	Zend_Captcha
		Zend_Config
		Zend_Controller
		Zend_Date
		Zend_Db
		Zend_Dojo
		Zend_Filter
		Zend_Form
		Zend_Http
		Zend_Json
		Zend_Layout
		Zend_Loader
		Zend_Locale
		Zend_Registry
		Zend_Server
		Zend_Service_ReCaptcha
		Zend_Session
		Zend_Text
		Zend_Uri
		Zend_Validate
		Zend_View
		Zend_Wildfire

Zend Framework Component	Dependency Type	Dependent Zend Framework Component
Zend_Progressbar	Hard	Zend_Config
		Zend_Exception
		Zend_Json
	Soft	Zend_Session
	Fix	Zend_Db
		Zend_Loader
		Zend_Server
	Sub	Zend_Captcha
		Zend_Date
		Zend_Dojo
		Zend_Filter
		Zend_Form
		Zend_Http
		Zend_Layout
		Zend_Registry
		Zend_Service_ReCaptcha
		Zend_Text
		Zend_Uri
		Zend_Validate
		Zend_View
		Zend_Wildfire
Zend_Registry	Hard	Zend_Exception
	Soft	Zend_Loader
Zend_Request	---	---
Zend_Rest	Hard	Zend_Exception
		Zend_Server
		Zend_Service
		Zend_Uri
	Fix	Zend_Http
		Zend_Loader
		Zend_Locale
		Zend_Validate
	Sub	Zend_Date
		Zend_Filter
		Zend_Registry
Zend_Search_Lucene	Hard	Zend_Exception
Zend_Server	Hard	Zend_Exception

Zend Framework Component	Dependency Type	Dependent Zend Framework Component
Zend_Service_Akismet	Hard	Zend_Exception
		Zend_Http
		Zend_Uri
		Zend_Version
	Fix	Zend_Loader
		Zend_Locale
		Zend_Validate
	Sub	Zend_Date
		Zend_Filter
		Zend_Registry
Zend_Service_Amazon	Hard	Zend_Exception
		Zend_Http
		Zend_Rest
	Fix	Zend_Loader
		Zend_Locale
		Zend_Server
		Zend_Service
		Zend_Uri
		Zend_Validate
	Sub	Zend_Date
		Zend_Filter
		Zend_Registry
Zend_Service_Audioscrobbler	Hard	Zend_Exception
		Zend_Http
	Fix	Zend_Loader
		Zend_Locale
		Zend_Uri
		Zend_Validate
	Sub	Zend_Date
		Zend_Filter
		Zend_Registry

Zend Framework Component	Dependency Type	Dependent Zend Framework Component
Zend_Service_Delicious	Hard	Zend_Date
		Zend_Exception
		Zend_Http
		Zend_Json
		Zend_Rest
	Fix	Zend_Loader
		Zend_Locale
		Zend_Server
		Zend_Service
		Zend_Uri
		Zend_Validate
	Sub	Zend_Filter
		Zend_Registry
Zend_Service_Flickr	Hard	Zend_Exception
		Zend_Http
	Soft	Zend_Rest
		Zend_Validate
	Fix	Zend_Loader
		Zend_Locale
		Zend_Server
		Zend_Service
		Zend_Uri
	Sub	Zend_Date
		Zend_Filter
		Zend_Registry
Zend_Service_Nirvanix	Hard	Zend_Exception
		Zend_Http
		Zend_Loader
	Fix	Zend_Locale
		Zend_Uri
		Zend_Validate
	Sub	Zend_Date
		Zend_Filter
		Zend_Registry

Zend Framework Component	Dependency Type	Dependent Zend Framework Component
Zend_Service_ReCaptcha	Hard	Zend_Exception
		Zend_Http
		Zend_Json
	Fix	Zend_Loader
		Zend_Locale
		Zend_Server
		Zend_Uri
		Zend_Validate
	Sub	Zend_Date
		Zend_Filter
		Zend_Registry
Zend_Service_Simpy	Hard	Zend_Exception
		Zend_Http
		Zend_Rest
	Fix	Zend_Loader
		Zend_Locale
		Zend_Server
		Zend_Service
		Zend_Uri
		Zend_Validate
	Sub	Zend_Date
		Zend_Filter
		Zend_Registry

Zend Framework Component	Dependency Type	Dependent Zend Framework Component
Zend_Service_SlideShare	Hard	Zend_Cache
		Zend_Exception
		Zend_Http
	Fix	Zend_Loader
		Zend_Locale
		Zend_Uri
		Zend_Validate
	Sub	Zend_Captcha
		Zend_Config
		Zend_Controller
		Zend_Date
		Zend_Db
		Zend_Dojo
		Zend_Filter
		Zend_Form
		Zend_Json
		Zend_Layout
		Zend_Log
		Zend_Registry
		Zend_Server
		Zend_Service_ReCaptcha
		Zend_Session
		Zend_Text
		Zend_View
		Zend_Wildfire
Zend_Service_StrikeIron	Hard	Zend_Exception
		Zend_Http
		Zend_Loader
	Fix	Zend_Locale
		Zend_Uri
		Zend_Validate
	Fix	Zend_Date
		Zend_Filter
		Zend_Registry

Zend Framework Component	Dependency Type	Dependent Zend Framework Component
Zend_Service_Technorati	Hard	Zend_Date
		Zend_Exception
		Zend_Http
		Zend_Uri
		Zend_Locale
	Soft	Zend_Rest
	Fix	Zend_Loader
		Zend_Server
		Zend_Service
		Zend_Validate
	Sub	Zend_Filter
		Zend_Registry
Zend_Service_Twitter	Hard	Zend_Exception
		Zend_Feed
		Zend_Http
		Zend_Json
		Zend_Rest
		Zend_Uri
	Fix	Zend_Loader
		Zend_Locale
		Zend_Server
		Zend_Service
		Zend_Validate
	Fix	Zend_Date
		Zend_Filter
		Zend_Registry
Zend_Service_Yahoo	Hard	Zend_Exception
		Zend_Http
		Zend_Rest
	Soft	Zend_Validate
	Fix	Zend_Loader
		Zend_Locale
		Zend_Server
		Zend_Service
		Zend_Uri
	Sub	Zend_Date
		Zend_Filter
		Zend_Registry

Zend Framework Component	Dependency Type	Dependent Zend Framework Component
Zend_Session	Hard	Zend_Exception
	Soft	Zend_Config
		Zend_Db
		Zend_Loader
	Sub	Zend_Captcha
		Zend_Date
		Zend_Dojo
		Zend_Filter
		Zend_Form
		Zend_Http
		Zend_Json
		Zend_Layout
		Zend_Registry
		Zend_Server
		Zend_Service_ReCaptcha
		Zend_Session
		Zend_Text
		Zend_Uri
		Zend_Validate
		Zend_View
		Zend_Wildfire
Zend_Soap	Hard	Zend_Exception
		Zend_Server
		Zend_Uri
	Fix	Zend_Loader
		Zend_Locale
		Zend_Validate
	Sub	Zend_Date
		Zend_Filter
		Zend_Registry

Zend Framework Component	Dependency Type	Dependent Zend Framework Component
Zend_Test	Hard	Zend_Controller
		Zend_Dom
		Zend_Exception
		Zend_Layout
		Zend_Registry
		Zend_Session
	Soft	Zend_Loader
	Fix	Zend_Config
		Zend_Locale
		Zend_Uri
		Zend_Validate
		Zend_View
	Sub	Zend_Captcha
		Zend_Date
		Zend_Db
		Zend_Dojo
		Zend_Filter
		Zend_Form
		Zend_Http
		Zend_Json
		Zend_Server
		Zend_Service_ReCaptcha
		Zend_Text
		Zend_Wildfire
Zend_Text	Hard	Zend_Exception
	Soft	Zend_Loader
Zend_TimeSync	Hard	Zend_Date
		Zend_Exception
		Zend_Loader
	Fix	Zend_Locale
	Sub	Zend_Registry
Zend_Translate	Hard	Zend_Exception
		Zend_Loader
		Zend_Locale
	Sub	Zend_Registry

Zend Framework Component	Dependency Type	Dependent Zend Framework Component
Zend_Uri	Hard	Zend_Exception
		Zend_Loader
		Zend_Locale
		Zend_Validate
	Soft	Zend_Date
		Zend_Filter
		Zend_Registry
Zend_Validate	Hard	Zend_Exception
		Zend_Loader
		Zend_Locale
	Soft	Zend_Date
		Zend_Filter
		Zend_Registry
Zend_Version	---	---
Zend_View	Hard	Zend_Controller
		Zend_Exception
		Zend_Loader
		Zend_Locale
		Zend_Registry
	Soft	Zend_Json
		Zend_Layout
	Fix	Zend_Config
		Zend_Uri
		Zend_Validate
	Sub	Zend_Captcha
		Zend_Date
		Zend_Db
		Zend_Dojo
		Zend_Filter
		Zend_Form
		Zend_Http
		Zend_Server
		Zend_Service_ReCaptcha
		Zend_Session
		Zend_Text
		Zend_Wildfire

Zend Framework Component	Dependency Type	Dependent Zend Framework Component
Zend_Wildfire	Hard	Zend_Controller
		Zend_Exception
		Zend_Json
		Zend_Loader
	Fix	Zend_Config
		Zend_Layout
		Zend_Registry
		Zend_Server
		Zend_Uri
		Zend_Validate
		Zend_View
	Sub	Zend_Captcha
		Zend_Date
		Zend_Db
		Zend_Dojo
		Zend_Filter
		Zend_Form
		Zend_Http
		Zend_Layout
		Zend_Service_ReCaptcha
		Zend_Session
		Zend_Text
Zend_XmlRpc	Hard	Zend_Exception
		Zend_Http
		Zend_Server
	Fix	Zend_Loader
		Zend_Uri
		Zend_Validate
		Zend_Locale
	Sub	Zend_Date
		Zend_Filter
		Zend_Registry

Appendix B. Zend Framework Coding Standard for PHP

Overview

Scope

This document provides guidelines for code formatting and documentation to individuals and teams contributing to Zend Framework. Many developers using Zend Framework have also found these coding standards useful because their code's style remains consistent with all Zend Framework code. It is also worth noting that it requires significant effort to fully specify coding standards. Note: Sometimes developers consider the establishment of a standard more important than what that standard actually suggests at the most detailed level of design. The guidelines in the Zend Framework coding standards capture practices that have worked well on the ZF project. You may modify these standards or use them as is in accordance with the terms of our license

Topics covered in the ZF coding standards include:

- PHP File Formatting

- Naming Conventions

- Coding Style

- Inline Documentation

Goals

Coding standards are important in any development project, but they are particularly important when many developers are working on the same project. Coding standards help ensure that the code is high quality, has fewer bugs, and can be easily maintained.

PHP File Formatting

General

For files that contain only PHP code, the closing tag ("?>") is never permitted. It is not required by PHP, and omitting it prevents the accidental injection of trailing white space into the response.

IMPORTANT: Inclusion of arbitrary binary data as permitted by __HALT_COMPILER() is prohibited from PHP files in the Zend Framework project or files derived from them. Use of this feature is only permitted for some installation scripts.

Indentation

Indentation should consist of 4 spaces. Tabs are not allowed.

Maximum Line Length

The target line length is 80 characters. That is to say, ZF developers should strive keep each line of their code under 80 characters where possible and practical. However, longer lines are acceptable in some circumstances. The maximum length of any line of PHP code is 120 characters.

Line Termination

Line termination follows the Unix text file convention. Lines must end with a single linefeed (LF) character. Linefeed characters are represented as ordinal 10, or hexadecimal 0x0A.

Note: Do not use carriage returns (CR) as is the convention in Apple OS's (0x0D) or the carriage return/linefeed combination (CRLF) as is standard for the Windows OS (0x0D, 0x0A).

Naming Conventions

Classes

Zend Framework standardizes on a class naming convention whereby the names of the classes directly map to the directories in which they are stored. The root level directory of the ZF standard library is the "Zend/" directory, whereas the root level directory of the ZF extras library is the "ZendX/" directory. All Zend Framework classes are stored hierarchically under these root directories..

Class names may only contain alphanumeric characters. Numbers are permitted in class names but are discouraged in most cases. Underscores are only permitted in place of the path separator; the filename "Zend/Db/Table.php" must map to the class name "Zend_Db_Table".

If a class name is comprised of more than one word, the first letter of each new word must be capitalized. Successive capitalized letters are not allowed, e.g. a class "Zend_PDF" is not allowed while "Zend_Pdf" is acceptable.

These conventions define a pseudo-namespace mechanism for Zend Framework. Zend Framework will adopt the PHP namespace feature when it becomes available and is feasible for our developers to use in their applications.

See the class names in the standard and extras libraries for examples of this classname convention. *IMPORTANT:* Code that must be deployed alongside ZF libraries but is not part of the standard or extras libraries (e.g. application code or libraries that are not distributed by Zend) must never start with "Zend_" or "ZendX_".

Filenames

For all other files, only alphanumeric characters, underscores, and the dash character ("-") are permitted. Spaces are strictly prohibited.

Any file that contains PHP code should end with the extension ".php", with the notable exception of view scripts. The following examples show acceptable filenames for Zend Framework classes:

```
Zend/Db.php
```

```
Zend/Controller/Front.php
```

```
Zend/View/Helper/FormRadio.php
```

File names must map to class names as described above.

Functions and Methods

Function names may only contain alphanumeric characters. Underscores are not permitted. Numbers are permitted in function names but are discouraged in most cases.

Function names must always start with a lowercase letter. When a function name consists of more than one word, the first letter of each new word must be capitalized. This is commonly called "camelCase" formatting.

Verbosity is generally encouraged. Function names should be as verbose as is practical to fully describe their purpose and behavior.

These are examples of acceptable names for functions:

```
filterInput()

getElementById()

widgetFactory()
```

For object-oriented programming, accessors for instance or static variables should always be prefixed with "get" or "set". In implementing design patterns, such as the singleton or factory patterns, the name of the method should contain the pattern name where practical to more thoroughly describe behavior.

For methods on objects that are declared with the "private" or "protected" modifier, the first character of the method name must be an underscore. This is the only acceptable application of an underscore in a method name. Methods declared "public" should never contain an underscore.

Functions in the global scope (a.k.a "floating functions") are permitted but discouraged in most cases. Consider wrapping these functions in a static class.

Variables

Variable names may only contain alphanumeric characters. Underscores are not permitted. Numbers are permitted in variable names but are discouraged in most cases.

For instance variables that are declared with the "private" or "protected" modifier, the first character of the variable name must be a single underscore. This is the only acceptable application of an underscore in a variable name. Member variables declared "public" should never start with an underscore.

As with function names (see section 3.3) variable names must always start with a lowercase letter and follow the "camelCaps" capitalization convention.

Verbosity is generally encouraged. Variables should always be as verbose as practical to describe the data that the developer intends to store in them. Terse variable names such as "$i" and "$n" are discouraged for all but the smallest loop contexts. If a loop contains more than 20 lines of code, the index variables should have more descriptive names.

Constants

Constants may contain both alphanumeric characters and underscores. Numbers are permitted in constant names.

All letters used in a constant name must be capitalized, while all words in a constant name must be separated by underscore characters.

For example, `EMBED_SUPPRESS_EMBED_EXCEPTION` is permitted but `EMBED_SUPPRESSEMBEDEXCEPTION` is not.

Constants must be defined as class members with the "const" modifier. Defining constants in the global scope with the "define" function is permitted but strongly discouraged.

Coding Style

PHP Code Demarcation

PHP code must always be delimited by the full-form, standard PHP tags:

```
<?php

?>
```

Short tags are never allowed. For files containing only PHP code, the closing tag must always be omitted (See the section called "General").

Strings

String Literals

When a string is literal (contains no variable substitutions), the apostrophe or "single quote" should always be used to demarcate the string:

```
$a = 'Example String';
```

String Literals Containing Apostrophes

When a literal string itself contains apostrophes, it is permitted to demarcate the string with quotation marks or "double quotes". This is especially useful for SQL statements:

```
$sql = "SELECT `id`, `name` from `people` "
     . "WHERE `name`='Fred' OR `name`='Susan'";
```

This syntax is preferred over escaping apostrophes as it is much easier to read.

Variable Substitution

Variable substitution is permitted using either of these forms:

```
$greeting = "Hello $name, welcome back!";

$greeting = "Hello {$name}, welcome back!";
```

For consistency, this form is not permitted:

```
$greeting = "Hello ${name}, welcome back!";
```

String Concatenation

Strings must be concatenated using the "." operator. A space must always be added before and after the "." operator to improve readability:

```
$company = 'Zend' . ' ' . 'Technologies';
```

When concatenating strings with the "." operator, it is encouraged to break the statement into multiple lines to improve readability. In these cases, each successive line should be padded with white space such that the "."; operator is aligned under the "=" operator:

```
$sql = "SELECT `id`, `name` FROM `people` "
     . "WHERE `name` = 'Susan' "
     . "ORDER BY `name` ASC ";
```

Arrays

Numerically Indexed Arrays

Negative numbers are not permitted as indices.

An indexed array may start with any non-negative number, however all base indices besides 0 are discouraged.

When declaring indexed arrays with the `array` function, a trailing space must be added after each comma delimiter to improve readability:

```
$sampleArray = array(1, 2, 3, 'Zend', 'Studio');
```

It is permitted to declare multi-line indexed arrays using the "array" construct. In this case, each successive line must be padded with spaces such that beginning of each line is aligned:

```
$sampleArray = array(1, 2, 3, 'Zend', 'Studio',
                     $a, $b, $c,
                     56.44, $d, 500);
```

Associative Arrays

When declaring associative arrays with the `array` construct, breaking the statement into multiple lines is encouraged. In this case, each successive line must be padded with white space such that both the keys and the values are aligned:

```
$sampleArray = array('firstKey'  => 'firstValue',
                     'secondKey' => 'secondValue');
```

Classes

Class Declaration

Classes must be named according to Zend Framework's naming conventions.

The brace should always be written on the line underneath the class name.

Every class must have a documentation block that conforms to the PHPDocumentor standard.

All code in a class must be indented with four spaces.

Only one class is permitted in each PHP file.

Placing additional code in class files is permitted but discouraged. In such files, two blank lines must separate the class from any additional PHP code in the class file.

The following is an example of an acceptable class declaration:

```
/**
 * Documentation Block Here
 */
class SampleClass
{
    // all contents of class
    // must be indented four spaces
}
```

Class Member Variables

Member variables must be named according to Zend Framework's variable naming conventions.

Any variables declared in a class must be listed at the top of the class, above the declaration of any methods.

The `var` construct is not permitted. Member variables always declare their visibility by using one of the `private`, `protected`, or `public` modifiers. Giving access to member variables directly by declaring them as public is permitted but discouraged in favor of accessor methods (set/get).

Functions and Methods

Function and Method Declaration

Functions must be named according to the Zend Framework function naming conventions.

Methods inside classes must always declare their visibility by using one of the `private`, `protected`, or `public` modifiers.

As with classes, the brace should always be written on the line underneath the function name. Space between the function name and the opening parenthesis for the arguments is not permitted.

Functions in the global scope are strongly discouraged.

The following is an example of an acceptable function declaration in a class:

```
/**
 * Documentation Block Here
 */
class Foo
{
    /**
     * Documentation Block Here
     */
    public function bar()
```

```
    {
        // all contents of function
        // must be indented four spaces
    }
}
```

NOTE: Pass-by-reference is the only parameter passing mechanism permitted in a method declaration.

```
/**
 * Documentation Block Here
 */
class Foo
{
    /**
     * Documentation Block Here
     */
    public function bar(&$baz)
    {}
}
```

Call-time pass-by-reference is strictly prohibited.

The return value must not be enclosed in parentheses. This can hinder readability, in additional to breaking code if a method is later changed to return by reference.

```
/**
 * Documentation Block Here
 */
class Foo
{
    /**
     * WRONG
     */
    public function bar()
    {
        return($this->bar);
    }

    /**
     * RIGHT
     */
    public function bar()
    {
        return $this->bar;
    }
}
```

Function and Method Usage

Function arguments should be separated by a single trailing space after the comma delimiter. The following is an example of an acceptable invocation of a function that takes three arguments:

```
threeArguments(1, 2, 3);
```

Call-time pass-by-reference is strictly prohibited. See the function declarations section for the proper way to pass function arguments by-reference.

In passing arrays as arguments to a function, the function call may include the "array" hint and may be split into multiple lines to improve readability. In such cases, the normal guidelines for writing arrays still apply:

```
threeArguments(array(1, 2, 3), 2, 3);

threeArguments(array(1, 2, 3, 'Zend', 'Studio',
                $a, $b, $c,
                56.44, $d, 500), 2, 3);
```

Control Statements

If/Else/Elseif

Control statements based on the `if` and `elseif` constructs must have a single space before the opening parenthesis of the conditional and a single space after the closing parenthesis.

Within the conditional statements between the parentheses, operators must be separated by spaces for readability. Inner parentheses are encouraged to improve logical grouping for larger conditional expressions.

The opening brace is written on the same line as the conditional statement. The closing brace is always written on its own line. Any content within the braces must be indented using four spaces.

```
if ($a != 2) {
    $a = 2;
}
```

For "if" statements that include "elseif" or "else", the formatting conventions are similar to the "if" construct. The following examples demonstrate proper formatting for "if" statements with "else" and/or "elseif" constructs:

```
if ($a != 2) {
    $a = 2;
} else {
    $a = 7;
}

if ($a != 2) {
    $a = 2;
} elseif ($a == 3) {
    $a = 4;
} else {
    $a = 7;
}
```

PHP allows statements to be written without braces in some circumstances. This coding standard makes no differentiation- all "if", "elseif" or "else" statements must use braces.

Use of the "elseif" construct is permitted but strongly discouraged in favor of the "else if" combination.

Switch

Control statements written with the "switch" statement must have a single space before the opening parenthesis of the conditional statement and after the closing parenthesis.

All content within the "switch" statement must be indented using four spaces. Content under each "case" statement must be indented using an additional four spaces.

```
switch ($numPeople) {
    case 1:
        break;

    case 2:
        break;

    default:
        break;
}
```

The construct `default` should never be omitted from a `switch` statement.

NOTE: It is sometimes useful to write a `case` statement which falls through to the next case by not including a `break` or `return` within that case. To distinguish these cases from bugs, any `case` statement where `break` or `return` are omitted should contain a comment indicating that the break was intentionally omitted.

Inline Documentation

Documentation Format

All documentation blocks ("docblocks") must be compatible with the phpDocumentor format. Describing the phpDocumentor format is beyond the scope of this document. For more information, visit: http://phpdoc.org/

All class files must contain a "file-level" docblock at the top of each file and a "class-level" docblock immediately above each class. Examples of such docblocks can be found below.

Files

Every file that contains PHP code must have a docblock at the top of the file that contains these phpDocumentor tags at a minimum:

```
/**
 * Short description for file
 *
 * Long description for file (if any)...
 *
 * LICENSE: Some license information
 *
 * @copyright  2008 Zend Technologies
 * @license    http://framework.zend.com/license    BSD License
 * @version    $Id:$
 * @link       http://framework.zend.com/package/PackageName
 * @since      File available since Release 1.5.0
 */
```

Classes

Every class must have a docblock that contains these phpDocumentor tags at a minimum:

```
/**
 * Short description for class
 *
 * Long description for class (if any)...
 *
 * @copyright  2008 Zend Technologies
 * @license    http://framework.zend.com/license    BSD License
 * @version    Release: @package_version@
 * @link       http://framework.zend.com/package/PackageName
 * @since      Class available since Release 1.5.0
 * @deprecated Class deprecated in Release 2.0.0
 */
```

Functions

Every function, including object methods, must have a docblock that contains at a minimum:

- A description of the function

- All of the arguments

- All of the possible return values

It is not necessary to use the "@access" tag because the access level is already known from the "public", "private", or "protected" modifier used to declare the function.

If a function/method may throw an exception, use @throws for all known exception classes:

```
@throws exceptionclass [description]
```

Appendix C. Zend Framework Performance Guide

Introduction

The purpose of this appendix is to provide some concrete strategies for improving the performance of your Zend Framework applications. The guide is presented in a "Question and Answer" format, and broken into areas of concern.

Class Loading

Anyone who ever performs profiling of a Zend Framework application will immediately recognize that class loading is relatively expensive in Zend Framework. Between the sheer number of class files that need to be loaded for many components, to the use of plugins that do not have a 1:1 relationship between their class name and the file system, the various calls to include_once and require_once can be problematic. This chapter intends to provide some concrete solutions to these issues.

How can I optimize my include_path?

One trivial optimization you can do to increase the speed of class loading is to pay careful attention to your include_path. In particular, you should do four things: use absolute paths (or paths relative to absolute paths), reduce the number of include paths you define, have your Zend Framework include_path as early as possible, and only include the current directory path at the end of your include_path.

Use absolute paths

While this may seem a micro-optimization, the fact is that if you don't, you'll get very little benefit from PHP's realpath cache, and as a result, opcode caching will not perform nearly as you may expect.

There are two easy ways to ensure this. First, you can hardcode the paths in your php.ini, httpd.conf, or .htaccess. Second, you can use PHP's realpath() function when setting your include_path:

```
$paths = array(
    realpath(dirname(__FILE__) . '/../library'),
    '.',
);
set_include_path(implode(PATH_SEPARATOR, $paths);
```

You *can* use relative paths -- so long as they are relative to an absolute path:

```
define('APPLICATION_PATH', realpath(dirname(__FILE__)));
$paths = array(
    APPLICATION_PATH . '/../library'),
    '.',
);
set_include_path(implode(PATH_SEPARATOR, $paths);
```

However, even so, it's typically a trivial task to simply pass the path to realpath().

Reduce the number of include paths you define

Include paths are scanned in the order in which they appear in the include_path. Obviously, this means that you'll get a result faster if the file is found on the first scan rather than the last. Thus, a rather obvious enhancement is to simply reduce the number of paths in your include_path to only what you need. Look through each include_path you've defined, and determine if you actually have any functionality in that path that is used in your application; if not, remove it.

Another optimization is to combine paths. For instance, Zend Framework follows PEAR naming conventions; thus, if you are using PEAR libraries (or libraries from another framework or component library that follows PEAR CS), try to put all of these libraries on the same include_path. This can often be achieved by something as simple as symlinking one or more libraries into a common directory.

Define your Zend Framework include_path as early as possible

Continuing from the previous suggestion, another obvious optimization is to define your Zend Framework include_path as early as possible in your include_path. In most cases, it should be the first path in the list. This ensures that files included from Zend Framework are found on the first scan.

Define the current directory last, or not at all

Most include_path examples show using the current directory, or '.'. This is convenient for ensuring that scripts in the same directory as the file requiring them can be loaded. However, these same examples typically show this path item as the first item in the include_path -- which means that the current directory tree is always scanned first. In most cases, with Zend Framework applications, this is not desired, and the path may be safely pushed to the last item in the list.

Example C.1. Example: Optimized include_path

Let's put all of these suggestions together. Our assumption will be that you are using one or more PEAR libraries in conjunction with Zend Framework -- perhaps the PHPUnit and Archive_Tar libraries -- and that you occasionally need to include files relative to the current file.

First, we'll create a library directory in our project. Inside that directory, we'll symlink our Zend Framework's library/Zend directory, as well as the necessary directories from our PEAR installation:

```
library
    Archive/
    PEAR/
    PHPUnit/
    Zend/
```

This allows us to add our own library code if necessary, while keeping shared libraries intact.

Next, we'll opt to create our include_path programmatically within our public/index.php file. This allows us to move our code around on the file system, without needing to edit the include_path every time.

We'll borrow ideas from each of the suggestions above: we'll use absolute paths, as determined using realpath(); we'll include the Zend Framework include path early; we've already consolidated include_paths; and we'll put the current directory as the last path. In fact, we're doing really well here -- we're going to end up with only two paths.

```
$paths = array(
    realpath(dirname(__FILE__) . '/../library'),
    '.'
);
set_include_path(implode(PATH_SEPARATOR, $paths));
```

How can I eliminate unnecessary require_once statements?

Lazy loading is an optimization technique designed to push the expensive operation of loading a class file until the last possible moment -- i.e., when instantiating an object of that class, calling a static class method, or referencing a class constant or static property. PHP supports this via autoloading, which allows you to define one or more callbacks to execute in order to map a class name to a file.

However, most benefits you may reap from autoloading are negated if your library code is still performing require_once calls -- which is precisely the case with Zend Framework. So, the question is: how can you eliminate those require_once calls in order to maximize autoloader performance?

Strip require_once calls with find and sed

An easy way to strip require_once calls is to use the UNIX utilities 'find' and 'sed' in conjunction to comment out each call. Try executing the following statements (where '%' indicates the shell prompt):

```
% cd path/to/ZendFramework/library
% find . -name '*.php' -not -wholename '*/Loader/Autoloader.php' -print0 | \
  xargs -0 sed --regexp-extended --in-place 's/(require_once)/\/\/ \1/g'
```

This one-liner (broken into two lines for readability) iterates through each PHP file and tells it to replace each instance of 'require_once' with '// require_once', effectively commenting out each such statement.

This command could be added to an automated build or release process trivially, helping boost performance in your production application. It should be noted, however, that if you use this technique, you *must* utilize autoloading; you can do that from your "public/index.php" file with the following code:

```
require_once 'Zend/Loader/Autoloader.php';
Zend_Loader_Autoloader::getInstance();
```

How can I speed up plugin loading?

Many components have plugins, which allow you to create your own classes to utilize with the component, as well as to override existing, standard plugins shipped with Zend Framework. This provides important flexibility to the framework, but at a price: plugin loading is a fairly expensive task.

The plugin loader allows you to register class prefix / path pairs, allowing you to specify class files in non-standard paths. Each prefix can have multiple paths associated with it. Internally, the plugin loader loops through each prefix, and then through each path attached to it, testing to see if the file exists and is readable on that path. It then loads it, and tests to see that the class it is looking for is available. As you might imagine, this can lead to many stat calls on the file system.

Multiply this by the number of components that use the PluginLoader, and you get an idea of the scope of this issue. At the time of this writing, the following components made use of the PluginLoader:

- `Zend_Controller_Action_HelperBroker`: helpers

- `Zend_Dojo`: view helpers, form elements and decorators

- `Zend_File_Transfer`: adapters

- `Zend_Filter_Inflector`: filters (used by the ViewRenderer action helper and Zend_Layout)

- `Zend_Filter_Input`: filters and validators

- `Zend_Form`: elements, validators, filters, decorators, captcha and file transfer adapters

- `Zend_Paginator`: adapters

- `Zend_View`: helpers, filters

How can you reduce the number of such calls made?

Use the PluginLoader include file cache

Zend Framework 1.7.0 adds an include file cache to the PluginLoader. This functionality writes "include_once" calls to a file, which you can then include in your bootstrap. While this introduces extra include_once calls to your code, it also ensures that the PluginLoader returns as early as possible.

The PluginLoader documentation includes a complete example of its use.

Zend_Db Performance

Zend_Db is a database abstraction layer, and is intended to provide a common API for SQL operations. Zend_Db_Table is a Table Data Gateway, intended to abstract common table-level database operations. Due to their abstract nature and the "magic" they do under the hood to perform their operations, they can sometimes introduce performance overhead.

How can I reduce overhead introduced by Zend_Db_Table for retrieving table metadata?

In order to keep usage as simple as possible, and also to support constantly changing schemas during development, Zend_Db_Table does some magic under the hood: on first use, it fetches the table schema and stores it within object members. This operation is typically expensive, regardless of the database -- which can contribute to bottlenecks in production.

Fortunately, there are techniques for improving the situation.

Use the metadata cache

Zend_Db_Table can optionally utilize Zend_Cache to cache table metadata. This is typically faster to access and less expensive than fetching the metadata from the database itself.

The Zend_Db_Table documentation includes information on metadata caching.

Hardcode your metadata in the table definition

As of 1.7.0, Zend_Db_Table also provides support for hardcoding metadata in the table definition. This is an advanced use case, and should only be used when you know the table schema is unlikely to change, or that you're able to keep the definitions up-to-date.

SQL generated with Zend_Db_Select s not hitting my indexes; how can I make it better?

Zend_Db_Select is relatively good at its job. However, if you are performing complex queries requiring joins or sub-selects, it can often be fairly naive.

Write your own tuned SQL

The only real answer is to write your own SQL; Zend_Db does not require the usage of Zend_Db_Select, so providing your own, tuned SQL select statements is a perfectly legitimate approach,

Run EXPLAIN on your queries, and test a variety of approaches until you can reliably hit your indices in the most performant way -- and then hardcode the SQL as a class property or constant.

If the SQL requires variable arguments, provide placeholders in the SQL, and utilize a combination of vsprintf and array_walk to inject the values into the SQL:

```
// $adapter is the DB adapter. In Zend_Db_Table, retrieve
// it using $this->getAdapter().
$sql = vsprintf(
    self::SELECT_FOO,
    array_walk($values, array($adapter, 'quoteInto'))
);
```

Internationalization (i18n) and Localization (l10n)

Internationalizing and localizing a site are fantastic ways to expand your audience and ensure that all visitors can get to the information they need. However, it often comes with a performance penalty. Below are some strategies you can employ to reduce the overhead of i18n and l10n.

Which translation adapter should I use?

Not all translation adapters are made equal. Some have more features than others, and some perform better than others. Additionally, you may have business requirements that force you to use a particular adapter. However, if you have a choice, which adapters are fastest?

Use non-XML translation adapters for greatest speed

Zend Framework ships with a variety of translation adapters. Fully half of them utilize an XML format, incurring memory and performance overhead. Fortunately, there are several adapters that utilize other formats that can be parsed much more quickly. In order of speed, from fastest to slowest, they are:

- *Array*: this is the fastest, as it is, by definition, parsed into a native PHP format immediately on inclusion.

- *CSV*: uses fgetcsv() to parse a CSV file and transform it into a native PHP format.

- *INI*: uses parse_ini_file() to parse an INI file and transform it into a native PHP format. This and the CSV adapter are roughly equivalent performance-wise.

- *Gettext*: the Zend Framework gettext adapter does *not* use the gettext extension as it is not thread safe and does not allow specifying more than one locale per server. As a result, it is slower than using the gettext extension directly, but, because the gettext format is binary, it's faster to parse than XML.

If high performance is one of your concerns, we suggest utilizing one of the above adapters.

How can I make translation and localization even faster?

Maybe, for business reasons, you're limited to an XML-based translation adapter. Or perhaps you'd like to speed things up even more. Or perhaps you want to make l10n operations faster. How can you do this?

Use translation and localization caches

Both `Zend_Translate` and `Zend_Locale` implement caching functionality that can greatly affect performance. In the case of each, the major bottleneck is typically reading the files, not the actual lookups; using a cache eliminates the need to read the translation and/or localization files.

You can read about caching of translation and localization strings in the following locations:

- `Zend_Translate` adapter caching

- `Zend_Locale` caching

View Rendering

When using Zend Framework's MVC layer, chances are you will be using `Zend_View`. `Zend_View` is performs well compared to other view or templating engines; since view scripts are written in PHP, you do not incur the overhead of compiling custom markup to PHP, nor do you need to worry that the compiled PHP is not optimized. However, `Zend_View` presents its own issues: extension is done via overloading (view helpers), and a number of view helpers, while carrying out key functionality do so with a performance cost.

How can I speed up resolution of view helpers?

Most `Zend_View` "methods" are actually provided via overloading to the helper system. This provides important flexibility to Zend_View; instead of needing to extend Zend_View and provide all the helper methods you may utilize in your application, you can define your helper methods in separate classes and consume them at will as if they were direct methods of Zend_View. This keeps the view object itself relatively thin, and ensures that objects are created only when needed.

Internally, `Zend_View` uses the PluginLoader to look up helper classes. This means that for each helper you call, `Zend_View` needs to pass the helper name to the PluginLoader, which then needs to determine the class name, load the class file if necessary, and then return the class name so it may be instantiated. Subsequent uses of the helper are much faster, as `Zend_View` keeps an internal registry of loaded helpers, but if you use many helpers, the calls add up.

The question, then, is: how can you speed up helper resolution?

Use the PluginLoader include file cache

The simplest, cheapest solution is the same as for general PluginLoader performance: use the PluginLoader include file cache. Anecdotal evidence has shown this technique to provide a 25-30% performance gain on systems without an opcode cache, and a 40-65% gain on systems with an opcode cache.

Extend Zend_View to provide often used helper methods

Another solution for those seeking to tune performance even further is to extend `Zend_View` to manually add the helper methods they most use in their application. Such helper methods may simply manually instantiate the appropriate helper class and proxy to it, or stuff the full helper implementation into the method.

```
class My_View extends Zend_View
{
    /**
     * @var array Registry of helper classes used
     */
    protected $_localHelperObjects = array();

    /**
     * Proxy to url view helper
     *
     * @param  array $urlOptions Options passed to the assemble method
     *                            of the Route object.
     * @param  mixed $name The name of a Route to use. If null it will
     *                            use the current Route
     * @param  bool $reset Whether or not to reset the route defaults
     *                            with those provided
     * @return string Url for the link href attribute.
     */
    public function url(array $urlOptions = array(), $name = null,
        $reset = false, $encode = true
    ) {
        if (!array_key_exists('url', $this->_localHelperObjects)) {
            $this->_localHelperObjects['url'] = new Zend_View_Helper_Url();
            $this->_localHelperObjects['url']->setView($view);
        }
        $helper = $this->_localHelperObjects['url'];
        return $helper->url($urlOptions, $name, $reset, $encode);
    }

    /**
     * Echo a message
     *
     * Direct implementation.
     *
     * @param  string $string
     * @return string
     */
    public function message($string)
    {
        return "<h1>" . $this->escape($message) . "</h1>\n";
    }
}
```

Either way, this technique will substantially reduce the overhead of the helper system by avoiding calls to the PluginLoader entirely, and either benefiting from autoloading or bypassing it altogether.

How can I speed up view partials?

Those who use partials heavily and who profile their applications will often immediately notice that the `partial()` view helper incurs a lot of overhead, due to the need to clone the view object. Is it possible to speed this up?

Use partial() only when really necessary

The `partial()` view helper accepts three arguments:

- `$name`: the name of the view script to render

- `$module`: the name of the module in which the view script resides; or, if no third argument is provided and this is an array or object, it will be the `$model` argument.

- `$model`: an array or object to pass to the partial representing the clean data to assign to the view.

The power and use of `partial()` come from the second and third arguments. The `$module` argument allows `partial()` to temporarily add a script path for the given module so that the partial view script will resolve to that module; the `$model` argument allows you to explicitly pass variables for use with the partial view. If you're not passing either argument, *use render() instead*!

Basically, unless you are actually passing variables to the partial and need the clean variable scope, or rendering a view script from another MVC module, there is no reason to incur the overhead of `partial()`; instead, use Zend_View's built-in `render()` method to render the view script.

How can I speed up calls to the action() view helper?

Version 1.5.0 introduced the `action()` view helper, which allows you to dispatch an MVC action and capture its rendered content. This provides an important step towards the DRY principle, and promotes code reuse. However, as those who profile their applications will quickly realize, it, too, is an expensive operation. Internally, the `action()` view helper needs to clone new request and response objects, invoke the dispatcher, invoke the requested controller and action, etc.

How can you speed it up?

Use the ActionStack when possible

Introduced at the same time as the `action()` view helper, the ActionStack consists of an action helper and a front controller plugin. Together, they allow you to push additional actions to invoke during the dispatch cycle onto a stack. If you are calling `action()` from your layout view scripts, you may want to instead use the ActionStack, and render your views to discrete response segments. As an example, you could write a `dispatchLoopStartup()` plugin like the following to add a login form box to each page:

```
class LoginPlugin extends Zend_Controller_Plugin_Abstract
{
    protected $_stack;

    public function dispatchLoopStartup(
        Zend_Controller_Request_Abstract $request
    ) {
        $stack = $this->getStack();
        $loginRequest = new Zend_Controller_Request_Simple();
        $loginRequest->setControllerName('user')
                     ->setActionName('index')
                     ->setParam('responseSegment', 'login');
        $stack->pushStack($loginRequest);
    }

    public function getStack()
    {
        if (null === $this->_stack) {
            $front = Zend_Controller_Front::getInstance();
```

```
        if (!$front->hasPlugin('Zend_Controller_Plugin_ActionStack')) {
            $stack = new Zend_Controller_Plugin_ActionStack();
            $front->registerPlugin($stack);
        } else {
            $stack = $front->getPlugin('ActionStack')
        }
        $this->_stack = $stack;
    }
    return $this->_stack;
    }
}
```

The `UserController::indexAction()` method might then use the `responseSegment` parameter to indicate which response segment to render to. In the layout script, you would then simply render that response segment:

```
<?php $this->layout()->login ?>
```

While the ActionStack still requires a dispatch cycle, this is still cheaper than the `action()` view helper as it does not need to clone objects and reset internal state. Additionally, it ensures that all pre/post dispatch plugins are invoked, which may be of particular concern if you are using front controller plugins for handling ACLs to particular actions.

Favor helpers that query the model over action()

In most cases, using `action()` is simply overkill. If you have most business logic nested in your models and are simply querying the model and passing the results to a view script, it will typically be faster and cleaner to simply write a view helper that pulls the model, queries it, and does something with that information.

As an example, consider the following controller action and view script:

```
class BugController extends Zend_Controller_Action
{
    public function listAction()
    {
        $model = new Bug();
        $this->view->bugs = $model->fetchActive();
    }
}

// bug/list.phtml:
echo "<ul>\n";
foreach ($this->bugs as $bug) {
    printf("<li><b>%s</b>: %s</li>\n",
        $this->escape($bug->id),
        $this->escape($bug->summary)
    );
}
echo "</ul>\n";
```

Using `action()`, you would then invoke it with the following:

```
<?php $this->action('list', 'bug') ?>
```

This could be refactored to a view helper that looks like the following:

```
class My_View_Helper_BugList extends Zend_View_Helper_Abstract
{
    public function bugList()
    {
        $model = new Bug();
        $html  = "<ul>\n";
        foreach ($model->fetchActive() as $bug) {
            $html .= sprintf(
                "<li><b>%s</b>: %s</li>\n",
                $this->view->escape($bug->id),
                $this->view->escape($bug->summary)
            );
        }
        $html .= "</ul>\n";
        return $html;
    }
}
```

You would then invoke the helper as follows:

```
<?php $this->bugList() ?>
```

This has two benefits: it no longer incurs the overhead of the action() view helper, and also presents a more semantically understandable API.